The Lord Carrington, with his humble duty

to Your Majesty, has the honour respectfully to

to submit for Your Majesty's approval that

Sir Nicholas Henderson GCMG, be appointed Your

Majesty's Ambassador to the United States of

America.

(CARRINGTON)

Foreign and Commonwealth Office

21 May 1979

MANDARIN

Books by the same author

Prince Eugen of Savoy (biography)
The Birth of NATO
The Private Office
Channels and Tunnels

MANDARIN

The Diaries of an Ambassador
1969–1982

NICHOLAS HENDERSON

To George Kanarek

With best wishes from

Nicholas Henderson

WEIDENFELD AND NICOLSON

LONDON

First published in Great Britain in 1994 by
Weidenfeld & Nicolson

The Orion Publishing Group Ltd
Orion House,
5 Upper Saint Martin's Lane,
London, WC2H 9EA.

A catalogue reference is available from the British Library

ISBN 0 297 81433 8

Filmset by Selwood Systems, Midsomer Norton
Printed and bound in Great Britain by
Butler & Tanner Ltd,
Frome and London

*The endpapers reproduce submissions to the Queen for
Nicholas Henderson's appointments to France and to the USA.
The Queen's approval is given followed by her initials.*

To Mary and other members of the Service

CONTENTS

List of illustrations   viii

Acknowledgments   ix

Introduction   I

A note on the published text of the Diaries   10

WARSAW 1969–1972   11

BONN 1972–1975   35

PARIS 1975–1979   91

WASHINGTON 1979–1982   263

Appendix   490

Index   495

ILLUSTRATIONS

Illustrations, which are taken from the author's collection, appear between pages 118 and 119, and 246 and 247.

ACKNOWLEDGMENTS

I would like to thank the following who have given me detailed help: Michael Pakenham who was in Warsaw and Washington in my time and who has the family gift of an excellent memory, not least for the comic and unusual; Julian Bullard who was Minister in Bonn when I was Ambassador there and whose eagle and scholarly eye has saved me from many blunders; Nicholas Bayne, formerly Financial Counsellor in Paris, where his powers of analysis were invaluable to me, as have been his comments on my account of our time together there; Peter Jenkins, who was my Private Secretary in Washington, his first overseas posting in the Foreign Service, and who has been generous with his time in giving meticulous examination to my text; Robert Kee who has given a magisterial overview to the whole book; and Alastair Forbes whose unique knowledge, particularly of the French scene, has been generously applied to my book thereby saving me from many solecisms.

As if subjecting my account to a litmus test of respectability, which I have thought necessary in view of the ban on the publication of my diaries explained in the Introduction, I have shown the text to Nicholas Gordon-Lennox, also a colleague in the Foreign Service, with an independent mind and a high sense of responsibility. He has reassured me that what I am publishing in no way constitutes a dereliction of trust – not that I would like his *nihil obstat* to be held against him by the guardian angels defending the pearly gates of the Radcliffe rules. Rohan Butler, for many years historical adviser to the Foreign Secretary, has also given me much specialist and wise advice.

The German, French and US Embassies in London have kindly checked names for me. Raymond Seitz has provided insights into many of those mentioned in the notes, though the responsibility for what appears is mine alone.

I also wish to thank the following for indispensable help in different ways: Michael Butler, Peter Carrington, Debo and Andrew Devonshire, Melville Guest, Roy Jenkins, Nigel Lawson, Patrick McDermott, Tony Parsons, Peter Payne, David Pryce-Jones, John Saumarez-Smith, Oliver Wright and Sabine and Nicolas Wyrouboff.

I am particularly grateful to Mary Cozens, Henrietta Davies-Cooke and Alice Temple Cox who have deployed their secretarial skills on my behalf over several years.

I owe a special debt of thanks to Gill Coleridge, the paragon of literary agents, to Ion Trewin, the nonpareil of publishers and to Douglas Matthews who has carried out with characteristic aplomb the difficult task of indexing.

Finally, as my dedication of the book attests, none of it would have happened in the way it did without Mary's constant and creative presence. Her frequent entreaties to me to be less bureaucratic in my drafting has I hope helped to lighten the text of the link-ups.

Nicholas Henderson

INTRODUCTION

In a book published several years ago, *The Private Office*, I gave an account of the workings of a central cog in the British machine of government. I did this, not by institutional analysis, but by drawing on personal experience to describe the manner in which the Private Office of the Foreign Secretary plays an indispensable role in mediating between different worlds, particularly those of diplomacy and politics; and I depicted the various ways in which several Foreign Ministers whom I had served had gone about their tasks.

My purpose now is to use the same method of personal narrative to relate what happens, not at the geographical centre, but at the periphery of government, so far as the conduct of foreign policy is concerned: to give an account of how an Embassy works, what an Ambassador does in the modern age, his relationship with his own government and the adventure of absorbing the culture of other countries; and to do so by writing about my time as the British Ambassador in a number of capitals.

I have found much mystification on the subject, and no little misrepresentation. An Ambassador, as I have learnt, is apt to be subjected to alternating currents of awe and hostility, curiosity and contempt; and like some strange creature who has escaped from a zoo he is rarely handled as a normal human being. Yet this is what he must remain if he is to discharge adequately his calling of go-between.

However that is but an occupational hazard. More important, and indeed a spur to the publication of this book, is the widespread current belief that modern inventions have rendered a diplomat's trade far less useful than it was in former times. Besides which, it is often supposed the decline in Britain's power has reduced the chances for our diplomats to play important parts on the world stage.

I am not, of course, suggesting that the life of a diplomat has been immune to the forces of change that have reshaped the activities and style of so many professions. What a diplomat today does, how he does it and even what sort of person he is are quite distinct from a mere generation ago. But that does not mean that at the fulcrum of the seesaw where he sits he is not capable of exerting considerable weight now on one side, now on the other, even if, for good reason, this influence is not noised abroad. This country's reduced role in the world has of course affected the scope for influence of a British diplomat. But whereas the geographical range may have been reduced, within a narrower compass his mission may have become more intense. No one who has observed the international scene since the end of the Second World War can doubt the extent to which some smaller countries have succeeded in getting their way, partly by reliance on the skills of their diplomats. As for big powers, it is arguable that diplomacy is more essential for them than ever before, now that the existence of nuclear weapons has mercifully reduced the risk of war between them.

The traditional game of diplomacy, as played for instance, by Talleyrand or Palmerston, has been rendered obsolete in the second half of this century (as incidentally has the children's war-game of L'Attaque) by the development of international institutions. Membership of the European Community, the IMF, the World Bank and the UN, and the existence of GATT have all affected the daily round of chancelleries. Nowadays there is less bilateral diplomacy and much more multilateral negotiation; diplomats play different parts than hitherto, though this does not necessarily mean that they are less numerous or regard themselves as less busy.

If heads of government and Foreign Ministers can now meet without difficulty what, it is asked, is the purpose of having permanent representatives? True, so the catechism continues, they may be needed to lay on the odd meal and to be at the foot of the steps with a reassuring smile when the minister's aircraft arrives, but that signifies that they have become little more than hoteliers or airport greeters.

Many aspects of diplomacy have, of course, been greatly affected by technological changes, particularly in communications; but so have other areas of international contact, whether those affecting private relationships such as tourism or public affairs such as defence, not to mention financial markets. Easy air-travel has brought more MPs to Embassies; and the first lesson for an Ambassador is to ensure that their needs are properly attended to.

The word diplomacy has many meanings, but it is used here to encompass the daily and nightly round of an Ambassador abroad; and in that sense it is concerned less with ends than with means, more with art than with politics, the lens being wide rather than focused on a single point. The often popular image of diplomacy as being concentrated upon a few great issues can indeed be accurate upon critical occasions; but the test of good diplomacy lies also in the ease and success with which an Ambassador is able to transact a whole range of practical everyday matters between states.

It was an axiom of Lord Salisbury's – and he was a theoretician as well as a practitioner of diplomacy – that in foreign affairs, the choice of a policy is as a rule of less importance than the methods by which it is pursued. This is because the many complex and changing forces at work make accurate forecast and reliable judgment difficult. While accepting the crucial importance of method I cannot help thinking that there are moments in international affairs when the choice of the policy itself is critical – and, as I will suggest below, I believe that what an Ambassador is capable of providing in the way of dispassionate advice and judgment may be essential to reaching the right policy decision.

Perhaps it is not for me to say so, but I have been personally very aware of certain hazards in an international negotiation to which a diplomat may be less exposed than a politician. He will not have to work in the limelight; he will know that the actual process of negotiation is nearly always slow and undramatic and that it will not be helped by a constant beam of publicity. Nor does a diplomat have to show personal success for the outcome. Nothing makes a negotiation more difficult than if one side fears that it is going to be made to look as though it has yielded too much by the other claiming that it has had a great triumph. Indeed, triumphalisation is the enemy of diplomacy.

The proper study of all diplomatic practice is man, the understanding and reconciliation of some of the deepest instincts of human nature; and these being unchanging it follows that the scope of an Ambassador's responsibility may be less subject to the forces of modern science than are the range and methods of many other professions, the armed services for instance.

The one invention that has had the most impact on the activities and power of a diplomat was the electric telegraph a century and a half or so ago. From then on he was subject to orders from home, as indeed was the military commander. The last diplomat to hold the issue of war or peace in his hands was Viscount Stratford de Redcliffe, 1786–1880, who for many years was a dominant influence at the Sublime Porte.

At the risk of spoiling the sport of those who like tilting at windmills or pricking supposedly false reputations, I cannot help thinking that the argument that modern communications have attenuated the diplomat's calling rests on a false premise. It presupposes that because political leaders meet frequently across international frontiers they will necessarily get on with, and understand, each other better; and that they do not require the continuing flow of information and analysis about another country that they need about their own and that a permanent mission abroad can alone provide. Many are the examples from recent history of the misunderstandings, misjudgments and antipathies that have been generated or aggravated by close contact. Hitler apparently reminded Mackenzie King of Joan of Arc.

I suppose the supreme example is the Hitler–Chamberlain relationship. There was no difficulty about meeting; but the effect of three meetings in quick succession did not bring about in the British Prime Minister's mind any sounder comprehension of Hitler's character or objectives. If it is argued that the Ambassador in Berlin at the time did not show any better judgment than the Prime Minister, I would rejoin that the great influence of the Ambassador in that situation demonstrates what a difference he can make – for good or ill; and that had Nevile Henderson counselled otherwise than he did the course of history might have been different.[1]

Anthony Eden told me years later that the greatest mistake he had made as Foreign Secretary was to have appointed Nevile Henderson to Berlin without even having seen him.

Eden's career also illustrates the possible downside of personal encounters between ministers. He and Dulles did not hit it off together and the friction created by their meetings may well have contributed to the breakdown in US–UK relations at the time of Suez in 1956.

Harold Macmillan, then Chancellor of the Exchequer, saw President Eisenhower at the height of the Suez crisis and came away with a completely false impression of the President's attitude, which compounded the disaster.

President Franklin Roosevelt had new-world scepticism of those with professional experience of old diplomacy. As he wrote to Churchill in March 1942, only three months after the USA had entered the war against Germany and when the Russians were bearing the brunt of the land fighting against the Nazis: 'I know you will not mind my being brutally frank when I tell you that I think I can handle Stalin personally better than either your Foreign Office or my State Department.' FDR's illusions about the value of personal diplomacy were shown in a message he sent on 30 August 1942 to William Bullitt, US Ambassador in Moscow: 'I have just a hunch that Stalin doesn't want anything but security for his country and I think that if I give him everything I possibly can and ask nothing from him in return, noblesse oblige, he won't try to annex anything and will work for a world of democracy and peace.' Of course, dictators were just as capable of misunderstanding democratic leaders as the other way round. Such a mistake was made by Khrushchev when he saw President Kennedy in Vienna in 1961 and thought him weak, which encouraged him to try to install missiles in Cuba.

A more recent example of the hazards of top-level personal encounters was President Reagan's meeting with Gorbachev in Reykjavik in

---

[1] See Richard Lamb, *The Drift to War 1922–1959*, W. H. Allen, 1989.

December 1987. The President appears to have been so carried away by the bilateral bonhomie of the moment as to have been ready to abandon the West's strategic nuclear deterrent. Of course I am not suggesting that ministerial meetings are to be avoided. They will continue to hold the centre of the international stage. The European Community could scarcely function without them. For heads of governments the recurring summits are clearly regarded by them as providing insights into the leadership and problems of the other main industrial powers. All I am asserting is that they are not an alternative to permanent diplomatic representation, a view supported by a recently retired senior member of the US Foreign Service, Mr Ronald Spiers, who has written: 'There is no substitute for on-the-spot knowledge of other cultures, languages, personalities and what buttons to push to get results.'[1] This reminder of the importance of the right buttons is linked with Mr Spiers's belief that 'professionalism is as important in the Diplomatic Service as it is in the military and intelligence services' and his plea for fewer political appointments to the top United States Embassies.

The intense public discussion of the causes of the First World War led afterwards to scepticism in this country of many features of the old diplomacy including the secrecy that surrounded it and the 'unrepresentative' character of those in the profession. From Lloyd George to Chamberlain there was a tendency for Prime Ministers to rely for advice on foreign policy on people outside the career. Chamberlain's dependence on Horace Wilson was the most notable and, in its consequences, the most disastrous example. I have said that I thought that Mrs Thatcher's attitude to the Foreign Office was the opposite of her attitude to the Church of England: with the latter she liked the institution but was not particularly drawn to the people at the top; as regards the Foreign Office she distrusted the place but liked the people, as shown by her employment of Tony Parsons, Percy Cradock and Charles Powell.

The account I give of my time as Ambassador in Poland, the Federal Republic of Germany, France and the USA is extracted from the journal I kept intermittently between the years 1969 and 1982. It is an uneven record because until my last year in Paris it constituted little more than occasional notebook jottings. It is much fuller for the latter than for the earlier period when my health was poor. It does not deal with my inner life or the state of my mind which Samuel Johnson said was the greatest thing to be recorded in diaries. It is concerned mainly with public affairs; and sometimes with personal, but not intimate, frivolity. A published diary can convey colourful details about food and entertaining, for

---

[1] Ronald I. Spiers, *Herald Tribune*, 28 July 1989. Besides serving as political Counsellor in the US Embassy in London, he was Ambassador to Pakistan and Turkey.

instance, or the content of casual conversation, which may not easily find a place in the broad sweep of an autobiography. I never meant it to be a comprehensive history of the public events with which I was concerned in the different capitals. I only recorded what particularly intrigued me at the time; and there was not always the energy or opportunity even to do this. I cannot say that I intended that what I wrote would later be published verbatim; but at the back of my mind was the thought that one day some parts of the journal might fill out the public record.

Keeping a diary became for me something of an indulgence. The chance of recording incidents or describing actors in some scene in which I had participated provided a benefit that had nothing to do with the possibility of publication. Events and people fell into sharper relief at the moment of impact in the knowledge that I was going later to describe them; and it was sometimes only when I came to look back, pen in hand, that I realised the full significance of the personality or occurrence. The practice also enabled me to enjoy, and sometimes suffer, experiences a second time. Like Browning's wise thrush I would sing each song twice over. As J.J. Rousseau has put it: '*En écrivant mes souvenirs je me rappellerai le temps passé, qui doublera pour ainsi dire mon existence.*'

My method was to write in longhand whenever the chance occurred, whether at home at weekends, or in aircraft at any time. I did not aim at a daily record or at anything systematic, so that, as I have said, the text I am publishing is inevitably uneven.

Unlike one Rector of the Sorbonne I never made a point of telling people I met that I kept a diary. Dr Robert Mallet informed me when I sat next to him at lunch on our first meeting that at every lunch or dinner he attended he notified his neighbours that he made a record each evening of what he had done and whom he had seen during the day. 'I have found,' he explained, 'that it improves conversation no end.'

Nervous of the stigma of frivolity that branded many traditional diplomatic memoirs in the past, rendering them by now an extinct literary species, I have nevertheless included accounts of episodes that were far from solemn. I hope that this will help to reflect the whole picture even if, in the telling, the lighter side comes to dominate the chiaroscuro. What gives a sense of transience, not to say superficiality, to any rendering of the career is partly the frequent shifting of scene, which is inherent in it, but also the sheer diversity of the subjects and people that come one's way. A serious negotiation with the Russians in Berlin could be followed within a matter of hours by a fancy-dress ball in Bonn. A presentation in Paris of the produce of Scotland, designed to titillate the palates of the French in favour of haggis as well as whisky, would give way to a computer exhibition held in the splendours of the throne-room of the Embassy. In two successive summers versions of the Chelsea Flower Show were held in the enormous garden there.

One aspect of my trade that I always liked was the chance it gave to meet people in different careers and with contrasted enthusiasms. Over thirty years ago I struck up a friendship with the skating fraternity during a championship in Vienna, particularly with the skating editor of *The Times*. Since then I have entered, however ephemerally, into the worlds of motor racing, show jumping, athletics, football, ballet dancing, medicine, aircraft production, motor car manufacture, cheese-making, textiles, the rag trade, sculpture, Hereford breeding – to name a few of the communities whose shop I have been able to enjoy. I realise that my contribution to these different professions and hobbies has been marginal.

I am frequently asked which diplomatic post I have liked best. It is not a question I can answer easily because they have meant such different things. It would be hard to say, for instance, that the long winters in Warsaw were joyous. Nevertheless our time there left a deep imprint on me and a feeling of having lived with and understood a different people and of having experienced travail with them; so that upon leaving Poland, more so perhaps than upon leaving any other country, we felt we were severing links that had been of intense and mutual value. Yet only a small part of it had been what is widely considered to be diplomacy.

What I am publishing here is in no sense a textbook. It is a personal view. But I hope that it manages to show how, in an Embassy, public and private life are intermingled. There is, to be sure, no separation, no green-baize door, between Chancery and residence. Nor should the impact be underestimated of what an Ambassador's wife can perform. I am not sure that this is adequately recognised. I do not simply mean her duties in running an Embassy and ensuring that guests are well fed and made to feel at home. What I wish to advance is that it is the Ambassadress, rather than the Ambassador, who at lunch or dinner parties will be placed next to the host or the most important guests, while the Ambassador will be seated beside their wives. Thus, when at the outset of the Reagan Presidency he decided, unlike his predecessor, to go out into the Washington world Mary, my wife, found herself next to him on many occasions. She had a far better chance to find out at an early stage what he was like and what he thought and how he acted than I could.

If I have dwelt upon the work of the Ambassador, let it not be thought that I therefore regard him as the only important member of the Embassy staff. This is far from the truth, as I know having worked at the coal face of many diplomatic missions; and it is far from my intention; it is simply that the Ambassador perforce is at the sharp end and it is he who has the most opportunity to glean information and exercise influence.

Why have I decided to make my chronicle public? Leaving vanity aside – without of course dismissing it – I think that my main motive has been the desire to redress the imbalance, to which I have alluded earlier, between how people are apt to perceive the role of a diplomat in the present age and the reality of what he is and the scope of his profession.

I would like to have published earlier. The choice of the best time is difficult. Guizot the French statesman and historian has analysed the dilemma. Explaining his decision to publish his memoirs he said that he preferred to speak of his times and of his own life from the edge rather than from the bottom of his tomb. This was more dignified for him and it meant that in writing of others he was more scrupulous in his judgments and descriptions. He went on:

> Most memoirs are published either too early or too late. If too early they are indiscreet or insignificant: one speaks of what it would be better to be silent about or one fails to speak about something of which people would be curious to know and of which it would be useful to talk. If too late, memoirs lose much of their pertinence and interest: contemporaries are no longer there to take advantage of the truth revealed and to enjoy a certain personal pleasure in reading about them.

When, in 1989, I, as a former member of the Foreign Service, sought authority, as is required by constitutional custom, to publish extracts from my diary, this was refused. Officials of the Foreign Office and the Cabinet Office considered that my text was in clear breach of the Radcliffe rules of confidentiality governing relations between ministers and officials. I had no wish to flout the Foreign Office, to which I owed loyalty. I recognised, too, the need for ministers to be able to feel that they could discuss things with officials without this being revealed later in a way that might harm them in the conduct of their business or jeopardise the public interest. It seemed to me a question of timing. A period of fifteen years was laid down in the Radcliffe rules as the time within which the obligations of confidentiality should apply. I therefore decided to wait.

Three years later I planned to go ahead. Publication would take place in the spring of 1994 by which time fifteen years would have elapsed since I retired from the Foreign Service in April 1979. My text in relation to my postings in Poland, Germany and France would therefore no longer fall within Radcliffe.

That left only the extracts of my diaries covering my time in Washington 1979–82. By then, however, I was no longer a member of the Foreign Service having been appointed there by Lord Carrington, just as my predecessor, Peter Jay, had been appointed by Dr Owen. In any case

I did not consider that what I was proposing to publish fell within the categories of infringement prescribed by Radcliffe. These were limited to disclosures of confidential exchanges between ministers, or of the views of, or official advice given to, the ministers of one government conveyed to the ministers of another government. Nowhere in my texts had I made revelations of this kind.

When I originally submitted my text I was led to believe that officials of the Foreign Office and the Cabinet Office thought that Mrs Thatcher would object to them, particularly over the Falklands conflict, and would regard them as a betrayal of confidence. She has now written a long account about the Falklands which covers much of the same ground as my own. Other former ministers have written and published their memories, some of which seem to me to pay scarce attention to confidentiality.

In submitting my text now for publication I think I would be lacking in a sense of proportion, and indeed, of humour, if I were to feel any sense of guilt that I was thereby jeopardising some national interest. On the contrary, I believe that it is high-time that there is a wider knowledge of what members of the Foreign Service do in their lives abroad in the modern age – the obligations, responsibilities and hazards that are incurred as well as the much-publicised glitter of entertainment and the indisputable advantages of discovering new peoples, countries and cultures.

My book is a long-overdue attempt to meet a long-felt need; and if, after this considerable lapse of time, I have published conversations of important people on matters of public interest, I hope that this will be judged, not as an irresponsible mark of indiscretion, but as a useful contribution towards the more open government to which our present leaders are keenly committed.

NOTE ON THE PUBLISHED TEXT
OF THE DIARIES

For the purpose of publication, I have not altered the original diary text –
other than to make deletions and grammatical corrections – even if, with
the benefit of hindsight, I might now judge or express things differently.
I have added sub-headings to each entry to serve as signposts.

Passages in italics are link-ups of the texts of the diaries.

The numbers in the text refer to notes usually set as footnotes. These
are given on first mention of a name.

Notes have not been provided for those who are adequately covered
in the text of the diary, or for those who are household names – except
to clarify what these latter were engaged in at the time I was writing.

WARSAW

1969–1972

A GLIMPSE BEHIND
THE IRON CURTAIN

The transfer in 1969 from the post of Minister in Madrid to that of Ambassador in Warsaw brought a change in every aspect of our life.

Within the continent of Europe there can hardly have been a greater contrast in climate, vegetation, culture and daily existence than that between Spain and Poland at the time. Everything was different in our new post: food, landscape, architecture, our relationship with people, the subjects which we talked about and what we did behind the grim barrier of the Iron Curtain.

Politically, both countries were dictatorships. Gomulka, the First Secretary of the Polish Communist Party and therefore the leader of Poland, was subject to the authority of Moscow, whereas Franco, who was a dictator all right, was beholden to no one and kept Spain in a cocoon of his own making, isolating it from the rest of the world. He did not seek to impose an ideological straitjacket on the economy of the country.

Architecturally the Warsaw Embassy Residence is a black marble cube. It was often referred to by the Poles as Tutankhamun's tomb. It was 'PSA modern' and the reception area on the first floor was aptly described by my predecessor as a cross between an airport lounge and the ground floor at Heal's. Unrelieved black on the outside, the Embassy was a pictorial riot within – twelve different colours in the reception area. There were shocks to the body as well as to the eye. The wall-to-wall fibre carpeting generated electric shocks in the frosty winter nights so that, when receiving guests, I had to earth myself by holding on to the banisters at the top of the stairs. However we had one exceptional aesthetic blessing in the Embassy: the collection of Beresford-Hope[1] silver with which we adorned the house whenever possible.

---

[1] Beresford-Hope was a member of the Diplomatic Service who had served in Berlin just before the First World War. There he fell in love with a Polish lady who, when she saw him one night at the opera with another partner, drew out a revolver and shot herself in front of him. In memory of this forlorn love he bequeathed his collection of Regency-style English silver and silver-gilt to a British Legation in Poland if such a mission were established within five years of his death. He died in 1917 so that when the British Legation was established in Warsaw soon after the war they received the bequest of the silver. Much of it was looted during the Second World War. But most has since been recovered thanks partly to the foraging activities of Aliki Russell.

When we arrived in Poland in March 1969, soon after the invasion of Czechoslovakia by the other Warsaw Pact powers, the permafrost of the Communist system seemed utterly enduring and impenetrable. The old guard of the party were entrenched in power, yet the system was palpably failing to deliver the goods, the criterion by which Marxism asked to be judged. Large numbers of Soviet troops occupied the country, however discreetly. Intellectual life was at a standstill, yet the Poles, whatever their inner despair, managed to skirt ideological orthodoxy in the arts, particularly in music, the theatre and cinema. It was impossible to remain unmoved by their spirit. They missed no chance of making cracks at the regime such as we witnessed in a production of Richard III when the translation of a passage used words very familiar to the Polish audience from government propaganda. This was greeted with derisory applause.

Their attitude to a new style from the West was that of a hungry seal to a bloater – to borrow a metaphor from Paddy Leigh Fermor. We made a practice of putting out for public consumption in the Embassy the newspapers and magazines recently received from London. Regardless of the frown of the authorities, the Poles devoured them immediately and we would often see, worn with extreme elegance in Warsaw, a dress copied from the latest fashion magazine and made up out of material from old family garments. Gift parcels containing clothes from Marks and Spencer were popular. When Mary commented favourably on a pair of boots worn by a young Polish girl, she replied, 'Your Marks is better than our Marx.'

Becoming an Ambassador for the first time, which was what my promotion to Warsaw meant, may not have been a turning point in the career in the sense that I would now be making a greater contribution to foreign policy. A junior officer at a desk in Whitehall or the Head of Chancery at a busy capital may make more of an impact on decision-making than the head of many diplomatic missions. But it marks a shift in both responsibility and panoply. You are in charge. You represent the government. You bear the Queen's commission. You suddenly find yourself living in a large house with servants and, of course, you have a car and a driver.

In a Communist country you are also a target. Every word you utter is, if possible, overheard. We had an experience of this in our early days in Warsaw. Our dalmatian, normally the mildest of dogs, was disturbed by the washerwoman searching our private rooms in the Embassy. He bit her severely in the right thigh. Such is the fear of rabies in that part of the world that anyone other than the owner bitten by a dog has to undergo a long and painful course of injections. This was the fate of our washerwoman and the news rapidly spread – which may have served as a cautionary tale to other would-be intruders.

Ironically our dalmatian, having rendered this disservice to the Polish state, managed to rub it in by winning the Warsaw Dog Show. This received much publicity and resulted in many – too many – propositions from the owners of dalmatian bitches.

The following extracts from my diary, starting three weeks after our arrival in Warsaw, give a glimpse, however fleeting and incomplete – for reasons I have explained above – of some of the features and incidents of our life behind the Iron Curtain.

1969

17 APRIL

WARSAW

DOUBLE TALK

After breakfast to the sound of Polish language tapes and much struggle with the headlines in the Polish press, I attend a morning meeting at the Chancery at 10 a.m. to run through the newspapers and discuss the day's events. It is Michael Pakenham's[1] hour. He has excellent Polish. He apologises for the length of Gomulka's speech. I say it isn't his fault. The press continues to be full of criticism of Britain for 'leading the pack in reviving the Cold War' after the recent Warsaw Pact invasion of Czechoslovakia. Radio Free Europa is described by the Polish papers as 'dirty slobs'.

At 11 a.m. I continue my round of calls on diplomatic colleagues. It is the turn of the Bulgarian. We sit either side of a shiny table in a large shiny room. A girl interprets. The Ambassador explains later that she is his daughter. I had guessed it as they both have the same dog-like eyes. He offers me cognac and blackcurrant juice. Out of politeness I cannot refuse. In a minute or two a waiter comes in with tea and coffee. We talk about the weather. We discuss roses. He tells me that a kilo of essence of roses – a great Bulgarian product – is equivalent in value to a kilo of gold. I rack my brains for some Bulgarian subject that we can discuss but can think of nothing but Gladstone's 'atrocities'. I tell him how well

---

[1] Michael Pakenham; third son of Elizabeth and Frank Longford who are lifelong friends. I proposed the toast at their diamond wedding party, given by Antonia, their daughter. Before I was married I shared lodgings in London with Frank, for whom I have always felt the greatest affection, admiration and respect. Michael had joined the Diplomatic Service in 1966. Warsaw was his first post abroad. He arrived there as Third Secretary in 1967.

his daughter speaks English. I ask him whether there is a close similarity between the Bulgarian and Russian tongues. His daughter puts this into Bulgarian. He gives his answer. She then says in English, 'He says, yes, because we have the same smell.' I think to myself how lucky I am to be able to hear such dialogue. What would Evelyn Waugh not have given for such an opportunity.

We have a lunch at home for Professor Barlow, formerly Professor of Electrical Engineering at London University. It is an electrical engineers' lunch. I take an extra glass of sherry beforehand to help me along but quickly realise that this may have been a mistake so soon after the cognac at the Bulgarian Embassy. Talk about laying down your liver for your country.

Seated on my right at lunch is Professor Groszkowski, President of the Polish Academy of Science. On my left is another professor, the Director of the Technical Institute of Electronics, who speaks nothing but Polish. Our Polish guests clearly take warmly to Professor Barlow, a jovial red-faced fellow who is wise enough to speak slowly, which cannot be said of most official English visitors abroad. Professor Groszkowski tells me that he regularly spends his summer holidays on the coast in Bulgaria where the government runs rest homes. He is a nice old boy who speaks English better than he understands it. I ask him which he prefers, the mountains in the south near Zakopane or the Black Sea. He smiles seraphically and says, 'Mountains very nice.'

After lunch I walk back to the office. People are sitting on benches with their faces turned up to the April sun. I am reminded of the scene in the Belvedere Garden in Vienna in the early spring when elderly people creep out from their apartments after the long winter's hibernation and come to life again in the rays of the sun.

We attend a dinner party at the Canadian Embassy. The Canadian Ambassador is a woman, very friendly and composed. The other guests include a correspondent from the East German press, a handsome Brazilian diplomatic couple and a Polish minister and his wife. The minister is of bourgeois background and it is difficult to believe in his dedication to proletarian values. He is easy to talk to. After dinner he gets on to the subject of Germany. I must understand what the Poles feel about it after six million dead and having had Warsaw wiped out. I ask him to believe me that I do understand but I also ask him to tell me why the Poles should trust the East Germans any more than the West Germans. 'Whoever said they did?' he expostulates.

I ask him about Czechoslovakia. I say that he should know how strongly people feel in Western Europe about the Warsaw Pact invasion. He says he knows. I ask him why, when even in East Berlin there were anti-invasion manifestations, no such thing happened in Poland. He tells me that I should distinguish between the attitude of the government and that of everyone else. The latter did indeed feel strongly but he explains that Dubček made things impossible for 'big brother in the East'. The post-January events in Czechoslovakia were due originally almost entirely to economic causes; only later did the movement become political. Dubček should not have allowed everything to have happened at once. He should have started with economic changes but the abolition of censorship and the political changes frightened 'big brother in the East'. Dubček was not man enough for the situation which required someone much tougher: 'Look at the way he used to cry and faint.' That was no good in such circumstances.

The minister says that the Czech economic situation is terrible. This has economic repercussions elsewhere. The chain reaction should enable East European governments to exert pressure on the Soviet Union to make a proper going concern of CEMA (the Council of Economic and Mutual Assistance). So far nothing has been done. There isn't even transferrable currency in Eastern Europe.

By the time I get to bed that night I feel I have had a long day, but the open way the minister has spoken – a minister in a Communist dictatorship – lifted my spirits at the end of it.

In contrast to the blight so evident in a Communist country the moment you enter it, as if it has touched everything in sight, I was witness in the first weeks after our arrival in Poland to a completely different experience, the sudden arrival of spring in a northern climate. Everybody we saw in the streets or public parks seemed to be proclaiming joy at their release from the grip of the long, grey winter; and people literally stripped to the waist whenever possible.

I felt like a theatre-goer when the curtain rises at the start of a performance and the stage is all at once bathed in light. Everything was coming to life before me: trees and flowers exploding, not gently as in an English spring where the primroses unfold slowly, but violently with a rush like the welling up and bursting forth of a river at its source. Nobody here could say that April was the cruellest month or that winter had kept them warm. Swept along in the torrent, we shared the feeling of renewal around us.

It was in this atmosphere that on an impulse I decided to make a grass tennis court in the Embassy garden, supplanting some of my predecessor's tomato beds. The court provided much summer amusement, not least for the snoopers of the Polish Secret Service in the surrounding flats. The tennis court was a good deal less level than most of Poland and often damp, features that flattered my game of spin and slice more than the classical strokes of the younger members of the staff.

During this first spring, Antonia and Hugh Fraser joined us and her brother Michael Pakenham to undertake a short tour of the south of Poland.

We picnicked by the River Donajec. As often happens on such journeys it was the occasion for much talk, particularly about the past. As we drove, much of the time was spent in discussing the Pakenham family. Antonia seemed to want to do this, greatly to my delight; and she showed much less interest in talking about the Fraser clan.[1]

Thanks to Michael's presence in the Embassy we had another Pakenham visit to Poland. With his mother, Elizabeth, and his sister, Rachel, we visited Hitler's headquarters in the former East Prussia. We gazed in awe at the remains of his lair, the Wolfschanze, where the failed assassination had taken place. We heard with horror how the vast concrete structures, now upturned and thrown about like colossal children's bricks, had been built by a large workforce every member of which had been executed afterwards to prevent any revelation of Hitler's whereabouts.

17 MAY

WARSAW

———

FEAR

Nobody denies that there is more fear about nowadays in Poland than for a long time. At least this fear, intensified by the reaction to the March 1968 student riots and then by the Czech invasion, has become a part of the Polish climate in the last year or so which it has not been since the days of Stalin. Many Poles are afraid to be seen to have close contact with Western diplomats.

Mary met the woman who runs the fashion house, Moda Polska. She invited her to dinner next week to meet Hugh and Antonia Fraser. The Polish lady was forthcoming and, speaking fluent French and English, accepted the invitation with enthusiasm. When, however, Michael Pakenham telephoned a day or two later to confirm, she said that she would very much like to see his sister when she came to Warsaw but, as for the dinner, 'there were difficulties'. Most of the other people from the university or artistic world whom we had invited have also declined. All observers of the Polish scene are shocked by this. My Swiss colleague

———

[1]See diary entry 27 October 1979.

says that it is wrong to assume that the Poles were always romantic and heroic. In their history they have at times been cautious, compromising and calculating. Their heroism goes in waves. A Secretary in our Embassy and an excellent speaker of the language comments on the two-facedness of some Poles: they say one thing to you in private conversation and then something quite different when in the company of other Poles. I cannot say that I find this either surprising or contemptible.

At one moment in my time in Poland I was having a conversation with Prime Minister Cyrankiewicz, a jovial, far from ascetic personality who embodied, almost to the point of parody, the Janus-like characteristics of many Poles who have managed to survive the twists in their country's history. We were talking, as happened so often in Warsaw, about Poland's unfortunate past, the result partly of her no less unfortunate geography. Cyrankiewicz was telling me how very different things were now and how lucky his country was to have 'big brother in the East'. I nodded, which I thought was polite, only to observe a look of horror coming over the President's face at the thought that I might be believing what he was saying.

During my time in Warsaw, often I reflected on the strange, two-tier relationship between Poland and Britain. Whatever the ideological divide there were links between the two countries that did not exist between others: Britain had gone to war with Germany in 1939 in fulfilment of its guarantee to Poland and had remained at war until the end, determined to restore an independent Poland; Polish troops had been stationed in the UK during the war and had fought alongside us with great gallantry; and the UK had been at the Potsdam Conference where the Oder-Neisse frontier between Poland and Germany had been confirmed.

Since the war, of course, the Polish government had become completely absorbed in the Soviet orbit and official relations with the British, as with other non-Communist governments had been seriously eroded. But Britain continued to be seen as an integral part of the West, to which the vast majority of Poles desired intensely to belong. We were an essential strand in their lifeline. Despite the ideological stagnation, cultural, academic and journalistic contacts had been maintained and had even been institutionalised by the regular Anglo-Polish Jablonna Conferences. So, although the inter-governmental landscape remained arid, there was much of an unofficial and lively kind that continued to flourish between the British and Polish peoples.

8 AUGUST
WARSAW

———

BREZHNEV'S VISIT

Brezhnev has been here for the twenty-fifth anniversary of the Polish People's Republic. This visit caused me to attend to one of the tasks I am meant to perform here, the observance of trifles: the attempt to gauge what is going on beneath the surface of events in Eastern Europe judged by the small area of the iceberg above the water. The Czechs were also invited. At the airport on departure I noticed that Brezhnev and Gomulka both embraced Svoboda,[1] but dismissed Husak[2] with a mere handshake. As for Gomulka, his hug-rating was evidently high in Soviet eyes. Brezhnev's attention to him was embarrassingly cordial. Throughout the visit Gomulka gave the impression that the Soviet leaders were the people he felt at home with, that he was proud and happy to have them there.

A look of sublime satisfaction was on his face as he wheeled Brezhnev round the diplomatic corps. His references to the Russians in his long speech to the Sejm were abject. Brezhnev was fulsome about him and the Poles. Gomulka spoke for about twenty minutes on the war and on Poland's sacrifices. Of course I fully understand why the Poles dwell on the past and their losses; they were proportionally so much greater than those of any other country but it is unreasonable that he should talk about the war and the struggle against the Germans and mention the Russians as the only opponents of Germany, avoiding all reference to the US or the UK. As for the Warsaw uprising it was described as an ill-timed misfortune, the responsibility of those working against the true interests of Poland and only for their own class purposes.

SEPTEMBER
WARSAW

———

POLICY ISSUES

In London recently I had meetings with several people in the Office to see whether there was any possibility of movement on the subject of

———

[1] Ludvik Svoboda, President of Czechoslovakia, 1968–75.
[2] Gustav Husak, succeeded Svoboda as President of Czechoslovakia.

European security and on the idea of a security conference proposed at
the Warsaw Pact meeting in Budapest last March. The Office view was
that they do not want to get into the position of pressing the Germans
to move faster than they wish over the recognition of the East German
regime and the Oder-Neisse frontier.

The main ingredient in HMG's present European policy is friendship
with Bonn. I discussed this with a senior official in the FO, a clever, dry,
unimpassioned man and asked him whether it was really impossible to
suggest anything – for instance, some further public move towards a
multilateral recognition of the Oder-Neisse frontier. The answer was that
the Federal German government might not like it and that we could not
at the moment afford to offend the Germans. We wanted their backing
for our application to join the Common Market and we depended upon
them financially.

I suggested that the West Germans seemed to be moving in the direction
of a new policy towards Eastern Europe; this would be hastened if the
SPD did well in the forthcoming federal elections. If the Bonn government went ahead and made some recognition of the frontier and of the
existence of the German Democratic Republic (DDR), they would gain
credit in Eastern Europe. Why should we deprive ourselves of the advantages of a positive policy? Nothing bound the Poles more to the Russians
than our failure to recognise their Western frontier. By not taking this
step of recognition we also ran a danger of encouraging the development
of revanchism in the Federal Republic of Germany. Here was an issue
on which HMG really did have a say. We were a Potsdam power; and a
European one. If we were to take our role in Europe seriously, now that
we had divested ourselves of foreign policy responsibilities elsewhere,
we could hardly behave as though this problem of an unsettled Central
Europe did not exist. We should bear in mind too that, unpromising
though it seemed to be, we should keep contacts with Eastern Europe
alive. We could not just dismiss those countries as lost for ever beneath
the Soviet yoke. There had been anti-Soviet revolts in three of them in
the past fifteen years; in Hungary and Poland in 1956, in Czechoslovakia
in 1968. Whether we were reconciled or not to the systems of government there, the people were not. Potentially this malaise in Eastern
Europe, and the problem of the proper relationship to those
countries, could cause us great difficulties: and could provide us with
great opportunities.

In the East European and Soviet Department of the Office I found
much sympathy with my view that we should try to respond favourably
to the idea of opening a dialogue with Eastern Europe. My thought was,
not that any immediate practical result would come from it, but that
politically it was unfortunate to give the impression, which we now did,

of being uninterested in the area, and of regarding the whole place as but the poodle of the Soviet Union.

I had also had a word with Teddy Youde, who has replaced Michael Palliser as the Foreign Office Private Secretary at Number 10. But I cannot say that he led me to think that the Prime Minister might see any political dividend to be gained from a new initiative on Eastern Europe.

Apart from the overriding aim of doing nothing that might upset the Germans there was another ingredient in the Office's policy that arose from the particular circumstances of the time.

As London saw it the satellite countries, by siding abjectly with the Soviet Union over the invasion of Czechoslovakia, had lived consummately up to their name. They were, therefore, not worth bothering about and any effort to be made towards the Communist world should be directed to Moscow. From the Warsaw Embassy we reacted strongly to this view which seemed to us to be a self-fulfilling policy of doom; and I think we helped to bring about a swing in the pendulum.

I NOVEMBER
WARSAW

THE PRINCESS BOILS

We went to Lodz for the day yesterday: an official visit to call on the municipal and university authorities. Accompanied by Michael Pakenham and Colin Budd who, like Michael, is a member of the Chancery in the Embassy, Mary and I set off in the Princess, driven by Karol, at about 8.30 a.m. We had some doubts whether we would ever get there as the Princess is not really to be trusted five kilometres beyond the Warsaw garage. I have been trying for a long time to get a new car as this unreliable hearse is becoming less and less of an advertisement for the new technologically up-to-date Britain. But the Treasury won't pay for the only cars that are available.

Michael, never at his best in the early morning, soon fell silent and it was clear that he was not feeling well. But he quickly recovered when the car began to show its expected paces and when we ran into the arms of the militia. The thermometer had started to soar and Karol had changed to driving very slowly. A militia car that had followed us in the last town perhaps with the intention of flagging us down, moved out into the middle of the road to overtake us. At that moment its bonnet flew open and the driver, completely blinded, came to a grinding halt whilst we chugged on regardless. However, within another kilometre or two the Princess began to boil. Karol decided he must stop and fill up with some more water. He drew up beside a farm and was busy pouring water into the radiator from an enormous bucket when the militia car passed us again. It stopped beside the road about half a kilometre ahead. We got under way again just after an enormous milk lorry had passed us. We followed this the short distance to the militia car. As it passed the militia man got out to flag us down. The milk lorry created such a draught that the militia man's cap was blown off and was crushed beneath the wheels of the milk van. However, bare-headed and a little short on dignity, he held up his hand to stop us. He examined Karol's papers after which we drove on, to be stopped a few more kilometres nearer Lodz by another militia car. Again there was the same inspection of Karol's papers. Just as we were about to be stopped a third time we thought of an idea. We would turn the tables on this militia car. So, after Karol had pulled up the Princess, Michael leapt out and called on the militia car to stop. He explained that all these halts had made us late and he asked if the militia car could guide us to the Mayor's office. The militia man had little alternative though he was not best pleased.

At Lodz we were struck by the liveliness of the polytechnic. We lunched at the Grand Hotel with an English teacher who has a post in the English faculty of the university. He was standing up to it well, I thought, though I could not imagine that it could have been an easy life in Lodz, not the most exciting of towns. His pupils were mostly girls wanting to learn enough English to get them a job that would take them abroad. Some no doubt hoped to marry him to obtain a foreign passport.

I was out of action in the UK for several months in the spring and summer of 1970 owing to a recurrence of TB. Thanks to modern drugs I recovered. I was not thrown out of the Service but was handled with exemplary consideration during the long and painful period of recuperation. I shall always feel deep gratitude and unreserved loyalty towards the Office for the way they treated me at this time, and particularly to Oliver Wright who was then Chief Clerk.[1] For the nearly two years more that I remained in Warsaw I managed to carry on but it was a struggle and I never felt well. Before I returned from the UK I called on Alec Douglas-Home who had become Foreign Secretary in

---

[1] Oliver Wright was an almost exact contemporary of mine in the Diplomatic Service. Ambassador to Denmark, he succeeded me in the Embassies in Germany and Washington. The Chief Clerk was responsible for all staff Matters.

Heath's government following the June 1970 general election, when the Conservatives had been returned after six years of Labour government.

We began our meeting by exchanging views on our common complaint. He spoke of the two years he had spent on his back with TB of the spine. The immediate impression he made on me now was one of extreme tiredness. He was in his shirt sleeves; his jacket was hanging in front of an electric fire drying. He had just walked over from the House of Commons and been caught in a storm. The effect was to make him appear even more than usually frail. He received me courteously, leaning back in his chair, putting his feet on the desk. I thought to myself of Duncan Wilson's story showing Home's perfect aristocratic behaviour. U Thant was calling on him. It was around teatime. Alec offered him a cup, took one himself, leaned back and put his feet up on his desk. Then suddenly remembering something, he moved forward, opened a drawer and pulled out a large packet of chocolate biscuits. He offered it to U Thant who refused. He then proceeded to eat the whole packet himself.

Now that I was before him, I thanked the Secretary of State for sparing me the time. It would make a difference when I returned to Warsaw to be able to say that I had seen him. We spoke about the heavy workload he had been carrying: firstly the election campaign and now the burdens of office. He said the latter burden had indeed become heavy. Then with a winsome smile he referred to the previous day's incident when smoke bombs were thrown in the Chamber of the House of Commons: 'They did their best to burn the awful place down yesterday ...'

I spoke of the importance of Britain's maintaining some sort of relationship with Eastern Europe. I knew he would not be able to come to Poland. He spoke about the idea of a security conference: 'I know there's going to be a conference sometime, so I see no point in opposing it. I never see any point in resisting something that you know is going to happen.' I suggested one or two positive purposes that I thought a conference could serve and he showed interest – but then he is invariably well-mannered.

1970

12 SEPTEMBER
WARSAW

A DIPLOMATIC CALL

On my return I called on the Cambodian Ambassador who lives in a dark little room in the Hotel Bristol while he awaits the favour of Pouma, the Polish government's official housing agency, to find him accommodation. He is painfully aware that the policy change of the government of Phnom Penh[1] means that he is not likely to have much luck in the near future. So he sits disconsolately at a small veneer desk opposite a large wardrobe in the hotel, waiting with Asiatic resignation.

The Ambassador apologised for the humble quarters in which he was receiving me. He beckoned me to an upright tasselled chair and offered me a Dubonnet and a cigarette. This confirmed the impression he had immediately made on me of being an oriental Michael Stewart[2] – the same physical smallness, gentleness, self-effacement, considerateness towards others and chain-smoking. A large blonde secretary appeared with a plate of biscuits, followed by an enormous butler bearing an ice-bucket containing a bottle of champagne. I wondered to myself how the diminutive Cambodian Ambassador and I were going to get through the bottle but I was grateful that he should have been generous enough to produce it. I asked him about the military situation in his country. He turned this by asking me what the BBC had said that morning. He confessed that he had no other source of information. I asked him about the conference of non-aligned nations in Lusaka. He enquired what the BBC had been reporting on the subject. So there we sat, the three of us – the Ambassador, myself and the champagne bottle – making small talk in the middle of the morning.

Neal Ascherson of the *Observer* comes to lunch. He is a specialist in this part of the world. He has been seeing many Poles while attending a

---

[1] In March 1990 Prince Sihanouk, who had ruled Cambodia since independence, was overthrown by a militarist revolt headed by Marshal Lon Nol who proclaimed a republic and was supported by the USA.

[2] Michael Stewart, Labour politician. Secretary of State for Education and Science 1964–5; Foreign Minister 1965–6 and 1968–70. I was his Private Secretary when he first became Foreign Minister and wrote about him in my book *The Private Office* in a chapter headed 'An Unsung Foreign Secretary'.

seminar on the Potsdam Conference. He says that there is a feeling that the British government, compared with the French, is holding back both over European security and over Brandt's Ostpolitik. We discussed the future state of Polish-West German elections. It looks as though the Germans will increasingly dominate the economies of Central Europe which will bring them greater political influence there. The British could do more to exert their influence but do not do so. We are overwhelmed by fear that if we take the slightest initiative towards Eastern Europe we will impair our position in Western Europe. We are so busy concentrating on not rocking the NATO boat that we may well fail to observe other countries are getting ahead of us.

1971

17 SEPTEMBER
WARSAW

ANOTHER EXPERIENCE IN
INTERPRETATION

Having enjoyed the interpretation of the Bulgarian Ambassador I saw no reason why Alexandra,[1] who had studied Russian at Marlborough and Oxford, should not also be usefully employed in the same way. The new Soviet Ambassador was due to pay a courtesy call on me. He had promised to bring his own interpreter but I had it in mind that Alexandra might be present to serve as a check. I mentioned this in passing to my Private Secretary who saw fit to pass it on to the Soviet Ambassador's office. He thereupon decided not to bring his own interpreter.

When, therefore, he arrived at the house I told Alexandra that she would have to cope. She ran into difficulties from the start. 'Would you please convey to His Excellency,' I said, 'that I am most grateful for the honour he has done me in making this call so soon after his Excellency's arrival in Warsaw.'

'Look here, Daddy,' Alexandra protested. 'I can't say that sort of nonsense in English, so how do you expect me to say it in Russian?'

The Soviet Ambassador asked me my view on the consequences of British entry into the European Economic Community. Alexandra was quickly out of her depth, not merely in Russian, but in English. She did

---
[1] My daughter.

not know the jargon of the Common Market and Comecon. However, the Russian ploughed on inscrutably and almost mechanically. He suggested that it might be helpful to my daughter to learn some of these terms.

'At least,' I hissed at her, 'get in a few "Your Excellencies" in Russian.'

'That's just what I can't do,' she snorted back. 'I don't know what it is and anyway I really can't go on in both languages. It's the worst thing you have ever done to me.'

But the Russian seemed quite happy. I deliberately ceased asking questions and just listened, hoping to bring the conversation to an end. However, he stayed for forty minutes, leaving Alexandra in a state of mixed exhaustion and fury.

'What a revolting man,' she said when he had finally left, 'he made no attempt to help. He just went on and on.'

'That's what Russians do,' I suggested.

30 SEPTEMBER

WARSAW

—

A SAINT TO STAY

I suppose Sue Ryder is as near to saint as is anyone I am likely to meet, unless it be her husband, Leonard.[1] The lives of both of them are dedicated to the same cause, that of helping those in such physical or mental distress that nobody else, or no other institution, will take care of them. They do not exactly work as a team as they have different homes that they look after in various parts of the world. But they have the same totally selfless aim to which their entire lives are dedicated.

Sue spends a great deal of time visiting her homes in Eastern Europe which is how we got to know her. She assumed the responsibility, for instance, for setting up a home for mentally handicapped children in Wroclaw; she relies on the local authorities to provide for day-to-day attention to the patients. Until recently one of her vans was going around with the depressing words on it; 'Sue Ryder Home for Incurables', but now this is changed to 'Sue Ryder Foundation'. The war and the suffering caused by the Germans gives her a particular rapport with the Poles. So much does she focus on the horrors of barbed wire and the wickedness

---

[1] Group Captain Leonard Cheshire, VC, OM, DSO, 1917–92. The most highly decorated and renowned RAF officer of the war. Married Susan Ryder, later Baroness Ryder of Warsaw in 1959.

of the Germans that one is apt at times to feel guilty because one was not in a concentration camp or killed in combat.

Sue felt guilty about coming to stay with us. She was working at one of her homes in Poland when she met with an accident. The doctors said that she must rest. She said that she could not possibly do that. There was too much work to be done. She was the only person who could do it. However, she was prevailed upon to come to the Embassy and take it easy for a few days. She said she would have to pay for her keep. When asked if she would like the curtains drawn so that she could sleep a bit in the daytime, as the doctor had suggested, she replied, no, she must make notes.

She was lunching with us one day in the little grey-coloured dining-room in the Embassy here. The dogs were kept well out of sight because it is clear that she does not like them. Not that she has ever said this because she would never be discourteous or inconsiderate, but I had the impression that she believes that when there are so many human beings in the world, so many souls, in need of food, it is wrong to divert time and resources to pet animals. She appears to feel some guilt about eating herself. She is inclined to let drop that she has not eaten all day as she has been too busy helping, for example, with the unloading of bricks, at the Constancin Home. Her commitment is to helping others in a particular way. If, because of this she makes others feel guilty this, I think, is subconscious but it serves a purpose because it may induce them to help in the same way. Good work cannot be done entirely covertly otherwise there would be no example for others to follow. At this lunch I mentioned that the other guest was a Protestant clergyman. Sue herself is a devout Catholic. Sue was telling us about some problem she has had with certain Polish officials. It was not quite clear, at any rate to me, what it was all about. But then Sue maintains an almost deliberate air of mystification which is linked with her pre-occupation about listening devices that she presumes, probably rightly, are positioned throughout the Embassy residence. I asked her whether she has difficulty in obtaining drugs for her homes and she responded with a fierce look as though I had committed some indiscretion and she pointed to the walls and hissed, 'Mind the decoration.'

The subject of Archbishop Wyszyński[1] arising in the conversation, I asked Sue if she had ever seen him.

'A very long time ago,' she answered, with the finality of someone slamming a door that should never have been opened.

By way of lowering the tone I asked about Leonard's tennis. Sue said she knows nothing about it.

---

[1] Stefan Wyszyński, Archbishop of Griezo and Warsaw and Primate of Poland 1948–81.

I am consumed with a desire to know about their private life. They have two children, but what time or attention I wonder can be given to them? I start at the beginning, as tactfully as I can, though Mary said afterwards that she didn't see where the tact came in: 'When you were first married did you immediately start working together on these homes?'

'Oh yes; you see we spent our honeymoon in India, firstly on the Ganges visiting a cancer home and then travelling every day having consultations about new projects.'

I am so mentally boggled by the account of this honeymoon that I lose my head and say to Sue, 'Wouldn't you, by the way, have something to drink, I mean some wine or something?'

'No, absolutely fatal,' she says emphatically.

Mary and I ask her about her children but while in no way dismissing them, or indicating a lack of affection, she does not seem to want to talk about them. As with so many topics it is as though she regards this one as a diversion from the true business of life, or at any rate her life – which is to help those in distress. It is this single-mindedness that is so astonishing. She does not appear interested in or to wish to devote time to any subject other than that of her homes.

While Sue is talking I start dredging my memory for details of Santa Teresa who would be my favourite saint if I knew enough about any others to have a choice, when she says, à propos the discussions she has been having with the authorities, 'But you have to make jokes. You would never get anywhere, would you, unless you were prepared for a laugh? We are always having jokes with the Poles. I pull their leg. They pull mine.' This seems to me to be in line with Santa Teresa.

Sue is a considerate guest, insisting on not putting us out or being in the way. She also has a wistful charm. It is impossible not to wish to help someone so frail-looking and self-sacrificing. Impossible not to try to prevent her going off at 8 p.m. with the intention of driving all through the night to keep some appointment in Czechoslovakia. Impossible not to try, but difficult to succeed, so strong is her will. She looked very much better after five days of rest and good food with us, but I am not sure that this made her feel any happier. She does not put on airs, not even those of sanctity; and I do not sense any falseness about her modesty. There is nothing of the grande dame about her. She makes no effort to dominate a gathering. She appears to be a very natural, very self-effacing little figure, with rather decided views and no wish to shine in any but a spiritual way.

1972

---

20 JANUARY
WARSAW

PING PONG WITH THE CHINESE

With the Warsaw winter diving into its second month yet without snow or ice to lure one out of doors for exercise, ping pong has come into its own. Several of us in the Embassy have become enthusiasts playing several times a week. I decided to challenge the Chinese Embassy to a match. Much publicity has been given lately to ping pong diplomacy, to the readiness of the Chinese to make contact across the ping pong table when they appear reluctant to do so otherwise. Why not, I thought, combine business with pleasure and see whether the Chinese in Warsaw would be prepared to be more forthcoming in this way?

At some national-day party – the stock exchange for the marketing of diplomatic issues in Warsaw – I proposed a match to the Chinese Ambassador. His reaction was to laugh unrestrainedly for several minutes. But I could not make out whether or not he accepted the challenge. I met him again a week or two later at the Chinese Embassy where he was giving a party to say goodbye. I renewed the proposal. He accepted but said that I would have to settle details with the Chargé after his departure.

I thereupon wrote to the Chargé suggesting a match in the Embassy residence, on a certain Sunday at 5.30 p.m., three players each side. About a week later a telephone message came through from the Chinese Embassy accepting the date and saying that seven Chinese would be coming, the Chargé, Lei Yang, the Third Secretary, Pei Yuang Ying, two interpreters and three players whose names, none of which appeared on the diplomatic list, were Len Aw Kay, Sen Tan Son and Wan Su Mee.

The Embassy asked for the names of the British team and I sent a message back saying they would be as follows: Mr J.N. Henderson; Mr Ian Chalmers; A. N. Other. The last name struck me as particularly suitable for the occasion.

A few days later, on the Thursday before the match, a further call came from the Chinese Embassy as follows: 'We have learnt that His Excellency Her Britannic Majesty's Ambassador is himself taking part in the event. We immediately realised that His Excellency could not be expected to play against common sportsmen. Our team has therefore been reconstructed as follows: the Chargé; the Third Secretary, Pei Yuang Ying; and Tzu Jung Szeng.'

In the last few days before the match we in the British Embassy went in for intense ping pong training. We selected Pete Talbot as the third member of the team, partly because he had served in Peking and had picked up the Chinese manner of playing the game, including the way of holding the bat and serving with oriental cunning. We thought it would give a more professional look. A number of other preparations were made. I purchased Chinese balls in place of the far-from-round Polish ones. I took up the carpet below the table. We tried to improve the lighting. We laid in plenty of China tea. I arranged for John Fretwell[1] to come along and help with his knowledge of the language. We were all set at 5.30 on Sunday for the arrival of our opponents.

As the cars drove up to the door and a large group of Chinese piled out I could not help wondering what the Polish security police must be making of the occasion. I could imagine some puzzled telephoning from one end of Warsaw to the other.

The Chargé and his retinue came smiling up our large staircase. They were all wearing the same tunics, buttoned up to the neck and black shoes such as they wear at national-day parties. They did not look like sportsmen of any kind, common or otherwise. I introduced my team. We offered tea and cakes with much subtle joking about it being Chinese, not Indian tea. Our guests smiled but I soon perceived that they smiled all the time. I explained how I thought we should organise the match: the order and number of games, etc. They smiled without demur. The struggle began.

In the first two encounters the Chinese made mincemeat of Ian and Pete. It was then my turn to play against the Chargé. He was evidently not much of an athlete and I won easily. He was very sporting about it, but said that he would not be playing any more. He frequently leant on the table with one arm, suggesting he might be suffering from heart trouble. I offered him Pilsner beer. He accepted willingly. From then on we all abandoned the tea and drank beer. The match then went entirely the Chinese way. I was taking part at the end against their best player. He said at the start of the match that he would give me an advantage by holding the bat the European way which he wasn't accustomed to doing. Somehow this did not help me much. It was a piece of gamesmanship I hadn't allowed for. We were one game all and he was leading 15–10 in

---

'John Fretwell, a member of the Diplomatic service who had served in Peking and Moscow and was at this stage Counsellor in Warsaw. When Assistant Under-Secretary of State, FCO 1976–9, he applied a cool but constructive mind to the problems of Britain's relations with the European Community. He was Minister in Washington 1980–1, Ambassador to France 1982–7. He and his wife, Mary, have been friends in and out of school.

the final. There was a shout in Chinese from the Chargé, following which my opponent started sending the ball back to me high in the middle of the table with encouraging words about giving me easy shots to hit. The effect was to make me quite unable to return the ball at all. He won 21–14 saying how much he had wanted to help me. The overall result at the Embassy was a defeat of one to eight, a serious loss of face for us.

We all shook hands. The Third Secretary, who in his last game had been prevailed upon to remove his jacket, put it on again. The uniformed figures trooped off in their black shoes expressing thanks. The Chargé asked if we would accept a challenge to a return match in the Chinese Embassy. They had a gymnasium where there were tables and space for volleyball. I accepted eagerly.

'Do most of you play every day?' I asked.

'Yes,' the Chargé said with an even more expansive smile than usual, one that was so pervasive and dominating that it seemed to hang about at the top of the stairs long after the grim tunic with the Mao badge had disappeared.

In order to prevent the above extracts giving a misleading, and at times an unjustifiably frivolous, impression of what was happening in Poland and of what I was involved in during my time there, 1969–72, I have to add one or two recollections.

It was impossible not to be aware of the discontent below the surface. People knew how much better conditions were elsewhere. Every foreign observer realised that Communism could not survive indefinitely in Poland with its Western traditions and strong Catholic Church. The only question was when and how it would break up. In December 1970, just before Christmas, the price of food was suddenly increased. This led to violent riots in the northern ports and demonstrations elsewhere. The authorities were paralysed. For a brief moment the people were sovereign, something unique in Communist history. Scarcely less significant for the future was the way the Russians simply looked on, without intervening. Not that they can have liked what they saw; but for them to have used force would only have exacerbated the trouble. Unlike the disturbances in Poland in 1956 or the events in Czechoslovakia in 1968, no overt anti-Soviet challenge or ideological threat was involved, which may have been decisive for them.

Discontent and disorders brought about the replacement of Gomulka by Gierek. At the outset Gierek made far-reaching promises of economic change but these came to nothing. They amounted to little more than tinkering with a system which was inherently flawed. Dedicated Communist that Gierek was, having imbibed the faith when working in the coal mines of northern France, he was not going to abandon Communism. I was having a chat with him once – it was in the interval at half-time in a football match at Katowice – and I said to him that he must be tired in view of all the work and pressures upon him. To which he replied in a matter-of-fact way: 'Communists are never tired.'

Without being clear who he was, Mary also spoke to him in the interval – in French. When she resumed her seat she said: 'I have just had a most interesting conversation with the French military attaché who talked about coal-miners in France and most courteously handed me cakes and other refreshments' (not something to be expected in a Communist country) – which reinforced my conviction that wives deserve to be briefed as much as Ambassadors.

Apart from the evident failure of the system to improve living standards and the unreadiness of the leadership to transform the system, with the consequences of ever-mounting public indignation, the public event that sticks out most vividly in my memory from this time was the signature of the Polish–Federal German Treaty on 7 December 1970. This helped to assuage understandable Polish fears over their western frontier for which they had for long been seeking international, particularly German, recognition. At the Potsdam Conference Poland had been given the right to administer former German lands 'pending a final peace settlement'. Such a settlement had never taken place. The new lands thus acquired amounted to a quarter of total Polish territory and produced 30 per cent of the country's manufactures, 40 per cent of its electricity and half its grain. No wonder therefore that Warsaw wanted to secure for their frontier as much finality as possible given their constant fear of a deal between Moscow and Bonn over their heads affecting their territories, at a time of Germany's growing strength. The treaty with Germany gave the Poles all that they could hope for in the circumstances. It also provided the promise of badly needed economic and technical help from the Federal Republic.

The treaty was one of the fruits of Brandt's OstPolitik which reflected a more forthcoming – and contrite – German attitude towards Eastern Europe, as manifested by the Chancellor's decision to kneel at the Ghetto in Warsaw when he came to sign the treaty.

When in the spring of 1972 the time came for us to leave Poland we were not sorry in many ways: we would not regret missing another winter there or the year-round blight of Communism; it would be a relief to escape the drumbeat of party propaganda, the attentions of the secret police and the narrow confines, mental and physical, in which life has to be conducted behind the Iron Curtain. But we would miss many features of our Polish life and the retention of a foothold in a hostile environment, useful for immediate commercial interests and perhaps future political relations. Also we would remember the lifeline to the West that we managed to hold out to many people who did not like the system and who wanted above all to feel that they had not been abandoned by the world to which they wished to belong. We left Poland with a pang.

BONN

1972–1975

TO BONN
AND INTO EUROPE

My transfer from Warsaw to Bonn came as a surprise to me. For two years I had been on a regime of anti-TB drugs which had greatly reduced my vitality and had led me to turn down two earlier proposals for posting. However, I was getting back to full strength and greatly looked forward to serving in a European Community country, particularly one of such importance to HMG.

The UK was about to join the Community and, as I soon discovered, expectations were high in Germany over the contribution our membership could make, thanks to our long parliamentary tradition. When, on some social occasion, I mentioned to Walter Scheel, the Federal German Foreign Minister, that our Foreign Minister, Alec Douglas-Home, would like to pay a visit to Bonn soon after our entry on 1 January 1973, he immediately took a diary out of his pocket and started discussing possible dates with me, which was not something I expected from a Foreign Minister. He was eager to show his government's enthusiasm over what they thought was a promising new step in the Community's evolution. Reflecting the mood in Bonn I told London that the German government now regarded the British government as the ally with whom they spoke first and whose views they expected to be closest to their own.

Alas, this was not to last even for the length of my tour in Germany. Even at the start of it, the conduct of the Anglo-German relationship was not entirely plain sailing. This was in part because of the ambivalent feelings of the British towards the Germans. There were no hesitations so far as the British government was concerned. It would have reciprocated the German sentiments, as expressed above, with the difference that now, nearly thirty years after the end of the war, it was the UK which was weak and Germany strong, at any rate economically (the GNP of the Federal Republic of Germany (FRG) was two and a half times that of the UK, with a labour force of about the same size). In many ways the UK needed German support more than the other way round. But the British people continued to have doubts and fears about the Germans, more so than about any other people, more so than did any other nation in the West, with the possible exception of the Dutch.

This tended to be the outlook not only of the older generation in Britain for whom the Nazi torchlights still flickered in the mind's eye, but also of many of the young who had been discouraged from any other view by TV films and comics portraying all Germans as 'baddies'.

The Germans did not readily understand this. They acknowledged the need, expressed by the Federal President, to be aware 'of the darkest phase in our history ... and not try to push it aside'. They believed, nevertheless, that they had put down deep democratic roots and had established a highly successful economic system based on market forces. Bulwarks against extremism and against the over-centralisation of power had been built into the 1949 constitution: in particular the rights accorded to the separate states (Länder) which would prevent any over-bearing authority, such as another Prussia, from emerging. To anyone coming to modern Germany it was important to take account of the deliberate devolution of power enshrined in the federal system. The corollary of this was the emphasis on variations in lifestyles and attitudes of the different Länder. The derogatory way in which a Bavarian talked of anyone living north of the Danube as 'a ghastly Prussian' was only to be compared with the contempt with which a Berliner spoke of someone from Munich. After all, Bismarck had described a Bavarian as being halfway between an Austrian and a human being.

At the time I reached Bonn Willy Brandt was Chancellor of a coalition government in which the Social Democrats held eleven posts and the Free Democrat Party five. His anti-Nazi record and trustworthy per-sonality were the most convincing expression the Germans could have found of their democratic credentials. As governing Mayor of Berlin, the post he had held before coming to Bonn to join the government, first as Foreign Minister, then as Chancellor, he had achieved a worldwide reputation for upholding democratic principles and resisting Soviet pres-sure. 'Dare to be more democratic!' was the Leitmotiv of his government, according to Günter Grass.

Brandt's touch as a leader reached far outside Germany. He had a burly, yet unaggressive presence, which he seemed to have no desire or need to assert. There was nothing self-seeking about him. Without any particular eloquence of language or originality of thought he had no difficulty in getting himself across as a sturdy fighter in the political ring at home and as a supporter of the underdog everywhere. He believed that Germany had to tread a new path on the European stage, which explains his commitment to Ostpolitik, a policy which brought about a profound change in Germany's relations with the Communist countries to the east.

In private he was warm, not given to small talk but nevertheless companionable. He was drawn to the company of intellectuals. There

*was nothing self-righteous or puritanical about him. He liked the good
things of life and had no social complexes. He enjoyed fishing and
when I presented him with a fishing-rod as a present from the British
government on his sixtieth birthday a beam transfigured his face.*

*The chance for a meeting between Brandt and Edward Heath occurred
soon after I reached Bonn. Heath came to Germany in September for
the Olympic Games which were to be held in Munich and Kiel. Before the
programme began he succeeded in carrying out some hectic sightseeing in
Munich which included an exhibition of Meissen at Lustheim and visits
to the palace of Schlossheim and the Pinakothek. The Prime Minister
had a large entourage: guides and directors, plain-clothes detectives,
his Private Secretary, Christopher Roberts, his Parliamentary Private
Secretary, Timothy Kitson, very much in the centre of the Number 10
inner circle, and a press officer whose far from complete self-confidence
was not fortified by Mary's frequent reference to her as Mrs Kitson. Then
there was the doctor, Dr Brian Warren. Since Churchill's time Prime
Ministers have seemed to regard it as de rigueur to take a doctor with
them on foreign travels. Harold Wilson did so. His health, like Heath's,
was robust. However, regardless of medical needs, Warren was a delightful addition to the company.*

*The programme of the games and countless meetings that Heath
intended were thrown into turmoil by the kidnapping in the Olympic
village at Munich of the Israeli athletes. Eventually it was arranged that
Heath would visit Brandt at Willy Daume's villa beside the Starnberger
See. My diary takes up the story from there.*

1972

---

10 SEPTEMBER

MUNICH – KIEL

THE OLYMPIC GAMES

We found Brandt very calm despite the crisis. He and the Prime Minister
sat talking on the terrace overlooking the lake. From time to time
someone appeared with a telex message about the state of affairs in the
village. Brandt remained composed and seemed able to switch his mind
completely to the political problem of the forthcoming summit meeting
and to the relations of the Federal German Republic with the German
Democratic Republic. Both Brandt and Heath were eager that the summit

should take place and were concerned about the possible reluctance of the French under Pompidou to go ahead with the meeting as planned. Some of us in the entourage tried to explain why the French were taking their present line. We were thereupon accused of taking the French side as usual. Often have I known this, that when trying to express a foreign government's reason for adopting such and such an attitude, one is accused of partisanship when all one was doing was trying to explain. On reflection, I have come to the conclusion that ministers rarely want things clarified. They know perfectly well what the issues are. What they do welcome is a chance to let off steam.

From Munich we flew to Kiel where the maritime part of the games was to be held.

Early the next morning we heard that all the Israeli hostages in Munich had been killed and that the games had been suspended for twenty-four hours. The Prime Minister went to the service for the victims and then visited the yacht club and *Morning Cloud*, his yacht which he had sent to Kiel to be there at the time of the games. I stayed in the hotel to do some drafting. Later that day after the Prime Minister and his party had returned to London the rest of us decided to visit *Morning Cloud*.

We found the crew on board. They invited us to look round. We went below and chatted. About the Prime Minister they said, 'He's no trouble. No trouble at all. Mind you, we wouldn't stay if he was. I mean we just do it for pleasure.'

I asked how they got on in races when the Prime Minister was not at the helm. They said it didn't make much difference. Sometimes they won. Sometimes they lost. 'Same as when he is on board ... but we never think of him as PM. He is just the skipper. He doesn't talk about work. Mind you, at the beginning he was inclined to be difficult about his tea. But now we hand him the mug and he just drinks it. No. He's no trouble.'

Subsequently I talked to Heath's old friend, Madron Seligman,[1] about the Prime Minister's interest in sailing. He does not sail for the sake of sailing. He just races. It was Seligman who introduced Heath to sailing. He had never been in a yacht before 1959 and did not start sailing seriously until 1965. I asked Madron why he was more successful than he, Madron, who had done it since he was a child. He said that Heath was more dedicated. He also had tremendous physical endurance and courage. I said, and Seligman did not disagree, that Heath likes to do

---

[1] Madron Seligman, was at Balliol with Heath where he shared his interests in politics and music. Conservative MEP for Sussex West 1979–1994. He has shown himself to be a man of many gifts and much good humour.

something that enables him to triumph over the elements and to prove himself to himself. He also likes the organisation involved and the fact that it keeps his mind off work. A doctor is said to have told him a few years ago that he must take up something that would distract him utterly from politics.

27 OCTOBER
BONN

―――

NEGOTIATING WITH THE RUSSIANS

In my absence in London for a meeting Reg Hibbert[1] has been conducting the British side of the Four Power negotiations on a quadripartite declaration. This is intended to reaffirm the continuing rights and responsibilities of the four victorious powers in Germany. He telephones me late in the evening to say that he must come round for a talk. There are urgent things to discuss as I have to attend a meeting with Egon Bahr[2] the following morning. He comes round and we talk until 1 a.m. One of the underlying problems of this whole negotiation is that Kissinger[3] appears to have done some deal with the Russians over the heads of the other powers. There is really little that we can usefully do round the negotiating table in trying to persuade the Russians to accept something when the American government has already reached an agreement with them bilaterally. This problem was to prove of increasing importance as the negotiations progressed in the following week.

At the end of the week we moved to Berlin for a quadripartite meeting and to give a lunch party for Prince Charles. With Germany divided, Berlin is theoretically under the control of the four occupying powers, the Soviet Union, the USA, France and the UK. Each of the last three has a diplomatic mission in West Berlin as well as in Bonn, and the Germans are most anxious that these should be kept going, whatever the cost to Berlin. They regard the retention of the Western missions at full strength in Berlin as a sign of continued commitment by the West to the independent status of Berlin and to its links with the West.

―――

[1]Reginald Hibbert, member of Diplomatic Service, Minister in the Embassy in Bonn 1972–5 where I had the benefit of his hard-headed advice. Ambassador to Paris 1979–82.

[2]Egon Bahr represented Federal government in Berlin 1969–72. Social Democratic Party (SPD) member of Bundestag 1972. Federal minister attached to the Federal Chancellor's office 1972–4.

[3]Henry Kissinger was at this stage Special Adviser on National Security to President Nixon who appointed him Secretary of State in September 1973.

The British Ambassador's house in Berlin is in the Grunewald and corresponds closely to the description of such a house, painted in Christopher Isherwood's novels of the thirties, where he used to teach English. Before the war the house belonged to the Ullstein[1] family. It is full of depressing furniture and decoration. Nothing much has been done to it for twenty-five years. It belongs to the British government so long as the occupation lasts. Mary intends to make it a showcase for British wallpaper – William Morris and Pugin.

The pattern of the negotiations has been similar each day as has been that of the social occasions. Meals with the Russians mean talk about the weather, chess, football and national characteristics. I ask Abrasimov[2] if there is any drink problem among the population in Russia, knowing perfectly well that there is; he says no, everybody in Russia is serving the state and happy to do so and does their duty and devotes their energies to the national cause. I ask him whether there are serious conflicts between the different republics of the Soviet Union, again aware of the acute nationality problem. He gives me the stock answer that there is no problem, that they are all happy to be citizens of the Soviet Union.

In one of the many lunches I had with Abrasimov I made a mistake. Leaning across the table, he said that there was a question he wished to put to me personally upon which he would be grateful for an answer. He wished to know how many racehorses I owned. He knew that 'Sir Soames',[3] who had been British Ambassador in Paris, owned a lot of horses. He was sure that I must do so too. I said truthfully that I owned no racehorses, a reply that clearly led me to lose caste in the Ambassador's eyes. Upon reflection I realised that I should have prevaricated and asked him in return for some revealing information about himself, his dacha and holidays.

The American Ambassador, Marty Hillenbrand,[4] a well-informed, clever, self-effacing man, who is very agreeable to deal with, appears to be under strange instructions, the result, I think, of the secret Kissinger–Russian deal. He hardly speaks at the quadripartite meetings, and at the

---

[1] Ullstein is a famous publishing firm in Germany. Gabby Annan, a member of the Ullstein family, and her husband, Noël, were staying with us in the house at this time. See diary entry of 5 April 1980 for note on Noël Annan.

[2] Pyotr Andreyevich Abrasimov, Soviet Ambassador to Poland, the German Democratic Republic, France and Japan. Order of Lenin (twice).

[3] Christopher Soames, Conservative MP 1950–66. Ambassador Paris 1968–72; Vice-President European Commission 1973–6. Governor of Southern Rhodesia 1979–80. Married Mary, daughter of Sir Winston Churchill.

[4] Martin Hillenbrand, US Diplomat. Ambassador to Hungary 1967–9. Ambassador to FRG 1972–6.

lengthy meals he conserves his energy. At the start of the talks when Reg Hibbert was representing us the Russian representative was inclined to single out the British as the least satisfactory of the negotiating partners and I am glad to say that he has not changed since my return. At the end of our last meeting Abrasimov said that he was pleased that the relations with his French colleague and the French government during the negotiations had been extremely good. They had also been good with the Americans. They were not so good with the British Ambassador but he hoped that they would be one day. Only with great forbearance did I refrain from thanking him for this bronze medal and from commiserating with the Americans and French for their silver and gold medals.

In the negotiations the French Ambassador adopts the tactic of saying that he wishes to address the Soviet representative on a personal basis. I find this odd because in dealing with the Russians I do not think there is much point in personal diplomacy, especially with Abrasimov who is clearly guided by strict instructions. There is nothing that can be said across the table that is going, by the brilliance of the advocacy or an appeal *ad hominem*, to persuade the Russians to be something against their will. Although I find the Frenchman's tactics odd I cannot say that he is difficult with his Western colleagues. He is rather proud of his languages and he is apt to speak in French or German or English interchangeably, and I must say he does speak them all extremely well.

At the first meeting that I attended the Soviet Ambassador, true to form, trotted out some Russian proverbs and I trotted some back, which were no less inventive than his. Later in the meeting he asked us for a dictionary of English quotations and I looked forward to hearing what it was that he was going to come out with, but he said nothing.

The lunch with Prince Charles went satisfactorily. Escorted by the British army he arrived on schedule and was taken upstairs to change from uniform into civilian clothes before coming down for a drink. We had been given elaborate instructions about the exact type of soft drink he likes before lunch. Needless to say he didn't then have this; he had something completely different. We had also been told of his likes and dislikes of food and that he hated hot rooms. So we had plenty of air in the dining-room, though later that day, when we had the reception at the Charlottenberg after dinner, it was incredibly hot and I noticed he moved from one room to another trying to find some air, not altogether successfully.

The function that night at the Charlottenberg was an ordeal. It began with a signing of the Golden Book ceremony, and speeches by the governing Mayor, and Prince Charles. He was then given a rifle with a telescopic sight. A reception was held after the dinner which, as I said, was conducted in tremendous heat. Prince Charles was introduced to various Berliners who were masquerading under such titles as the Honorary Consul of Uruguay or the Honorary Consul of Burma.

The next few days and nights were taken up with negotiations before flying off to Munich to visit the plant where the multi-role combat aircraft (MRCA) is being assembled, to meet the head of the German Secret Service and to preside at a dinner for Prince Philip.

The dual responsibility for Berlin and Bonn gave an extra spice to life in Germany. We frequently spent the week on the Rhine and then went to Berlin for the weekend where there was first-class theatre and music and a glittering night-life. Without much imagination it was possible to see Sally Bowles scurrying down the Kurfürstendamm. A grand party was given by the city of Berlin every New Year's Eve to which we were invited. One year we were in a group with a prominent businessman from the Ruhr. Handsome and self-confident, he boasted to me, as one after another beautiful woman, dressed, or half-dressed in the latest fashion, swept into the ballroom, that he would be able to get off with anybody he wished, and he asked me to single out whoever I chose for his attention. Whereupon, I pointed to someone of strikingly alluring appearance and told him that that was his challenge. He immediately made the approach which was not rejected. The two of them disappeared and I did not see them again the whole evening. It was the practice for all the guests at the party to assemble the following morning to have breakfast together. I waited for my friend from the Ruhr to join us, eager to find out how he had got on. He arrived looking haggard. He sat down, put his head in his hands and muttered, 'It was terrible. The worst evening of my life. Never again. Ugh.' I asked him what had happened. He looked up and said with a groan, 'It was a man.'

Regular air services connected the Federal Republic with Berlin. There was also a daily British train which trundled through East Germany with the blinds down at the insistence of the East German authorities. The train served an excellent English breakfast at 1945 prices. There was nothing economically viable about the train but it had symbolic significance, demonstrating the continuity of transport links between Berlin and the West.

IO NOVEMBER
BONN

THE GERMAN PRESIDENT VISITS THE QUEEN

President Heinemann has been on a visit to the UK, an official state visit at the invitation of the Queen. Accompanied by his suite he was asked to stay at Windsor Castle; Mary and I were invited to stay there too, and to attend on the President and Mrs Heinemann throughout their tour.

In my experience the opening phase is all-important and can set the tone of the entire official visit. The Heinemann party were treated on arrival to a glittering pageant at the Royal Pavilion, just below the castle, where they were greeted by the Queen and other members of the royal family, and by the Prime Minister and the Foreign Secretary in morning coats and by the Service Chiefs in full ceremonial dress.

To the sound of patriotic music seven carriages drew up, drawn by beautifully matched black and white horses. We climbed into them – the Queen and the President alone in the first carriage with an interpreter; Mary and I in the last accompanied by two members of the German party. We trotted off for a spectacular drive through the streets of Windsor. Looking back, this was, I think, the most amusing, certainly the most extraordinary, event for me of the whole visit because we seemed so enormous in these coaches with these vast horses, in the narrow, beautiful, old streets of Windsor, which were lined with crowds of people having a lovely time on a beautiful sunny autumn morning, there, I think, largely to see the royal family and the coaches, and little interested, I suspect, in the foreign guests. I gave a wave with the palm at the royal angle because for all they knew I was an important person and anyhow they waved at me so I waved back at them and was tickled to observe the children and the dogs, some of the latter barking, others just sitting and wagging their tails as we passed.

We trotted all the way up to the drive to Windsor Castle, quite a pull up. Several of the party commented to me what marvellous horses we had, so strong, so beautifully matched, so wonderfully disciplined – such as only the English could breed. I learned afterwards that they were nearly all German horses, as the Germans alone produce this particular horse which is half a carthorse.

On arrival at the castle we were met by Martin Charteris who showed

us to our room, a beautiful suite that we later discovered was used by
Princess Margaret and Lord Snowdon when they stay at Windsor. Mary
had an enormous bedroom with two beds. I had a comfortable room to
myself with bed, chest of drawers, dressing-table, desk, and writing
paper, a bowl of white peppermint creams, a glass jar of digestive biscuits,
a cornucopia of fruit, apples, bananas and grapes. There were decanters
of whisky, sherry, and gin; and bottles of many varieties of mineral water.
We had a large bathroom with the toilet delicately screened off. There
was a separate loo.

A valet was already in our suite when we arrived. His name was
revealed to me by a little notice on the dressing-table. Mary, meanwhile,
was being attended to by no less than two lady's maids and it was not
long before she was ringing the bell for a special hairdresser who was
also in attendance.

We made our way to one of the many drawing-rooms for drinks prior
to lunch. I should say that for this and the whole visit the most elaborate
plans and programmes were produced. In our rooms, for example, there
was a foolscap table plan of the lunch headed 'Luncheon Sitting List,
Tuesday, 24th October', showing the entrance, the windows and seven
tables with the places of everyone at the lunch party. To this was attached
an enormous sheet of paper headed Windsor Castle with a red crest on
it, giving the names of the fifty-nine people at the lunch arranged in
different categories. For the members of the British suite in attendance
and various members of the royal household, including the Palace
Steward, a memorandum from the Master of the Household, Brigadier
Sir Geoffrey Hardy-Roberts, was also supplied, headed with a red crest
and Buckingham Palace. The text of this memorandum gives some idea
of the detailed work that goes into arranging the programme of an
official visit. It was headed German State Visit, and read as follows:
'With reference to page 1, paragraph 7 of my Administrative Instructions
and the second paragraph on page 21 of the Lord Chamberlain's Office
Ceremonial, it has now been decided that the President of the Federal
Republic of Germany will present his Suite to the Queen and the Duke
of Edinburgh in the Green Drawing Room, *not* the White Drawing
Room.'

I am not quite sure to which administrative instructions this memorandum referred, but before we reached Windsor, several days before
the visit began, we all received a beautiful programme bound in blue
with a gold crest and gold lettering. This contained a brief itinerary
showing the main daily items followed by many pages indicating the
detail of the programme. Each day had a separate section of the programme which you could take out from the clip fasteners to use separately. Each moment of the day was clearly explained and defined and

delimited as to what you were meant to do, where and who with at every turn.

There were also elaborate alternative plans. For example, there was an alternative arrival plan that took seven foolscap thick pages headed Lord Chamberlain's Office, with the usual red crest. This gave plan one or plan two, depending upon delay in arrival, diversions to Gatwick, alternative motor car processions and also alternative arrangements at the Royal Pavilion in Windsor Park in the event of the ground there being waterlogged. Several members of the German suite who spoke extremely good English asked me what on earth the word waterlogged meant. This alternative arrival plan, which incidentally never needed putting into practice for us, had a distribution list of enormous length, as I presumed did all the administrative arrangements. I only mention this to show again the incredible detail, the elaborateness and trouble to which the people organising these programmes have to go. It is partly because every single possibility and snag is foreseen and everything is worked out that things run so smoothly. Contrary to widespread belief, I think the very tightness of the protocol really makes it work the more easily because everybody knows what they have to do and there is no struggling, no anxiety, no feeling that people are being left out.

There was another document which was rather less beautifully produced than the others but none the less interesting for that. It had the names of all the German party including the President himself and Frau Heinemann. In the left-hand column was the full name, thus His Excellency the President of the Federal Republic of Germany, Doctor Gustav Heinemann. In the second column was the suggested pronunciation of the name in English, so it put HY/NE/MANN (HY as in my). The third column gave an abbreviated form of names for use in conversation, i.e. Your Excellency or Mr President. A final, fourth column indicated linguistic ability. The President listing, for example, was given as 'very slight', as was Frau Heinemann's.

After Frau Heinemann on the list appeared His Excellency Herr Walter Scheel, Vice-Chancellor and Federal Minister for Foreign Affairs. The pronunciation of his name was given as SHALE (as in 'ale'). As for the German Ambassador to London, Karl-Gunther von Hase, we were told to pronounce his name like HARZE. Scheel's Private Secretary, Dr Harald Hofmann, Minister Counsellor, was ascribed a short 'o' as in *Tales of Hoffmann*. We were told to pronounce as KASPARY Herr Professor Doctor Fritz Caspari, Deputy Head of the Federal Presidency, and to express the first syllable 'a' as in cat. Dietrich Spangenberg, State Secretary, the Head of the Federal Presidency, had to be pronounced SCHPANG as in bang.

I wondered what the Germans themselves made of this guide to pronunciation if, as I imagined, it was included among the documents in everybody's rooms.

The afternoon programme included the exchange of presents, the presentation of addresses on behalf of the Royal County of Berkshire and the Royal Borough of Windsor and tea with the Queen Mother at Royal Lodge. The state banquet in the evening was held in St George's Hall.

I was sitting next to Sue Hussey[1] on one side and Mrs O'Sullivan, the wife of the Irish Ambassador, on my other side. Mary was sitting between the Irish Ambassador and Mr Harold Wilson, the Leader of the Opposition. Wilson made a good remark at the end of the dinner when a troop of pipers entered. He muttered, 'Here comes the deterrent.' I had an enjoyable time with Sue Hussey.

Before the state banquet we had been issued with another booklet giving details of the evening and the menu and wines to be served. One of the German party told me an amusing story that when Chancellor Adenauer had been to Buckingham Palace a number of years ago, the Queen had served him what she thought was rather a good Moselle and she had turned to him and said, 'Mr Chancellor, I hope you like this wine,' to which he had answered, 'No.' However he made up for this apparent discourtesy by sending a couple of cases of a wine that he thought was good. I heard later that the royal family considered it disgusting, more like syrup than wine.

At the banquet the orchestra of the Coldstream Guards played throughout. They began with a march, Old Comrades; then Mozart, Lehar, Schubert, more Léhar, followed by a Strauss waltz.

The Queen's bodyguard of the Yeomen of the Guard stood round the banqueting hall as we dined. On the table, which somebody told me was so large and so wide that people had to stand on it to iron the cloth, which they had been doing throughout the day, there was a display of porcelain. A card, one for each guest, recorded that the Royal Minton dessert service had been made for Her Majesty Queen Victoria; it had a turquoise border with panels of flowers and rich gilding and painted centres of the royal monograms, Crown VR Sèvres Style 1876. For the sweet course there would be the Tournai Dessert Service called the M. de Buffon after the great French naturalist, Comte de Buffon circa 1770–89. The glass we used was Royal Waterford Table Glass, George II, 1788.

The President, who has a good voice, made, I thought, an effective speech, both on this and on many other occasions. It struck the right

---

[1] Susan Hussey, Lady-in-Waiting to the Queen since 1960. Daughter of 12th Earl Waldegrave; married to Marmaduke Hussey.

note, both about his own country and about Britain. He said, for example: 'We admire Great Britain's creative power which has enabled it at all times to preserve traditional values and yet to perceive new developments and respond to them by reform. The German people consider themselves happy to count Great Britain among the partners with whom they can jointly tackle the tasks ahead of us in Europe.' The fact that we were about to enter the Common Market, which created a new relationship between us and Europe, was emphasised in speeches on both sides throughout the visit.

Afterwards in the Waterloo Chamber and the Grand Reception Room guests were introduced to the royal party. One member of the royal suite explained to me that they did not sit down because there was always a danger of getting stuck. But quite a large number of the household had lists of people, ten to twenty names, who were to be brought up and presented to the royals and to the members of the President's party. So there were quite a lot of busy-bees going about the room moving people from one place to another. There were also various people in uniform bearing long sticks like billiard cues. This excited the curiosity of the German party.

Official life began the next day at 10 a.m. with a reception by the President for Heads of Missions of the Diplomatic Corps. This was followed by a discussion on the environment, lunch at Hampton Court, a tour of Westminster Abbey and dinner at the Guildhall where there were several processions and speeches.

After the dinner we drove back to Windsor Castle. Following our long day it was like going home. When we arrived at about 11.15 p.m. we went upstairs, rather the worse for wear I thought, but to my surprise there were the Queen and Prince Philip and the rest of the royal family all in evening dress waiting to welcome the party back and give them nightcaps and show friendliness. I thought it an achievement that they should have done this, the sort of personal touch that the President and Frau Heinemann must have admired and appreciated.

At one moment during the visit I recalled how Roy Jenkins had told me of an incident when Adenauer came to the UK on an official visit. He went to Chequers where the Prime Minister, Harold Macmillan, went out of his way to show him round and make him feel at home. He pointed to the pictures, saying, 'Mr Chancellor, I am sure you would like to see this rather fine Rembrandt.' To which Adenauer replied, '*Das ist kein Rembrandt*'. Not daunted by this Macmillan went on and said, 'Chancellor, here is a Holbein which I am sure you would like to see.' '*Kein Holbein*', was Adenauer's only comment.

Most of the morning of the following day, Thursday, 26 October, was taken up with a service of the Most Honourable Order of the Bath at

Westminster Abbey at which the President was made an honorary member of the order.

In the afternoon the President was taken to visit the Palace of Westminster to have tea with the Speaker, Mr Selwyn Lloyd, and to call on Scotland Yard. The President, however saintly, was apparently particularly intrigued by the museum of horrors and by the exhibition of sawn-off shotguns. The President gave a dinner that night at the German Embassy. It was attended by the Queen, the Duke of Edinburgh, Princess Anne and members of the Cabinet and Opposition.

The programme ended with a flying visit to Scotland at the President's personal wish. In charge of the flight was the Captain of the Queen's Flight, Air Commodore Archibald Winskill. He is a person of great charm and radiant personality. Susan Hussey tells me confidentially that he is just the man for the job. He combines buffoonery with great and concealed expertise and devotion to duty. I noticed that he is well in tune with the customary pitch of royal banter. He and Sue Hussey chatted together, mostly matter-of-fact raillery. Once again I was impressed by the importance that everyone in the royal entourage seemed to attach to keeping well and truly down to earth.

The President visited John Knox's house. It was too small for all of us to enter so the rest of us went on to Edinburgh University where President Heinemann was to receive an honorary degree.

At lunch at the university I found myself sitting next to the wife of a senior economics don. I asked her how many students there are at the university. She told me. I asked her what proportion of these were foreigners and she said, 'Oh, about 40 per cent.' I expressed some surprise at the size of this number and asked where most of this 40 per cent of foreigners came from. 'Oh well, I suppose most of them come from England,' she said.

Mary and I had an agreeable flight back to Germany with the President's suite which gave me the chance of a chat with Caspari. He was a Rhodes scholar and he retains a house in England where his children are at school. He told me one or two rather amusing stories. We were talking about the problem in Adenauer's day arising from his resentment against the British because they sacked him from being Mayor of Cologne immediately after the war. Caspari admitted that this continued to rankle with Adenauer. On one occasion Johnnie Herwarth, who was German Ambassador in London in the fifties, returned on a visit to Bonn. He saw Adenauer who complained to him saying, you've become so British, why you even have your hair cut like an Englishman.' To which Herwarth made the rapid reply, 'It's not too easy to find German hairdressers in London.'

Caspari tells me that President Heinemann said to the Queen, at some stage at the end of the visit, how personally delighted and flattered he had been by the attention that the royal family had shown to him and Mrs Heinemann. He had told the Queen that he had found her quite unlike what he had expected. Apparently the Queen took this well though she was a bit mystified by it.

We had a *Kalte Aufschnitt* and some drinks on the plane and as we landed at Bonn everybody clapped as if giving vent to a sense of relief! There is a general feeling that the whole visit has been extremely successful which I think is true.

1973

HEATH VISITS GERMANY

10 MARCH

A backward glance may reveal the problems confronting an Embassy before the arrival of a VIP; and a brief account may also say something about the present state of relations between England and Germany and the situation in Western Europe generally, and perhaps give clues to the personality of the Prime Minister and of Chancellor Brandt.

A great deal of preparation went on in all spheres, that is to say over what the two men were going to talk about, what the Prime Minister wanted to get out of it, and the public relations side. In the Embassy we applied a good deal of thought to how to put the Prime Minister across to public opinion in advance of his arrival. The Prime Minister had indicated that he wanted to see some of the churches in the south of Germany. We took this up and it became, before long, an important, and not the least difficult, feature of our preparations.

I went to London about three or four weeks beforehand to take part in a meeting of John Hunt's[1] committee of Permanent Under-Secretaries, known as the European Unit, the main item on the agenda of which was the preparation for the Prime Minister's visit. It was not an encouraging meeting. I found that the top civil servants in Whitehall were hardly enthusiastic about Europe. John Hunt himself said that he found himself invariably facing a row of hard-headed anti-Europeans. It was made the

---

[1] John Hunt was the very model of a modern civil servant. In the Cabinet Office and the Treasury 1960–79; he was Secretary to the Cabinet 1973–9. His smiling countenance belies strong convictions including his long-held belief that the UK has to become a whole-hearted member of the European Community.

more unsatisfactory because Derek Mitchell,[1] who should have been representing the Treasury, had had to fly to Bonn that morning to deal with a currency crisis – with the problem of the rising Deutschmark following the flood of dollars into Germany, a subject that came to dominate not only the preparations, but the visit itself.

I attended several meetings with the Federal government, including the Chancellor himself, about the visit and our shared intention to build it up into an extremely important event. It was to set the tone for the way in which two of the largest members of the Community hoped that the Community would decide upon its main policies, as well as to enable a bilateral discussion to take place of the substance of those policies.

There was considerable advance publicity. The Prime Minister gave an interview to *Spiegel*; and German television broadcast a long programme about the Prime Minister's life. The Chancellor briefed the British press two days before the visit, with, as I shall show, somewhat disastrous results; and the Federal government spokesman also briefed some of the political correspondents in Bonn in the week before the Prime Minister's arrival. The press of both countries dilated on the great significance of the visit and what the two men would talk about.

The impending visit also had an impact on our own lives in the house. From the moment of our arrival here last summer Mary had wanted to do all sorts of redecorating but it had been going slowly and we found that it was handy to be able to invoke the Prime Minister's visit as a means of spurring on the Department of the Environment to install wallpapers and have long-overdue painting carried out before the Prime Minister's arrival. We kept saying, which was in fact true, that the Prime Minister was extremely observant and choosy about the way Embassies looked and that, if things didn't appear adequately representational and an honour to Britain, there would be a good deal of hell to pay. Under this threat I secured the erection of a greenhouse in place of the broken-down structure beside the house – an innovation that over subsequent years has cast not shadows, but sunlight, upon the Embassy, providing them annually with an abundance of grapes.

Many administrative arrangements had to be made. Two of the rooms downstairs on the ground floor – the small sitting-room and the winter garden – had to be turned into offices; additional desks, extra telephones and copying machines and several enormous typewriters installed.

We worked out with the Germans the details of the social side of the

---

[1] Derek Mitchell at this stage of his career was Second Permanent Secretary (Overseas Finance) Treasury, having previously been Principal Private Secretary to the Chancellor of the Exchequer 1962–3 and to the Prime Minister 1964–6; and Deputy Under-Secretary of State, of Economic Affairs 1966–7 and Economic Minister in Washington 1969–72.

programme. Who was to give a meal to whom and when. We even got down to the *places à table*: who would sit next to the Chancellor and the Prime Minister at the two meals. It was agreed that the Chancellor would give a dinner the first night at Schloss Gymnich where the initial meeting was to take place and the Prime Minister would give a lunch in the Embassy the following day.

The reason why the Chancellor decided to receive the Prime Minister and to have the first meeting at Schloss Gymnich was because 1 March, the day of his arrival, was the festival of Weiberfastnacht, when the women of the Rhineland are accustomed to getting their own back on the opposite sex by cutting off the ends of their ties. Herr Brandt may have been worried about the attentions they might pay to Mr Heath and his neckwear were he to arrive in Bonn. It was therefore arranged that the Prime Minister and his party would be flown by helicopter from the Cologne airfield to Schloss Gymnich, which is a fifteen-minute flight, and that a dinner party would be given by Brandt after the first meeting which would be held *unter vier Augen* (i.e. confined to four eyes). As things turned out many people cried off at the last moment from Brandt's dinner, as they did from the Prime Minister's lunch the following day – a practice to which we had to become inured during our time in Bonn.

It was a stroke of luck that among the guests invited to Heath's lunch was the acting head of the Bundesbank, Emminger, a man who had much impressed me when I had visited him earlier in Frankfurt, by the clarity of his mind and his readiness to express it. We could not have foreseen that because of the financial crisis that blew up Emminger was to emerge as the key figure at the time of the Prime Minister's visit. Schilling, the Chancellor's Secretary, asked sardonically how on earth we could have known that there was going to be a crisis requiring Emminger's presence. The Germans had not invited him or anybody else from the Bundesbank to the Chancellor's dinner.

I have mentioned that during the briefing meeting in London Derek Mitchell had been away because of a financial crisis. This had, to all appearances, been resolved by about the middle of February, but then, suddenly, just before the Prime Minister was due to arrive in Bonn, the same old story started up again, of people selling dollars and buying Deutschmarks. The flow of money into Germany became much greater on the Wednesday, the day before the Prime Minister was due to arrive, and it reached a crescendo on the morning of the day of his arrival, 1 March, presumably on account of speculation about exchange-rate changes. At the press briefing given by Brandt shortly before Heath's arrival he had spoken of the need for the Community to reach some lasting way of handling the monetary problem. He had given the impression that there was an acute problem for which there had to be new solutions. This had the effect of undermining confidence in the dollar.

This financial crisis also impinged on the planning for the Prime Minister's visit to southern Germany. We realised that it might look bad if the Prime Minister was gallivanting about in Bavaria when the British housewife was in difficulties securing the fuel to cook her Sunday joint. However, by the morning of Thursday, 1 March, the situation was no worse and Tom Bridges,[1] with whom I had been in frequent telephonic contact at Number 10, said, 'Well, we are coming.'

As we waited on the tarmac at Cologne airport for the Prime Minister to arrive, figures kept being handed to us on little slips of paper about the amount of money that the Bundesbank had been taking in. We were assured that the Prime Minister's party were being given the same information.

Heath arrived looking his usual sunburnt self and came down the stairs of the Comet on to the red carpet. After introductions he made for the two helicopters that were to fly the party to Schloss Gymnich. The atmosphere was still sufficiently unaffected by the overhanging currency crisis for Max Podewils, the Head of German Protocol, to suggest that we might do a detour and fly round Cologne Cathedral. The Prime Minister was delighted at the idea which proved to be the last and only non-political event of the visit.

We descended vertically at the Schloss to be greeted by the Chancellor and his entourage. Only at this stage did I catch sight of Derek Mitchell who was by now playing such a key part at the Treasury. I had known him years ago when he was Private Secretary at Number 10 and when I was Private Secretary at the Foreign Office. He had been included in the party at the last moment because of the evident intention of the Chancellor to lay so much stress on monetary matters. I said to him that the Germans wanted us to join a float to which he replied that that was all very well but that they would not be prepared, he thought, to give us the financial backing that we needed. The Federal government could make all sorts of optimistic statements about this but he knew from Emminger that in fact the banking authorities were not ready to give sterling the support it would need, according to the British authorities, if we were to enter a joint float.

At the castle the Prime Minister and Brandt went immediately into a

---

[1] Tom Bridges, member of Diplomatic Service. Private Secretary to the Prime Minister 1972–4. Minister (Commercial), Washington 1976–9; Ambassador to Italy 1983–7. An impeccable public servant with an irrepressible sense of humour, made the more infectious by his usually solemn expression, he was not without worldly wisdom. Asked for his view on how a young member of the public service could best advance his career he replied that he should do a good draft for his superior who could sign it with pride as if it were his own.

huddle, accompanied only by the latter's Private Secretary and Robert Armstrong.[1] A crowd of pressmen and photographers filled the outer rooms. Members of the two delegations occupied a room nearby where we were served tea. The party included von Wechmar, the FRG spokesman, and his opposite number on our side, Donald Maitland. Christopher Audland, the Head of Chancery in Bonn and, of course, Derek Mitchell, were also with us.

It was revealed quite soon, somewhat to our surprise, that a meeting of a committee of the German Cabinet was going to be held that evening at Schloss Gymnich. This would mean a curtailment of the Prime Minister's talk with the Chancellor. As we sipped our tea and ate little cakes people started to come into the room. Obviously they were not press people, but who were they? Several were wearing polo-neck sweaters. I did not know their identity but doubted whether, dressed like this, they could be members of the Cabinet committee. How wrong I was. They had indeed arrived at the castle for the meeting and were wearing polo-neck sweaters because they were afraid of losing their ties to the female surgeons of Weiberfastnacht. Their appearance gave a musical comedy air to the proceedings which had hitherto been solemn. Among those who arrived I spotted Karl Otto Pöhl, State Secretary in the Ministry of Finance, deputising for Helmut Schmidt who was still in hospital. Pöhl was meant to be on leave but he had been hauled back from Zermatt where he had been on a skiing holiday. He was sunburnt and relaxed and wearing tweeds. We, the British delegation, provided a reception committee for these high-level Germans. Light-heartedly we suggested that perhaps what was needed was a joint German–British Cabinet meeting. Such a gathering might indeed be able to make real progress towards a European union.

When the time arrived for the meeting of the German Cabinet committee the Prime Minister went up to his room where the rest of us joined him. We seized a bottle of whisky and discussed what the Chancellor had been saying. He had apparently been taking the line that there must be some European solution to this problem but he had not indicated the way it might be reached that would be acceptable to the British if, as he wanted, we were to join the European float.

At dinner the Prime Minister was seated between Frau Vocke, the Minister in Brandt's office, and the Chancellor. Mary sat on the Chancellor's left; Egon Bahr was on her other side. I was opposite the

---

[1] Robert Armstrong, who at this time was Principal Private Secretary to the Prime Minister. Later Secretary of the Cabinet and Head of the Home Civil Service. Music is his *violon d'Ingres*; he has been a dedicated public servant whom Roy Jenkins has described as having 'a Rolls-Royce mind'.

Chancellor and had Frau Bahr on my right and Frau Annemarie Renger, the Speaker of the Bundestag, on my left. We had a good dinner and excellent wine. The atmosphere was agreeable. The room was beautifully decorated and the service excellent. I leant across the table and got the conversation with the Chancellor round to the Middle East. He had just seen a deputy minister from the Egyptian government and gave his views on the Federal government's policy towards the Middle East. He said that the Federal government, however much it might like, for reasons for instances of oil, or generally in pursuit of its foreign policy, to play more of a role in the Middle East, just could not afford to do so. The Germans could never, in view of their recent past, get into a remotely anti-Jewish position. They must play a purely intermediary role without however being prepared to become mediators.

I had an agreeable time at dinner talking to Frau Annemarie Renger and Frau Bahr. Mary, meanwhile, was getting on like a house on fire with both the Chancellor and Egon Bahr. She said afterwards that she found them very easy and charming to talk to.

Then the Chancellor got up and tapped his glass, produced a few sheets of paper from his pocket, and, as is his practice, read out his speech without giving it much feeling. He then gave a toast to the Queen. The Prime Minister rose and also began by reading a speech which had been written out for him. It contained a reference to the Chancellor as the President which was not too happy. When he had finished reading he put the text down and started to speak impromptu with his two hands held out at his sides. He said that we were now at a crucial stage in Europe where key decisions had to be made. He recalled how in 1940 Churchill had offered the French joint citizenship, which had been an act of vision. If Churchill had asked a lot of clever, wise and experienced advisers about it before doing so they would no doubt have found all sorts of reasons why it was inexpedient, impractical and ought not to be suggested. However he had gone ahead with it and it had had an important effect. Likewise, the Prime Minister said, he thought that this was a moment in which a financial crisis was hanging over us when it was time for big decisions without too much heed to the detail. He made an amusing aside to say that he had noticed a certain note of anxiety, not to say terror, in the eyes of a few of his officials sitting around him, but nevertheless this was what he thought. The impact of this impromptu appeal to vision was considerable and he sat down to loud applause. I feel sure that the way he had spoken helped greatly to create the favourable atmosphere in which the meeting took place after dinner between the two heads of government.

At this meeting, so it was reported to me, Pöhl took an extremely forthcoming line saying that he was sure that the German government could give sterling all the backing it needed. It would be prepared to carry responsibility for the sterling reserves and would undertake any steps necessary to prevent a flight from sterling. All this would be done without any limit, without any condition, without any payment and without any interest. Brandt had apparently shown no hesitations or wish to disagree with what Pöhl had said. No wonder then that when we left the Schloss and returned to the Embassy the British party were in a state of euphoria.

We sat around in the drawing-room downstairs with whiskies, the party then comprising the Prime Minister, Robert Armstrong, Tom Bridges, John Hunt, John Robinson[1] and myself. The main thought was that it would be necessary to get the German side to indicate categorically that they were prepared to go as far as this. We could then tell the British Chancellor of the Exchequer about this because it was suggested that there should be a meeting of the Finance Ministers of the whole Community the following weekend.

At about 1 a.m. the Prime Minister said that he was going off to bed. The rest of us were left to draft telegrams to London reporting what had happened and how we proposed to handle the situation the following day. The secretaries at Number 10 were their usual uncomplaining selves, taking everything down and incorporating it in telegrams which were then sent off. We went to bed at about 4 a.m.

The next morning the house was busy early. The hall downstairs, as is always the case during these high-level visits, was full of people going to and fro or hanging about waiting for something to happen. There was plenty for them to look at in the way of flowers and decoration; and Zorba[2] was inclined to turn up from time to time as if part of the team. The Prime Minister's Private Office had been established in the downstairs drawing-room and in the conservatory. I made sure that they were plied frequently with coffee and that they had a permanent tray of drinks on hand as well as flowers. They seemed quite happy though were much looking forward to getting away and seeing something of Germany as part of the Prime Minister's sightseeing team. Alas, this was not to be.

The PM and I set off in the Rolls at about 9.30 a.m. for the Chancellor's office. We were preceded by the customary group of white mice on motorcycles and a police car. The purpose was for the two heads of government to sign a document on the Anglo-German Foundation, an

[1] John Robinson, member of Diplomatic Service, was the key Foreign Office official in negotiations on British entry to the European Community. Ambassador to Algiers 1974–7. Minister, Washington 1977–80. Ambassador to Israel 1980–1.
[2] Zorba, my dalmatian, who had been with us in Spain and Poland where he won the Warsaw Dog Show. He was to accompany us to Paris after Bonn.

organisation designed to help promote industrial relations between the two countries. After this had taken place the bilateral talks were resumed. The discussion touched on the conference on security and co-operation in Europe at Helsinki, the Mutual Balanced Force Reduction talks in Vienna, East–West relations generally, the Middle East and oil. Pöhl then joined. The Chancellor immediately called upon him to say what was the latest state of play about discussions with Brussels and the idea of a meeting of Finance Ministers over the weekend. Pöhl spoke with great authority. He seemed a dashing fellow, not at all overawed by the occasion or by the absence of his minister. On the contrary he seemed to be enjoying himself, to be very relaxed and to have distinctive ideas of his own, without, however, being at all boastful. I thought that he played a most interesting and fascinating role. John Hunt said afterwards that there was nothing like a bit of illness to help someone along.

I did not attend the final round on finance later that afternoon but I was led to believe that the rats had got at Pöhl's forward proposals of the night before and that qualifications were already being made about the extent to which the Germans could help. Perhaps Schmidt, who, although in hospital, was still as it were in operation, had entered caveats. He also had undertaken to attend the Finance Ministers meeting in Brussels. So the outcome on the financial side was better than it had looked before the Prime Minister's visit from the point of view of a joint European solution involving considerable German help to prop up sterling, but nothing like as wonderful as it had looked late on the first evening.

The financial situation had, however, totally stultified the whole purpose of the heads of government meeting because, far from being able to devote themselves to the future of Europe or how to give Europe a new dimension to bring about European union in the next few years, they had really been so held down by the present crisis that they had not been able to lift their eyes to the distant horizon at all. The elaborate briefings for the Prime Minister on what to say about regional policy, how to deal with the need for a better relationship between the Community and the United States of America, or how to create and then conduct a policy towards the Mediterranean – none of these subjects had been dealt with except in the most cursory way and then only in the margin of the financial problem. The meeting could not therefore be said to have succeeded in its original purpose.

The entire sightseeing trip to Bavaria had to be cancelled as Heath had to return to London to deal with the forthcoming meeting of Community Finance Ministers.

1974

CALLAGHAN WEEK[1]

---

24 MARCH
BONN

This has been Callaghan's week for me. The problems inherent for officials when they have to adapt themselves to a new government have been rendered even greater than usual by the arrival in power of a party bent on reversing the foreign policy of its predecessor. Heath's government made Europe the focus of its foreign policy. This in itself had been something of an innovation given the traditional blue water tinge of our diplomacy. It did more than change course. It took the lead, or at any rate, Heath did, in stressing the need to create a European union governing all aspects of relations. As the summit meeting in 1972 Heath, Pompidou and Brandt declared that this union was to be achieved by 1980. Now, only two years after this resounding declaration, the new Labour government has made it clear, through the mouth of their Foreign Minister, Callaghan, that it does not accept this concept of union at all. Indeed it will only accept the customs union and common agricultural market aspects of the Community; and it will only accept these if the terms for Britain's membership are renegotiated to give Britain more financial benefit.

Callaghan has left no doubt of his agnosticism about the idea of union if this means going beyond the limited economic sphere which I have defined above. Agnosticism is his own description. He has said that he intends to pursue a more traditional type of British diplomacy. He has told the Office that 'he wishes to put more muscle into the United Nations'; he attaches great importance to the Atlantic Alliance and he wishes to have closer relations with the Commonwealth. He favours global rather than regional solutions, and America is, of course, vital to any global approach. Europe comes after this and the policy towards it is to 'renegotiate British entry to the EEC in keeping with the Labour Party's manifesto'. He takes it for granted that we officials know that it is our duty to implement the manifesto and nothing but the manifesto. He has indicated that he expects to find support from the fellow socialist government of the Federal Republic of Germany. He recognises that he

---

[1] Following the general election in February 1974 in which Heath failed to win a majority, Harold Wilson became Prime Minister on 4 March as head of a minority government. Callaghan was Foreign Secretary.

may have difficulties with France. His hope is that the outcome will be an agreement that will enable Britain to stay in the EEC.

Heath's decision to throw in our lot with, and indeed help to lead, Europe was widely welcomed on the Continent. It fitted in with the conviction, common amongst most modern European leaders, that if Europe is to stop tearing itself apart and to play the role and exert the influence on the world stage that its talents and tradition deserve, this can only come about if the countries join closely together in all aspects of life, political and economic. The new government's complete reversal of this policy looks like causing concern to our continental neighbours. I think that many of the leading members of the British Cabinet are unaware of this, or would scarcely care even if they were aware. Peter Shore, for instance, the Secretary of State for Trade, does not conceal his intention to work for withdrawal from the EEC by negotiation.

A problem of credibility is posed for those who represent Britain abroad in present circumstances. Over the past three years our duty has been to spread the gospel of Europe and the UK's whole-hearted dedication to it. Now we have to preach the opposite. A diplomatic colleague has suggested that there ought to be a special psychological disturbance allowance payable to representatives abroad on such seismic occasions. Callaghan told Brimelow,[1] who has communicated it to FCO officials at home and abroad, that he does not want what he describes as 'zealotry' over Europe. When later I discussed this ukase with Norman Statham, the Economic Minister in the Bonn Embassy, he recounted how he had been involved with the abortive entry negotiations under George Brown in 1967. George Brown, an enthusiastic pro-European, had been in the habit of peering at the faces of people assembled for meetings in his room at the Office. He would point at one or two of them, saying, 'Your trouble is that you don't have enough zeal for Europe.' Apparently he, Statham, and Con O'Neill[2] had been singled out from time to time for such censure, unfairly they thought.

Many Labour ministers, including, I think, Callaghan, are determined to assert their authority right from the outset. It has not taken much perception for them to realise that members of the Foreign Service are convinced that Britain would not count for much in the world or provide a comprehensive framework in which its citizens can fulfil all their talents

---

[1] Tom Brimelow, Permanent Under-Secretary at the FCO from which he retired in 1975. A highly respected Soviet specialist. In Warsaw where I succeeded him as Ambassador he had applied the same thoroughness to making a beautiful garden as to mastering the political scene.   .

[2] Con O'Neill, a distinguished but intermittent member of the Diplomatic Service since 1936, his career interrupted by service in the army and journalism. Ambassador to Finland 1961–3, to EEC 1963–5. Leader of British delegation to negotiate entry to EEC 1970–2.

if it remains an offshore island without participation in Europe. I find myself recollecting often about the events of 1964 when Wilson's government took over from the Conservatives. What happened then was that officials bent over backwards to adjust themselves to their new masters, even to the extent of refraining from saying things which they feared, if they said them, might have given the impression of trying to dictate policy even though such a course would have enabled the government to avoid committing mistakes, at any rate of tactics. I am thinking in particular of the way the Wilson government announced an import surcharge immediately on assuming office. This excited much hostility abroad and was counter-productive. Better results could have been achieved by a different method of going about it. Governments, of course, have the right to introduce new policies and the Civil Service has the duty to implement them but officials have the obligation to draw ministers' attention to the likely consequences of their acts and to advise on the manner in which the government's aims are most likely to be achieved. At any rate, this applies certainly to foreign policy.

When they came to power in 1964 Labour leaders had much faith in socialist solidarity. They were convinced that the socialist governments of Scandinavia would rally behind them. But when they clapped on the import charge that I have just mentioned they quickly found that this was not so. The Labour governments of Europe were among their strongest critics. Now, in 1974, I found that Callaghan, who is chairman of the Labour Party, is confident that he can rely on support from Brandt's government because of its similar ideology. Personally I am sure that while there will no doubt be sympathetic noises there will be no governmental backing from Bonn that goes beyond what the Germans conceive to be their national interest, something that will be assessed by a coalition in which the FDP holds the Foreign Ministry.

My Callaghan week began on Tuesday when I flew to London for a meeting the following day for Heads of Missions from EEC countries. The man who drove me from London airport was depressed about the general situation at home. I asked him what worried him in particular. 'Well,' he said, 'you wouldn't mind if it was an increase of 1p but when there's an increase of 2p or even 3p on a pound of dog biscuits it really does make things difficult.' Later, when I was trying on a new suit, the tailor said that the coal strike had frightened Americans away from London because they were worried that they would find it too cold there. He also thought that 'many gentlemen from Europe who used to come to London for their clothes no longer do so.'

The next day I found little of the light-heartedness and banter that usually punctuate Office meetings. A senior official counselled us to avoid appearing hostile towards the new government's foreign policy. It would be premature to tell them what the consequences would be of pulling out of the Community or to try to explain the possible political development of the Community.

Callaghan explained that the Labour Party manifesto was the guiding light of the government's foreign policy. It had only been cobbled together with difficulty. He would be renegotiating our terms in accordance with the manifesto. 'If they don't like it, they will have to think about it, won't they?' (I was to hear this phrase several times in the course of the next few days.) Callaghan said that he did not have much experience of diplomacy but he had plenty of experience of trade union negotiations and he would apply the same principles. What mattered there was to toughen up in the last fifteen minutes. This predilection for last-minute toughening up was also expressed several times in the next day or two. At a meeting for the British press held in the FCO later in the same morning, the Secretary of State said that those of his audience who had played rugby football would know of the importance of the last fifteen minutes of the game. The Welsh rugby team was careful always to pace itself throughout the match so as to be able to be at their toughest in the last quarter of an hour. Callaghan, I know, has always been a great believer in pacing himself.

Speaking to us representatives from abroad Callaghan said he wanted us to know that the government were not '*demandeurs*'. He thought that that was the word that people used when they were acting from a position of weakness – which did not apply to the Labour government. If the subject of staying in the Community or not were put to the British public today they would vote for withdrawal. But he was not negotiating to withdraw. It depended what new terms were reached and what the club looked like at the end of the day. There was everything to play for. He quoted Groucho Marx's saying about the sort of club to which he would not wish to belong but there was not much mirth amongst those worldly people seated around the mahogany table in that fine old conference room of the India Office, beset with trophies of past glories.

On his negotiating tactics Callaghan said that he believed in telling the truth. He had a bad memory which is why he believed in telling the truth – again a phrase to be repeated several times in the next forty-eight hours.

The Secretary of State went on to say that on renegotiating he would keep his objectives clear. But he would leave a way out for the other side. More flies were caught by honey than by vinegar. He said that his policy would amount to a return to a more traditional and pragmatic British policy. The timetable had to be related to the next election. September 1974 might be too soon for the renegotiations to have been completed. He was thinking more of the end of the year.

Someone else asked what he meant by renegotiation. He replied that he did not know enough about it yet but he thought that there would have to be structural changes. He did not see how there were going to be fundamental renegotiations without changing the Treaty of Accession. To this Michael Palliser[1] reacted by saying that he hoped we would not try to reopen the treaty which would require unanimous agreement. We should be able to improve our terms of membership, particularly as regards our budget contribution, without renegotiating the treaty.

The British representatives from Community capitals gave their views to different ministers on the likely reaction of European governments to the new British government's stance on Europe. What they had to say was not popular and they tended to be treated like the message-bearers of bad news in ancient times who were held responsible for them. Ministers left us in no doubt that their colleagues in the Cabinet would expect them to show resistance to the élitist, pro-European attitudes of the Foreign Office.

I returned to Bonn early the next day so as to be ready for Callaghan on his arrival. This was to be his first visit abroad since becoming Foreign Secretary.

We dined that night as Scheel's[2] guests. Apel[3] and Frank[4] were there, as well as leading officials from the Auswärtiges Amt. Scheel sat opposite Callaghan. I was on Scheel's right. The dinner passed off pleasantly enough with badinage and joking as is Scheel's style.

Scheel made a speech, friendly in manner and substance. Callaghan replied, so far as I could tell without much preparation. It is the sort of thing he does excellently, with humanity and humour. I began to think that all was going to go well with the visit right up to the end. However, as soon as dinner was over and we moved elsewhere for a discussion my optimism was rudely dashed.

We were seated in armchairs. Coffee, liqueurs and cigars circulated. Callaghan raised the problem of machinery of consultation between Europe and the USA. This has become acute since the end of last year, largely owing to the 'adversary relationship' between Kissinger and Jobert[5] (to use Kissinger's phrase to describe the attitude he fears that

---

[1] Michael Palliser at this stage in his career in the Diplomatic Service was Ambassador and UK Permanent Representative to the European Communities. The following year he became Permanent Under-Secretary of State, FCO and Head of the Diplomatic Service.
[2] Walter Scheel, Free Democratic Party (FDP) member of the Bundestag 1953–74; Vice-Chancellor and Foreign Minister 1969–74; President of the Federal Republic 1974–9.
[3] Hans Apel, Social Democratic Party (SPD), member of the Bundestag. Parliamentary Secretary of State, Ministry of Foreign Affairs 1972–4; Minister of Finance 1974–8; Minister of Defence 1978–82.
[4] Paul Frank, official of the German Foreign Office.
[5] Michel Jobert; French politician. Secretary-General of the Presidency 1969–73; Minister of

the French are trying to make the EEC adopt vis-à-vis the USA). There is little difference between Bonn and the new London government on the importance of the US Alliance. This part of the discussion therefore was amicable, if inconclusive. It was when we got on to the EEC questions and the British government's attitude to Europe that the atmosphere deteriorated. Callaghan showed that he had little belief in the idea of political union. He insisted that there must be a thorough renegotiation. The touchstone was what would please the British housewife.

Scheel hardly spoke. Apel made one moderately critical intervention. Most of those present gave the impression of having been hit on the head, which they had been in a way.

The next afternoon a briefing was given by the Foreign Ministry to the representatives of Community countries in Bonn. The German side had been left very pensive by the Callaghan visit. They had known that the Community were in for a difficult time. They had not, however, realised quite how difficult it was going to be.

I heard from other sources how disturbed the Germans had been by Callaghan's performance that evening. There was even some discussion of asking von Hase[1] to call at the FCO and make this clear. Von der Gablentz[2] told me that he had proposed this and had discussed it with Van Well. Typically it had not materialised, the German Foreign Ministry's policy being to avoid a collision course with everyone. This is partly because of concern about their past. They are not prepared to risk doing anything that might cause others to say that the Germans are throwing their weight about. The result is that they try to placate everyone and exert far less influence than their true power and wealth would justify.

On the drive to the airport for his departure Callaghan said that he thought his visit to Bonn had not made things worse. With sycophantic expediency, I agreed; but I went on to say that I hoped he would not mind if I referred to a problem. He was wanting to get something out of the Germans – and the other members of the Community. This related, for example, to agricultural prices and budgetary contributions. If we wanted to win support it would help if we showed that we understood what mattered to the other members of the club. For the Germans – and others – this was the political aspect. To them the idea of working towards European integration was highly important. I knew the difficulties in

Foreign Affairs 1973–4. See also diary entry 13–16 March 1975 on his friendship with Edward Heath.

[1]Karl-Günther von Hase, German Ambassador to London 1970–7 where he made a lasting impact.

[2]Otto von der Gablentz, joined Foreign Service of Federal Republic 1959. Department of European Political Co-operation 1973–8. Later Ambassador to the Netherlands and Israel.

the Labour Party and the Secretary of State's own scepticism, but we would make it much easier for the Germans to accept our particular needs if we could show some comprehension of their concept of Europe. Otherwise it looked to them as though we were trying to get the rules of the club changed to suit our convenience while continuing to say that we thought it was a lousy club and that we did not want it to develop.

Callaghan reacted brusquely. He did not believe that the German leaders attached any importance to the European idea I had been talking about. After all, neither Brandt nor Scheel had spoken in these terms to him. NATO existed and we could always have bilateral contacts with the German government. What more was wanted? He apologised for being rude to me and for the abrupt way he had spoken.

I continued by talking about the division of Germany and the newness of German political institutions compared with ours. The Germans had to belong to something and their people must be made to feel that they had some new identity now that their nation state had been divided. The European Community provided this. It was also a political lightning conductor against extremism or temptations to pursue adventurous policies in the east.

The Secretary of State said that he would think about it. But I must also understand the political position at home. We went on to talk about Eastern Europe. Callaghan said that he was interested in doing more there. He thought that the Tories might have had a blind spot about Eastern Europe, just as I thought he had a blind spot about Western Europe.

Finally I produced the emotive card of Ernest Bevin's name, recounting how Bevin had supported and even inspired the concepts of the Marshall Plan and NATO without knowing in detail how they would work out or what exactly they would achieve. I suggested that that sort of vision was needed in Western Europe now. Callaghan repeated the word vision without animosity as if to say that that was a good idea.

The following weekend I was in Edinburgh for the Königswinter Conference.[1] Speaking to several pro-European Labour politicians I was aware how worried they were. As if to console themselves they were persuaded that Callaghan would become so infuriated by the extreme

---

[1] Anglo-German conferences, attended by politicians, journalists and diplomats, had been held annually since 1950 when they were instigated by a remarkable German woman, Lilo Milchsack, the wife of a Düsseldorf barge-owner. They were held originally in the small Rhineland town of Königswinter. The idea had been to instruct the Germans, who were then threadbare, economically and politically, in the ways of democracy. By the time of this entry the Federal Republic had outstripped the UK economically, and they needed few lessons from London in how to run a democratic society or market economy. Nevertheless the conferences have continued, meeting alternately in the UK and Germany.

anti-Marketeers that he would be driven to defending his position as
Foreign Secretary and thence to defending the cause of Europe.

II JUNE
BONN

———

WILSON WEEK

Well, if last time it was Callaghan week I was writing about, now it is
certainly Wilson week. I went to London a few days ago to attend a
meeting called to take stock of how we are getting on in our effort to
renegotiate the terms of our membership of the Community and to
prepare for the Prime Minister's visit to Bonn to see the Chancellor,
Helmut Schmidt.[1] He would begin by attending the Scotland-Brazil
football match in Frankfurt and then come on to see the Chancellor in
his office.

Michael Palliser spoke strongly about the extent to which Britain was
now regarded as an unreliable partner in Europe. Our unconcerned
readiness to tear up our treaty commitment to the Community merely
to meet the internal political problems of the Labour Party had produced
a profound shock.

We, representatives from abroad, received an unpleasant warning
about our reporting; this amounted to being told that we must temper
our reporting on how London's new policy looked from the European
capitals so as to avoid giving offence to our present political masters. We
must not give the impression of being too pro-European. It was for
ministers to decide policy. I bridled at what seemed to me to be a form
of suppression upon which I was given a personal reprimand about being
too outspoken in what I said to ministers and too pro-European.

Then I flew to Berlin for the night where we were entertaining Peter
Hall[2] who was giving the annual Queen's Lecture. We gave the usual
sort of Berlin buffet lunch – a mixture of military government personnel
and journalists with one or two people from the theatre included. After
the lecture we took Peter Hall to dinner at Boubou in the Kurfürstendamm and from there home for a prolonged theatrical gossip.

---

[1]Helmut Schmidt, Social Defence Democratic member of the Bundestag since 1953. Minister
of Defence 1969–72. Succeeded Brandt as Chancellor 1974–82.
[2]Peter Hall, theatre director who, after thirteen years running the Royal Shakespeare Company,
had become Director of the National Theatre in 1973 and was Artistic Director of the
Glyndebourne Festival 1984–90.

Early the next morning the RAF flew us to Kiel for the Kieler Woche – very comfortable VIP service on board with weather charts and a large breakfast. A day's sailing with the British Kiel yacht club in the Baltic confirmed the previous view I had formed of the uninvitingness of that sea: the water cold and polluted.

I attended an official dinner that evening and had a private talk afterwards with the Minister-President of Schleswig-Holstein, Gerhard Stoltenberg, who was on the point of going on a visit to the UK.

The next morning the same VIP RAF aircraft took me to Northolt where I was met and driven to London airport just in time to meet Genscher[1] who was coming over to England for a talk and lunch with Callaghan. This took place at Dorneywood which was looking extremely attractive on a beautiful sunny midsummer day. Genscher was accompanied by senior officials from the German Ministry of Foreign Affairs who were impressed by the beauty and informality of the house and garden. As we walked on the lawn or lunched off fresh asparagus from the garden, and as I overheard the remarks of some of our German guests, I reflected that they must find it ironical that though the Federal Republic of Germany might have twice Britain's GNP and a far better economic prognosis, it could not match a place like Dorneywood or the atmosphere of effortless and unshattered peace and affluence that surrounded it.

The discussion with the Germans followed the usual European course: inflation, oil money, CSCE, MBFR, European political co-operation, European union and of course the inevitable water-jump of British renegotiation. Genscher was very reasonable and very clear. He explained the importance of the goal of European union. Callaghan was benign, beaming like the successful farmer he is, happy to be host in the country but not concealing that he would rather be getting down to real work with real people on the real earth of his farm. Luckily we had no last fifteen-minute toughening up such as the Germans had experienced at the first meeting with Callaghan in Bonn. But nor did they sense much resonance from him to their ideas of European union.

After seeing Genscher and his team off at London airport I was driven to Chequers where I was due at 5 p.m. to brief the Prime Minister on his forthcoming visit to Germany.

The housekeeper who had been at Chequers in October 1973 when Brandt had been there for the weekend greeted me warmly. She asked after Alexandra who had picked me up there in the Mini after Brandt had left. The housekeeper left me in the hall talking to the golden

[1] Hans-Dietrich Genscher, member of the Free Democratic Party (FDP) in the Bundestag since 1965. Minister of Foreign Affairs 1974–92.

labrador, Paddy. I was getting on very well with him when the Prime Minister appeared in his shirt sleeves.

'Oh, it's mine is it?' he said in his characteristic throwaway style. 'From the way you were talking to him I thought it might be your dog.'

He led me to the study overlooking the rose garden at the back. Mrs Wilson and one or two friends or relations were in deckchairs outside. There was the usual P.G. Wodehouse atmosphere that hangs about Chequers: French windows leading on to large lawns and rose beds, many people hanging about apparently not doing very much; a feeling that somebody is on the point of perpetrating some practical joke; and the shimmering presence, if not of a Jeeves, at any rate of a servant or two ready to meet any need. One of these brought tea with scones and butter and jam. The Prime Minister and I helped ourselves. He sat in a high-backed chair smoking his pipe. He told me that this was the first free weekend he had had since the election. He seemed relaxed; indeed this was the main change I noticed in him since I had seen him in the early days of the previous government. He was less prickly, less on the defensive, with scarcely a chip visible on a frame that was now distinctly more portly.

'Well, what are the Germans thinking?' he began. I explained to him what I wanted to talk to him about before his meeting with Schmidt. Or at least I began explaining, when he interrupted to ask me what the country-side was like round Düsseldorf. He had a guest staying at Chequers, some distant relation whose precise kinship he described with that passion he has for detailed and often irrelevant information. This relative was going to take up some job in Düsseldorf. I gave him some encouraging news about the attractive countryside bordering on the Ruhr and the Prime Minister said he would pass it on. The trouble he was taking in attending to the wishes of his distant relation by finding out about the countryside near Düsseldorf was an example, I reflected, of Marcia Williams's[1] dictum that Wilson is an extraordinary ordinary man. It was decent and considerate of him to be bothering about this matter.

We discussed German politics and German politicians. We talked about renegotiation. He seemed to me over-optimistic about what we might get out of it. He appeared to believe that it would be possible to amend the Treaty of Accession. I left him in no doubt about the weakness of our bargaining position. The Germans did not think that we had any alternative to membership. He listened attentively. I was struck the following week to hear extracts from my cassette played back in some speech he made. Even quite small iron-filings of information that I had

---

[1] Marcia Williams, Private and Political Secretary to Harold Wilson 1956–83 (at 10 Downing Street 1964–70 and 1974–6). Created Life Peer 1974, as Baroness Falkender.

let drop had been drawn into the magnetic circle of his mind.

I stayed about an hour at Chequers. The Prime Minister accompanied me to the door when I left. It was a beautiful evening. I drove off across country to Combe, rather tired after a day that had started in Kiel. But I nourished the hope that my talk with the Prime Minister might have been some help.

I met the Prime Minister again the following evening when he arrived by special plane at Frankfurt to attend the Scotland v Brazil World Cup football match. Displaying the tartan tie he was wearing, he stepped jauntily on to the tarmac. He seemed in high spirits with scarcely a care in the world except to be present when Scotland won. We flew by helicopter to the ground and then went by car escorted by policemen on motorbikes. Obviously he enjoyed the panoply of his reception. After the match, which was a draw, we went downstairs below the stand for sandwiches and drinks. Wilson, the polymath, was full of advice on how Scotland could have won. 'I would have moved Bremner in from the left wing where he was wasting his time,' he said. He continued to hold forth in this confident way when he met the team. He soon found himself giving a series of press conferences full of advice on how Scotland should have played. It was, therefore, no surprise to me to read in a British paper shortly afterwards some equally categorical advice for the Prime Minister on how he should stick to his last and not ventilate his views on things he knew little about.

I had assumed, and hoped, that after a long day that had included questions in the House of Commons the Prime Minister would spend most of the two-hour drive to Bonn asleep. How wrong I was. He talked ceaselessly. There was a lot of traffic on the Autobahn. We were escorted by a police car with a flashing light. The Prime Minister seemed neither tired nor put out. Puffing away at his pipe or lighting it with a fuel-injector lighter like a flame-thrower, he seemed impervious to all stress. Nothing stopped the flow of talk. I cannot recall the detail but it was mostly about the past. The nearest we got to the present was when he talked about Stafford Cripps and the pre-war Popular Front. The name of Wedgwood Benn cropped up. Wilson dismissed him with a few scathing epithets. He had just had him in to a 'headmaster's talk' to use his own phrase. His lack of judgment about people and things was on a par with that of Stafford Cripps and it would be difficult, he thought, to be more crushing. The talk dwelled for a long time on the period between 1945 and 1950 – an account of some FAO delegation which Wilson had led to Washington and another delegation to Moscow. The negotiations had all ended in success. Dates of arrival and details of the successful completion of the negotiations were given without hesitation. I heard about how he had been offered his first ministerial post and how he had been made a Cabinet minister at thirty-one, the youngest since, well I forget who, but Wilson knew. He talked about Bevin and Attlee. He spoke of Gaitskell – as though he had been his strongest supporter.

I asked him what he thought about the Crossman diaries, the publication of which I knew the government was trying to stop. Wilson was appalled by the idea of publication. It would set a serious precedent. 'Crossman was a great teacher,' Wilson said, sliding rapidly back to his own past, to the time when he had been a don at Oxford.

When we got home to Bonn, which was I suppose around midnight, Mary greeted us with a large supper. Robert Armstrong, Tom Bridges, Haines,[1] Donoughue,[2] and the Prime Minister's doctor, Dr Stone,[3] and the rest of the Prime Minister's considerable entourage fell upon the feast eagerly. The Prime Minister confined himself to whisky. He said that he ate little nowadays. He had lost a lot of weight. His doctor was happy with him. Wilson sat on one of the sofas with a glass in one hand and a pipe or cigar in the other and continued his life in the past. We were back at Oxford before the war, how he had won the Webb-Medley, the three books he had read on economics that had helped him most (these included *Supply and Demand* by my father); his hard work with Beveridge; his successes in various exams and fellowships. Norman Statham and Reg Hibbert sat beside him. They had no chance to say anything. It was a Wilson monologue. He looked older and more tired as the night wore on – as did we. The more exhausted he became, the greater the flow of talk.

Eventually we got him to go to bed. On the way we put the dog out. Wilson accompanied us in this task. He has a rapport with dogs. He started telling Mary and me about his labrador, Paddy, a beautiful dog. 'Alec Home,' Wilson began, and then, dodging off at a tangent as is his way, said, 'you know we called our son after Alec's brother-in-law, Giles Alington, a don at univ. The only don, I believe, who got a third. But a first-rate teacher. Alec,' Wilson repeated, getting back on course, 'asked me if Paddy had a good pedigree. I told him that compared with Paddy the Homes were social upstarts. Alec then asked me if he was a working dog. "Of course he is," I said. Now your dog, your dalmatian,' Wilson continued, 'you can see he has more beauty than brains. He belongs to the Foreign Office in the Whitehall of dogs ... beautiful but stupid.'

The next morning Wilson was spry. We assembled on the terrace overlooking the Rhine at about 9.15 a.m. Haines and Donoughue dis-

[1] Joseph Haines, Chief Press Secretary to Prime Minister 1969–70 and 1974–6. Political Editor Mirror Group Newspapers 1984–90.
[2] Bernard Donoughue, Senior Policy Adviser to the Prime Minister 1974–9. Life Peer 1985.
[3] Dr Joseph Stone, knighted in Harold Wilson's dissolution honours 1970.

cussed the line to be taken by the Prime Minister in some debate in the House of Commons that night. Haines looked uncannily like the *Private Eye* caricatures of him. Getting the house ready for Wilson's visit, we had tried, out of courtesy, I hope, rather than sycophancy, to prevent the too conspicuous display of copies of *Private Eye*.

Wilson paced to and fro on the terrace. It was a lovely morning. The barges were moving up and down stream. The view of the Siebengebirge was like crystal. So far as I could observe Wilson was oblivious to these enchantments.

We drove together to the meeting with Chancellor Schmidt. Obtusely, I had somehow expected that he would wish to talk about the forthcoming meeting, but no, he was off again down memory lane.

The meeting with Schmidt went well. Whereas Brandt received guests in sofas and armchairs placed round a low table, Schmidt favours upright chairs round an office table. He was friendly to Wilson. There was no criticism of the Labour Party's line about Europe. I wished there had been because I knew how Schmidt felt. Apart from European problems the two heads of government talked about the difficulties likely to arise from the enormous financial surpluses that will accrue to the oil-producing countries following the rise in the price of oil.

At about 12.15 Wilson drove back to the Embassy to meet the British press. He was in excellent form. Nicholas Colchester of the *Financial Times* put to him a rather ticklish question implying inconsistency in Wilson's policies. He received a flow of words and innuendos in reply. Later Colchester telephoned the Embassy to ask us whether we thought the Prime Minister had answered his question, because, reading his notes through afterwards, he could not make head or tail of what Wilson had said. I was not surprised. This is part of Wilson's technique. Long before the listener has realised that the flood of words is not answering his question the Prime Minister is a long way downstream and dealing with some quite different subject.

Following the press conference we drove to the airport to the tunes of the same monologue. Wilson flew off home to meet with a series of defeats in the House of Commons. In Bonn he had not behaved at all as though he was in any domestic political difficulty. He had exuded confidence and serenity. The officials close to Wilson, however much they may disagree with the line he is taking, particularly on Europe, seem happy to be serving him. They respond to his warmth and confiding personality.

Wilson was a considerate and courteous guest. He thanked Mary profusely for her hospitality. I kept thinking to myself how different he was from the much more abrasive head of government that he had been in 1964. I also realised the extent to which he was living in the past. He did not seem to see himself in any creative political role.

He was quite frank to me about his main objective, which was to keep all the clashing balls of the Labour Party in the air at the same time. Although I was concerned by the smallness of his appetite, he showed plenty of stamina. I was reminded of what Marcia Williams had written in her book, that what you need in public life is 'faith, hope and stamina and that the greatest of these is stamina'. Wilson was realistic about his position in the Labour Party. 'They keep me there,' he told me, 'not because they love me but because there is no one else who can keep the party together.' Wilson kept saying that his doctor was pleased with him. Yet I was struck that Michael Palliser, who shares the same doctor, is sure that Wilson will not be in office in six months' time even if Labour wins another election. I wonder what Michael is basing himself on.

24 NOVEMBER
BONN

PSYCHOLOGICAL ADJUSTMENT[1]

The need for psychological adjustment pay persists. It is difficult and depressing representing the UK abroad these days: because of our appalling internal situation – strikes, inflation, balance of payments difficulties, poor growth – and because of our shaky policy towards Europe. Hailsham, whom I met at London airport the other day, said, as he bewailed the loss of traditional virtues amongst his compatriots, that representatives abroad had no alternative but to maintain a stiff upper lip. A member of my staff said, apropos our continued demands at Brussels for exceptions to be made to meet our difficulties, e.g. at the moment over sugar and beef, while at the same time our ministers continue to make derogatory remarks about the Community, that we have no alternative but to grow a thick skin.

The trouble does of course stem from the lurch to the left in leadership of many trade unions: they are against a reasonable wages policy, and at the moment look like wrecking Wilson's 'social compact'; they are also against Europe. The leadership of the Labour Party dare not have a confrontation, such as brought Heath down. At a recent meeting at Gymnich, Callaghan, discussing a possible reference to European union

---

[1] Since the February 1974 election Wilson had governed in accordance with a 'social compact' with the trade unions whose membership was now eleven million. In the October 1974 election Wilson won a slender majority.

and the 1972 summit, made a long speech about the attitude of the Labour Party, ending up with a statement: 'Well, at any rate, we won't have it. So that's that.' He took the same intransigent line on direct elections to the European parliament.

I did not think that the Gymnich meeting helped much. Callaghan arrived by private plane on the Saturday afternoon. He was taken by helicopter to Gymnich. He had a private meeting with Genscher that lasted about forty minutes. These meetings without officials are rather like the discussions that parents have without their children. There is the same *'pas devant les enfants'* atmosphere. The children were admitted later, in various stages.

Callaghan's main aim at Gymnich was to try to secure German support for our budgetary formula on renegotiation. It is essential to secure some formula and some mechanism which will enable us – and other countries whose contributions to the Community budget are disproportionate to their GNP – to get back money from the Community so as to prevent an unfair transfer of resources from the poor to the rich. It is not difficult, but tedious, to describe the atmosphere of these meetings. I remember Gerry Young, then head of the Foreign Office News Department, being asked at a press briefing about some conference: 'What subjects were discussed – the usual or something new?'

'Same old subjects.'

'What was the atmosphere like?'

'Same old atmosphere.'

The ministers sit opposite each other at a long coffin-shaped table. They are flanked by officials, a few of whom take notes, some of whom listen, and all of whom are bored. They know the subjects all too well. Each minister makes a statement, let's say on the subject of the CSCE, or the Community-Arab dialogue. Then there is a question or two. The officials rarely intervene. Occasionally if the minister is getting something entirely wrong one of his officials will lean forward over the table and say something like: 'Secretary of State, if I may say so, I think that that is entirely right. But I would also suggest that you have in mind as well another aspect of the problem, namely ...'

After the meeting we assembled upstairs for drinks in a room, allegedly set aside for the British delegation, where there was a TV set. Genscher said that he had heard that they would be showing pictures of the dress show that we had had that week at the British Embassy. He and his wife had attended. He had gone out of his way, in front of Callaghan, to say what a good party it had been. I noticed that Callaghan did not react particularly favourably. I wondered how he would react to the TV film. I needn't have wondered. Predictably, he said that it was a good thing that the Chancellor of the Exchequer had not seen it. He then muttered something, half jokingly, to the effect that he noticed that he hadn't been invited. Genscher, however, seemed determined not to leave the subject alone. In his speech later at dinner he referred, in customary fashion, to the splendid work of the two countries' Ambassadors. He went on to say that it was really something for an Ambassador to arrange a dress show to help his country's exports; but he thought that it was an unusual triumph then to ensure that it was watched on TV by his own Foreign Minister.

During our time in Bonn we gave a fancy head-dress party which the Germans appear to have found strange and enjoyable and which certainly livened up the Bonn routine. Mary made me a head-dress representing our dog in which his black spots were reproduced exactly where they were in reality. I greeted the guests wearing this head-dress with Zorba beside me looking rather shy. A photograph was taken of us which was subsequently carried prominently in the German press under the matter-of-fact heading: 'British Ambassador receives his guests'.

7 DECEMBER
CHEQUERS

VISIT WITH CHANCELLOR SCHMIDT

I was at Chequers last weekend for a visit by Chancellor Schmidt. It was only a little over a year since I had been there with Brandt when he was Chancellor. Everything was different, the atmosphere, the arrangements, the substance of the talks. Heath, who had been Prime Minister then, would sit with Brandt in long periods of silence. Neither was a master of small talk. Wilson and Schmidt on the other hand are both talkers.

Having given up golf, Wilson is now very much an indoors man. The afternoon of our arrival he had gone by helicopter to open a new sports centre at Crawley. 'I promised them I would do this,' he said. 'I had had it put off once. I couldn't disappoint them again. I made a speech of course. Then I had to open the bowling green. I know a bit about bowling. I was determined not to bowl short, otherwise they would have said something. So my first ball went right out the other end. Then it was the others' turn. When I came to bowl my second ball I took it in my hand like this. I took account of the bias. I know about bias. And I knelt down and delivered the bowl right down the middle. It went between all the other ones and ended up second closest to the jack.'

Those of us in attendance – Haines, Robert Armstrong, Tom Bridges and myself – drinking pre-dinner gins and tonics expressed suitable admiration for this athletic feat. The Prime Minister nowadays has as little to do with the press as possible – very different from the almost total preoccupation with the media at the beginning of the 1964 government when he paid constant attention to the lobby correspondents, not without short-term advantage, though of course the press could not take the over-exposure for long and eventually turned against him. The Prime Minister's two favourite bugbears at the moment are the press and officials.

He and Chancellor Schmidt were able later to make common cause on the awfulness and irrelevance of officialdom both at home and in Brussels. So much so that they seemed even to overlook their value as scapegoats. They waxed indignant about all the briefs put up in preparation for this particular meeting. These were matters that only politicians could decide, not the 'moles', 'weevils' or 'faceless bureaucrats' as the officials in Bonn, Brussels and Whitehall were variously described. The PM said it was 'intolerable of officials to prepare a summit communiqué in advance of the meeting'. He followed this by asking rhetorically, 'Who do they think we are?' We forbore to answer. There was something of a Churchillian ring about the way he said it.

The Chequers meeting last year took place on 6 October, the day the Yom Kippur Israeli-Arab war started. Heath said that one of the main international problems was how to deal with the large quantities of Arab money that was apt to move from one place to another, disrupting the money markets but the sums Heath was talking about then were trivial compared with present Arab surpluses. Even so I remember that no one had a solution to the problem then beyond saying that 'it would have to be considered by the group of twenty.' Although the weather last year was foggy we did manage to move outside for a time. But this year we were closeted indoors without a break. When Schmidt literally staggered out of Chequers around noon on Sunday to drive to the airport he complained that he was 'badly in need of air'. The hospitality at Chequers ran no danger of excessive finesse. I heard afterwards that Schmidt told someone that he had been received in the UK in 'characteristic down-to-earth British fashion'.

I must record something of the reception Schmidt had after arriving at Heathrow on Saturday morning and how he spent his first few hours in the UK. Callaghan as chairman of the Labour Party had asked him if he would attend a Labour Party Conference to be held in the Central Hall, Westminster. He thought that this might help to give Labour members a better understanding of the realities of Europe. I was at Heathrow to meet Schmidt. After a cup of coffee in the temporary bungalow that continues to serve inadequately as the VIP lounge for particularly important visitors, the Chancellor drove into London. There was no police escort beyond the perimeter of the airport. There were hold-ups on the Cromwell Road where rubbish was piled up on the pavements as a result of a labour dispute in the Cleansing Department of the Kensington Borough Council. Upon arrival outside the Central Hall, Westminster, the Chancellor was greeted by hostile posters, boos, angry faces and shaking fists, the message of which, though in sharper language, was that Britain wished to have nothing to do with Europe and that Schmidt should immediately go home. The Prime Minister received him at the entrance and led him upstairs along many corridors, past innumerable doors bearing the names of Methodist ministers, to the hall, where the delegates, preoccupied by a debate on Clay Cross,[1] paid little attention to the arrival of their distinguished visitor as he took his seat in the front row on the platform.

The meeting which Schmidt joined was in turmoil over a demand, expressed by frantic card-waving delegates and to the accompaniment of slow hand-clapping, that there should be a vote on the motion about Clay Cross rather than it should be decided, as Callaghan the chairman had ruled, upon the basis of a show of hands. The card vote held up the proceedings for ten to fifteen minutes. When order was restored the meeting moved on to the next subject which was the state of affairs in Chile. Mr Jack Jones and Mrs Judith Hart both spoke. The burden of their speeches and those of others was that a message should go out loud and clear from the hall that the British people would not tolerate the continued activities of the fascist dictatorship in South America. The speeches and the unanimous resolution were greeted with loud applause.

Then the Chancellor's turn came. He had a difficult task: a conference that had shown itself before his own eyes to be unruly and responsive to extremism, that only the day before had passed an anti-European resolution and that contained prominent members who had expressed their intention of walking out in the middle of his speech, a speech to be delivered in an alien tongue.

Callaghan gave the Chancellor an encouraging introduction. He said that he was being welcomed there not with the formality becoming to a head of government but informally as a fraternal delegate from the Socialist Party of Germany.

I have rarely seen anyone change the mood of an audience so radically

---

[1] Clay Cross, long-rumbling dispute arising from the refusal in July 1972 by the Clay Cross Council, Derbyshire, to raise rents under the Conservative Government's Housing Finance Act 1972. Two of the ten councillors were brothers of Dennis (Beast of Bolsover) Skinner MP. The councillors were fined and disqualified.

as Schmidt did on that occasion. He was neither patronising nor hec-
toring. He struck exactly the right note. There was no doubt he made a
considerable impact on the audience and I could not help wondering
whether leading British socialists who believed in Europe could not
succeed in having the same effect were they to be as straightforward and
courageous as Schmidt had been.

But to return to Schmidt at Chequers. He told me that he remembered
how dark it was. He noticed now that the panelling in the main reception
hall had been scraped. The Prime Minister said that he thought this had
been an improvement. Not so the 'fussy' wallpaper that Heath had
installed. As we stood about drinking before dinner the Prime Minister
gave his account of how Churchill had painted in the scarcely visible
mouse in the painting by Frans Snyders that hangs over the fireplace.
After dinner on our way to the long library for the meeting, the Prime
Minister showed Schmidt and the rest of us into the bedroom that he
and Mrs Wilson are occupying. He told us that this was where Churchill
had spent much of the war. Lots of people thought, quite wrongly, that
Churchill had been at Number 10 most of the time: this was untrue; he
knew this because he had been on Churchill's staff. Some of us on the
British side, as we crowded into the small bedroom and looked at the
bed on which the Prime Minister's and Mrs Wilson's pyjamas were laid
out, winced just a little as the Prime Minister's account rolled on. The
Germans said nothing.

At one moment in the course of the weekend I found myself before
the fire with Mrs Wilson. She said that she did not regard Chequers as
home. She went to their house nearby whenever possible. Paddy the dog
was there. She would be going there that afternoon. We talked about
Oxford. 'Did you know the Methodist minister who had married us?'
she asked, adding that he had just died.

'No, I am sorry I didn't,' I said. I then countered with: 'Did you know
Cyril Connolly? He has just died.'

'No,' she said.

I then referred to a book review by her that I had just read in the
Guardian. It was about the Scilly Isles. I said that it was typical of the
Guardian to make no boast of the fact that they were publishing a review
by the wife of the Prime Minister. She said that she thought that was
how it should be. I interjected, paraphrasing Dorothy Parker, that one's
highest praise must go out to those who refrain from doing what they
have every right to do. Mrs Wilson asked after Miss Taylor who used to
be at Chequers and who now works for us in Berlin. I was struck by
what a gentle, totally natural unassuming person she was. *Private Eye*'s
rendering of her is not right, I found myself saying to myself.

I had a little personal exchange with the Prime Minister at the dinner table. Schmidt sat between the Prime Minister and Healey.[1] The latter, pointing to me one place away, said to Schmidt, 'You know we were at Oxford together. He was very right wing – a member of the Social Democratic Party.'

Upon which I said, 'Yes, I think I was probably a social democrat before anyone else around this table.'

It was a little unwise and immodest to have said this in that galère even though I added that I had ceased any such loyalty to social democracy twenty years ago. I say, unwise, because I knew perfectly well how touchy the Prime Minister is about his pre-war political credentials at Oxford. He immediately chipped in: 'Of course I had nothing to do with those people. I came from the north. I watched those young men from public schools wearing hunting pink and holding forth about socialism in the Bullingdon Club.'

Wilson's affinities at Oxford were with the Liberal Party of which he was an unprominent member. Denis Healey said that his father had been an Asquithian Liberal. He did not mention his own membership at that time of the Communist Party, though, so far as I know, he never makes any attempt to hide it.

After the dinner party was over on Saturday evening and Schmidt had gone to bed the Prime Minister, puffing away at his pipe, stayed on in the long library talking to the inevitable entourage of Haines, Armstrong, Bridges, John Hunt and me. He spoke about what he had to get out of Europe to satisfy the British people. His starting point was what would be necessary to enable him to persuade the electorate that he had kept his word and done better than the Tories. Joe Haines said that he had an aunt who thought that food prices were high because of our membership of the Community. He thought Mr Wilson would have to be able to show the public that he had got the Community to bring down the price of food for the British housewife. The Prime Minister said that he thought this was a good idea. He also thought that New Zealand and Australia were important. The British people minded a lot about them. The Tories had let them down. He did not believe world food prices would stay high indefinitely. The British people must be able to buy food wherever it was cheapest. I made a mild attempt to draw attention to the fact that we now got cheaper food as a result of our membership of the Community. I also mentioned the meat/sugar deal by which the Community was going to subsidise the cost of sugar to the British

---

[1]Denis Healey, at this stage in his career Chancellor of the Exchequer where he remained until 1979. Secretary of State for Defence 1964–70. Opposition spokesman on Foreign and Commonwealth Affairs 1980–7. His book, *The Time of My Life*, has sold more copies than any other contemporary political memoir.

consumer. But the Prime Minister was not impressed. The sugar deal done by the Tories in 1971 had been a bad one. The Prime Minister waxed enthusiastically about the old Commonwealth much as he had done in a recent speech in which he had spoken of his forty-three close relatives in Australia.

During this and other discussions at Chequers I was impressed by how little the Prime Minister seemed to have been following the European story. 'I'm leaving that to Jim,' or 'Leave that to Jim,' were words that were frequently on his lips. Clearly he sees no political advantage in becoming too personally involved in European questions. The Prime Minister, when the budgetary problem had been explained to him, said that he thought a mistake had been made in attaching so much import-ance to it. There were other things that we ought to get that were much more crucial. He referred to Michael Foot and sovereignty which was a real difficulty.

Whatever the Germans may have felt about the weekend – and I had some doubts about this – it struck me that it must have been useful for the Prime Minister to have had to focus his mind on the Community. He must have seen that his own political and personal future could not be separated from the negotiations and from the subsequent need to secure the acceptance of the British people to whatever came to be agreed.

1975

28 JANUARY

BONN

SEDUCED BY SHIRLEY WILLIAMS

When I met Shirley Williams at the Königswinter Conference in Edin-burgh last year I urged her to come to Germany to help leaven the dough of anti-Europeans who looked like descending on us under a Labour government. She said that she would like to come, but she would need some camouflage. We would have to find a 'consumer reason' for her to visit Germany. She is Minister of Prices and Consumer Protection.

For one reason or another the visit did not take place until last week; and even then the camouflage was pretty thin because at the last moment she had cancelled a visit to Berlin where she was expected to attend some European consumer conference. However she stuck to her plan to come here where we had arranged a comprehensive programme.

I managed to see and talk to her quite a lot. She is wonderfully unspoilt by fame or office.

When we reached the house from the airport and were discussing the programme in front of the fire she said, 'Do you mind if I sit on the floor? I like it much the best.' She seemed remarkably independent of the sort of support most ministers need or, rather, demand. She never asked for briefs or biographical details. She brought with her a Press Secretary, a Political Adviser, Lyttle,[1] and a Private Secretary. But she did not seem to expect much of them.

She makes no fuss and seems to take little out of herself and to have great endurance. Soon after 7 p.m. she gave an interview to the British Forces Broadcasting Service. She asked me beforehand what the attitude of the average member of the British Army of the Rhine and his wife would be towards continued membership of the Community. She was surprised, agreeably so, when I said that I was sure they would be pro. She is neither ascetic nor hedonistic. She is musical rather than visual. I am not making the slightest criticism; she is so clever in what she says, and how she says it, that it matters not at all if she is relatively unobservant.

We had a galaxy of varied talent to meet her for dinner – politicians, journalists and trade unionists. She sat between Egon Bahr, with whom she got on well, and Rohwedder[2] with whom she got on less well because he is so outspoken. I made a short speech of welcome at the end of dinner, to which she replied brilliantly. She has a way of putting things together in a speech so as to make the whole appear original, although the parts are not. Her main theme was that the UK was now having to pay for not having lost the war, and that we had a lot to learn from Germany which had learned a lot as a result losing the war. Put down baldly like this it sounds banal, but, as I say, she strung it together to make a beautiful sequence. She spoke the following morning to members of the Embassy staff about the British government's internal and external policies. I have never heard a better or more revealing summary; and I know I was not alone in being so impressed.

After dinner we adjourned into small groups. Shirley conducted a seminar with Emminger, the Deputy Governor of the Bundesbank, Dech-amps, the Foreign Editor of the *Frankfurter Allgemeine Zeitung*, and a

---

[1] John Lyttle worked closely at different times with Mark Bonham-Carter, Shirley Williams, Roy Jenkins and Archbishop Runcie. He was wise and witty. Although a non-believer, his funeral service in the Chapel of Lambeth Palace was attended by three Anglican Archbishops (two of Canterbury, one of York). Roy Jenkins has suggested that there was a touch of Harry Hopkins about him.
[2] Detler Rohwedder, Secretary of State in the Federal Ministry of Economic Affairs; President of the Treuhandanstalt August 1990–April 1991 when he was assassinated.

representative of the DGB, the Deutsche Gewerkschafts Bund. The last
had incomplete mastery of English but this hardly mattered as Shirley
speaks quite good German, learned, so she told us, in socialist camps.
Later van der Vat, *The Times* correspondent here, also joined the group.
He was much taken with Shirley, later asking me, 'Is there a Shirley
Williams society?' adding, 'If not, I'll found one.'

When the guests had gone we stayed on chatting with Shirley. We did
not get to bed until about 2 a.m.: the usual sort of topics – domestic
politics, the differences between the Germans and the British, and the
age gap.

She was not too pessimistic about current trade union attitudes.
Scanlon[1] was losing ground rapidly and the moderates were gaining, not
only in the TGWU but also in the AUEW. This was relevant to the
referendum on continued membership of the European Economic Community. Trade union leaders might for the most part campaign against,
but they probably knew the result would go the other way and may well
be content that this should be so. The new attitude that was emerging in
the trade unions was concerned more with unemployment than with
wage demands. She was insistent that industrial unrest was limited to
about twenty firms in the UK, though from the press you would think
it was much more widespread. She believed that public opinion was
developing a desire to go back to the ideas of austerity, partly because
they identified these with egalitarianism. There was a failure of communication between management and workers for which our social
structures, so difficult to change, were partly responsible. Strikes, she
considers, are as much the result of frustration and as much concerned
with status as wages.

On the subject of Europe Shirley spoke about the lack of interest
amongst the British people. There was no emotion about the idea of
Europe. It did not represent anything as important for us as did the
Adenauer–de Gaulle reconciliation for the French and Germans. She
thought there might be a low poll in the referendum. The young were
more enthusiastic about continued membership than the old. She did
not think that the anti-Europeans in the Cabinet would resign if the
referendum came out in favour of continued Community membership.
Her belief and hope was that, although there would be a very difficult
and acrimonious five months or so, differences would soon be patched
up within the party after the referendum and, given the total disarray of
the Tory leadership, Labour was likely to be in unchallenged power for
some time.

---

[1] Hugh Scanlon, President of Amalgamated Union of Engineering Workers, 1968–78.

As I watched Shirley talking during her visit to various people and audiences I could not help wondering whether she had the calibre of a Prime Minister. It seemed to me that she had, even though her judgments tended towards the rosy and over-optimistic. But since the visit we have heard the news of Mrs Thatcher's election to leadership of the Tories. This could make Shirley's way to the top much more difficult. It was hard to imagine Mrs Thatcher and Mrs Williams being leaders of the two main parties at the same time. I am struck incidentally by the enormous enthusiasm roused among the wives and female secretaries in the Embassy by Mrs Thatcher's appointment; nothing to do with politics, but a feather in the cap for women in the pursuit of important posts.

23 FEBRUARY
BONN

WARNING FROM THE TUC

I have been in Düsseldorf to attend a dinner addressed by Mr Len Murray, General Secretary of the TUC. It was organised by the British Trade Council for a mainly German audience including the chairman of the Deutsche Gewerkschafts Bund (DGB). From the way Murray spoke you would have thought he believed that he was addressing a recalcitrant gathering of shop stewards at home were it not for the frequent interjection of the words 'You Germans'. He complained that part of the trouble arose because Britain had an able lot of industrial correspondents whose job it was to write up every labour disturbance however small or fleeting. One of Britain's main strengths, he asserted, was a way of life that had nothing to do with figures of growth or productivity. He concluded with the words: 'You Germans better look out. When the British do get going again, you had better look out for your pants.'

13–16 MARCH
BONN

THE KÖNIGSWINTER CONFERENCE

We had a large weekend party for the twenty-fifth anniversary of the first Königswinter Conference, the brain-child and constant ward of Dame Lilo Milchsack: Jennifer and Roy Jenkins, Ted Heath, Shirley Williams, Jo Grimond and David Ennals are all staying in the house.

When Roy spoke at the conference he paid tribute, humorously and gracefully, to the twenty-five years of Königswinter: 'It is the first time we have ever had a speech from Dame Lilo Milchsack; it is the first time we have nearly had a speech from the Bundeskanzler' (Chancellor Schmidt had cancelled at the last moment). Referring to the building where Königswinter had always been held he described it as 'this inelegant, uncomfortable, but memorable old Adam Stegerwald Haus'.

Commenting on this to me later, Jo said, 'It's a bit thick, Roy complaining about the discomfort of the Adam Stegerwald Haus. He has scarcely spent five minutes in it. He is always with you in the Embassy guzzling caviar.'

Ted seemed to enjoy the weekend. We put him into the Rheingold Suite. The Jenkins were upstairs in the Blue Room. Caroline Gilmour had been with us ten days before and Mary had discussed with her the problem of which rooms they were to have. Within hours of her departure I had a telephone call that reached me in Hamburg. It was Roy to say that he thought it would be appropriate to put Ted in the Rheingold Rooms even though protocol-wise he, Roy, might be entitled to them. He would be perfectly happy in the Blue Room. Jennifer spoke about this later to Mary. She said that Roy had the best of both worlds by this arrangement: he could please Ted by waiving rank in his favour; and he could have the room he preferred, which was the blue one. Apparently memories of a night he spent in the Rheingold rooms when he had to prepare an emergency budget as Chancellor are apt to produce nightmares. Roy was also insistent that we should give his Private Secretary, Hayden Phillips,[1] a good room and treat him with the respect due to his rank. He said that people in the Diplomatic Service had the reputation of treating home Civil Servants as though they were inferior beings. We duly took note of this, aware as we are how ready people are to take umbrage as soon as they step inside an Embassy. It is partly in order to counter this that we leave quantities of drink and fruit in all the bedrooms.

We took a lot of trouble with the buffet dance we gave on the Saturday evening. There were over two hundred guests including twenty-three British Members of Parliament, six editors or deputy editors of leading

---

[1]Hayden Phillips, a civil servant who held important Whitehall posts before and after working for Roy Jenkins in Brussels; Permanent Secretary, Department of National Heritage since 1992; married (second) Laura Grenfell. A serious and brilliant man whose humorous attitude to life has not impaired his official career.

papers and six professors. Robin Day[1] came up to me at one stage of the evening and, beaming through his headlamp glasses, said, 'Well, as one who contributes about 60p in every pound to tax. I would like to say that I don't at all regret the expenditure tonight.' I thanked him. A bus left fairly soon after the buffet supper was over but a number of guests stayed on for the dancing. These included the Jenkinses, Shirley Williams, Robin Day, Jo Grimond, Erik Blumenfeld,[2] Ted Sommer,[3] Carlotta Geyr,[4] Charles and Carla Powell[5] (she a great attraction of the dance floor) and several of the glamorous female translators from the Embassy. John Mackintosh,[6] whom I had had most in mind when deciding that we would have dancing after dinner, unfortunately took the bus back to Königswinter at an early stage of the evening. He complained afterwards that it was one of the worst mistakes of his life. Everyone took to the floor boisterously. Roy was in the highest spirits. He told Mary, when he started to dance with her, that he had not danced for nine years and that he was afraid he might fall over. However, he soon got the hang of it and was still gallumphing around at 2.30 a.m.

On the last evening when the rest of the party had gone, Ted said that he would like to take Mary and me out to dinner in a restaurant. We said that we would not be wanting to eat much and anyway we had a lot of work to do, but Ted was graciously insistent and we went off with him to a Greek restaurant, the Dionysus. Ted also said that he did not want much to eat but when it came to the point he ordered dolmades and stuffed olives and lamb from the charcoal grill. He shovelled them away after a fashion that would have made the army clearance men now working in Glasgow to remove the piles left by the strike look as though they were playing spillikins.

During the weekend Mary and I had been with Ted in the car on many occasions. Mary had been worried by the frequent silence during these drives, but I persuaded her to accept them as part of life with Ted. It was not meant to be rudeness. It was just that he saw no need to talk unless the spirit moved him. Well, at this dinner in the restaurant he suddenly

---

[1] Robin Day has told me subsequently that this Königswinter evening was the best party he had ever attended. One of the prominent Germans present had told him what a privilege it had been to dance with a Cabinet minister – Shirley Williams.

[2] Erik Blumenfeld had been educated in England 1935–9; incarcerated in Auschwitz and Buchenwald; CDU member of the Bundestag 1961–80; he was a frequent and entertaining attender at Königswinter Conferences.

[3] Ted Sommer, editor-in-chief of *Die Zeit*; also a key and diverting Königswinter participant.

[4] Carlotta Geyr, a naïve painter whose artistic and dancing talents had been developed by long residence in Spain.

[5] Charles Powell, First Secretary in Bonn, later Private Secretary to Mrs Thatcher; ably supported by his Italian wife, Carla, whose talents were outstanding.

[6] John Mackintosh MP, historian and politician, a brilliant and courageous, pro-European member of the Labour Party whose life was tragically cut short in 1978.

became loquacious, thanks only partly to the ouzo but more to the subject of the past to which we moved. He became animated in talking about the negotiations in 1961–2 for Britain's entry into the European Economic Community, giving long accounts of Couve's[1] and Wormser's[2] tactics. He was neither critical, nor bitter, except about one moment when they had studiously avoided shaking hands with him. Words poured forth, and nothing would stop him, so much so that when we had arrived back at the house and he had reached the climax, de Gaulle's veto, he made no move to get out of the car, but just went on talking. We remained opposite our house pinned in the car until the General's veto had been finally cast.

Talking of the more recent entry negotiations which had finally succeeded, Ted said that he was sure that his friendship with Jobert had played an important part. They had first got to know each other on holiday in Spain many years ago and their friendship was maintained through the years on annual holidays that they spent together at Hythe. Ted was certain that this had made it possible for him to get on to terms with Pompidou. This in turn had been decisive in securing our entry.

I hit upon a way of getting more of a response from Ted than just yes or no during our many car drives. There were several Tory MPs in the British Königswinter delegation. Mere mention of one of their names was enough to stir him and to produce an effect like a sea-lion surfacing. 'What do you think of X?' I would ask innocently.

This produced an explosion: 'No good at all. No bottom to him, all over the place.'

I thought I could perceive the glimmer of a clue about how X must have voted in the Tory leadership election. On another occasion I invited comment on Y.

This produced a reaction that was more like a whale spouting: 'Utterly useless. Quite useless. Can't bear him.'

---

[1] Maurice Couve de Murville, diplomat and politician. Foreign Minister 1958–68; Prime Minister 1968–9.
[2] Olivier Wormser, French official and diplomat; Governor of the Bank of France. My colleague in Bonn. See diary entry for 13 March 1976.

15 JUNE
BONN

POST-REFERENDUM EUPHORIA

We are still in a state of post-referendum[1] euphoria attenuated only by disappointment with the limited nature of Wilson's Cabinet reshuffle.

Harold Lever[2] was here mainly to see Schmidt just before the referendum. He is a great talker. He was interesting on the subject of Wilson, whom he knows well personally and whom, he says, he loves 'because he has been so good to me' – he meant that after he had had his stroke he would have given up public life had Wilson not told him how to overcome his handicap and carry on. He is critical of Wilson's failure to tackle the left. I muttered something about Wilson's overriding aim being to keep the Labour Party united. He exploded at this, saying that on the contrary 'it suits Wilson to have the Labour Party split. If they ever get together they will get him out.'

Schmidt had set considerable store by his meeting with Lever. He is a man searching after the truth in public affairs and he inclines to think that there are specialists – financiers and economists – who can reveal to him with some degree of absoluteness and much objectivity the causes of problems and possible solutions. He does not believe in magic or panaceas; nor that complicated issues can be solved by single or simple means. But he does believe that the right answers depend upon a correct analysis of the facts. He is responsible for the answer; he does not have the time to find out about the facts for himself. This explains the initiative he has recently taken to try to get experts from the main oil producing and consuming countries together to give him, and other leaders, a sound factual basis upon which they can take the necessary decisions. It also lies at the heart of his ready response to a proposal that the Prime Minister made to him last summer that he should send over to talk to him the financial wizard he had in his Cabinet, Harold Lever. Hence last week's visit here.

I was glad that Lever should have heard directly from Schmidt what he thinks of us in present circumstances – inflation, balance of payments, strikes, trade union extremism, poor management. 'If you telephone someone in the City of London at 9 a.m. there is never anyone there,'

---

[1] A referendum (the first in British history) was held on 5 June 1975 in which 67 per cent of voters favoured British membership of the European Common Market.
[2] Harold Lever, Chancellor of the Duchy of Lancaster 1974–9, brought practical financial knowledge to Wilson's Cabinet.

Schmidt had said to him. He had also manifested a poor opinion of British products, saying, 'I was brought up on the tradition of British quality but what you turn out now is old-fashioned in design and poor in quality.'

At a dinner in the Embassy Lever expressed his enthusiasm for deficit spending. Governments, he declared, should not bother about getting into debt. The only danger to the world lay in their being afraid to overspend. The German guests who heard this were both surprised and troubled. Ted Sommer was in the party and intervened with characteristic humour. He is a close friend of Schmidt's and may well have reported to him what Lever said, which will have confirmed Schmidt in his view that Britain is a country run by financial rakes.

Lever told him that he thinks he is useful to Wilson because of the respect in which he is held in the City. His friends in the Square Mile know that he would not go along with anything that was really outrageous. Schmidt said to him just before he left that he had been told that he was a millionaire. Lever answered that with today's rate of inflation and prices it did not do one any good with one's creditors to be called a millionaire. It was really rather insulting. He had made his money in 1945 on the Stock Exchange. He had been a barrister by profession. Then his first wife died and he had done nothing for five years but play cards. He completely neglected his constituency and the Commons. He could not understand why they had not got rid of him.

About his second wife he went into some detail in conversation on the terrace of our house overlooking the Rhine just before his departure. Diane was present. Harold said that he had met his 'little Arab girl' one evening when playing cards. 'I met her once or twice again and realised I was in love with her. I managed to make it financially beneficial to her husband and we are now on quite good terms with him.' The Arab girl listened inscrutably and less nervously than did Mary and me as the account went on. Subsequently I heard Lever say that when somebody had accused him of marrying Diane for her millions, he had riposted, 'Oh, I would have married her if it had only been one million.'

The day after the referendum result became known I went to Brussels to talk things over with Michael Palliser and Eddy Tomkins.[1] We had agreed that this might be desirable whichever way it went. But as it had gone the occasion inevitably became a celebration with champagne in the garden before lunch. Marie[2] was present and in fine form. I

---

[1] Edward Tomkins, member of the Diplomatic service, at this time Ambassador in Paris where I succeeded him.

[2] Marie Palliser, daughter of Paul-Henri Spaak. Married to Michael in 1948. We first knew them in Athens where Michael and I were Junior Secretaries. Marie is unconventional, independent-minded and alluring.

congratulated her on becoming the mother of the Service, Michael having just been appointed Permanent Under-Secretary.

Eddy said that the Quai d'Orsay were pleased with the referendum result, not least because the Embassy in London had been predicting a different outcome. I asked him how Mrs Thatcher had gone down in Paris on her recent visit. He said, 'Surprisingly well, particularly with Chirac.'

When the time came to leave the Federal Republic in August 1975 I reflected on the latest accomplishments of the Germans against the setting of their recent history. They had established an extremely effective system of democratic government. They had achieved an economic miracle. They were now a most unmilitaristic people who no longer seemed to be spellbound, as their forebears had been, by the concepts of Geist and Macht, or by mythological heroes singing of fate and doom. Recently they had brought about a shift in foreign policy by promoting normal, and even friendly, relations with the Soviet Union and Eastern Europe, the full impact of which was not to emerge for many years.

The great success the Germans had had in restoring their economy and overtaking the British was evident to anyone making the briefest journey in the Federal Republic. Unfortunately my diary does not record the travels we made to the Länder or the visits we paid to many German companies, e.g. chemical, steel, motor vehicle, aircraft or jam-making. At Stuttgart I was impressed by the trouble taken with the foreign workers, many of whom were of Turkish origin. They had their own schooling. At the Volkswagen plant at Wolfsburg I asked the chief executive to tell me, on the basis of his successful experience, what tip he would give British motor vehicle manufacturers to enable them to compete more effectively on the world motor vehicle market. He threw his hands into the air and said that it was not a question of one tip. At least ninety changes were needed, some of them extending well beyond the vehicle-production line, to enable Britain to produce motor cars successfully. A senior manager involved in the electrical industry put it to me, by way of illustrating the reasons for Germany's achievement: 'We were all on the floor together in 1945. There was no them and us.'

The reasons for the gap between the industrial performance of Germany and the UK seemed to me to include the following:

a) The quality of management in Germany where a career in industry attracts people of the highest calibre;

b) the small number of trade unions (16 were affiliated to the German Trade Union Federation as compared with 108 affiliated to the TUC) and the fact that membership was based not on craft or occupation but on the industry in which the person worked;

*c) The greater discipline of the German people, a characteristic which, in
Chancellor Schmidt's view, had, more than anything else made the labour
situation much easier to handle in Germany than in the UK.*

No less impressive was the seriousness with which the Germans
took their democratic institutions. Aware of their lack of long-standing political traditions, many Germans appeared to outsiders to be
protesting too much about their new-found beliefs. But this was
understandable; and in most important respects, e.g. sovereignty of
parliament based on universal suffrage, freedom of press and opinion,
and respect for the rule of law, there could be no question about the
thoroughly democratic nature of their system. I talked about this
with Helmut Schmidt who, in personality, was the exact opposite to
his predecessor as Chancellor, Willy Brandt. Whereas Brandt retained
a bear-like hold on the affections of the mass of the German people,
Schmidt had won nationwide respect for his intellectual ability,
courage and capacity for decision. He was also noted for his supreme
self-confidence. This was felt acutely in Bonn where to the question,
'What is the difference between God and Schmidt?' the answer was,
'God knows everything, but Schmidt knows it better.' Among his
outstanding qualities as a statesman, so it seemed to me, was his
ability to see immediate problems in a wide setting, to be able to
analyse and conceptualise, somewhat in the manner of Henry Kissinger whose birthplace, incidentally, was not very far from his.

Schmidt's overriding view was that the Germans, as a result of very
heavy and painful inoculation, had been so immunised that they were
less likely than other Europeans to swing to extremism.

This also was my conclusion. Nor did I think that they would
be likely to do anything rash in the realm of international affairs.
Ostpolitik, certainly a highly original step, had only been possible
because Bonn continued to stick firmly to the foundations upon
which their post-war policy had been based: the Atlantic Alliance
that ensured US support, and European union that embodied reconciliation with France and provided a much-needed overall goal,
even a holy grail, for the Federal Republic.

It was no longer true by the time I left Bonn that the Federal
government regarded us, as it had done three years earlier, as the ally
whose views they expected to be closest to its own. This change had
been brought about by our economic weakness and because of our
lukewarm attitude to the European Community. There was no
Schadenfreude over our economic decline; and they would have liked
us to have been full-hearted members of the Community, to serve as

a counter-weight to the French, and because of the contribution that our political tradition could bring to Brussels. The Chancellor still referred proudly to his refusal to vote in the Bundestag for the ratification of the Treaty of Rome because Britain was not a signatory. While they were disappointed, the Germans nevertheless realised that we were important to them politically, economically and militarily. We were, after all, the most important military partner in NATO.

Towards the end of my time in Bonn we had a visit from Mrs Thatcher. It was, I think, her first journey abroad after becoming leader of the Tory Party in February 1975 and she showed much interest in finding out all she could about the Germans. She was also eager to get on to good terms with them.

PARIS

1975–1979

The move to Paris was also a surprise. I had never served in the Embassy there and knew little about it except that the house and furniture had been purchased by Wellington from Napoleon's sister, Pauline Borghese, and had great architectural, aesthetic and historical value. Its situation was also prestigious – on the rue du Faubourg St Honoré, hard by the Elysée, the President's palace. The garden was on the same grand scale as the house.

When we reached Paris at the end of 1975 the French were riding high, particularly in comparison with the UK, and Valéry Giscard d'Estaing, the President, lost no opportunity of spelling this out. His line was that the age-long competitive struggle between France and the UK was over for good with France the victor. Certainly the French were confident in themselves, particularly about the management of their economy which had been relatively successful. Giscard was satisfied that he could continue to govern from the centre to achieve what he called 'change without risk', notwithstanding the deep-seated Bourbonism, whether of the right who wanted no risk of change or of the left, where 20 per cent of the voters were Communists, who sought a transformation of society.

Giscard was a most active performer on the world's stage. He saw and exploited a role for France wherever a lacuna was left open by the Great Powers. He saw such a gap in the Third World, particularly in Africa. He spoke much of France's rayonnement *which was his way of describing the country's traditional* mission civilisatrice. *Towards the Americans he adopted a much less prickly tone than his predecessors had done. With their support he had managed in November 1975 to call an economic and monetary summit at Rambouillet. This was to be the first of a series of such meetings which have continued to this day.*

He also showed initiative in developing the European Council as the chosen instrument for running the European Community. He was the first leader in France to promote the idea of direct elections to the European parliament. There was no doubt about the validity of his European credentials and his determination and ability to get a move on in a way he believed that served both France's and Europe's interests.

This was one of the reasons for his scepticism about the United

Kingdom at this time. The British government had cancelled the Channel Tunnel in January 1975 which he regarded as an act of insularity. The renegotiation of UK terms of membership of the Community and the referendum about continuing to belong to it had been further examples of the UK's half-hearted commitment to Europe. Besides which, Britain's economy seemed to be in chronic decline; its GDP was two-thirds that of France.

Giscard was on warm personal terms with Helmut Schmidt and his policy seemed to be increasingly directed to working closely with the Germans. His relationship was different with Callaghan who was the undoubted voice of Britain abroad for the next few years, firstly as Foreign Minister and then as Prime Minister after he succeeded Wilson at Number 10 in April 1976. The contrast in personality and outlook between Giscard and Callaghan epitomised many of the considerable differences between France and Britain at this time. I realised that it was the task of the British Ambassador in Paris – as of the French Ambassador in London – to do what he could to help bridge this divide.

1975

14 DECEMBER

PARIS

ARRIVAL AT A PALACE

We arrived here last Monday evening. The change from our life at Fairholt Street in London and our cottage at Combe in the country to that of the British Embassy in Paris in the rue du Faubourg St Honoré is characteristic of the violent oscillations involved in the career.

One day we were busy doing odd jobs to the house, having a row or rather several rows with the Gas Board in an attempt, unsuccessful throughout most of our three-month stay in England, to get hot water for the bath; and then in the evening we were packing and loading up the Mini and Rover prior to setting off for France. We left at dawn the next day for Dover, took the ferry and were then met at Calais by the British Consul, by the head of the French docks and by a representative of the Mayor. A chauffeur and Rolls-Royce were waiting to take us to Paris and two chauffeurs had come to Calais to drive our private cars. We arrived at the Embassy in state to be met by all the resident staff lined up in the hall. Our luggage was immediately taken care of – so thoroughly that the valets ceremoniously removed from the cars all the rubbish and papers that had accumulated on the floor and in the pockets over the years, transported them up the marble stairs and then spread them out, whether in our bedroom, or in the tented Diana Cooper marble bathroom or in the library. My broken penknife from the glove pocket, the half-eaten plastic bags of peanuts and raisins and the peremptory summonses for parking offences that had littered the car floors were laid out beside Duff Cooper's beautiful leather bindings or beneath the frown of the caryatids on sentry duty round Pauline's bed or clashing with the swan-neck gold fittings of the bathroom.

It seems to be a law of the house that everything has to be kept constantly on the move from one end to the other. Thus no sooner have I taken my clothes off than they are wafted away to some distant room. I was staggered by the size and grandeur of the Embassy even though I have been here several times before and stayed in the house. I see immediately why it creates such a strong and often resentful reaction in the bosom of so many British visitors: the indignation that mounts within many a breast as the visitor is led by some liveried footman up the enormous marble stairs and through the grand Empire reception rooms until he at last reaches his host and hostess seated comfortably beside a log fire.

The head butler, Giovanni, showed us upstairs, but not before we had had a rapturous greeting from Zorba in the hall. I had half expected him merely to give us a peremptory wag of the tail before asking to go out and lift his leg because that's his customary way of showing his feelings. But no, he was most welcoming and has been reluctant to leave my side ever since. I have already found what seems to be a perfect constitutional for him and me, up and down the Allée Marcel Proust in the Jardin Marigny, just the other side of the Avenue Gabriel at the end of the garden. I can let myself out through a small gate, instead of having to leave the Residence by the main entrance in the Faubourg.

Before leaving London I gave an interview to French radio. I was asked very solemnly whether, in view of all the kidnapping that goes on, I was worried about my own security in Paris and whether I had taken any precautions on this subject. Briefed by Andrew Palmer,[1] I answered equally solemnly that I had indeed taken the most elaborate precautions. I had sent in advance to Paris my dog, a dalamatian. Exceptionally fierce, he had had as many victims to his credit as spots. I warned all would-be kidnappers who might be listening to look out. It is amazing how many people in France heard this programme. Nobody refers to what I said

[1] Andrew Palmer, member of the Diplomatic Service and Press Officer in the Paris Embassy at this time. Ambassador to Cuba 1986–8; at the Holy See since 1991.

about the future of Europe, etc, but everyone speaks of '*autant de victimes que de tâches*'.

At seven o'clock all the ministers, Service Attachés and Counsellors turned up at the house with their wives to meet us. The purpose I think was to try to ensure not that we would be able to remember all of them but that they would at least recognise us.

We just had time for a bath before the Wyrouboffs[1] came to dinner. They were full of kindness and sympathy, even going so far as to send a vast picture round the next day to fill one of the gaps on the wall of the Salon Vert.

And so, eventually, to bed, to Pauline's bed. A magnificent *lit de parade* in the Empire style. Mary showed me Napoleon's looking-glass incrusted with bees in ormolu that makes you look thinner. I drew her attention to Wellington's desk in the library on which much of the impedimenta of our cars was by now displayed.

As I went to sleep I felt some sense of relief that we were at last here, in the Embassy in Paris, a place in which I had not, even in the wildest of my dreams, ever expected to find myself.

20 DECEMBER

PARIS

20 DECEMBER CALLAGHAN AND HEALEY IN PARIS

Within days of my arrival in Paris Anglo-French relations plummeted and British diplomacy suffered a diplomatic rebuff. This came about following the calling of a conference in Paris for the third week in December, a north-south conference on energy and raw materials. Callaghan wanted Britain to have separate representation from that of the European Community at the conference, and said so publicly. The other governments had decided to be represented there by the chairman of the European Council and the President of the Commission and to comply with the terms of an agreed mandate. They turned Callaghan's proposal down. If Britain were to have a separate seat other countries would press for the same. True, Britain was a producer of oil and the other countries were not but the latter were producers of different sources of energy, e.g. North Sea gas.

Domestic politics probably caused Callaghan to go out on a limb on this subject: the need, with a Cabinet divided on Europe, to present a suitably St George image abroad in defence of British interests; and the chance of dishing the Scottish Nationalists and Tony Benn who was Secretary of State for Energy. When Callaghan finally realised that he was not going to get his way he decided to arrive late at the conference; and when he came to speak he departed from the agreed Community line.

He gave a dinner at the British Embassy for Commonwealth representatives attending the conference. Later in the evening he held a meeting with officials at which he read out a message Kissinger had given him after his speech congratulating him upon it. He was in ebullient form and it was impossible not to admire his resilience in the face of setbacks that others might have found humiliating.

The following extract from the diary takes up the story at this point.

Callaghan returned to London the next day instead of staying to the end of the conference. There were rumblings about his speech in the French press. The Foreign Minister, Jean Sauvagnargues,[1] telephoned to say that the President wished me to know of his concern about Callaghan's speech which had not been in accordance with the Community mandate, particularly as regards the Minimum Selling Price (MSP). He would be issuing an official public statement to that effect later that day. I sent a telegram to London to warn them. That night I received a telephone call to say that a telegram was on its way containing a message that Callaghan wanted me to deliver the same night to Sauvagnargues. This message refuted the French view. It would be made public immediately. I telephoned Sauvagnargues at his home at about 8.30 p.m. He indicated that he thought that this whole public altercation was unprofitable. The least said now the better. Unfortunately, however, the story had already been given to the press which made as much of a meal of it as they could. Indeed the row between ourselves and the French became far and away the most prominent outcome of the North-South Conference.

The French decision to issue public criticism of Callaghan's speech from the Elysée was surely taken on Giscard's initiative. I suspect that he saw in it a means of pleasing the oil producers – who hated the idea of an MSP – and of maintaining France's particular relationship with those countries. Callaghan's public counter-attack, while it added fuel to the fire, was understandable. I have had a letter from him since; what might be called a political bread-and-butter letter. He referred to the robust line he was taking in response to what he regarded as a rather

---

[1] Jean-Victor Sauvagnargues, Foreign Minister 1974–6. Specialist on German questions, he was Ambassador to Bonn 1970–4 and to the UK 1977–81.

intemperate reaction by President Giscard. This might give us some uncomfortable moments in the weeks ahead but it was essential that the French should know what it is that they can and cannot get away with. We shared their fundamental interests and in the longer term it was essential that we should work very closely together. But the prospects for this would be improved if they knew that we would always be prepared to stand up to them.

At the end of 1975, which is very soon after my arrival in Paris, UK-French high-level relations can be seen to have reached a low ebb; and it was in this atmosphere that I presented my credentials to President Giscard on 23 December. In the course of a short talk I said I hoped that he would feel free to talk to me whenever he wished about political affairs in London, as well as about any particular problems between the two countries. I had had such a contact with Chancellor Schmidt. I said that I knew personally several of the leading political personalities in the UK. He asked me who, and among other names I dropped Roy's. He sparked at this, showing no interest in anyone else I had mentioned. He said that he had a great regard for Jenkins. He had read his book on Charles Dilke with admiration. I said that Roy would be visiting Poniatowski, his opposite number, in a few months' time, upon which the President commented that he would like to have a private meeting with him.

He went on to say that it had not been possible to visit the UK last October because the Queen's and his programmes did not permit it.

I have been struck in recent conversation with British ministers by their pessimistic prognosis of Harold Wilson's health. The widespread opinion amongst those at the top is that he is not as perky as he was. The *Daily Mail* has just carried a long piece of political gossip by Dempster about the tiredness and ill-health of the PM. The story gave the impression that it had been inspired by some authoritative source. Callaghan was mentioned as the most likely person to step into Wilson's shoes if, as the article suggested, he were to resign.

The PM asked Callaghan to see John Dickie[1] of the *Daily Mail* who was in Paris for the meeting to try to get him to write a story correcting the impression of the PM's rapidly failing powers. He duly saw Dickie, but the article published the next day amounted to a violent attack on Callaghan for his mishandling of the conference and for leaving Paris less than twenty-four hours after arriving.

---

[1] John Dickie, diplomatic correspondent of the *Daily Mail* for three decades. Never without a carnation in his buttonhole, he brought to his paper both panache and a probity in reporting such as was more usually to be found in the 'heavies'. Nor can anyone say that the bestowal on him of the OBE has blunted his edge.

I noticed that Callaghan had brought with him for bedtime reading Robert Blake's book, *The Office of Prime Minister*. 'God forbid I should ever have to be in Harold's shoes,' Callaghan protested when he saw that I had caught sight of the title.

Relaxing with Mary and me before the Commonwealth dinner Callaghan said what a relief it was not to be Chancellor of the Exchequer with responsibility over the exchange rate. A couple of nights later Denis Healey, sitting in exactly the same spot, made the same remark the other way round: what a relief it was not to be dealing with foreign affairs.

The night before, Healey, helped by a good dinner and an entourage of Treasury officials, had criticised the Foreign Office for not stopping the Foreign Secretary from getting into such a difficult position over the separate seat issue. I protested at this, which Healey did not like. He retorted by asking me how I justified the high figure of my *frais* that had recently been published in answer to a parliamentary question. I rejoined that it was necessary for entertaining people like him. Later the same evening he flattered Treasury officials in contrast to Foreign Office ones. Derek Mitchell, who was sitting next to him, was singled out for particular praise.

Healey was more agreeable in private with Mary and me over, and after, dinner on Saturday night, having failed to leave by air as planned on account of fog. He became more indiscreet and interesting as the evening wore on.

We talked a lot about the Prime Minister's health, a subject that seemed no further from the forefront of his mind than it was from that of the Foreign Secretary. He began, of course, by saying that he did not want to leave his present job. He needed another two years to get the country's finances straight. But the Prime Minister was showing extreme weariness. A Cabinet colleague who was close to him had told him in great confidence that Wilson would be likely to go sooner rather than later. I said that I knew who that colleague was because he had said the same to me in a similar spirit of confidence. Healey was surprised when I guessed the name correctly. The effect was to make him even more indiscreet.

Inevitably we got on to the succession. Healey thought that if it occurred now Callaghan might just beat him to it. He, Healey, was certainly in the top bracket. At the moment Wilson was far and away the most popular Labour politician in the country. Everything, of course, depended on the Parliamentary Labour Party. He thought that Roy Jenkins had quite a strong following. People rallied to him though he did little to encourage them. He also had a big following in the country.

Healey indicated that there were many other things that he would be happy to be doing in life than politics. He had spent the afternoon poking about in the antique bookshops on the Left Bank. He said that he was glad that none of his children wished to pursue a political career. He was not sorry that he had not been a civil servant or a diplomat. 'They lack the ultimate power of decision,' he said.

1976

---

3 JANUARY
PARIS

TROUBLES AHEAD

An unpleasant parliamentary and press campaign is being conducted against the overmanning and high allowances of the Diplomatic Service. Paris is under particularly strong attack because the *frais* here are high. The figures of my salary and *frais* are frequently published. I agree with much of the criticism, at any rate so far as the overmanning of the Office is concerned, and I have written to London suggesting I be sent an order to cut the staff by 20 per cent. The costs of running the house is a different and more difficult matter. Soames set up an establishment designed to push out the boat and put Britain on the map in Paris, regardless of cost. I am uncomfortable with the four footmen and major-domo in the house. They spend much time hovering to show how busy they are.

We attended a lunch party at the Wyrouboffs on New Year's Day. They are great friends of the Pierre-Brossolettes (he is the Secretary-General in the President's office). Sabine's sister, Philippine de Ganay, is a great friend of Madame Giscard's sister. So between them they know quite a lot about Giscard's reactions and background. He was not pro-British. Recently at a dinner at Rambouillet to which he had invited some aristocrats following a day's shoot there, the subject of the new British Ambassador was raised. Giscard said that he thought it extra-ordinary that the British government should send someone to Paris whom none of the people round the table knew. Philippine de Ganay, who was sitting next to him, interjected, 'But I know him.' Only to have Giscard dismiss this by saying, 'Oh well you would, of course, because you are such a well-known Anglophile.'

It was suggested at the above-mentioned lunch that I would be wasting my time if I thought I was ever going to make any impact on, or have much personal contact with, the President. No amount of charm would make any difference.

I asked whether it was not perhaps that Giscard just disliked foreigners. To which the answer was that this was not so. He had no hostile feelings towards the Germans, for instance.

Coming on top of Callaghan's recent diplomatic efforts I could not help thinking that my task of promoting Anglo-French relations was going to be even harder than I had realised.

6 JANUARY

PARIS

———

A DESCRIPTION OF GISCARD

The following extract has been amended so as to avoid disclosing, for reasons of confidentiality, the name of my interlocutor.

At dinner last night we met a senior official from the French government. I talked to him about the President. He said that he was so quick that he picked things up without difficulty. If he saw someone his purpose was, not to derive information, or to weigh the pros and cons of some action, but to seduce his listener.

His decisions were taken according to political criteria exclusively. He had attained power, and his main, or perhaps sole, aim was to retain it. I asked him whether he did not think that Giscard had been fortunate so far in his Presidency. He had not had any serious difficulties. Was it not possible that he would run into them one day? The answer I got was that he was an extremely skilful tactician. It was not an accident that he had avoided trouble so far. He could see in advance how difficulties might arise and the most appropriate action to avoid them. He did not like being overladen with detailed work, preferring to keep his mind free for important political decisions. He was like a highly bred racehorse. He wished to conserve himself for the big races. In response to my question about how much of his time he spent on foreign policy the reply was: 'Less than 20 per cent – he doesn't need to spend more. It is the political scene at home that occupies him.'

My interlocutor said that Giscard was not at all anti-American: 'He likes them; he finds them energetic and interesting and, of course, they are powerful.' I refrained from touching on Anglo-French relations or what the President thought of the British. However from others I have talked to I have come to realise how uphill will be the work of anyone from London trying to influence Giscard. It may be some help that he has people around him, like Pierre-Brossolette, who is far from anti-British. After his father's arrest by the Nazis in 1943, the British had managed to smuggle him and his mother to England where they had spent the rest of the war. He would never forget this, so he has said.

5 FEBRUARY
PARIS

HEATH AND MENUHIN AT
THE SORBONNE

Ted Heath has been here for the night to receive on honorary degree at the Sorbonne. The porter who handled his luggage at the Gare du Nord pointed at him and said proudly, '*Je vous connais, n'est-ce pas. Vous êtes Mr Harold Wilson.*' Not the best of starts.

We gave a grand dinner for Heath. The guests included Chirac,[1] Mendès-France,[2] Madame Pompidou,[3] Yehudi Menuhin (also here for an honorary degree), Peter Ustinov and another forty or so people seated around the enormous dining-room table bedecked with Wellington's *surtout de table*, garlands of flowers and cornucopia of fruit. It looked like Aladdin's cave elevated above the ground. Somebody asked Alexandra who our interior decorator was. Mary in fact had spent forty-eight hours on the arrangements, including flowering up the whole house.

Madame Pompidou said something which reinforced my view on the odd idea the French have of us. She told me how nervous she and her husband, who was then President, had been when they had paid their official visit to London. 'You English make one frightened. Georges's and my knees shook at Buckingham Palace.'

I asked why.

'Well, it's all your traditions. We are so frightened of putting our foot in it,' she answered.

A Frenchman with whom I discussed French formality and solemnity

---

[1] Jacques Chirac, member of National Assembly since 1967. President, Rassemblement pour la République (RPR). Prime Minister 1974–6 and 1986–8. Mayor of Paris since 1977.
[2] Pierre Mendès-France, active in the French resistance and the Free French Forces. Prime Minister 1954–5 when his government terminated the war in Indo-China. Long-time leader of the non-Communist left.
[3] Madame Georges Pompidou, widow of the President, she took an interest in the arts. A loyal political supporter of Chirac.

said that he thought the seriousness that pervades everything nowadays is a recent phenomenon dating from May 1968.

I have hit on one way of getting a laugh: to announce well in advance that you are about to make a joke. This worked in Toulouse a fortnight ago where I went to address a large gathering of the Chamber of Commerce. I said, 'We have a tradition in England of introducing jokes into speeches on quite serious occasions. However at a recent dinner I made a speech without any joke in it. When I resumed my seat my hostess, a charming lady, asked me why I had not given them any example of this English humour. I said that it was so difficult to make a joke if one spoke with a strong English accent, upon which, she retorted, *"Monsieur l'Ambassadeur, avec votre accent vous n'avez pas besoin de plaisanteries."* '

I think they got the hang of this and once they had started to laugh they continued to do so. Next day's Toulouse press referred to my deployment of English humour.

To return to Ted Heath, I think that he enjoyed the dinner. He loves a bit of theatre and does not at all mind being at the centre of the stage. Without exactly thanking us he did say that it had been a good party. He spent some of Saturday morning rehearsing with my Private Secretary in the Embassy, Howard Davies,[1] the speech that he was to make in French at the Sorbonne. Despite Howard's coaching his pronunciation remained defiantly un-Gallic with the result that the English members of the audience understood it better than the French.

His performance at the end of the ceremony in conducting the Sorbonne choir and orchestra in the 'Hallelujah Chorus' went down very well.

Menuhin behaved like a saint throughout his visit. Instead of a speech of thanks to the Sorbonne, he played them something on his violin.

---

[1] Howard Davies; my Private Secretary in Paris 1975–6 where he showed a singular combination of originality and responsibility. He then joined the Treasury before switching to industrial consultancy. Since 1992 he has been a highly active and creative Director General of the CBI.

22 FEBRUARY
PARIS

PITFALLS IN THE PROVINCES

On official visits to the French provinces, of which I have just made two, one to Toulouse, the other to Strasbourg, pleasure and pain are closely matched. I find myself frequently comparing such journeys to visits to the Länder in Germany, and am impressed by the similarity, however much people talk about the sharp differences between the French and the Germans. An official lunch with a Minister Präsident in Hanover or Saarbrücken or Wiesbaden is like a parallel occasion in a Préfecture in France, at any rate on the basis of my admittedly limited experience so far. Conversation with the wife of a Préfet runs on much the same lines as one with the wife of a Minister Präsident though there is inclined to be more attack. The food is good, but no better, so far as I can judge on these official occasions, in French provincial towns than in similar ones in Germany.

Before going to Toulouse I had been warned that the Préfet had been ill and that indeed he was making a great effort to be up and about for our visit. Upon arrival at Toulouse airport I was met by his Directeur de Cabinet and I enquired tenderly after his master's health. He explained to me confidentially that it was intestinal trouble. We drove into the town, our journey being made much quicker, but also noisier, by the motorcycle escorts. We drew up at an imposing building, bedecked with the Tricolor and the Union Jack. A huissier opened the door of the car, another showed me up the steps. Guards on duty at the entrance presented arms. After our climb we found ourselves in front of a portly middle-aged couple, evidently there to greet us. I shook the man's hand saying how sorry I was to hear that he had been suffering. He raised his hand to his neck and explained that it had been bad but was now much better. It struck me that there had either been something awry in my briefing or that I had got hold of the wrong end of the stick. It was soon apparent to me that I was being received, not by the Préfet but by the Maire – who may well have been feeling quite well until that moment, suffering from no more than a stiff neck, and who was, no doubt, somewhat perturbed by the gravity of my enquiry. Had I learnt some sinister secrets about his health in Paris? he may have wondered.

Then when, a few minutes later, we met the Préfet I asked tenderly after his health also, Mary, I think, began to wonder whether I had gone off my head. However the Préfet was quite pleased to respond to my solicitations.

Almost immediately upon arrival at a regional capital one is expected to give a press conference. Before reaching Toulouse I had tried to prepare for questions on Anglo-French relations, the Channel Tunnel, Concorde, direct elections to the European parliament, etc. But the press in Toulouse were not at all interested in my admittedly scarcely stimulating replies on these subjects. They wanted to know what I thought of Toulouse and its beautiful churches. It did not seem to matter, or they rendered no account of the fact, that I could not possibly have had time to see them properly, if at all; but I should have been forewarned because the same thing had happened to me in Strasbourg. At Toulouse I was asked what I thought of the local wine. Here I made another gaffe. I said that I had never drunk it. 'Was it,' I asked, without any wish to be polemical, 'like wine from Bordeaux?' The journalists were discountenanced; and there was much shaking of heads. 'Well then,' I asked innocently, 'is it like the wine on the other side of the border, like Spanish wine?' This produced expressions of incredulity. The next day there was critical press comment under headlines in the *Dépêche du Midi* about my ignorance of the produce of the region. The day after the press conference I had to make a speech at a luncheon given by the Toulouse Chamber of Commerce. I was assured that it was their biggest gathering since Pompidou's visit in 1971. Monsieur Cavaillé, the Minister of Transport, who is in charge of Concorde, was present. In the course of my remarks I admitted that I had caused offence the previous day by showing ignorance of Toulouse wine. It seemed to me, however, I said, that my strategy had been effective because I noticed that at the lunch my hosts had come forward with a particularly wide selection of the most delicious local wines. In fact, as a result of my gaffe, there was a noticeably comprehensive display at the table of all the produce of the region.

I had been warned about the inherent rivalry between Préfets and Maires; the former have the power and panoply of the central government, which they represent; the latter are elected and are usually more popular local figures. I had expected our plans to be thrown out of joint by friction between these two authorities. But at Toulouse we were given a grand lunch by the Préfet which caused the Maire to give an equally sumptuous dinner for us in the evening. We had requested him to forbear from doing so because we had to attend a concert given by the English Chamber Orchestra, under Raymond Leppard, that was due to begin at 9 p.m. However he insisted, with the result that we found ourselves still in the middle of dinner by the time the concert started. The Maire said that he and I would have to make speeches so there was no possibility of getting away early. We did not therefore arrive at the concert hall until halfway through the second half of the programme and we made our way, far too conspicuously, down the gangway to our reserved seats.

The British Council had arranged to give a party for the orchestra after the concert. On emerging from the hall I was told that they would not be coming because they were insulted by my behaviour in turning up late. The manager approached me and said, 'You are obviously a worthy representative of the Queen in your interest in music.'

I had no alternative but to grovel and to explain exactly what had happened. I said that I was in the hands of the French authorities. I apologised profusely. In the end the orchestra turned up. I was abject in apology to the conductor, the first violin, the second violin, to everyone in fact. To make amends for our late arrival at the concert we stayed right to the end of the party and did not get to bed until 2 a.m., having started the day in Paris at 6 a.m., and in the interval having attended two official meals, made four speeches and visited five factories. I was kept going by Poire Williams liqueur and by the sense of occasion that a visitor from Paris seemed to give the people of Toulouse. Mary wore an intriguing fur hat and high fur collar. The Préfet's wife whispered to me late at night – or rather early the following morning – that when she had seen her on arrival on the steps of the Préfecture she had said to herself, 'Here's a typical English lady with her lovely blue eyes.' Mary is Greek and has brown eyes.

13 MARCH

PARIS

———

SUNDAY LUNCH AT LIPP

Mary and I have just had Sunday lunch at the Brasserie Lipp, which has been our favourite Paris restaurant since we first went there some twenty-five years ago. We made personal contact with the proprietor, Roger Cazes, and he is happy to reserve us a table, a privilege for which many Parisians envy us.

Our table was next to that of Françoise Giroud[1] and her companion Alex Grall who owns and runs the publishing house of Fayard. He said that he had just been in London, his favourite city. He was thinking of buying a house there. It was a city for men. Was there any other street in the world like Jermyn Street? 'I love London,' he repeated. 'One has

———

[1] Françoise Giroud, French journalist and politician. Secretary of State for Women's Affairs 1974–6 and for Culture 1976–7. Co-founder of *L'Express* 1953.

the impression that it is the ultimate. It is decadent, yes, the end, that's
what I like about it.'

13 MARCH
PARIS

———

ONE OF THE CLEVEREST PEOPLE I HAVE KNOWN

Olivier Wormser looked in to see me the other day. He had been my
colleague in Bonn and had given me a lengthy and brilliant briefing there
about his native land. One of his main points had been the extent to
which the French defeat of 1940 continued to dominate people's minds
however much this was suppressed on the surface. He had also told me
that I should never forget that France had had a revolution (the effects
of which still coloured their lives) and that we had not. When I reached
Paris I was able to realise how wise had been Olivier's briefing. He is in
fact one of the cleverest people I have known.

I admire his modesty of manner and independence of mind. He is
unseduced by flattery. He is human and frank in his likes and dislikes.
He is a paragon of gratitude. In the early days after the fall of France he
was in London attached to de Gaulle's mission there; and he found
himself on some occasion in the Reform Club where my father was living
during the week. They met and, according to Olivier, became friends,
seeing each other regularly, my father giving Olivier what he regarded,
so he told me thankfully, as invaluable instruction on economics. Olivier
said that he would never forget his kindness and wisdom.[1]

Visiting me now in the Embassy, Olivier asked how I was getting on
and how relations were going between Paris and London. Had I had a
warm reception upon my arrival? I replied that I could not complain at
all about the way I have been received. But relations between our two
countries left a lot to be desired, particularly at the highest level. Giscard,
I elaborated, did not seem to have much time or respect for Britain in
present circumstances. Olivier hesitated for a minute in his reflective way
and then said, 'I wonder if he is aware what Britain's contribution is on
the defence side. After all, you're spending a bigger proportion of your
GNP on defence than we are.' I said that that seemed to be an excellent
approach. Giscard might well not be aware of this point. I repeated to

---

[1] Many years later I learnt that Wormser had given a painting by Vuillard to the National
Gallery in London in acknowledgment of France's debt to the UK after the 1940 débâcle.

Olivier a remark that Giscard made recently to a group of journalists when he had launched his *ballon d'essai* about a directory for Europe. He had dismissed British defence measures as trifling and had said that if a war came France would have to defend Britain.

Olivier was bored in Bonn. He has nothing to do except report on the internal scene. 'I am busy, but not occupied,' was the phrase he used, gazing wistfully out of the window of my office upon the large garden and beyond that to the Pavillon Gabriel and the Champs Elysées. 'I like that much better than the Rhine,' he said.

14 MARCH

PARIS

A VISIT BY ROY JENKINS

Roy was here for a weekend last month. Ostensibly on Home Office business he was more bent on his own private problem of whether or not to seek the post of Presidency of the European Commission. The French won't have Soames in that post. Unfairly, in my view, some of them dislike what they see as his excessive desire for public recognition for his achievements. They do not see diplomacy as something that calls for or justifies personal publicity, nor as a realm of activity in which dramatic successes can be sought and chalked up. They see it much more as the humdrum inconspicuous pursuit of small steps. By contrast, the French have unanimous admiration and affection for Mary Soames.

Roy wants to get out of British politics. Short of some catastrophic event and a realignment of political forces he does not see himself getting to Number 10. He does not like the Home Office. He would not want to return to the Treasury. He explained all this recently to the Prime Minister, indicating that he would probably be thinking of pulling out before long. Wilson said that he understood this but Roy should understand that he could not very well move Callaghan. Wilson went on to say that he supposed Roy would not be interested in the Presidency of the Commission. He hoped he would not be because he wanted him to stay in the government but he mentioned it, he said, in the same way as he had offered the Mastership of Trinity to Rab, not at all thinking that he would accept. Roy followed up the meeting with a letter which he told me was one of the best he had ever written. This asked the Prime Minister to bear Roy's name in mind for the post but without commitment. Despite the Welsh complexity of the letter Wilson appears to have taken it as a green light. He immediately communicated with Schmidt who got in touch with Giscard.

When, therefore, Roy called on Giscard during his visit here the President, without any beating about the bush, immediately offered him the post, saying that Schmidt and he both very much wanted him to accept.

Talking this over with Roy afterwards I said that I did not understand why Giscard was so keen on appointing him because it was French policy to continue to keep highly restricted the powers and influence of the Commission. Surely Giscard must see that Roy would give it too much weight. Late the first evening, lubricated by several bottles of Gevrey-Chambertin 1969, and uninhibited by any reservations from Jennifer who had gone to bed to help recover from flu, Roy revealed to Mary and me his inner feelings on domestic politics and on much else. He was confident that Wilson was going to retire very soon and this of course would affect his decision about the Presidency.

10 APRIL
PARIS

MORE ABOUT ROY

Since my last entry it has been a time of inner Labour Party politics, focused on the election of a successor to Wilson and of a continually falling pound. In France the right have suddenly lost faith in Giscard and in themselves, whereas the left have increased their popularity, judged by the cantonal elections and opinion polls. There is much talk of what will happen internally and externally if the alliance of the left secures a majority in the next legislative elections which are due in the spring of 1978, which is what they look like doing at the moment.

After Roy's bid for the leadership of the party failed he hesitated some time between going for the Presidency of the European Commission and becoming Foreign Secretary, assuming Callaghan was to offer him the post. In the event Callaghan did not do so. Roy has told me on the telephone that Callaghan said that the reasons were political – implying that it was the objections of the left and of the anti-Marketeers that had prevented him making Roy Foreign Secretary. The British press have been almost unanimous in their criticism of Callaghan for putting

Crosland[1] into the job instead of Roy. I have been impressed by Crosland's capacity for rudeness coupled with his complicated character, his unpredictability and his manifest personal charm. Robert Kee[2] once told me of a weekend that the Croslands had spent with them in a cottage in the country. At Tony's request they invited to dinner Hugh Dalton who was living near by. They thought the evening a success and that Dalton had much enjoyed himself. Tony had taken a normal but not leading part in the conversation. After ferrying Dalton home and returning to the house he immediately complained of the triviality of the dinner-time talk, which he said had not been worthy of such a distinguished visitor. A great row ensued. Early the next morning, Sunday, the Kees heard the noise of people on the stairs. They looked out to see the Croslands leaving surreptitiously. Tony explained hurriedly that he could not bear to stay any longer in view of the humiliating failure of the evening before.

Great friends at Oxford, Tony and Roy appear to have become cool towards each other recently. Rivalry may have a lot to do with it but Roy also resents Tony's unmannerliness and what he thinks to be his lack of principle, as over Europe where he has taken an attitude of aloof detachment.

The European press tend to see in Callaghan's failure to appoint Roy as Foreign Secretary a mark of lukewarm Europeanism. Domestic Labour Party politics appear once again to have been dominant. This will not help our position in Europe. In our present economic plight we need all the help we can get from our partners in Western Europe.

Roy told me on the phone that he would now definitely be seeking the Presidency. Once he had made up his mind he admitted that he was beginning to think that he would regret having to leave British politics.

I have paid visits this week to St Malo and Lille. Many speeches. Jokes about cabbages went down well in Brittany where, with the French Minister of Defence, I inaugurated a new car ferry between St Malo and Plymouth. Lille was its usual industrial self. But I was interested to meet Mauroy, the number two in the French Socialist Party. I was much impressed by him.

---

[1] Anthony Crosland, politician and writer. Callaghan made him Foreign Minister in 1976. Roy Jenkins, close friend and rival, has written of his exceptional intellect and personality flawed by 'some uncontrolled demon of discontent'.
[2] Robert Kee, scholar, author and broadcaster. A close friend since Oxford. Champion of victims of injustice. Has written and broadcast much about Ireland. His book, *The Laurel and the Ivy*, is a life of Parnell. In 1991 he married Kate Trevelyan, General Manager, *Burlington Magazine*.

18 APRIL
EASTER SUNDAY

A NEAR GAFFE

I nearly committed another gaffe, not totally dissimilar from the Toulouse one, on a recent visit to Lille.

Howard Davies had told me that I would be meeting the wife of the Préfet on my visit there and that I would quickly be able to identify her because she spoke excellent English, indeed she preferred to speak English to French. I would also be able to spot her because she was pregnant.

I had not been in Lille many hours when, after giving a TV interview in the library of the Consulate General, I was introduced formally to Madame X whose name I did not catch. However, it did not matter. She spoke excellent English and seemed keen to do so. This must be the Préfet's wife, I decided. As our conversation continued I cast my eyes down to her figure. Although not an expert on these matters it seemed to me that she was remarkably thin, though you can never tell these days because people seem to wear pregnancy-type clothes whatever their condition. On the other hand she spoke with authority about Lille where, she indicated, she was engaged on important duties to do with student exchanges and referred to her husband as someone engaged on crucial work in the area. I was wondering how to clarify the issue and whether, for instance, to ask discreetly if she was going to continue with her own duties much longer or if there would have to be a gap when I was wafted away for another encounter elsewhere in the town. This time there was no mistake about it. The wife of the man to whom I was introduced was not merely a perfect English speaker but also demonstrably pregnant. Indeed she talked of almost nothing else. It was as if she had had some inkling of the doubts in my mind. Usually I am not particularly enthusiastic about pregnancy talk or the evident signs of it; but on this occasion I was grateful.

Someone once got their own back on me when I failed to take proper notice when being introduced to a stranger. This happened in Germany. I was in Bremen on some official visit, accompanied by Francis Mac-Ginnis,[1] a large man who was a paragon of a diplomat according to

---

[1] Francis MacGinnis, member of the Diplomatic Service; Director-General British Information Services, NY 1968–72; Counsellor, Bonn 1972–6. Minister, Berlin 1977–83.

many people in Germany and indeed the epitome of an Ambassador. Going round the room being presented to the local dignitaries I was shaking hands and smiling affably when a lady said, 'You have already shaken hands with me, you are starting to do the circle a second time round. Now would you please introduce me to your Ambassador.' She nodded in the direction of Francis who was standing in dignified fashion in the middle of the room.

19 APRIL

PARIS

—

IN A GILDED CAGE

Recently, one beautiful spring morning, a budgerigar appeared at the window of my office. It sat on the balcony rail and gave every impression of wanting to come in, of wishing to return home, which was not surprising I suppose, given the fact that my office resembles a gilded cage – even more gaudy than anything he could have escaped from. I opened the window and in it flew, perching on the ornate cornice just below the multicoloured ceiling depicting Cupid and Psyche, Bacchus and Apollo and indeed various other gods in varying states of nature.

I had forgotten all about the budgerigar when my secretary announced the arrival of an official diplomatic visitor, the Ambassador of Mauritius. He was ushered into the room and I asked him to sit down on the blue satin settee. I offered him coffee and biscuits. We were chatting amicably, and even constructively, about the organisation of the Commonwealth Club in Paris when the budgerigar started to show interest. It began flying in circles around His Excellency's head. The Ambassador, trained in the British tradition, remained inscrutable; and when the budgie started doing the loop-the-loop just in front of his eyes he merely blinked while continuing his exposé of the kind of way he thought the Commonwealth lunches should be organised. I found it difficult to interrupt him by saying, for instance, that I was sorry but that I had just let a budgerigar in through the window. Besides, it seemed to me that he was getting used to it and it enabled him to show a truly Alec Guinness-like phlegm as the bird did a particularly tight turn round his ears. The Ambassador spoke about the importance of providing signed silver trays for all departing Ambassadors, and, as the budgie showed its appreciation by a well-timed fly-past, it occurred to me that this representative from Mauritius might regard the presence of the bird at our meeting as simply a manifestation of traditional British eccentricity. Perhaps he assumed that I always had a budgerigar flying about in my office. I decided, therefore, to continue our meeting without making any reference to it and to see whether he continued to do likewise. He did.

However as he was about to leave I turned the conversation to the flora and fauna of his native island. 'I suppose,' I said, 'you have birds like this flying about everywhere in Mauritius?'

'Well, not quite everywhere,' he replied.

6 JUNE

PARIS

LOCKED OUT OF THE EMBASSY

How pleased the terrorists would be if they knew the tiresome impact on daily life of the security precautions that have been introduced against them. We have a security officer at the front entrance of the Embassy who is Maltese. He speaks neither good French nor English and seems to aim at being disobliging. He is known widely as the Maltese Falcon. He can scarcely communicate with us but he manages to make himself understood, or at any rate, he conveys his resentful attitude towards us. He achieved a gold medal for this last night.

It was a serene summer evening and after supper in the gallery overlooking the garden Mary and I went down the lawn to turn on the sprinklers. When we returned to the house we found that the glass doors had been locked on the inside. 'I bet the Maltese Falcon has locked us out,' Mary said. He had. We tried the bell that has been fixed outside against precisely such an eventuality. I had been told that with this bell there was no need to worry if the door was locked because the ringing would arouse the security guard. However, no amount of ringing made any impression this evening on the Maltese Falcon. We tried hammering on the panes. No response. We shouted to the top of the house where the staff had rooms but they were either out or engrossed in television. I tried to open the office doors on the garden side next door but they were all locked. Mary said that she was beginning to feel cold. I felt in my pocket for my keys with the idea of letting myself out by the garden door into Avenue Gabriel and walking round to the front entrance. But I had left them in my jacket pocket which I had thrown off when leaving the house to deal with the sprinklers. Mary began to talk of breaking windows. It occurred to me, however, that we would never get them mended in time for the Queen's birthday party due to take place the following week. I then remembered that, when picking blossom in the spring, I had been struck by how low at one point the garden wall was between the Chancery garden (which was accessible to ours), and the garden of the club next door, the Centre Inter-Alliée. Perhaps I could climb over the wall and make my way through the club and round into the street to the front of the Embassy.

I crept through the bushes and looked over the wall. There dining demurely outside in the warmth of the summer evening were members of the club being served by many waiters. It looked to me as though the wall was negotiable. Given my very informal attire I realised however that I might have difficulty in negotiating the company beyond – in passing myself off as a respectable citizen making his way between the dining-room tables rather than a cat burglar which is what I more realistically resembled. It so happened that I was particularly shabbily dressed. Having been playing tennis earlier I had simply put on a button-up pullover without any shirt beneath.

Having crept through the bushes on the other side of the wall I straightened myself up, and started walking towards the diners and waiters with as much insouciance as possible. It was difficult not to feel self-conscious because a good many eyes were upon me and they struck me as flickering between surprise and hostility.

I went up to the nearest waiter and explained my plight. I was the neighbour of the Centre and had been locked out of my house. Could I please make my way through the club to the road and thence to my front door. The waiter was unabashed, polite and understanding. He ushered me through with the wave of a white glove. The nearby diners who had obviously heard my statement seemed to understand my predicament.

But this was not the end of the problem. Having arrived at the portal of Number 39 rue du Faubourg St Honoré, the Embassy, I pressed the bell marked *Appel* and waited until the voice of the Falcon came croaking through the grille asking me to identify myself. 'I am the Ambassador,' I said, 'Would you please let me in.'

'Who?' came the response.

'It's the Ambassador,' I repeated, realising that the Falcon was baffled and that he was merely performing his security duties conscientiously, making sure indeed that no interloper entered either on the garden or the road side of the house.

'Ambassador in bed,' he replied, evidently convinced that I was an impostor since he knew, having locked the garden side of the house, that Mary and I were safely upstairs. Who was it then outside in the road clamouring to enter, using my name?

I repeated my identification and request for admission, this time in

French. I listened while the little cogs in the Falcon's mind clicked into place. Eventually they did so and there was a parallel click of the lock of the door which then opened. I stepped into the courtyard and made my way to the front door. This opened just a chink and I could perceive the Falcon peering out nervously. He was reassured at the sight of me, but at the same time astonished.

After we had liberated Mary from the garden the Falcon explained that indeed he had thought we had come in from the garden and were upstairs. That was why he had locked the garden door. He had seen the dog earlier and he had supposed that we must have preceded him. He was certainly in the house. The Falcon seemed amused by the incident. It was the first time I had ever seen him laugh. 'But how,' I asked, 'did you not hear us ringing?'

The Falcon did not understand, so I pointed first to the bell, then to his ears, at the same time assuming a look of interrogation. He grasped the point and then showed us proudly that the bell rang in the pantry and that he made a point of shutting the door between the pantry and the hall. I began asking him what in that event he thought the purpose of the bell was, but I realised that it was absurd.

The Falcon was very pleased with his night's security work. I have never seen him so happy. He had done his best to keep me out of both sides of the house. We went upstairs to bed leaving him wreathed in smiles.

12 JUNE
PARIS

PRESIDENT GISCARD'S STATE VISIT
TO THE UK

I called on the President in preparation for his state visit to the UK. When I had first put the idea of a call to Pierre-Brossolette, the Secretary-General in his office, his reaction was negative. It was in what I call the French *'Je m'en fiche'* mode. The President was very busy; and in any case he did not see diplomats. I pointed out that he was seeing plenty of British journalists. Pierre-Brossolette undertook to do his best, which indeed he did, because I was given an appointment shortly afterwards.

I did not think Giscard would be forthcoming with me in conversation, partly because he had not yet applied his mind to the programme but also because of his current – or perhaps not just current – lack of enthusiasm for Britain and the British. As Pierre-Brossolette had bluntly reminded me, he also had scant regard for diplomats as such. I was determined, however, to avoid appearing in any way defensive when I saw him. I would be as matter-of-fact as possible and certainly avoid giving any impression that our present economic difficulties meant that the meeting would be taking place with us in a position of inferiority.

My doubts and fears proved to be unjustified. My driver wanted to take me in the Rolls. He likes sweeping into the courtyard of the Elysée to salutes all round. But I preferred to walk the step or two up the road. The manner of receiving guests at the Elysée is grand. There is a huissier on every floor in white tie or uniform. The French attach so much more importance than we do to all aspects of ceremony. After waiting a few minutes in an ante-room I was shown through several highly decorated, gilded halls, in two of which secretaries were working, to the end of the building where Giscard greeted me in his study, asking the huissier to bring some tea. He proceeded to have a friendly run over the programme for the visit. I was struck by Giscard's capacity to captivate while keeping his distance. A large bitch – named Jugurtha, so I learned later – lay on the floor asleep. Only subsequently did I identify its race as a braque but it was evident that it was not a labrador so would not do as the wife of the male labrador puppy that the Queen was proposing to give him.

Back now to record some of the preparations for the visit beginning with the Queen's dog. I had suggested a dog as a present, undeterred by my previous experience when a dog had been handed over as an official gift in Germany. In the course of a visit to Bonn, Alec Douglas-Home had given his German opposite number, Walter Scheel, a beagle puppy, handing it over on the terrace of the British Embassy in Bonn, overlooking the Rhine. Beautiful though the Scheels found the puppy they were uncharmed by its attentions to the aubussons and by its habit of leaving bones in the Foreign Secretary's bed. The beagle was not declared persona non grata but was handed over to the local pharmacist who lived near the Scheels' chalet in Austria. As I say, notwithstanding this unhappy precedent, I was sure that a dog would be the most suitable present for the Queen to give President Giscard on his forthcoming state visit to the UK. I discussed the subject with Nicky Gordon-Lennox,[1] the Head of Chancery, who said, 'Obviously. It's just the thing.' He agreed to discuss it with Jean-Paul Anglès, the Head of Protocol, to find out how such a gift would be received. Having got a positive answer I telephoned Martin

[1]Nicholas Gordon-Lennox, member of the Dip. Service. Counsellor and Head of Chancery Paris 1975–9. Ambassador Madrid 1984–9. A free-spirit, he and his wife, Mary, have been life-long friends. In retirement he has managed to combine being a Governor of the BBC, an investment adviser, a Director of Sotheby's and a successful water-colourist.

Charteris[1] at Buckingham Palace and he thereupon undertook to go into action. This was several months before the date of the visit, and, as the time wore on, Charteris telephoned to ask me to confirm that the President would be pleased to have the dog. The final training stages, including some pretty basic French, were due to start and Martin wanted to be quite sure before proceeding.

I had an appointment to see Claude Pierre-Brossolette to discuss the idea of a joint declaration on future high-level consultations between the two countries, and realised that I would be able to tackle the dog question at the end of that meeting. Claude, no more enthusiastic than usual, nevertheless undertook to discuss the idea of a declaration with the President, leaving me with a clear impression, that I conveyed to London, that it would be advisable to keep this subject between the Elysée and the Embassy, and not throw it to the wolves of the Quai. I must say I thought this was right because although the President has no love for the British he is not governed by the Gaullist reflexes of the Quai which cause them to jerk into a negative response when anything is suggested to them from across the Channel. When, at the beginning of June, Michael Palliser, on an official visit to Paris, raised with Geoffroy de Courcel,[2] the Head of the Quai, the idea of a joint declaration, the latter was exceptionally cool towards it: 'It will be frowned upon by the other EEC countries,' Courcel objected, showing a sudden, newfound French sympathy for the smaller members of the Community. This hostile reaction contrasted with the positive one that the President was to show towards the project.

Our initial discussion of the declaration concluded, I moved on to the matter of the dog, saying, 'Before Buckingham Palace gives the green light for the final stage of training to be started I would like to be sure that a dog, a black labrador, from the Queen's own kennels at Sandringham, would be a welcome present for the President.' Claude gave a shrug and said dismissively, '*Quelle idée absurde. Il possède déjà plusieurs chiens. Je suis sûr qu'il n'a pas besoin d'un autre.*' I said that he and I had already cleared the idea in principle some time ago. More shrugs. More sighs of despair. No, Claude was sure that the President would not want yet another dog.

I knew I had to reckon with the fact that the lack of enthusiasm, let

---

[1] Martin Charteris. A devoted and independent-minded courtier. Private Secretary to the Queen 1972–7. Later Provost of Eton and Chairman of the National Heritage Memorial Fund.
[2] Geoffroy de Courcel, distinguished diplomat in the highest traditions of the French Diplomatic Service, concluding his career as Secretary General, Ministry of Foreign Affairs 1973–6. He showed courageous readiness to flout tradition when in 1940 he accompanied de Gaulle to London. Ambassador to UK 1962–72. His wife, Martine, was much admired there for her looks, wit and intelligence.

alone grace, over the dog, was no different from what it had been as regards the visit itself whenever I had discussed it with Claude during the preceding months. He had taken the line that the President was not really interested in the visit at all. He realised that he had to go through with it. It would have very little political interest for him and must be kept as short as possible. This coldness and utter lack of zeal were, I was all too aware, merely a reflection of the temper of relations between our two countries, at any rate in the upper reaches. The whole thing was described to me explicitly as a frightful bore. I tried not to reflect this in reporting to the FCO. However, Buckingham Palace must have come to sense the mood in Paris when the programme kept on being changed so as to make it shorter. The President, having said initially that he would arrive before lunch on Tuesday morning and leave on Friday evening after a day's visit to Scotland, subsequently said that he intending arriving late on Tuesday afternoon and that he would skip the visit to Scotland altogether. These changes were conveyed by the French Embassy in London to the Lord Chamberlain's Office who pointed out that they would mean cancelling the state drive from Victoria station to Buckingham Palace on arrival and causing considerable offence in Scotland, where the Queen's plan to invite the President to Edinburgh had become widely known. Martin Charteris telephoned me asking me to take the matter up directly with the Elysée. The Queen on her own initiative had been giving exceptional attention to the programme. The response from Paris, so Martin left me in no doubt, seemed to London cavalier. 'Would you,' Martin asked, 'try to find out what it is all about and see what you can do?'

So along I went once again to see Pierre-Brossolette. He was by no means out of form. 'Well,' he said, 'it's like a loaf of bread. If it's too long you cut it off at both ends.'

I avoided following him down that lane and said that the President might think it a pity to miss the TV coverage that he would get from the coach drive through London. I had had the impression that he might like the experience of a *bain de foule* in London. This would certainly be his best chance. As for Scotland, I pointed out the awkwardness of cancelling now that the arrangements had gone so far, with, so we thought, the President's approval. The French, after all, had a special relationship with the people of Scotland. I did not say anything about the Queen's involvement or feelings. I refrained from giving any impression that we were seeking a favour. It was the success of the visit from the standpoint of both countries that mattered. I asked Claude to have a word with the President which he undertook to do. I must explain that despite his theatrical casualness Claude was never anything but friendly personally. I was sure that in his attitude he was reflecting the

Mary's Christmas card from Warsaw,
December, 1969.

Gomulka, Cyrankiewicz and Willy Brandt after signing the Polish-Federal German Treaty on December 7, 1970.

NH in the Old Square, Warsaw.

Pingpong against the Chinese.

Hugh and Antonia Fraser, and Mary picnicking by the river Donajec in south Poland.

Mary in Dolna Market, Warsaw.

Mary's Christmas card from Bonn just before UK entry to the EEC.

With Willy Brandt in the German Federal Chancellery.

On the Rhine. Photograph above by Cecil Beaton of Princess Alexandra and Mary with
NH and Ann Fleming in background. Below: Beaton, NH and Mary.

Koenigswinter conference, March 1975: Shirley Williams, Edward Heath, Lilo Milchsack, NH, Johnny von Herwarth, Roy Jenkins.

With Alec Douglas-Home, Foreign Secretary, when giving a Beagle puppy to his German opposite number and Frau Walter Scheel.

Hostess, Commonwealth Ball, Bonn.

Author at masked ball, Bonn.

Zwei hohe Tiere:
Sir Nico Henderson,
der gemeinsam mit seinem
Dalmatiner Zorba („Zwei
Dalmatiner beehren sich") zur
Maskerade der Bonner Köpfe
geladen hatte, versucht
seinem Vierbeiner klarzu-
machen, daß man sich
als Gastgeber nicht vor seinen
Gästen aufs Büfett stürzen
darf, und Zorba begreift:
Botschafter führen ein
Hundeleben

**Masken-
ball der
Bonner
Köpfe**

With President Valéry Giscard
d'Estaing and Foreign Minister
Jean Sauvagnargues at the
Elysée Palace after NH
presented Credentials.

At Concorde assembly plant,
Toulouse, following the
investiture of a British
decoration on chief test pilot,
André Turcat.

feelings of the President, at any rate at this stage before the start of the visit.

Mary and I remained on close terms throughout with Claude's wife. A word now and then with her has enabled us to maintain things in perspective, to keep in the forefront of my mind how exceptionally busy Claude is.

In the end the President reversed his decision. He would arrive on the Tuesday morning as planned; but he would only spend half a day in Scotland. I should stress that no suggestion was made that the President had agreed to go back more or less to the original plan out of deference to British wishes. It was the President himself who had decided, according to his own wishes and interests, what the best programme would be.

Another irritation in the planning stage of the French President's visit occurred over the exchange of decorations, a subject that frequently begets drama. Giscard had been annoyed that when Eddie Tomkins, my predecessor, left Paris, he had not been allowed to accept the Grand Cross of the Légion d'Honneur that the President had wished to bestow on him. Eddie had told him that he could not receive the decoration because of the rule that forbids British Ambassadors from accepting foreign decorations except during state visits. It is a rule that goes back to Queen Elizabeth I's injunction: 'My dogs shall wear no other collars but mine.' When he was consulted about the awards to be given to the British party at the time of his official visit to London some eight months later Giscard said that he wanted to give Eddie his Grand Cross and me something less because I had only recently arrived in Paris. On our side this was thought rather unfair as I had done all the work preparing for the visit. Anyway, after a great deal of toing and froing both of us received French decorations but of a lower order than the Grand Cross. There were difficulties over other awards, Giscard insisting on higher decorations for his own people than he was offering to give ours. Senior members of both governments became involved in the subject. When I showed impatience over this to Nicky Gordon-Lennox he pointed out that this was the sort of thing that dominated all state visits. They were about panoply not substance.

For the sake of the visit and to maintain some degree of cordiality it all ended with Giscard getting his way. Mary and I set off from Paris with a view to accompanying Princess Margaret by train to Gatwick to meet the President who was arriving there by private plane.

The royal train was most agreeable. Our places were marked and we occupied a table with the French Ambassador and Madame Jacques de

Beaumarchais.[1] Colonel Johnnie Johnston[2] of the Lord Chamberlain's Office was in charge of the party. Dressed in uniform and bearing a sword, he had that mixture of efficiency and light-heartedness that is the hallmark of present-day royal impresarios. He told us that during the journey we would be asked to go along and be presented to Princess Margaret. In due course the four of us filed along the corridor to the royal presence. Princess Margaret asked me if I would join her for the return journey with the Giscards. 'So much easier,' she said, 'for four people to talk rather than three.'

So there I was, an hour or so later, seated next to Madame Giscard in the royal carriage. Princess Margaret was on her left and Giscard the other side of the Princess.

The Giscards were on their most gracious behaviour. Madame Giscard was positively chatty – about gardens, her sister and travel. Princess Margaret offered drinks. The conversation became general and, through some turn that I cannot recall, the name of de Gaulle cropped up. Giscard said that he thought that it would be wrong to regard the general as anti-British. 'I remember,' he said, crossing his legs, smiling and enunciating the words with pursed lips as he does when he wants to be even more seductive than usual, 'I remember a French Cabinet meeting in the early sixties when the Concorde aircraft project was discussed. I was the Minister of Finance and I spoke against Concorde because of the high cost that it would entail. The Minister of Industry put the case in favour. When the general came to sum up he said that of course I was right. On financial grounds the project was indefensible. But nevertheless he would decide upon continuing with it because it was a collaborative project with the British. It was the only one of its kind and it was most important to keep something going in which the French and British were both working practically together.'

In defiance of chronology I must record here something else about Concorde and the state visit. In the speech that the Queen was going to deliver that evening at the state banquet at Buckingham Palace there was mention of Concorde. The Queen asked Martin Charteris to clap loudly when she came to this point and to encourage others in his vicinity at the banquet to do likewise. All went according to plan. I do not think that it is usual for royal speeches to be interrupted, even by applause, but with Martin Charteris leading the clapping

---

[1] Jacques de Beaumarchais, French diplomat of unusual flair. Ambassador to UK 1972–7. His wife, Marie-Alice, is renowned for her exceptional elegance and intellectual vitality.
[2] Johnnie Johnston; Comptroller, Lord Chamberlain's Office 1981–7. Always cheerful and never pompous he made the conduct of even the most protocolaire piece of business an occasion of pleasure.

everyone else was encouraged to join in so that the response was thunderous. When he came to give his press conference at the end of the visit Giscard said that before his arrival he had been led to think that the British were not very enthusiastic about Concorde. He realised now that he had been wrong. When the Queen had referred to Concorde in her banquet speech there had been spontaneous and loud applause.

I regard this story as a tribute to the Queen's understanding of the workings of guided democracy.

To return to the royal train, we rolled into Victoria station to be met by the Queen, Prince Philip, the Prime Minister and most of the Cabinet. Tony Crosland was conspicuous by not wearing a morning coat. (Roy says Tony always dresses one notch down from what is prescribed; thus if the invitation states white tie, Tony will wear a dinner jacket, if it indicates dinner jacket he will wear a lounge suit.) We were shown to our carriages. It was a brilliant sunny morning. The place seemed alive with bands, horses and cheering crowds. We set off down Victoria Street in what, for me, was the most enjoyable part of the whole visit. Mary and I were in the last of the five carriages. Our companions for the drive were Anglès and Philippe Sauzay, who had been Giscard's Chef de Cabinet since the time he became President. As the procession proceeded through the crowded streets, the French seemed inhibited from responding to the cheers. I found that with a mere raise of the hand it was possible to produce an instantaneous response from both sides of the street, the British public no doubt taking me for a member of the French delegation. I suggested to Anglès and Sauzay that they should try to secure the same reflex action. So they raised hands and received a thunderous response. Our carriage came to be met by a welling roll of applause along the street. But I was more reticent in my royal behaviour when we reached Whitehall as I spied one or two long bureaucratic faces scowling from the pavements by the entrance to the Home Office and Treasury. It was all very well, their expressions seemed to be saying, for members of the Diplomatic Service to deport themselves ostentatiously abroad, but to have them acting in that manner at home in London, well ...

When Giscard had first studied the programme in Paris and seen that it was to begin with a private lunch at Buckingham Palace with his hosts he believed, so I was told, that he was going to have a very small intimate party with the Queen and Prince Philip and perhaps one or two other members of the royal family. It was explained to him that the lunch would be rather a bigger affair than that. Nevertheless I am not sure that he realised quite how large such a family lunch could be. I sat between

Susan Hussey and the Duchess of Grafton,[1] opposite the Queen and Giscard. Princess Margaret was on Giscard's other side. I was able to observe that the Queen and Giscard got on like a house on fire. I think they spoke English most of the time. It seemed evident to me that they were both out to charm the other and neither is bad at doing so. I was sure that this first lunch, like the journey to London from Gatwick on the royal train, was highly important in getting the visit off to a good start.

After lunch came the exchange of presents. These were laid out in a small ante-room and the guests filed past them. As with the exchange of decorations so with the gifts, the British side were the more generous. Giscard's present was a modern Sèvres service. In addition to the insignia of the Order of the Bath, a beautiful gilt jewelled box was also given to the President by the Queen and Prince Philip. Then there was the lengthy pedigree of the dog and a fine dog whistle.

The Queen led Giscard out on to the terrace at the back of Buckingham Palace where a healthy-looking man in knickerbockers was in attendance, waiting to present Sandringham Sambo, a two-year-old labrador. I must say I thought it looked on the stout side but was immediately reassured by its athletic performance. The handler had a machine that shot an object some distance into the garden. Sandringham Sambo dutifully ran after it and brought it back to the terrace. Although there were plenty of duck about round the lake in the garden the labrador had stuck to his appointed task. He posed with the President for a photograph which, as it turned out, was the most publicised photo of the whole visit.

When I went to the Elysée a fortnight later for the customary 14 July party, I asked Michèle Gay of the President's staff, with whom I play tennis regularly, if she could help me to track down Sandringham Sambo. I said that I had sent to London an account of the President's visit seen from the official angle but that I was sure that there were certain people who were eagerly waiting news of how the dog was getting on in his new home. Silly, I know, but the English are like that about animals. She agreed willingly and mobilised another member of the Presidential Cabinet who thought the dog was probably in the kennels on one side of the garden. Leaving the throng of guests busy picking up political gossip or pursuing some official duty we made our way through dark undergrowth to the two gloomy, prison-like kennels, one of which was empty, the other occupied by a surly-looking braque. 'That's Jugurtha,' Michèle explained, 'she bites people.'

---

[1] Fortune Grafton, Mistress of the Robes to the Queen since 1967.

'But where is Sandringham Sambo?' I asked.

'Oh, he must be somewhere,' was the answer. Then, seeing that this left me little upon which to construct a report to London, Michèle added, trying to be helpful, 'Perhaps he is in the President's study. He is often there.'

This cheered me up. The thought that Sandringham Sambo at least shared some of his new master's working hours would be a comfort to London.

'Well, let me know,' I said. 'If, when you see him, you can give me a reassuring account of his health so that I can tell London, that would be most useful.'

I have seen Michèle several times since for tennis and she has been to dinner with us but there has been no word about the dog. I have wondered at times whether he was going to be cast out like Scheel's beagle; but then I have quickly reminded myself that he is not a down-holsterer like the beagle but a working dog needed to help the President on his hunting trips. Later I heard that he had been absorbed happily into the household (see entry for 11–12 November 1976).

This account of the President's state visit to the UK avoids any assessment of the political consequences. I was in no doubt at the time that the trouble taken to put together an entertaining programme, the personal attention shown by the royal family, and the panache with which it had been carried out had made an impression on the President. I do not say that they overrode the opinion he had been forming of the country's rapid and irreversible economic decline; but they made him think better of us in a number of ways and this was to become evident to me as time went on.

Relations between the two countries in the higher echelons were not to reach the low ebb they had plumbed in the previous year; and this was thanks to the changed attitude, or at any rate sentiment, of the French President, partly as a result, I think, of the visit.

The declaration on high-level consultations that had emerged from the visit as planned was not just a high-sounding expression of hope. It signified an earnest intention to give to relations between London and Paris something of the importance attached to those between Paris and Bonn; and for a time it certainly succeeded in having this effect.

Whenever subsequently I have been asked, as has happened frequently, whether official visits which are usually costly, time-consuming and, in many ways, such as the consequent traffic congestion, tiresome to the public, can be regarded as doing any good from the standpoint of the national interest, I have replied emphatically that they certainly can be

*as I have seen from my own experience – and in saying this I have had
in mind in particular the impact of Giscard's visit to London in 1976.*

SUMMER
PARIS

REGGIE MAUDLING AND LES MISÉRABLES

Les Misérables was founded just after the war so that those living in Paris
who had been involved in the war on the French and British side could
continue to meet each other over dinner. It has been a problem for British
Ambassadors for some time. The Ambassador is the President. It is his
club. He has to organise the dinners. By the mere passage of time the
membership has become somewhat geriatric, yet nobody is prepared to
kill off the club, nor to let it die because it does serve as some sort of
link. The leading figure on the French side, Monsieur Durand Reville, is
convinced that the club provides British Ambassadors with a distinguished
ready-made list of contacts; and, to be sure, there are famous names among
them, e.g. Mendès-France, Joxe,[1] Raymond Aron,[2] Geoffroy de Courcel –
but these are people one would probably meet anyhow. The age-old
problem of what to do with the club has usually been solved by getting a
large number of Embassy staff to come along and bring guests from among
their regular French contacts. So Les Misérables has stumbled on.

Its name comes from the fact that the first meeting-place was the house
in which Victor Hugo had lived. Kenneth Rose[3] who was here the other
day asked me if it was true that the club was named after Zola's house.
Gently I corrected him to Hugo. 'My word that was a good one', he
said, the old school master's love of a howler bursting to the surface.

Howard Davies, my Private Secretary, is the chief organiser. He suggested that for the first dinner under my chairmanship we should have a
distinguished visitor. I invited Reggie Maudling, Shadow Foreign Secretary, who told me some time ago that he would like a pretext to visit

---

[1]Louis Joxe, diplomat and politician. Secretary-General of the Committee for National
    Liberation 1943–4 and of the Government 1944–6. Ambassador to USSR 1952–5; to
    Germany 1955–6. Minister of State in charge of Algerian affairs 1960–2.
[2]Professor Raymond Aron, author. Edited *La France Libre* in London 1940–4. Held various
    Chairs 1955–78. A universally accepted sea-green intellectual of the right.
[3]Kenneth Rose; biographer, columnist and friend. His column in the *Sunday Telegraph* has
    been widely read as respectable Sabbath eavesdropping for over thirty years. He has
    written a brilliant portrait of Curzon. His life of King George V is a model of a readable,
    unreticent royal biography.

Paris. Howard met him at the airport and I gave a lunch for him to which I invited leading members of the UDR, e.g. Olivier Guichard[1] and Debré.[2] The conversation became general towards the end of lunch and Debré held forth. I was astonished, as was Maudling, by the unregenerate nationalism of his views, expressed with vehemence amounting to fanaticism. He was particularly vexed by the idea of a directly pre-elected European parliament which would impinge upon the pure sovereignty of the nation state. He did not like the idea of a European union at all. He worked himself up into a state of high indignation over the threat that all these newfangled ideas posed to the manhood of France and to the spirit of France. Somehow the recent divorce and abortion laws came to be included in his long indictment, delivered with such burning passion and sincerity that nobody round the table dared to interrupt, not even Guichard who could not have gone along with much of it. In his few remarks at the end of Debré's tirade, Maudling sounded in comparison like a long-committed European, instead of being what he is, a recent convert to something that he does not believe in very deeply. But he was astonished by Debré's uncompromising nationalism, though less so than by the realism he later ran into with the Foreign Minister, Sauvagnargues. Maudling was, I think, a little shocked because Sauvagnargues had nothing good to say about Europe which he described as nonsense and 'eye-wash'. He spoke scathingly of those who favoured a directly elected European parliament. 'You British are quite right in regarding it all as "eye-wash"' – a favourite term.

However, before the Sauvagnargues meeting there was a long afternoon of siesta for Maudling. Howard Davies commented how satisfactory it was when the picture of a public personality as depicted by *Private Eye* turned out to be, if anything, an understatement. I also thought that the description of Maudling as an 'unmade bed' was particularly appropriate.

After the dinner that evening, which like the evenings of many dining clubs was a mixed blessing depending largely on drink and conversation, I asked one or two of the Misérables to come back to the Embassy for a nightcap. These included Philippe de Rothschild,[3] who, when I offered

---

[1] Olivier Guichard, politician. Principal Secretary to de Gaulle 1947–54. Minister of different departments of State 1967–77.

[2] Michel Debré, politician. Ardent supporter of de Gaulle, whom he served as Prime Minister 1959–62. Also Minister of Economic Affairs, then Foreign Affairs 1966–9, and Defence 1969–73.

[3] Philippe de Rothschild; a somewhat unusual scion of the great family; with literary interests and a gift for translation, particularly Elizabethan texts; owner of Château Mouton-Rothschild, he brought about the upgrading of its status to 1er Cru Classé, the only wine to be reclassified to First Growth since Bordeaux wines were classified in 1855. He commissioned paintings for the labels of each vintage.

to open some excellent claret, implored me not to open anything from his château as he knew it all too well. I cannot recall what the conversation was about, probably the past, and certainly it was not very serious. But I know that we sat in the library and that we had not got through a bottle – Pétrus 1953 – before Maudling was asleep. He was in one of the high-back leather chairs and from then on contributed nothing to the party except loud snores. I calculated that it was his third sleep of the day leaving out of account what may have happened in the aeroplane.

In talking to me about himself Maudling seemed relaxed to the point of detachment. He supposed that Christopher Soames was after his job as Shadow Foreign Secretary. He was convinced that he would do it very well. He had a high opinion of Callaghan whom he believed the Labour Party would have done better to have chosen as their leader rather than Wilson. Callaghan had great authority in the House of Commons.

17 OCTOBER

PARIS

———

THE THINK-TANK INVESTIGATES THE

EMBASSY

Much indignation in the Embassy, shared by me, over the visit this past week of the Central Policy Review Staff (CPRS), a group appointed at the end of last year by the Prime Minister and Foreign Secretary to investigate the conduct of foreign policy. This is the third such enquiry in the past fifteen years. True, Plowden[1] and Val Duncan[2] did the service no harm but the setting up of yet another and outwardly more hostile enquiry has not been good for morale.

Apart from the leading member of the group, Sir Kenneth Berrill,[3] there are three investigators: Mr Young, a middle-ranking official from the Ministry of Defence. John Odling-Smee,[4] an economist, and Tessa

---

[1] Edwin Plowden, a great public servant in the category of Oliver Franks, he chaired a committee on overseas representation 1963–4.
[2] Val Duncan, Chairman and Chief Executive, the Rio Tinto-Zinc Corporation, since 1964. Chairman Review Committee on overseas representation 1968–9.
[3] Kenneth Berrill, economist, public servant and financier. Head of Central Policy Review Staff, Cabinet Office 1974–80 (CPRS) when he chaired an enquiry into the conduct of foreign policy.
[4] John Odling-Smee, fellow in Economics, Oriel College Oxon 1966–70. Economic Adviser to CPRS 1975–7; to HM Treasury 1977–80. Under-Secretary and then Deputy Chief Economic Adviser HM Treasury 1982–90. Director European II Department IMF since 1992.

Blackstone,[1] who was on the national executive of the Labour Party until her appointment to the CPRS. Berrill himself is head of the think-tank and before that was Chief Economic Adviser to the Treasury. He dined with us alone one night and talked exclusively about the state of the British economy. He takes the view that on present estimates there is no reason to suppose that we are ever going to pick up economically. He foresees irreversible decline; and with this decline an inevitable reduction in our standard of living, both in relation to other countries and to that of our own past. The key lies in our poor industrial production. The organisation of, and attitude of mind in, many of our trade unions is partly responsible. Berrill gave an example of our malaise, drawn from the motor industry. A plant working for Chrysler may be making exactly the same car with the same assembly-line and machinery in the UK and on the Continent. The output of the factory in the UK is 50 per cent less than that elsewhere. As he talked depressingly about the poor state of this and that section of our manufacturing industry I could not help wondering why the CPRS were not focusing on them rather than devoting their time to the relatively inexpensive and successful process by which our foreign policy is conducted.

Berrill took a very moderate line in talking to me about the objectives of his review. His enquiry would not be an 'inspection', with the exception of the defence set-up in Washington. No single Embassy would be singled out for cuts. It was the broad canvas of the conduct of British policy abroad, including the interests of the Department of Trade, that was the focus. However, he was less reassuring in talking to other members of the Embassy staff. He admitted to being critical of our 'lifestyle' and targeted the drinks trays Mary leaves in guests' bedrooms adding that he did not get through a bottle of gin in three months in his office.

In conversation with Ronald Arculus[2] on the way to the airport upon his departure, Berrill explained that the middle classes at home were being so hit by inflation and taxation that there was great resentment at anyone abroad living on a grander scale. His idea, and that of the other members of his team, was that if you represented a tatty country you should accurately reflect it by being tatty also. There was complaint apparently about our Rolls-Royce image. It was suggested that we should give up the Residence and live in a small house in the suburbs. I intimated that the French would regard this as a sign of sharp decline, just at the moment when we were trying to persuade them, and others abroad, that

---

[1] Tessa Blackstone; Adviser CPRS 1975–8. Master Birkbeck College since 1987 when created Life Peer. Opposition spokesman on education and science in the Lords since 1990.
[2] Ronald Arculus, member of the Diplomatic Service; Minister (Economic) Paris 1973–7. Ambassador to Italy 1979–83.

despite all the terrible trade figures, productivity rate, etc, we were not down and out but determined to recover.

Ms Blackstone said that in London she thought it appropriate that the representatives of Third World developing countries should entertain on a very modest scale. She believed that English people liked to be given simple food and drink by foreign embassies. She asked me if the French were different from the English in this respect. I said that I thought they were. I also said that even if we were in a parlous economic condition we had not yet reached the status of a Third World developing country. At a large buffet lunch that I gave for the CPRS team and for a visiting delegation of Members of Parliament, Mary served her most austere menu. I had implored her to make it as simple as possible and to insist on people serving themselves. There had to be no excessive waiting. However, this did not prevent Ms Blackstone complaining afterwards – not to me personally – about the over-lavish style in which we entertained. To me she said that she had heard that the French resented the extravagant scale of entertaining at the British Embassy because they could not return it in their homes and this embarrassed them. At her request I had put her at lunch next to Monsieur Ripert, who is head of the Plan. She talked to him and, without any beating about the bush, asked, 'Tell me, do you think this sort of entertaining does any good?' Somewhat flabbergasted he told her that he thought it was both agreeable and useful.

Although they said nothing to me about it, the team apparently disapproved of the respectful way the Embassy staff treated me almost as much as they did of my lifestyle. 'Why,' they asked, 'do they call the Ambassador sir? Why do they get up when he comes into the room?'

The odd thing is that my Private Secretary, Howard Davies, who hitherto has hardly been regarded as a pillar of the establishment and who to some has appeared downright bolshie, has reacted strongly against the prejudices of the CPRS team. As part of their process of eliminating the 'Rolls-Royce image' of the Embassy they have suggested the need to wipe out my private office altogether. But neither Howard, nor Joan[1] – also in my private office – reacted favourably when, working late one evening – I was away in London for a meeting – they were spotted in the office by Ms Blackstone who sniffed that their presence there at such an hour was a 'typical example of over-administration'.

The French gave us wonderful support. They insisted that the British

[1] Joan Hopkins, Private Secretary in the Paris Embassy to Edward Tomkins and then to me. Later Vice-Consul and Second Secretary in New York. She subsequently served in several departments of the office. Nobody could have been better at dealing in French with awkward visitors and telephone callers.

and German foreign services were the only ones for which they had any respect. They were on the point of introducing reforms to make their service more like that of the British. To us they confessed privately that they could not understand what the enquiry was all about unless it was to bring about the same decline in the British Diplomatic Service as seemed to be taking place in so many other areas of British life. There is something in this. Mr Young says that the Service should have people in it of lower quality. Mr Hurrell, who arrived halfway through the week and who has been seconded to the team from the Overseas Aid Department, thinks that at least thirty Ambassadors should be appointed from his department with corresponding reductions in those appointed from the Foreign Service. Ms Blackstone does not seem to believe that a separate Diplomatic Service is necessary at all. The work should be done by home civil servants and by people sent out from Whitehall on special missions. Mr Odling-Smee believes that it might be better to remove all trade-promotion work from the Diplomatic Service and create either a separate service (as existed before 1945) or leave the work to Chambers of Commerce. Members of Berrill's team are clearly determined to get their swingeing views into print, whatever he may think. I have been thinking about how the Service could defend itself. I believe that our staff associations should become mobilised for the task. We should canvass MPs and must prevent the report holding the field. Here abroad we sense a tendency at home to favour rolling with the punch. That is not our stance.

25–28 OCTOBER

PARIS

VISIT BY THE QUEEN MOTHER

For a long time it has been planned that the Queen Mother would come to Paris at the end of October to open the new British cultural centre. A great deal of work has gone into the detailed arrangements. Sir Martin Gilliat, her Private Secretary, came here on three separate occasions to go through every item of the programme.

Her Majesty could scarcely have arrived at a moment when Britain's reputation in France was lower. The morning when she reached here, the pound, having slipped badly for weeks, registered a record fall. The French press were full of the '*effondrement*' of '*la livre sterling*', the '*effacement*' of the UK and of the '*dégringolade*' of our economy. For days I have found listening to the news on the French radio, and hearing the French commentaries upon our '*déclin*' unbearably humiliating. The pound has come to have the same place in registering our collapse as a thermometer has in recording the health of a hospital patient. To me the almost constant attendance at the bedside during the prolonged, seemingly irrevocable, malaise, has been so depressing that I have lain awake at night wondering how we can possibly go on like this and how we should best comport ourselves abroad. It has seemed impossible to go on making those brave speeches that I have delivered for so long, not entirely convinced myself of their validity, about our situation not being as bad as it looked.

Well, from the moment the Queen Mother descended the steps of her aircraft of the Queen's Flight at Le Bourget on Monday afternoon, dressed in her usual powder blue Norman Hartnell attire, and wearing her beaming smile, we felt our spirits rise. She is a great enjoyer and radiates happiness. I have a rendering now of the word that Giscard favours so often and that we find untranslatable, '*rayonnement*'. The word describes the Queen Mum's effect on those around her.

As we walked from the aircraft to the airport lounge, the Queen Mother said how lovely it was to be back in Paris. 'The air's so delicious here,' she said, twinkling, though in point of fact the pollution in the Paris air has been particularly bad of late when autumn fog is descending. However, nothing was going to dissuade the Queen Mother from enjoying herself and saying so.

She arrived, as is the wont with royalty, accompanied by an enormous entourage. Apart from Gilliat there was Viscountess Hambleden (Lady-in-Waiting), Miss Gosling, a secretarial assistant who dealt with the presents and typed out little speeches, and a footman (whose role appeared to be to put a tartan rug over HM's knees whenever she entered the Rolls and to help serve her at the table; he wore a Windsor tailcoat of hunting pink cloth which the French found 'very chic'. He got on famously with our footmen, such is the bonhomie of this particular international whose Mecca, I suppose, is Buckingham Palace). There were also two ladies' maids, a hairdresser and a detective.

The visit coincided with that of the King of Spain.[1] His life is threatened by Basque terrorists. We were frequently crossing Juan Carlos's motorcade and I suggested to the Queen Mother that it would be such a pity if our car was mistaken for his and she found herself dying for Spain. She said she quite enjoyed this bad taste joke, as she described it – not so the detective who was sitting in the front of the Rolls.

---

[1] Juan Carlos I became King of Spain in November 1975.

Staying with us also were the Graftons who are close friends of the Queen Mother. But that was not all, because another friend, Ruth Lady Fermoy[1] and Her Majesty's Treasurer, Sir Ralph Anstruther, were also 'in attendance'. They stayed in a hotel nearby and, at Queen Elizabeth's request, were invited to dinner the first evening and to the Embassy reception. Nor should I forget Air Commodore Archie Winskill, the Captain of the Queen's flight, who stayed throughout the visit and whom we managed to fit in to all the parties. It was not possible to imagine that he could be more skilled flying the plane than he was graceful in the social life of the Embassy. He has a French wife and was Attaché in the Embassy in Paris some time ago.

It is the size of the tail of these royal parties that makes these visits so much more complicated for the house than those of other VIPs. They all have to be at the beck and call of Her Majesty and therefore lodged and fed close at hand. A special bell had to be installed between Her Majesty's bed and the room of one of her lady's maids in case she wanted her at night. It was difficult to believe that the Queen Mother can have had many sleepless moments, such was the serenity of her temperament and the evident soundness of her constitution.

A second aircraft of the Queen's Flight had to bring the luggage, which arrived earlier the same afternoon so that it could all be unpacked by the time the visitors arrived.

In the drive to the Embassy from the airport I found the Queen Mother easy to talk to. The only awkward moment was when she asked me about the English church. Not yet having been inside it, I prevaricated, replying that there had been an unfortunate split.

'But I presume you go to St George's,' she said.

'Oh yes,' I assured her.

Luckily the conversation changed. So far as I know she never reverted to the subject of the English church in Paris during her stay. To prevent any possible renewal of it, however, on that initial drive I got quickly on to the subject of politics upon which I knew that the Queen Mother was outspoken.

She did not seem to take a close interest in what the English papers were saying during her visit. However, one afternoon we were asked to send out our head butler to buy her a copy of *Sporting Life* so that she could read about the latest racing form and results. She explained to me in the course of one exchange of confidences in the car that the Queen (she always refers to her by her title, never as 'Elizabeth' or as 'my daughter') was 'flat' and she was 'steeplechase'. From her attitude to our

[1] Ruth Lady Fermoy, Woman of the Bedchamber to Queen Elizabeth the Queen Mother 1960–90.

dalmatian dog I got the hang of her feeling for animals. She was not at all worried by his omnipresence during her visit. Martin Gilliat had told me beforehand that there would never be any complaints about the dog. I avoided dog-talk with her, however, as she owns corgis for which I would have been unable to express adequate enthusiasm.

During our several car rides in the three days of her stay, and on odd occasions when we were together, as just before her departure when we sat chatting in the Salon Vert following the President's lunch, I came to understand something of her talent for drawing people out, of showing interest and of exerting charm, without having to say anything very memorable. Indeed I can recall little of the words she used, but a great deal of the warmth of her personality and her infectious *joie de vivre*.

11–12 NOVEMBER
RAMBOUILLET
———
BILATERAL SUMMIT

The Prime Minister has been here for a bilateral visit this week. He could not have arrived in more inauspicious circumstances. The pound has been falling headlong. Our economy has been doing worse than ever. Politically the government at home, having just lost two by-elections and having been beaten in the House of Commons, looks irretrievably weak. Yet our relations with the French have been better than for a long time. This is not perhaps surprising as the French want us to be down even if they do not want us to be out. So they will take trouble to help us – within limits. They fear that a complete collapse by us would be bound to affect them adversely. They are very sensitive to the growing relative strength of Germany. It is indicative that in Giscard's book,[1] which has sold one and a half million copies in less than a month, largely through clever marketing, with copies on sale next to the cashier at food shops, the only mention of the UK is when reference is made to France's superior GNP. This is described as 'marking a decisive advantage in the greatest rivalry in European history'. The significance of the FRG, according to Giscard's book, is that France must make sufficient effort to catch up with them economically by 1984.

Giscard's state visit to the UK in June of this year laid the basis for our new and better relationship. He even felt paternal about the idea of

---
[1] *La Démocratie Française*, 1976.

regular high-level ministerial meetings between us – of which this week's meeting in Rambouillet was the first in the series. Wilson's departure from office has also helped. I think Giscard has quite a liking and respect for Callaghan whom he regards as being like a politician of the Fourth Republic. Because of parliamentary difficulties at home and the refusal of the Tories to grant pairs, the Prime Minister arrived at Rambouillet accompanied only by Crosland. Healey, Dell[1] and Silkin[2] turned up the next morning. There were many last-minute changes. Nevertheless there were many signs before the visit that the President was determined to put himself out and to make the most of the occasion.

I drove with Callaghan from the airport to Rambouillet, about a half-hour's drive, so there was plenty of time for talk.

He said that he was glad to get away, to escape from the pressure, and not to have the Chancellor of the Exchequer asking to see him every half-hour about some crisis. He wished he was back in the Foreign Office. That was the best department. The trouble with Number 10 was that you had the political burden. It took about half his time. Then people were always getting at him over honours. He could see the look on their faces when they approached him in the lobby of the House of Commons. You could read the words OBE written upon their features. He said that Harold was much better than he was as Prime Minister in a number of respects, particularly in his capacity for keeping several balls in the air at the same time. I said that it was this very facility that had undermined credibility. Callaghan did not comment on this.

I was impressed by Callaghan's joviality. He was confident that sterling would not collapse entirely. Other countries would not let that happen. Likewise Healey when he arrived the following morning, was buoyant, for all the world as though he had nothing at all to bother about. He had the effrontery to begin his remarks to the plenary session under Giscard's chairmanship with a comparison between the present British and French economies that suggested that our difficulties were on a par with theirs. 'We have got one advantage over you,' he said in his immodest way, 'and that is that we have got an incomes policy, and you have not.' He proceeded to give figures of our present rate of strikes that were highly favourable.

Giscard replied that he did not think our economic situations were comparable. He refrained from drawing attention to our low growth, balance of payments difficulties, poor productivity, etc, but pointed out

[1] Edmund Dell, Secretary of State for Trade 1976–8. Member of Committee of Three, appointed by European Council to review EEC procedures 1978–9.
[2] John Silkin, Minister for Planning and Local Government 1974–6. Minister of Agriculture, Fisheries and Food 1976–9.

that the French public sector borrowing requirement would be reduced by about 50 per cent over the next year.

I suppose that the French may be impressed by the sheer brazenness of our attitude, by our apparent unawareness of defeat. I am reminded of Marshal Soult's despatch to Napoleon after the Battle of Albufera: 'I had the English beaten. They were such fools. They did not know it and they declined to run.'

On the journey back to the airport at the end of the visit when we had the chance for another long chat, Callaghan said that he no longer had the vitality of former times, to which I replied truthfully that this was not apparent. I reminded him of the ability he had expressed to be able to pace himself. 'Yes, but I get tired now,' he repeated. I asked him if it was the consequence of his operation and he said that he supposed it was. He slept well. Nothing interfered with that. He did not worry as he had done when he was Chancellor. On the Thursday afternoon he had managed to have a nap between the House of Commons and taking off for Rambouillet. He found that having to make speeches took it out of him.

On the first drive Callaghan had raised the subjects he would be discussing with Giscard. I was struck then and later at the meeting by how different he was from two and a half years ago when he first became Foreign Minister. I rarely got into the car with him then without some sort of row, usually about European union which was dismissed as 'cloudy mysticism'. However nowadays it is all light and understanding. He also expresses personal gratitude to me. I cannot help thinking also that he may be finding that foreigners, however undesirable, are better than his own left wing. I asked Callaghan about his weekend with Schmidt at Chequers just after the German election. He said that they had got on very well.

At the plenary meeting later in the morning Callaghan and Crosland comported themselves well. How much better Callaghan is at this sort of gathering than Wilson who had invariably given the impression of trying to outsmart the other side.

On the all-important subject of sterling, the French were hopeful, an attitude that was not inevitable. They could have been lukewarm or distant. They were neither. They were both sympathetic to us about our plight and afraid for themselves. They are not, for the moment, envious. Giscard gave expression to their support in his press statement; so that when the Prime Minister came to say goodbye to me his final words were: 'Well, I think they have helped sterling.'

Madame Giscard attended the lunch on Friday at the Elysée as did Sandringham Sambo. I do not know whether he is always there or whether he was trotted out for this British occasion. He was much in evidence, coming into the dining-room where he nuzzled up to the guests hoping for scraps. Two liveried servants made unsuccessful attempts to persuade him to lie down in the corner of the room. Rather surprisingly, Giscard appeared to take no notice of him.

1977

FEBRUARY

PARIS

THE DUCHESS OF WINDSOR

On arrival in Paris I was told that the Duchess of Windsor would be one of my responsibilities, or, to be more precise, that she would become so when she died, an event that then looked imminent. When this occurred an elaborate programme would have to be implemented so that her body could be flown to England and buried at Frogmore, alongside the Duke's. I should also in the meantime maintain contact with her and her secretary so that I would be able to keep the royal family informed about the state of her health, a subject about which there was the closest interest. After all, questions of the disposal of what many regarded as the inheritance of the House of Windsor could be at stake.

Soon after reaching Paris, therefore, I made contact with Miss Schultz, the Duchess's secretary, who has recently ousted an American, John Utter, who looked after everything while the Duke was alive. I do not know what the cause was of this court rebellion but suspect that it had a lot to do with the vexed question of money and inheritance. Miss Schultz, a sensible Swiss lady in her thirties, seemed eager to maintain a link and she undertook to let me know when the Duchess was well enough to receive Mary and me. In the meantime I sent the Duchess presents on stated occasions and passed on the occasional message.

We had been here more than a year before Miss Schultz telephoned one day to say that the Duchess's health had improved so much that she would like to see us. We were summoned for 4.30 one afternoon to her house in the Bois de Boulogne. Nothing very special at the entrance: a gate opened by a porter, then a short drive past laurels and cedar trees to the gravel before the front entrance. A butler greeted us, looking a little sinister. Miss Schultz was at the door with a friendly smile. Beyond her in the hall I caught sight of the royal standard flying from the balcony. 'The Duchess much looks forward to seeing you. She is very much better.

But if she offers you tea, which she will do, would you please say no, that you have had it already, because it would tire her too much if you stayed with her for tea. I shall give you tea downstairs afterwards.' I thanked Miss Schultz for this briefing and we were led upstairs past large drums of the Welsh Guards to the ante-room to her bedroom. It was full of pictures of the Duke and of cushions covered in petit-point. Miss Schultz told us afterwards that the room was where everything went on when the Duke was alive. It was between their two rooms. 'They discussed everything there. You noticed the petit-point. That was all done by the Duke himself.'

We had hardly had time to notice before the butler showed us into the Duchess's bedroom. As we entered a nurse shimmered out of the room. The Duchess was lying on a couch by the window. Her hands, which caught the eye immediately, were badly contorted in shape, and paralysed. Our handshakes were perfunctory. Unless we had known before whom we were meeting I do not think that we would have recognised her. There is nothing in the face to recall that very distinct and dominating look known to the whole world. We had an exchange of small talk about how long we had been in Paris, about the Embassy and such arrangements as we were making for the Jubilee. We said that we hoped to be able to invite her one day. She said that she was hoping she would be able to go to America. She offered us tea. We knew our part and declined. We spoke about the arrival of spring. She did not speak of the flowers we had sent her before our visit. I was conscious of the butler hovering in the room next door. The door to it had remained open. I do not think that she was in a condition to talk about anything seriously. Every now and again she took a deep breath which seemed to require considerable effort. She kept her hands under the rug. She was perfectly compos mentis but it was as though living was a big task and could only be coped with for short intervals at a time. She did not strike one as being comfortable or at ease with herself as she lay beneath those blankets.

Later we discussed the Duchess with Miss Schultz who said that one of her troubles was that she still had a great deal of nervous energy but that her feet and hands were too paralysed for her to be able to work it off. She sometimes asks Miss Schultz how she could get rid of all the tension that builds up within her. She has a good appetite but has to be fed by a nurse because she does not have sufficient use of her hands. The Duchess has a nurse in constant attendance. There are three on duty who work in eight-hour shifts. The house has a staff of six reduced from twenty-four when the Duke died.

Miss Schultz said that the Duchess was very worried about money. They had sold quite a few things already. The French authorities had allowed them to occupy the house rent free so long as the Duke was alive; but since his death they had charged rent. The French, however, were very helpful about taxes. Miss Schultz gave the impression that even though the Duchess might wish to leave Paris and go and live in America she would not be able to afford to do so – meaning, of course, at her present standards that include a chef and three nurses. The chef, apparently, is in danger of going to seed because he has nothing to do but cook invalid food. I asked Miss Schultz who were the friends whom the Duchess saw. She said, practically none. She has very few French friends and those she had when the Duke was alive no longer seemed interested. She has American friends who came over and then her eyes light up. She much prefers talking to them than to anyone else. She is really only happy now with Americans, but, of course, many of her friends have died.

Miss Schultz showed us over the ground floor, saying that the Duke and Duchess had taken a great interest in the interior decoration. Frances Donaldson's book[1] makes this clear. The dining-room is in a Chinese style, very elaborate and pretty. Miss Schultz said that in the Duke's day the house was always full of orchids, his favourite flower. Now they could not afford to heat the greenhouses which, like the garden, were getting very run down.

I could not resist asking Miss Schultz if the Duchess had read Frances Donaldson's book. She explained that the Duchess could no longer read to herself but she read out to her. She was careful in her choice of books. No, she had not read out the Donaldson book. The Duchess was interested in the royal family: what they were doing and what their plans were, for the Jubilee, for instance. She liked things to be straightforward. I did not press the point. I gathered, however, that Miss Schultz's reading-out regime was not onerous.

Miss Schultz lead us into the hall to say goodbye. She pointed out the red leather box that stands on the hall table, perhaps the most conspicuous of all the objects to be found there. The words, 'The King', are inscribed on it. 'It's always been here,' she said.

'Is there anything in it – papers, I mean?' I asked.

'Do you know I have no idea, nobody has ever asked. I don't even know who has got the key,' she answered.

As we drove away from this moribund scene I thought to myself what a fine story it would make if, upon the Duchess's death, this box were unlocked and found to reveal some quite unexpected and dramatic

---

[1] *Edward VIII*, 1974.

records kept by the King relating to his public or private life or to the abdication.

25–26 FEBRUARY

PARIS

———

DR OWEN'S VISIT

There was great interest in the arrival here this week of Dr Owen[1] who was only made Foreign Secretary on Monday, four days before the visit, at the age of thirty-eight, younger than any Secretary of State this century except Eden. It was Owen's first journey abroad as Foreign Secretary. He had arranged to come here as Minister of State before his appointment. He decided to keep to the programme. The French, persuaded already that Owen is an '*Européen convaincu*', were delighted. We could do with a bit of this delight as bilateral relations have recently gone back to the good old bad days.

At the end of their meeting Owen and his opposite number, Guiringaud,[2] held a press conference at the Quai d'Orsay. The throng was such that the French Foreign Minister was moved to remark that he had never before seen so many journalists and cameramen present for such an occasion. Owen conducted himself with effortless aplomb, both then and throughout the visit. I find remarkable his self-assurance which is such that he does not seem to have to boast. He shows no signs of the need to prove himself; nor of anxiety. His temperament is as good as his physique. A neurologist, he does not seem to have any nervous system at all. Nor, unlike many politicians, with the notable exception of Callaghan, does he drink more than a very occasional glass of wine. He is ascetic, whether on medical or moral grounds. He is not after the good things of life. Nor after panoply. I ask myself why he abandoned medicine for politics and find the answer in his evident desire 'to do good' without being priggish about it. His wife Debbie, an American, the daughter of a German Jewish immigrant to New York, has been a successful literary agent. She told me that not long ago they had both spent a week on a kibbutz in Israel, staying with a couple they knew well in a tiny apartment

---

[1] David Owen had been appointed Foreign Secretary in succession to Callaghan when the latter became Prime Minister upon the sudden death of Tony Crosland.

[2] Louis de Guiringaud, member of the French Diplomatic Service, 1938–78. With the Free French Forces and in the resistance in France. First Secretary in London 1946–9, Ambassador to Japan 1966–72; to the UN 1972–6. Foreign Minister 1976–8.

and eating in the local canteen. The food had been bad, the conditions uncomfortable. They had loved it. 'You see,' she said, rather cryptically I thought, 'we are not like the Hendersons, we do not like to surround ourselves with beautiful things. We like events.'

I do not think that she meant this hostilely. She is a most engaging person. Her aim was to describe him. She said that she thought Americans discussed politics in a less profound way than did the British. She herself had never been much interested in politics or politicians in America. 'I think that's why I liked David,' she added uninhibitedly, 'You see we talked about things deeply.'

The *Herald Tribune* has quoted her as having vowed when young – she is scarcely old now – never to marry an Englishman, a doctor or a politician. She found that she had done all three at once.

Owen's high-mindedness inclines him to sympathise with President Carter, particularly over dissidents, at present a burning issue. When I introduced him to Professor Raymond Aron he was ready to contradict him, saying that he could not agree that detente was meaningless. When he first arrived in Paris, having attended a long and indecisive Cabinet on direct elections to the European parliament, he gave me, as we drove from the airport, an account of the discussion from which he deduced that the chances of meeting the Community deadline of May/June 1978 for direct elections were slight. I said that I thought that this would be very serious for our standing in Europe. Readiness to meet the direct elections deadline was increasingly seen as the touchstone by which a country's European good faith was judged. Owen thought I was wrong. Direct elections were not really important. He could not make out where the Prime Minister was trying to go on the issue. Some of the things said in the Cabinet by the anti-Europeans had been dreadful. Rather to my surprise, when we were driving out to the airport the following day, prior to his departure, and the subject of direct elections arose, Owen took a different stance. I said that I realised he attached less importance to direct elections than I did. 'Oh no,' he interrupted, 'I regard them as of the utmost importance.'

I talked about this later with Roy Jenkins who arrived to stay the weekend. He is a great friend of Owen, one of his staunchest supporters in the Parliamentary Labour Party.

Telling us of his loyalty Roy said that he could almost use of him the words spoken by a general of his batman: 'He is one of the bravest men I ever knew. He followed me wherever I went.'

Roy says that this is Owen's method. He is apt to lead off with some extreme point of view then he swings back and is always all right in the end, absolutely all right. I said that I was a little disturbed by Owen's statement to me that he was in the centre of the Labour Party and that it was very important for him to show this. He was by way of explaining the significance he attached to the lunch he had just had at the Embassy with young French socialists. Roy said that I should not worry too much about that. Perhaps he thought that such a stance was necessary to him as he had just become Foreign Secretary, but Roy could assure me that Owen was well and truly right wing.

'Then,' I said, 'I was a little taken back by the way Owen, upon looking at the photograph of Ernie Bevin that stands in one of the rooms in the Embassy had said, "I can't think why all you Foreign Office people were so keen on him, except for reasons of inverted snobbery." '

Roy admitted that there was a 10 per cent streak of inverted snobbery in Owen. But he wasn't to be drawn in any criticism of him. He thoroughly supported his appointment as Foreign Secretary. I thought this a great tribute, not so much to Owen, as to the magnanimity of Roy who must have been turning over a hundred times in his mind whether he had made the right decision in going to Brussels or whether he might not have become Foreign Secretary upon Crosland's death had he not left British politics. He said nothing to me of this kind. He has shown not the slightest resentment of Owen's great good fortune.

I was not quite sure that Owen reciprocated such loyalty in equal measure. There had been some discussion in meetings with the French about participation or otherwise of the President of the Commission in the forthcoming summit meeting. Vice-President Mondale had said to Roy during his visit to Europe that the US government would favour this but that of course the French were against. Callaghan also did not want Roy there. The attitude of the United States was that they would accept the consensus of the Community on whether or not the President of the Commission should be present. Guiringaud told Owen that the French objected but Owen decided not to pass this on to Roy. He also told me that I must not do so. I rejoined that Roy would want to know the French attitude as well as that of the British government. Owen insisted that we must not tell him, I am not quite sure why except that it fits in with his determination to do nothing that might displease Callaghan to whom, after all, he owes his promotion.

Owen conducts himself extremely well. He is charming without appearing to be out to please. He expresses gratitude without being effusive. He is not at all shy, but nor is he assertive. He is unself-conscious – and he is very handsome. It is surprising, given the relatively short time he has been in politics, that he is such a good speaker. He spoke well after dinner in reply to a very serious speech by Guiringaud. He said that with him, Owen, as President of the Council, and with Roy Jenkins as President of the Commission, there was talk on the Continent of English domination of Europe. It was in fact of Welsh domination that the people should be frightened. The French, he had perceived, seemed to prefer the Welsh to the English. I passed Owen notes of what Guiringaud was saying because he does not understand French. He managed to read and remember these and make suitable use of them. Altogether very impressive.

When we got back home after the dinner Owen came to the Salon Vert and chatted with the staff – not drinking anything – and he was very unpompous and friendly. I suppose we got to bed at about midnight. He was up early and after some work on his boxes embarked upon a series of press and television interviews and a reception to meet British members of the Embassy staff. He was first class at talking to people. He did not seem to think there were too many people in the Embassy, or at any rate he did not say so. We are sensitive about this after all the fuss of the think-tank. Being so young and vigorous and perhaps because he is new to the Office, Owen is unparsimonious with his time. As I have mentioned, he attended a lunch for young French socialists whom he impressed with his openness. He told Rocard[1] that foreign affairs were by no means his prime interest; indeed he had been disappointed when first appointed to a junior post in the FCO. He was much more interested in social, economic and medical questions.

Following the lunch he had a private chat with Roy Jenkins. Roy had been a little complicated, or should I say Celtic, in not joining us for coffee after lunch to meet the socialists. He sent in a message saying that he had arrived at the house and I suggested that he should join us. But he did not do so, saying afterwards that he thought it might have been a bit awkward though it had nothing to do with wanting Owen to come to see him first in his room, rather than the other way round, something that apparently had occurred to Roy though it had not to me.

I found Mrs Owen a most agreeable companion at lunch. We had a good deal to talk about as she is a friend, indeed the literary agent for Tom Matthews;[2] and they have a house at Buttermere, near us in the country. She has not had her head turned an inch by her sudden turn of fortune. She appears to have wished to continue with her work as literary agent. She is unaffected and full of enthusiasm.

As we said goodbye to them at the airfield, Owen said that he felt completely refreshed and reinvigorated by his stay here; and I think that he meant it. He had told me in the car how interested he had been to

[1] Michel Rocard, an *énarque* par excellence, i.e. an alumnus of the Ecole Nationale d'Administration which since 1945 has produced many rulers of France whether in politics, government, finance or industry. Prominent member of the Socialist Party since 1974. Prime Minister 1988–9.
[2] T.S. Matthews, American author and journalist. Editor of *Time* magazine. Biographer of T.S. Eliot. Mary had worked for him on *Time* in New York.

talk to the socialists. He had not wanted to spend his time in Paris looking at beautiful things, or reflecting upon his sudden promotion, or relaxing by himself. He is as sincere as he is serious, though I should not give the impression that he is without humour. Not least of all had I been impressed by his resilience because after all he had had a strenuous, and, for him, a strange twenty-four hours at the end of only his first week as Foreign Secretary.

Driving back in the car I asked myself, and Mary, whether he would be another Anthony Eden. Would he eventually become party leader and perhaps Prime Minister, posts which, by reason of his age and the position he now holds, are obvious possibilities? Much depends, I suppose, on whether he has the toughness to overcome all the attacks that will be made upon him by all those within his own party who, for various reasons, not least envy, will be out to pull him down from his present pedestal. It is much too early to make a reliable forecast. Judging from his performance here, he obviously has many of the qualities necessary for the highest political office.

3 DECEMBER

PARIS

——

A VISIT BY MRS THATCHER

Mrs Thatcher came to Paris to see Chirac, the former French Prime Minister. I had persuaded her to see Barre,[1] the present Prime Minister, as well, if only to avoid the impression that the Tories regarded the RPR as their sole counterpart. She reached the house in Paris before I did and I found her sitting demurely in the Salon Vert chatting to Mary. She was accompanied, as usual, by John Stanley, a young Tory MP. My impression of her now, as always, was how considerate and uncomplicated she is. There is no side about her. She does not put on airs or assert herself. She is not aggressive or cocky. Nor is she like Barbara Castle who always seems to be trying to mark her personality on the occasion.

Mrs T is keen on her femininity. She takes trouble both with her hair and dress. We had to get a hairdresser to come to see her at the house on Saturday afternoon. She tipped him handsomely, saying to Mary, 'I

---

[1] Raymond Barre, economist, politician and international civil servant. Vice-President of the European Commission 1967–72. Prime Minister 1976–81 under Giscard, to whose Republican Party he belonged. His wife, Eve, who came from Hungary, relished the good things of life, and we found that her enjoyment enhanced ours.

don't want them to think we are mean.' That evening we had a purely domestic dinner at her request. I am not sure that she is altogether happy being with people who speak French, of which she does not appear to have much command. Apart from Mary, me, Mrs Thatcher and John Stanley there were the Kenneth Jameses[1] and Fitzroy Maclean[2] who was accompanying her to Yugoslavia the following day. Despite the ungrandness of the party she wore an elaborate, long, décolleté dress. There was nothing casual about her attire. I kept thinking how unkind the British press are to go on about her provincial clothes and appearance. True, she does not have any of the downright, down-to-earth dowdiness of the British upper classes such as Lady Dorothy Macmillan, the supreme wearer of tweeds and sensible shoes.

In the morning I had taken Mrs T to call on Barre. They had a serious talk about inflation and unemployment, subjects on which they see eye to eye. Barre did most of the talking, all of it in excellent English. They also discussed nuclear reactors. Barre appeared momentarily taken aback when Mrs Thatcher, sitting beside him, with crossed legs and looking her most feminine in her light blue suit, suddenly looked at him intensely and asked; 'Mr Barre, what do you think of fast breeders?'

She lunched with Chirac. Couve was also present. It lasted from 12.15 to 3.45. When Mrs Thatcher got back to the house I suggested a spot of sightseeing but she declined. Obviously Chirac is a good deal more exhausting than most people she has had to meet in British politics. She clearly has great qualities of brain and character and despite understandable exhaustion by Chirac I think there is no doubt about her stamina.

12–13 DECEMBER
CHEQUERS

VISIT BY PRESIDENT GISCARD

Despite the winter weather the atmosphere of Chequers impressed the French party favourably. I recalled Helmut Schmidt's visit there when Wilson presided. Somehow that had not gone well. It had not been much

---

[1] Kenneth James, member of the Diplomatic Service. Minister in Paris 1976–81. His previous service was in Tokyo, Rio and Moscow. Later Ambassador to Poland and Mexico. A close friend.
[2] Fitzroy Maclean, renowned Commander British Military Mission to Yugoslav Partisans 1943–5, described in his famous book, *Eastern Approaches*. MP and author.

better when Heath had entertained Willy Brandt in 1973, a visit that had coincided with the outbreak of the Yom Kippur War, not because Heath was inattentive but because Brandt, like Schmidt, is not one to be influenced by surroundings. With the French it was different. The shadows of the past impressed them more. I suppose it is understandable that they respond more enthusiastically than do the Germans to accounts of the big decisions in the war that Churchill took at Chequers and of the great speeches he delivered from there. Callaghan acted as guide to the French party showing them Churchill's bedroom and pointing, just as Wilson had done with the Germans three years before, to the mouse that he had painted into a corner of the enormous Snyders canvas in the central hall.

It occurred to me too that Chequers, while redolent of Britain's past, is not strident in its memories of anti-French triumphs as are so many places in London. Nor is there any need to go through Waterloo station or Trafalgar Square to reach it.

Giscard arrived at Chequers by helicopter from Windsor where he had lunched with the Queen. This had got the visit off to a good start, highlighting Giscard's position as head of state as well as chief executive.

I have had to exercise unwonted discretion over a piece in *Private Eye* about Giscard's private life. This carries all the old stories about him, with the difference that it mentions his girlfriends' names. The article, published as a letter from Paris from 'Lunchtime O'Boulevards' and headed by a photo of a girl lounging longingly on a bed, asserts that the French electorate has become disdainful of him because of his taste, 'which runs towards social-climbing, man-hungry, over-the-hill tarts'.

Private Eye produced this just before Giscard arrived for his visit to England. I had not seen it myself. John Hunt drew it to my attention, saying with a wry smile that he hoped the French party, and particularly the President himself, had not seen it. I was glad to notice that no one on their side mentioned it to me. Since getting back to Paris I have had to exercise great restraint in refraining from mentioning the piece to anyone. There are many Parisians who would be fascinated by it. It would never do, I realise, if it were to be said that I was going about Paris advising people to read the salacious contribution to Anglo-French understanding made by Lunchtime O'Boulevards.

Mrs Callaghan, with whom I had a chat at Chequers the afternoon of our arrival, is a warm-hearted, apparently uncomplicated person who does not feel inhibited from enjoying the pleasures and comforts Chequers offers the wife of the Prime Minister. She looks forward to spending Christmas there with the children and grandchildren who love the swimming pool.

I talked with her over tea in the vast central hall. She seemed at a loss what to do, exactly like the rest of us, cast aside by our political masters as they indulge in private talks. She asked whether she might not join us for supper when the ministers had decided to dine alone without officials. She said it had been suggested that she might like to have dinner upstairs on a tray, but it would amuse her more to be with us. Michael Palliser, who had joined the conversation, and I generously welcomed her to take part in the hospitality of her own house; and, sure enough, there she was later in the evening helping herself with us to the buffet supper. She sat between François-Poncet[1] and Sauvagnargues and gave every appearance of enjoying herself enormously. Equally, the two Frenchmen seemed to enjoy her company, intrigued at any rate, I suspect, by the lack of pomp about the whole affair.

The Chequers visit began with the usual difficulty that afflicts French delegations when invited to the English countryside – what to wear. I was told that when Pompidou had visited Chequers he had worn enormous checks. The British side had been dressed in ordinary dark suits. He had therefore taken the first opportunity to disappear and change back into normal working clothes. Meanwhile the British hosts, with consummate tact, had decided to put him at ease by changing into country clothes. So that when everyone reappeared they were still sartorially ill-matched, but this time the other way round.

Well, on this occasion, I was able to observe, as I began my vigil in the central hall waiting for the great men to appear, that the PM emerged wearing a blue pullover, but no jacket. When Giscard arrived and observed the PM's attire he immediately took off his jacket and handed it to an attendant – almost as though he felt guilty of having committed some social solecism. What the two men did or where they went once they had aligned their attire, I have no idea. But one moment I think they went for a stroll. Certainly they spent the best part of the afternoon together. They were joined for dinner by other ministers from both sides. Some of us officials were allowed on to the scene after dinner for a talk in the Long Gallery.

This took place before an enormous fire with everyone seated on sofas and armchairs. The combined effect of the excellent wine and the heat were naturally unconducive to wakefulness, at least in everyone accept the PM who heaped more logs on the fire and himself handed round the brandy. He doesn't touch alcohol himself and must have been proud of the effects of his attentions upon his guests. Giscard, I must say, stood up to it well, and certainly better than Brandt had done on a similar occasion a few years before. I recalled to myself that he had gone straight

---

[1]Jean François-Poncet, joined Ministry of Foreign Affairs 1955. Secretary-General to the Presidency 1976–8. Foreign Minister 1978–81. Elected to the French Senate 1983.

to sleep, leaving Pöhl to hold forth to Heath upon Germany's views on the world economic situation.

Certainly the rest of us found attentiveness difficult that evening as our leaders talked about the need to do something to induce a reduction in Japan's enormous trade surplus. There was also a good deal of talk about Africa, with a long intervention by Owen. By about 11.30 p.m. Giscard had had enough and stood up, saying that it was time to go to bed. The Prime Minister held a meeting in the central hall to discuss the programme for the following day. He prefaced this by saying that he and Giscard got on extremely well together. They had seen eye to eye over Europe and he found Giscard just as anti-communautaire as he was. Some of us raised our eyebrows at this. The PM would have none of it, adding that Giscard had told him that the British gave in too easily even when some point of great national interest was at stake.

When I called on François-Poncet this week to have a post-mortem on Chequers I told him how the PM interpreted Giscard's mind on Europe. He said that there must have been a terrible misunderstanding. Callaghan, to be sure, is anti-communautaire; but Giscard is very much the opposite.

There was a useful plenary at Chequers on the second day which dealt with industrial co-operation, the Franco-British Council and all sorts of odds and ends including student exchanges. Industrial co-operation has been the bee in my bonnet for some time. I was delighted to hear that Giscard and Callaghan sang a similar tune and agreed to set up a special bilateral committee. They spoke encouragingly and harmoniously on this subject at the concluding press conference. This conference followed the last ceremony at Chequers which was the planting of a tree by Giscard.

I reflected afterwards upon the great improvement in relations between the two countries and between Giscard and Callaghan personally compared with two years previously when the Elysée had issued a communiqué denouncing the PM. Such a step was unthinkable now. This owed something to Callaghan's masterly handling of Giscard at Chequers: just the right combination of respect and informality, and of humour and seriousness; and without giving an impression that he was handling him at all. Rather, he just seemed to be himself, a bluff, jolly, very pragmatic fellow who disdained all expertise outside politics but who wanted to help things along in the right direction, which, at the moment, is also the direction that France seems to want to take. At the plenary session when the tricky subject of civil aviation had arisen, Callaghan had referred to a Tory deputation he had just received and had then drawn Giscard's attention to an article in *The Times* that morning by a Tory MP suggesting that we were in danger of being taken

for a ride by those wily and grasping European aeronautical engineers.
He handed a copy of *The Times* across the table to the President saying,
'You see, there is a picture of you on page one, and of your beautiful
daughter on page five. No wonder people are saying the French are
taking us over.'

Giscard joined in the chortling. I noticed that what really intrigued
him was the photo of his daughter. She had just been married in private
in Palermo to a divorcé. The Giscard family do not approve and did not
attend the wedding. I think that *The Times* published the photo ahead
of any French paper. Giscard took possession of the PM's copy and
folded it away carefully below his other papers. I imagined that he
intended showing it to Madame Giscard later that day.

I was left with the following main conclusions from the Chequers
meeting. It had done wonders for Franco-British relations, a subject that
needs constant attention and can never be taken for granted. It was
made possible by Callaghan's demeanour, and by the transformation in
Giscard's attitude towards Britain, brought about partly by his official
visit to Buckingham Palace in June 1976. The atmosphere of Chequers,
even in mid-winter, played a useful part. True, some of the French guests
had to be housed for lack of space in the Shoulder of Lamb in a nearby
village. But on the whole the French party were intrigued, as well as
interested, by the Chequers meeting and its ambiance.

Finally, the effects of the understandings there will radiate outwards
and influence all sorts of other things, particularly, I hope, the creation
of an Anglo-French Königswinter and the development of collaboration
in high technology to meet the manifold threats to the industries of our
two countries.

1978

I APRIL

PARIS

HEATH CONDUCTS THE EUROPEAN
YOUTH ORCHESTRA

With my birthday today I start my last year in Paris and in the diplomatic
career. The prospect of retirement concentrates the mind like a death-
sentence. Each moment is heightened. Nothing will happen again in the
same way. Relief and doubt cast their shadows before as retirement

throws every passing event and thought into sharp relief.

We have been entertaining the members of the European Youth Orchestra, founded by Ted Heath, and now on its first tour. He had asked me, to give a supper party afterwards, so I wrote to various VIPs,[1] including Barre, Guiringaud, Simone Veil, Françoise Giroud and Artur Rubinstein, inviting them and explaining what the European Youth Orchestra was. They nearly all accepted.

The concert was in two parts, Ted conducting the overture to *Die Meistersingers*, and Claudio Abbado the Sixth Symphony of Mahler.

We all felt proud of Ted's performance and he beamed at his thunderous reception. We heard tributes to his versatility, and whispers about the relative ease of conducting an orchestra compared with a Cabinet. This was certainly Barre's line. Guiringaud said how much he would like to be able to do something, one thing really well, whereas Heath excelled in sailing and politics as well as music.

From the first note of Mahler, Abbado seemed to lift and direct the movements of those one hundred and twenty young musicians from the nine countries of the Community. It was inspiring. I asked him afterwards how conducting the very young compared with conducting a mature orchestra. He said that they were more enthusiastic and energetic. They were like a very young horse, magnificent and fiery, but apt to take off. Ted, with whom we discussed this later, said that they were prepared to rehearse for hours. He, like Abbado, was laudatory about them. He went on to say that the only problem of the tour had been that of national anthems. There was the European anthem, the Ode to Joy, which was always played; no difficulty about that. But what about the anthem of the country visited? Abbado said that they should not be played. However, he, Ted could not imagine the Queen turning up at a performance in London and not having God Save The Queen played. The members of the orchestra were eager for their national anthems to be heard. In Italy, if Abbado insisted upon the Red Flag rather than the Italian national anthem he would let him conduct the orchestra for it.

Last night Heath opened the proceedings by announcing that the orchestra would play the Marseillaise and the Ode to Joy. The audience were asked to remain standing for both. Surprisingly, at the end of the Marseillaise there were boos and whistles. I perceived that Barre was disconcerted by this. *Le Monde* today describes the incident as an anti-Barre demonstration which I am sure it was not. It was more an anti-nationalistic reaction from a crowd that contained many enthusiastic

---

[1] All these people have already been mentioned except for Simone Veil who, at this time, was Minister of Health and Social Security and in 1979–82 was President of the European Parliament, and Artur Rubinstein, the famous pianist, then living in Paris.

Europeans. These had responded warmly when Heath, in his opening remarks, had spoken of the European mission of the orchestra: 'Europe is not just for the European Commission, or for Ministers' – pause – 'or ex-Ministers ...' he proclaimed.

We had some trouble with the *places à table* at the supper after the concert. We focused on three of the dozen tables and tried to make sure that the VIPs came to them. It worked more or less, though of course some of the more pushing guests made a beeline for these although they were not intended for them. I have learnt to take great trouble over the *places à table*, a subject I priggishy despised when I started in the career. I recall how shocked I was when the Minister Counsellor in the Embassy in Athens, Moore Crosthwaite, consulted me about how people should be placed at a dinner he was giving. It seemed to me odd that he should be spending time or trouble on such things. How wrong I was. A great friend of ours, prominent in Paris life, whom I shall here call Catalina, was upset at a recent dinner with us because Rosamée Henrion had been better seated than she felt she had been. This was because Rosamée is the sister-in-law of the President. I made sure at this dinner that Catalina was at the same table as Barre and Heath. She was delighted and said to me afterwards that she had never before been seated between two Prime Ministers. She telephoned various friends in Paris to say what a pity it was they had not been invited to the party.

Barry, our butler, personally looked after Barre at the supper party. He made sure that he received copious helpings of the sumptuous buffet. There was a lot of wise shaking of heads round the room about it being unsurprising that the Prime Minister was so fat. He was there to enjoy himself, and his vanity is not the sort that is concerned with his appearance. So he ate salmon and roast ham, followed by curry, and ending up with ice-cream. But despite Barry's attentions he managed to resist the cheese and brandy-snaps. I have noticed how much more rotund Barre has become since he moved to the Prime Minister's office. It was Heath's size, however, that struck most people. He does not seem to worry about it. Kenneth James took him out to lunch at Allards. He began by saying that he never ate any lunch, but he proceeded to have a hearty meal.

After all the other guests had left last night he sat on at one of the round tables and chatted until about 3 a.m. I think that is what he enjoys doing most. He liked recounting amusing incidents of the orchestra's tour and about this particular dinner party and the other guests. Going up to bed in the lift he became even more confiding, revealing what a nervous strain the concert had been for him.

Artur Rubinstein was one of the stars of the evening. He came both to the concert and to the party. Claudio Abbado was delighted to meet him. Rubinstein came accompanied by Miss Annabel Whitestone,[1] but not with his wife. Rubinstein's recent behaviour has been a source of secret stimulus to many older men in Paris – as it is of concern to women of the same age group. At ninety-one he has eloped with his English secretary, the blonde Annabel, who had come to help him in his blindness with the writing of his memoirs. They first went to Venice together and we were told that she alone could provide the stimulus and literary help that he needed to complete the work. On their return to Paris a ménage à trois was established. This has broken up and Madame Rubinstein has departed to their house in Marbella. She is deeply upset.

Earlier in the day I had taken Heath along to a reception given by Chirac in the Hôtel de Ville. I was struck by Chirac's bonhomie and reasonableness. He showed great attention to Heath. There was none of the abrasive metalicness that I have seen so often recently in his TV appearances. People are apt to say that Chirac has become bearable because he is so tired.

◆

2 APRIL

PARIS

———

A PARTY ON THE SEINE

A party last night given by Philippine de Rothschild[2] for her sixteen-year-old daughter. It took place on a boat on the Seine. Nearly all teenagers and a few grown-ups who made a striking contrast to a parallel party in London. Here the young are demure, sober, conservatively dressed and well behaved. Nobody is drunk or amorous or combative. The music was provided by tapes and one drummer and was fairly stereo-type rock and roll. I am struck by how young and pretty they all look and am reminded of a malicious remark Françoise Giroud reported to me. Someone had said, speaking of a woman they had just met, *'comment elle a dû être vilaine.'*

Philippine greets us with theatrical enthusiasm. She manages, in between welcoming other guests, to tell me how disappointed she was not to have been invited to our party last night, saying, 'I could not have

[1] Annabel Whitestone was a distinguished musicologist who was the English representative in Madrid of Rubinstein's concert agency. In 1992 she married George Weidenfeld.
[2] Philippine de Rothschild, daughter of Baron Philippe de Rothschild. An actress by profession until, upon her father's death, she took over the management of Mouton-Rothschild vineyard.

come, but I would like to have been invited.' I say how sorry I am. She says that she is sad, but not bitter. She had heard that it was my birthday. News of such parties spreads like a prairie-fire in Paris. She gives me a present of a bottle of Mouton-Rothschild 1921. We embrace again. She points to the Eiffel Tower and says that she has managed to persuade the Paris Municipality to leave on the floodlighting for two hours longer than usual. It looks like a great toy across the river. The water-level is so high that boats are unable to pass beneath the bridges.

Ludo and Moira Kennedy[1] are with us for the night as well as the Zervudackis.[2] Ludo once again astonishes me by his charm and responses. I suppose they lie at the heart of his television success. He is handsome, but not too so. He is interested but not intellectual. He is like a man looking for something, he does not quite know what. His reactions are those of Mr Liberal Everyman. 'Such a pity Princess Margaret is threatening to let down the royal family,' he said. His passion is backgammon. He is one of the former members of St James's who, having been taken on by Brooks's, have transformed the nature of the club by their constant attendance at the backgammon boards. I often see him there. Indeed I have sometimes seen him playing before dinner, after dinner and again the next morning at breakfast time. He assures me that it is his only form of gambling. Obviously he feels a bit guilty about it. I think Moira finds it a harmless vice.

Ludo does not feel well at the end of dinner so Moira alone accompanies us to Philippine's boat party. A photographer takes a photograph of us waltzing together and whispers to me afterwards how pleased he is to have a picture of me with Rita Hayworth.

A few visits to the garden in the course of the day. No sign of spring except that the birds shriek suddenly as if they think one has no right to be in the garden; and having done so they hide beneath the first leaves, the prettiest of the year. The shrubs are preparing to burst. In the afternoon the croquet club of the Embassy puts up its hoops in the adjoining garden.

---

[1] Ludovic and Moira Kennedy. Ludo is a writer and broadcaster and a popular television personality. He fights sturdily and steadily to rectify miscarriages of criminal justice. His autobiography, On My Way to the Club, has been a great success.
    In 1950 he married Moira Shearer, the exquisite ballet dancer, who can never escape, however much she tries, from her worldwide fame as the ballerina in The Red Shoes. In an effort to do so she describes herself in Who's Who simply as a writer, which indeed she is.
[2] Nolly Zervudachi, assistant to Stavros Niarchos.

4 APRIL

PARIS

———

ODETTE POL-ROGER

I lunched recently in the Travellers Club, an extravagant building in the Champs Elysées that used to be the home of La Païva, one of the great *horizontales* who lay across the Paris scene in the last century. It appears to be in economic difficulties, like many clubs. Members play back-gammon in the afternoon. Someone has suggested the idea of selling the premises for their historic interest and to build a modern club elsewhere. The building would be snapped up by a rich outsider for its amazing decorative features: the colossal wall paintings of Apollo, Hecate, and particularly of Aurora asleep on a pink cloud; its staircase of alabaster, and the bathroom in marble and onyx, decorated with Venetian tiles; the bath itself adorned with silver-gilt taps encrusted with semi-precious stones. Nor would a wealthy would-be buyer find it possible to resist La Païva's bedroom with the frescos of the Goddess of Dawn soaring in the empyrean.

An odd mixture for supper yesterday evening. Odette Pol-Roger,[1] Costa,[2] Alan Maclean[3] and his wife and ten-year-old son. Odette radiated friendliness and interest. She tends to criticise the French so far as public life is concerned and to praise the British and their politicians. Her great-grandfather was English – Wallace, of the Collection. Winston Churchill was her great hero; and by several accounts I have heard, he adored her. The British Embassy in Paris has served no champagne but Pol-Roger since the war. Odette says that Churchill once confided to her that he hated privilege but liked inequality. Once they were dining tête-à-tête in London soon after the war. 'Tell me,' Churchill said, 'when did you first know that the Allies were going to win the war?'

'I always knew it,' Odette replied.

'Brave girl,' Churchill retorted, gracefully laying his hand on her forearm.

Last night Odette expressed predictable joy over the elections[4] in

[1] Odette Pol-Roger, one of three Wallace sisters of English descent. She married into the eponymous champagne family.
[2] Costa Achillopoulo, Greek photographer and traveller. Collaborated with Patrick Leigh-Fermor in *The Traveller's Tree*.
[3] Alan Maclean, publisher with Macmillan, he married Robin Empson, the daughter of Sir Charles Empson.
[4] The left did not win as Giscard and his government had feared.

France. 'You know,' she said, 'I am beginning to think that my compatriots aren't such political fools after all.'

5 APRIL

PARIS

———

THE MAIN PROBLEM IN MIND

Howard Davies, who used to be my Private Secretary here, and now works for the Treasury, called yesterday morning. His current work concerns the financing of Concorde. He seems to know a good deal about British industry generally. The outlook he thinks is appalling. We are slipping back inexorably as an industrial power. By the early 1980s we will be a net importer of industrial goods. I asked him whether the industrial outlook of France and of Germany was not also grim in the face of Japanese, South Korean and other Asian competition. He said, yes, though not nearly so bad as ours because our productivity was so low and there seemed no likelihood of improving it. Bad management and appalling labour relations would continue to dog us.

I had a similarly gloomy talk the other day with someone from the National Economic Development Council. A clever, if paradox-prone man, Bernard Asher marked his originality by dismissing 'productivity' as an irrelevant criterion by which to judge the efficiency of industry. He told me that he would be leaving NEDDY shortly and returning to ITT, whence he had come. This may explain his hostile reaction when I tried to insist that Britain must retain certain indigenous industries, aviation and motor cars for instance, rather than be entirely dependent on outside sources. Asher said that our big firms were quite competitive. Their trouble was that they tried to produce too wide a range of goods. Where we were weakest was in the smaller firms. We had far fewer of them than our main competitors and they were inefficient. In marketing, the British were poor in the big markets; for instance we had barely 5 per cent of total French imports against the Federal Republic of Germany's 18 per cent. We did well in the tiny markets, like Gibraltar.

Asher did not appear to believe much in the idea of industrial collaboration with our European partners. Few people in Europe do. He thought it might serve to rationalise our production efforts so that we did not all produce the same wide range of goods.

I record this because it affects the main problem on my mind these days – one that has been mounting over the past few years. I find that the question of peace or war, or East–West relations, or what we do about disarmament, or our impact in NATO, or the residual problems of empire and Africa that take up an inordinate amount of the Foreign Secretary's time – these questions of traditional diplomacy are all secondary to that of our economic and industrial decline and the ways to arrest it.

I have sent several despatches on this subject over the past two years. My sphere of responsibility is obviously limited. I can point to the way the problem of the threat to Western European industry presents itself to the French (and Germans) and how they are thinking of meeting it. The airbus is a typical example. We pulled out of this Franco-German project in the early stages. We can never make up our minds whether to be junior partners of American industry or equal partners in European industry. My fear is that even if a great many people in Whitehall are thinking and worrying about this issue, the decisions when they are taken will be ad hoc and piecemeal.

I wish I thought I could do more about it than merely be a gadfly. It is interesting that leaders of British Aerospace and Rolls Royce have asked to fly out to see me. They have, I am sure, heard of my despatch on the future of the aircraft industry and industrial co-operation.

6 APRIL

PARIS

THE NEW FRENCH GOVERNMENT

The new Barre government has just been formed. Another anticlimax. Everyone had been assuming that there would be a lot of new faces. Giscard had promised this in his eve-of-the-poll speech whatever the result of the elections. As it turns out it is very much the mixture as before.

Personally I am delighted that Guiringaud is Foreign Minister. He is a man of character, prepared to say things to the President. The President is already irritated by Barre, by his lengthy way of saying the obvious and by his independence. For the moment he needs him.

There must be an atmosphere of *triomphisme* at the Elysée. The President had always been sure that right was on his side even when, as a year or so ago, everyone in Paris was decrying him. Now he had been vindicated by the electorate.

8 APRIL

PARIS

POST-ELECTION EUPHORIA

Euphoria prevails in Paris after the election. There are no left-wingers at seizième dinner parties. Even Giscard is acknowledged everywhere to have done well, not least in circles in Paris where recently he was execrated. It is one of the most amazing turn-rounds of public favour that I have witnessed. At the beginning of last year everyone was repeating Pierre Viansson-Pontet's epithet, 'fragile' to describe Giscard. The Gaullists of course loathed and despised him. It was striking too the way all the well-to-do in Paris – less so in the provinces – who can usually be relied upon to let their material interests dictate their politics, refused to consider that Giscard was on their side. '*Il est complètement fichu*', was the expression a friend of mine used about him as we discussed over one lunchtime the low ebb into which his reputation had fallen. Now all that is forgotten. Success has succeeded in proverbial fashion. Françoise Giroud does not share the prevailing euphoria. I saw her the other evening at a party. Emphasising that she was speaking to me as a friend, not as British Ambassador, she said, 'You will see; *il va tout lâcher.*'

Today is Philip Nelson's[1] birthday. The girls in the private office give him a tape of the latest pop music. It is called 'Blood, Sweat and Tears'. I ask them if they know where the title comes from. They have no idea. Nor has Philip. Overcome with sic transit thoughts I tell them. It makes me feel, not so much that I am very old, as that they are very young.

I give a farewell lunch to the Air Attaché, very similar to other departing lunches for Service Attachés that I have given over the years. I wonder whether, when I retire and look back on my career, it will be a long procession of farewell lunches that will swim into view, rather as visions of Osborne and Balmoral filled the mind's eye of Queen Victoria on her deathbed, at any rate according to Lytton Strachey. There is one feature that makes these ceremonies wholly worthwhile: neither the Service guests nor the departing Attachés are ever in the least blasé. They are always delighted to be there and grateful for what one says in the stilted little speech that coincides with the ice-cream and brandy snaps.

---

[1] Philip Nelson succeeded Howard Davies as my Private Secretary. His quiet confidence and ability were immediately impressive. He has served subsequently in Rome, Manila and Budapest.

9 APRIL

PARIS

———

A DAY OF MONDANITE

Lunch with Paul-Louis Weiller[1] in his luxurious house in the rue de la Faisanderie, and dinner with the Aga Khan. Paul-Louis had a good royal story.

When Queen Salote of Tonga was in London for the coronation she had a private audience with the Queen. She said how delighted she was to be received by Her Majesty, particularly because she had British blood. The Queen looked somewhat astonished and asked how that was. 'Well,' the Queen of Tonga explained, 'when my grandfather was King, a British expedition landed and the invaders were all defeated and eaten.'

At the Aga Khan's dinner I had expected to find the jet-set there. Not at all. It was a party given to celebrate a prize he has awarded for a work of architecture that best promotes the idea of Islam. I sat next to a woman who was an architect from Pakistan who resented the fact that she and everyone else in the profession in her country had been trained in the West where the needs of Pakistan, and the rest of Asia, were not at all understood. What was needed was housing as cheap and plentiful as possible. Aesthetics would have to come after.

Mary sat next to Hugh Casson[2] who told her about his ideas for the Islamic building that is to be put up opposite the Victoria and Albert Museum.

We were dining in a beautiful setting in an old house on the Ile de la Cité. The dining-room and closed-in cloister were full of white lilies and white blossom and were lit by candles.

---

[1]Paul-Louis Weiller, wealthy industrialist and engineer. Director Air France. An admirer of Diana Cooper upon whom he lavished expensive gifts, including a superb mink, which, in her uninhibited way, she always referred to as her 'coat of shame'.
[2]Hugh Casson, President of the Royal Academy 1976–84. He popped up at our different posts, always enthusiastic and enlivening the occasion.

12 APRIL

PARIS

FAVOURITE BISTRO

I lunched alone yesterday at my favourite bistro, Chez Gérard, in the rue de Mail. I read a volume of Claire Bretécher's cartoons given me as a birthday present by Simone Veil. They appear regularly in the *Nouvel Observateur* and are apparently very much the thing at the moment. The captions are in the latest slang with words like *mec, phalo, mazo* and terminations in os such as *collabos*. The characters in the cartoons frequently break into English. They keep saying, 'of course'. I am told that the young have now extrapolated this to the expression: 'of course de cheval'. I also chat with the proprietor, Madame Leonetti, about dogs.

14 APRIL

PARIS

ANTI-SEMITISM

It remains a mystery to me why the Académie Française, to which neither Malraux, Sartre nor de Gaulle deigned to belong, should retain such prestigious cachet.

An election to fill vacant seats has just taken place. Neither candidate received enough votes to be elected. There is speculation why. Thus *France-Soir*: '*Les académiciens français ne sont absolument pas anti-sémites mais ils se montrent toujours soucieux d'un certain "dosage"; il y a actuellement trois Israelites sous la coupole – un règlement non-écrit peut parfaitement interdire l'arrivée d'un quatrième*' – about the most anti-semitic remark I have read for a long time. No English person nowadays would admit to being anti-semitic though they may well be so. Some French would be unabashed at admitting it.

17 APRIL
PARIS

———

DILEMMA OVER AIRCRAFT

The following entry is the first account in my diary of the subject that was to engage much of my attention during the next six months – whether and how we should rejoin the Airbus Industrie Project (AI).

We had been original participants in AI to produce the airbus; and Rolls Royce had secured the contract to supply the engines. But we then pulled out in 1967 because Rolls Royce decided instead to make the RB 211 engine for the Tristar. In the event, this bankrupted them. My belief at this stage was that if we did not now get back into AI, our chances of ever doing so would become slim. The French and Germans were bent on going ahead on their own without us if necessary, convinced that they had a project that was viable in itself and good for the future of European technology generally.

I wrote a despatch strongly in favour of re-entry and followed it up with persistent pressure which, I was told, caused irritation in London. There was too much passenger-seat piloting from Paris. The idea of collaboration on the airbus was part – and at that time the most import-ant part – of a policy that I was pushing for promoting Anglo-French industrial co-operation. The outlook became cloudy when the French insisted that the British Aircraft Corporation (BAC) could only be admitted to AI if British Airways (BA) undertook to buy planes from AI. BA's wish, however, was to buy planes from Boeing rather than AI; and in this they were encouraged, to put it mildly, by Rolls Royce. The latter were confident that they could win a contract to supply Boeing with an engine for the B757 provided they could bring along two purchasers of the aircraft – which they hoped to have found in British Airways and Eastern Airlines.

Allen Greenwood[1] and Peter Fletcher[2], deputy chairman and member of the board of British Aerospace, flew over to lunch with me today to

---

[1] Allen Greenwood, deputy chairman British Aerospace (1977–83); deputy chairman (1972–5) and chairman (1976) British Aircraft Corporation (BAC), which came to be incorporated in British Aerospace.
[2] Peter Fletcher, a former Air Chief Marshal. Director, Corporate Strategy and Planning, British Aerospace (1977–82). Director, Airbus Industry Supervisory Board (1979–82).

discuss aircraft. I have had a similar request from Kenneth Keith[1] of Rolls Royce but have managed to fend him off and will lunch with him early next week in London. Both British Aerospace and Rolls Royce have heard, I suspect, of the pressure I have been putting on London to choose the European rather than the American option. Ministers have to decide soon whether to support a deal between British Aerospace and Boeing providing for joint construction of a new medium-size aircraft (the B757), or whether to back British Aerospace in the agreement they want to make with Airbus Industrie to join the French and Germans in a reduced version of the airbus (the B10) and in the construction of a new European aircraft jet. As a corollary of this decision ministers will have to decide whether British Airways should be allowed to replace their Tridents with Boeings, as they wish to do, or whether they should be forced to buy European.

A great debate rages in London on this subject and my despatch has added to the blaze.

Greenwood and Fletcher have told me that the airbus is in operation with ten different airlines, all of whom are delighted with it. Of course I cannot enter the lists on the subject of aircraft qualifications. I know that if the US option is chosen it will have an effect well outside the realm of civil aviation: it will not help the attempts being made to co-ordinate defence procurement in Western Europe. I doubt whether we would in such circumstances get much of a share of a new European aircraft; and it will not help industrial co-operation generally in Europe. Another theme I emphasise is that civil aircraft have an importance beyond the plane itself, just as railways did in the last century. The danger of going in with Boeing is that you become a junior partner and are eventually reduced to being a components manufacturer. Whereas the European option would enable us to remain a major, independent aircraft manufacturer. At the moment, our aircraft industry is larger than all the rest of Western Europe put together. The problem is to retain it on the same scale. I have had a talk on the subject with General Mitterrand,[2] the head of Aérospatiale. He is impressive, perhaps not always ready to tell everything he knows but never speaking an untruth. He is direct and even matter-of-fact. The British aircraft industry is so large that I think he would like us in. He fears the countervailing pull of Rolls Royce towards the USA.

His wife is sociable and pretty. We have seen a lot of them lately. I

[1] Kenneth Keith, merchant banker and industrialist. Chairman Philip Hill Investment Trust 1967–87. Chairman and chief executive Rolls Royce 1972–80.
[2] General Jacques Mitterrand, served in Air Force 1937–75. Chief of Staff of the Armed Forces 1968–70. Chairman and chief executive Société Nationale Industrielle Aérospatiale (SNIAS) 1975–81.

have sent her a book and attended a memorial service for the Aérospatiale representative in London who has just been killed in a helicopter crash. I went simply to please Mitterrand. The French attach enormous importance to *actes de présence*. We tend to dismiss such gestures as superficial and hypocritical. I think the French are more honest in their assessment of human nature, or at any rate of their own.

Though strongly tempted to discuss his brother, François Mitterrand, with the General I always resist doing so. He would not like it if he thought I was more interested in his famous brother than in him.

20 APRIL
PARIS

———

MORE CHAT FROM LIPP

I lunched yesterday at Brasserie Lipp with Jean Marin,[1] a delightful, large jovial man with nothing petty about him. I asked him if he could help find a job for Sam White.[2] He was sympathetic but said that he was already helping Sam's daughter.

Inevitably we spoke to Roger Cazes, the proprietor of Lipp. Although extremely right wing he likes to have politicians of all complexions at the brasserie. I said that I had been there first with Mary in 1950. We had been going there intermittently ever since. The extraordinary thing was that Cazes himself was always there and always the same, lunch or dinner, weekdays or weekends. I said that I loved the place. It was a sort of club for me.

Jean Marin echoed the prevailing Paris view that the results of the elections had been a surprise to everyone (except the Préfets who had forecast a majority victory in messages to the Ministry of the Interior). France was now extremely stable politically with a promising economic outlook, whereas, if less than half a millon votes had gone the other way, France would now have been in near chaos.

———

[1] Jean Marin, pseudonym of Yves Morvan, journalist well known for his broadcasts for the Free French from London during the Second World War.
[2] Sam White, journalist, who had for long written for the *Evening Standard*. He had an uncanny nose for a story. Reputed to spend much of his time at the Crillon bar and later the Travellers Club. His friendship with Nancy Mitford turned litigious when he libelled her and she returned the compliment by portraying him as the unsavoury Mockbar in *Don't Tell Alfred*.

21 APRIL

PARIS

DUNCAN GRANT'S FAREWELL VISIT
TO PARIS

We have given a dinner party for Duncan Grant[1] who, aged ninety-two, is staying with us, having expressed a wish to come to Paris to see the Cézanne exhibition at the Grand Palais. Guests: Loulou de Waldner, the Beaumarchais, the Daninos, Colette Modiano, Eric de Rothschild, Mary Dunn, Maurice Dumoncel, one of the Feray brothers, as well as the home team of Duncan Grant, Roche and Quentin Bell.[2] Duncan wore a beret and had a tartan rug over his knees. I knelt down to talk to him while he was having a drink before dinner and said that I hoped that it had not all been too exhausting.

'Why should it have been?' he asked indignantly with a flash of the eyes.

'Oh well, it must be rather a change.'

'Why do you think that?'

'Well, I just thought that it must be rather different.'

'You have no right to presume any such thing,' he replied, putting an end to that passage of our conversation.

I must say I was a little discouraged by this effort at friendly conversation.

Everyone else at the party was chatting animatedly when he pointed to Loulou and addressed her as Ottoline (Morrell).[3] Then, turning to me he asked angrily, 'Why can't you get them to stop making all that noise?'

'Oh I can't do that,' I said. 'They are here to meet each other.'

'Well, if you can't do that, you are not much good as an Ambassador.'

There was nothing for it but to agree. It was an eye-opener to me of

---

[1] Duncan Grant, painter and friend of mine since early days.

[2] Dinner party guests: Loulou de Waldner, Baronne Geoffroy de Waldner de Freundstein, a great gardener. Pierre Daninos, writer best known in the UK for his books on Major Thompson. In *Who's Who* gives as a recreation, collecting British hobbies. Colette Modiano, writer. Eric de Rothschild, in charge of the vineyard Lafite-Rothschild. A close friend. Son of Mary and Alain R., Nephew of Cecile and Elie R. Mary Dunn was one of the brightest young things of Nancy Mitford's world. She was first married to Philip Dunn, then to Robin Campbell, then to Charles McCabe, and, finally, again to Philip Dunn. Maurice Dumoncel, publisher. The Feray brothers, Thierry and Jean; of a Protestant family, they are both knowledgeable in the field of art. Paul Roche, friend of Duncan Grant. Quentin Bell, art historian, painter and sculptor.

[3] Ottoline Morrell, hostess and patron of the arts, striking in appearance, and in her unconventional interests and attitudes.

the discontent and frustration that must build up within old people. I remembered Duncan as a gentle person when he was young. I would have expected him to have become benign with age. Not at all. Roche treats him like a child, which of course in a way he is. I wished Roche would have attended more assiduously to Duncan's elemental needs. This was a recurring problem during the visit.

The next morning Quentin appeared in Mary's study to say goodbye. 'I'm afraid Duncan fell out of bed in the night,' he said. 'Roche says he won't be able to be moved for twenty-four hours. They won't be able to leave today.'

Roche seemed very happy at the thought of staying on. There was a problem over the postponed flight. We would have to get a medical certificate that Duncan was fit to travel. So that afternoon the doctor came round to the Embassy. Luckily he gave suitable clearance. The next day when all was set for the departure Roche announced that Duncan and he had colds. 'I wish it were pneumonia,' Roche said, 'then we could stay on here a long time.'

We grinned politely. I had made up my mind by then that the whole visit had been Roche's idea. I am sure that Duncan had never thought of such a thing; and when, as eventually he was lifted into the car to leave, I said that I hoped he had enjoyed it, he gave me the least enthusiastic of replies. I managed to get a photograph of Duncan in his chair with straw hat and feather taken in the courtyard as they left for the airport.

If my thoughts were not always of the sweetest, this occurred, I think, because I felt I had been deceived. Roche had never given me any inkling of Duncan's parlous condition. The old man was scarcely in a state to be moved from one room to another, let alone taken abroad for a strenuous time of sight and gallery-seeing. However, Duncan had achieved his dying wish, as Roche expressed it, to see this exhibition of Cézanne's last works.

My final thought, as they drove away, was not of Cézanne, but of euthanasia and my own wish to avoid the humiliation of a decline such as Duncan's.

I had little time for morbidness, as Silkin, the Minister of Agriculture and Fisheries, was arriving in the courtyard just when Duncan was leaving. Here to talk about fish, he was coming to me for a private lunch. He is not aggressive in character and more agreeable than his public anti-European persona led me to think. I find it odd that someone who so obviously likes European life – at any rate restaurants, wine, etc – should be a professional anti-European. Politics tend to follow tastes. Not so with him. He talked about the thirtieth anniversary of his wedding which had occurred that day, and how they had spent their three weeks' honeymoon in Paris.

For some reason we talked about bread and I managed to light a spark of interest in him for the wholemeal bread shop that is one of our favourite resorts in Paris. Silkin decided that he must visit it on his way to the airport to take his private plane back to England. He told me that he thought his talk with the new French minister had been worth it. He had clearly got on well with Le Theule. Silkin's officials were less sure that the meeting had been all that fruitful. Certainly the fish problem is with us for a long time. It will be one of the dominant problems in Anglo-French relations.

I have just written an article for *Le Monde* on the subject. It is to appear tomorrow. I doubt whether it will have much effect on official French thinking. It seemed worth while to try to give the historical perspective.

24 APRIL

PARIS

THE SECRETARY-GENERAL AT

THE QUAI

I saw Soutou,[1] the Secretary-General at the Quai, this morning. He is one of the most delightful people in the world to see. Kenneth [James] says that, coming as he does from a quite humble background, he is the pet of the Quai who proudly show him off to all those, and there are many, who accuse the ministry of upper-class domination. He is a great contrast to his predecessor, Courcel, who though perfectly polite, found it necessary to find something to complain about whenever one saw him. I suppose it was part of his Gaullist philosophy, that no occasion must be lost to put the other fellow in the wrong for the sake of France. I found that, before calling on him on whatever subject, I had to arm myself with counter-charges about French misdeeds against the moment when he came out with some inevitable criticism of a British transgression. I very much liked Courcel and respected him. But it was a little nerve-racking, as it was intended to be, to have to go through this one-upmanship on every visit.

Now that he has retired I find Courcel positively cosy, partly because he evidently feels bitter about the way Giscard put him out to grass.

[1] Jean-Marie Soutou, French diplomat since 1943. Secretary-General, Ministry of Foreign Affairs 1976–83. A French official with whom it was always a pleasure to do business.

I went to see Soutou about the outstanding claim by the families of British victims for damages from an air crash that occurred near Nantes over five years ago. He listened with characteristic courtesy, moving as quickly as possible to discuss the Soviet shooting down of the South Korean civil airliner. This is indeed the international topic of the moment. He regarded it as a useful corrective for those who have been inclined to believe that Russia was becoming rapidly much more civilised. He went on to speak of the Belgrade Conference and of Soviet motives both there and earlier at Helsinki. Their aim was, he was sure, to avoid all serious commitment on human rights while getting the West to recognise all their conquests and the new frontiers of Eastern Europe.

I asked him whether he agreed with the frequently expressed view that President Carter had at least succeeded in making the world more conscious of, and responsive to, human rights. Soutou said that he did not believe this at all. Carter was surrounded by the same sort of people as had surrounded FDR. The earlier Democrats had been naïve about the USSR, so were the present ones. It was a dangerous naïvety that carried the belief in a bipartisan world such as could settle the fate of all other countries.

5 MAY

PARIS

___

CONTRASTED MEETINGS WITH TONY BENN
AND KENNETH KEITH

I have been at home for a few days to attend a dinner of the Lord Mayor's on Anglo-French Industrial Co-operation and to be present for meetings between the new French Minister of Industry, Monsieur Giraud,[1] and Varley[2] and Benn.[3] I was also asked to lunch by Kenneth Keith to be brainwashed on Rolls Royce's case over the aircraft choice.

Calling at the Department of Industry at 6 o'clock for Varley's meeting with the French minister I was met in the hall by the usual frayed notices that adorn government offices: injunctions about switching off lights and looking out for window cleaners, and warnings about the lifts not

___

[1] André Giraud, mining engineer and politician. Administrator General Commissariat for Atomic Energy 1970–8; Minister of Industry 1978–81.
[2] Eric Varley, Labour MP 1964–84. Secretary of State for Energy 1974–5; for Industry 1975–9. Life Peer 1990.
[3] Tony Benn, at this stage of his career Secretary of State for Energy (1975–9).

working. I was struck by the same mixture of informality bordering on casualness and cordiality when, the next morning, I arrived to see Tony Benn. I arrived at Thames House South, Millbank. At the entrance I was greeted by a notice telling visitors to go next door. I obeyed and was then sent by the security guard to a door marked enquiries. Inside was a battery of broken-down furniture and ashtrays. The walls were plastered with posters enjoining one to save fuel. From this I deduced that at any rate I was in the right place, in the Department of Energy. The receptionist had rung a bell after I had said whom I wanted to see, upon which another woman entered. 'Tony Benn,' the receptionist shouted, ''E wants Tony Benn.' I followed a pair of escorting sandals that slapped on the linoleum of the long corridors.

Benn greeted me in his usual friendly way. He was about to take his place in the middle of a long table. In front of him stood a large mug of tea. He asked me if I would like a cup and I accepted. We were drinking away happily and chatting: 'What shall I say to Monsieur Giraud? What is the purpose of the meeting? How are Anglo-French relations at the moment? How much energy is France producing now from nuclear reactors?' These were the questions we were discussing when the French minister arrived.

Benn welcomed him in most amicable fashion and said how good of him it was to call, particularly as he had only been minister for a few weeks. He was most grateful to him for having come such a long way to see him. In point of fact Giraud had not come to London with the purpose of seeing Benn but to attend a dinner. There were introductions all round and we took our places. Benn continued to be at home with his mug of tea. My less proletarian cup stood in front of me. I was feeling a certain sense of inhospitality, not to say rudeness towards our French guests, when, without a word or a knock, a trolley came trundling into the room laden with cups and coffee pots. The visiting minister was served in the take-it-or-leave-it fashion that seems to be de rigueur nowadays, as if in keeping with some deep-seated national belief that frills must be avoided, and that too much trouble over presentation is a mark of insincerity.

I hope the French minister found Mr Benn's office was as much worth the detour as I did. The visitors were seated opposite an enormous representation of a mining town with smoke belching from chimneys and a large wheel turning at the head of a mine-shaft. At the top of a banner appeared the words: 'National Union of Mineworkers'; at the bottom 'Labour for unity and strength'.

Covering the side wall was another colossal banner hung on a curtain rod with a tassel at one end. It was headed: 'The Worker's Union, Witley Branch. Unity is Strength'.

There was a representation of a man and woman shaking hands with a seraphic look on their faces. Below them were these words: 'United to obtain the just reward of our labour'. Tony Benn's image was maintained at his very elbow. Beside him stood a miner's lamp.

The meeting went well. Benn is exceptionally courteous and convincing – as long as he keeps off certain subjects, for instance Europe. He lauded the idea of closer Anglo-French bilateral relations, largely because it was a means of keeping the Community at bay. The French rather liked this. Benn must have said at least a dozen times that his main aim was to stop Brussels interfering. If they had their way they would hand everything back to the international oil companies.

Benn was more forthcoming than I had expected on the fast-breeder. It would be in production in the UK in the early eighties.

Lunch on Tuesday with Kenneth Keith at Rolls Royce's headquarters in Buckingham Gate was an experience I will not soon forget. He is determined to bring off a deal between Rolls Royce and Boeing. He is afraid that a decision by British Aerospace to enter Airbus Industrie will ruin his chances, largely because he thinks the European deal can only come if BA are forced to buy airbuses instead of Boeings. He knows that I am protagonist of the European solution.

He was accompanied by John Russell (formerly Ambassador in Madrid), and Peter Thornton (a former civil servant, turned tycoon). They hammered at me to try to make me understand the importance of saving Rolls Royce from a further bankruptcy. Naturally I agreed with this objective but suggested that Rolls Royce should avoid the anti-European image that it seemed to be acquiring.

The upshot of a long and acrimonious lunch was that Keith agreed to come to Paris to try to improve relations between Rolls Royce and the French.

9 MAY

PARIS

———

A VISIT BY TRADE UNIONISTS

Late supper last night for a party of British trade unionists here at the invitation of the Confédération Française Démocratique du Travail (CFDT): Len Murray, General Secretary of the TUC; Jack Jones, former General Secretary of the TGWU; John Macgougan, General Secretary of the National Union of Tailors and Garment Workers; and F.F. Jarvis, General Secretary of the National Union of Teachers. The French side was led by Edmond Maire who has been the General Secretary of the CFDT since 1971.

They were the sort of visitors to whom HMG wants Embassies to pay a lot of attention. We diplomats abroad must realise how important they were. Having seen them at work elsewhere I am not sure that the British trade unionists will either learn much from or make much of an impression on their hosts here.

Maire is a reasonable and agreeable man. He had originally contemplated becoming a priest but decided instead to join Pechiney as a laboratory assistant. I placed him next to Len Murray with a girl in between as interpreter. Unfortunately I did not hear much of Maire's views, largely because Murray did all the talking. However, he evidently believes that the French unions should avoid becoming too involved in politics at the present time and that they should see whether the Patronat[1] are prepared to respond to the government's call for 'ouverture' and more social justice. None of the French visitors brought their wives. I asked Maire why. He said that it was not the custom in France for wives to accompany their husbands at official or business dinners. Then he added with a disarming smile that if he had known that there were going to be such charming ladies present he would have brought his along.

I was depressed to hear the British trade unionists playing the old record: strikes in Britain were not so widespread or frequent as people thought: 98 per cent of British industry was without any strikes; it was all the fault of the headline-writers; anyway what mattered was the quality of life about which no other country had any lessons to give us. The arrival of so many people from overseas to live in the UK was proof that the quality of our life was superior to anybody else's.

We had taken a lot of trouble with the arrangements – to produce food and drink that would prevent the trade unionists accusing us of the extreme of either extravagance or meanness. I do not know if we succeeded. I was sure that we were right to entertain the British trade unionists rather than neglect them, however much they might later complain about the luxury of the Embassy. They would have had stronger and more justifiable grounds for complaint if we had ignored them. Personally, I have never found trade union leaders ungrateful or petty so far as social relations are concerned.

---

[1]Patronat, the body of French employers, somewhat similar to our CBI.

I saw Kenneth Rose last night. He is staying with Nicky Gordon-Lennox. He told me how George V had visited an exhibition of Cézanne with Queen Mary. At the end of the room he stood transfixed before a picture and said, 'Come here, May, this'll make you laugh.'

Alas, Kenneth Rose did not know which picture it was.

I worked all day yesterday on a despatch about the new French government. I also had to prepare for the Heads of Mission meeting in London tomorrow. For this purpose I called on the Elysée to try to elicit the views of the President on the enlargement of the Community. I am sure that the President has enjoined everyone in his circle to be discreet at all times with everyone. This makes the higher reaches of the French government a stony source from which to try to draw blood. One of the joys of talking to and dealing with most French people is that they tend to be '*bavard*'. There is no trouble in getting them to talk. Not so with anyone who is under the close eye of Giscard. If, for instance, you ask at the Elysée what the President's views are on enlargement you are apt to be told that he has not reached a view and that your interlocuter does not know his provisional thoughts. The only hope, I have found, is to say something like this: 'Such and such a subject is coming up in London this week. I want to be sure that in communicating with London about the likely French attitude I am being more or less accurate and will not be leading England astray. Would I therefore be right in saying that the President's opinion is more or less as follows . . .' I then make a slightly exaggerated statement of what his view might be in the hope of provoking some reaction. This tactic is by no means perfect. It is, nevertheless, the only one I know. My diplomatic colleagues suffer no less than I do from the taciturnity of the Elysée. However, I do not suppose French interests suffer thereby.

The Gordon Richardsons[1] were here for the weekend. He is most agreeable – very handsome and charming with an interest in books. On his previous visits here he has always been accompanying Denis Healey to some secret meeting and we have had a hurried official lunch at which Denis has boomed away informatively. I have never known what Gordon thinks of him as he always listens politely and avoids argument. He says that when Denis first became Chancellor he always clicked his heels, bowed and said 'Sir' upon meeting Gordon. The latter was not quite sure why he had done this. Whether or not it was intended to be ironical, it had certainly mystified foreigners

---

[1] Gordon Richardson, Governor of the Bank of England 1973–83, married Peggy, daughter of Canon Dick Sheppard.

who deduced from it that they must have got their idea of the rank of the two men the wrong way round.

14 MAY
PALAIS DE MONACO

—

A WEEKEND WITH THE RAINIERS[1]

Princess Grace was our guest in the Embassy here for the fashion show last autumn. She may have been impressed by Mary's flower arrangements there, designed to reflect in silver the spirit of the Jubilee. Anyway, she wrote a month or two later inviting her to take part, either as a judge or a participant, in the annual Concours International de Bouquets in Monte Carlo in May. Mary accepted, saying that she would like to participate. The two categories of the competition for which she entered were *'Fleurs Imposées'*, where they give everyone the same collection of leaves and flowers, and, secondly, *'Un Petit Déjeuner'*, an arrangement that, according to the rules, has to be *'réalisé sur un plateau'*, but is otherwise up to the whim of the exhibitor.

So we took down with us from Paris the raw materials for this breakfast setting. We had with us cardboard boxes containing jars of various sorts of flowers. It had been a problem picking them at the right time in the garden in Paris. We packed them in ice which kept them fresh on the long drive down. From time to time as he drove, Jacques (the chauffeur) would lift the layers of sopping newspaper beside him to peep, with a certain air of disdain, at the little plastic containers of lily of the valley, pansies, euphorbia, sweet williams and black tulips, peopling the leather front seat of the car. '*Ça va*,' he would reassure us. Tommy, the night guard at the Paris Embassy, had been most eager the previous evening to help with the packaging of the flowers for their long journey. He could not suppress his surprise that we should be taking flowers from Paris to the Côte d'Azur. 'You will find plenty of 'em down there,' he assured us. We would, but Mary was quite right that they would be shop flowers, like iris or birds-of-paradise, not at all what she needed for the arrangement she had decided upon.

We also had with us on the journey a large silver tray and the lustre

---

[1] This account was published in the Autumn 1988 issue of *Antaeus* magazine.

tea-set that we collected from the cottage at home last weekend. These were essential props for the exhibit.

We were greeted and treated at the palace with great hospitality. Our initial worry was how the flowers would weather the night. Mary snipped off the ends of their stems and, resorting to the gold mosaic hand basin in our bathroom, changed the water in the plastic containers. Sensing a crisis, the English housekeeper at the palace rose to the occasion and insisted that we leave the flowers in the passage where they would be cooler and she could keep an eye on them.

I had an interesting talk with Princess Grace at dinner. She said that her father, an Irish politician, had preferred her elder sister to her. She had been very conscious of this and it had hurt her. I wondered, though did not ask, whether this had had anything to do with her decision to go on the stage. Feeling insufficiently appreciated, as she thought, by her parents, had she sought to compensate for this by looking for attention elsewhere? I was not sure that this was so, because she seemed so undemonstrative, almost self-contained, with no apparent wish to strike a pose or seek the limelight. That may be because she has had so much notice taken of her without having to make a great effort.

She said that her mother had brought her and the rest of the family up very strictly. She had tried not to spoil her own children but it had not been easy. I asked when they did the washing-up and the housework. She said Rainier, which is how she calls him in conversation, had begun with big yachts, but they had got smaller and smaller so that there was now no crew to look after them on board. It was there that the children had to do the chores.

As we sat beside each other at another dinner, one which was held at the Hôtel de Paris following the Flower Exhibition, the conversation got round to wine. She is an enthusiast. I said that Mary regarded me as a wine bore, indeed my nickname now in Paris was WB. She said that she did not agree. She would love to own a vineyard. I asked myself why not. It is difficult to gauge the extent of their wealth. I also found it hard to judge with her, as it is with other minor royalty, what was the correct degree of formality or informality to maintain. In doubt I plumped for being formal.

She and the Prince are extremely free and easy and unpompous. Neither of them puts on airs at all. He took part in the flower competition, in two categories, one of which was 'One of the Twelve Months of the Year' and the other 'Adventure and the Sea – Illustration of a text from Jules Verne'.

He worked away at his exhibits just like all the other competitors with no extra help and no ceremony, clad in an open shirt and espadrilles. I was not even sure that the Japanese ladies alongside him, bent over their contorted little creations, were aware who he was. He had a nom de guerre for his presentations which was 'Monsieur Louis de Rosemont'. He arrived and left in a Land-Rover, driving himself. It was piled high with garden equipment as well as large bits of rusty iron to help recapture Jules Verne. Apparently one of his many hobbies is welding. Whenever any metal breaks up at his farm behind Monaco he insists on doing the smithy work himself. His naturalness and enthusiasm are engaging. There is nothing remotely ceremonious or blasé about him.

Certain court formalities are in contrast with the Rainiers' personal informality. For instance before meals the guests have to assemble before the arrival of the Rainiers, and then to curtsey and bow, for all the world as though they were attending a formal ceremony at Buckingham Palace. It is the same before setting off to the town in convoy. The non-royals, i.e. the guests, have to foregather at some predetermined point ten minutes before the Prince and Princess are due to appear. They have, as it were, to be in attendance – in waiting.

Yesterday I went for a swim in the palace pool before lunch. The meal was to be served alongside the water, beneath the palm trees, mimosas and nisperas. I was about to get into the water when an elderly courtier approached me to say that we would be lunching in ten minutes' time. I said that, given the coldness of the water, I would have plenty of time. In fact I was not ready on the dot, was not wearing a tie and was putting everyone into stitches of embarrassment when the Prince arrived before me. Mary rushed over to say that I really must behave and that I could not possibly appear without a tie. So I hurried to my room, followed all the way by my valet who seems to have a ceaseless vigil to watch over me to try to ensure that I am turned out correctly and punctually. I found it odd that, eating beside a swimming pool, one has to be dressed as in a restaurant. However, I see that appearances must be maintained. The palace has to avoid becoming like a jet-set pleasure-dome such as the Marbella Club for instance. That would be fatal. So I agree that it is I who must conform. From now on I shall be on time and with a tie. But for the visit to the zoo? Will it really be necessary then? Will the baby tiger, and the diminutive seal – the Prince's pets – show their bare teeth if I show my bare neck? I shall soon find out.

All yesterday morning Mary worked at her flower arrangements. I was employed as a runner and, when she saw the paraphernalia used by the Japanese and other competitors, she asked me to do some shopping for her in Monte Carlo. Firstly I was asked to fetch some croissants; then to buy a bunch of dark grapes; and finally a flower holder, because one of the rules was that each flower had to be in water and she wanted to tuck a flower under the breakfast plate. As a finishing touch she grasped the daily newspapers that I had under my arm and slid them under the corner of the tray. Thanks to her talent for design and, I hope, of mine for delivery, she won two prizes. One of them was a first prize for harmony of colour; the other was for the breakfast arrangement.

There was heavy Japanese competition, twenty-six of them having flown from Tokyo to take part. They went to enormous pains in their presentations. I was told that many had been on three-year courses devoted exclusively to flower arrangements. No wonder the products were so unspontaneously awful, so far removed from the wayward changeability of nature. Three Japanese ladies were already in the exhibition hall, which was decorated elaborately but unconvincingly to simulate the world of the sea, when we arrived at 7.45 a.m. They started cutting up and contorting the leaves and flowers provided by the *Fleurs Imposées* competition. They were still at it four hours later when the exhibits had to be finished and the judging started. None of them won a prize; indeed the Japanese invasion was beaten off all round. They did not win a single medal. One received a *mention honorable* and her name was called – after a fashion – at the prize-giving, but to her evident disappointment she had nothing to take back to Tokyo to mark the distinction. As I watched those inscrutable, but unmistakably downcast, faces I could not but wonder whether the Japanese contingent would be quite so numerous next year. (I have been reminded subsequently of their hari-kari commitment on this occasion by a line spoken in characteristically sardonic jest by Maggie Smith: 'If you think squash a competitive activity, try flower arrangement.')

We made a lot of new friends over the weekend, including the Montague Meyers.[1] At the first dinner in the palace I sat between the Princess and Mrs Meyer, alias Fleur Cowles, an old friend of the Rainiers. When the ice-cream was served she said, 'I don't know what it is, but at least it will make us fat.'

She talked about the Prince. One of his passions is the circus. He takes a special interest in clowns and animals. He had planned once to follow a circus throughout its summer tour and had had a Mercedes adapted as a caravan for the purpose. Alas, at the last moment, he had been dissuaded. He has a zoo at the foot of the rock which he has promised to show me round before I leave.

Fleur complimented me on Mary's dress and on her appearance generally. She continued to do this throughout the weekend, whether in relation to her *petit déjeuner*, her straw boater, or her performance of the charleston, saying, with a thrust of her face towards her hands, that she just couldn't stand such competition. Indeed Mary's charleston and

---

[1] The Montague Meyers. He is an industrialist, she a painter who works under the name of Fleur Cowles.

the late nineteenth-century decor of the Hôtel de Paris dining-room were
the highlights of the ball for most of us.

With Meyer I had an agreeable talk about Ernest Bevin who had been
a great friend of his father, the owner of a successful timber company
that had always done a great deal of business with Russia. After Bevin's
death, as I remembered, Meyer had been generous to his widow, Flo,
who had been left almost penniless.

Another friend we made was Rory Cameron who lives in Provence –
about which he has written a book. I had the impression that the Princess
was delighted he was there. People kept telling me that he was Lady
Kenmare's son, as though that would explain everything. Mary and I
both found him delightful, liking and hating all the same things as we
did. Recently he has sold his mother's beautiful house and garden, La
Fiorentina, just west of Monte Carlo. The crowds had become impossible. He has now established himself near Avignon. From his personal
accounts and those in his book, *The Golden Riviera*, describing inter-
war visitors and neighbours like Somerset Maugham, I gained the
impression that his life must have been like that depicted in Cyril Connolly's *Rock Pool*, before this part of the Riviera had turned from gold
to concrete. I suppose those towering blocks are essential to the livelihood
of Monaco, but they do present a horrifying picture to the eye. One can,
of course, have a lovely view of the sea from them, but it is the view
from an aeroplane.

A courtier came to my room on Sunday morning to tell me to be in
the Cour d'Honneur at 11.30 where Son Excellence would join me to
take me to see his motor museum and his zoo.

He arrived and we shook hands. 'Good morning, sir,' I said.

'Good morning, sir,' he said.

Showing me round the lovely old cars, he told me which were his
favourites, and which Grace's. He intends starting a museum open to the
public.

He then drove me in a Ford Fiesta down to the zoo. There was no
nonsense about a police escort. The Prince observed the traffic lights and
the instructions of the policeman on point-duty. The only departure from
the ordinary was that the policeman saluted the Prince as he drove past.

The zoo is in the hands of an Austrian who was formerly a bear-
trainer until he got mauled, and of a French couple, of whom the woman
was a former dentist's assistant and the man previously an employee of
the estate. His face wore scars that did justice alike to his courage and
inexperience with animals. 'The trouble is,' the Prince confided to me,
'that they got too confident.' He told me of a particularly nasty accident
when the female of a pair of ant-eaters, who had been as docile as a
lamb for years, suddenly attacked the keeper and took a joint out of his

thigh. I asked knowingly whether this had happened when she had been on heat and the Prince confirmed that this was so, though the keeper had not known it at the time.

We stared at an enormous young gorilla bleeding from its paws. 'The trouble here,' the Prince explained, 'is that she will eat her feet. We cannot think why.'

I asked – again with extreme sagacity – whether she had had children and was told that she had not. I also enquired whether the Austrian and his wife and the French couple had children. They had not either. They certainly had plenty on their hands with all these shrieking animals. The monkeys seemed particularly talkative that morning.

As we went round the zoo, built on the edge of the rock below the palace, the Prince gave instructions to the attendants. He pointed to a light that needed mending. He suggested putting those two chimpanzees together. He asked for a bucketful of carrots and apples to be brought for the elephant. He then fed the elephant tenderly by hand, inserting the food deep into its mouth while it thrust back its trunk. 'She's got a very good character,' he explained, 'never complains.'

I asked the usual question about its private life and was told that there was no room for more than one elephant – 'but she seems quite happy.'

In fact we left Monaco after our weekend feeling that everyone there, whether visitors or staff, were bound to be happy – so long as they were not too involved with the female ant-eater or a Japanese flower arrangement.

20 MAY

PARIS

VISIT OF THE LORD MAYOR

OF LONDON

We are in the middle of a visit to Paris by the Lord Mayor of London, Sir Peter Vanneck. He is Francophile and is the owner of a house in the Corrèze. This makes him persona grata with the Maire of Paris, Chirac. He wears his official garments well and obviously enjoys leading the little processions composed of the Sheriffs, the Chief Commoner, the Sword Bearer, the Sergeant-at-Arms and the City Marshall, all of whom accompany him everywhere wearing furs and feathers, frills and medals. The Parisians are delighted by the sight of these quaintly dressed visitors, particularly by the Lord Mayor himself wearing his triangular hat covered with feathers and his splendid uniform. There is flippant talk whether Chirac should not be encouraged to institute a uniform specially designed by Yves St Laurent for the elected Lord Mayor of Paris which would certainly enable him to upstage President Giscard.

The Lord Mayor is a handsome outgoing personality, very much a product of my school [Stowe], with plenty of panache and no inhibition about displaying it. He made a good speech at the Town Hall in very adequate French. In a speech at dinner at the Embassy the following evening he told a good story about Edward VII's visit to Paris in 1903 when he had come here to prepare the way for the Entente Cordiale. When the King first appeared in Paris he encountered a good deal of hostility. People made snide remarks about Fashoda and recent conflicts between the two countries in Africa. One of the King's staff said to him, 'It doesn't seem as though they like us much.'

To which the King replied laconically, 'Why should they?'

I did not think that historical enmity was far in the background during the visit we all paid to the museum of the Légion d'Honneur. Inevitably most of the trophies shown mark some passage of arms with the British. The French were at pains to show us the painting of Churchill receiving the Légion d'Honneur in the court of Les Invalides, and the portrait, hardly a flattering one, of the Queen. Although the French did their best to conceal it, the British party, particularly the Embassy members, were intrigued by a picture of Philip le Bel and his naked mistress. The picture showed him putting a collar round her neck.

22 MAY

PARIS

MORE MINISTERIAL MEETINGS

ON AIRCRAFT

We have also had a visit to Paris by Ministers Varley and Dell for talks with their opposite number, Le Theule, about aeroplanes. The meeting had two purposes, at least I think so: to find out whether the French (and the Germans whom they visited earlier the same day) had anything more to offer by way of co-operation than that already discussed with British Aerospace; and to be able to show in the event of the American option being chosen, that effort at the highest level had been made to try to probe the possibilities of co-operation on aircraft with the Europeans.

I thought that Le Theule handled himself well, particularly as he is very new to the post of Minister of Transport. Varley was good. If there was no divine spark he was clear and courteous as I have always found him to be. He sticks to his brief and creates an amicable impression.

Dell was gruff with the French. He said that British Airways wanted to buy American aircraft, not European. The government had no powers to make them buy what they did not want. There was no hint that he would be prepared to ask British Airways to have another look in the European direction, though Le Theule clearly sought this. As Dell was speaking Varley passed me a note: 'You are listening to the next Labour Chancellor of the Exchequer.'

I said that I did not doubt it.

When the meeting was over we all had drinks in the house, that is to say all the members of the sizeable British delegation from London and a few people from the Embassy who had been helping by making records and administrative arrangements.

Varley's head civil servant, Ronald Dearing, a Deputy Secretary in charge of the air division of the Department of Industry, said, 'Well, Secretary of State, I think we can say, mission accomplished.'

I asked him what mission, and he listed seven points of which I remember little, except that they did not seem to me to correspond to the outcome of the meeting. I noticed that neither Varley nor Dell were inclined then, or at any other time, to talk about policy on aircraft in front of officials. However, later, when Varley and everyone else had retired and I was left alone with Dell I confronted him on the central issue. He made no bones about it: the question was not whether we should support a European or an American option but whether there was any option that could stand up against Boeing. He did not think there was. He was therefore 100 per cent for the Boeing deal. I said that in the long run that could mean the disappearance of an independent British airframe industry. Dell said that he did not deny this but it did not matter. I rejoined with profound disagreement. I said that there was a limit to the wisdom of letting British industrial production decline. What would the large labour force in Britain be doing in five to ten years' time if a lot of manufacturing industry was terminated? I thought it was lamentable that a British Cabinet minister with responsibility for these things could contemplate with equanimity the eclipse of an independent British capability in this high-technology field.

Denis Howell,[1] the Minister of Sport, who was also staying in the

---

[1] Denis Howell, first elected as Labour MP 1955. Minister of State, Department of Environment which included responsibility for sport, 1974–9. A life-enhancing guest.

house to attend some conference, had joined us for a drink. He said that he was inclined to agree with me.

Dell argued that it was nothing to do with whether he was a Cabinet Minister or not. He thought that in a few years' time we would all have to protect ourselves in the face of cheap labour competition. The European Community would have to create an enormous wall around itself to protect our industry.

I said that I thought this might well be so but why did we wish to exclude the aircraft industry which employed over one hundred thousand highly skilled people? Did he also think that we should cease to be an independent car producer? Dell said that that was different.

Just as our exchanges were becoming acrimonious, the lights fused. This did not extinguish our spirits. Our row became even more outspoken. We went on arguing while the security guard brought candles in great number which he arranged as if he was decorating a birthday cake.

After the party had left the next day I wrote to the two ministers summarising my impression of the visit. I do not suppose that they will have liked it much, or indeed my attitude throughout. I get the feeling that home civil servants are increasingly inclined to say what they think their ministers will like; or, to be more precise, they tend to take account of their masters' political views in suggesting what should be done.

I remember Rab saying that he wanted officials to indicate what they thought was required in the national interest. It was for him to look after the politics. This is not an attitude that permeates Whitehall at the present juncture.

1 JUNE
PARIS

MIDSUMMER MISCELLANY

We gave a little dinner last night for Douglas Wass,[1] Head of the Treasury. Nicholas Bayne[2] and I were chatting with him in the garden before the

---

[1]Douglas Wass, Permanent Secretary HM Treasury, 1974–83. Subsequently held several business appointments including chairmanship Equity and Law Life Assurance Society. Reith lecturer 1983.

[2]Nicholas Bayne, member of the Diplomatic Service. Financial Counsellor, Paris 1975–9. Ambassador to OECD, Paris, 1985–92; High Commissioner to Canada 1992. An exceptionally brilliant and modest economic adviser who later gave me much help over my valedictory despatch from Paris.

arrival of the French guests. We were talking about the scale of inflation at different epochs of history. Prices in the UK never rose between the end of the Napoleonic Wars and the First World War. 'But you know,' Wass said, 'one of the periods of the most rapid inflation was the fourth century AD under Vespasian.'

Bayne's brow furrowed: 'I thought it was Diocletian,' he said quietly.

Wass admitted his appalling error. I felt proud that the FCO could hold its own with the Treasury in such matters.

I attended a lunch yesterday in the Louis XIII Room at the George V given by the magazine *Historia*. It was a distinguished gathering. Dumoncel was host. Alain Peyrefitte,[1] Edgar Faure[2] and Maurice Druon[3] were among the guests. There was much talk of precedence. Peyrefitte called for silence while he asked me about precedence in the House of Lords. I confessed to ignorance and some indifference. There was also heated discussion about the filling of two empty seats in the Academy. Amongst the lunch guests was a spry ninety-three-year-old maître. Dumoncel asked me if I could follow what was going on. I assured him that I had no difficulty. I did not add that it was not a new subject to me. People have talked of nothing else for months.

There was then the business of considering books for the *Historia* annual prize. This was a random affair. I was struck by how unsystematic the French can be. They preferred to use instinct and extraneous criteria. What happened was that one or two people suggested titles and the others then said they knew this or that author well – that he was a '*bon garçon*'.

At one moment Dumoncel said that he was proposing to extend the group and bring in foreigners. He wished to put forward my name. He referred to what I had written. He said, to my embarrassment, that I was about to embark on a book about 1940 (this was a passing idea that I had thrown out in conversation with him). There were approving noises. Peyrefitte said that not only did I occupy a beautiful house but that I was capable of showing people round and telling them all about the pictures. Edgar Faure said that he has never been shown round the Embassy. He suggested that not only should I be

[1] Alain Peyrefitte, politician, member of the Académie Française, Lord Privy Seal, Minister of Justice.
[2] Edgar Faure, lawyer and politician, leading member of several governments in the Fourth Republic. From being a radical socialist he came to represent the 'Gaullistes de Gauche' and served in several Fifth Republic governments under President de Gaulle.
[3] Maurice Druon, author and politician, member of the Académie Française. Joined the Free French forces in London. Minister of Cultural Affairs 1973–4. Prolific writer of romantic and historical novels. Has devoted much enthusiasm and charm to Anglo-French relations.

admitted to the club but that they should choose my book on 1940 here and now for next year's prize!

I said that I was confused and flattered, which was all too true. The lunch ended because Peyrefitte had to answer questions in parliament. No book had been chosen. Druon confided to me that he thought I would enjoy it because the atmosphere was like that of the common-room of an Oxford college.

A waiter in white tie ushered me with great punctilio through the marble halls of the George V to the front door. The members shook me by the hand, whispering 'Your Excellency'.

3 JUNE

PARIS

———

OUR LAST QUEEN'S BIRTHDAY
PARTY

About sixteen hundred people turned up for the Queen's birthday party. It is the tenth and last QBP we will give. To paraphrase T.S. Eliot, the life of a British diplomat is measured out, not in coffee spoons, but in QBPs. Marcel, the gardener, rightly predicted that it would not rain, something that he said he knew from the state of his kidneys.

Before coming to Paris I had heard about the annual garden party and its importance in the social scene of Paris. Scepticism about this was deepened when I saw the list of regular invitees. Our first year we cut the list down a lot, producing great ill-feeling amongst those eliminated, but a sense of heightened pleasure in those retained. One aim was to stop people thinking that they were doing a favour to the British government or to the Embassy by coming. I think we achieved this, an invitation to the party no longer being taken for granted. Last year we were subject to the worldwide ban on such parties on economic grounds, but we managed to have an exception made for us, partly because it was Paris and partly because of the Jubilee. We released a lot of hot-air balloons.

This year the numbers have crept up. There were few refusals. The turnout of hats was impressive. The consumption of champagne and strawberries colossal. The hungry guests even ate Mary's decorations.

The pipers were in evidence but not over-obtrusive on eye or ear. They stayed two nights in the house to save money.

The first guest to arrive, and almost the last to leave, was de Gaulle's son[1] who made a speech as he shook hands with me about the importance of the occasion and his awareness of what it represented.

The Hartmans[2] brought Kissinger[3] along with them. He was, of course, a great draw. Many French people expressed surprise that he should be there. Marie-France Garaud,[4] éminence grise of the Gaullist Party, solicited an invitation to the party in a roundabout way. She approached someone on the *Financial Times*, asking him to call to see her. When he arrived she asked if he could get her an invitation as she very much wanted to attend. She explained that neither he, the *Financial Times* man, nor she must telephone the Embassy because the lines were tapped and she would not want it to become known to the government that she had been a *demandeuse* in this way. I was, in fact, delighted to invite her. Dark horses, like her, are like glow-worms at a party. I have noticed too that with Giscard looking set fair for a long innings, the Gaullists are feeling a bit out of things at the moment and, like the socialists, are grateful for attention.

Most of our personal friends arrived towards the end of the party and well after we had left the receiving line. Our hands were mangled. Some members of the British community appeared to wish to demonstrate their loyalty by giving Mary and me a particularly firm grip.

There has been a rapturous reaction to the party which has been described as 'the best ever' – the great event of the Paris scene – and, to quote Johnny Faucigny-Lucinge:[5] 'If only the Queen herself could have seen it.' All this was some return for all the hard work Mary devoted to preparing for the party. She spent literally days and nights doing the flowers, which were greatly admired; and she made red, white and blue bows and rosettes, all of which were stolen. I think she secretly feels a

---

[1] Philippe de Gaulle; son of the President, he had the same christian name as Marshal Pétain who was his father's patron early in his career and with whom, at the time of Philippe's birth, the family were on the closest of terms; see *The Last Great Frenchman* by Charles Williams, Little Brown & Co 1993, p 61.

[2] Arthur Hartman, member of the US Foreign Service. Ambassador to France 1977–81, then to the USSR. A glowing exception to the rule that US career diplomats do not reach the highest posts. Helped by Donna, his forceful wife.

[3] Henry Kissinger, by now out of office, but still a colossus on the world stage where he has remained ever since.

[4] Marie-France Garaud; Magistrat at the Audit Office; in Pompidou's office when he was Prime Minister and President; a brilliant lawyer and political adviser. Too colourful to be an éminence grise.

[5] Jean-Louis de Faucigny-Lucinge, known as Johnny to his friends; a cosmopolitan aristocrat who mingled with artists and writers. He served as impresario for the annual holiday visits to France of Queen Elizabeth, the Queen Mother.

little sad that this is our last party and that she will never do it again.
However we have had photos taken so that we can recapture it in the
scrapbook in years to come if we so wish.

I must say that we felt tired at the dinner party afterwards given by
the Mentzelopoulos. He is the main owner of Felix Potin and has recently
acquired Château Margaux and a large part of the wine firm, Nicolas.
A retiring personality of Greek origin he shows little drive or dynamism
on the surface. He speaks glowingly of the loyalty and hard work of his
French employees. Perhaps he has the gift of gaining people's confidence
by giving it. I am intrigued by the contrast between the magnificence of
his possessions and the modesty of his person. There seems to be no rule
for tycoons, they come in all different shapes and sizes. I always used to
think that evident vitality must be a sine qua non, but I no longer think
so. Vernier-Palliez,[1] the head of Renault, is, I suspect, the modern boss
prototype: wise, cautious, hard-working, unflashy and dedicated.

A rumbustious senator was at the dinner, ready to attack on all fronts.
He said that his life as a member of the European parliament was made
impossible by the British members whose attitude and behaviour were
insupportable. My trouble with this attack was that I would probably
have shared his sentiments had I known which anti-European MPs he
was talking about. As it was, I felt bound to retaliate. I could not be
browbeaten across the dinner table.

4 JUNE
PARIS

——

MENDÈS-FRANCE, RAYMOND ARON
AND ROY JENKINS

We lunched with Mendès-France on the 2nd. I always expect from him
more than I get, being impressed by his sea-green reputation, his pallor
and his courtesy. I tend to be disappointed by what he says. Nowadays
he is always a little banal. The other guests were the Bettencourts[2] (she

---

[1] Bernard Vernier-Palliez; Chairman and Chief Executive, Renault, 1975–81; Ambassador to
Washington 1981–84 where we were colleagues.
[2] André Bettencourt, politician, member Chamber of Deputies 1951–77. Minister in various
departments of state 1966–72. Senator 1977.

is a scent millionairess) and the Pierre Dreyfus[1] (he was formerly boss of Renault). The latter has just been to Israel. Mendès-France wanted to hear about it. He said that they were obsessed by danger in Israel.

I changed the subject to Zaire[2] and asked Mendès-France for his reaction to French intervention there. This and French military action in Chad[3] are the main topics of news here at the moment. Giscard has hoisted himself and France into the world's headlines. France has suddenly become the arbiter of Africa, a role he has long sought. Giscard's view has been that Africa is unstable, is the source of essential minerals and is an area outside the traditional preserve of the two superpowers. The European powers have historic connections with Africa. They should make their presence felt more there so that Africa does not fall under Communist domination, and in order to protect their essential interests – economic and strategic.

Mendès-France gave a delphic reply to my question. Bettencourt said to me later as we left the lunch that it was impossible to know whether he would have intervened or not. He is like an old prophet, though with honour in his own country. He lives simply. Lunch was served by a coloured maid and was not good. There was one bottle of wine between us all, a 1955 burgundy – Clos Vougeot. Neither of the Mendès-Frances drank. But nor, I noticed, did they drink milk.

He apologised to me as we left that he could not come to the Queen's birthday party and that he would be unable to attend the next dinner of the Misérables. As to Mendès-France's personality there is nothing remotely grand about it. He wears a Légion d'Honneur buttonhole. I felt that I really wanted to talk to him about the distant past where he seems to belong – to the Fourth or even the Third Republic.

When, later that afternoon, Hélène David-Weill[4] telephoned and I tell her that I have been lunching with Mendès-France, she says, 'That must have been interesting.' I have to confess that it had not been. Once again I am struck by the expectations that Mendès-France arouses amongst his compatriots.

I go to a reception for Jacques de Larosière[5] who is just off to the IMF.

---

[1] Pierre Dreyfus, eminent public servant and industrialist. President and Chief Executive Renault, 1955–75; Minister of Industry 1981–2.
[2] French and Belgian airborne units had been despatched to the mineral-rich Zaire province of Shaba. They were sent to restore order there following massed killings and anarchy.
[3] French forces were sent to Chad to help the Government there suppress Libyan-backed rebels.
[4] Hélène David-Weill, wife of Michel David-Weill, Senior Partner Lazard Brothers New York since 1971; Deputy Chairman Lazards London since 1991. Their friendships and interests, including patronage of the arts, straddled the Atlantic.
[5] Jacques de Larosière, French official and international civil servant. Managing Director International Monetary Fund 1978–86. Appointed head of European Bank of Reconstruction and Development 1993.

I met his sister last summer on a boat between Istanbul and Piraeus. We sat up on deck as the ship glided at sunset between the Dardanelles. We clicked immediately and our friendship has been translated to her brother whom I greatly like.

We dined that night with the Casanovas.[1] He is one of Barre's right-hand men. Among the other guests are the Raymond Arons. Again, as with Mendès-France, I am impressed by his reputation, his intellectual brilliance and the strength and serenity of his character. We talk about France's new dynamism in foreign affairs. He favours the African intervention in Chad and Zaire, but not participation in the UN force in the Lebanon which he regards as nostalgic imperialism. I say that I have ceased to follow the domestic political scene very closely since he wrote in *L'Express* that there would be no domestic politics of any interest for three years. He tells me that I should not take him too seriously.

Roy and Jennifer arrived on Friday night. Roy says that since he went to Brussels he has been keeping a diary and has already written one hundred and fifty thousand words. He says that he loves reading other people's diaries. He likes to know what people have to eat. Some years ago he showed me a diary he had kept of a visit to China. At one point it had the following entry: 'This was the first occasion upon which we dine later than 7 p.m.' There were many accounts of the meals, few of which apparently came up to expectations.

The four of us lunched together on Saturday. Roy was satisfied, I think, with the Lynch-Bages 1960. He brought his own cigars with him so we did not have the usual trouble arising from inadequate hospitality in this respect on my part. After lunch we sat in the garden in the shade chatting. It was a beautiful afternoon.

Early the next morning I saw Roy jogging round the garden. This is his new addiction. Last time he was here he sprained his ankle doing it.

---

[1] Professor Jean-Claude Casanova, lawyer and economist. At this stage in his career Counsellor to the Prime Minister.

5 JUNE

PARIS

———

L'AMOUR DES ANIMAUX

I began the week by taking Zorba to the vet. He had to have a growth removed from his neck. It was a harrowing experience taking him there, though Dr Tourbien is kind and gentle. Waiting, as I have frequently done lately, in the vet's ante-room, I have gained the impression that the French are just as dotty as the English about animals and birds. I was surrounded by people nursing kittens, rabbits and dogs, sometimes in baskets, more often held close to the bosom. A girl next to me was clasping a pigeon which had damaged its wing. I was sure that Tourbien would handle it with the utmost care.

8 JUNE

PARIS

———

THE CHATSWORTH OF FRANCE

We dined last night at Vaux-le-Vicomte, described by some as the Chatsworth of France. It is certainly very impressive, even though the evening was damp and foggy which encouraged the other guests to say cheerfully how much this must have made us English feel at home. I find I can no longer conjure up even a weary smile in response to outmoded clichés about our national climate and character. Paris nowadays is, I believe, more prone to fog than is London. I have to admit, however, that most of the unchanging generalisations about the British are more flattering than they are true: that we are phlegmatic, self-disciplined, good-humoured, class-ridden, unsexy and rich, with great knowledge of wine, hunting, lawn-making and parliamentary democracy.

The Vogües had a gathering of the young *gratin*[1] and near-jet-set to meet us. At least, I suppose that is who they were. I was seated next to the young Duchesse de Rohan, the daughter of a diplomat. She is immensely charming. We talked about the Jubilee party we gave last

———

[1] *Gratin*, French slang equivalent of upper-crust and like that term not used by those it describes. There is no café society ring about the term which smacks rather of the landed nobility of earlier times.

autumn for British fashion. She had been seated at a table with Princess Caroline of Monaco and Jacques Chazot.[1] She said it was the first time she had met him. He could not keep his eyes off the Princess. I asked whether he was not also interested in talking to a young Duchess. 'Not really,' she replied. 'You see I am not *gratin*.' I was interested in this contribution towards a correct understanding of that term.

Her husband is an *Enarque*[2] and works in some government department which certainly does not square with being *gratin*, despite the great title.

9 JUNE
PARIS

A BRILLIANT FOREIGN SECRETARY

The Zaire debate continues, having suddenly become more bitter as a result of attacks on the French government's action by the Gaullists and the socialists. Rocard told me privately, not long after the French sent in their paras, an action which has been criticised by Mitterrand, that the socialists would have been readier to show solidarity if the slightest attempt had been made by Giscard to take them into his confidence. That is not his way. He likes dramatic, personal initiatives. Consultation is not his strong suit. It already looks as though *ouverture*, the theme of this government's tenure just after the election, is already a thing of the past.

Nicky Gordon-Lennox comes in to the office to tell me of a Namibia crisis.[3] I listen patiently but without much sense of anxiety. Namibia has been dominating the telegram traffic for the past year. It is one of the subjects in which the Foreign Secretary has engaged his abundant energies in the hope of achieving some clear-cut settlement. African problems seem to me to be inherently unsuited to such solutions. They are likely to continue to be messy and unresolved. Chirac sees in the subject an opportunity to pick a quarrel with Giscard and to thump the anti-American drum.

---

[1] Jacques Chazot, ballet dancer, choreographer and orchestra director; created a ballet for Françoise Sagan, a close friend; spiritual father of Marie-Chantal; said to be the only male dancer to have danced on his points.
[2] *Enarque*, see footnote on Michel Rocard, diary entry 25–26 February 1977.
[3] Namibia crisis occurred in the long-frustrated attempt to implement UN-backed proposals, initiated by five powers including UK, for elections leading to an independent Namibia (since 1948 under South African administration).

Guiringaud was guest of honour at a small private dinner given the other night by the De Roses.[1] He told me that, having just been in Washington where he represented France at the NATO summit dinner, he was convinced that the US government was more preoccupied by the Communist putsch in Afghanistan than by events in Africa. It was the main reason for its change of line on East–West relations – for Carter's less woolly attitude towards the Russians.

I find Guiringaud quite exceptional: he is dry, matter-of-fact, straightforward, with an excellent command of the facts, great stamina and a serene nervous system. Roy says that he did brilliantly in explaining the case for intervention in Shaba to the Community Foreign Ministers meeting in Denmark a fortnight ago.

His wife does not like social life and rarely accompanies him. She hankers after New York. Certainly the first time I sat next to her, which was at a lunch at the Elysée given for the Queen Mother, her eyes only lit up when we talked about New York. She is very handsome and wears beautiful clothes and has an independent spirit. I wish she did not shun all official functions, though I certainly understand her reason for doing so.

10 JUNE

PARIS

FRICTION IN THE AIR

Kenneth Keith came here for a lunch on Tuesday to meet the French heads of the aircraft industry – except for Ravaud,[2] the boss of SNECMA, whom he refused to see. I find it worrying that Rolls Royce, a great international company, should not be on speaking terms with their French opposite numbers. I suppose it was something that Keith was prepared, albeit against his will, to come here to talk to the other chiefs of the French aircraft industry.

I went to Le Bourget to meet him. He arrived in an enormous private plane, bringing with him Pepper, the head of one of the divisions of Rolls Royce. We travelled into Paris together and discussed how the meeting

---

[1] François and Yvonne de Rose. A French diplomat, he was Ambassador to NATO; a specialist in defence matters.
[2] René Robert Ravaud, president of the main French aero-engine manufacturer, the Société Nationale d'Etude et de Construction Moteurs d'Aviation (SNECMA) since 1971. Since 1977 president of Groupement des Industries Françaises Aéronautiques et Spatiales (GIFAS).

at lunch could most usefully go. His language was less salty than it had been during our recent lunch in London. It had moved to what George Weidenfeld describes as city-baby-talk. He told me that the problem was to get British Aerospace off the pot. I am glad to say that he did not ask me to define precisely what it was that the lunch was aiming to achieve. I did not really know myself beyond the need to get Rolls Royce off its pot so far as the French were concerned, which would be quite a difficult and important task. However, Keith seemed in a much better mood than when I had lunched with him in London. He was completely confident that HMG would take the American option, because it could not dictate to Rolls Royce or let them down.

As it turned out the lunch with the French went quite well. General Jacques Mitterrand, chief executive of the Société Nationale Industrielle Aérospatiale (SNIAS), had told us previously that he would need a translator for Keith because he could never understand a word he said. In the event Keith spoke slowly and clearly and with a minimum of city-baby-language, so that Mitterrand had no difficulty in following him. Philip Nelson gave Keith a simultaneous whispered translation of Mitterrand's statements. I discouraged recriminations. Keith had told me beforehand that there would be no point in raking over the past, which was murky on both sides. We are exposed, in this aerospace problem, to the chronic French complex that they will not show themselves to be 'demandeurs'. They, like the Germans, would certainly prefer us to join them in aircraft production rather than see us throw in our lot with Boeing. They do not, however, wish to show too much enthusiasm because they think that this is bad tactics and would weaken their bargaining position. I told Froment-Meurice[1] that there was a danger of British ministers concluding that the French were not interested in our participating with them in Airbus Industrie, and that it would therefore be best to go where we were wanted, i.e. with the USA. I believe the penny is beginning to drop here on this. The French have asked my advice on a paper they are going to submit to their ministers.

I cannot say that any tangible result flowed from the luncheon discussion. Keith agreed, at any rate, to look more closely at the possibilities of co-operation with the French industry, and the French were a little more forthcoming than they have been hitherto about the possibilities for Anglo-French cooperation. Relations previously were so bad that the lunch cannot have made them worse, and it may lead eventually to some improvement.

Keith presented his case well, I thought. He is very realistic and has

---

[1] Henri Froment-Meurice, French diplomat. Director Economic Affairs at the Quai 1975–9. Ambassador to USSR 1970–81, to the FRG 1982–3.

maintained good relations with many leaders on the Labour side. His sympathies and tastes do not lie with Europe. He is a powerful personality, not the sort of Englishman the French take to naturally. Lack of sympathy is common to both sides. There was, I have to admit, nothing abrasive between the French and British at our luncheon table. Mitterrand was particularly friendly to me.

That afternoon I called on François-Poncet[1] at the Elysée. I try to see him fairly regularly because he is after all nearer than anyone to the Presidential sun whence in France all influence flows. I know how busy he is and how little inclined to gossip so I am grateful for the way he agrees readily to see me when I ask. He knows, I think, that I do not waste his time: and I always try to have something interesting to tell him besides asking him for information. I find it best not to put general questions on wide subjects in the hope that he will take off because I know that he won't. I avoid asking him, for instance, what the President's views on Africa are at the moment, because he will reply with a shrug of the shoulders that it is a big question and that he has not had the chance of a talk with the President about it recently, though of course I will be able to find a good deal in the public statements the President has made.

That afternoon I said to him that my personal view was that the President had not so far shown any enthusiasm for British participation in Airbus Industrie. Both he and Callaghan had hardly touched on the subject at their last bilateral meeting at Chequers in December. There was a danger of British ministers concluding that the French were not interested. I then gave figures about the considerable size and importance of the British aircraft industry in relation to that of France and Germany combined. François-Poncet did not disagree. He said that he had taken note of what I had said.

12 JUNE

PARIS

———

STRUGGLE OVER TURF

We lunched yesterday with the de la Haye Jousslins[2] in Normandy in a château that has been in the family for three hundred years. Like the

———

[1] Jean François-Poncet, see footnote for entry 12–13 December 1977. He had succeeded Pierre-Brossolette as Secretary-General to the French Presidency 1976–8.
[2] De la Haye Jousslin, Bertrand and Laure, both of distinguished French families; she is the daughter of Charles de Noailles, a famous gardener.

present owners, it is distinguished and very thin. It is only one room thick, *entre cour et jardin*, as the French call it, with no connecting corridor. Apparently that's how they built and lived in the seventeenth century. Our hostess, the daughter of Charles de Noailles, has a beautiful garden. Odette Pol-Roger, who was also a lunch guest, accompanied us in guessing the names of the shrub roses and in complaining in her leg-pulling way that we only visited grand châteaux in Normandy, never places like her humble little house.

The hostess said that the only trouble with the house was that you could not sit out in front or behind it because of the gravel. I retorted that it was the same at the Embassy in Paris when I arrived. I could understand the need for the gravel courtyard on the Faubourg St Honoré side because of the traffic. I had not seen why it was necessary to have gravel in the courtyard the other side looking on to the garden. I then told her a little of the following rather painful story.

With the help of the Commonwealth War Graves Commission, I decided to remove the gravel and to have turf laid in the garden courtyard of the Embassy. One fine day the Commission people arrived with a truck piled high with turf in swiss rolls. They set to work to remove the gravel, to put down topsoil and then to lay the turf. They had not got very far before I realised what an enormous improvement it made. Alas, also not before I received a telephone call from the Department of the Environment in London. The official the other end of the line said that he had heard that I was in the process of turfing in the garden courtyard. He asked me to stop the work immediately because I had not sought or received permission to carry it out. I said that I would do no such thing. It was not costing HMG one penny. It was greatly improving the look of the place. The official became agitated and insistent. I must stop the turf-laying immediately. I was, he said, changing the character of the property and doing so without authority. I said, 'Sorry, but I wouldn't dream of it.'

Half an hour or so later the head official of the Department of the Environment dealing with government property abroad telephoned me. He made the same appeal that I should abandon the turf-laying until I had put up a case for making the change. I said that I did not see why I had to seek permission. If they wished to do so, they could lift the turf and restore the gravel on my departure. It was all carefully stored at one end of the garden. Meanwhile I could assure him that a grass courtyard was a great improvement on the gravel and would add to the pleasure of the place for official entertaining.

The high official said that eighteenth-century palaces in France were always surrounded by gravel. That was the tradition. I had no right to change, thereby fundamentally altering, the character of the property. I said that surely the garden was a little different from the house which I was most eager to maintain in its traditional splendour unlike some of my predecessors. I asked him whether Lord Gladwyn had obtained permission for the ugly little urn that he had had erected in the garden, a monument which, as if in eternal defiance of the DOE's insistence upon deciding upon everything in the garden themselves, bore an inscription in Latin saying that the garden had been entirely reconstructed by Gladwyn. I said that I would undertake to stop turfing and submit the whole thing to an enquiry if he agreed that the continued presence of Gladwyn's urn in the middle of the main lawn of the garden could also be included in the investigation.

The official repeated his request which had by now become a demand that I should cease the turfing forthwith. I expressed regret that I could not do so. The work was making rapid headway. It would be completed by nightfall. We would have a beautiful grass courtyard resembling an Oxford quad, a fine example of that English grassmanship upon which the French are always congratulating us. The receiver was slammed down the other end and I returned to survey the progress being made in the unfurling of the turf swiss rolls. My pride and pleasure at the rapidly evolving lawn were disturbed by a message reaching me that the Chief Clerk in the Foreign Office wished to speak to me urgently on the phone.

I returned to the office where I was put through to Mr Curtis Keeble. 'It's about your lawn,' he said to me. 'I have just had the head of the Property Services Agency [PSA] on the line. He is in a terrible state.'

I explained what had happened. Curtis was most understanding about it. He even saw the comic side, but he asked me whether I would take account of the overall relations between the Diplomatic Service and the PSA. These could be jeopardised if I persisted in defying them. I said that I really could not accept the fact that I was unable to undertake a little, costless operation in the garden without applying to the Department of the Environment for permission. I added that if an Ambassador did not even have the right or authority to put down a spot of grass there was not much point in having him.

Curtis was extremely sensible about this. I said I was sorry on personal grounds to have to resist him. I said that the problem was getting out of proportion. He should not have to be bothered with it. The others were putting him in an absurd position. He agreed. He was apologetic at having telephoned me. He said, however, that the PSA were in such a state about it. I said that I was sorry for that but it would be equally absurd for me to go back now on what I had decided upon as an improvement to the garden. That was how we left it.

It was not quite how the Department of the Environment left it. They decided to take their revenge by refusing to carry out any work on the house for an indefinite period of time. This meant that for a year or so they refrained from attending to countless tasks that the maintenance of a house like this and of this size and age requires. They have stopped sulking by now and we are back to normal in our relations with the PSA. I suppose that they may have the last word and that the day I leave they will decide to remove the turf and put back the gravel. You can never win against the machine, though you can throw grass in the works from time to time.

The lawn was in fact completed by nightfall on the day in which I had had all those telephone entreaties from London. It was a moonlit night. In the middle of it Mary woke me up to say that she had peeped out of the window and seen hundreds of little gnomes rolling up the turf and carrying it away. I said that they must all be Principals in the PSA.

So far as I know the gravel has never been restored. In retrospect I'm not proud of my role in this story which shows a high-handed contempt for the place of gravel in the surroundings of eighteenth-century palaces.

17 JUNE
PARIS

CHELSEA ON THE SEINE

We decided to repeat last year's exhibition of garden equipment, a sort of Chelsea on the Seine, with the difference that I also invited Hillier[1] to stage a show of shrubs. This he did with great effect. He was the centre of attraction throughout the two days and sold all the shrubs he had brought over.

He and his wife arrived on Monday night and stayed with us until Wednesday when they moved to the Volkonskys – Prince Pierre and his daughter, Isabel. She has found her vocation in life. She passed some time a year or two ago in Winchester with the Hilliers where she did a course in gardening. She hopes to set up business in France as some sort of Hillier's agent. Her presence here was invaluable for the exhibition, as she, with the help of Marcel, my gardener, did all the fetching and carrying. Hillier was a delightful old boy with a profound knowledge of trees and shrubs. Contrary to what I had imagined, he also showed himself to be very business-like.

---

[1] Harold Hillier, horticulturist. President Hillier Nurseries, Winchester, which he joined 1932.

I asked Hillier where, if he had a choice, he would ideally like to make a garden. Would he choose a Mediterranean, rather than a more northern climate? He said that he would choose Winchester. He added that he was responsible for a garden at Ventnor in the Isle of Wight, where he could grow practically everything that grows in the Mediterranean. Mary asked him about olives. He admitted that they would not do there. It is the very occasional hard frost that makes the growing in the UK of certain Mediterranean plants impossible – not the lack of sun or heat.

The big gate of the Embassy garden that gives on to the Avenue Gabriel opened at 8 a.m. on 13 June. Outside was a queue of trucks and vans bearing GB plates, their drivers waiting patiently to unload and set up their stands in the garden. Philip Broad and Peter Gregory-Hood of the Commercial Section of the Embassy had been working for months to prepare for their arrival and for the attendance of over a thousand representatives of the trade and press who were asked by special invitation to come any time on the 14th and 15th. I also gave a reception for about two hundred people on the 14th which included in addition to members of the trade, all the Amateurs de Jardin.[1]

A chart had been produced showing every exhibitor's site; a line of guide-girls in Laura Ashley dresses was trained to check all exhibitors and visitors and to provide name-tags; a bar was set up; a telephone installed; and lunch for all exhibitors, numbering about one hundred and fifty, provided in the dining-room. It took some organisation, not to say diversion of effort from other more humdrum commercial activities. I am sure, however, that our trade will benefit enormously. It did so after last year's exhibition. We are already having a lot of publicity. One of the television channels, FR3, showed it on the screen the first evening. The British press are displaying uncanny interest. The *Financial Times* and *The Times* both have prominent pieces and the BBC interviewed me. Alexandra telephoned afterwards to say that she had been highly embarrassed, particularly by my pseud remark that while others started the day jogging, I did so digging. I suggested that she should make allowances for what Rab used to call the 'impressionist technique' that has to be applied to public affairs.

The Times's report included an interview with Marcel.[2] He spoke proudly of the Embassy garden. According to *The Times*: 'Monsieur Pihée spoke disparagingly of the garden of the President of France in the

---

[1] The Amateurs de Jardin were members of a club who paid regular visits to gardens in France and elsewhere. They did not spurn the interiors of houses and what might be seen – and offered – therein.
[2] Our gardener.

Elysée Palace a few doors along the Faubourg St Honoré. "That," he said, "is not up to much." '

In point of fact I do not believe that Marcel has ever seen the Elysée garden. He has obviously been brainwashed by someone. It occurred to me to wonder whether the French Embassy in London, which no doubt monitors the English press as assiduously as we do the French press, would be sending back this particular tribute.

While the garden was being laid out with mowers, greenhouses, forks, spades, teak furniture, sprayers and even gnomes, I spent a most unhorticultural day. I attended exhibitions of plastics and carpets (most disappointed in our carpet designs and the unimaginative way of displaying them, compared, for instance, with the Finns). I attended a lunch at the Automobile Club, given by the chairman of BP, Sir David Steel. I received a junior British minister from the Department of the Environment, Robert Cryer, to whom I showed the preparations going on in the garden. Finally, I attended a seminar organised by *Les Echos*[1] at which Raymond Barre spoke.

We gave a dinner party for the Hilliers on the eve of the garden exhibition. Other guests:[2] the Douairière Duchesse de Mouchy, the Elie de Rothschilds, Cécile de Rothschild, Philippe Michel Dominik (gardening correspondent of the television channel, Antenne 2), the Volkonskys, the Wyrouboffs, the Sean-Louis de Ganays, Odette Pol-Roger, Roy Hay, Vincent Labouret – apart from people from the Embassy.

At 1 a.m. the following morning I set off for the airport with Philip and Patrick McDermott[3] to meet the Foreign Secretary who was arriving in an RAF aircraft, having attended a banquet at Buckingham Palace given for President Ceauşescu of Romania. He was coming to Paris to attend a working breakfast at the Quai d'Orsay on Namibia and Zaire.

Considering what a day he must have had David Owen was quite debonair on arrival. In the car driving to the Embassy we chatted, mostly about Africa. He was surprised when I said that despite the differences between us on Zaire our relations with France were good. 'That's what

---

[1] A French newspaper specialising in economic matters, later taken over by the Pearson Group.
[2] Many of these names have already had a mention. The Duchesse Douairière de Mouchy was the mother of Sabine Wyrouboff and Philippine de Ganay; she cultivated a beautiful garden near Paris. Elie and Cécile de Rothschild, brother and sister, are also dedicated gardeners. Cécile is also known for her talent for collecting paintings and for her friendship with Greta Garbo. Liliane, Elie's wife, is an Egeria. Philippine and Jean-Louis de Ganay live in the romantic château, Courances, where Field Marshal Montgomery was quartered when Deputy Supreme Commander of NATO forces in the early fifties. He left behind a piano as parting present. Roy Hay, a well-known gardening broadcaster. Vincent Labouret, formerly a member of the French Diplomatic Service, at this time in the oil business.
[3] Philip Nelson, my Private Secretary. Patrick McDermott, a member of the Diplomatic Service who was with us in Bonn and Paris where, in both posts, we benefited from his efficiency; his beautiful wife Christa had been a translator in the Bonn Embassy when I was there.

I like about the French,' he interjected, 'you can have quite a row with them about one thing, but it doesn't really affect other things.' I thought to myself how much this owes at present to the forbearance of Guiringaud and the wise understanding and tolerance of Soutou. Things weren't always so easy and won't necessarily be so again.

We talked about the relevance, or as Owen sees it, the irrelevance, of the East–West issue as regards Africa. Owen said that he thought people exaggerated the extent of Soviet success in Africa. He also said that, thanks to our careful policy over Zaire, we are now the heroes of the Third World. I was impressed by his buoyancy, notwithstanding the battering he now gets in the British press. His capacity to disregard personal criticism, or at any rate, to appear to do so, is a great quality for public life.

The next morning I made sure that the car picked him up at the Avenue Gabriel entrance so that he could see the garden exhibition due to open at 9 a.m. I cannot say that he showed much enthusiasm or interest in it. His mind was on some telegrams about Africa that he was clutching and that had come in during the night. I had more or less the same reaction the following morning when I took Edmund Dell to his car via the garden. He also had arrived in the middle of the previous night, this time after a vote of confidence in the House of Commons. Being Secretary of State for Trade I somehow hoped that he would evince enthusiasm for what we were doing to promote British exports. Never the most communicative of men, he certainly wasn't forthcoming at 9 a.m. in our garden. He merely asked whether all that the Embassy had done had been to provide the ground.

Ted Heath, who came later that morning on his way to a meeting of Insead [European Institute of Business Administration] at Fontainebleau, showed much more interest. He chatted with many of the exhibitors who were evidently delighted to see such a familiar face. 'Where are you from?' was his stock question. They were happy to give him the information. Later in his speech at Fontainebleau he explained that a businessman's activity lies in taking decisions, whereas a politician's lies in talking and getting people to vote for him.

That night we dined with Philippe de Rothschild. Ted loves good food and drink of which there was plenty. Indeed he loves a dinner party and relies on us to take him to one every time he visits Paris, which is frequent. I must say I enjoy doing so. He is one of the political leaders whom I find I wish to please.

The following night we attended a ball given by Jean-Marie de Broglie[1]

---

[1]Princesse Jean-Marie de Broglie, at this time Christie's representative in Paris.

for her son who has just got married. It was held under a marquee in her courtyard in the Avenue Washington. It was described as a ball. But, whether because of the cold or because of the inhibition of French men to make fools of themselves on the dance floor, there was precious little dancing. Mary went home early, as did many others. I stayed on, largely out of curiosity.

18 JUNE
PARIS

THE THREAT TO LIVING STANDARDS

In the past week I have heard speeches by Giscard, Barre and Heath. They have all spoken in remarkably similar terms about the threat to Western European living standards and stability caused by:

a) the breakdown of the world monetary system which was established at Bretton Woods;
b) the failure of existing institutions – UN, World Bank, IMF, etc – to achieve the tasks for which they had been established;
c) the five-fold increase in oil prices since the end of 1963;
d) the emergence of the developing countries – Brazil, Iran, India, Hong Kong, Singapore, Korea – as efficient and cheaper producers of many of our traditional manufactures, e.g. steel, textiles and ships.

22 JUNE
THE AUVERGNE

MONSIEUR FRANÇOIS MICHELIN[1]

I have just been on a visit to the Auvergne, a region of unspoilt country renowned for cheese, extinct volcanoes, dark satanic buildings, the Michelin Tyre Company and a population famous for its craftiness and toughness that has produced many politicians including Laval, Pompidou, Chirac and Giscard.

Briefing me over breakfast, the first morning, the Préfet, a young dynamic Enarque, told me that when I left the Préfecture to walk about

---

[1]François Michelin, a French industrialist. Joint managing director Michelin et Cie since 1966.

the streets of Clermont-Ferrand, I would find myself amidst a stocky people with big square heads and bodies covered with hair. Others have told me, I do not know with how much ethnic precision, that the people of the Auvergne have Mediterranean blood in their veins, many of their ancestors having travelled north in ancient times and then remained in this mountainous region somewhat cut off from the outside world. The Préfet said that it was only now when he had come to live in Clermont-Ferrand that he was able, retrospectively, to understand Pompidou, in whose Cabinet he had worked earlier. They were an amazing people, extremely intelligent, but with no interest in the truth. They did not exactly lie. They were so keen to get the best out of any situation or out of any person that truth became irrelevant. *Rouler*, was the word he kept using to describe their behaviour, which I think can best be translated by manoeuvring. They have only to enter his office and they start trying to *rouler* him. This attitude prevails over any principles they may have, though traditionally the region is a radical one. The Préfet considers Laval to have been a typical Auvergnat. He had always tried to manoeuvre rather than to take sides. I expressed surprise at this. He assured me, however, that Laval had attempted to work with the Gaullists at one time. The Préfet thought that there was much in Giscard's approach to politics, by which I think he meant his belief in trying to work from the centre outwards to manage people rather than confront them, that was typically Auvergnat.

However, it was when we came to talk about Monsieur François Michelin and the tyre company that the Préfet took off. The tyre company dominates the local scene. It employs twenty-five thousand people, or 70 per cent of the labour force and Monsieur Michelin is the master of Michelin. He told me himself later that this is not so and that shares in the company can be bought on the market though they accord no voting rights. He said that he himself did not favour paying his labour force in securities. He takes all the decisions himself, without however being a patrician. He is too authoritarian and austere for that, so the Préfet thought. He starts each day by going to mass at 6 a.m. He watches over the morals of his employees so intensely that if it comes to his ear that anyone has been unfaithful to his wife he is thrown out of the company immediately. Joining Michelin is like joining a religious order, a very strict order but one in which you are well paid. No employee, whatever his status, is allowed to lunch away from the factory. Nor are they permitted to speak about the company. There is a vow of silence as in a Cistercian monastery. François Michelin himself takes the same oath. He never sees the press or makes an announcement – with one exception. He gave an interview to *Paris Match* a few months ago. This was because he had run into labour troubles, practically for the first time. He had tried to introduce twenty-four-hour working in the plant. This had never been done before in Clermont-Ferrand and there was strong objection, even though it meant that there would be more jobs. Indeed this latter point was what made it unpopular with the unions who thereby saw a reduction of the social unrest upon which their hold is based. François Michelin had not reversed his decision but had just not put it into effect because of the persistent opposition. He had been sufficiently shaken to change the habits of a lifetime and to give an interview to a newspaper.

He turned up occasionally at meetings of the Conseil Economique et Sociale de la Région but never spoke, except again on one memorable occasion when he disarmed everyone by saying, 'You see I've got two feet.'

François Michelin rarely buys a new suit. He dresses in overalls. He never buys a new car but drives himself about in an old 2-Chevaux. He does not travel except on work. He avoids going out socially. When the Préfet had invited him to dinner that night to meet me he had not replied for three weeks and had then said that he would come without his wife.

He did all the recruiting himself. The Préfet told how some highly qualified scientist had applied for a post. He had turned up for an interview with Monsieur Michelin as arranged and been installed in some small waiting-room. He waited there a long time before anyone came to see him. Somebody eventually appeared and asked him a lot of questions about his career and qualifications all of which he fully answered. He was then left alone again for a long interval before someone else appeared and put to him more or less the same questions. This was followed by another wait before a third person came to see him with identical questions and he also disappeared. None of the interviewers introduced themselves and the applicant had no idea which of them was Monsieur Michelin. He decided, however, not to enter that particular monastery.

The Préfet said that his relations with Monsieur Michelin were correct but not close. Michelin had never invited him to anything. So far as he knew he had not invited anyone to his house. There was something of a mystery here because he had quite a big house – unlike his car – and no one had any idea what was inside. I asked whether it could turn out that he was another Howard Hughes and be revealed as having great possessions. The Préfet did not know, except that Michelin must indeed be very rich. He added that neither he, nor anyone else, so far as he knew, had been allowed to visit the factory. When de Gaulle had come to Clermont-Ferrand on one occasion he had called on Monsieur Michelin but had not been permitted to penetrate beyond his office.

Despite these eccentricities Monsieur Michelin ran the company extremely efficiently, the Préfet was sure of this. He employed first-class people. He paid well. He delegated extensively to those whom he trusted. The product, judged by the market, was highly successful.

'You could find,' the Préfet concluded, 'that he will talk to you, or he could be silent. But he won't be rude.'

Naturally my curiosity was aroused by this briefing and I was impatient to meet the great man upon whom I was due to call in the afternoon. Accompanied by the Consul General and by Philip Nelson my Private Secretary, I turned up at 3 p.m. at the factory gates. The entrance to this world-renowned enterprise was theatrically unworldly in appearance. No name, no grille, no gate, just a shabby entrance with one or two people walking about. We gave our names to a man behind the guichet and were shown along a grey linoleum-floored corridor to a cell-like room. This was furnished with simple, upright chairs and a table on which lay a trade magazine of the engineering industry dated 1963. A window gave on to the road. There were no pictures and not even a calendar on the walls. So far everything complied with the reputation of asceticism that we had been encouraged to expect.

We were exchanging some not very serious remarks when the door opened and a tall, gangling figure entered. The Consul General had met him before so we were not subjected to the uncertainties that had afflicted the engineering applicant. My first impressions of Monsieur Michelin were of his height, the size of his ears, his bulbous eyes and his new suit. The last was a blow after we had been told that he would be wearing overalls and patched trousers. He apologised immediately for the modesty of the room saying that his office was being redecorated. There was no difficulty about starting up or maintaining the conversation. I began by saying that I lived in London within a few hundred yards of the Michelin building at the top of Sloane Avenue which, I believed, was preserved as a building of outstanding architectural interest. Did it not date from before the First World War? Monsieur François Michelin said that it did. I cannot say that he showed outstanding interest in this artistic heritage, merely expressing regret that there was no room to expand the building because of the neighbouring streets.

Michelin appeared obsessed by the Russians. For example in answer to my question whether he thought that the outlook on the labour front was satisfactory, he replied that it all depended on Brezhnev. He controlled things at Michelin as elsewhere in Western Europe. He was working for the downfall of the West. It was he who had decided that the majority would win the last French elections.

With the Préfet's remarks about Monsieur Michelin's authoritarianism towards his staff in mind I asked him whether he could get rid of people whose political activities inside the firm were disruptive. 'Only if they fall down on the job,' he replied, adding, 'I can't remove them for political reasons or there would be an outcry.' This was a good deal less autocratic than the Préfet had led me to expect.

Michelin did not make much distinction between Communists and socialists, regarding them all as equally bad. Later, when I talked to him just before dinner that night, I was surprised when he said that the trouble with the European Community was that it was turning Europe into a socialist/Communist community. I expressed disagreement with this point of view. Michelin said that he was in favour of fixed and immovable exchange rates. Trade unions, he insisted, were simply a manifestation of bad management. All labour legislation was pointless. Industry would have reformed itself of its own accord and stopped over-long hours and child labour, etc. Later when we were in his car together he said that government expected too much of industry. The latter's job was to provide employment and produce good things at a fair price – nothing else. '*C'est ça le fond du problème*,' he concluded. It was a phrase he was to use frequently during our talks.

I had expected him to launch into a diatribe about Britain's economic decline. On the contrary, he was polite and tolerant. He found the workforce in Scotland perhaps a little better than that at Coventry. Even the latter, however, were, so he put it, '*épatant*'. To Philip Nelson he said after dinner that night that he had been disappointed by one incident at the Coventry plant. A draughtsman had spent his tea-break working on a design. When his mates discovered that he had been working in the tea-break they tore it up.

After he had chatted for some time I thought it better to withdraw rather than outstay the very warm welcome he had given us. I therefore said that I did not wish to detain him any longer. He leant forward and said that he was delighted to receive the 'representative of a country which I respect and like'.

He asked how much time I had available. My heart leapt, thinking that perhaps he was going to show me the Forbidden City. I said that I was not as busy as he was. He wondered whether I would like to see the test-track. I said I would. Anything to give me more time with this remarkable man. So Philip went to telephone the editor of the local paper, *La Montagne*, to say that we would be late. I accompanied Monsieur Michelin to the road.

'I hope you don't mind my little car,' he said, pointing to an old 2-Chevaux across the street. He held the door open for me as I climbed in. There were many passers-by in the street. I supposed they must have recognised the car and its owner, between them obviously the most famous landmarks in Clermont-Ferrand but there was no stopping and staring, perhaps because they are too well known, not to say famous. Monsieur Michelin drove the car himself. I was beside him. The Consul

General and Philip sat behind. He drove quite a long way past a number of his plants. 'That one was bombed during the war,' he said, pointing to a row of chimneys behind one of the many high walls that surround his factories. I asked him about the war. 'Pre-war,' he replied, 'we produced thirty-five thousand tons of tyres annually. Our wartime production was five thousand tons. We only made tyres the Germans didn't want.' He went on to mention various relatives who had been deported and killed. From the way he spoke and from what I knew of his character there seemed little likelihood of his having collaborated – unlike, for instance, the Renault car family.

He chatted away easily, more easily than he drove which was rather like someone in middle age who has suddenly been able to save up enough money to buy a small car and is uncertain of the gears yet eager not to damage them. He said that his percentage of the labour force in the area was much too high. It meant that if there was trouble in Michelin the whole population were affected.

I asked about diversification, saying that Dunlop had branched out into many non-tyre products in accordance with the tendency of much modern industry. Was he thinking of doing the same? His answer was an emphatic, no. He believed that one of the reasons for the success of the Michelin management was that it had concentrated on a specific product with undivided attention. Later he explained that they did not even try to produce aeroplane tyres which were quite different and would create new problems on which the Michelin staff were not experts. I asked him about the inventiveness of his employees. Did he have difficulty in getting brilliant engineers or scientists? 'That is the most difficult problem,' he replied, 'the French are not inventive. Their education does not encourage them to be inventive.' I rejoined that I thought the British were rather inventive even if they had fallen behind in many aspects of industrial production. Monsieur Michelin did not demur.

When at last we reached the gates of the test-track, Michelin carefully produced his pass to the man at the entrance and explained whom we were. We were allowed through. We drove past a number of nondescript sheds and hangars and looked at a test slope equipped with a rough surface (exactly what you would expect in a tyre-testing establishment) before coming back to the entrance gate. Monsieur Michelin then said to the attendant that he wished to drive us round the test-track. He was told that he could not do so in his car but must drive a rather bigger, but no less battered, one, a Fiat into which we then all climbed. I commented that even Monsieur Michelin had to stick to the rules. 'Particularly me,' he replied in somewhat masochistic vein.

We drove round the track on the left-hand side, going anti-clockwise. One or two other cars were doing the same. I asked why we were all driving on the left-hand side. He said that he didn't know, it had always been the rule of the test-track.

I began to wonder why he had driven us all this way to witness a number of oldish cars driving round and round at a not very high speed. Philip suggested later that it may have been to kill time, to kill our time, so that we could not, even if we had wished, have been able to see over the plant before our next engagement. Some weight was given to this interpretation by the way, on our return to the main gates of the factory, Monsieur Michelin said to me that it was a pity we did not have more time, confessing that it was he who had used it up. He did not specify what he would suggest that we did had we more time, and I suspect that this remark, like the visit to the track, was a way of avoiding the charge that he was deliberately refusing to let us see the process of tyre-making. If de Gaulle had been refused I could hardly complain that a visit over the plant had been denied us. It struck me as odd that Monsieur Michelin must regard his process of tyre-making as more susceptible to industrial espionage than did the bosses of other great enterprises their products. The only other plant where I have ever been denied admission was the Pilkington Glass Company in the north Midlands where, shortly before my visit, they had perfected a new float-process of making sheet glass that they thought was susceptible to plagiarism by even an ill-trained eye.

Having completed our uneventful circuit of the track we returned to base and changed cars back to the 2-Chevaux. Monsieur Michelin asked the attendant to convey his apologies to some guard near the track to whom he had omitted to show his pass.

That evening Monsieur Michelin came to dinner with the Préfet whose guests we were. All the local worthies were there including the editor of *La Montagne* who had never been at a party with him before. They stood around chatting before dinner but none seemed to dare to approach the great man. It was the same after dinner. None of the other guests came near him as if they were too much in awe of him. So Philip, the Consul General and I had him more or less to ourselves, except during dinner when I noticed he sat in almost perpetual silence. To say that he had no small talk would not be carrying understatement too far. However, I found that he liked talking about serious subjects.

I asked him if he travelled. He replied, 'As little as possible.' He said he particularly disliked Paris. Sometimes he had to visit his other plants but he left Clermont-Ferrand as rarely as possible. I suggested that this was because he had to control everything himself. He demurred, saying, as he pointed to his eyes and ears, that he didn't control he just watched and listened. I suddenly realised why both features were so pronounced.

In the article in *Paris Match* which I read later Michelin is reported to have said as regards his power: '*Je ne sais pas si j'ai pris le pouvoir à 33 ans. Disons que j'ai pris des responsabilités.*' The *Paris Match* article appears in a number incongruously devoted to Peter Townsend's memoirs relating to his '*romance avec Margaret*'. The article makes a good point about the contrast between the austerity of Monsieur François Michelin and the hedonism of Monsieur Bibendum who advertises Michelin tyres and the *Guide Michelin*.

By the end of the day, after watching him at close quarters and hearing the many things other people said about him, I thought I had acquired some idea of Monsieur François Michelin. Certainly he was an unusual person, but, like so many unusual people, what was odd about him was the way certain very ordinary qualities have become exaggerated within him: his austerity; his simplicity and his one-track mindedness. I was not convinced that they would have been sufficient to create the Michelin empire, but they certainly produced the sense of mission and sacrifice necessary to keep it going, at any rate up until now. It was the aura surrounding him, rather than Michelin himself, that I remember most clearly as the shining light of that Clermont-Ferrand visit.

23 JUNE

PARIS

THE BIRTH OF THE EMS[1]

Roy looked in yesterday afternoon. He had travelled from Brussels to see Giscard and came along the road afterwards, not to tell me all about it, because that would be incorrect, but to give me the general feel. He said that Schmidt and Giscard have worked out a plan for a European Monetary System (EMS) and they were determined to press ahead with it, whatever Britain's reservations. This would be their message at the Community summit in Bremen on 6–7 July. Roy said that he had got the feeling from both the French and the Germans that they were heartily sick of the endless foot-dragging by the British in the Community.

This piece of information was very useful to me. It confirmed my own hunch, and enabled me to send with conviction a pretty scarifying

---

[1]The purpose of the EMS was to create monetary stability by narrowing the range of exchange-rate fluctuations in the currencies of the members of the European Community. It looked at the time to be a highly promising step towards monetary union. Britain did not join the exchange rate mechanism until 1990 and withdrew two years later as the entire mechanism came under severe strain.

telegram. Our leading European partners were fed up with us – with our reluctant Europeanness; and they were determined to go ahead in creating a new monetary system for the Community. We would not be able to divide or break them even should we wish to do so.

30 JUNE
PARIS

THE COMPANY OF HAROLD
MACMILLAN

I have just passed a delightful twenty-four hours with Harold Macmillan.[1] His memory remains formidable despite his eighty-four years. His faculties seem to be intact; and his style is undimmed. True, his sight is not good. He is apt to get launched on some story of a rather lengthy kind about the past. I have subsequently seen Debo Devonshire[2] at the Royal Show. We talked about her uncle, as she refers to him. I expressed enthusiasm over his company. She told me that her children groaned at the way his stories went on. One of them had invented a riddle: 'Why is Uncle Harold like a pig caught in a traffic accident?' Answer: 'Because they are both crashing boars.'

Macmillan remains remarkably alive and interested in all that is going on around him. He appears saddened rather than embittered by many features of modern Britain. In no doubt about our present decline, he nevertheless sees no reason why we should not recover. 'The British have always been lazy people,' he said, 'but there is a lot of good in them.' He gave some account of a group of ladies who were doing good works in his village. He appears worried by his poverty. We talked a lot about taxation and what it had done to the professional classes. As for the great estates they were in dire peril. His spiritual home is a Whig country house of the eighteenth century. 'You can always tell a Whig house, even now – the chequered marble floor, the columns and statues, the library, the pictures picked up for a song on the Continent. And the general atmosphere.' In a theatrical aside he added, 'We can hardly blame those now who have the money and buy from us.' He recounted how Lord Chandos, when he was owner of Stowe, had run into financial difficulties

[1] Harold Macmillan, created Earl of Stockton 1984.
[2] Debo Devonshire, dutiful restorer and efficient manager of the Chatsworth estate, including farm, restaurant and shops, notwithstanding which she has retained all the Mitford beauty and wit.

and had been told that he must make economies. He had a head chef and a special chef for meat. Why must he maintain a patissier as well? some adviser asked him. Protesting, Lord Chandos had wondered what on earth a man could do if he could not even have a biscuit with his glass of port. Macmillan thought that compared with the Whigs the Tories had historically been dull dogs. They had lived in the country and hunted 'and that sort of thing'.

'Poor Andrew,'[1] he went on. 'Every time there is a sale and the price of old masters goes rocketing up he realises that he will have to pay even more in transfer tax.'

We had many long chats, an activity that he enjoys. On the afternoon of his arrival at around 4.30 p.m. we met in the Salon Vert. He took a whisky and soda. Alexander,[2] his grandson, who was accompanying him, never touches alcohol so he had tea. Later, before changing for dinner, we strolled on the lawn. After the dinner party was over and the speech at the Cercle Interallié was delivered we returned to the house and he reminisced for an hour or two. Some members of the Embassy staff who had been at the dinner joined us. They said afterwards how much they had enjoyed hearing him talk privately.

He and I talked again before and after lunch the following day. It was a lunch given him by Ambassador Massigli[3] whom Macmillan looks upon as being somewhat doddery and even old. He is over ninety but clearly Macmillan has strong feelings of affection for him, not least because of his part in the war.

When, the first afternoon, we were walking in the garden he turned to his grandson and said, 'Have you seen that my things are all right upstairs?' Alexander said that he had, upon which Macmillan said, 'Just go up and have a look, would you.' It must have been as apparent to Alexander as it was to me that his grandfather wanted him out of the way for a moment so he took the heavy hint and disappeared. Putting his arm in mine and with his stick in his other hand, Macmillan led me off down the lawn. I wondered what on earth it was that he wanted to divulge confidentially. He explained that he had heard that I was thinking

---

[1] Andrew, 11th Duke of Devonshire, nephew of Harold Macmillan, in whose last government he served as junior minister. Patron of the arts; widely regarded as the noblest living duke.
[2] Alexander, son of Maurice Macmillan, Harold's son and heir. As a journalist he had been a *Daily Telegraph* staff correspondent in Paris.
[3] René Massigli, Commissioner for Foreign Affairs, French Committee of National Liberation 1943–4. Ambassador to London 1944–55. His wife, Odette, was noticeably distinguished, not least in her dress. Indeed her reputation for dress was such that she had made Nancy Mitford feel like 'Cinderella in the Cinders'. In December 1944 Nancy Mitford wrote, 'I am kept awake at night by her clothes', later adding, 'luckily all the other English are in the same boat ... they all look incredibly moth eaten.' *The Letters of Nancy Mitford*, Hodder and Stoughton, 1993.

of writing a book when I retired. He asked me what subjects I was considering. I mentioned one or two things that I had been turning over in my mind. He said that he thought that they would all be interesting. He would like to give the subject further thought. I must realise that such a task would mean a lot of work for me.

I said that his autobiography must have meant a lot of work for him. 'No,' he replied, 'I just had my diary. The main help of that was that it gave authenticity to what I wrote. People could not say that I had made it all up afterwards. I spent ten years on the work, five hours a day, and when Dorothy died it became like a companion to me.' He continued in this vein, seemingly turning ideas over in his mind, speaking very deliberately. I drew his attention to the trees in the garden, one of which he had planted many years before. He was not in the least interested. It struck me that he was not particularly visual, at any rate as far as nature was concerned. Having spoken about the writing of his autobiography he became reflective and seemed to be lost in the question of what book I might best embark upon.

I was touched that he should take the trouble and to be so sympathetic in the way he did so. There was nothing in the least patronising about it. Nor was he doing it as a matter of form or out of politeness. He indicated at one moment that Alan Maclean, who works for the publishers, had spoken about it to him. Of course, although this was not necessarily intended, he does attach importance to courtesy and it was certainly human and considerate to discuss the subject with me in so intense and detailed a way. He told a story to illustrate courtesy. A friend of his had invited him to some small luncheon party where one of the other guests had used rather strong language. 'You can imagine that from my time in the war,' he said, 'it didn't mean much to me, but my friend was upset about it and wrote me a letter afterwards apologising for the bad language. Now that's good manners, isn't it.'

It was a criterion that he used about many people whom we discussed, whether or not they had good manners. De Gaulle, for instance, whom he had obviously found difficult, was described as always having 'very good manners'. He referred to the General's visit to Birch Grove. He had insisted on going there rather than to Chequers, which was not easy because it is quite a small house. The General always had to be accompanied by a supply of blood in case an assassination attempt against him was made. 'There it was at Birch Grove,' he said, 'set up in the middle of the squash court, like a temple of Mithras.'

I noticed Macmillan was careful to avoid criticising people though I was certain that he had his likes and dislikes. There was nothing woolly about him. It was simply that he preferred discussion to criticism. He said nothing whatever about Mrs Thatcher. He was in general very reticent about all active politicians. When Harold Wilson's name was mentioned he said that he was very clever. When Dr Owen was mentioned he referred to the doubt some foreign statesman had expressed whether he was a very good medical doctor.

I was surprised that he was a little critical of the Americans, while explaining carefully that he was half American and therefore not at all anti-them. He was obviously bitter over the US attitude to Suez. He had little sympathy for John Foster Dulles.[1] He considered that FDR had been fundamentally anti-British and had never liked Churchill. I reported a remark that Lord Moyne[2] had once made to me concerning WSC's tolerance in listening to FDR's long stories, which he had done not because they amused him in the least, but because it would incline FDR to be more disposed towards the Allied cause. Macmillan seemed to resent the fact that the UK had been forced to sell all its overseas assets to pay for the war. He thought that this was the decisive cause of our decline. To which I replied that the West Germans had ended the war in physical as well as financial ruin but that had not prevented their recovery. As with the name of some person whom he did not wish to discuss, so with an argument that was either embarrassing to him or uninteresting, he simply changed the subject. The theme of the United States of America in recent times was dropped from our agenda.

During the first afternoon he tried out on me various themes that I discovered later were to appear in his speech to the Misérables.[3] He believed that the Soviet threat was unique in history because it combined military power with ideological appeal. Not realising at the time that this was to be the central theme of his speech for the evening I queried the force of Communism's ideological appeal at the present time. I suggested that it had lost much of its impetus. The young of Western Europe were no longer lured by Marxist-Leninism, as they had been in my youth. Nor were they now in Africa or the Middle East. The love affair between the Jews and Communism had been shattered irremediably. Macmillan listened but said nothing.

His speech to the Misérables made a great impact. There were about eighty of us dining. I invited Simone Veil, and then to match her with another woman, I invited Odette Pol-Roger. Otherwise, it was a mostly male company. René Massigli sat beside me. At ninety-one years of age he is just as agreeable as ever and just as incomprehensible in both French and English.

---

[1] John Foster Dulles, US Secretary of State 1953–9.
[2] Walter Moyne, Deputy Minister of State Cairo 1942–4 where I was his Private Secretary. Assassinated there 1944.
[3] Les Misérables, the Anglo-French dining club.

Macmillan began his speech with a few words in French. He read from a text held close to his eyes. Nobody could hear. I was a little anxious. But then he moved to English. His voice became firmer and he stood increasingly upright. I have seen before this theatrical unfolding of his person from weakness to strength.

This occurred at a dinner in Oxford. At the start of his speech one wondered whether he was going to be able to complete it. As he went on he threw off the feebleness and ended vigorously. At one moment he gave his famous definition of what Oxford does for its pupils. 'It teaches you about quality,' he said. 'It teaches you to identify rot when you see or hear it.' After the speech was over I turned to one of my neighbours at the table who was a contemporary of Macmillan's and asked him what he had thought of the speech. 'A lot of damn rot,' he replied.

Macmillan's speech at this dinner in Paris was a plea for European unity. He ended up declaring that old men had dreams. It was for the young to have vision. Some of the guests were near to tears.

In one of our many long communings together Macmillan talked about domestic UK politics and the outlook for Britain. 'The Conservatives cannot manage it by themselves,' he said. He thought that recovery would require a coalition government. Hence the speech he had made recommending it. The trouble was that he had spoken too early. I reported this afterwards to Roy Jenkins who thought that, on the contrary, Macmillan had spoken too late.

Macmillan told me how he had appointed Ormsby-Gore[1] to Washington. 'You see Kennedy had three lives. There was the social; then the intellectual, and there was politics. David belonged to all three. So when Kennedy asked me if I could send him to Washington I really had no alternative, had I?'

The morning after the speech, Macmillan stayed in bed until about noon. Alexander told me that he was reading *Vanity Fair*. Despite the pull of Thackeray he could not resist coming down for a chat before lunch.

Macmillan and his grandson went off by train to Deauville in the afternoon where they were to spend a week in some hotel by the sea with Alexander's wife and children. I gave them some wine to help keep out the cold. I could not help fearing for them in the appalling weather. When, before leaving, Macmillan was asked to sign our visitor's book, he tripped towards the console table, taking very short steps as is his custom; and he then put his eyes very close to the page to sign. I was sorry to see him go.

---

[1]David Ormsby-Gore succeeded to title as 5th Baron Harlech 1964. British Ambassador to Washington 1961–5.

14 JULY
PARIS

A POT-POURRI

We are blessed with a benign British community in Paris. Fortunately there is no British Embassy church, thanks apparently to Christopher Soames who took advantage of a deadly theological dispute between the high and low Church congregations to decree that in future there would be no Embassy church as such.

One day I visited the SNECMA aero-engine plant outside Paris where the Director-General, Ravaud, showed me round and gave me lunch. Unfortunately I did not emerge with any conviction that co-operation with the French in aircraft production is going to be any easier. They look upon us more as rivals, inclined to work with the Americans, rather than as partners for the future. Even though Concorde was a success as an example of high technological partnership it does not seem to have provided a model for collaboration. All those promising sentiments about Anglo-French industrial co-operation uttered at the beginning of 1976 at the time of Concorde's inaugural flight seem now to sound hollow; and I think the fault lies on both sides. Initially the British were to blame for pulling out of the airbus project – in the late sixties – and more recently for our sour and insular attitude to closer European unity as a whole. For a year or so now I have had the impression that the French want to go ahead on aircraft with the Germans and without us – unless we are prepared to eat our words and grovel for having made our initial mistake in withdrawing from the airbus. The pro-Boeing sentiments of Kenneth Keith and McFadzean (head of British Airways)[1] do not make this likely.

But to return to Ravaud. He is outspoken and self-confident and I could quickly understand the clash of personality that had occurred between him and Kenneth Keith. He said that the difficulty about co-operating industrially with Rolls Royce was that they were too big (Rolls Royce employ about sixty thousand people to SNECMA's twelve thousand). I mentioned this later to François-Poncet with whom I had a tour d'horizon on our relations, including industrial co-operation, and he commented that it was 'absurd'. He said twice, and he is not a man inclined to repeat himself, that the French would welcome us into Airbus

[1] Frank McFadzean, created life peer 1980. Chairman and chief executive British Airways 1976–8. Chairman and chief executive Rolls Royce 1980–3.

Industrie to produce the airbus and the B10 – but it must not be as 'wreckers'. The French, I find, are increasingly suspicious that we only join things in order to undermine them from within. 'If you can't beat them join them' is a favourite British guide to action at the present time and I have heard Callaghan use it with the French. It is hardly more flattering or reassuring as a basis for partnership than another favourite British tenet, 'Divide and rule' which they are apt to pronounce as though it was some spiritual dogma that will give comfort to others. I am sure that our attitude towards Europe since joining the Community in January 1973 is grist to the mill of those in France who see our intentions as being those of wreckers from within – and these fears certainly prevail now over aircraft.

I gave a press conference for British correspondents just before going off on leave. Every one of them senses how un-European our policies and tactics look to our European partners. They are quite bitter about it. One correspondent asked me if any Frenchman had ever asked me what single thing the British government had done to help towards creating the unity of Europe as required by the Treaty of Rome. I tried to make a joke of it by saying that I was on good terms with the French. Although I sympathised with the sentiments that had prompted this and several other hostile questions, I said that I thought one had to keep a sense of proportion in Paris. The French might give the impression nowadays that they were the good boys of Europe. It must not be forgotten that they had pursued an empty-chair policy in the sixties before we were members, nor should one think that in all capitals of the Community the French were regarded as the saints and we the sinners in the Community. I suggested that the French attitude on wine and Mediterranean products must be kept in mind when censuring the British over fish.

I discussed with the British correspondents the Bremen meeting and the Franco-German plan for a new European monetary system where again we give the impression of foot-dragging. My own feeling is that when, before Bremen, Schmidt and Giscard came forward with their plan which we did not like we should have put forward an alternative. Instead of this we disassociated ourselves from the idea.

I am glad to say that Roy Jenkins is getting some of the credit for the new scheme. He certainly took a very forward line last autumn on the need for a leap towards economic and monetary union. His initiative was dismissed at the time by all the experts at home as impracticable and premature. He is now getting a favourable press, even if, as I suspect, British ministers resent him all the more for it.

We attended a large dinner at the Federal German Embassy in honour of the Mayor of Berlin who has come to Paris for an exhibition on

Paris/Berlin in the twenties. I sat between the Duchesse de La Roche-foucauld[1] who likes being invited to Embassies, and a former Private Secretary of de Gaulle's who had been with him right at the end of his career. He said that de Gaulle became self-conscious about his age and the decline in his powers. He was particularly afraid that intellectually he might be slipping. In consequence he learned even more things than usual by heart, partly to prove to himself that he could do this and partly to ensure precision in what he said.

On the morning of 14 July I attended the défilé – the 14 July parade which is part military display and part popular fête. The day begins with soldiers marching down the Champs Elysées and ends with the Parisians dancing en masse in the streets. We left Paris before the dancing began. I was struck at the morning parade by the turnout and discipline of the troops as they marched past President Giscard, thinking to myself to what extent they exemplified modern France, its seriousness and sense of public duty, just as their forebears in the 1940s, who had appeared dispirited, had represented the France before the fall.

9 SEPTEMBER

PARIS

———

THE AIRCRAFT CRUNCH

At Farnborough I had a meeting with Allen Greenwood and Peter Fletcher of British Aerospace about the problem of British re-entry to Airbus Industrie (AI) and then attended an official lunch.

On returning to Paris I sent off three telegrams analysing the French, FRG and UK views on the aircraft problem and suggesting what might be done to break the log-jam.

I have heard subsequently that after much inter-departmental wrangling the Cabinet have agreed to provide the financial backing for British Aerospace to join AI. The Treasury and Department of Trade were against, the Department of Industry and the FCO in favour. I was told that nearly all the talking and certainly the loudest was against. The PM listened quietly and then summed up by saying; 'Well, it seems to me that the consensus is in favour of joining AI so we will go in.' Callaghan is continuing to show excellent qualities as PM.

The Cabinet, however, said that the decision was taken on the assump-

---

[1] La Duchesse de la Rochefoucauld, a literary hostess, who much enjoyed social life.

tion that no pressure would be exerted on British Airways (BA) to buy an AI plane. BA have become fanatical adherents of Boeings and are also threatening to make a political fuss – which could be awkward for the Labour Party before an election – if forced to buy a plane they do not want. They have been supported – or more true to say, cajoled – by Rolls-Royce.

The French are furious over BA's decision to go for Boeings. They say that it precludes British Aerospace participation in AI.

The French Minister of Transport, Le Theule, went to London last week for a talk with Varley which I attended. He was very tough. The French press are being critical, saying that the British are trying to have their cake and eat it and to face both ways. Varley was equally adamant that HMG could not force BA to buy the European aircraft against their will.

A message has now gone from the PM to Giscard. I am not certain that the latter really wants us to join AI so I don't expect a quick and easy outcome. I have heard indirectly that Giscard was furious with the message – with the way it referred to BA's purchases of the Boeings at the same time as the offer to join AI. HMG believes that it has a useful bit of leverage in the fact that British Aerospace are the only European airframe manufacturers who can make the wing. If, therefore, we are not in the project and the others have to make the wings themselves this will hold up production and mean that AI loses important markets to Boeing. My fear is that AI might turn to the Americans to make the wing or hire British technicians to engage on the project. It would be another Suez-type miscalculation on our part.

There has been another problem in Anglo-French relations arising over the proposed purchase by Peugeot-Citroën of Chrysler's overseas interests, particularly their extremely unprofitable UK operation. Goodness knows we ought to be thankful to anyone who is prepared to take over plants like Linwood where productivity is exceptionally low and the labour force extremely difficult. They can be seen nightly on TV insisting on their right to strike about anything at any time, but also on the absolute obligation that will fall to Peugeot-Citröen to maintain the workforce intact. Needless to say HMG's bargaining position for trying to get an employment commitment from the French is weak. Chrysler do not want to let their other operations be taken over without the inclusion of the UK plants because otherwise they will be left with heavy financial commitments, such as severance pay, in the UK. So we have the Chrysler management on our side.

If it all goes through it will be fascinating to see whether the French can make the British car industry work better than the British themselves or than the Americans have been able to do.

10 SEPTEMBER
PARIS

SUNDAY IN PARIS

Listening to the BBC World Service this Sunday morning, which remains a wonderfully balanced source despite persistent inaudibility, I could not help saying to myself that there seemed to be even more violence and turmoil than usual: Rhodesia; Iran; Beirut; and Nicaragua (not a continent without some serious disorder); time-bombs in Israel if the current Camp David talks between Begin and Sadat fail; continuing horrors in Cambodia; and the threat of terrorism hanging over all of us. How right Hobbes was about the life of man being 'nasty, brutish and short'.

Writing this journal causes me to step back a little from the immediate scene, or rather to see it in some sort of perspective. It means that things don't fly past my life without a second look. I am not one of those who can think or even imagine without a pen in the hand, so I find that the requirement to write regularly encourages reflection about people and ideas, more than I would otherwise do. It enables me to collect myself. It gives me ideas and it even squeezes out of me an occasional phrase. I like to think that it loosens up my otherwise somewhat official prose style. I felt much happier yesterday, when, having written nothing much for some time, I was able to devote time to the journal. It would be going too far to say that I think that it has produced anything creative but at least there has been some sense of fulfilment. Events have greater significance for me when I have written about them, which reminds me of a remark Isaiah Berlin[1] made about Frederick Hoyer Millar[2] when they were both serving in the British Embassy in Washington during the Second World War. Frederick was Head of Chancery at the time and therefore was much involved in reporting to London on many aspects of US-UK wartime relations. Isaiah said that Frederick conceived of the war solely in terms of the telegrams he drafted and despatched.

One of the pleasures of staying in Paris for weekends, rather than racketing around, is that it gives me time to think back and write down

---

[1] Isaiah Berlin, President British Academy 1974–8. President Wolfson College 1966–75. Fellow All Souls College Oxon. Philosopher and historian of ideas. The most renowned Oxford figure since Benjamin Jowett and rivalled only by Maurice Bowra as the university's greatest wit in living memory.

[2] Frederick Hoyer Millar, Member Diplomatic Service. Washington Embassy 1939–44; Minister there 1948–50. Ambassador to Germany 1955–7. Permanent Under-Secretary of State 1957–61.

what remains after going through the sieve that only time and reflection can provide.

Marcel is a wonderful gardener. He is industrious and ingenious. He appears to take pride in making our garden look better than the Elysée garden which is not a reflection on his patriotism but simply the fruit of his personal loyalty and addiction to his '*boulot*' – a favourite word of his for work. I have difficulty only in his attitude to cutting the lawn. He is quite at home seated on the large mowing machine but seems to fear that too frequent cutting will do the grass harm. I try to persuade him that the more he cuts the denser it will become. It is not laziness on his part. I have never seen a readier worker. Naturally, he likes me to know of his labour. '*Il n'y a plus de chômage ici,*' is his favourite phrase at the moment as he tries to bring order into the beds after the neglect of the four-week holiday. No sooner do I sympathise with him over all the *boulot* involved than he dismisses it by saying that it is his duty.

17 SEPTEMBER

PARIS

GISCARD AND SCHMIDT IN CAHOOTS

I have had a very agreeable lunch with Soutou at the Travellers. He confirmed something of which I was convinced already, that Giscard and Schmidt would persist in creating a new monetary system in Europe, however much officials and bankers told them that it would not work and whatever the doubts of the British. Giscard and Schmidt see the EMS, not simply as a means of helping intra-Community trades, but as the only way of making progress towards European unity. They also think that with the EMS Europe can create a stable monetary system that will serve as a reserve currency for world trade.

My own feeling is that not only has Giscard written us off as a partner who can contribute to the creation of Europe, but that he does not mind this. He is by nature inclined to view us more as a rival than a partner; and I suspect that he thinks that the smaller part Britain has the better, e.g. in aircraft production, motor cars, not to mention intra-Community collaboration in the politico-economic sphere. The less London's role the greater the scope for Paris.

I am sure Callaghan does not want to be left out in the cold, hence his support for participation in the airbus and hence also, I believe, the likelihood that he will ultimately join the EMS, though of course he will throw away any political advantage he might gain on the Continent if, as seems likely, he gives the impression of half-heartedness.

I OCTOBER
PARIS

___

CLOSE FRENCH–GERMAN COLLABORATION
ON EMS; MORE AIRBUS TROUBLE

The appalling impasse we have reached over British entry to Airbus Industrie could have been averted, I think, if the PM and Giscard had been on easy telephoning terms, such as those that run between Schmidt and Giscard. I don't think that it is mainly a language problem though it may be that Giscard feels in a slightly inferior position speaking English to someone who is English. The main handicap is the lack of confidence and sympathy. With Schmidt, Giscard feels that he is dealing with someone who does not have a large anti-European extremist wing of his political party always tugging at him. They obviously get along very well and have complete trust in each other. Callaghan can inspire trust more than did Wilson but he always displays an unequivocally non-Continental attitude. He is too English, too involved with his own domestic affairs and too uninterested in unanchored political speculation, particularly about the future of Europe, to make much personal appeal to Giscard.

Partly as a result of this, but more because of our persistent economic weakness and refusal to have a coherent European policy or show any warm-heartedness towards Europe, Schmidt and Giscard are increasingly establishing a bilateral lead; and because of these same factors the other Community countries which at one time looked to London to play a useful role in standing up to French nationalism and in serving as a counterweight to possible German assertiveness, no longer have much faith in us. Europe is going ahead without us. Giscard and Schmidt, for instance, are pressing on with the creation of a European Monetary System. Following the Copenhagen meeting in the spring when Schmidt rallied to the idea which was one that Giscard had been favouring for a long time, a tripartite group of experts that included the British was set up to work out details. We more or less pulled out of this before the next European Council meeting because Callaghan had doubts. He had been encouraged by the scepticism expressed by officials and bankers regarding the feasibility of the scheme so long as there continued to be such discrepancy in the economic performances of the different countries. I have consistently told London that Giscard (and Schmidt) regarded the EMS primarily in political terms and that they would stick to it whatever the doubts and fears of the experts. Politicians in London and the Treasury have not wanted to hear this.

Then, as regards the airbus, the French are saying, with some reason, that we must either buy some aircraft from the consortium which would be an earnest of our interest in the project and indicate that in future we would not be tempted to favour an American producer under pressure from Rolls Royce at the expense of the development of Airbus Industrie, or we must forsake our right to thwart the future development of the programme, e.g. by giving up a veto. Giscard himself is insisting on this. He is indignant at what he regards as Callaghan's 'bizarre' attitude on the subject by which he means his authorisation to BA to buy Boeings, saying that he cannot make them buy what they do not want, and then applying for British Aerospace to get into Airbus Industrie.

I had a session yesterday with François-Poncet which left me in no doubt about the strength of Giscard's feelings on the subject. It is indicative that Schmidt has left it to the French entirely to play the hand over the airbus entry negotiation. They are fed up, and say so frankly, with trying to pull our chestnuts out of the fire. They will accept whatever the French require. So much for our special relationship with Bonn.

During the long airbus week, Varley was here for a meeting with Le Theule (his opposite number on this subject). He continues to strike me as an agreeable, honest, unforceful man. The meeting was running late on Wednesday evening and Le Theule asked whether we could continue the following morning, adding that the difficulty was that he had to be at the Council of Ministers at 9.30 a.m. I immediately intervened, inviting him to breakfast with his delegation. I added that we were practically next door to the Elysée so that he would waste no time in travel. Le Theule's eyes lit up at the prospect of an English breakfast. He accepted with alacrity, as did his staff.

By the time we got back to the house the chef had left for the evening. I arranged for Christoph[1] to drive out to his house in the country to ask him to be in by 7.30 a.m. the next morning and to prepare a large breakfast for fifteen people by 8.30 a.m. Meanwhile Mary and I went to work on Giovanni, the Italian head butler, to get him to prepare the table for breakfast in the gallery. He is not sound on breakfast, thinking

---

[1] Christoph Houngbedji, Mary's chauffeur, born in Dahomey, now Benin, he was the best of drivers; always courteous, he did his best to stop her overspending at the flower market.

it enough to place a cup in the middle of a plate then serve coffee with a piece of dry bread. However, by next morning everything was in order: the large hotplate was groaning with scrambled eggs, bacon, tomato and fried bread; and the table was well supplied with toast, brioches and marmalade. Le Theule was delighted with the spread. He said he would have to exercise restraint and not eat all he was offered or he would fall asleep in the Council of Ministers.

We made excellent progress with our discussions over breakfast. Indeed we reached agreement on practically everything. It was only later that Giscard put a spanner in the works by saying that he could not accept the agreement. He insisted that either BA must buy some of the Airbus Industrie aircraft, or the powers of British Aerospace in the consortium, and in particular their veto right, must be diminished. I was disappointed by this setback when we seemed so near to agreement. Later I had a wrangle with François-Poncet about it but doubt whether it did much good. One result of my talk with him was that it enabled me to telegraph to London a detailed analysis of Giscard's attitude.

Unfortunately, as if in accordance with Newton's law, this move by Giscard has produced an equal and opposite reaction on the British side. A good deal of ill-will is developing on both sides. Alas, relations at the highest level are not such as to assuage this; on the contrary. I happened to see Giscard today at the Grand Palais for an opening of an exhibition of paintings by the Le Nain brothers. The Queen has lent some pictures which was why I was in the select band invited to accompany the President on the tour of the exhibition. He nodded graciously when informed that such and such a picture had been lent by Her Majesty. I was thinking of aeroplanes when one of Giscard's aides spoke to me to say that he dealt with culture in the Elysée and with aircraft. He had heard that the PM's adviser was arriving for a meeting (I presumed that this was K. Berrill). He said that he hoped we could reach agreement soon. I said that I did too but that it was not going to be easy. In fact the difficulty is now British suspicion that Giscard is trying to alter everything.

I was intrigued by the way at one moment Giscard beckoned to his guide to say that he would like a reproduction of one of the pictures. It struck me as monarchical until, upon reflection, I realised that Louis XIV would have insisted on taking possession of the picture itself, not of a mere reproduction. The paraphernalia and guards of honour for Giscard's arrival were certainly regal. The gallery was closed until he had completed his viewing, even though many people, invited to the opening, had to queue up outside. Louis XIV could not have done better than that. Everyone stood in awe and in full respect for *la fonction du Président*. I am continually astonished by the deference shown to him,

totally unlike the attitude, possessive but fraternal, of the Americans
towards their President. At Truman's Inauguration Ball in Washington
nearly thirty years ago I had watched the way the American public,
admitted to the party in thousands, thought that they had a right to
touch him and treat him as one of them. Giscard sets himself on a
pedestal distant from the people who are encouraged to see in him the
embodiment of everything that is grand and traditional in France. The
US President is one of the people; Giscard not at all. He is clearly above
them, conscious that they want to look up to him rather than to feel him
to be on their level.

We dined at Lipp's on Sunday with Françoise Giroud and Alex Grall.
She said that her only doubt was about how the trouble would come
about: that there would be a social outbreak soon in France she was in
no doubt. I said that my impression of France at the moment was that
of a country extremely rich economically and no less extremely stable
politically. She acknowledged that it was a very rich country.

3 OCTOBER

PARIS

THE ROTHSCHILDS

A party last night chez Cécile de Rothschild. Ostensibly for Alan Pryce-
Jones[1] it was in fact an excuse to entertain all the members of the family.
The evening gave me a chance to say to Cécile that there was no need
for me to study Victor Rothschild's complicated chart of the family when
you could see them all here in person.

I chatted with Liliane de Rothschild whose conversation is as bright
as her eyes. She is amusing about Les Amateurs de Jardins and their
secrecy each year about where they are going for their annual outing.
None of us can understand whom the security precautions are directed
against. Lilian says there are three great mysteries in France: the identity
of the Man in the Iron Mask, the fate of Louis XVII and the next
destination of Les Amateurs de Jardins.

---

[1] Alan Pryce-Jones, editor of the *Times Literary Supplement* 1948–59; Trustee National Portrait
    Gallery 1950–61; director The Old Vic Trust 1950–61; member Council of Royal College
    of Music 1956–61; book critic *NY Herald-Tribune* 1963–7. A man of exceptional
    versatility.

5 OCTOBER
PARIS

———

WHITEHALL'S ATTITUDE TO EMS

In London for a meeting of Permanent Under-Secretaries in Whitehall to consider the pros and cons of British entry to the European Monetary System.

Douglas Wass made a long but clear analysis. He did not deal with the political side; on the economic he said that there should be no danger in the short term; the longer term would be more difficult. On the whole, in his view, the economic arguments should not be decisive. Kenneth Berrill intervened in much the same sense, adding that if we were to remain in the Economic Community the political arguments must be strong in favour of joining the EMS. This was the general view of the meeting. Nobody had many illusions about the readiness of the other eight members to make many concessions to us to persuade us to join. Michael Palliser referred to the growing tendency of Britain to find itself in a position of one against eight in the Community.

15 OCTOBER
PARIS

———

ESTABLISHMENT CONTACTS

One evening this week Chaban-Delmas[1] gave an enormous reception at the National Assembly in honour of President Giscard d'Estaing. The ambition of everyone present was to be seen by the monarch, and if possible to shake him by the hand. His monarchical demeanour becomes more marked, but he carries it well, moving about greeting people graciously and not patronisingly, nor heartily. He is ready with a remark and remembers faces as effectively as he does figures. His stamina strikes me as inexhaustible, a quality I have never heard commented upon, though nobody repeats the absurdly inappropriate epithet 'fragile' that was used about him frequently until his success in this year's elections.

———

[1] Jacques Chaban-Delmas, Mayor of Bordeaux since 1947; leader of Gaullists in National Assembly 1953–6; Minister National Defence 1957–8; Prime Minister 1969–72; president of Regional Council, Aquitaine 1974–9. A very fit, elegant and likeable politician.

I had an interesting lunch on Friday with Madame Beytout,[1] the owner of *Les Echos*. She had her young editor with her, otherwise no one else. She began by saying that she had just been to the USA for a fortnight. This had confirmed all her suspicions about the growing lack of interest in the USA concerning the outside world. 'And,' she said almost provocatively as she poured me out a glass of port, a pre-lunch apéritif that continues to strike me as odd although it is quite frequent in France, 'you are responsible for their lack of interest in Europe.'

She explained that whenever she had talked about Europe and the need for progress to be made towards unity the Americans had said that the British were against it so they supposed that nothing could be done.

Madame Beytout lamented Britain's decline. She said that we were like a sleeping cat, though goodness knows when we were going to wake up. It was essential that we should do so before Germany became too powerful.

I started today attending a conference of the International League for Animal Rights held under UNESCO auspices. Some Moslem religious leader was on the platform, his head covered in white linen. I suggested to François Valéry[2] who was beside me that it was Brigitte Bardot in disguise. I find it strange that no one had taken their dog along with them to the meeting. Then we drove to Epernay for lunch with Odette followed by a visit to the *vendange*. Highly agreeable. She showed me correspondence from Churchill, mainly about his horse which he had named Pol Roger after her and which, judged by the messages, did not appear to have been very successful.

We heard a rumour this week that Alexandra is engaged. Her friend is coming here with her next weekend and we are told that they are going to divulge it to us then. They have been practising with much laughter and imitations how they are going to break the news. Mary and I have also been rehearsing our responses. So it should be a gloriously spontaneous occasion.

---

[1] Jacqueline Beytout, president and chief executive of the daily paper *Les Echos*; always stimulating company.
[2] François Valéry, son of the poet, Paul Valéry, member of the French Diplomatic Service; at this time Ambassador to UNESCO. Prominent in the social and literary world.

22 OCTOBER
PARIS

___

A MIXTURE OF OFFICIAL AND SOCIAL ACTIVITIES

At a tête-à-tête lunch with François-Poncet on Monday I said that I was unhappy about Anglo-French relations. The spirit of Chequers where Giscard had met Callaghan last December had not been maintained. In contrast, Franco-German relations had been getting markedly closer. François-Poncet spoke of HMG's half-hearted commitment to Europe in general and its evident doubts about EMS in particular. Our attitude towards Europe did not help with either bilateral or Community problems. I told him that we wanted to be in an EMS provided it could last and be effective; but we did not want just to join the old snake; nor indeed had this been the French aim when discussion about the new system had first arisen.

I also spoke about the airbus and the need to surmount the present unreal difficulties. François-Poncet, who appeared to listen attentively, said he would inform the President of our conversation.

Before we parted François-Poncet repeated his previous warning to me against relying on opinion picked up in Paris as being a trustworthy source for what France stood for. *La vraie France* was to be found in the provinces and nobody ought to pay any heed to the tittle-tattle talked by journalists and *le beau monde* in the capital.

I think François-Poncet would have been a little shocked had he known about the way we were to spend that evening. We attended a gala at the Théâtre des Champs Elysées organised by Valentino to launch a new perfume named after him. It was an extravagant occasion. Le tout Paris was there: ministers, diplomats, *le gratin* – all dressed in black ties and highly sophisticated evening costume. I spotted Curt Jürgens with some tall young girl. His presence, more than that of anyone else, gave a jet-set, glitzy-magazine aura to the evening. I was seated next to Madame Deferre.[1] Niarchos was a few places along, an Italian Princess beside him. George Weidenfeld[2] was also in the official loge. He had come from London especially and stayed the night with us. For the gala he was the guest of Ira Fürstenberg who seemed to have some particularly

___

[1] Madame Gaston Deferre, writer; member of the renowned diplomatic family, Charles-Roux; wife of the socialist politician who held ministerial posts and became Mayor of Marseilles.
[2] George Weidenfeld, chairman of Weidenfeld and Nicolson since 1948. He has remained my friend and publisher through fifty years and five books. His flair as a publisher does not lie in reading manuscripts but in spotting potential authors and then giving them encouragement and finding worldwide outlets.

extravagant role in helping to launch the perfume. She, I suppose, almost vies with Jürgens in the ability to invest any event with the atmosphere of high and fast living. The Fürstenberg party went on afterwards to dine at Maxim's.

Last week the house was turned over to an exhibition of British carpets. At 8 a.m. on Monday morning the gates at the end of the garden on Avenue Gabriel were thrown open and a party of carpet sellers started humping their wares up the lawn to install them in the ballroom. They took a lot of trouble. The resultant display was varied and excellent. There seems to be a law according to which carpets with the most garish colours and loudest designs sell best. I liked David Hicks's[1] products but they cost thirty pounds per yard.

Harold Caccia[2] has been here to speak at the annual Oxford dinner. He described how he had been a member of the Oxford rugby football XV that had played three matches in France in the twenties. The teams had made a rough crowd in the evening and were liable to be rowdy and destructive. However the manager of the XV had anticipated any difficulty by equipping each of the players with a piece of paper that they were to brandish if they ever got into trouble. This contained the phrase: *N'ayez pas peur, Monsieur Thomas Cook vous payera.'*

I said a few words to thank Harold, whose character I described as a living translation of the French word *'débrouillard'*. Referring to his early posting to Peking I recounted his valiant efforts to learn Chinese. The time had come for him to take the exam. 'Tell me,' the mandarin had asked him, 'how do you say in Chinese, "Come here, boy"?' Harold thought for a minute and then said a few words of Chinese which the examiner said were correct. 'Now,' the examiner asked, 'tell me how you say; "Go there, boy".' Harold did not have the foggiest idea how to say it so he got up from his seat, went to the other end of the room and gave once again his Chinese rendering of 'Come here, boy,' beckoning suitably with his finger. Apparently this succeeded in impressing the mandarin.

The Oxford dinner was not the end of our evening. From there we went on to a supper party given by Guy and Marie-Hélène de Rothschild[3] following the first night of a Françoise Sagan play. I have always wanted

---

[1] David Hicks, interior and garden designer of exceptional originality. He was to redecorate the library in the Washington Embassy in our time there.
[2] Harold Caccia, member of the Diplomatic Service. Ambassador to Washington 1956–61. Permanent Under-Secretary FO 1962–5. Provost Eton 1965–77. A colleague and close friend since we first served under him in Vienna in 1953. His skill in clarifying issues for ministers is decribed in my book, *The Private Office*.
[3] Guy and Marie-Hélène de Rothschild. He was president Compagnie du Chemin de Fer du Nord 1949–68; of Banque Rothschild 1968–78. A highly respected gentleman of the Turf. Marie-Hélène, his second wife, is distinguished for her stylish dress and grand parties.

to meet Françoise Sagan and was disappointed that the Oxford dinner prevented me going to the play and meeting her afterwards. However Marie-Hélène said that we must come to the supper in any case. So we went at 11.30 p.m. The narrow street of the Ile St Louis where the Palais Lambert is situated was already blocked with Rolls-Royces dropping guests who were dripping with diamonds. They had come on from the theatre. It proved to be an enormous party of over a hundred. Everyone was seated. The Palais Lambert exudes both luxury and exquisite taste. The table plan, a drawing on which each name was inscribed in beautiful calligraphy, is a work of art of unabashed *mondanité*. We had been to their house-warming there in the summer of 1977 when there had in fact been two parties as they could not fit everyone in on one night. This had led to feverish anxiety amongst many of the *beau monde* of Paris in case they had been invited to the less chic evening.

As we mingled with the guests it became apparent that the Sagan play had been a disaster. 'You didn't miss a fing,' Hélène David-Weill said to me with her particular pronunciation of 'th'. Elie Rothschild was sure that even the Oxford dinner must have been preferable. There seemed to be no sign of Françoise Sagan herself at the party.

I was seated at the supper on Marie-Hélène's right; on her left was Baryshnikov, the Russian ballet dancer. The others at the table were Madame Deniau[1] next to Chirac and Mrs Peter Townsend[2] who was on my right. I did not think that Chirac was quite *dans son assiette* in that *galère*. He made a valiant effort, leaning over Madame Deniau and saying to Baryshnikov; 'I like your dancing very much. In fact I think you are a better dancer than Nureyev.'

To which Baryshnikov replied, 'Thank you very much but you know it's not the Olympic Games.' He went on to explain to Chirac that he danced quite differently from Rudi. It was not possible to compare their two styles or say that one was better than the other. I must say that Chirac took this rebuff very well.

Halfway through supper Marie-Hélène disappeared, saying that she was going to bring Françoise Sagan to our table. She came back with a shy, unpretentious person with tow-coloured hair that she kept sweeping back from her eyes. She sat in Marie-Hélène's place, saying that she had been seated previously next to Philippe Tesson[3] of the *Quotidien* so

---

[1] Madame Deniau, wife of Jean-François Deniau, economist and diplomat. Ambassador to Spain 1976–7, Secretary of State for Foreign Affairs 1977–8; Minister of Foreign Trade 1978–80.

[2] Mrs Peter Townsend, wife of Group Captain Peter Townsend, Equerry King George VI 1944–52; Deputy Master of HM Household 1950; Equerry to the Queen 1952–3; Air Attaché, Brussels 1953–6.

[3] Philippe Tesson, journalist, diarist and drama critic, *Canard Enchaîné* 1970–83. Director and editor-in-chief, *Quotidien de Paris* from 1974.

she knew all about me. Baryshnikov, she and I then had a triangular
conversation. To begin with, it was about nothing in particular. We were
all three finding our bearings. We spoke of Leningrad and the amount
of ballet to be seen in New York. We did not speak of the play. Baryshnikov had not seen it either. He then said that he wanted to know
whether French wives slept in the same beds as their husbands. This was
obviously a fertile field. I managed to get in a remark about the odd idea
Françoise had of Englishmen, judged by her stories. She said that fiction
was different from reality.

We were getting on very well, the three of us, when I felt a nudge in
the ribs. It was Marie-Hélène who had inserted a chair the other side of
me. She said she had had enough of my back. Françoise Sagan said that
she supposed she must be going back to her proper place. I must say I
felt rather proud of my charge as I escorted her to her table but I noticed
that no one else in the large crowded rooms through which we walked
seemed particularly interested in her. It had not been her evening, though
I must say it had been mine, having been given the chance to meet her
on such a splendid stage.

What struck me most about her in our few minutes of conversation
was her defencelessness and her lack of pretention. There was nothing
remotely grand about her. She was not the great writer stooping to her
public. She was more like a gamine who had somehow found herself and
was bordering on happiness. She told me that she had given up drink
three years ago but that many of her friends had not. I did not tell her,
but I will if I see her again, about the effect that one of her books had
had on me. We had been in Paris a few months, participating in the
inevitable round of official functions and involved in that sort of thing
so intensely that I began to wonder whether Paris was any different from
any other city and whether I would ever be able to feel that I was leading
a Parisian life. I decided one day to lunch by myself at Lipp, to buy the
latest Sagan novel beforehand and to read it as I lunched. The effect on
me was considerable. Monsieur Roger Cazes[1] had obliged as usual by
providing me with an excellent table. The waiters were attentive without
being insistent; the ladies at the *caisse* looked down authoritatively.
There was the usual slight pressure at the entrance where Monsieur
Cazes stood, pad in hand, ticking off the names of those who had
booked, a privilege more difficult to come by than membership of the
Jockey Club, so much so that I do not admit to anyone that I have been
granted it. Monsieur Cazes is not a man to trifled with. I recall the time
when someone dining there referred to him as Monsieur Roger which

[1]Roger Cazes, see reference to him on entry for 13 March 1976.

produced the rebuke: '*Roger ou Monsieur Cazes, mais jamais Monsieur Roger.*' Françoise Giroud, who was seated beside me, said that Monsieur Cazes did not like being treated like a *coiffeur*.

Seated there at Lipp eating the Alsacien speciality and reading Sagan I suddenly felt myself a person as distinct from a functionary. Her book and the atmosphere of Lipp had combined to lift me into another world and I felt that I belonged to Paris.

28 OCTOBER
PARIS

DIARY JOTTINGS;
AIRBUS SETTLED

After supper on Sunday evening we did a little tour of Paris by night before going to the Deux Magots for a drink. It was a balmy evening and we sat outside watching the pavement performers. A fair young girl started to play the guitar and sing. 'You can never mistake those American features,' James Fox[1] said to me, 'that protuberant chin and those glistening teeth.' Later when the girl came round with the hat James asked her where she was from. He assumed a slight American accent in putting the question. 'I'm from southern England,' she replied.

A grand dinner chez Goulandris[2] for Karamanlis[3] on the 23rd. I had an interesting conversation with Raymond Aron about the importance of the Sino-Japanese Treaty, very much his sort of subject. I sat between Madame d'Ornano[4] and Madame François-Poncet. The former bubbles over, the latter would like to do so, I think, but is under Elyséen restraint. Karamanlis said that he was going on to Dublin. There was no need to stop off in London. He had no problems there. His relations with Jim Callaghan were excellent.

Lunch the next day with Kenneth James, Geoffroy de Courcel and Daudy[5]

---

[1] James Fox, writer, son of a great friend, Dinah Bridge. The author of *White Mischief*, Jonathan Cape, 1982.
[2] Basil Goulandris, shipowner and art collector.
[3] Konstantinos Karamanlis, Prime Minister of Greece almost continuously 1955–63. Then lived abroad. Returned to become PM 1974, restoring civilian rule after the collapse of the 'Colonels'. Became President 1980. The most widely respected Greek politician since the Second World War.
[4] Madame Hubert d'Ornano. See description in diary entry for 17 November 1978.
[5] Philippe Daudy, essayist, novelist and journalist. Agence France-Press 1946–61. A founder of the Franco-British Council to promote relations at all levels. In 1989 he published a book, *Les Anglais*. An ebullient, talkative, impulsive promoter of the Anglo-French Entente.

to discuss the Franco-British Council and the idea of launching an Anglo-French Königswinter. 'You know the French are not like the Germans,' Geoffroy de Courcel kept reminding us. He called Daudy by his surname. Whether for that or for some other reason Daudy was somewhat aggressive.

A terrible diplomatic call that afternoon from the Syrian Ambassador who delivered a diatribe against Sadat whom he called 'that traitor', which made me think afterwards how much Sadat had earned his Nobel peace prize.

Dinner that night chez Thérèse de Saint-Phalle,[1] Baronne Drouas. She always collects interesting people. She had Claude Pedriel, PDG of *Le Nouvel Observateur* who became involved in an unequal argument with Pierre Hunt[2] in defence of Nixon. From this unpromising theme he went on to deplore the encirclement of the Soviet Union.

After dinner I had a heart-to-heart talk with Hunt about Anglo-French relations. He did not pretend that they were good. He spoke of the British half-heartedness towards Europe. I hit back by referring to the spokes the French were putting in the wheel of industrial co-operation. I also spoke of Giscard's recent TV interview in which he had talked proudly of his role as Minister of Finance as having been to ensure that France overtook the UK. He added that France's aim now was to overtake the FRG within ten years. There was plenty of the spirit of competition in the broadcast but precious little to help strengthen bilateral relations. Hunt said that the broadcast had been exclusively intended for a domestic audience. I said that it had nevertheless been taken note of abroad.

The next day, 25 October, we attended the opening of the Magasin du Louvre, now, strangely, the property of the British Post Office Pension Fund. They have modernised it and converted the bottom three floors into an antique market. I flew to London to give a speech the following day to a conference for industrialists organised by the British Overseas Trade Board; and to make a broadcast on the BBC on the same subject. Kenneth Rose rang me a day or two earlier to ask if there was anything I could tell him about my activities that would be suitable for his *Sunday Telegraph* column. Had I, for instance, a vivid memory of dining with the new Pope at Cracow in the course of my duties as British Ambassador to Poland? I said that alas I could not help him over that. I mentioned my trade promotion speech. 'That,' he said, 'comes in the category of activities that are essential but not exciting.' I could not but agree with him.

I returned to Paris to hear that the airbus business had been settled. It

[1]Thérèse de Saint-Phalle, writer, prominent in Paris social life.
[2]Pierre Hunt, French Diplomatic Spokesman for the French President 1978–80.

is a great relief. Had it not gone through the political repercussions would have been considerable; and I think that within a few years British Aerospace would have become a mere hewer of wood and drawer of water for Boeing. Immodestly I think that we in this Embassy have played quite a role in keeping the political aspects in view throughout the protracted negotiations. It was never to be taken for granted that British ministers would approve the project.

5 NOVEMBER

PARIS

THE PROMISE OF WEDDING BELLS

Alexandra telephoned Mary on Tuesday evening saying, 'Hello Mummy, Derry and I are thinking of getting married.'

Mary immediately rang me on the internal line with the words, 'wedding bells'.

Since then much of our time has been taken up with plans for the wedding which they want soon as Derry has to go off to India. Complications have arisen from the disturbing news that Alexandra has to have an operation for the removal of a 'cyst the size of her fist'. Naturally she and we were very worried. However, as usual, Bodley Scott,[1] into whose hands we have confided ourselves frequently, says that there is nothing to worry about: 'These things are not unnatural in girls of that age and she is obviously very strong.'

Mary and I had a meeting with Monseigneur Meletios of the Greek Orthodox Church to see if His Grace could marry them in December. He raised no difficulties but knocked the stuffing out of me and of my purse by saying that the choir alone would cost five thousand francs (equivalent to about six hundred pounds) and that a similar amount would be needed for the officiating clergy. Mary has dropped him a line saying that I will be coming to see him, that we are not Greek shipowners and that we are merely passing occupants of our house, the splendour of which had no doubt impressed him.

We have taken a helpful European step recently that I emphasised when talking to Froment-Meurice and later to Soutou. HMG has said that it wants to try to settle the fish problem before the end of the year.

---

[1] R. Bodley-Scott, physician to the Queen 1952–73. Physician to many hospitals. In 1979 he published *Cancer the Facts*. A doctor whose manifest knowledge, patience and wisdom inspired in his patients confidence in him and in themselves.

In order not to sour the atmosphere it has decided to postpone the implementation of a new regulation relating to the fish net sizes which would certainly have produced an outcry in France. Froment-M asked me why it was easier for us to be conciliatory on fish now than it had been a few weeks ago. To which I replied that it was still difficult, but perhaps we wanted to show that degree of European faith for which our partners were always asking. I also think privately that the PM feels that we are under attack on too many fronts at once just at the moment. You have to be an Israeli politician to be able to endure such embattlement for long.

On All Saints day we lunched, as we have done before, at Royaumont with the Elie de Rothschilds. Their son and daughter-in-law were there; also Odette and her sister. I tried to get Elie and his son, Nathaniel, who now runs the business, to be philanthropic and to promise to keep running the Tramway Mont Blanc.[1] The continuation of this line is said by Patrick Reilly and Jeremy Lever to be essential to the maintenance of the famous Sligger Urquhart chalet.

It has been a week of anti-semitic heart-searching in France following the publication by *L'Express* of an interview with Louis Darquier de Pellepoix who was Vichy minister in charge of Jewish affairs. Living now in Spain, he is an unregenerate anti-semite and has said that the only things gassed at Auschwitz were fleas; all the rest were a Jewish invention.

I am not sure that the French are particularly anti-semitic but they get very worked up about it, pro and con, another consequence, I believe, of their national psychosis over the events of 1940. The Rothschilds are somewhat immune, much as the King of Jordan, or the King of Saudi Arabia are felt to be outside the target of those who are habitually anti-Arab. I suspect that the eastern seaboard of the USA or the provinces of the UK are no less anti-semitic than France, but they would keep quiet about it. As regards anything to do with 1940–4 the French cannot let sleeping dogs lie.

We went to an amusing film the other night, *La Mort Sur Le Nil.* It was not dubbed and had French subtitles. At one moment Ustinov (Hercule Poirot) breaks into French and quotes Molière, upon which David Niven, who plays a typical English colonel, protests. 'My God, can't you speak some civilised language?' Those responsible for the French subtitles lost their nerve and rendered this: 'Would you please translate.'

---

[1] Tramway Mont Blanc; to the best of my knowledge it is still running.

15 NOVEMBER
PARIS

THE GREEK CHURCH; JOHN GRIGG AND
CÉCILE DE ROTHSCHILD

I went to see Monseigneur Meletios who received me in his living quarters behind the church, his coal-scuttle well down on his head. He took the initiative in saying that he entirely agreed that it would be a bad idea to have the chorus from the opera. Instead he would have a few Byzantine songs at the end of the service. I said that the man whom my daughter would be marrying had been divorced. I wanted to avoid any last-minute difficulties. Would he please tell me what particular papers he would require relating to the divorce?

Monseigneur Meletios placed the tips of the fingers of his hands together and asked, 'What church was he married in?'

I replied, 'Anglican,' though indeed it was only a guess.

'Then, so far as the Greek Church is concerned,' he said, 'he was never married. Therefore there is no question of divorce.' He hesitated a moment before adding, 'Would you like a coffee?'

I declined, saying that I must not take up his time, upon which he rejoined, 'Well, I shall show you the church.'

He led the way into the church which indeed I already knew quite well; and he disappeared behind the altar whence came a sound of clicking as he switched on all the lights.

The church looked beautiful. I felt very warm towards the Monseigneur.

John Grigg[1] came to lunch one day: a most enthusiastic, life-enhancing man. He is interrupting work on his life of Lloyd George, of which he gave us the second volume, to write something about the Second World War. For this he had come to Paris to interview General Billot. Among other subjects, we talked about Tony Benn whom he insisted on calling Anthony, having known him at Oxford under that name. He denied that Benn was possessed of hare-brained ideas. However, he went on to tell us how, just after the war when bread had been rationed, Benn, then an undergraduate at Oxford, had proposed that all the undergraduates at New College should forgo their bread so that it could be sent to China.

---

[1]John Grigg, writer, columnist for the *Guardian* 1960–70; more recently for *The Times*. Chairman of the London Library 1985–91. Is engaged upon a full-length biography of Lloyd George. He and his wife, Patsy, are close personal friends.

John said that fortunately the proposal had been rejected by the JCR, not least on the grounds that the Chinese didn't eat bread anyway. I asked John how in the light of that story he could really maintain that Benn was not hare-brained. He agreed that perhaps he would have to withdraw, but he insisted that Benn was not a prig and that he had a good sense of humour.

'Does he have a sense of humour about himself?' I asked.

'Well,' he quipped, 'you must admit that humour is not the longest suit of people in politics.'

John has certain ideas to which he adheres fanatically rather as Ian Gilmour, a great friend, also does. I recall his stand against the monarchy and his renunciation of his title. He is unequivocally pro-French. He thinks that the British are no less nationalistic than the French. 'Of course we are very like each other. That's why we get on so well,' was his comment which perplexed me not a little. But John is so enthusiastic that I did not want to start an argument.

I lunched this week with Cécile de Rothschild a few doors down the Faubourg. Other guests included John Foster[1] and Bertrand Goldschmidt[2] who, when the subject of Clemenceau was raised recalled his remark that: 'There are three unnecessary things in life, Poincaré, the prostate and the Italians.'

Cécile has beautiful pictures and a wonderful chef and cellar. She is a most agreeable companion. People tell me how beautiful she was and how her love for her brothers prevented her from ever marrying. They also speak of her great romance with Greta Garbo. I don't know anyone less boastful and it is rare to meet someone living alone who speaks so little of themselves. Among other interests that we have in common is gardening. We have both just acquired an excellent rose, Margaret Merrill, of which we had a display during the Garden Exhibition this summer. We exchange plants in the same way as others exchange wine.

---

[1] John Foster, barrister, Fellow of All Souls, Recorder of Oxford 1938–51 and 1956–64. MP 1945–74.
[2] Bertrand Goldschmidt, a French scientist. With the Commissariat à l'Energie Atomique since 1946.

17 NOVEMBER

PARIS

___

MORE EMS AND MORE PARTIES

I had a bad day yesterday trying to do too many things at once. It began with a meeting at 9 a.m. with Ken Couzens[1] of the Treasury, Kit McMahon[2] of the Bank of England and Michael Butler[3] of the FCO to discuss our attitude to the EMS. They are all against our joining and I showed my disagreement and, I fear, my irritation. The question at the moment is whether the pound will be more stable inside than outside the new system. I regard the decision to be largely a political one where the advantage certainly lies in entry.

The London team made much of the argument that no central bankers or experts in the UK, France or Germany believed that the scheme was appropriate for Britain. I countered by mentioning three heads of clearing banks who were in favour. They pooh-poohed this, saying that they had inadequate experience in this field. Later in the morning I attended a seminar organised in Paris by a firm of stockbrokers. A young economist spoke. He was pessimistic about the UK economy unless the trade unionists could be brought to their senses. Asked whether he was in favour of Britain joining the EMS he said emphatically, yes, partly because this would require us to maintain the necessary disciplines to keep inflation in check.

There has been too much mondanité this week. A Community dinner was given by the Germans in honour of Guiringaud. The Bettencourts gave a dinner for Edgar Faure. I can rarely understand the significance of what he says while realising that his compatriots find him brilliant. I am sure it's lack of comprehension on my part.

At the Embassy we gave a farewell dinner for the departing Cypriot Ambassador. In honour of Mentzelopoulos, who has recently acquired Château Margaux, I served magnums of his wine. Mary and I went on afterwards to a party given by Stavros Niarchos who had insisted on us

___

[1] Kenneth Couzens, at this time was Second Permanent Secretary (Overseas Finance) 1977–82 in the Treasury. Permanent Under-Secretary of State Department of Energy 1983–5.

[2] Christopher McMahon, after an academic career entered the Bank of England as adviser 1964. Executive Director 1970–80. Deputy Governor 1980–5. A man of wide interests which include looking at pictures and, in good weather, gardening (he was born and brought up in Australia which may explain this qualification).

[3] Michael Butler, Member of the Diplomatic Service. Department Under-Secretary of State, FCO 1976–9. Ambassador and Permanent UK Representative to EEC, Brussels, 1979–85. An expert on financial and Community matters. His principal recreaction is collecting and writing about Chinese porcelain.

looking in to see some Greek dancers flown here from Athens. Peter Payne[1] played a near-host role. He said that Niarchos had not given a big party for years and he was delighted to be doing so. I was as impressed by the sight of Niarchos's impressionist paintings as by the dancers.

One night, after dining with André Faure[2] of Twinings, to meet Garry Weston[3] of Fortnum and Mason, we went on to the Hubert d'Ornanos. She is the daughter of a former Polish diplomat, Count Potocki and his Radziwill-born wife, whom we had known in Madrid – a man who bore political exile with nobility. People enjoy going to their apartment, the walls of which are lined with paisley patterned fabric. They are personal friends of Giscard.

18 NOVEMBER
COURANCES

BOAR SHOOT

We are staying the night with the Jean-Louis de Ganays at Courances. The rest of the party have gone off boar-shooting. The ladies and I will join them for lunch in the forest. In the meantime I can spend an unvirile morning catching up with non-shooting activities. It is tempting to spend time sending off to friends picture postcards of the château.

I am not quite sure why, given that I do not shoot, we were invited. Philippine is a great friend and I believe she thinks that we would like to experience this segment of French life. She says that this sort of thing won't last much longer so I had better see it.

We dined the first night at the Château de Fleury where Jean-Louis's brother lives. There are five Ganay brothers, all handsome and Anglicised. At the outbreak of war Jean-Louis volunteered immediately and joined up as an agent of SOE.

At the lunch in the forest after the first shoot the men arrived with their rifles and in various states of mind depending on how they had shot during the morning. Everyone agreed that the first battu had been épouvantable. Sherry, vodka, taramasalata and Baltic herring on brown bread were served by men wearing letter-box-red outfits, the same, so I

---

[1] Peter Payne, of Greek and English parentage; worked for Niarchos; helped by his tri-lingual charm, he then established his own highly successful insurance business with a large shipping and cultural clientèle.
[2] Andre Faure, tea importer with wide business and social contacts.
[3] Garfield Weston, Chairman, Associated British Foods since 1967; Fortnum and Mason since 1978; British Sugar 1991.

was told, as those worn by the beaters, who needed to make themselves conspicuous in case they might be taken for boars as they groped their way through the undergrowth. The guns stood in *miradors* which are a form of elevated butt. There were eighteen rifles in the shoot.

As they cast aside their weapons and reached for refreshment a plastic container swung from the neck of each huntsman. It contained a chart of the forest, of the *miradors* and an instruction to each gun on where he was to go for every drive. It also included tags and an instrument like a small gimlet. I was asked if I could guess what it was for and suggested it might be for hanging up their clothes in the *miradors*. This was thought to be rather an urban reaction though I never heard what the purpose was. I took some photographs of the breadwinners and their ladies who were tactful not to ask how their spouses had performed, knowing full well that they would soon tell them if they had been successful.

We sat down to lunch at a long wooden table beneath a giant cloche. One of the men opposite me asked me whether I ever shot. I said, never. 'I hope not for ecological reasons,' he said. Someone else muttered, 'How strange for an Englishman. I thought everyone hunted in England.' A little later my neighbour, the Princesse de Ligne who had not heard this conversation turned to me and said; 'I suppose that you confine your shooting to smaller birds.' The Princess had herself been shooting in the morning. This was evident from the plastic envelope that hung like a necklace round her neck. I found out that she had not shot a thing. Nor had the two men opposite me.

It was a delicious lunch: hot smoked salmon, frankfurters and sauer-kraut – much as Lipp would have served. There was also soup, salad and plenty of wine and vodka. Jean-Louis announced: 'Five minutes more.' The huntsmen swallowed brandy, stuffed chocolate biscuits into their pockets and staggered from the table. The ladies, which included me, but not the Princesse de Ligne, returned to the château where I spent an agreeable afternoon reading Uhlman's little récit, *L'Ami Retrouvé*.[1]

At about 6.30 p.m. all the dead boar were laid out on the drive before the château. There must have been fifty of them, all lit by *flambeaux* held by the beaters. We were invited to go outside and to prod and admire them. Jean-Louis said that he would be getting twenty francs a kilo for them. Restaurants and hotels were eager to buy. The day's work would bring him in three thousand pounds, a sum earned mostly by the visitors who received nothing more for their labours than the animals' tusks. At supper that evening the main dish consisted of livers cut from the boars at the moment of death, apparently a great delicacy.

---

[1] Fred Uhlman, *L'Ami Retrouvé*, Gallimard, 1978.

22 NOVEMBER

PARIS

TONY BENN IN PARIS

Tony Benn has been here to talk about energy with Giraud, the French Minister of Industry. He did not brag about Britain's oil wealth. I suppose he could hardly do so, when you think of it, given the strident appeal of the anti-Europeans at home about the UK's poverty which requires a revision of our budgetary terms of membership of the Community. Benn was delighted when the French minister said that he thought that Community energy questions should be handled by ministers rather than left to the European Commission. This chimed in with Benn's psychosis – shared by many members of the Cabinet – about Brussels. It is one of the topics upon which, at the moment, it is easiest to make common cause with the French. I gather, however, that at the lunch, which I was unable to attend because I was entertaining a large group of MPs, the two ministers did not see eye to eye when Benn dilated on the importance of generating public discussion on energy issues. Giraud, as Benn admitted to me later, had been horrified by the idea. So far the French had had little trouble with public opinion. He was not going to do anything to stoke up interest. Is it a sign that I have been brainwashed by several years in Paris that I find there is a lot of hard-headed sense in this attitude?

Benn, of course, is one of the main troublemakers so far as entry to the EMS is concerned. At their last meeting in October the PM told Schmidt frankly about his political difficulties, leaving him in no doubt that on account of these the UK would not be able to enter the exchange-rate mechanism of the EMS, at any rate at the outset. Schmidt has told many people about this, saying that he is darned if he will make concessions just to enable Callaghan to keep Benn in his Cabinet.

23 NOVEMBER

PARIS

THEATRICAL GAFFE

We gave a lunch for Kenneth Macmillan, the choreographer, who is doing some ballets for the Paris Opéra. I had decided to make it a musical lunch and had invited, among others, Bernard Lefort, the new head of the Paris Opéra.

All the other guests had arrived and we were waiting for Monsieur Lefort. Giovanni appeared and announced his name, but the man he presented was not the Monsieur Lefort whom we all were expecting. Kenneth James, Richard Auty[1] and I looked at each other in wild surmise. In a whisper I asked them to try to find out who our visitor was. It struck me that the real Bernard Lefort might arrive at any moment. After some surreptitious confabulation we discovered that the unexpected visitor was indeed Bernard Lefort. But he was not our man, he was a journalist, a political journalist who worked for RTL.[2] Kenneth wondered whether we should not come clean and confess that an awful mistake had been made. I said no, we must not make him feel awkward. So I went over to talk to him about the political scene, asking him how he saw it in the present climate just before the Anglo-French summit.

I must say that M Lefort behaved impeccably. True, he was sweating a little. But I was not convinced that he had tumbled to our mistake. He said that he had known people in the Embassy in the past and mentioned Michael Palliser's name. We clutched at this as if at a raft. We all made a lot of Lefort. But it was not exactly easy at lunch. Mary was on his left. On his right was Nadia Nerina who has nothing to do with anything except ballet. Opposite him was our choreographer guest-of-honour who can never have been a great one for discussing politics. Certainly that lunchtime, which was a few hours before his first performance in Paris, he could think of nothing but dancing; and it was the same with the rest of the company. We were all ballet-orientated.

After lunch M Lefort drank up his coffee, said how much he liked the Embassy and had enjoyed himself that day and left. We had got to like him very much but felt a slight sense of relief when he was gone. I continued to hope that he had not realised what had happened. But this was shattered that evening when Mary received a bouquet of roses with a card headed: Bernard Lefort and underneath these words: '*Je regrette de ne pas pouvoir vous accompagner au ballet ce soir.*'

We have been thinking since how to make amends. At any rate one of the guests, Mlle Violette Verdy, Directrice de la Dance à L'Opéra was delighted. She had just been sacked by the right Monsieur Lefort. We had invited her without knowing this. It would have had the makings of a nasty confrontation. So, in making one gaffe, we had avoided another.

The three ballets did not meet with favour from the audience, most of

---

[1] Richard Auty was on the staff of the British Council 1949–80. Their representative in France and Cultural Counsellor, British Embassy Paris 1976–80.
[2] RTL: Radio-Télévision Luxembourg.

whom were there because they have *abonnements* to these gala occasions rather than because they like the opera. They were shocked because the dances were new and different. They booed. Mary and I were confused. Luckily in one of the long intervals during which the duchesses stride about in the foyer Mary lost her temper with a group who were running down the whole performance. This made us feel much better. It restored our morale and, in fighting form, we went on to the David-Weills' supper party in the rue Saint-Guillaume.

26 NOVEMBER

PARIS

———

THE FRENCH PUSH OUT
THE BOAT

Our Franco-UK summit took place in Paris on 24 November. This is the third in the series of such visits which were instigated in the course of Giscard's official visit to London in June 1976. Normally they involve an overnight stay, but this time the PM let it be known that he wanted to return the same day. So a lot had to be crammed in to quite a short time.

A week before the meeting was due to take place Giscard telephoned the PM. His purpose apparently was to impart an atmosphere of friendliness to the visit. Relations have not been good lately: unanswered letters between the two; resentment in London at Giscard's ever-closer relationship with Schmidt; resentment in Paris at what they regard as the persistent non-European stance adopted by HMG as reflected in the PM's Mansion House speech; Silkin's obstructions on fish and our generally negative attitude to EMS.

I don't know whether this Embassy played a role in bringing it about, but, at any rate, the French came to realise quite recently that there was just as much resentment in London towards Paris as the other way round. This coincided with a sudden feeling in France, such as comes over them from time to time but in this instance was stimulated by statements in Bonn suggesting support for increasing the powers of the European Assembly once it is directly elected, something that is anathema to a broad spectrum of French political opinion, that Germany is getting a bit above itself. There only has to be a touch of this anxiety in the air for the French to begin thinking of their ally on the other side and to wonder whether they should not reinforce the UK–France relationship.

It was in this spirit that Giscard rang Callaghan. However I believe that, in keeping with the seesaw movement that invariably governs the interplay of sentiment between the two countries, it was now the turn of the British side to play hard to get. Would the PM not be able to stay the night? the President asked, saying that he would like to offer him hospitality. Callaghan replied that he wanted to get back to his own bed for the night.

'Well,' the President explained, 'I would like to give you a large dinner party, to mark the importance of the occasion.'

The PM said that this was all right by him so long as he could get away in time. To the French, of course, the offer of a grand dinner is a sign of favour; to Callaghan it looks more like a waste of food. The President then asked whether there was anyone the PM would particularly like to have invited to the dinner. To which the Prime Minister answered that there was no one.

When I saw Callaghan he asked me what I thought that the President was getting at. I replied that this pushing out of the boat was not meaningless. The President wanted to show that the meeting was important to him. He probably thought that he had been leaning too far towards the Germans and must now redress the balance.

From the moment that the Prime Minister's TriStar touched down at Roissy in a fog there was no doubt that the French intended to make a fuss of him and his party. I was reminded a little of the Russians whose social graces exactly mirror, not respect, nor affection nor historic ties, but their degree of interest in the visitor at that particular moment. The numbers of police motorbikes put at the PM's disposal reflected Giscard's concern to demonstrate interest.

As usual I had useful chats with the PM in the car drives at the beginning and end of the visit. I was a little surprised that he was taken aback by my telling him about France's greater economic strength compared with Britain's. 'Their GDP is now nearly 50 per cent above ours,' I said.

I think the visit fulfilled its main purpose, which was to make the two political leaders focus on each other and on the bilateral relationship between the two countries. This should not really have been necessary but it was and there is no doubt that personal contact can help. The British ministers who participated apart from the PM – Healey, Owen, Varley and John Smith[1] – said how much they had valued the ministerial lunch given by Giscard when they had let their hair down over EMS.

'Best discussion I have ever had with the French,' I heard Healey say.

---

[1] John Smith, Labour MP. Minister of State Department Energy 1975–6; Secretary of State for Trade 1978–9. Leader of the Labour Party and Leader of the Opposition since 1992.

Later someone said to me that Healey had done most of the talking.

Owen told our office meeting that for the first time he had been able to see what Giscard was getting at over the EMS. I do not, however, think the visit will have helped to secure us much public acceptance here of our half-in half-out approach to the EMS. The French will go along with our decision because it suits them to be able to say that the EMS is a Community system. But they will ensure that we are criticised for our lack of faith in Europe and I expect that they will do their best to see that any pressure on the weaker currencies is directed against the pound rather than against those in the system.

2–3 DECEMBER

PARIS

———

MOUNTBATTEN TO STAY

Lord Mountbatten has been on a visit here this week to discuss Prince Charles's programme for his visit next summer for the United World Colleges.

What was odd in talking to Mountbatten was the way, on the first evening, he held forth about what interested him without showing the slightest interest in what others said. He would declaim for instance: '... and that is something upon which I would greatly value your view ...' I would begin to answer but soon realise that he wasn't listening at all. Indeed he was proceeding to talk about the next point on his mind. Not that he is rude. He has an old-world courtesy and takes trouble with those serving him, e.g. at the moment the Naval Attaché at the Embassy. All Naval Attachés to Paris find they have to dance attendance on Mountbatten on his frequent visits here. They do it willingly.

I had three receptions that night: at Perkins Motors to show interest in the sale of their engines here; at Maurice Druon to say goodbye to the Cypriot Ambassador; and to the Princesse de Polignac[1] for what purpose I do not exactly know. Then out to dinner.

I lunched yesterday with the Midland Bank who have just opened a branch in Paris. I was most impressed by the local chairman, Carmoy,[2] who has worked for years for the Chase Manhattan, as also with the brilliant young men he had around him. They were multilingual and it

---

[1] Princesse Edmond de Polignac was prominent in Paris society.
[2] Hervé de Carmoy, vice-president and director-general Chase Manhattan Bank, Paris 1970–78; general manager Midland Bank plc 1979.

was impossible to detect their nationality. Carmoy agreed that one of the great differences between us lies in the area of compromise, something that to the Frenchman appears synonymous with defeat but that to the Englishman is a sign of success.

François-Poncet has just been on the line. I have been drafting a character sketch of him to send to London. I emphasised the cool, clinical, éminence-grise nature of his personality. On the telephone he had been affable and forthcoming.

Although last week's bilateral summit has restored Franco-British relations to an even keel we are getting a very bad press here as a result of our reluctance to join fully the EMS.

The PM has given a good interview to the *Observer* which conveys well and honestly the make-up of his character. Asquith said that a man's career depends on his capacity to develop in his forties. With Callaghan what is amazing is the way he has emerged as a rounded person during his sixties. He says in the interview that no one should be able to become PM unless he has either had a serious prostate operation or reached sixty. By this I think he means that it is only under such circumstances that personal ambition can be kept properly in check.

I am thrilled by the tribute he pays in the interview to Nicholas Davenport,[1] though it is in the context of saying now let us all praise famous geriatrics.

4 DECEMBER

PARIS

――――

INDUSTRIAL CO-OPERATION

Today I sent off a despatch on the airbus negotiations. It is a great relief that we have won that battle.[2] As I've already indicated I feel no inclination to be falsely modest about the role played by the Embassy in helping to push it through.

During their summit talk last week the PM and the French President

――――――――――

[1] Nicholas Davenport, an intellectual city broker with a wide range of friends and interests; a regular writer for the press, latterly for the *Spectator,* he was adept at making financial matters comprehensive, and even exciting, to those who later came to be apostrophised as 'the chattering classes'. Author of *Memoirs of a City Radical,* 1974. He never aged and was the best octogenarian tennis player I have played with.

[2] The airbus fleet now has a 30 per cent share of the world market for large civil aircraft. Since production began in the 1970s Airbus Industrie have delivered well over one thousand aircraft.

referred to the airbus negotiation as an example of industrial co-operation, though it had only gone through with great difficulty and much acrimony.

17 DECEMBER
PARIS

ALEXANDRA'S WEDDING

Last week was wedding week. A great deal of time was devoted to the list of people to invite to the church and to the Christmas wedding party in the evening and to the places at table. We seated all the two hundred and eighty guests at thirty-three round tables in four rooms. Arranging them was a massive task right up to the kick-off, in which Philip Nelson helped me enormously. In the end only four people failed to turn up. Inevitably many were offended by one thing or another. Madame Massigli was incensed. At Garrett's[1] suggestion we had only invited her to the church and not to the party. She was deeply offended when I telephoned to apologise. This happened after she had poured her heart out to Garrett. I said that it was all my fault; it had been an appalling error that I had made in the list. 'Don't you think you ought to check the list,' she suggested.

I agreed and implored her nevertheless to come to the party.

She said she could not do so because she had no suitable dress and added, 'As someone who has a certain reputation for dress I could not come unless I was properly dressed.'[2]

Mary spent days and nights over the menu and the flowers including baskets of mistletoe and Christmas roses for the church. The house also was hung with mistletoe provided generously by Liliane de Rothschild.

Visitors came from all directions. There was a charter plane from London. Christine[3] came from Bonn with Zorba. I took him walks as I always used to do and he stopped at exactly the same places as usual in the Champs Elysées including a special area where I had always given him a biscuit, just as though there had been no gap of eight months. It was very sad when he left on Monday morning.

---

[1] Garrett Drogheda, Alexandra's future father-in-law.
[2] Madame Massigli's reputation for dress was long-standing, as described in the diary of 30 June 1978.
[3] Christine Bischler, our social secretary in Bonn, who had become owner of Zorba as retirement to the UK drew near for us.

House guests were the Droghedas, Zervudachis, Kees, Diana Phipps,[1] Carla Powell and Ted Heath. The party really began on Friday evening when we had a large buffet supper including roast pheasant. Many of Alexandra's friends who had come by the charter plane that evening clearly assumed that we had open house at the Embassy for all meals. They started pouring in so that the staff were swamped with fetching and carrying and washing up. I had to put my foot down gently the following two days and say that we could not entertain them all for lunch. They seemed surprised, as though denied what was theirs by right. The Droghedas were appreciative of everything. Garrett watched Mary arranging the flowers with great fascination, expressing frequent wonderment that she took such trouble. Joan played the piano. Robert blew up balloons. All this took place on Saturday morning.

Ted Heath arrived on Saturday afternoon. As he stood about in the Embassy courtyard in his metal-blue suit it was clear that he had no intention of travelling to the church with the other house guests. So he accompanied Mary and Garrett just ahead of Alexandra and me. I gather that he walked up the aisle with Mary and played the role of official greeter. He stood beside her in the church. Frank Longford was in the row behind. I must say we were very touched that Ted should have come here specially, though we knew that he loved a party provided it was lavish and star-studded. I asked him how he had enjoyed Madron Seligman's sixtieth birthday party. 'Oh it was quite good fun,' he replied with enthusiasm, adding, 'but it was funny. He gave a cinema show in the middle. I suppose he was bored with the guests. Typical Madron.' I realised we had to be on our toes in entertaining Ted at our party that evening.

I had placed him for the dinner at a table with Madame Barre, Madame Simone Veil, Princess Firyal[2] and Diana Phipps. The other men at the table were Alastair Burnet,[3] Claude Pierre-Brossolette and myself. Neither Madame Barre nor Simone Veil seemed inclined to speak a word of English; and neither Heath nor Burnet had much French so conversation was not easy. However Mary insisted that they would prefer to be well placed for a sticky evening than badly placed for an amusing one. Anyway they were intrigued by the decor of the rooms and

---

[1]Diana Phipps, born in Czechoslovakia, married an American and after his death moved to London where, with her dramatic looks and stylishness, she quickly acquired a coterie of devoted and mainly literary friends.

[2]Princess Firyal, of Jordan, formerly wife of the brother of the King of Jordan. Lives in London.

[3]Alastair Burnet, broadcaster for Independent Television News from 1976; editor the *Economist* 1965–74, of the *Daily Express* 1974–6. A journalist with gravitas as shown by the firm anchorage of ITN *News at Ten* when he was presenter 1982–91 and by the way this slipped after he left the programme. With authority he 'fronted' ITN's general election broadcasts.

by the elaborate fare. Before anyone attacked the long buffet table groaning with dishes Madame Barre asked if she could inspect it in its pristine state. She proved to be fascinated by the idea of *pâté de faisan fermière*, by the *œufs vert-pré* (eggs served on artichoke hearts), by the *pie de dinde*, the *cochon de lait* (which reminded her of Hungary), the sauce Cumberland and the cheeses which were English, Scottish and French. Of course at that early stage of the saturnalian evening she did not realise that this was just a start and that the desserts were going to be just as breath-taking: plum pudding with a brandy butter mountain, mince pies, *glacé Gladstone*, *sauce gingembre* and *gâteaux de nöel et de mariage*.

Eventually Madame Barre was to try them all. There is nothing blasé about her. She hates to miss a party.

Truly the chef had excelled himself. He and his pantry boys had worked literally for days and nights. Towards the end of the evening they all came to celebrate with us in front of the towering wedding-cake. Returning for a minute to our table where Madame Barre was in the best of spirits, Simone Veil, seated between Ted and me, appeared tired and worried. She does not like the corner into which the Gaullists keep trying to push her, with Chirac at the moment playing a frenetic wrecking game aimed at undermining Giscard. I had heard a rumour that Madame Veil was intending to resign her ministerial post and stand for the European Assembly as a UDF (i.e. Giscardian) candidate. I adopted my usual tactic and indicated to her that I assumed she would be doing this. To which she replied that no decision had yet been taken. I had the clear impression that office has lost a lot of its appeal for her. I like talking to her and she kindly said how sad she was at the prospect of our leaving Paris. She has been a great help with us over the Hertford British Hospital. One of the things I am most pleased to have done during my time in Paris has been to get the hospital incorporated in the French social security system. Its modernisation should now take place without difficulty. I made a point of not thanking Simone Veil too openly for the help she has given because I think it might make it difficult for her with her officials if I gave the impression that she has done us a great favour. Nevertheless we ought to feel grateful because I am not sure that we would have got the hospital on to the right footing without her personal intervention.

When Jackie Bamboo[1] started to play a waltz the floor became crowded with devotees from the homeland throwing themselves about like dervishes. This was to be a feature of the whole evening, the eagerness of the

---

[1] Jackie Bamboo, dance band leader.

British contingent to dance uninterruptedly and without inhibition until dawn. As usual the French, particularly the men, were reluctant to take the floor. Not surprisingly Johnny Faucigny-Lucinge was an exception. As he swung into action he shouted to me over his shoulder how much he regretted his compatriots' inhibitions. Alex Grall also enjoyed himself dancing, as did Claude Pierre-Brossolette. Far and away the best dancers were the Joël de Rosnays.[1] Stella apparently goes to dancing classes three times a week. People tended to sit watching them in amazement, the British full of admiration, the French less so except for Eric Rothschild who was clearly enthralled.

I have been told that the upbringing of the French tends to make them think of dancing as synonymous with effeminacy. *'Il est danseur'* is apparently a term of abuse to use about someone whom we might describe as a fly-by-night. However, I persuaded Jackie Bamboo's merry men to play Zigeuner music which evidently transported Madame Barre back to Budapest; and I asked her to dance. We waltzed. We even turned both ways. Madame Barre wrote a very nice letter afterwards. Alas, Simone Veil was not prepared to dance. But Françoise Giroud danced as if she meant it. Ted danced with Diana Phipps.

With the arrival of the Christmas puddings in flames and the opening of the crackers the party started to escalate. The English surged on to the floor like the crowd at Twickenham invading the ground after a varsity match. There was a momentary hiccup when Jackie Bamboo had to take time off for a drink and the tape recorder failed to work. The dancing went on until the morning when Jackie Bamboo stood his drum in the middle of the floor and struck up God Save the Queen. Her great-grandmother, Queen Alexandra, and her great-great-grandmother, Queen Victoria, looked on from their marble busts in recesses on either side of the room.

The remaining guests settled down to onion soup and sausages. We ate our way through several of Mary's fruit decorations before going to bed.

---

[1] Joël de Rosnay, Research Attaché, Pasteur Institute 1962–6; with MIT 1967–70; Attaché French Embassy, Washington 1968–70; since when he has held many high-level scientific posts and written learned works on the origin of life and biotechnology. Married Stella Jebb, December 1959. In the litheness of his physique there is something of Mark Boxer about him.

29 DECEMBER
PARIS

THE CHANGING ROLE OF THE EMBASSY;
OUR LAST CHRISTMAS PARTY

I have not been so busy lately, which reflects, I think, the changing role of an Embassy now that we are in the European Community. Officials in the various ministries do an increasing amount of work directly with their opposite numbers in the Community capitals. It is the same with ministers. Owen, as is his wont in speaking about the role of the officials serving him, has explained in public once again the limited part that he sees for diplomats abroad. Not long ago he said that he did not see any point in having an Ambassador in Paris when all he had to do was to pick up the telephone and speak to the French Foreign Minister. He has said that he finds himself taking a much closer interest in a problem if he has to handle it himself rather than simply sending an instruction to an Ambassador.

I think that there will inevitably be some reduction of Embassy work as the Community develops. My own feeling is that officials tend to fly about and meet too often. We had a brief discussion of this problem when the Chief Clerk had a meeting earlier this month with the Heads of Missions from Community countries. Donald Maitland[1] said that for a recent meeting on agriculture in Brussels sixty officials had come from Whitehall, including two for potatoes – he supposed one for new, the other for old potatoes.

I suggested that we officials in Embassies could be used more often, and not simply for providing a car service. I do not think that this is happening, at any rate at the moment, because it is easier for someone in Whitehall to step into a plane and fly here than to sit down and draft a comprehensive brief for an official in an Embassy to use.

Much of the work that has kept me busiest here this past year or so – Airbus Industrie negotiations, or industrial co-operation – has been at my own instigation. Nobody from London has suggested that I do anything in particular; on the contrary I have had something of the

---

[1] Donald Maitland, member of the Diplomatic Sercice. Head of News Department FO 1965–7. Principal Private Secretary to Foreign Secretary 1967–9. Chief Press Secretary 10 Downing Street 1970–3. Ambassador and UK Permanent Representative to EEC 1975–9. Permanent Under-Secretary of State Department of Energy 1980–2. A man of great energy and adaptability badly needed for his varied and distinguished career.

impression from time to time that they think that I am doing too much back-seat driving and should pipe down a bit.

Alexandra had the operation yesterday in Sister Agnes. It was worse than they had expected. There were two cysts, not one. All rather worrying. Mary is with her, perching at night in our half-decorated apartment in Dorset Square. We only hope that it is nothing worse and that it will not prevent her having children. Somehow it makes it much harder that she has never been ill before in her life. I have terrible thoughts about the Olympic girl runner[1] who was suddenly struck down with cancer. However, I have just spoken to Alexandra on the phone and she sounds quite cheerful. She says she is surrounded by flowers and is being read out to by Mary – John Pearson's *Life of Ian Fleming*. She also says that the nurses seeing her name on the door thought she must be some old dragon.

Our last Christmas staff party, our last Christmas children's party, our last British luncheon have come and gone. I had to make a speech at this last event and suddenly felt myself quite moved when saying that I would not be with them next year, a combination, I realised afterwards, of tiredness and self-pity. Mary enjoys the children's party. She makes them all dress up. This year they had to be a fruit, vegetable or flower. Nicholas Bayne was Father Christmas. He dressed up in the Chancery and then walked up the Faubourg St Honoré with his sack to Number 39. The traffic was brought to a dazzled standstill as he entered the Residence courtyard.

1979

11 JANUARY

PARIS

A VISIT TO VAL D'ISÈRE AND

GRENOBLE

I attended the British Ski Championships in Val d'Isère. The night train from Paris to Bourg St Meurice, a station in the heart of the Alps, was warm and cut one off cosily from the outside world. I read Somerset Maugham's *A Writer's Notebook*, and I slept. In the early morning, as the train wound its way through the icy valley via Moutiers, I mapped

---

[1] Lilian Board.

out an outline for my valedictory despatch. Everything seemed clear and easy in that pristine mountain atmosphere.

Philip Nelson and Lord Congleton, the President of the Ski Federation of Great Britain, were at Bourg St Meurice to meet me and we drove up the Val d'Isère in a taxi, talking all the time of how the championships were going and about the skiing conditions. I enjoyed entering into the heart of the skiing world. Happily, I found that my friends of two years before, Joan Raynsford and General Reggie Leathes, were still in charge of the British Championship. Philip whispered to me later what a wonderful skier she was 'despite her age'. Philip and she had done a run together from the top of one of the téléphériques while Reggie and I, who had accompanied them up the mountain, sat in the sun drinking *gluhwein* and watching all the skiers start their descent. He is seventy but has been coming to Val d'Isère for eighteen years without interruption to help with the administration of the championship, as has Mrs Raynsford. The work, of course, is demanding. So many things have to be attended to – the entries, the training facilities, the finances, judges, slalom courses, timing devices, not to mention the prize-giving. General Leathes played a necessary but humble role in handing the correct prize to Mr John Ritblat[1] for presentation. I said afterwards to Mrs Raynsford, as we dined in the excellent little hotel, the Kern, that I doubted whether the young skiers appreciated all the hard, voluntary work that she and others had to put into it for the championship to work. 'No, probably not,' she said, 'but why should they?' I could not help wondering what would happen when she, Reggie and their like gave up their labour of love. They are the descendants of a great British skiing tradition. The young skiers of today seem more professional, and many of them are financed by public bodies. There is plenty of spirit in them, but it is not quite the same.

I was amused by one incident. During the women's slalom one of the girls was disqualified for missing a gate. Standing at the finishing post with the trainers and organisers I sensed considerable disappointment. 'Poor Kirstie,' someone muttered, 'she's only thirteen; it's her first championship; her father's made a big sacrifice sending her to Austria to help her training ...' Such was the pathos surrounding little Kirstie that the judges reversed their ruling and allowed her to make another run which she did without further disqualification.

When the time came for the prize-giving that evening I was amazed to hear Kirstie Cairn's name being read out repeatedly as the winner of this and that prize. At one moment two of the burly male skiers hoisted her

[1] John Ritblat, chairman and managing director, the British Land Co since 1970. Sponsor, British National Ski Championships 1978–91.

on to their shoulders to help her fetch the weighty trophies. Far from being a poor little suppliant, she was the most successful skier.

Philip and I went to Grenoble by train the next morning. We had a fascinating visit to the Institut Laue-Langevin, on the outskirts of Grenoble, a Franco-German-British research organisation. Dr John White,[1] an Australian who has studied and taught at Oxford has been director for several years. He gave us an account of what the institute does for research and he showed us round, including the reactor.

For the visit to the reactor we had to wear plastic galoshes and white overalls. We entered what seemed to be a lift. After the heavy door shut behind us we waited inside for a few seconds without anything moving until a similar door opened at the other side. This was to maintain a constant pressure in the reactor. We entered the enormous rotunda where the reactor is housed. Dr White told me that the dome was said to cover a bigger span than Santa Sophia.

Then began the explanations given by various experts in white overalls. We crossed what looked like a miniature railway line before peering down into a large well. 'That's the reactor,' I was told. I peered at an object that was giving off a blue light. I asked what the piece of string was that was dangling in the water. 'That's a piece of string', was the answer. It was explained to me that to produce neutrons you need extremely enriched uranium; and when after forty-four days it has ceased to be productive the uranium is taken out of the reactor and put 'in this bath alongside'. We went to a similar well adjacent and there in the water was an object suspended by a crane giving off a similar blue glow. In answer to my somewhat naïve question of what would happen if you fell into the water a scientist pointed to two life-buoys smaller than those on a ship but reminiscent of what you might see on the stage set of a musical comedy. We were taken up and down various gangways and passed indefinable objects. Dr White told me that many people found that the reactor resembled a ship, and I don't believe that he was thinking of the life-buoys. We were introduced to a learned serious-looking French scientist who was invited to describe his duties. He began by saying that he was concerned with research on 'large biological objects'. He explained later that he was using neutrons for research into viruses that were a little bigger than molecules. He said that his findings which affected plant life were published in specialist journals. The director was proud of a hovercraft air cushion system that had been developed at the

[1] John White, university lecturer, Oxon 1963–85. Assistant director 1975, director 1977–80, Institut Laue-Langevin, Grenoble. Professor of Physical and Theoretical Chemistry, Canberra, since 1985. The UK had to withdraw from the Institut in 1991–2 because of financial pressure.

With the Queen Mother and Mary
at the British Embassy, Paris.
Below: at Château Lafite, with
Elie and Philippe de Rothschild.

With Princess Grace of Monaco and Princess Alexandra at British Embassy dinner.

Odette Pol Roger in her vineyard.

Chelsea on the Seine.

After the wedding; Alexandra and Derry Moore with NH and MH below the portrait of
Pauline Borghese.

Received by President Carter, at the White House July 1979.

Mary with Michael Deaver and Leonard Cheshire at fundraising dinner for Cheshire Homes in the British Embassy, Washington.

Mrs Thatcher's first visit to President Reagan in Washington. *Above*: meeting at the White House. NH, Michael Palliser, Peter Carrington on Mrs Thatcher's right. Al Haig and James Baker on President Reagan's left. *Below*: dinner at the British Embassy showing Iona Carrington between the President and Al Haig, and Vice-President Bush on the Prime Minister's left.

To Nicko — A superb Ambassador — a man for all seasons. May your roses make life sing — May your wit and character continue to lift up your friends, always! With respect Ceg Bush

With Vice-President Bush.

Mary with Harry Simpson, the British
Embassy chief.

Katherine Graham, proprietor of the
Washington Post, and Meg Greenfield,
one of her editors.

WASHINGTON TALK

British Ambassador: Days in Crisis

By LYNN ROSELLINI
Special to The New York Times

WASHINGTON, April 20 — Chuck telephoned Nicko the other afternoon. They talked about Al.

"Hello, Chuck, I haven't any developments," said Sir Nicholas Henderson to Senator Charles Percy, referring to the Falkland Islands crisis. The two men chatted briefly about the peace-making efforts of Secretary of State Alexander M. Haig Jr.

Then Sir Nicholas said goodbye. "It's a great advantage," he observed a moment later, "being on friendly terms with people."

As British Ambassador, Sir Nicholas, Nicko, to his friends, is on a first-name basis not only with Mr. Haig and Senator Percy, the chairman of the Senate Foreign Relations Committee, but also with nearly every other important Government official, member of Congress and columnist in Washington.

He breakfasts with Joseph Kraft, the columnist. He plays tennis with Katharine Graham, the chairman of the Washington Post Company. He dines at the home of Lane Kirkland, the labor leader. And he studs his Embassy parties with the best and brightest of Washington's political scene. Now, he is calling in some of those chits.

'A Different Role'

"Once the invasion had occurred," said Sir Nicholas, "we here in the Embassy had a completely different role."

Until just a few weeks ago, Sir Nicholas filled his days with a quiet routine of meetings, luncheons, speeches and dinner parties, aimed at the Washington diplomat's main task, making friends for his country. The biggest events on his calendar were a party next month to unveil the newly decorated Embassy and his planned retirement later this year.

Then Argentina attacked the Falkland Islands and suddenly, the Ambassador was everywhere: calling on Mr. Haig at the State Department; meeting at the White House with top Presidential aides; giving live interviews on television news shows; rushing to Capitol Hill in his silver Rolls Royce to confer.

"Suddenly, our role was not just the usual one to tell London of how opinion here was being shaped," he said, "but also to shape opinion, to bring home to our friends in the U.S. how something that was our problem could impinge on America's own interests."

By his position alone, the British Ambassador, like the Israeli Ambassador, is one of a small number of Washington diplomats who enjoy instant access to anyone in town.

"There's no dividing line between your private life and your public life," he said. "When I see X, Y or Z for dinner or drinks or tennis, I don't think

The New York Times/Teresa Zabala
Sir Nicholas Henderson in his office.

whether this is useful or not."

The Ambassador is a tall, likable man with shaggy gray hair, a shambling gait and the eccentric air of an Oxford don. On the tennis court, he maintains a running, often humorous patter and a mischievous arsenal of slices and drop shots. In the drawing room, he personally escorts his guests around by the arm.

But these days, the Ambassador has had little time for entertaining. When he does go out, he has to be careful not to show up at parties where the Argentine Ambassador, Esteban Arpad Takacs, will also be present.

"We don't exactly salute each other," said Sir Nicholas, chuckling. "People try to avoid asking us together, like in private life where two people have just separated."

In his more than 30 years as a diplomat, Sir Nicholas has been known for his outspokenness. Just a few weeks ago, he publicly criticized the United States Representative at the United Nations, Jeane J. Kirkpatrick for attending a dinner at the Argentine Embassy on April 2, the day Argentine troops seized the Falklands.

Now he is sitting at his Embassy desk, beneath a picture of Queen Elizabeth II. As he bends over a steno pad, drawing lines and circles with a blue fountain pen, he comments on his past three years here.

"Washington is enormously different," he says. "You don't have a system of government. You have a maze of government. In France or Germa-

ny, if you want to persuade the Government of a particular point of view, or find out their point of view on something, it's quite clear where the power resides. It resides with the Government.

"Here, there's a whole maze of different corridors of power and influence. There's the Administration. There's the Congress. There are staffers. There's the press. There are the institutions. There's the judiciary. The lawyers in this town. You know, it's difficult not to believe that the Mayflower was full of lawyers. People think that it was a lot of high-minded characters. I think that it was lawyers.

"Here, because of your Constitution, because you never wanted another George III to arise in your country who could boss you around, you made quite sure that the executive didn't have ultimate power. So it's entirely George III's fault."

"So," he went on, "that makes life in Washington for a foreigner very much more exciting, difficult, varied than anywhere else. A familiar sight of Washington is to see some bemused diplomat pacing the corridors of the Capitol, trying to find out where decisions are being taken. And when he's found that out, he may find it isn't on the Hill at all. It's somewhere else."

Does Sir Nicholas understand Washington now?

"No, I don't think I understand it," he says. "I promise I don't."

Falklands crisis: *New York Times* feature.

To Nicko & Mary - With warmest friendship & Regard - Sincerely

Nancy & Ron

Farewell party at the White House.

institute for moving heavy equipment about. As a result the floors everywhere were highly polished.

I began to feel that I was taking part in a Charlie Chaplin film, so incompatible was I with my surroundings. Once or twice the director stopped to ask little groups of people, some French, others English or German to explain to me what they were doing. They did so, but I cannot say that I was left much wiser. However it was apparent to me that they were happy and totally involved in this self-contained world. I found it difficult even to ask questions, feeling like the character in one of C.P. Snow's unconnected cultures. I wanted but did not dare to ask if I could catch a glimpse of some heavy water.

We left the reactor by the same pressure-lock system through which we had entered. We removed our special clothing. We did our best to comply with a notice telling all those who had entered the reactor to 'control themselves'. We washed our hands on leaving, and stood in front of what looked like an X-ray machine. I was told to hold my hands up in front of it and not to leave before the red light was extinguished. This happened within a few seconds. I was not told what would happen if the light stayed on. I was reminded of the time thirty years or so ago when George Jellicoe[1] and I visited Oak Ridge, the atomic energy plant in the USA. We were made to carry about with us little packets which we had to deliver up upon leaving. 'We'll let you know in a fortnight,' said the man to whom we gave them. We looked quizzical. 'We'll let you know whether you are impotent or not,' he explained.

---

[1] George Jellicoe, after exceptionally gallant war service in which he liberated my wife from hitherto-occupied Greece, joined the Diplomatic Service and was posted to Washington at the same time as I was there. He left the Service and entered politics 1961. Minister of State, Home Office 1962–3. First Lord of the Admiralty 1963–4; Lord Privy Seal and Minister in Charge, Civil Service Department 1970–3. Leader of the House of Lords 1970–3. Since when he has had a successful business career. Chairman Tate and Lyle 1978–82. A man of rumbustious energy and of wide interests which he shares with his wife, Philippa. As Roosevelt said of Winston Churchill, but perhaps with more conviction, we are glad to have lived in the same century as they have.

29 JANUARY
LONDON

———

COMMISSION BASHING; PERFORMANCE ART

I have just attended a meeting of officials in London to discuss where we are to go in the Community. The main question was what we do about the large deficit in our net contribution to the Community budget. My main intervention was focused on saying that our present half-hearted or hostile attitude to the Community makes it impossible to get sympathy for any of our demands. In the immediate future France's sole concern, so far as Britain is concerned, will be to await the outcome of the election.

John Fretwell, with whom I had a most useful talk yesterday – he understanding better than anyone the arcane subjects of the European Community, e.g. EMS and MCAS[1] – told me that he had included recently in a brief the suggestion that we should refrain from abusing the members of the European Commission because their views could have a direct effect on our interests. Commission-bashing, i.e. attacks on the faceless men of Brussels, is a favourite pastime nowadays. A minister minuted alongside this suggestion: 'Officials are getting uppity.'

Michael Palliser stayed with us last weekend. I told him of the horrific exhibition of British art that was on show in Paris at the time, thanks to a subsidy of seventeen thousand pounds from the British government. I was invited in an official capacity and found my arrival at the exhibition blocked by a man who took off all his clothes and walked up and down naked. The British Council Arts Adviser told me that it was Performance Art. I have written, perhaps somewhat humourlessly, to Sir J. Llewellyn, head of the British Council asking whether he approves of such expenditure of government funds.

---

[1] MCAS: Monetary Compensation Amounts – part of a Community system of artificial exchange rates for agricultural products, designed to offset the effects of currency fluctuations on farm prices. Michael Butler, the guru on the arcane workings of the Community, has admitted that 'The MCA system is not easy to understand.' See Michael Butler, *Europe: More than a Continent*, Heinemann, London, 1986, pp 36–7.

9 FEBRUARY

PARIS

———

GLOOM LIGHTENED BY BURNS NIGHT

Sir Arthur Knight,[1] chairman of Courtaulds, was lunching with us in Paris on Monday. I asked him whether he thought a change of government could turn the country round and bring about a new attitude leading to economic recovery. His enormous eyebrows went down like aeroplane flaps and he replied: 'Yes, I think so. At least one must think so because there is no alternative and anything else means despair.' He agrees with me that it is difficult to understand the Armageddon thesis of those who delight in the depth of the crisis and who chant that things have got to get worse before they can get better.

I spend time working on my valedictory despatch which will deal with the state of our decline over the past quarter of a century and the contribution that our foreign policy has made to this. It makes me feel slightly better that I am no longer playing games of make-believe, and that, on the contrary, I may be contributing to a candid understanding of where we have got to so that Newton's words can be heeded: 'the important thing is not to teach but to learn.'

That night I had to attend a Burns' night dinner. Mine was the only frivolous speech. I had been able to draw copiously for it from that admirable compendium of after-dinner stories, *Pass the Port*.[2] When the time came to dance reels I was intrigued to see that the best dancers were French, who also wore the trimmest kilts. There is nothing the English can ever do in their relations with France, including a benign attitude to the tunnel if they ever come to adopt it, that can enable them to catch up with the intimacy the Scots have with the French in their Auld Alliance.

---

[1] Arthur Knight, Chairman of Courtaulds 1975–9. Chairman National Enterprise Board 1979–80. He was a businessman whom I saw frequently, always with interest.

[2] *Pass the Port*, a collection of after-dinner stories, not too risqué, and, some of them, not too universally known, published by Christopher Brann Ltd, 1976.

I I FEBRUARY
PARIS

___

OWEN CRITICISES THE FRANCO-GERMAN
RELATIONSHIP

Owen has given an interview to the *Nouvel Observateur* in which he makes hostile references to the closeness of Franco-FRG relations. He has elaborated on this in a lengthy interview with the Foreign Press Association intended to set his criticisms of the closeness of the Bonn–Paris relationship in the context of the decisions taken on EMS. It may be true that we suffer from the extent to which Giscard and Schmidt get together and decide things on their own; but I am not sure that it's much good expressing annoyance about it, particularly when the fault lies partly with us for our lack of European-mindedness and for our economic weakness which makes us a dispensable partner.

On Friday the Quai issued a communiqué expressing in lofty fashion its disdain for Owen's intervention. It ran: 'We have a tradition which makes us refrain from the exercise of disproportion in the comments that we make on countries which are friends and associates of France.'

25 FEBRUARY
PARIS

___

A JOINT VISIT BY TED HEATH
AND KAY GRAHAM

Ted Heath's secretary rang up this week and asked if he and Kay Graham[1] could come and stay Saturday night with us. They would be attending the first performance of the new production in Paris of *Lulu* and they hoped we could go to it with them. I said, yes, though we already had Christine Bischler, plus Zorba for the weekend, as well as Rohan Butler.[2]

___

[1]Katharine Graham, owner of the *Washington Post, Newsweek,* several TV stations and over fifty cable TV systems. Co-chairman board of *International Herald Tribune.* She is said, though not by herself, to be the most powerful woman in the USA. A close friend since my time in Washington in the late 1940s and a tennis partner 1979–82.
[2]Rohan Butler, Fellow Emeritus All Souls College, Oxon. Historical Adviser at the FCO 1963–82. The leading scholar on modern British diplomacy.

Kay was tickled in a way to be travelling with Ted and she enjoyed the VIP treatment that went with it. But she did not like the contumely with which newspaper people are treated in Europe compared with the attentions paid to them in the USA; nor, as she found out, did the *Washington Post* ring the sort of bell to which she is accustomed whenever it is mentioned in America. Kay said to me ruefully, 'Pam [Hartwell] is always saying to me: "You don't know how spoilt you are in the USA. Here in Europe newspaper people count for nothing."' Kay added, 'It's rank and status that count here.'

She arrived at our house with only a short dress for the opera. This obviously caused a certain sense of inadequateness. She and Ted had come from a meeting of Willy Brandt's Third World Commission near Geneva to which they would be returning after their night out at the opera. 'People think I am Ted Heath's tatty Third World girlfriend,' Kay complained. Indeed, as they moved about together that evening it was naturally assumed by attendants and huissiers that they were literally together. They were frequently introduced as Mr and Mrs Heath; and when, at the end of the evening, Ted and I arrived back at the Embassy, much later than Kay and Mary, Michel, the Polish night security officer on the front door informed Ted confidentially, 'Your wife has gone to bed.'

The party at the Austrian Embassy after the opera upset Kay. They had asked far too many people for the size of the house and for the scale of entertaining that was possible there, with the result that only a small proportion of the guests could be seated. This included Ted, Mary and me, but not Kay. 'They obviously don't know who I am,' Kay protested and she was right. I don't think that even Raymond Barre, or Madame François-Poncet showed that they understood Kay's importance. Certainly the arrangements were inadequate. There were no tables or chairs and not much food for those not placed. Ted was quite happy next to Madame Pompidou and close to Helmut Schmidt. Kay hung about in an ante-room getting cross until Mary realised that she had to be taken home. Back at the Embassy they found precious little food in the refrigerator. The trouble with the Embassy kitchen is that everything is locked up except at authorised mealtimes so that Bohemian life is impossible.

When Ted and I got back to the house around 3 a.m. we wandered into the Salon Vert and started chatting. We must have gone on for over an hour. He appeared to have no wish to return to the conference. He helped himself to whisky. The subject he wanted to talk about was the state of the nation – he was extremely pessimistic. He thinks it is going to be very difficult for the Conservatives to turn it round.

16–17 MARCH
CHÂTEAU LAFITE

SERIOUS TASTING

This was a long-planned weekend. Eric de Rothschild in his smiling way told me one evening when we were having a drink together that he had a theory about the phylloxera saga. It was a myth, he thought, to believe that wine since the outbreak of the disease had never been so good. What's more, he could prove it with a tasting. We agreed there and then that we would, with the help of one or two experts, spend a weekend at Lafite tasting some pre- and some post-phylloxera wine; and that I would turn our findings into an article for which Derry would take photographs.

So there we were on Friday evening – Mary, Alexandra, Derry and I, accompanied by Odette Pol-Roger whom Eric has also invited for the weekend – catching the train at the Gare d'Austerlitz for Bordeaux. Eric was at Lafite to greet us. The only other guests were a young couple, the Abdys.[1] She is French. He is the son of a rich English baronet famed for his furniture collection and friendship with Joan Drogheda. We had a few glasses of Lafite before going to bed.

The next morning was bright but cold. We devoted it to visiting the *chais* and the cellars. I did a little boning up on the phylloxera problem. I read Cyril Ray's book on Lafite and a good deal of a major work on the château by R. Pijasson that Eric has recently commissioned. It rather looked to me as though the phylloxera legend had already been exploded, but perhaps we would be able to lay its ghost with our panel of experts. Meanwhile the tasting room was being prepared with glasses; and wines were being brought up from the cellar.

Over lunch we limbered up with a few bottles from the better, if not the best, *millésimes*. The only thing to do after this feast was to make for the Atlantic coast and go for a brisk walk along the strand. This we did and all of us enjoyed it intensely.

The tasting began at 7 p.m. Derry had installed his cameras and lights. The bottles were lined up at one end of the table like a sports team before the kick-off. The experts – from Bordeaux and the manager of Lafite – were already in their places. A sommelier appeared in an apron to give the final touch of professionality to our proceedings. He poured out the first bottle and we all made our comments on the forms provided. Some, or rather the experts, then spat out rather than swallowed the wine they

---

[1] Valentine Abdy, European Representative Smithsonian Institution, Washington, since 1983.

had tasted. It was difficult for me from the outset to keep a straight face for the camera and to avoid cribbing what the connoisseurs either side of me wrote about the wines. I was short of jargon, but quickly picked up words like '*charnu*', or '*court*' or 'full-bodied'.

The outcome of our *dégustation* is recorded in an article that I have written for an American paper for which Derry has produced the pictures. Basically, we all agreed that good post-phylloxeras were just as good as good pre-phylloxeras, i.e. that the grafting of vines on to new stocks (from the USA) which had had to be carried out as a result of phylloxera had not impaired the taste of the wine.

24 MARCH

PARIS

———

LAST WEEK IN PARIS

This has been our last week in Paris. The French use the expression I am told, '*rompre l'établissement*', literally to break up the house, to describe what a diplomat has to do when his time comes to an end at a post. It just about describes our feelings faced with the enormity of sifting through all our things.

We dined with my diarist friend, Recteur Mallet[1] of the Sorbonne. Philippine de Rothschild and Odette Pol-Roger were the only other guests. He was insistent that one's diary should not be published for fifty years. I felt less sure about this. He is a most amiable man. Separated from his wife, he lives alone, which he says gives him plenty of time. We talked about Ireland, where he has a house, and the ways of getting to and from there. He seems to enjoy his annual drives across England and Wales to reach it. He lives in considerable style at the Sorbonne. We were waited upon by two footmen in white gloves. I asked Geoffrey Warnock,[2] who happens to be staying with me at the moment, whether this would not be unheard of in present Oxford after a decade and a half of egalitarian rule. He said that he thought that this was so but that white gloves might still put in an appearance at Cambridge from time to time.

As we descended the enormous stone staircase to be shown something

———

[1] Robert Mallet, Rector University of Paris 1969–80. Poet, playwright and novelist.
[2] Geoffrey Warnock, philosopher, Principal Hertford College, Oxon 1971–88. Vice-Chancellor, Oxon 1981–5. A profound but unpedantic scholar who breathed fresh life into Hertford College.

of the Sorbonne I saw, to my surprise, the unexpected and bearded figure of Hugh Arbuthnot[1] coming into the entrance hall from the street. He approached me and told me, in a low voice, that following Richard Sykes's[2] murder by the IRA in The Hague that morning there were reports that the terrorists were planning to strike elsewhere and that the Ambassador in Paris was said to be one of their targets. There had been an anonymous telephone call etc. He suggested that for my return journey I should abandon the Rolls-Royce and follow him. Showing as much sangfroid as we could we completed the tour of the Sorbonne. We then dismissed our driver and returned with Hugh. We left the Rolls for Odette so that she could be taken home in it, a service she told me afterwards that she greatly appreciated, interpreting it as a sign that we had no worry that she might be assassinated in mistake for us.

Since then the Préfecture of Police have attached three security men to guard me whenever I set foot outside the Embassy. Two accompany me and one drives their car which they describe as *banalisée*, i.e. not looking like a cop's car. The Commissaire also told me that their dress would be *banalisée*, by which I assumed he meant that they would wear mackintoshes.

I went for a walk this afternoon and was surprised by how closely they followed me. It was like being pursued by a double-shadow. It makes an otherwise simple stroll through Paris a somewhat self-conscious affair.

François-Poncet has given a large men's lunch to say goodbye. He tried to get people from different walks of life. For instance I sat next to Madeleine Renaud[3] whom I have never met before. Her husband, Jean-Louis Barrault,[4] was also present. When I came to make a speech I was able to refer to the fact that Gladstone's favourite audience had been one of actors.

François-Poncet made a long and extremely eulogistic speech. I thought it very good of him to take such trouble because he really has got an awful lot to do at the moment. Though slightly elegiac the speech did not have in it quite the forebodings of the one made at my farewell dinner given by the Misérables. After I had spoken, the club's oldest member got up and said, '*Je vous souhaite une bonne fin de la vie.*' Philip

---

[1] Hugh Arbuthnott, member of Diplomatic Service. Paris Embassy 1978–83; Ambassador to Rumania 1986–91; to Portugal since 1989–1993, to Denmark 1993–.
[2] Richard Sykes, member of Diplomatic Service. Deputy Under-Secretary FCO 1975–7. Ambassador to The Hague 1977–9 when he was assassinated.
[3] Madeleine Renaud, French actress and author. Comédie Française 1921–47; co-director Compagnie Madeleine Renaud-Jean-Louis Barrault since 1947.
[4] Jean-Louis Barrault, French actor and producer. Founder and Director Théâtre d'Orsay 1974–81.

Rothschild who was at the dinner apologised to me profusely afterwards.

I made quite a long reply, heavily prepared, in answer to François-Poncet. I spoke a bit about the system *de pensée Cartésienne qui inspire la politique étrangère de la France*. (Courcel has alluded to this subsequently in a speech of his own.)

I also expressed sadness about leaving which was genuine. Jean-Louis Barrault came up to me afterwards and embraced me on both cheeks. One or two British guests, whilst saying that they also liked the speech, promised that they would not try to kiss me.

President Giscard's farewell lunch for us was full of drama. I received a call on Monday morning, rather early, around 9 a.m. from Jacques Wahl, the Secretary-General at the Elysée. He said that he had tried without success to reach me on Saturday. He wished to convey an invitation from the President for a lunch in our honour on 22 March which was in three days' time. I expressed regret that I would have difficulty in accepting as I was giving a lunch myself that day. There was silence at the other end of the line as if Wahl was waiting for me to say that I would cancel my lunch and come to the President's. I interjected that unless the President specifically asked me to do so I would have difficulty in getting out of my lunch as I was entertaining the President's parents and Madame Brantes who was Madame Giscard's mother. Another silence down the line before Wahl asked, 'Well, what do you suggest then?' He added that the President was very busy and that he would be leaving for Moscow on 29 March. I proposed as one solution that the President should take over my lunch party. Wahl agreed that this was an idea and he undertook to consult the President about it.

He rang me back in a matter of minutes to say that the President liked the idea. He would be inviting his parents and Madame Brantes to the lunch on the 22nd in my honour. I told Mary of this change of plan. She was quite pleased to get out of giving a lunch party ourselves so soon before our departure. I gave the Elysée the names of the other invitees to my lunch which included the Minister of Transport and amounted to a total of twenty-seven. The party has for long been known in the Embassy as the 'geriatrics' soirée'. I thought that the President might at any rate like to invite some of our guests such as the de la Hay Jousselins who were friends of his. Wahl was shortly on the line again. The President had decided that it would be difficult for us to cancel all our guests. He could not invite them all as he had his own list. Could I manage Wednesday 21 March instead? I said that I already had an engagement but that I would make myself available, so it was fixed for that day. Later at our lunch, which we stuck to, and which went off quite well, the oldsters seemed delighted to be there and were in blissful ignorance that they had at one time been on the point of being dropped. Edmond Giscard said that his son had telephoned about the idea of switching lunches and he had advised against. At our lunch I sat next to the president's mother, Madame Giscard, whom I like very much indeed. A great admirer of Beatrix Potter, I detect in her both sensitivity and resilience, qualities that her son has inherited. She told me, apropos of what I no longer remember, that she had been a lifelong liberal unlike Edmond (her husband) who had always been a royalist. 'When Vally was elected President I asked him whether this did not reconcile him to republicanism.' On my other side was Princess Paul, widow of Prince Paul of Yugoslavia.

For the President's party we were summoned to the Elysée at 12.50, which meant a rush for me as I had a decoration ceremony that morning. I had taken some trouble preparing a speech that I had committed to memory and that I repeated to myself in the car as we drove round the block to the President. The other guests were: the Geoffroy de Courcels (but conspicuously not the Beaumarchais), Wahls, Mérillons, Robins, Bourges (Minister of Defence), Hargrove (*Times* correspondent) and the Jean-Louis de Ganays.[1]

We were placed in file round the edge of the room by Humbert de Lyons to await the arrival of the President and Madame Giscard. They both shook hands all round before the President, who is always extremely courteous in manner, came over to have a word with me about the early age of retirement in our service and about the posts at which I had served. We talked about Poland. I got off on the wrong foot by saying that I knew he often went to Poland shooting. He said that that was the excuse. Such visits gave him the chance to talk to Gierek who told him many interesting things about the Russians. For instance, the last time he had seen Gierek he had said how nervous Brezhnev had become in the face of the US-Chinese rapprochement. This had greatly affected Giscard's attitude. I thought to myself of Choiseul's advice to Talleyrand: 'A minister who moves about in society is in a position to read the signs of the times even in a festive gathering, but one who remains shut up in his office learns nothing.' (This is quoted by Bernard in his *Life of Talleyrand*.)

While we were talking, Giscard's two dogs, Jugurtha, a braque and

---

[1] Guests: Jacques de Beaumarchais had displeased the President in the course of Giscard's state visit to London in 1976. Jean-Marie Mérillon, French diplomat. Ambassador successively to Jordan, South Vietnam, Greece, Algeria, NATO, Switzerland and the USSR. At this time he was Director of Political Affairs at the Quai d'Orsay. Gabriel Robin, French diplomat. Adviser at the Elyseé 1973–9; Director Political Affairs at the Quai 1979–81. Ambassador and Permanent Representative to NATO since 1987. Yvon Bourges, politician and overseas administrator. High Commissioner in various African countries 1948–61. Minister of Defence 1975–80. Charles Hargrove, *Times* correspondent in Paris 1966–82.

Sambo,[1] a labrador which had been the Queen's present, were scrabbling at the French window asking to be let in out of the rain. The President gave orders that Sambo be admitted. He came in like a tornado and stayed with us throughout lunch. The President twice got up from his seat to direct him now to one, now to another, corner, but to no avail. He went up and down amongst the legs of the guests.

The rest of the the guests went in to lunch and we remained behind to accompany the Giscards. He went in ahead of her and was served before anyone else – all very monarchical. I was on her right. Madame Wahl was on my other side which delighted me. Madame Giscard and I chatted about this and that: travel, fishing, gardens. She said that they were hoping to go to Greece this summer. They have a bit of land there, but no house. She thought things would be fixed up in the course of President Tsatsos's forthcoming official visit to Paris. She said that official visits were tiring, one was either waiting or rushing. Sympathetically she said that it was quite impossible to sightsee if someone was shouting into your ear and showing you everything. Giscard leaned across the table to ask me if I had been at the Jean Monnet funeral and whether Lever (who had represented the British government) was in the Cabinet. I said that he was and explained that he had no department.[2] This rather baffled the President. Giscard also asked me if I ever visited the provinces and, like a good boy, I was able to assure him that I did. I know that he attaches much more weight to provincial than to Parisian opinion which indeed is often critical of him.

The President made a generous quite short speech that began particularly well. He said that there was something he did not understand. He was asked to give his *agrément* to the accredition of new Ambassadors. Nobody asked him if he agreed to an Ambassador leaving. Had he been asked if he agreed to my going he would have said no.

I was not able to be so elegant in my reply. I had expected the President to speak rather longer which meant that I had to cut down mine and this meant a certain amount of mental juggling. I did not want to lose some of the best balls I had been planning to throw into the air but would obviously have to drop some. However I stuck to my joke about dogs which went down well so I decided to plough on with another joke. This is more or less what I said: 'Mr President, there was one moment when I feared for our relations (I noticed a look of surprise and even alarm come over his face). This occurred when a British journalist interviewed my French gardener. Patriot though he is, he, like his coun-

---

[1] Sandringham Sambo, the Queen's present to the President at Buckingham Palace. See entry for 12 June 1976.
[2] Harold Lever was Chancellor of the Duchy of Lancaster 1974–9.

trymen, easily identifies himself with his work, and he said that the Embassy garden was the most beautiful in Paris. The journalist asked him if it was really more beautiful than the garden of the Elysée. Though I was sure he had never seen the Elysée garden he said that it was. His remarks were reported in the British press and I was worried to think of reports on this that the French Embassy in London had been sending to Paris.'

Giscard gesticulated as if to say that he had not minded at all and even said something like, 'It's quite all right' so as to reassure me.

We had coffee afterwards in the ante-room where we had gathered before lunch. Giscard was again at his most charming. He asked tenderly after Palliser whom he said he had known well in earlier times. (I passed this on later to Michael who said that he was pleased.) I was not sure whether it was up to me to make a move to leave and I was hesitating about what to do when Giscard himself said goodbye and we all trooped out. I felt quite happy as we walked the few yards home. I felt that the lunch had put some sort of seal on my Paris posting which I suppose was what it was meant to do; and I even thought that Giscard had gone above and beyond what mere courtesy required in such a situation.

The Prime Minister has been here for the European summit held on 12–13 March. I have never known him so benign. Before driving in from the airport I had suggested that he might wish to be accompanied by Donald Maitland who knew much more than I did about the meeting. He asked Donald if he had anything special to tell him and when the latter said no he suggested that I should join him, adding, 'After all it's your car.'

He was very considerate and asked me how much longer exactly I had in Paris. Before the arrival of the party on Monday we had been told that they might require lunch before their departure on Tuesday. On the other hand they might not, as they could want to rush back to London. If possible I wanted to avoid preparations for lunch for forty people if it was not going to be needed so I asked the Prime Minister whether he thought he would be staying. 'I've got out of questions in the House tomorrow,' he replied, adding, 'I don't see why I shouldn't enjoy some of that food I read about.' He was presumably referring to a piece by Kenneth Rose in the *Sunday Telegraph* the previous day, reproducing one of Mary's menus. 'No, if you can have me, I would like to lunch with you. I look forward to it,' he said graciously.

As we drove between the Grand and Petit Palais he asked me what they were for, and I replied for art exhibitions. 'How I look forward to being able to do that sort of thing,' he said, 'to look at a few pictures for a change . . .' Then, almost as an afterthought, as if he sensed a political audience, he said, 'But I must win the election first.'

Callaghan asked to be shown over the house after lunch, expressing great interest in the history. All very strange because he must have been here countless times before, though I remember a terrible gaffe by the Embassy in 1964 just after Labour had come to power. There was a meeting in Paris that Callaghan, as Chancellor of the Exchequer, had to attend. Nobody from the Embassy took any notice of him. Nick Fenn[1] of the Private Office had to give him dinner. I am sure it took him a long time to forget this snub. Now, on this visit, you might almost have thought that he was casing the joint against the time when he was appointed Ambassador here. Certainly he was showing a very different attitude to that of Helmut Schmidt at breakfast-time that morning.

Schmidt came to the house for a bilateral breakfast with Callaghan. As they went upstairs together Schmidt gasped, saying how grand and luxurious the Embassy was. 'Would you like to buy it?' Callaghan asked, with a laugh.

'Not only would I not like to buy it,' Schmidt replied in his most Schmidt-the-lip manner, 'but I wouldn't even like to live in it.'

Later, when I was showing Callaghan some of the splendours of our house about which the French have none of the puritanical inhibitions that afflict the Germans and the British government at the present time, he asked me what the Federal German Embassy was like. To which I answered that it was even grander than ours, though not as nice. Callaghan showed surprise. He seemed to suspect that Schmidt had been reacting out of envy. I said that Schmidt was a puritan. He demurred saying that he was not like Stafford Cripps.

15–16 APRIL

COMBE

FAREWELL TO FRANCE

The last weeks in Paris were such a rush that I had no chance there to record what happened. The Office gave a farewell party in which Kenneth James made a moving little speech and presented me with a dog-token on behalf of the staff, that is to say for the purchase of a dog of any race in the United Kingdom.

---

[1] Nicholas Fenn, member of the Diplomatic Service. Assistant Private Secretary to the Foreign Secretary 1963–7. Head of News Department FCO 1979–82. Ambassador to Burma 1982–6; to Ireland 1986–91; High Commissioner in India since 1991.

Sabine and Philippine[1] organised a farewell party for some of our French friends at which they had intended to give us a present, a Fontaine Wallace such as can be seen in the streets of Paris. I have always had a penchant for these fountains and I suppose lots of people in Paris knew this. Chirac had promised that the City of Paris would meet half the cost, perhaps to be seen as part repayment of the debt they owed to Sir Richard Wallace who had given the city the original fountains. Without this contribution a fountain would have been beyond the means of our friends. However, at the last moment, some official in the Hôtel de Ville with considerable financial responsibility and with no less considerable animus against Chirac, said that he could not approve the gift. If Chirac persisted in going ahead with the idea he would organise hostile publicity about it. Chirac said that he was prepared to meet the cost out of his own pocket. When, very belatedly I heard this, the whole story having been kept from me, I said that, touched as I was by the thought, I could not possibly accept. Apparently no second-hand fountain was available and they were having to have a copy made at the enormous cost of fifty thousand francs which was equivalent to about six thousand pounds. When, therefore, the party took place on the last Thursday evening all our friends were there but not the fountain; nor Chirac which was perhaps as well because many of those present were Giscardians, including close relations. Philippine made a nice speech in which she unveiled a photo of a fountain. I replied saying how touched and sad I was but that the event had produced a new fable de la Fontaine which began:

Maître Corbeau sur son arbre perché
Tenait en son bec un Wallace ...

I put finishing touches to my valedictory despatch. The main subversive tenor of this document has been leaked to Sam White in Paris who wrote quite a sensational piece about it in the *Evening Standard* with the result that some people in the Office have been getting rather hot under the collar. Someone has written a minute, so I have been told, saying that it is most unfortunate and that it will make enemies of many who supported us over the Berrill Report.

The Chancery, under the direction of Nicky Gordon-Lennox, gave me a farewell lunch at the bistro, the Louis XIV. It was one of the most enjoyable lunches I had in the whole of my time in Paris. I was surprised when one of the members of the Chancery said at lunch; 'Do you know we are four grammar school boys to three public school ones?' It had

---

[1] Sabine Wyrouboff and her sister, Philippine de Ganay.

never occurred to me that this question of class education featured in the minds of those self-confident and able young men whom I had observed daily at the morning meetings at the Embassy. My only complaint is that the new members of the Service speak so indistinctly – nothing to do with accent, but simply without clarity of diction.

On our last but one evening in Paris we were entertained by the Private Office, plus the Gordon-Lennoxes. We started off at Philip's flat in Montmartre. From there, accompanied by the security guards, we went to the Escargot restaurant. Mary baled out after that, but the rest of us proceeded to the Crazy Horse. I asked Carol[1] if she had been there before. She said that she had. I asked her if she had enjoyed it. She said that she had. She had liked the music. She sat through the show as inscrutably and impassively as usual, but no doubt appreciating the music! I appreciated the pretty girls, and, for the first few numbers, the elegant way they stripped from wearing practically nothing to absolutely nothing.

Our last day was spent packing and clearing up. I wrote reports on many members of the staff and signed innumerable letters. I was still signing as we crossed the Channel the following day. Most of these were letters seeking money in support of the British Hospital.

The chef did us unproudly for our last supper in the house. Somehow we had expected a great spread but in fact it was a rather meagre meal. Derry, who was spending the night with us, suggested that he had acted out of kindness, out of a wish to break us in gently into the austerity we would find at home.

We set off for Calais at 8 a.m. on Sunday 1 April. The Consul was at the ferry-port to meet us, as were the Mayor and the chairman of the Chamber of Commerce. They came on board with us to say goodbye. We were given a cabin by Townsend Ferries where we all drank champagne and where we were served bacon and eggs during the crossing.

It has all been too much of a rush to think of regrets and of what we would miss. Yet I was heartbroken at having to say goodbye to all those who had worked with us. In future everything would be so different that it would be like entering a new world, so dissimilar that it would be difficult to make comparisons and even to look back. Yet I knew that one day recollection would be a source of great pleasure and I dared hope that this journal might serve as a colourful reminder.

---

[1] Carol Schumann, my Private Secretary in Paris and then in Washington; she was married with a child but managed to look after us all with unobtrusive and gentle efficiency.

WASHINGTON

1979–1982

1979

16 MAY
LONDON

APPOINTMENT TO WASHINGTON

Paris, I thought, was my final destination in the diplomatic caravanserai. Having reached the retiring age of sixty on 1 April 1979 I returned to England where I began the process of adjustment to a very different life lived at a very different pressure. However dissimilar the circumstances I had the sensation which Winston Churchill has described when suddenly bereft of office: he felt like a diver too quickly hoisted. Not that for me there was any surprise. The date had been fixed for the ending of my career. Nevertheless, I cannot say that I had given much thought in advance to what I would do in retirement. I had a vague idea that I might write a biography or some work of history, hoping that the knowledge and experience I had acquired en route would make up for the erudition that an academician can accumulate in a lifetime of reading and research. But this prospect came to a sudden and unexpected end.

On the 4–5 May I was attending an election night party of Pam Hartwell's.[1] Her parties were a traditional and enjoyable feature of elections. The guests, many of whom arrived direct from their constituencies where they had just been elected or re-elected to parliament, were drawn to the political-social honeypot that Pam managed to create. In the early hours of the morning, by which time it was clear that the Conservatives were going to win the election, I ran into Peter Carrington.[2] 'If things go all right,' he said, 'I shall be wanting to get into touch with you quite soon.' From this remark it was easy to deduce that he assumed that he was going to be Foreign Secretary in Mrs Thatcher's government,[3] but I had no idea what he might be thinking of for me. This, however, became apparent a few days later as related in my diary.

---

[1] Pam Hartwell, daughter of 1st Earl of Birkenhead. Wife of Michael Berry, created Baron Hartwell, 1968, chairman and editor-in-chief the *Daily Telegraph* 1954–87. With verve she conducted a salon in London for journalists, politicians and latterly for theatre people until her untimely death in 1982.

[2] Peter Carrington, Foreign Secretary 1979–82. Despite the brevity of his tenure he stamped the office with his personality and achievements. His resignation over the Falklands War did him honour but was a loss to the nation.

[3] Mrs Thatcher won the 4 May 1979 general election giving her an overall majority in the House of Commons of 43.

18 MAY
COMBE[1]

CARRINGTON'S CALL

At 9 a.m. on Thursday 16 May George Walden,[2] the Foreign Secretary's Private Secretary, telephoned me at our flat in Dorset Square[3] to say that the 'boss would like an important word with you in twenty minutes' time'. Would I be there? I said that I would be.

Mary and I continued to hang up pictures and talk about what should go into the day's shopping list when Peter rang, asking, 'How are you?'

'How are you?' I retorted.

'Very tired,' he replied.

'I'm not surprised.'

'Nicko, I want you to go to Washington.'

'Aren't I too old? Am I allowed to?'

'I can do anything.'

'Well, will you let me give it a little thought? I will ring back.'

'Yes, of course. Nicko, you should know that the offer was made first to you know who. It was a Num question'.

'No, I don't know who.'

'Yes, of course you do.'

'Yes, I get you'.[4]

'I wanted you to know this because you may hear later that you were not the first choice.'

'Thank you. I quite understand.'

Mary and I discussed the surprising news. She said of course I must accept. What was I hesitating about? I would have been the only man who hesitated, as I had done, before accepting Bonn, Paris and Washington. Anyway she liked Americans and I was too young to be planting sweet peas all day (as I had been doing the previous weekend). It wasn't as though books were flowing from my pen and I wasn't really suited to the City.

---

[1] Combe, village in Berkshire where I have a cottage. Michael Stewart, former Ambassador to Athens and Kingman Brewster, US Ambassador to London, also lived there – hence the remark of the sporting fraternity that it is easier to shoot an Ambassador in Combe than a partridge.
[2] George Walden, MP, member of the Diplomatic Service which he left to enter parliament. Resigned as junior minister and took up journalism with the *Daily Telegraph*. An attractive and brilliant man of decided views and uncertain métier.
[3] Dorset Square, where we had a small apartment.
[4] It was Heath.

I rang George Walden back later in the morning and said that I accepted. He replied that Peter would be seeing Peter Jay[1] over the weekend. They did not want to give him the bum's rush. The general feeling was that he had done quite well. The present government did not want to give the impression that they were hounding him out in a hurry. Nothing would be announced until they had talked with Jay to find out his wishes.

Michael Palliser, now Permanent Under-Secretary in the Foreign Office, also called: 'May I be the first, as they say, to add my ...'

'Thank you. It was a great surprise.'

'So it was to me. It was nothing to do with us. It was entirely the Secretary of State's doing.'

He went on to say that I must keep the news very secret and that he did not know when I would have to go. It depended much on Jay. Did I have any particular wishes?

I said that I was easy.

Roy [Jenkins] telephoned me last night saying, 'I've known about it since last Friday.' He said that he was delighted but added; 'I'll tell you who will be furious: all the ex-Ambassadors, Gladwyn[2] for instance. Not that it matters.'

I agreed on both points.

He was most friendly and thoughtful as always. He is so capable of putting himself in someone else's shoes. He is a wonderful friend. We agreed to meet as soon as possible.

This is the best moment of a new appointment, when it remains secret to you and you can indulge in a few daydreams while talking and ostensibly thinking about something else. Not that I was quite so thrilled about Washington as I had been about Paris. I was less anxious about it also; and not at all sorry to abandon retirement so soon.

[1]Peter Jay, Ambassador to USA 1977–9.
[2]Gladwyn, member of Diplomatic Service 1924–60. Permanent Representative UN 1950–4; Ambassador Paris 1954–60. Deputy Leader of the Liberal Party, House of Lords 1965–88. He has been noted for his intellectual energy and his grand, rather than diplomatic, manner.

24 MAY
LONDON

____

CALL FROM HEATH; TALKS WITH JAY
AND CARRINGTON

Ted Heath telephoned me this morning.

'I hope you did not think I was standing in your way,' he said.

I laughed. He went on to say that we had always planned to have a dinner after our return from Paris. It would have to wait now until the European elections were over.

Almost immediately afterwards I saw Michael Palliser. He said that he wanted to scotch the rumour that was rife that my appointment had been unpopular in the Service. On the contrary he, and everyone with whom he had discussed it, were delighted. It would help towards breaking down the rigidity of the sixty-year-old retirement rule.

I had a long talk yesterday with Peter Jay. He came to Brooks's for tea and a drink. It began as a threesome with Isaiah Berlin serving as a go-between. I heard later from Andrew Knight,[1] a great friend of Jay's, that the latter has great admiration for Berlin. Jay talked about the book he was planning to write. It was intended to show that neither capitalism nor socialism had the answer. He described his life in the United States with great gusto; there had been much travel including thirty speeches a week and visits to fifty states a year.

He told me that they would be staying on in Washington after he left the Embassy. He hoped that this would cause me no embarrassment. I said that I would welcome his company and counsel. Later, I thought to myself how I should best reply publicly if asked whether I minded Jay staying on in Washington and perhaps commenting on the American scene for the British media and for that matter for the American press. Above all I would have to stop myself giving a flippant answer.

I took to Jay's openness and exuberance. I was struck, and said so, by the time he devoted to talking to me about the organisation of the British governmental machine in the USA. He said that his interest in this subject might have owed something to his naval background.

When I saw Peter Carrington the next afternoon I noticed how tired he was. George Walden told me that he had not expected to find quite

____

[1] Andrew Knight, journalist and newspaper executive. Editor the *Economist* 1974–86; the *Daily Telegraph* 1987–9. Chairman Times Newspapers since 1990. His flexibility, courage, good looks and success have inevitably led to controversy.

such a heavy load of work. He was having to start the day at 6 a.m. to get through the papers. The Office hours so far, George commented ruefully, were just as bad as under David Owen. But morale in the office has rocketed since the appointment.

Referring to my appointment to Washington Peter said, 'You're a brave man. It is very good of you. I can see that you might well have preferred to become a tycoon.' He went on to explain why he had chosen me. He wanted someone who would not be inferior intellectually to Jay ('who had done quite well. I like him') and yet would not be a run-of-the-mill official. He wanted someone with panache.

He told me that Rhodesia was going to be a problem. He got on well with Vance.[1] He doubted whether Mrs Thatcher would become buddies with President Carter.[2] He said that she was proving very dynamic. She got on well with Schmidt who had asked him, Peter, what to call her. In the event he had said 'Prime Minister' the first three times, then no appellation for a while and finally Margaret.

Peter said that my valedictory despatch had been identical with his election programme. He asked me what Andrew Knight was doing about publication of it in *The Economist*. I said that Ian Gilmour[3] had asked him to hold it up. So had I. He had led me to think that he had received the text from three different sources. Peter didn't seem to attach a great deal of importance to whether or not it was published.

Mary and I drove to our cottage on Friday after attending Faith's[4] funeral at the Putney Vale Crematorium. It poured all day yesterday. Despite that, I did not succeed in getting down to the task of doing any background reading on the USA, nor even to the answering of the many letters and telegrams that I have received. Cynthia Kee[5] says that my address must now be Combe-les-Deux-Eglises.

---

[1] Cyrus Vance, US Secretary of State 1977–80, a high-minded public servant who resigned from the State Department in 1980 over the US hostage operation in Iran.

[2] Jimmy Carter had been President since January 1977.

[3] Ian Gilmour, writer and politician. At this stage he was Lord Privy Seal and a member of the Cabinet; he represented the FCO in the House of Commons. Since dismissal from office by Mrs Thatcher he became one of her most trenchant Conservative critics. He and his wife Caroline are close friends.

[4] Faith Henderson, my mother, who died aged eighty-nine.

[5] Cynthia, wife of Robert Kee.

25 MAY

LONDON

—

MORE ABOUT THE APPOINTMENT

Marie Palliser[1] has just telephoned to congratulate me on the appointment and said how much she had liked my valedictory despatch which has now been published. She is both a highly realistic and unstuffy person; and is also extremely loyal to Michael.

The news of the appointment broke when I was in Dorset for the night staying with Freddie Warner,[2] having spent the day helping him with his European election campaign. We reached his home for dinner at 10 p.m. where Simone was awaiting us with a delicious meal. As we arrived, there was a call for me from George Walden who told me of the toing and froing over the announcement of my appointment. Vance, the US Secretary of State, had approved. Also the Queen, with delight. Vance was now communicating with the President by telephone. The odds were that they would have to issue a communiqué in the night because Apple, the *New York Times* correspondent in London, had apparently got hold of the story and was intending to publish it.

After a rather short night I set off the next morning for London at the same time as Fred departed to resume his election campaign. I switched on the car radio to hear the news of my appointment.

By the time I reached Dorset Square the place was under siege with press men wanting to interview and photograph us. Mary had been answering the phone non-stop since early in the morning.

Later at the FCO I was photographed and interviewed by the press. Ham Whyte, the head of News Department, gave me much helpful advice, putting my mind into a transatlantic groove rather than the much more inhibited European one to which I have been accustomed.

Mary and I managed to go to the Chelsea Flower Show that evening. We had a celebration dinner with Alexandra at the White Tower. I was sad to see John Stais[3] looking so much older and less active.

I have had a wonderful press and will have the greatest difficulty living up to it. It is strange that the Washington post should engender so much more publicity than the Paris Embassy. It certainly does. Already I am

---

[1] Marie Palliser, wife of Michael Palliser.
[2] Freddie Warner, member of the Diplomatic Service. Ambassador to Tokyo 1972–5. MEP 1979–84. He was a contemporary of mine in the Service, which meant, inevitably, that, posted to different parts of the world, we saw little of each other until retirement.
[3] John Stais, proprietor of the White Tower Restaurant where I had lodged forty years before. He remained a friend. I wrote an obituary of him published in *The Times* on 14 September 1983.

beginning to see that I will have to work out a few lines and ideas for public statements. The first essential is to learn a good deal more about my own country. Fourteen years abroad have not helped me to be able to speak authoritatively on what the British are thinking and doing. In France they did not care much, aware how much better they were getting along than we were.

8 JUNE

LONDON

HULLABALOO OVER THE LEAKED DESPATCH

The hullabaloo over the leaked despatch published by the *Economist* has gone on all week. Many people, e.g. Rees-Mogg,[1] Marcus Sieff[2] and David Harlech, have taken the line that the leak was a public service as it was high time that the jolt for which the despatch called was given. George Walden telephoned to tell me the line the PM had taken in an unattributable press briefing in Paris after her meeting with Giscard. The following is her answer to one of the questions:

I must say that I found it a very, very interesting despatch. If I might say so, some of the things which Peter and I have been saying with much less panache and much less style were said in that. As you gentlemen know, it is not only what is said but who says it that gives things some particular significance. One could not quarrel with that analysis I'm afraid. It's all written there in the figures. What I am determined to do is to get the position turned. That after all is why, I believe, we were elected at the general election.

There is another view that confidential documents should not be published. Alec Home and Harold Caccia adhere to this. But others, e.g. Robin Hooper,[3] have written in enthusiastic terms about the leak and the substance of the despatch. Fortunately, Tony Benn has described it as 'pessimistic nonsense' (though he has not criticised the fact of the leak) and David Owen has said that I am out of touch with things in Britain.

---

[1] William Rees-Mogg, at this stage, editor of *The Times*.
[2] Marcus Sieff, joined Marks and Spencer 1935, Chairman 1972–84.
[3] Robin Hooper, member of the Diplomatic Service. Deputy Secretary Cabinet Office 1968–71; Ambassador to Greece 1971–4.

The head of the Security Department in the Foreign Office inter-viewed me. He took the line that it wasn't really a security problem at all. There was nothing secret in the material in the despatch. His only criticism was that it had been over-classified.

The counter-attack is beginning. Anthony Sampson[1] in today's *Observer* asks how the FCO dare criticise others, e.g. the Tory and Labour Parties for pusillanimity towards Europe when the Office themselves were just as blind on the subject. Friday's *New York Herald Tribune* published most of the text of the despatch in the middle page. The *Economist* must be pleased to have stoked up so fierce a debate on the subject.

I called on Kingman Brewster,[2] the US Ambassador, a delightful man, broad-minded, good-humoured and detached. He has rented a house in Combe where we joined them for a drink one evening. She is as enchanting as he is.

16 JUNE

COMBE

AUDIENCE WITH THE QUEEN; BRIEFING FOR
WASHINGTON

Mary and I had an audience with the Queen at 12.30 on Thursday. It is the fourth of these kissing of hands that I have done. Once again I thought to myself how bored she must be having to see every new Ambassador accredited to London as well as those going abroad bearing her commission. She showed no sign of it. Extremely natural, surely one of her outstanding qualities coupled with great self-discipline, she was obviously wanting to find something to laugh about. When she laughs her whole face creases, and this is particularly noticeable because otherwise it is very composed.

An equerry told us what we should do on reaching the Royal Room; bow, walk forward, shake hands. On leaving we should bow again, turn and walk away, but not backwards. The Queen would make it very clear when the audience was ended.

---

[1] Anthony Sampson, writer and journalist. Editor of *Drum* magazine 1951–5. Staff of *Observer* 1955–66, 1973–4. Author of *Anatomy of Britain* 1962, and subsequent updates.
[2] Kingman Brewster, US Ambassador to UK 1977–81. Professor of Law, Harvard 1953–60. President Yale 1963–7. Master of University College, Oxford 1986–8.

We went past large pots of lilies and even larger ones of fuchsias before being shown into the presence. I had rather hoped that we might have been offered a sherry, but I suppose she couldn't start that sort of thing or people would never leave, or be so nervous that they spilled it all over the carpet.

The Queen spoke of our change of plan, i.e. from prospective retirement to the Washington post. We referred to the difficulties of unpacking and packing within so short a space of time. I did not get the impression that this was a very profitable subject and we went on to talk of other things: the energy problem; the fate of the Shah; the materialism of the British people; Mrs Thatcher; my despatch (Why did you write it, the Queen asked, though I must say I thought that the content had made that pretty clear); and her wish one day to visit the west coast of the USA.

At dinner with the Kees we met Conor Cruise O'Brien.[1] Brilliant and funny, he seemed inspired by Susan Crosland's[2] somewhat plodding and naïve questions about politics and history. 'You must be,' he said at one moment, as she waded through some long theory, 'the mistress of the subordinate clause.'

He also talked very solemnly about Ireland. He is a fervent opponent of the IRA and a disbeliever in facile solutions. He is worried by the attitude of Senators Moynihan and Kennedy which he says is music to the IRA. He points out that the Scottish Protestant settlers have been longer in Ulster than most of the population of the USA have been in America.

In the course of my briefing I saw Keith Joseph[3] who was accompanied by officials. I said that the Americans would be interested to hear about the new British government. They would want to learn about its industrial strategy and what he proposed doing to increase productivity. I hoped to be able to enlighten them on the basis of what Joseph could tell me. He flung his hands in the air but revealed little.

He also spoke of my despatch, as did Jim Prior,[4] whom I saw at the end of the week. Prior thinks that they will have more difficulty over wage negotiations than over the proposed legislation on Trade Unions.

[1] Conor Cruise O'Brien, official of Irish Foreign Ministry and of the UN 1944–61. Editor the *Observer* 1979–81. Prolific author.
[2] Susan Crosland, second wife of Tony Crosland, she has written spicy and successful novels.
[3] Keith Joseph, Conservative MP 1956–87. Secretary of State for Social Services 1970–4; for Industry 1979–81; for Education and Science 1981–6.
[4] Jim Prior, Conservative MP 1959–87. Secretary of State for Employment 1979–81; for Northern Ireland 1981–4; chairman GEC since 1984. A non-monetarist, he was soon singled out as not being 'one of us' in Mrs Thatcher's government.

He is very agreeable. I look forward to seeing him in America where he has many connections.

8 JULY
COMBE

A VISIT TO NORTHERN IRELAND

I started the week visiting Northern Ireland. Belfast offered a predictably grisly scene. The army gave me a comprehensive briefing. The GOC, General Sir Timothy Creasey, summed it up by saying that it was ten years since the army had first arrived. His solution is to revert to preventive detention of the five hundred or so terrorists, all of whom are known to the army and the Royal Ulster Constabulary (RUC). The success of this would depend upon the Irish Republic taking the same action as regards suspected terrorists in their territory. The second part of his solution would involve taking the prime role for combating terrorism away from the RUC and giving it to the army. He also favoured appointing a supremo in charge of the whole Northern Irish operation – not a minister, who inevitably has to spend half of his time at Westminster.

From the way he spoke I got the impression that the army did not think they should be asked to go on bearing their present burden much longer in conditions which do not provide for a solution of the terrorist problem. It was a surprise to me to learn that the authorities know where all the terrorists are and that they are hamstrung from bringing them to book because none of the Catholic population dares testify against them.

I visited the Maze prison where the governor, a genial, straightforward fellow, told me with pride about the up-to-dateness of his prison and the high cost of keeping every prisoner. We first visited one of the blocks of the conforming prisoners where there are facilities for learning a trade and exercise. Life there is not too bad. From there I went to the 'dirty prison' where there are about three hundred and fifty convicted terrorists who refuse to conform. They won't wear prison uniform so they go about naked, except for an occasional blanket. They refuse to use the toilet or washing facilities. They cover the walls of their cells with excrement. They pour their urine beneath their doors so that it flows into the corridor. They won't read or have any communication with the prison authorities. When we entered the block, let in by a series of warders bearing keys and whose morale seemed remarkably high, the governor told me not to mind if the prisoners shouted rude things at me.

What in fact happened was that the sound of my arrival was accompanied by a crescendo of shouting and banging on walls and doors. The governor had two of the cells opened and he went in to speak to the terrorists. The rest of us hovered outside overcome by the stench. Fortunately I was not invited to enter a cell and confront the naked and furious-looking prisoners.

That night I slept badly thinking of the appalling physical and moral degradation of these people.

The next day I visited Londonderry and met John Hume[1] and other Catholic politicians. Commander Johnson, the head of the RUC there, was a balanced and informative guide. He said that his security problem would be solved if he could arrest six leading terrorists whose where-abouts he knew. I was surprised to hear that he had regular contact with his opposite number in the Garda in Donegal. From there I went by helicopter to Dublin where I dined and spent the night with the Ambassador, Robin Haydon.[2] A number of Irish officials were present at the dinner. (No minister came, for fear, I gathered, of being contaminated with the British in American eyes.) They deplored the misunderstanding of the problem in the USA.

14 JULY

WASHINGTON

INITIATION TO AMERICAN LIFE

The Secretary of State for Defence, Francis Pym,[3] was expected to fly to Washington in July. It was therefore decided that Mary and I should arrive there beforehand and then return home in late summer to complete our holiday and briefing.

At the time when we reached Washington Jimmy Carter was President and Cyrus Vance was Secretary of State. Carter's standing with Congress, press and public opinion was low, though by no means at its nadir. Shortly after our arrival, after a much-publicised period of reflection at Camp David, he descended from the mountain-top to give a television

---

[1]John Hume, MEP for Northern Ireland since 1979 representing Social Democratic and Labour Party; MP (SDLP) for Foyle since 1983. An influential, moderate yet uncompromising Irish politician.
[2]Robin Haydon, member of the Diplomatic Service. Head FCO news department 1967–71. Chief Press Secretary 10 Downing Street 1973–4. Ambassador to Ireland 1976–80.
[3]Francis Pym, Conservative MP 1961–87. Secretary of State for Defence 1979–81. Secretary of State FCO 1982–3. His book, *The Politics of Consent* (1984) gives a fair account of the early years of the Thatcher government.

performance in which, as if in the confessional before the American public, he admitted to failings. He pleaded for understanding. It was not the sort of leadership that the Americans were looking for when they were still smarting from the humiliation of Vietnam and when there was much criticism that they were not exerting sufficient influence throughout the world to deter the Russians. Confusion, rather than confidence, was created by the surprising resignation of all members of the Cabinet, a step intended to leave Carter free to appoint anybody he wanted to help meet the energy crisis.

In this stifling weather (it is over ninety degrees Fahrenheit and about the same in humidity) we are like luxurious prisoners, able to see, but not to go out. The doors into the garden are all locked, as are the windows. The only living thing that moves in and out of the house is the cat, a seventeen-year-old creature, rather mangey and with only half a tail, but blessed with almost divine authority in this house, judged by the way the servants kowtow to it. They say that for long it was thought to be female, but at some moment in its long history it was diagnosed as male. It was the gift of a member of the Kennedy family, so naturally we treat it with the reverence it clearly expects. The Embassy is its shrine and it knows it. We had a reception this evening for a visiting TUC delegation, led by Len Murray. The cat took up a strategic position in the middle of the Tabriz carpet in the ball room where we received the guests, but, as apparently is its custom, it slunk away soon after people arrived.

This morning when I woke up in my air-conditioned room I could not even see out – such was the condensation formed on the inside of the windows. However, I can perceive enough through the misty panes to realise that it is not my sort of garden, though everyone here raves about it: the grass is thick rye grass, the roses are hybrid teas growing in rectangular beds surrounded by pavements and there are begonias everywhere. The herbaceous borders are full of Juniper trees instead of shrubs and flowers. The two greenhouses have nothing in them but potted ferns.

I have spent most of the day preparing for Francis Pym's visit (he arrives on the 15th) about which I am probably over-fussy having an ideé fixe about the attention MPs and ministers expect from Embassies. What ministerial, parliamentary and official visitors require of an Embassy is not only advice or analysis about the political scene or expertise on this or that topical subject, but transport, food, drink and newspapers. I imparted this tip, at once cynical and schoolmasterly, to the staff when I spoke to them en masse the morning after my arrival; and I got them to re-do Pym's programme.

The main American preoccupation at the moment is energy. In Europe there is intolerance of the USA for gas-guzzling and for the continued low price of oil, half that for gasoline compared with the UK. The Americans are obsessed by the gas-lines and by the fact that the price has gone up by about 60 per cent since the start of the year.

When Alexandra telephoned from London today to ask to speak to me the guard on duty at the Chancery desk disclaimed all knowledge of the existence of such a person. I do not find this surprising. After all Heads of Missions come and go frequently. When Brzezinski[1] telephoned a few months ago to ask to speak to my predecessor the guard at the Chancery reception desk asked him to spell his name and then, predictably, made heavy weather in getting his tongue round it ... 'B..r..z. Spell it again please.'

Brzezinski was apparently surprised by the insouciance of the Chancery guards in not knowing him. But then Zbig may have been unaware of the age-long practice at British Embassies throughout the world of having a particularly qualified band of night-watchmen on duty at their portals and switchboards at all times of the day and night out of office hours. These men rarely know the language of the country in which they are serving, let alone the names of the people running it – which, of course, keeps many tiresome callers from the outside world at bay and provides a unique safeguard against any danger of contamination with the locals, let alone the risk of going native of which the British Foreign Service has a paranoid fear.

But the insouciance *may go too far. One Saturday afternoon when the Washington Embassy telephone switchboard was off duty the Chancery guard took a call from someone with an Irish voice who said that he wanted to come round to murder the Ambassador. The guard reported this to the security officer who asked him how he had reacted to the call, to which the guard answered, 'Oh, I told him that the Ambassador was out and that he should ring later.'*

A crisis arose one weekend when I was in Washington about the international force for Sinai. The Italian Ambassador telephoned the Embassy to speak to me. The security guard acted extremely promptly. He put the Ambassador straight through to the kitchen, no doubt having spaghetti on his mind. The Ambassador had some difficulty in disengaging himself from the chef and getting back to me. That particular guard was in good form. The same day the Greek Chargé d'Affaires

[1]Zbigniew Brzezinski, born Poland, came to USA aged twenty-five, having been at McGill University. Research on Russian and international affairs Harvard 1953–60. Professor at Columbia 1962–77. Assistant to President Carter for national security affairs 1977–81. Promoter of the idea of a 'quick reaction force' – a term which admirably describes him.

called at the Embassy in person to speak to someone. He was immediately
shown up to the canteen, presumably on the gounds that he had come
to the Embassy to talk about moussaka. Henry Kissinger has told me
that he always has difficulty in getting through to someone at the British
Embassy during the weekend. He was inured to this but needed to
summon up all his humour to avoid being upset by the suspicion that
his calls always seemed to rouse.

22 JULY

WASHINGTON

———

PYM, THE CONGRESS AND
THE HARRIMANS' DINNER

Three days and nights of weapons, or, rather, their acronyms, GLCMS,
SLCMS and ALCMS, not to mention MX and the AV8B. Pym acquitted
himself extremely well and he and his wife Valerie were delightful guests.
He did not seem to be overawed by the need to master the details of
these technical subjects. To me these weapons are strange and difficult,
but Pym seemed able to answer questions about them as well as about
Northern Ireland and Rhodesia. The questioning was particularly testing
at a long session at the National Press Club, an event which gave me
pause personally as I myself shall have to address the club in the near
future.

The programme started with a call on Monday morning on the House
of Representatives Armed Services Committee. We found a group of
people, mostly in shirt sleeves, some with ties loosened, helping themselves to coffee in paper cups from a large tin urn. These it turned out
were the Congressmen upon whose every whim and word the Western
world depends. They greeted us in unceremonious but friendly fashion,
the sort of reception we were to receive throughout Pym's visit. They
offered us coffee and we stood about for a while drinking it while men
came in and out of the room bearing files. There was a long table down
the middle of the room and seats either side at three different levels. We
were eventually asked to take our places and the chairman, the Majority
Leader, Congressman Price,[1] a man of seventy-four, opened the proceedings. He did not belie his age. Alternating between the two parties

---

[1] Congressman Melvin Price. First entered the House of Representatives as Democrat for
Illinois 1945.

he then asked each of the Congressmen present, numbering about eighteen, to put questions. The Congressmen were all very polite and welcoming to Pym. Their questions were inoffensive. The whole event was marked by informality. Congressmen came in and out of the room frequently.

This same atmosphere of extreme informality masking, however unconsciously, great power, characterised the lunch we had two days later with the Senate Foreign Relations Committee. Their room was quite small and unimposing: photos of past Senators and Senatorial groups on the walls, a desk at one end, lunch laid on a long central table and a clock on the chimney-piece equipped with a buzzer that rang like a division-bell. It was active during our lunch because of the four votes of the Senate that took place. The Senators had to keep leaving the room to vote which made coherent discussion difficult. Senator Javits[1] asked a detailed question about East–West relations. Before Pym could reply he rose from the table muttering that he had to go off to vote. He never returned. I sat between Senator Mathias,[2] a delightful man who introduced himself as a friend of Kay Graham's, and Senator Claiborne Pell[3], a former State Department official who is a friend of George Jellicoe's and was around in Washington when I was here before, but in a very different capacity. He looks like a character actor playing the part of an Edwardian Englishman at the Henley Regatta. He is vice-chairman of the Senate Foreign Relations Committee and could become chairman if the present incumbent, Frank Church who, incidentally, was only present for a few minutes during the lunch, fails to be re-elected, which is quite possible. Lorraine Cooper[4] tells me that Claiborne Pell adores being a Senator. It is his whole life. He says it is the only place in the world where you rise higher just by being there.

Pym is the least self-important of politicians but I could not help wondering at times during his visit whether he did not think he was being treated just a trifle too unceremoniously. At the end of lunch with the Secretary of Defence, Harold Brown, who is a physicist by training and without any of the politician's arts, Pym turned to him and said, 'Well, I look forward to seeing you this evening.' He was referring to the dinner that was to be given that evening in the Embassy to which he supposed, as it turned out wrongly, Brown would be coming. It was a

[1] Jacob Javits, Republican senator from New York since 1957.
[2] Charles Mathias, Republican Senator from Maryland 1969–87.
[3] Claiborne Pell, Democratic Senator from Rhode Island since 1961 who became chairman of the Senate Foreign Relations Committee 1987.
[4] Lorraine Cooper, wife of John Sherman Cooper, former Republican Senator from Kentucky and Ambassador to India and the GDR. She brought a sophisticated touch to political entertaining in Washington.

return dinner for the one Brown gave on Monday night for Pym. In fact Brown had refused our invitation. He said to Pym, 'No, I won't be coming. I have got a lot of papers to read.' This was not a model of tact but Pym took it philosophically. The Americans are certainly interested in the new British government and its ministers but after several years of Labour government, which they regarded as soft towards the left and trade unionists, they have lost a lot of respect for Britain.

I hoped that Pym did not conclude that just because the Washington scene was messy and their capacity for public spectacle so poor (for example the guard of honour for Pym outside the Pentagon was a feeble little show, the band inaudible owing to jets flying overhead) the USA is weak. This would be a false conclusion. It is just their way of going about things; the democratic process at work in the post-imperial, post-Vietnam, post-Watergate climate.

Sitting next to Brzezinski at a dinner given for us by the Harrimans[1] I was struck by a remark he made. We were talking about the decline in respect for authority in the United States, and more particularly about the lost influence of the Wasps (White Anglo-Saxon Protestants). Gone were the days when the country was run by people like Dean Acheson[2] or – and Brzezinski was about to say Harriman but then hesitated despite the latter's stone deafness. 'To put it crudely,' he added, 'neither Kissinger nor I would have got where we did if the old forces had maintained their influence.'

It was an interesting evening. The other guests were Frank Church whom I have already mentioned, Senator Sarbanes,[3] Clark Clifford,[4] Senator Percy[5] and George Vest[6] of the State Department. When the ladies had withdrawn Harriman said that if Kay Graham had been there she would have insisted on staying behind with the men. We discussed the burning topic of Carter's long-awaited TV broadcast which had taken place the previous evening. It had been part sermon and part ukase on conserving energy; there is great excitement and uncertainty caused by the handling of the Cabinet resignations. A general feeling prevailed

---

[1] Averell and Pamela Harriman. Ambassador on special missions to London and Moscow in Second World War; Ambassador UK 1946. Married 1971 Pamela Digby Churchill Hayward, who had first been married to Randolph Churchill. She was appointed US Ambassador to Paris 1993.

[2] Dean Acheson, US Secretary of State 1949–53.

[3] Paul-Spyros Sarbanes, Democratic Senator from Maryland since 1977. He was a Rhodes scholar, Balliol College, Oxford 1954–7.

[4] Clark Clifford, lawyer and special Counsel of President Truman. Secretary for Defence 1968–9. He was a paragon of the Washington establishment until the BCCI imbroglio.

[5] Charles (Chuck) Percy, Republican Senator from Illinois 1967–85. Chairman, Foreign Relations Committee 1981–5.

[6] George Vest, member of US Foreign Service. Appointed Assistant Secretary of State for European Affairs 1977.

among the guests that whatever good the President's TV speech might have done in restoring confidence to his waning leadership it would have been undermined by the confusion created over the Cabinet resignations. (Kissinger had telephoned me the previous evening and told me that the Iraqis were saying that there had been a coup in Washington but Carter had managed to retain control of the TV.) This has been the theme of a flood of press comment. There is much talk of the incompetence of the Georgia mafia and of Hamilton Jordan's[1] appointment as Chief of Staff at the White House which has done nothing to restore confidence.

Brzezinski thought that the way the matter had been handled had been a mistake. The trouble had come when Jody Powell[2] had announced the resignations of the entire Cabinet, whereas it had been intended as something quite different, that is to say an offer of resignation by Vance, made at the meeting, on behalf of all members of the Cabinet, so that the President should feel free to dispose of all the offices as he wished. Brzezinski had to leave the dinner party early because of a demonstration on behalf of boat-people outside the White House. He was very cheerful and buoyant, not at all what I had expected. Indeed the *New York Times* had an article on Friday saying that his whole style had undergone a transformation recently. He was no longer trying to compete with Kissinger. He had gained much more self-confidence. When I saw him the following day at the White House he was a paragon of frankness and friendliness. We would call each other by our Christian names. We would see each other as necessary but I must not be offended if, at any time, he was too busy to give me much time; and we might even have a game of tennis together.

I had to speak to him about Ireland, a subject that relates more to domestic American politics than to international affairs. I also asked him if he could do anything to ensure that Carter would receive me for credentials the following week. He seemed surprised that credentials mattered at all. I said that they were a mere formality but nevertheless Vance could not see me until I had presented them.

To return to Harriman's dinner, Pam Harriman read out an extract from Mary Soames's[3] life of her mother. I gather that Pam often makes a speech on such occasions. She is very pretty, charming and seductive and, notwithstanding her English appearance and accent, nourishes political ambitions in the USA.

---

[1] Hamilton Jordan, campaign manager for Jimmy Carter 1975–6 and 1980. White House Chief of Staff 1979–81.
[2] Joseph (Jody) Powell. Appointed Press Secretary to President Carter 1977.
[3] Mary Soames, married to Christopher Soames. Biographer of her mother, Clementine Churchill.

25 JULY
WASHINGTON

———

FIRST CONTACTS

This entry on initial contacts shows how much the problems of Northern Ireland dominated the UK's relations with the USA at this time. The British government protested at the refusal of the US to authorise the sale of American handguns which had been ordered by the Royal Ulster Constabulary (RUC). They also resented the amount of financial and moral support, whether direct or indirect, that the Provisional Irish Republican Army (IRA) continued to receive from the USA, without which terrorism in Ulster would have had difficulty in surviving.

Yesterday was credentials day. As we drove to the White House the Head of Protocol explained that Mrs Carter never attends these ceremonies. The President, however, likes to have families present. The Saudi Arabian Ambassador who was presenting his credentials a few minutes before me – our cars were stacked outside the White House like aeroplanes waiting to land at a busy airport – had said that his wife could not come unless Mrs Carter was there. That was the practice in his country. Instead he brought four of his sons with him.

We waited first of all in a room on the ground floor of the White House. The walls were covered in a scenic paper chosen by Mrs Kennedy whose hand was evident everywhere. We were then led away along a veranda to the Cabinet Room. Apparently Presidents can choose the paintings of their favourite predecessors to be hung there and Carter had chosen Jefferson, Lincoln and Truman. A large oval table filled the room. We were told that on resignation, or at any rate on departure from office, ministers are entitled to purchase the chair they have sat on during meetings of the Cabinet. The chair is inscribed with the name and office of the occupant.

We were then shown into the Presence. The President shook us by the hand and said some welcoming words. He then led us over to his desk, at which moment a group of photographers rushed towards us, like a hurricane. The President made a few more remarks about there being no need to introduce 'the Ambassador of our greatest ally'. We exchanged documents and the cameras fired.

Mary was then taken away to chat with the Head of Protocol while the President said that we should have a few words together and he beckoned me to the sofa. The others present were Brzezinski and George Vest.

The President spoke about the importance of US–UK relations and he was laudatory about Mrs Thatcher and in particular about her contribution at the recent Tokyo summit meeting. Subsequently I reported this to London, not only out of sycophancy but because the new government wanted to think that the relationship, whether special or not, has not been impaired simply by the disappearance of Jim Callaghan who, by all accounts, had got on well personally with President Carter. We then had a word on Ireland, and Rhodesia. Carter was much more impressive, I thought, than on the TV screen. His smile is endearing and natural, his gentle manner of speaking and his unobtrusive personality seem more appropriate to private than to public intercourse.

Before our few minutes were up I mentioned the Prime Minister's wish to come to Washington in September. The President said that he would have to look at the proposed dates. 'When is the Pope coming?' he asked. Brzezinski replied that he was not coming till October but that there might be difficulties in the idea of Mrs Thatcher coming in September because of certain internal commitments. 'Well, I'll look at it,' Carter said.

When I came to draft a telegram reporting this, my Private Secretary, Nick Witney,[1] asked whether I could not add that the President, while expressing reserve about the dates, had welcomed the visit in principle. I rejoined that I could not very well do this because the President had not done so. I suspect he has domestic politics in the forefront of his mind and does not particularly welcome the prospect of any interruption. Vance told me later that he thought a visit in September would be very necessary. (I have heard subsequently – 5 August – that the President has replied that he cannot manage to receive the PM before mid to end November. I am sure that he is totally preoccupied in trying to restore his domestic image before the Primaries early next year.)

On my initial call on Vance we quickly got on to the subject of Ireland. The particular issue was the State Department's proposed ban on the sale of arms to the RUC. Vance is a reasonable and agreeable man. I suspect that he may have made some commitment about Ireland to Tip O'Neill,[2] the Speaker of the House of Representatives, which is going to sour our relations. I did not want a showdown at our first meeting. The issue is not one in which reason is going to prevail; and I did not wish to invoke emotion at this initial encounter. I was told of a recent discussion

---

[1] Nick Witney, at the time a member of the Diplomatic Service. He was my Private Secretary in Washington. A first-class public servant he decided to move from the Diplomatic to the Home Civil Service. His place as Private Secretary was taken by Peter Jenkins who immediately showed the adaptability the career demands. He subsequently became First Secretary in Paris and Minister in Brasilia.

[2] Thomas (Tip) O'Neill, Democratic Majority Leader Congress 1973–6. Speaker 1977–87.

between the Irish Ambassador and Governor Carey[1] in which the former, who, like his government, takes a very definite line against the IRA, was explaining what the trouble was in Ireland, e.g. the problem of terrorism and the irreconcilability of Catholics and Protestants, when Carey interrupted to say, 'The problem is not there but here.'

London is as worked up as is the USA on the subject of the sales of arms to the RUC and I foresee much bitterness. The PM feels particularly strongly after the murder of Airey Neave.[2] My own view is that discretion is the better part of valour on this subject of arms sales. They should never have been ordered specifically by the RUC in the first place but by HMG or the British army. As it is, the aim should be to avoid giving the IRA the chance to say that they have won a famous victory and one which shows that the USA are on their side. It would be expedient therefore to withdraw the order in return for a promise that there will be no publicity about it and nothing to suggest that we have been turned down. However, I do not think that Mrs Thatcher in her fighting mood is likely to play it that way.

I reminded Teddy Kennedy[3] of the problem when I saw him. Quite quietly he replied that there was no need to remind a member of his family of the horrors of terrorism. I was intrigued to meet Kennedy who is being increasingly tipped in the USA as likely to secure the Democratic nomination in the place of the discredited Carter and then perhaps to become President. There is much talk of the charisma of the Kennedy clan and of his handsome and winning appearance; all this in marked contrast to the homeliness and lack of glamour of Carter. My first impression was a physical one, of Kennedy's large size. I had not expected to find such a middle-aged, jowly-looking person. My next impression was that of the absence of sparkle in what he said and how he spoke. It was of course the early afternoon and therefore an unpromising time for such a meeting. However, having made all allowances, I said to myself that it would surely be wrong to assume that this man was going to be the Presidential candidate, particularly with Chappaquiddick behind him.

The Republican Minority Leader had told me the day before when I called on him on the Hill that he thought Kennedy would run into Chappaquiddick trouble if he tried to stand. He referred to unpublished

---

[1]Governor Hugh Leo Carey, elected Governor New York 1975. Democratic Congressman from New York 1958–75.
[2]Airey Neave, Conservative MP 1953–79. Head of Mrs Thatcher's Private Office and Opposition Spokesman on Northern Ireland 1975–9. Assassinated 1979.
[3]Edward Kennedy, Democratic Senator from Massachusetts since 1962. Youngest brother of President Kennedy, his career was seriously impaired by involvement in the Chappaquiddick accident in 1969.

tapes of the trial and he implied that it would be Carter, rather than the Republicans, who would see that the dirt became public.

Over the past week or so I have met many Congressmen. My overriding impression is of their great friendliness and warmth. I have only to enter a Senator's room for him to say, 'Welcome. Well, I sure do wish you a good time in Washington representing your great country.' Uninhibitedly they go more than halfway to meet you which is not exactly what happens in many European countries.

There was a savage piece of journalism in the *Washington Post* last week by Sally Quinn,[1] headed 'Rosalynn's Journey'. It began with Mrs Carter supposedly saying: 'He is the Patient. I am the Nurse.'

It described Mrs Carter's tour and speeches intended to reassure the American public that the President is sound in mind and body. We are strongly advised in the Embassy to steer clear of giving an interview to Sally Quinn.

The press set-up at the Embassy is practically non-existent. Peter Jay wiped it out on the grounds that everyone should do his own PR. A First Secretary is supposed to devote a third of his time to 'information'. That is the sum total of it whereas there are forty-five people in British Information Services in New York.

I saw the British correspondents soon after I presented credentials. I made a few off-the-record remarks about the state of US–UK relations at the present time. I said that the queues for petrol had brought home to the man in the street in the USA that the USA was no longer of decisive influence in every part of the world. Reuters reported this in rather stark terms and the following morning John Robinson, the Minister in the Embassy, was telephoned by David Aaron, who is on Brzezinski's staff, with a request for the text. He appeared worried by the Reuters account, thinking it may have indicated that I was belittling the importance of the USA. I told Robinson that there was no text, to which he replied that the incident showed how touchy the administration were at the present time. I can see that I shall have to be very careful on this score when I make any public pronouncement.

I had an interesting talk with James Schlesinger,[2] Minister for Energy, who is shortly to be replaced. By reputation a bluff, taciturn man, Schlesinger began by talking about my father[3] at Oxford. He had been his pupil. He had admired him greatly. Such good ideas as Keynes had

[1] Sally Quinn, journalist, reporter *Washington Post* since 1969. Married the editor, Benjamin Bradlee, 1979.
[2] James Schlesinger, Secretary of Defence 1973–5. Secretary Department of Energy since 1977. A brilliant scholar who served both Republican and Democratic administrations.
[3] Sir Hubert Henderson, Fellow and Warden of All Souls College, Oxford, Professor of Political Economy, Oxford, 1945–51.

had came from my father. He was often in our house. He remembered seeing me then, or did I have a brother? He remembered the jugged hare that my mother had served for lunch. It had been disgusting, how could anyone have thought of eating jugged hare?

When we eventually came to speak about energy Schlesinger said that he thought that one day the USSR would threaten Middle East oil supplies. They would need the oil. The USA's credibility as protector had been undermined by events in Iran. It would be necessary to establish a presence over the horizon in the form of aircraft carriers. He did not think that the US government would have the will to do this and he was therefore pessimistic in his prognosis about the future.

Schlesinger also said how much he hoped that the UK would maintain its present rate of oil exports to the USA. It was low in sulphur content which was what the USA most needed.

13 AUGUST

DORSET SQUARE

MRS THATCHER'S PRIORITIES

Back in England I called on Mrs Thatcher at Number 10.

As I was walking through the hall, and before the front door had shut, a taxi drew up outside and who should step out from it but the unmistakable Mr Denis Thatcher. He was rather younger-looking and more alert than I had expected but then the picture of him that had been forming in my mind's eye owed a great deal – too much – to *Private Eye*. He passed me on his way to the lift where he was still waiting when I caught up with him. Although I was being led down the corridor beyond the lifts I could not resist the impulse to stop and shake him by the hand. I introduced myself and added that I hoped that he would be accompanying the PM to Washington.

He said that he did not think he would be coming to Washington but I would find this out from 'her'. He made a movement of the hand in the direction of the PM's office.

Mrs Thatcher apologised for having kept me waiting. I congratulated her on Lusaka.[1] She replied modestly, saying that they were only just starting. From this we went on to talk about the aborted plan to visit

---

[1] Lusaka, Commonwealth Conference in August 1979 attended by Mrs Thatcher. Rhodesia was the main subject.

Washington in September. She said that she was much relieved. She could not have left London while the Rhodesia Conference was going on here. This and Europe were her first priorities. She did not really see what the point would have been of an early visit to the USA. You could only tackle a limited number of things at a time. It was no good trying to take on everything. What was there to discuss now with Carter? At some time she would want to talk about Rhodesia with the President but it was impossible to tell now when that would be.

I said that the USA administration and public were greatly interested in the new British government. 'I can't help that,' she interrupted rather unexpectedly. 'I can't be expected to take account of that in working out my priorities. Rhodesia and Europe come first.' Eventually we agreed that she might think in terms of a short visit in early December. She might want to talk to Carter then about Rhodesia.

She spoke of the terrible amount of money we were giving to Europe. 'I have the money and they won't get their hands on it,' she insisted with some animation. I interjected that the Europeans have difficulty in seeing us as a poor country when we had the oil. She rejoined that figures of GDP per head spoke for themselves.

When I passed through the door of Number 10 on my way out I was conscious of the large crowd that is always there now, particularly in this holiday season. I wondered if they knew what she was like. I thought to myself that she certainly excites great curiosity and that this is in no small part due to the very downrightness of her views and her categorical way of expressing them – to both of which characteristics I had just been directly and uncompromisingly exposed.

CONTRAST FOR A DIPLOMAT BETWEEN PARIS AND WASHINGTON

Life for a British Ambassador in Washington is very different from that in Paris, not least on account of the need in the USA for the Ambassador to make frequent speeches and press and TV appearances. In Paris these are not expected of him. Indeed it would be thought odd and might prove counter-productive with the French government for a foreign diplomat in Paris to appear to be advancing his country's cause in public or to be thought to be pressurising Congress or public opinion. An Ambassador in France is called upon from time to time to make speeches; but he is not expected to use them as a means of exerting influence on the French authorities.

In Washington it is quite different. Lobbying is an essential part of life there for foreign diplomats as for Americans wanting to secure governmental or Congressional support. It would be regarded there as a sign of lack of conviction in his country's case if an Ambassador did not go out of his way to promote it publicly. Congressmen do not take it at all amiss to be solicited by a foreign diplomat on some piece of legislation in which his country has an interest.

Because of the common language the British Ambassador is probably more sought after for speeches than his diplomatic colleagues. He does not need to be particularly eloquent. The Americans devour speeches, it has been said, as goats do waste paper. It is no good, in response to some press or TV enquiry, for the British Ambassador to reply that he has nothing to say, or nothing new to say. Such a response would not be taken, as it might be in the UK, as a mark of honesty or integrity but as a sign of lack of conviction. It is essential in the USA, given the fact, as James Bryce has expressed it, that in that country the people are sovereign, to proselytise for one's case publicly if one is to win support on Capitol Hill or in the Administration.

16 SEPTEMBER
WASHINGTON

FIRST ORDEALS

The Washington ordeal of a speech to the National Press Club (NPC) is behind me. All new British Ambassadors are exposed to this trial which takes place before a large audience and is broadcast live on radio.

I cannot say that the Embassy staff helped me all that much in my preparation for the Press Club. When I asked for advice, for instance, on what I should say if I got a question on this or that subject, the answer was invariably on the lines: 'Well, I should be extremely cautious; better say nothing if you can; if you have to say something I should stick to generalities.'

I pointed out, quietly to begin with, but my voice and indignation rising perceptibly, that faced with the press, you cannot just say nothing and that one of my responsibilities as the new Ambassador to Washington is to put across to the United States as best I can what the new London government stands for.

The next line of retreat of the officials is to suggest that I refer the audience to some statement that was made in the House of Commons some time ago: 'That will show that you are saying nothing new,' they say triumphantly.

I tried to explain that whereas I am not trying to propound something entirely new, I cannot simply repeat what has been said before, and that indeed Mrs Thatcher does represent a change and wishes this to be known and understood.

I spend some time thinking of ripostes to hypothetical questions recalling Peter Jay's not totally happy comparison of Callaghan to Moses at his NPC speech. I was determined to avoid all biblical allusions in speaking of Mrs Thatcher. Conscious of the Sackville syndrome,[1] or perhaps booby-trap, as it would be better described, I also worked out various ways of dealing with questions about US domestic policy and what I thought about them. If necessary I would use Ernest Bevin's mixed metaphor about the need to avoid opening up a Pandora's box and finding it full of Trojan horses. I also decided to repeat a reply that President Eisenhower was fond of using, according to Tom Griffith[2] who came down to spend the night with us. When confronted with a question that he did not wish to, or could not, answer, he would content himself with saying: 'That is a subject that has been discussed before me.' Tom Griffith, incidentally, a wise and unself-important man, said that Harold Nicolson had taught him how the traditional wisdom of British foreign policy lay, not in trying to find solutions, which was almost always an impossible task, but in seeking adjustments. I decided to preface my speech by recalling my earlier attendances at NPC lunches a generation ago. I could not recall a single thing that had been said at any of the functions I had attended, but I could remember, as I sat in this or that corner of this large room, the sympathy that I felt for the speakers who had the danger either of being so cautious that everyone fell asleep or of being so incautious that they themselves were unable to sleep for nights.

Continuing bronchitis contracted in Corfu at the end of August has

---

[1] Sackville syndrome. As described in my book, *Channels and Tunnels*, just before the Presidential election of 1888 the British representative in Washington, Mr Sackville-West, received a letter from an American asking for guidance that would help him in making up his mind how to vote. He asked what seemed to Mr Sackville a fairly harmless question, whether he thought that the incumbent President, Grover Cleveland, would, if re-elected, continue to maintain friendly relations with Britain. Mr Sackville replied, he thought innocently enough, that he thought he would.

This reply was rapidly leaked to the press; and equally rapidly exploited by the rival Presidential candidate, the Republican, Benjamin Harrison, as being a serious interference by a foreign diplomat in America's political affairs. President Cleveland insisted upon Mr Sackville's immediate recall and Mr Sackville left Washington with his tail between his legs.

[2] Thomas Griffith, an editor of *Time* magazine 1943–67. Editor *Life* magazine 1968–72. He and his wife, Caroline, were close friends of ours.

not helped work. I had to go to the opening of the exhibition of Treasures from Chatsworth which took place at Richmond last Monday. This involved a two-hour drive, a speech and a long attendance in the receiving line. The dinner was prolonged and hot. None of this did my cough any good, nor indeed did the large glasses of bourbon that I drank chez my hostess, Mrs Walter Robertson, who invited a number of people back to her beautiful house overlooking the James River after the official ceremony. I may have been led astray by the bourbon, but I found myself enjoying Mrs Robertson's gentle but lively company surrounded by people who were proud of their British origin. Fortunately I think their minds are focused mostly on the past because they seem to be little aware of the economic difficulties through which we have been going in recent years. As in characters out of *Gone with the Wind*, these people are living delightfully anachronistic lives, waited on by black servants and reading English glossy magazines.

The young Hartingtons,[1] who were also present for the Chatsworth exhibition, were making themselves very popular by their good looks and evident curiosity. Lady Hartington is astonished at the way all Americans meet you more than halfway, greeting you effusively by saying how much they want you to have a good time, or a good dinner, or whatever. I must confess that I had rather forgotten this particular pleasure of being in the south and how reassuring it is.

Coughing badly on my return to Washington where I had many engagements to fulfil before Friday's NPC lunch, I decided to give up all antibiotics. This made me feel much better in myself even if it did not mean the disappearance of the virus.

When the time came for me to speak, I opened my remarks by craving for indulgence. I feared that my voice was not as strong as it should have been. I therefore sought the audience's charity, reminding them of Oscar Wilde's remark that: 'None of us is perfect; I myself, for instance, am peculiarly susceptible to draughts.'

Tom Bridges, who is leaving the Embassy after three years, has told me that he has been brainwashed by the United States in two respects. He accepts without question the consumer orientation of society. The USA aims at selling anything and everything. Nothing is spared in trying to titillate the potential buyer. The other dominant feature to which Tom, the most prudent of men, senses that he has succumbed, is the absence of any confidentiality. There are, he insists, no secrets. Everything becomes public.

---

[1] Stoker and Amanda, he, the Marquess of Hartington, eldest son of 11th Duke of Devonshire.

We had Bernard and Laura Ashley[1] to stay for two nights this week. They were here for the opening of a shop in Washington, the seventy-eighth in all. They were delighted with the main guest room where they stayed. Mary has had it decorated entirely in Laura Ashley paper and materials. The Ashleys are unlike most people I have met in the rag or decorating trade. They seem more like a healthy, middle-aged couple on their way to attend an agricultural show.

I gave a lunch during the week for David Steel,[2] chairman of BP – a gathering of ministers and Senators, fairly predictable, as it turned out, including the non-appearance of one of the Senators.

Heavy pressure in the office preparing guest lists and programmes for the many visiting British ministers who are descending on us.

I have heard that after he had been here a short time Peter Jay, complaining of the high cost of entertaining (apparently he said he spent three thousand dollars per month of his own money) asked the Office: 'Where is the profit?' Rather a good question, I have come to think. Having served the government for long I know, of course, that there is no profit. But with our present exertions and our poor health I am inclined at the moment to ask: 'Where is the pleasure?'

Incidentally we ran into the Jays at the party given by *Time* magazine. He said that he was now going to get down to writing his magnum opus. I gathered he was surprised that people had not expected him to stay on in Washington after ceasing to be Ambassador here. Personally I see no reason why he should not continue to live in Washington – so long as he does not in articles or speeches lead people to think that he is still representing HMG.

23 SEPTEMBER

WASHINGTON

EXCITING EVENTS

We are both struggling with ill-health. Mary has had a very high temperature and is suffering from a patch on her lung. I still have not thrown off my virus which the doctor diagnoses, as he does Mary's, as

---

[1] Bernard and Laura Ashley, founders of the Laura Ashley fabric and garment firm which is established today worldwide. They became close friends. After our retirement, Mary was appointed a consultant.
[2] David Steel, managing director 1965–75, chairman 1975–81 BP. Director Bank of England 1978–85.

pneumonia. The pills I had to take for high blood pressure had a debilitating effect. My motto at the moment is better death than tablets. I have to be well enough to get to New York tomorrow to see the Secretary of State and join him for his talk with Vance.

Mary was too ill to join me one night at dinner with the Bill Moorheads.[1] It was a party in our honour. Other guests included the House Majority Leader James Wright,[2] the Rowland Evanses,[3] the Clayton Fritcheys,[4] Joe Alsop[5] and the Brademases.[6] I sat between Lucy Moorhead and Mrs Brademas who turned out to be a doctor, not that her profession was what struck me most in her company that evening. It was her dress that dazzled me. It was not just décolleté but de-everything, with gaps either side. At one moment in the evening I was delighted to find her left breast resting on my plate. My only reaction was to tell her what a pretty dress she was wearing. I also said that I hoped that she would come to dinner with us soon and wear it at the Embassy. She said that she would come, even if her Congressman husband could not do so. I have now got them both coming on 4 October, a dinner for Jim Prior.

I gave Joe Alsop a lift home. He had not done so well as I had from Mrs Brademas's company – except that he had received free advice from her on how to deal with acne. He asked me in for a nightcap. I was struck by the beauty of his house which in my earlier time here was occupied by the owners, the Johnnie Walkers.[7] Alsop told me that he was bequeathing his library to Wolfson College, in honour of Isaiah Berlin. We gossiped about the Joyces[8] and Max Hayward.[9] Henry Kissinger telephoned to ask where Nancy[10] was. Joe said that she had been

[1] William Moorhead, first elected Democratic Congressman from Pennsylvania 1956. His wife, Lucy, was a writer and excellent party-giver.
[2] James C. Wright, first elected Democratic Congressman from Texas 1952.
[3] Rowland Evans, widely syndicated columnist since 1963; beholden to no party or cause, he was highly respected and read for his views and the information he gleaned and divulged.
[4] Clayton Fritchey, columnist and special assistant to US Ambassador UN 1961–5. Married at this time to Polly, widow of Frank Wisner – old friends.
[5] Joe Alsop, newspaperman and author. Served with the air force in the Far East and on staff of General Chennault 1943–5. With his brother, Stewart, wrote a syndicated column 1945–58, then on his own 1958–74. Subsequently art historian. By nature combative and intolerant he was an engaging personality and was a glittering star in the Washington firmament who lit up our lives throughout our time there. Reston described him as 'one of the bravest and most opinionated columnists of his time ... who ... seldom allowed the facts to interfere with his prejudices'.
[6] John Brademas, Democratic Congressman from Indiana 1956–80: President New York University 1981–91. A Rhodes scholar who gave helpful advice over Oxford's current appeal.
[7] Johnnie Walker, Chief Curator 1939–56, director 1956–69, National Gallery of Art Washington. Married Lady Margaret Drummond.
[8] Bob and Jane Joyce; he was formerly a US Foreign Service officer.
[9] Max Hayward, gifted linguist and translator from the Russian. A Fellow of St Anthony's College, Oxford.
[10] Nancy, Henry Kissinger's wife; a keen gardener.

with him for a drink around 6 p.m. but he had not seen her since.

One day this week I began by breakfasting at the White House with Anne Wexler[1] and her husband. 'It's difficult not to have a feeling of paranoia,' she said, as the coloured waiter served us. She was reflecting the widespread malaise in Washington over Carter's poor prestige. I was surprised by the size of the breakfast-room and the numbers of people there. Presumably, as Carter starts the day so early, his staff tend to take breakfast at the White House. There were lots of cries of 'Hi, Anne' and 'Hi, Joe' as other White House staffers passed the table. We talked about Carter's problem. Later that day I received from the Wexlers a two-volume biography of Jefferson.

I lunched that day at the Senate with the Mathias's. It was fascinating. I joined them for sherry before lunch in his office, an agreeable room containing old furniture and a fairly old labrador. It was not altogether unlike lunch at the House of Lords.

The next morning I called early on Ambassador Henry Owen.[2] He is the President's special assistant for summitry. His office is in the old Executive Building beside the White House. It was difficult getting in there owing to security. I had the identical problem on another day when I called at the same building on Ambassador Strauss.[3] Driving home with Fortescue,[4] who belongs to the Embassy Chancery, I was saying how friendly Strauss had been, and indeed how agreeable and easy it was meeting American ministers or officials. Fortescue said that that was of course true. But one had to remember that although the Americans spoke a lot they might not always tell you everything, or even the essential. Their friendliness could be deceptive. We both mused about the delights of Paris where he had, as I well knew, broken many hearts. He had worked as Private Secretary to Christopher Soames and had adored the job as well as his boss.

Owen greeted me by referring to my valedictory despatch from Paris and saying that he was looking forward to our talk more than to anything he had done for a long time. 'I hope you don't mind,' he said, after we had had a word or two on the oil problem, 'if I take a telephone call in a minute or two from Germany. I must speak to Horst.' He seemed in a fair state of agitation and buzzed his secretary to ask if the call was

---

[1] Anne Wexler, adviser and official working for President Carter and Vice-President Mondale. Joe Duffey was her second husband.
[2] Henry Owen, State Department official 1946–69. Appointed 1977 personal representative by President Carter to prepare for summit meeting.
[3] Robert Strauss, Chairman Democratic National Committee 1972–7. Appointed 1977 special representative for trade negotiations in the office of the President. Appointed Ambassador to Moscow by President Bush.
[4] Adrian Fortescue, member of Diplomatic Service. At this time First Secretary in the Washington Embassy.

coming through. This occurred before we had got our conversation going again and he started talking to Horst (presumably the sherpa in Schmidt's office preparing the way for the next summit) about his objections to the FRG's idea of having an imprecise ceiling on oil imports in 1985. He continued to expound his objections. Indeed he went on and on, and Horst seemed to have no chance of getting a word in. It was all very polite, even charming, but I began to wonder whether Owen was not a bit unbalanced, at any rate on this subject. The time was slipping by. I realised that I was going to have very little chance of a talk as I had to be at the New Zealand Embassy punctually at 11 a.m. for the opening of their new building by Vice-President Mondale and the New Zealand Prime Minister, Robert Muldoon. I must have been half an hour listening to Owen's telephone call when his secretary entered to say that my office was on the line urging me to depart at once for the New Zealand Embassy. So there was nothing for it but to get up and leave. Owen was still speaking on the phone, his eyes closed, as if he was talking in his sleep, so I do not think he saw me go.

However, he telephoned me twice that afternoon to apologise and resume our conversation. I was reminded of Maynard Keynes's account of the difficulties he had experienced in Washington at the time when he was negotiating the loan just after the end of the Second World War because of the way everyone upon whom he called in person immediately became involved in a prolonged telephonic conversation. He came to the conclusion that there was no point in visiting people. It was much better to stay in one's office and ring them up.

I gave a lunch on the Friday for Conor Cruise O'Brien. None of the four horsemen (O'Neill, Moynihan,[1] Carey, Kennedy) nor any of the Congressmen involved in Irish affairs was prepared to come to meet him. We had mostly officials and press. Conor was brilliant as usual. He said that the best thing for the Americans to do was to keep quiet on the subject of Northern Ireland because there was nothing at the moment that could be done about it. No initiative that they, at any rate, could usefully take would help to promote any solution.

---

[1]Daniel Patrick Moynihan, Elected Democratic Senator from New York 1977. Ambassador to India 1973–4; Permanent Representative to UN 1975–6.

6 OCTOBER
HOT SPRINGS, VIRGINIA

A VISIT TO THE HOMESTEAD

We drove here from Washington yesterday, looking at Monticello on the way, to help Mary recuperate from her terrible attack of viral pneumonia. Joe Alsop had suggested the place, saying that it was old-fashioned – 'the sort of place our parents went to' – and that the food was as good as the air.

The sight of this enormous pile of a hotel crowded with people for conventions, bearing identity tags on their lapels, their first name in large letters, set Mary back badly. We felt we would be more suited to the place if we were golfers and could make use, for instance, of the attractive little electric cars, the pride of the hotel, which transport the players and their clubs between shots. However we have been on little constitutionals in the mountain air along clearly demarcated 'trails', sometimes accompanied by a black labrador. I hope and think that the therapy will work.

We agree that we are having a useful insight into one aspect of American life. To the question frequently cast at us as we pass people in the corridors of the hotel, or on the path leading to the various play-grounds – golf, tennis, bowls, buggie-rides or horseback riding – 'Hi, folks. Where you from?' we feel disinclined to respond in the required cheerful tone. Mary wants to reply, 'From nowhere.' I tell her that her accent will give her away.

I have just read a life of Philip Lothian,[1] who was British Ambassador in Washington at the outbreak of the Second World War. Looking like a successful businessman he went down well in many circles in the United States. He enjoyed engaging strangers in conversation – and he played golf. We find there is nowhere to sit outside at this hotel except in front of the tennis courts where we spend hours, our heads buried in books, no name discs proclaiming our identity.

I paid a visit last week to New York where I stayed with the Heinzes[2] and occupied a lovely penthouse overlooking the East River. I had a chance to see Peter [Carrington] and get his mood. He is very open in what he thinks and feels. He is the least pompous of politicians. I don't

---

[1] By T. R. M. Butler, Macmillan, 1960.
[2] Jack and Drue Heinz. Appointed chairman of H. J. Heinz and Co 1959; involved in many community and cultural activities. Drue has a special interest in literature and sponsors the Hawthornden Literary Prize. A most generous benefactor of the London Library.

really know his likes and dislikes because he is very tolerant when it comes to the performance of official duties. Evidently he likes being active but he is not unborable and is, I would guess, quite sensitive to pressure and criticism. In this respect he is unlike Ted Heath or Jim Prior, to pick two examples of men who, in my view, have impervious nervous systems, which make them suited to the rough and tumble of politics.

Peter was extremely considerate to me while I was with him in New York for which I was doubly grateful as I was still not feeling my best and because he was obviously tired. After a meeting with Vance we adjourned to his suite in the hotel, helped ourselves to drinks and sat down for a chat. 'Wouldn't it all be ghastly if it wasn't for this,' he said to me, meaning, I think, if it wasn't for the chance of a laugh and a bit of gossip. A few minutes later when I had said something serious he said, 'Nicko, you're looking very Ambassadorial this evening.' Peter's attitude to politics may be patrician but it is not die-hard. He made an excellent speech to the Council for Foreign Relations and answered questions admirably. Afterwards he said to me that he thought the audience had been a bit long in the tooth. I retorted that in this country they make a cult of elder statesmen. Carter has just called in fifteen wise men to advise him on the handling of the Cuba/SALT II ratification crisis. Their average age is seventy-two. Harriman, aged eighty-six, is the eldest; James Schlesinger, whose hair is even whiter, the youngest.

Peter told me that when they were flying to Lusaka[1] for the Commonwealth Conference on Rhodesia, Mrs Thatcher, who was trying out some special glasses, suddenly asked him if he was worried about Iona[2] who was also in the party. He asked what she meant and she explained that she had been told how an unruly crowd of thirty thousand people was going to greet her, and that it was quite likely that acid would be thrown into her eyes – hence the glasses.

When the plane touched down at Lusaka there, sure enough, was the unruly crowd. Without the slightest sign of fear Mrs T stepped forth from the plane – almost as if she owned the place which indeed she almost did from the moment of her arrival, such was her impact. Peter told the story as an example of Mrs T's unflinching courage.

I was back in New York a few nights later to attend a dinner given by Barbara Walters[3] for George Weidenfeld's sixtieth birthday. I offered George a lift from the hotel and he accepted, provided we could pick

---

[1] Lusaka Conference, see diary entry for 13 August 1979.
[2] Iona, wife of Peter Carrington.
[3] Barbara Walters, the most famous TV interviewer at this time. Author of *How to Talk with Practically Anybody About Practically Anything*.

up Princess Fürstenberg who was staying at the Pierre Hotel. I agreed, and while I waited in the car outside the hotel he disappeared upstairs for a moment to help her with her dress. She came down, large and voluptuous.

George, who apparently had been lionised in New York throughout the week, greatly enjoyed Barbara's dinner for him. He adores New York. Among the other guests were Nancy Kissinger (Henry could not be there as he had to attend Carter's wise men call-up at the White House), Dr Kurt Waldheim, the Israeli Ambassador, Mrs Javits, an array of tycoons from real estate and Wall Street, none of them names to me, and Pat Lawford who has all the characteristic Kennedy gift for challenge. I was telling her how well I used to know her sister, Eunice, in years gone by, and how many people had been after Eunice's hand, when after speaking about Eunice for some time I was interrupted by Pat who said, 'Look here, when are you going to stop talking about Eunice and start talking about me'.

The apartment shone with glass and metal. The furniture was white. There were squiggles for paintings on the wall; in the corridor photos of Barbara with famous men. We were seated at glass-topped tables. I was on Barbara's right. From time to time she glanced at notes. She then got up to speak. Someone shouted out, 'Unaccustomed as you are to public speaking'. She paid a glowing tribute to George, with a generous reference to me as the new British Ambassador and to other VIPs present. Then George spoke, fluently and confidently, referring to three of his oldest friends who were present – the Israeli Ambassador, Waldheim and me. Waldheim followed with a long and singularly graceless speech. The Israeli Ambassador spoke, also at considerable length. As he got up, Pat Lawford leant across the table to me and said, 'It will be your turn next.' I suddenly realised that my god it would be. What the hell was I going to say? I felt my heart pounding as I racked my brains. Some jokes that came to mind were, I realised, quite unsuitable. Others were destined for a speech I had to make shortly at a large public dinner in New York. However, such was my predicament that I decided that it was first come first served and that I had no alternative but to blow some of my Pilgrim's-dinner jokes.

I enjoyed the evening and the chance of meeting New York's jet-set. The party was made easier for me by my pleasure in wine and I was amazed, once again, by the way George seems to get through such events without a drop of alcohol.

I was back at the hotel where I was staying – the Carlisle – at about 1 a.m. I woke up in the middle of the night and got out of bed to go to the bathroom. I opened a door which closed behind me, only to find that I was not in the bathroom but in the hotel corridor and that my door was locked against me. I was in my pyjamas. Calls of nature were pressing. What could I do? There was no telephone. The entrance to the staircase was shut. So I rang the lift just in case there was a lift-boy on duty. By great luck there was and, when he arrived, he seemed not at all surprised to see me in my pyjamas. He disappeared to the ground floor to fetch a master-key as if this was a regular part of his duties, which, indeed, it may well have been.

I had two British ministers, David Howell[1] and Jim Prior and their wives to stay at the Embassy this last week. Mary was still not well enough to take part. For me the task of organising dinner parties is not the least onerous part of such visits. I have to think out whom to invite and then when someone cries off, which happens almost invariably, whom to ask, often at short notice, to replace them.

Howell struck me by his intelligence and coolness. He and his wife were most appreciative and sensitive guests. What surprised me about him was his apparent belief that American leaders would come to see that they must take unpopular measures to restrain energy consumption and that this would not jeopardise their prospects in the next year's elections. He took the line that Mrs Thatcher's unpopular policies had not prevented her getting votes. I cannot say that I think US politicians will respond to this line of argument.

Jim Prior made some very good speeches. He is an excellent performer with a clear logical mind. I also liked his objectivity and insistence on the need for moderation. He told me that 'the trouble is that I am not a monetarist'. He clearly does not expect the tight money policy to stick as the only weapon. Nor does he think that an improvement in the economy or a rise in productivity can be expected before the government has secured a second term in office.

He has an ideal temperament for a politician: imperturbability, patience and stamina. He also seems difficult to bore and does not waste too much time or energy on non-political matters. I think, also, that he can see the wood from the trees. If something were to happen to Mrs Thatcher my guess, on the basis of the admittedly small amount of time that I have passed with him, is that Prior would be a serious candidate for the leadership, particularly if there were to be a move towards the left.

I arranged a dinner partly for him to which I had invited Meany,[2]

---

[1] David Howell, Conservative MP since 1966, Secretary of State for Energy 1979–81. Exceptionally intelligent, he was one of the first members of Mrs Thatcher's government to be victimised for not being 'one of us'.
[2] George Meany, President of American Federation of Labour and Congress of Industrial Organisations (AFL-CIO) since 1955.

Kirkland[1] and his wife Irena, apart from a few Congressmen and journalists. Meany and some of the others cried off at the last moment. I have ceased to worry about this, but it made me view the prospect of the evening with growing gloom. However, as things turned out, it all went swimmingly. Two of the guests were an hour late. We did not wait for them. The food was excellent and for some reason I had decided to serve a particularly good wine, Lafite 1970, little thinking that anyone would notice. Kirkland, however, and his wife were most knowledgeable and appreciative. No less enthusiastic were the Carter Browns.[2] He belongs to the Johnnie Walker tribe of Americans with elegant manners and accent, a dwindling tribe as Joe Alsop never ceases to lament. I was struck, incidentally, by how warmly Mrs Kirkland spoke of Joe Alsop.

In between looking after the two ministers I have been busy on Ireland. I have had to field another telegram from London calling for staff cuts and to attend a reception of the Washington branch of the English-Speaking Union where I shook hands with four hundred people all of whom said, 'Welcome to Washington. Glad to see you,' and where I had to make a speech. In thanking them for their warm greetings I said that I could not help wondering how different must have been the experience of my opposite number in London, Kingman Brewster, when he arrived there as Ambassador. Instead of hearing: 'Welcome to London. Have a wonderful time,' he would have been greeted with proverbial and dampening understatements by my compatriots such as: 'Hope it's not too bad,' or 'You'll get used to it.'

11 OCTOBER
CHICAGO

PRINCESS MARGARET IN CHICAGO

I am here for a night to attend a dinner given in honour of Princess Margaret to raise money for doing up the backstage of Covent Garden, not, to my mind, an altogether straightforward piece of fund-raising given that we are in the heart of the Middle West. HRH admitted this in her speech before the showing of a film about the dilapidated state of

---

[1] Lane Kirkland, since 1969 Secretary-Treasurer AFL-CIO. A trade union official with wide interests and contacts. His wife, Irena, was a 1949 refugee from Czechoslovakia who adapted quickly to Washington life.

[2] Carter Brown, director National Gallery Washington 1969–92. Pamela, his wife, helped to inspire the grand soirées given by the gallery.

the theatre behind the scenes. She said, 'You may well wonder why I am here.' I think that the audience, of whom a high proportion were millionaires, was indeed a bit puzzled. Nobody, however, was so crude as to mention the word money, let alone that the aim of the evening was to get people to take out their cheque books and contribute large sums. I had to admire the confidence that enabled HRH to be there in that particular capacity.

The function took place in the casino, a delightful Edwardian-decorated building. The film about the state of Covent Garden was long, but it was not easy to square the circle of showing how awful everything was and, therefore, how necessary it was to raise money for it, and at the same time to hold the attention of the somewhat sophisticated people present, few of whom were greatly interested in opera or ballet. Prince Charles did the commentary in the film and when he first appeared on the screen there was a flutter of applause.

I arrived in Chicago yesterday afternoon and was immediately struck by the glittering modernity and wealth of the place, utterly changed from when I was last here over thirty years ago. The shoreline drive along Lake Michigan is almost beautiful, as are the curved skyscrapers, seemingly made of glass. Along with my gasp of wonderment went a sigh of realism over yet another example of the wealth-creation of the USA compared with that of the UK.

Many of the rich women in Chicago leave the city during the winter. They go to Florida where they play bridge and golf and attend women's lunches. Their husbands join them for weekends. I have noticed the prominence in Chicago of the Playboy Club and Playboy Towers and of bunnies generally – in response presumably to a promising market. Chicago has confirmed my view of the solidarity of American women. It is they who cause the problem for Kennedy over Chappaquiddick, not the men. When I am on safari in the United States and find myself seated next to some lady at lunch or dinner she will say at an early stage how much she looks forward to meeting my 'dear bride' – and she means it.

Barely had I written the above than scandal broke over remarks made by Princess Margaret about the Irish being 'pigs'. She has of course been deeply moved by Mountbatten's murder. It was surely very bad luck that her words were picked up and quoted. I am told that she now has to be guarded by five policemen in case some infuriated Irish-American should seek to stone her.

20 OCTOBER
COMBE

REFLECTIONS

Reflecting on the following entry, I regret the irritation displayed over the company of Joe Alsop. He did go on a bit, as described. But this did not prevent him being an original, erudite and loyal friend. Mary and I saw a great deal of him throughout our time in Washington. Many of the most stimulating social occasions we attended took place in his house. In manner he was downright and domineering. Kay Graham, a lifelong friend of his, said that he behaved like an Englishman, by which I think she meant that compared with the kindness and warmth of so many Americans, he was eccentric, selfish and not too considerate of other people's feelings. His accent and intonation were not English even if they had a WASP sting about them. Polly Fritchey, also a great friend, told me how some American who had met Joe for the first time asked her afterwards, 'Why does your friend speak funny?'

As the diary entries reveal, Joe was obsessed by the Vietnam War and by the pusillanimity of all those who had failed to support US military involvement there consistently and whole-heartedly. For him there was no question of forgetting or forgiving in this respect. His attitude reflected his intense patriotism and his hard-headed approach to public affairs, however much his tastes veered towards the aesthetic and humanitarian. To us it was a useful reminder of the trauma of the Vietnam War that continued to affect the American psyche.

Having returned to the UK to attend various meetings I have come to Combe for a night's rest and reflection.

Looking back over this past fairly hectic fortnight from the quiet of Combe I recall a dinner given by Joe Alsop. It was a masculine occasion including Bob McNamara,[1] Paul Volcker,[2] and Mike Blumenthal.[3] Joe was in his most obstreperous form, shouting, as he is inclined to do when there are more than two people present, and coughing and going 'Err ... err ...' between sentences and resorting to predictable abuse of anyone

---

[1] Robert McNamara, with the Ford Motor Company 1946–61, ending up as President. Secretary of Defence 1961–8. President of the World Bank 1968–81. He was one of the most influential figures in public life over two decades.
[2] Paul Volcker, Chairman American Federal Reserve Board 1979–87. A large man who exuded intelligence and goodwill.
[3] Michael Blumenthal, US Secretary of the Treasury 1977–9. Since 1979 chief executive Burroughs Corporation.

who had been what he called 'soft' on the Vietnam War. He monopolised the conversation. The dinner itself was excellent, beginning with smoked salmon, smoked eel and vodka. When I saw McNamara the next day for lunch in the Embassy (for Denis Healey and Nigel Lawson)[1] I muttered something about the problem of social life with Joe and he dismissed it with the remark, 'Yes; but we all know Joe.' Some had in fact known him so well that they had left the dinner party as soon as the meal was over, turning aside with tact, but determination, his entreaties to continue the one-sided conversation in his library.

The talk, when Joe had not monopolised it had been about money, about the sort of salaries that those present thought reasonable in the modern world. I was staggered by the sums they were talking about. Blumenthal had just that day been appointed chief executive of the chemical empire, Burroughs. His salary was going to be several hundred thousand dollars a year. He also said that when he had left the Treasury he had been approached by some firm that organises lecture circuits and been offered ten thousand dollars each for ten lectures.

I found myself wondering what on earth these people, like the millionaires I had met in Chicago, wanted to do with their money. What did they spend it on? I found within myself a seed of revulsion that I knew would grow fast if I heard much more talk about money. In Chicago the millionaires clearly looked down on academics and journalists, not to mention government employees, for the simple reason that they earned little money. When at such gatherings the conversation goes round the table with people revealing their salaries I remain resolutely mum. If I was to say what I earned as a diplomat my reputation would plummet.

I am finding that the unending social round, the need to travel about the United States, as well as to be present in Washington and entertain there, are proving exhausting. I have been told that my blood pressure is too high and that this could bring on a heart attack or stroke. My overriding concern is that I should not let Peter Carrington down. He had trust in sending me here. Would that I felt a little fitter and more dynamic. Mary feels the same. There is no doubt that we should have had more of a gap between finishing up in Paris and coming here.

I enjoyed an evening with bankers in New York at the Morgan Guaranty; also the lunch the following day with New York editors. At both I had to assume omniscience and answer questions on literally anything from anti-trust legislation in the USA to HMG's attitude to the control of immigration, via the inevitable subjects of SALT II, Northern Ireland and the current attitude of British trade unionists.

---

[1] Nigel Lawson, at this time Financial Secretary to the Treasury. See diary entry for 27 October 1979.

Last Sunday I attended a two-hour service in Washington Cathedral conducted by the Archbishop of Canterbury, a performance that was compared with the Pope's recent appearance on the US scene. Mary went off to carry out some function in Dallas that afternoon. David Steel[1] arrived. We talked about Jo Grimond[2] and his new book, an autobiography. We both agreed, rather unoriginally, about the waste of Jo's life. I suggested that he might have been taken more seriously and given some establishment job after he had given up the leadership had he not been so charming, modest and unambitious. We also talked about Jeremy Thorpe[3] who, according to Steel, was a talented fund-raiser. Steel is highly agreeable personally and a delightful companion for a chat about politics and people.

27 OCTOBER
WASHINGTON

POWER TALK WITH ZBIG

I invite Brzezinski to breakfast – the most popular meal for members of the Administration, or, at any rate, the only one to which one can be sure that they will turn up.

Talking of power politics and imperialism he referred, as he had done when I had sat next to him at the Harriman dinner, to the years he had spent at an English-type prep school (presumably in Canada soon after leaving Poland) and to the pride the headmaster had taken in pointing to the large portion of the map of the world that was painted red. He said that the Americans had never had that feeling of empire.

He did not think that it would be a sensible way, even if practical, which is was not, to try to stop further Soviet-Cuban expansion by drawing a line on the map and saying to the Soviet government that they must not overstep it. Nor did he believe in the idea of a code of conduct. He thought that there was no difficulty in letting the Russians know that there were limits to American acquiescence, and he implied that there was much more regular contact between the Kremlin and the White House than meets the eye. 'They can be made to understand,' Brzezinski

[1] David Steel, MP since 1965. Leader Liberal Party 1976–88. Co-founder Liberal and Social Democratic Party 1988.
[2] Jo Grimond, Liberal MP 1950–83. Leader Liberal Party 1956–67. With his leonine looks, good humour and original cast of mind, he was a fine Liberal Party Leader, apparently free from any hankering after personal gain or advancement.
[3] Jeremy Thorpe, Leader Liberal Party 1967–76.

assured me. He also hinted at various steps that the US government would be taking to show the Russians that they were not soft, e.g. by military exercises and fleet movements and by increases in the defence budget for MX.

Zbig has a reputation for seeing things in black and white and for being anti-Soviet to the point of intransigence, partly to distance himself from Kissinger, whose reputation he is said to resent. I did not find him like this during last week's conversation. He was cautious in his ideas of what the Quick Reaction Force might do. His enjoyment of the position he holds is infectious. 'I love it,' he says, without inhibition. He said at one moment that he did not think he would return to academic life, or 'academe' as he called it, though he might write a book. Much less, he thought, had happened during his time at the White House than when Kissinger had been there, so his book, he surmised, would inevitably be less interesting.

He is very pleasant to talk to, ready to express views and lively in his manner of expression. I decided that I would try to repeat the breakfast idea, so much more satisfactory than bearding him in his office in the middle of a busy day.

I also saw Marshall Shulman,[1] the Sovietologist who is now installed at the State Department, a quiet, erudite man whose very tentativeness is impressive. He does not expect direct Soviet military threats to occur and he is sceptical about the mid-eighties strategic inferiority window theory.

I think that Shulman also sees the situation in Eastern Europe as being very unstable for the Russians. Rather to my surprise, Zbig had spoken of possible revival by the Russians of the threat to West Berlin. I said that I thought that the present German situation suited the Russians well. He did not demur, but one day in the future . . .

During these hectic briefing days I had Healey staying in the house and I gave a lunch for him and Nigel Lawson, Financial Secretary of the Treasury. I also invited Paul Volcker, Bob McNamara, Clark Clifford and Larosière. The lunch became a monetarist seminar. Volcker disclaimed all title to being a monetarist which rather took the wind out of Lawson's sails. My task was to promote a stimulating debate and to stop Healey and Lawson having a dogfight across the whole length of the table. My success, I think, was only partial.

I had an interesting conversation with McNamara. He sees the main problem for the world in the future as arising from the increasing birthrate in the underdeveloped world. I said how ironical it was that

---

[1] Marshall Shulman, since 1977 Special Adviser on Soviet Affairs to the Secretary of State.

the Pope should be becoming a popular world figure once again when he stood against the one thing that could control the population problem.

That evening we went with Healey to a performance of Stoppard's *Night and Day* at the Kennedy Center. Maggie Smith was the star; and what a star she was. Without her the play would, I think, just have been an argument. She lifted it into drama.

I went by Concorde to London the next day. After the tripartite meeting on the Caribbean I ran into Ian Gilmour and went and had a chat with him. Apparently Prior is in Mrs T's bad books. He insists on being heard in Cabinet even if it means shouting. Ian said that he had not succeeded so well. She had interrupted him after he had only managed to say 'I believe ...'

Peter Carrington asked me to see him. He told me that he had to go over to Number 10 to see the Prime Minister. The problem was to explain the complexity of the issues and the need for subtlety in dealing with them. He, like everyone, admitted to her indefatigability.

Roy Jenkins, with whom I dined one evening, had spent two hours with Mrs T that morning talking about British insistence on reducing their contribution to the EEC budget. Her view is that because we consider that we are being hard done by, others should think so too. Clearly Roy foresees a terrible summit meeting ahead in Dublin.

The Foreign Office are trying to cook up some package to put to ministers to give us a better European image and therefore ease the way towards making progress on the budget. This would include something on defence and our joining the EMS. Goodness knows if Mrs T will buy it. One of the troubles, as Peter C himself admits, is that a great deal of the time of ministers continues to be taken up, as it has been for years, with the problem of Rhodesia. So, other subjects of far greater long-term importance to Britain get neglected.

In London I went to an evening party given by George Weidenfeld to launch Kissinger's book.[1] It gave me the chance to see a great many people in a short space of time and to find out the sort of things people are hating or loving at the moment and what they are talking about. Predictably their predilections had not changed much since I last saw them, only a few months ago. Antonia Fraser[2] was very friendly. She intends coming to Washington shortly. Mark Boxer[3] was in search of

---

[1] Kissinger's book: *White House Years (Memoirs)*, 1979.
[2] Antonia Fraser, writer; daughter of Frank and Elizabeth Longford. Married, first, Hugh Fraser MP, second Harold Pinter. Prolific author; entertaining and eloquent TV and radio performer.
[3] Mark Boxer, cartoonist; appointed editor the *Tatler* 1983. Worked for *Sunday Times* 1962–79. Cartoonist: *The Times* 1969–83; *Guardian* 1983–6; *Daily Telegraph* 1986 until his premature death in 1988, only six years after marrying the TV presenter Anna Ford, his second wife. An artist of singular talent and charm.

new prey. Marigold Johnson[1] buttonholed me about her British-Irish Association. Elizabeth Longford was eager to know about Michael's[2] American girlfriend. Frank spoke about the two innings he had had with Kissinger. He said that Kissinger agreed with him that Nixon was a genius manqué. Pam Hartwell was indignant with Courcel over the Franco-British Council. Grierson[3] invited me to the opera in Washington. George Weidenfeld said that he would be coming to Washington for Christmas.

In fact it was very much the usual sort of George evening with even greater names than usual being dropped, including Sir Harold and Lady Wilson. Princess Ira Fürstenberg was there. She is known locally as the IRA. She telephoned me the next evening to ask me to join them for dinner but I said that I was going to the country. She then put Niarchos on the line to talk to me. He said that they had only invited me because they couldn't find anyone else in London. I thanked him for his generous thought.

I flew to New York for a dinner of the Pilgrims where I had to make a speech.[4] This was an ordeal for me, not least because I had to wear white tie and decorations, all of which I have difficulty in putting on – and keeping on. It did not turn out to be an evening to be remembered except for the warmth of our American hosts and the friendliness of the Pilgrims. New York was at its best, cold and sparkling. Spending the night at the Knickerbocker Club I had a delightful walk in Central Park where I watched the seals surfacing in the late afternoon sun. The leaves were all turning, the sun dancing. I came across the statue of a sledge-dog commemorating support for some Polar expedition. The dog's copper back was shiny from being sat upon by decades of children. The four biggest statues nearby were of Columbus, Shakespeare, Robert Burns and Walter Scott. I tucked this observation away in my mind in case I was called upon to say a few words at the Scottish ball to which I was bidden that evening.

Barbara Walters telephoned. She wanted interviews with Princess Margaret and Mrs Thatcher. She invited me to join her table that evening at a party for the New York Opera. In accepting I found myself entering a new world – glittering, theatrical and, of course, rich. Everyone seemed to have known Freddie Warner when he was in New York. Everyone –

---

[1] Marigold Johnson, wife of the author, Paul Johnson (see diary 31 May 1980), has organised British-Irish Association conferences with charm and persuasion.
[2] Michael Pakenham, member of the Diplomatic Service now in the Washington Embassy.
[3] Ronald Grierson, since 1968 director GEC. Director, S. G. Warburg 1958–86. Executive chairman South Bank Centre 1985–90.
[4] All new British Ambassadors have to address the Pilgrims, whose president since 1955 was Hugh Bullock, a distinguished and dedicated proponent of close Anglo-American relations.

except me – seemed to know Beverly Sills[1] for whom the party was being given. Rather ashamed, but unresisting, I felt myself drawn like a moth to these lighted candles.

We lunched with the Wrightsmans[2] in New York. They have an apartment on Fifth Avenue full of priceless furniture and pictures. Jayne said that she had given all the good things to the museum. She was lamenting her failure to buy a painting, a landscape, or rather an iceberg-scape, which had been sold at Sotheby's that morning for two and a half million dollars. It was by Church, an American nineteenth-century artist. The Annenbergs[3] were among the guests. He gave a toast to 'the autumn return to New York of the Wrightsmans'.

We journeyed back to Washington by train, rather a treat after all the flying we have been doing lately. At each station the train announcer expressed wishes to the departing passengers for a happy evening. The track was uneven and the train bumpy so I was not able to read but I was quite happy daydreaming and snoozing, taking stock and recharging batteries.

The Gordon Richardsons were in the Embassy in Washington when we arrived. We found them as agreeable visitors as they had been in Paris. He combines good looks with great plausibility. She is round and jolly. They were full of appreciation of the Laura Ashley room.

One morning I called on Senator Byrd,[4] the Majority Leader. I had been waiting for an opportunity to see him and this came when I received a telegram from London asking me to arrange for Mrs Thatcher to meet Congressmen during her visit here on 17 December. I took the opportunity of my call to speak to him about SALT II ratification, and the importance HMG attaches to it. He said that he might arrange an informal meeting with Senators at which I could put that view across. I said I would welcome it. Senator Byrd was surprisingly dressed; at least I, who am used to the image of Senators as serious figures eager to appear typical representatives of their countrymen, was surprised. He wore a red jacket and a silk smock. Perhaps, as Majority Leader, he finds it necessary to show some panache, not to say flamboyance, and I have

---

[1] Beverly Sills, leading soprano New York. With New York City Opera since 1979. General director 1979–88. Has appeared in most major opera houses in Europe and Latin America.

[2] Charles and Jayne Wrightsman. He was president Standard Oil Company of Kansas 1932–53. Jayne is a connoisseur and generous benefactor of the arts. She is trustee of the New York Metropolitan Museum.

[3] Walter and Leonore Annenberg. A company executive, he is president Triangle Publications. Appointed Ambassador to London 1969–74 he triumphed over an initially somewhat mocking reception. President Reagan appointed her Chef du Protocol 1981. See diary entry 8 January 1990 for description of their property and art collection at Palm Springs, California.

[4] Harry Byrd, Democratic Senator from Virginia 1965–83.

noticed the tendency of some Congressmen to behave nowadays a little like Charles Laughton in *ruggles of red gap*.

On Saturday, while the Richardsons dined happily by themselves at home in front of a log fire in the library, we had to endure a characteristically curate's egg-like diplomatic evening. It began with a concert at the Kennedy Centre at which Rostropovich conducted a violin concerto by Mendelssohn and a symphony by Dvořák, both very moving and beautiful. Then we drove to the Hilton Hotel for an enormous dinner-dance given, like the concert, in honour of the UN Association. There must have been a thousand people in the low-ceiled, hotel diningroom where we sat at a table with a party of businessmen from some Chicago finance corporation. They were very friendly. Mary was very tired. We listened to speeches and applauded the arrival of distinguished guests before settling down to the predictable conversation with our table neighbours: 'Where are you from? I hope you like Washington ... Mrs Thatcher is doing very well, isn't she. We wish we had her here ...'

A rather distinguished dinner was given last Saturday night at the National Portrait Gallery by David Rockefeller[1] and Ripley[2] of the Smithsonian. Despite several speeches I was not clear even at the end of the evening what it had been in aid of. I was seated on the right of the wife of a Republican candidate for the Presidency who was emphatic and loquacious about the nuclear bomb.

Mary did better. She was seated next to Henry Kissinger. We saw a lot of him last week. The Bradens[3] gave a cocktail party for him and his book on Tuesday and this was followed by dinner given by Joe Alsop. The former was marked by the presence of Danny Kaye, the latter by an outburst the other end of the table by Wendy von Staaden, the wife of the departing German Ambassador. Mary was witness to it. There are several versions of what happened, though all agree that it was unexpected. Apparently she talked of the dire consequences that might occur if the USA installed the cruise missile on FRG soil, or, according to some accounts, if the USA didn't install them. Susan Mary Alsop,[4] who has one of the best intelligence services in Washington to which she contributes a good deal of material herself, was not present at the dinner, but this did

---

[1] David Rockefeller, banker. Joined Chase National Bank, New York City, 1946. Chief executive Chase Manhattan Bank 1969–80.
[2] Dillon Ripley, Secretary Smithsonian Institution 1964–84.
[3] Tom and Joan Braden. He was a journalist, having served in Africa and Italy in the war with the King's Royal Rifle Corps. Joan was described to me by Joe Alsop as being somewhat unique in Washington because she was flirtatious.
[4] Susan Mary Alsop, wife of Joe Alsop with whom she was on the best of terms since separation from him. She was no less of a star than he was in the social cosmos of Washington; and was author of several books including *Lady Sackville: A Biography*, 1978.

not deter her from talking a lot about it at her house the following evening.

At the end of Alsop's dinner I had a long and useful talk with Kissinger about Rhodesia. He said that he was four-square behind us and would do everything possible to help. He rang me up two days later to say that he had had breakfast with twenty Senators who were unanimously behind us.

I am reading Kissinger's book with intense pleasure and admiration. I asked him to what he attributed the great improvement in style compared with earlier books. He could offer no explanation – about the only thing I found he could not explain – except perhaps that he had not read a book for eight years. Not only is he immensely interesting to talk to but I am intrigued by the contrast between him and his wife, Nancy. I sat next to her at Joe's dinner. She is much taller than he is and evidently has a highly sensitive nervous system, whereas I wouldn't think that he has any nerves at all. She is very conscious of her surroundings and likes looking for antiques. I would guess that he is oblivious to them. She said that she had liked Tony Crosland. I asked her about this, adding that he had been a friend of mine since Oxford. She said that she had sat next to him at some dinner. On his other side was a woman who talked to him endlessly about the Queen and her admiration for Her Majesty. Exasperated, Tony Crosland had turned to Nancy and said, 'If this woman mentions the Queen again I am going to empty my glass down her bosom.' Clearly Nancy had liked Tony's unconventionality.

On my other side at dinner was Irena Kirkland, also the most agreeable of companions. It would be odd to think that Joe Alsop is a good friend of America's leading trade union boss if one did not have always in mind how different from ours are American trade union leaders. They do not consider themselves as engaged in class war; nor are they wedded to any political party.

Next morning I paid a call on Speaker O'Neill on the Hill. My purpose was to speak about Mrs Thatcher's wish to see some members of Congress during her visit here in December, to fill him in on Rhodesia, and to leave him in no doubt, following a request for information from his office, that we were still wanting more revolvers for the RUC from the US supplier.

The meeting started in very friendly, almost hilarious, fashion. He came into his outer office where I was waiting, wearing a thick white pullover that someone had just brought him from County Mayo. We exchanged pleasantries and he was most obliging. He exuded Irish charm and flattery. We discussed the first two subjects without difficulty, but when I came on to talk about arms for Ulster he stiffened up. He did not at all like what I had to say and our meeting ended on a very different note from that of the start. Fortunately Representative Foley[1] was present. He had just come from London where he had experienced at first hand the strength of feeling there on this subject. He intervened usefully, but this only made O'Neill more taciturn.

13 NOVEMBER
LOCUST HILL FARM, MARYLAND

DOBRYNIN

We are spending a lovely quiet night in the country at Polly Fritchey's farm.

I called on Dobrynin[2] last week. He was jolly, as I had expected. I asked him how he reacted to the present Iranian situation in which a group of students have occupied the US Embassy in Tehran and are holding the staff hostage until the Americans hand over to their mercy the Shah who is undergoing treatment in a New York hospital for terminal cancer. He shrugged his shoulders and said that the Iranians seem to dislike the Americans, the British and the Russians equally. I was rather comforted by this. (The Iranians have now abrogated the Persian-Soviet Treaty of 1921, as well as the Persian-American Treaty.)

When Dobrynin came to the door to see me off he commented, in a way that did not reflect admiration, on the fact that I did not have a Rolls-Royce.

The following day I called on the Chinese Ambassador. Very dull. He made the set speech about the threat we all face (i.e. from the Russians). He commented favourably on Hu's recent visit to London. I was reduced to asking him about the meaning of a large poster on the wall opposite us in the waiting room where we sat. He explained that it was a poem by Mao ('a very good poet'). I then found myself recounting the story of the ping pong matches in which I had played against the Chinese Embassies in Warsaw and Bonn. Ping pong seems to serve the same life-raft role in small talk with the Chinese as does chess with the Russians.

---

[1]Thomas Foley, Democratic Congressman from Washington since 1962. Majority Leader 1987–9, Speaker House of Representatives since 1989. An exceptionally well-informed and dispassionate politician.
[2]Anatoly Dobrynin, Soviet Ambassador to USA 1962–86.

20 NOVEMBER
SHUTTLE NEW YORK/WASHINGTON

RAB IN NEW YORK

To New York to speak at a lunch organised by Barclays International and to attend a lecture by Rab organised by Sotheby's.

Rab gave a characteristic performance, except that his diction has deteriorated. He spoke in one and the same breath of his own aims as a painter – 'I painted with Churchill' – of his membership of various Cabinets, of Plato, Keats, Proust, Seurat, the Post-Impressionists and many other authorities whose words he cited with a brilliant connecting sweep but often inaudibly.

Afterwards we dined as Peter Wilson's[1] guests at the house of a certain Mrs Thew whom nobody knew (by which I mean that Nin Ryan,[2] Brooke Astor[3] and John Pope-Hennessy,[4] among the other guests had not heard of her). I sat between Mrs Doug Dillon[5] and Kitty Carlisle Hart.[6] The latter stayed behind afterwards to talk to Rab and me. I think she could only half gather what it was that Rab was getting at. He spoke of his involvement in English domestic politics and of his time as Master of Trinity as though they were subjects of universal interest. 'If I had been less of a gentleman,' he said, 'I could have become Prime Minister,' and then added with a chuckle, 'or if Alec had been less of a gentleman.'

Without any introductory explanation but with a good deal of scratching of his chronically dry skin he suddenly said to Kitty Carlisle, who is a singer and an actress, her life not having been concerned with politics or with Britain, 'I was able to avoid trouble at Trinity. I stopped the rowing men throwing the others in the water. I said, "You know the water is cold. It will hurt their chests." So they understood and didn't throw them in the water.'

---

[1] Peter Wilson, chairman Sotheby's 1958–80.
[2] Nin Ryan, widow of John Barry Ryan. For some years she has been at the heart of political and cultural circles in New York and London; the mother of Virginia Airlie.
[3] Brooke Astor, widow of Vincent Astor. Member executive committee of New York Public Library; chairman Women's Committee, New York Zoological Society; member Council Pierpont Morgan Library. A vibrant personality, she is a generous benefactor and considerable author.
[4] John Pope-Hennessy. Professor of Fine Arts, New York University since 1977. Director of Victoria and Albert Museum 1967–73; of British Museum 1974–6.
[5] Mrs Doug Dillon, Phyllis, wife of former Secretary of the Treasury and managing director, Dillon Read and Co since 1971.
[6] Kitty Carlisle Hart, author and actress on stage and screen including a prominent role in the Marx Brothers film, A Night at the Opera. Widow of the director, Moss Hart.

He recounted how he had always gone out in society, as had Talleyrand. Kitty Carlisle was mesmerised by the way he talked.

'Are you going to write another book?' she asked, to which he replied, 'Well yes, you see I would like to, so that I could describe Nicko ...'

Kitty C was baffled.

Mary and I spent some time walking about New York. It was a brilliant day and we were awestruck by the city. I do not feel tempted to buy anything but I love the sight of the shops, the mixture of people in the streets, the vendors of hot chestnuts and those great glass rectangular edifices reaching into the sky almost out of sight.

24 NOVEMBER
WASHINGTON
———

USA HOSTAGE CRISIS

The crisis precipitated by the taking of US hostages in Tehran continues and has been compounded this week by the occupation of the Grand Mosque in Mecca and by the student incursion, connived at by the Pakistani authorities, into the US Embassy in Islamabad. We have been involved, as refuge-provider and message-passer. I hope that the USA realises the value of allies but I am not convinced of it. They have for so long been accustomed to pre-eminence that they have difficulty in adjusting to dependence. Vance, however, has been passing warm thanks to Carrington, however much, for tactical reasons, it may be as well not to draw attention publicly to the help we are giving in Tehran. It could only have the effect of inflaming the students, already in a state of frenzy.

30 NOVEMBER
WASHINGTON
———

MORE TALK WITH ZBIG; MALFUNCTIONS IN
SILICON VALLEY

Before I set out for California I saw Brzezinski. Much though I was tempted to do so I refrained from making a joke of the fact that his photograph had appeared in the press showing him at some film-star party the very night he had cancelled at the last moment coming to dinner with us to meet Mary Soames – on account, so he had averred, of pressure of work.

We talked about arms for the RUC, the AV8B, the danger of Islamic revivalism taking on an anti-American form, Mrs Thatcher's forthcoming visit to Washington and, of course Iran. I played my usual record about how much help we were giving the USA there, hoping that this would contribute to our stock of diplomatic capital upon which we should be able to draw for use elsewhere. I had said the same to Cy Vance over the weekend. Vance had been more unstinted than was Zbig in his thanks for this help. He has subsequently expressed them publicly. Zbig wanted us to give increased public support for the American position. I said that we were always expressing our indignation at what the Iranians were doing. We have, incidentally, joined in European Community and Commonwealth pronouncements on the subject since I saw Zbig.

When I am with Zbig I keep thinking of the frequent speculation that he is hoping to become Secretary of State in succession to Vance. The latter has said that he will not serve a second term even if Carter is re-elected. Somehow I don't see Zbig as Secretary of State, any more than I see Kennedy as President. But it is pure hunch and may prove utterly wrong. He lacks that indefinable and essential quality for top political office, gravitas.

Zbig led me to think, more than Vance had done, that the US government might be contemplating military action over the hostages in Iran. But then he is an activist by nature. He asked me whether I thought US policy over the Iran hostages was on the right lines. I told him I thought it was – firmness and restraint seemed to be the only guides.

Our California trip had some highlights which admittedly shine less brightly in retrospect.

On a visit to Silicon Valley, just south of San Francisco, which is the home of the semi-conductor industry, I was given a briefing by a Mr Wells the vice-president of one of the leading companies in this line of advanced technology. He happened to be a Scot, a living example of the brain-drain. He obviously knew all the technical jargon and details but he was not too good at explaining the elementary problem of what semi-conductors can and cannot do. He showed a diagram on a blackboard covered with scientific words – iods, dopants, diodes, integrated circuits – linked by arrows to unscientific words like memory and water and yield. He assumed that we understood how these minute objects are used to store and transmit information, for example to control the consumption of petrol in an internal combustion engine. I was left entirely convinced that all these things would happen but much in the dark as to how.

Rather typically – and satisfactorily – Mr Wells's gadgets all failed to work, though he had assured me, with a spate of figures, that there was nothing that could go wrong with semi-conductors because there was none of that expansion and contraction caused by heat in pre-semi-conductor systems. He wanted to illustrate something by showing a series of slides but the projector behaved liked a bad case of St Vitus's dance. In answer to my question about the future application to industry of this advanced micro-processing technology, Mr Wells gave the telephone as an example. 'You see here,' he said, leaping to his feet and seizing hold of a receiver, 'it is in operation. You see these buttons. They have been programmed. You only have to press one against someone's name and his phone will ring.'

'Let's try,' I said, taking the receiver, and reading out some of the names, I said, 'Let's ring Mr Zoblinsky.'

'Certainly,' said Mr Wells, pressing the button opposite his name. Nothing happened. I suggested another name with the same lack of result.

'There seems to be a malfunction,' I suggested, proud of my high-tech jargon, and Wells (a latter-day H.G.) shrugged his shoulders in agreement. It really didn't seem to be his day until he came on to talk about his daughter's success in the local Highland dancing competition, an activity about as far removed from chips and Silicon Valley as could be imagined. I could see that Highland dancing was going to be less important than semi-conductors for the future wealth of mankind but I was convinced that it was going to provide more immaterial benefit.

3 DECEMBER

WASHINGTON

ANN FLEMING[1]

I have telephoned Ann Fleming who has just had an operation and is recuperating chez Goodman.[2] In cracking form, as she always is in adversity, she said that when Pam Harriman had had some female operation in New York the surgeon had said to her afterwards: 'Well,

---

[1] Ann Fleming, widow of Ian, an enthralling entertainer with rapid repartee, a loyal friend. Her letters, edited by Mark Amory, were published in 1985.
[2] Arnold Goodman, solicitor and the most celebrated go-between of his time. Confidant of Harold Wilson at Number 10, he was described as the 'oil-can' of the government. Chairman Arts Council 1965–72. Director Covent Garden 1972–83. Master of University College Oxon 1976–86. His memoirs Tell Them I Am On My Way were published in 1993.

dear, we have taken away the nursery, but left you the playpen.'

I have just given a lunch for the intelligence community, in honour of Brooks Richards.[1] They could throw no light, only a flood of clichés, on why the Islam world is turning so strongly against the USA, or how to stop it, or what is going to happen next. It was difficult to believe that they were meant to be a bunch of the best-informed people in the USA. But perhaps they were being intentionally tight-lipped.

23 DECEMBER
WASHINGTON

MRS THATCHER'S FIRST VISIT TO WASHINGTON AS PRIME MINISTER

Mrs Thatcher has just paid her first visit to Washington as Prime Minister. Since the idea was first mooted in the summer the wind has blown hot and cold from both sides over the timing. When eventually it came about last week it took place just after British ministers had been heavily engaged in negotiations about Rhodesia and when the US President and government were still intensely absorbed, as was American opinion, by the seizure and retention in Iran of US Embassy hostages. Each side was highly interested, even if not directly involved, in the preoccupation of the other.

The visit gave me surprises on the personal plane. Gloomy had been the foreboding in London and Washington on how the two heads of government would get along together. Mrs Thatcher was seen as having to get over an inherent difficulty arising from the close relations her predecessor, Callaghan, had had with the President, based partly on a common political outlook that she certainly could not share. So the rest of us watched eagerly as the two came out of their corners. It soon became apparent that they were hitting it off well together; and so it continued throughout the visit.

I surmised that the Prime Minister respected the President's matter-of-fact mastery of the very varied subjects under discussion as well as his quiet unpolemical manner of exposition. Carter himself, hailing from a southern state and thus harbouring no atavistic anti-British feelings, was ready to meet the new Prime Minister more than halfway and in a spirit

---

[1]Brooks Richards, member of Diplomatic Service. Ambassador to Greece 1974–8. Deputy-Secretary Cabinet Office 1978–80.

of allied solidarity that was much needed on his side at that juncture owing to the crisis over the Iran hostages.

Also intriguing in the empyrean of personalities to which we were suddenly exposed was the rapport between the Prime Minister and the Foreign Secretary. For various reasons, above all because of the crucial nature of foreign policy decisions and the way the conduct of such policy is bound to attract the limelight, with inevitable domestic consequences, some degree of friction is inherent in the relationship between the holders of the two offices – as indeed in that between the President and the Secretary of State in the US government. The first relationship between a Prime Minister and Foreign Secretary that I was able to observe directly for any length of time was that between Attlee and Bevin in the first post Second World War Labour government; and it was evident to me, as it was to every witness, that the avoidance of strife then depended not upon any clear-cut constitutional division of authority, but upon the forbearance and unobtrusiveness of the Prime Minister. Coming now to the present day, it did not require any profound perception of character to realise that, self-effacement not being Mrs Thatcher's long suit, any more than disregard of his proper responsibilities was Carrington's, tension must be expected. Politicians rarely like listening to each other's speeches which often sound to them over-simplifications. Carrington had to listen to a good many of the Prime Minister's in Washington and New York. His stance in politics is that of a patrician; Mrs T's is certainly not. It was not surprising then that there was irritation. What to me was unexpected was the manner in which Mrs T went out of her way to attribute to Carrington much of the credit for the outcome of the Zimbabwe negotiations. She was also sympathetic towards him personally – understanding in a very human fashion – when, tired towards the end of a long day, he began to worry whether the Zimbabwe agreement would stick. In talks with me, or rather in frequent asides, Carrington paid tribute to her courage. He told me that he liked her very much as a person. He had not always done so; and it had not been easy to begin with because after all he was a Heath-man. But he thought that she was very nice as a human being.

A key moment occurred the first evening at the Embassy. We were discussing the attitude the Prime Minister should adopt on the question of the USA's intention to go to the Security Council under Chapter VII of the UN Charter over the seizure of US hostages in Tehran. The official briefs had recommended caution, emphasising the possible difficulties that might result from too resolute a stance. Mrs Thatcher herself expressed doubts whether she should come out categorically in support of the Americans. Leaning forward on the sofa, Peter Carrington said, 'Margaret, you have got to say, yes. You have got to do so.' He was very decided about this. He swept away all the reservations in the official briefs. I know that he was influenced by the great and consistent help we have had from the US government throughout the Rhodesian negotiations.

However, it was still not clear to me, when our Sunday evening briefing finished, how Mrs Thatcher would play the hand the following day either with the President or the press. I did not have long to wait. In the first few minutes of the first meeting at the White House she announced unequivocally HMG's whole-hearted support for the USA, should they go to the UN under Chapter VII; and she stated this to the press on the White House lawn. The effect of this was like a trumpet-blast of cheer to a government and people badly in need of reassurance from their allies. It got the visit off to a perfect start. Peter's lead on Sunday night had been an important contribution.

Mrs Thatcher was tired the first evening in Washington, one of the few times I have seen her in something less than dynamic form. She explained to me later that she had been taking antibiotics for five days to counter an infected tooth and this had pulled her down. I had noticed at the private dinner in the Embassy on Sunday evening how she had yawned a good deal, which is very unlike her.

In addition to talking to the PM that first evening about Iran we discussed the speeches prepared for her for the following day. The one for the White House dinner was inadequate, so I and others thought, as it did not allow for the seriousness with which the Americans are regarding the hostage problem. Peter said that I had better write an alternative which I did later that night. When Mrs Thatcher came to read it in the car the next day she seemed pleased and said that if I ever needed a job she would take me on as a speech-writer. She folded it up and put it in her bag as she does any document she values and wants to keep handy.

Apropos her handbaggery, I have been told a story from Lusaka. One day when the less affluent members of the Commonwealth were complaining about their economic plight and their need for help from the UK, Mrs T turned to the official beside her and asked, in a stage whisper which everyone could hear, for the sheet of paper setting out the details of aid HMG was providing. Only with difficulty was she prevailed upon not to read this out. However, she put it in her purse and brought it out threateningly whenever any delegates started lecturing her on the need for more British economic assistance.

Mrs Thatcher began her official programme with an interview early on Monday morning with Barbara Walters. Then at 10 a.m. she was standing on the dais in front of the White House whilst honours were done to her by the US armed forces. I was rather moved as she stepped out of the car to be greeted by the President and Mrs Carter, the first woman from the Western world to be received in that fashion. She told me afterwards that she had not somehow expected such a solitary, yet splendid, reception as she had experienced when she drove up alone in front of the White House, the TV cameras whirring and the drums poised to beat.

The two hours of talks went well. The President was quiet, but clear and well briefed. There was only one subject about which he obviously did not wish to speak – arms for the RUC. He admitted to Mrs T that he agreed with her: the licence for the export of the arms should be granted by the USA, but the trouble was that the Congress would not allow it. He advised Mrs T to 'speak to Tip O'Neill about it'.

I told Mrs T beforehand that Carter reacted best to dispassionate argument. Whether because of this, or because she sensed the atmosphere herself, she certainly adopted an unpolemical tone with him. She takes in everything that one says which means that one has to be very precise in the advice and information one gives her.

We had lunch at the Embassy where the Prime Minister was hostess to sixty prominent people. The house and Christmas decorations looked very pretty. Mrs T took a glass of whisky. She had another during lunch as well as half a glass of red wine. I have noticed that whisky seems to be her favourite tipple and, as Peter said to me later in New York, 'Thank God she likes the stuff.' She is disciplined without being puritanical, at least so far as the small pleasures of life are concerned.

Just as we were going in to lunch Mrs T received news that the Rhodesia settlement had been initialled. With her sense of occasion she decided to announce this to the assembled company before they started eating.

We served smoked salmon and game pie. Alas, there was inadequate time for the lunch but many guests, including Peter and Walter Annenberg, said afterwards how much they had enjoyed it. George Walden commented on what a good chef we had, to which Peter retorted, 'It's all Mary.'

The meeting on Capitol Hill was a great success. Mrs T harangued them for ten minutes and then answered questions. They liked what she said and her forthright way of expressing it. Her retinue was somewhat worried by the detailed way she described our budgetary problem with the European Community. Americans like the black and white style in which Mrs T paints everything as well as her candour and lack of reserve. One Congressman rose and asked if she would accept the Republican nomination for President.

The President gave a wonderful party at the White House. We were received by him and Mrs Carter in the Yellow Room on the second floor.

The only others present were the Vances and the Kingman Brewsters. Ushered downstairs, we shook hands with the President again at the head of the line of all the guests – over a hundred I would say – invited for the dinner. Each had been given a little envelope enclosing a card showing the seating place at table – except for those, and they were numerous, for whom there was no room, with the result that they were expected to sit in some ante-room. They opened their envelopes to find nothing inside.

It was an elaborate evening. There were many events and a lot of trouble had been taken with them. The President himself acted as master of ceremonies. He started off with a set speech before the dinner. He was generous about the bilateral relations and about Mrs T, more so, it occurred to me, than mere courtesy required. There was the usual slightly embarrassing joke about the burning of the White House by the British at the beginning of the last century. Mrs T followed, reading out the speech I had prepared for her. It went down well enough and there was sufficient titter, I thought, at the jokes. Both speeches were filmed by a battery of TV cameramen.

As dinner ended we were serenaded at our tables by a troupe of gypsy-like violinists. They played sentimental central European music but neither this nor their costume, which smacked more of the Police than of the Blue Danube, nor the geometrical pattern in which they moved succeeded in creating a romantic atmosphere. The bright lighting was not helpful either. Afterwards we returned to the ballroom in which other guests who had not been invited to the dinner were assembling. The President introduced the playing of some Berlioz and the singing of carols.

The placing at table was odd and not such as to flatter Carrington. Mrs Carter sat on the President's left (no other couples were placed together) Mrs T was on his other side. Somebody quite insignificant sat on Mrs Carter's left. Peter was seated at a distant table. So there was no chance of them all talking together about public affairs. When I described the *places à table* later to some American he was at first surprised then said that Mrs Carter would not have wanted a political discussion at dinner. She wasn't really interested in politics. It was Jimmy she was interested in.

Tuesday morning began for Mrs T at 7 a.m. with a live appearance on TV. At 8.15 a.m. she received the British press correspondents at Blair House. Then to New York where she addressed over two thousand people at a lunch given by the Foreign Policy Association. She then answered questions in a most confident way. The Americans loved it when, as if inviting interrogation, she thrust her head back and exclaimed, 'I like questions,' not to mention her confession that she was an Iron Lady. 'I have to be,' she said. After she had been at it some time she received the usual request from a member of the audience that she should offer herself for the Presidency of the USA.

That evening, after a further round of functions, she spoke at a dinner organised by David Rockefeller. It was for about one hundred and fifty of the leading bankers and businessmen from all over the United States. Mrs T looked her best in a black velvet dress which showed off her blonde hair, still remarkably soigné despite the rigours of the day. When she came to speak she thrust aside her notes and said that she would tell them in as direct a way as possible what she was trying to do and where the difficulties lay. She proceeded to do so in a manner which appealed enormously to her audience who, it must be admitted, were longing to hear her free-enterprise message and were doubly delighted to have it expressed in such ringing tones.

Again there were questions which she answered fluently. Her speech was very ordered with plenty of signposts, and a clear sense of overall direction.

I waved goodbye to them at Kennedy airport with a considerable sense of relief that it had all gone so well; and with the conviction that Mrs T had made a remarkable impact. Before saying goodbye to Peter I said that I would be sending a telegram on the visit.

'Bet you it's pretty oily,' he said.

The telegram I sent rounding up the visit was certainly oleaginous but then I think the visit deserved all the praise I could impart. I reported that there had been great interest in the Prime Minister before the visit and plenty of goodwill had piled up in advance. The results had disappointed no one. One senior Senator who had been present for the meeting on the Hill said at a social gathering I attended, and he said it three times, 'I do not recall any visitor to the USA who has made such an impact.' I asked whether he was referring to visitors to Congress. 'No,' he replied, 'I mean any visitor anywhere to the United States.' He went on to explain to the company that he was not speaking only for himself because he had discussed the Prime Minister with many other Senators and that what had struck them all was 'the candour, the direct simplicity of the language and the process of thought imparted with the orderliness of soldiers in the line'.

1980

―――

8 JANUARY

PALM SPRINGS, CALIFORNIA

―――

STAYING WITH THE ANNENBERGS; DINNER WITH
RICHARD NIXON

I went to Phoenix, Arizona, to address the annual convention of the American Farm Bureau, a gathering of about eight thousand American farmers from all over the country. It might well be asked – and many did ask – why on earth I was invited to speak to the farming community of America. The reason was that the directors of the American Farm Bureau are trying to make their members more internationally-minded, and they came to see me in Washington to ask me to talk about how the USA looked from outside. I am not often invited to address eight thousand people so thought I should not turn down the opportunity. I spent considerable time over the Christmas holiday preparing the speech which I then had to bring up to date to fit the latest developments in Iran and Afghanistan, including the highly topical and pertinent subject of grain sales to the Soviet Union. I also worked out a few jokes, some of them original.

So there I was entering the vast Convention Hall in Phoenix packed with farmers. A woman at the organ struck up a rousing fanfare whenever applause was required. When I arrived the president of the meeting was making a long and fairly inaudible speech. I noticed that the microphones gave a blurred sound that echoed back from the distant wall. Seated in the front row I studied the programme and noticed that my speech, described as an 'address', was to be preceded by 'Tribal Dances', which were under the heading of 'Entertainment'. The convention's programme was to end two days later with another item of 'Entertainment' filled by Bob Hope. Whereas I was to be preceded by Tribal Dances he was to follow an address on 'Soya Bean Production'. My neighbour in the reserved seats whispered to me that Bob Hope would be receiving thirty-six thousand dollars for his appearance.

When I came to speak I was aware immediately of the physical problem of sound and echo in that enormous auditorium. One had to wait for the words to bounce back before one went on. I was even more aware of what was of interest to the farmers and what was not. When I spoke of President Carter and the combination of restraint and firmness that the US had to show in dealing with the Iran problem, there was silence, or rather that sense of hostility, barely suppressed, that is so distinct to anyone making a speech. When I mentioned Mrs Thatcher there was an immediate and enthusiastic response that was very eloquent to me on the podium. She has become a 'cult' figure in the USA as the Governor of Arizona put it to me when I sat next to him at the lunch that day, a party given by the editor of the local newspaper, the *Arizona Republic*.

From Arizona we flew to Palm Springs to stay with the Annenbergs. Their property is particularly luxuriant with oleanders, olives, eucalyptus, citrus and decked out with lakes, swimming pools and a golf course. Shown to our room we were waited upon by an English maid who immediately offered to press our clothes and to provide Mary with hair-rollers. Driving us around his private golf course in his little electric car, Walter shouted cheery greetings to the numerous American-Mexicans mowing and watering.

'I behave,' he said to us with a guffaw, 'as though I were seeking election afresh each day.' We laughed and he went on, 'Yes, I mean it. I've learnt that in life. The more fortunate you are the nicer you have to be to people.'

We were duly impressed by the amazing transformation he had brought to the desert in the space of only sixteen years, as by the masterpieces he had assembled in the house – Toulouse-Lautrec, Gauguin, Renoir and Picasso. 'I cannot resist beautiful things,' he told us, as he showed us some photos of the nine-dragon wall in Peking that he wishes to have copied for erection in his park at Palm Springs.

Tomorrow a marble seat, a copy made in Italy of one he saw at Delos, will be delivered from Los Angeles by helicopter – 'to avoid damaging the lawn'. There were statues and objects everywhere, interspersed among the trees and greens and flagpoles. It is an odd mixture. 'I'd like it better,' Mary whispered, 'if there were no golf course.' The setting of an oasis, which Palm Springs is, in the desert surrounded by bare, rose-coloured mountains, some tipped with snow, is magnificent.

Waking up in the morning was dramatic: the mountains looking pink, seen through the enormous window, and the sprinklers coming on all over the golf course; opposite us the swimming pool was steaming. I was astonished to find that its temperature was over eighty degrees. 'I hate cold water,' Lee Annenberg said to me later. Personally I found it too hot and was exhausted after a few strokes. Walter keeps in touch all the time by phone and telex with his far-reaching business interests. He also manages to play nine holes of golf a day. When the weather gets hot in May they move to Sun Valley in Philadelphia.

He showed us his 'room of memories', a study lined with photographs, nearly all of himself in various groups. A high proportion were devoted to his time as Ambassador in London which lasted five and half years.

There were few pictures of his life before then, yet he was sixty-one years of age when he went there. It had been the highpoint in his, and even more in Lee's, life.

Driving us to the airport she told us about their appointment to London. Walter had always been a friend of Nixon's (I noticed that he always referred to him as Mr President, never as Richard or Dick). He had made the suggestion to him when he came to see them at Palm Springs in November just after being elected President. The appointment was not to be announced for several months. During the interval great pressure had been brought to bear on the President and on Walter himself to cancel the appointment and, when it had become public, there had been great criticism which Lee obviously was still sensitive about. The point was, so she stressed, that Nixon had stuck by it, despite the opposition. He had shown great loyalty and she thought that this quality had been the cause of his undoing with Ehrlichman, Haldeman, John Mitchell[1] etc. He had not been prepared to remove them even when he knew that they were guilty of wrongdoing.

I was bowled over by their warmth and spontaneity. He calls her 'Mother'. Joe Alsop says that I have been 'reached', a word he prefers to 'corrupted'.

We knew that Nixon was coming to dinner that evening. Annenberg had telephoned me in Washington a week or two earlier saying that he assumed we would want a quiet evening. He had mentioned to President Nixon that we were coming and he had shown a wish to meet us. He would therefore be dining with us. Would there be anyone else we would like him to invite? I could not think of anyone, not being a habitué of Palm Springs. Various people to whom I spoke afterwards said that I should have asked for Bob Hope, a close friend of Nixon's.

Before dinner the Annenbergs explained that they had invited another couple from Kansas and that Nixon was not able to arrive by helicopter because of the weather at San Clemente. He would, therefore, be coming by car which took about two hours. They had thought of taking us to Bob Hope's ball that was taking place in Palm Springs but realised that we would be tired. So we would be spending the evening with Nixon and the couple from Kansas – 'her father was in the food business.' I rather wished that we were going to Bob Hope's ball but said of course that we would much rather stay at home. Lee said that Bob Hope travelled around so much that his wife, Dolores, advised them to say 'Hello' to Bob when they caught sight of him.

When we emerged from bathing and changing, Nixon was already

---

[1] John Ehrlichman, Bob Haldeman and John Mitchell were all implicated in Nixon's Watergate downfall.

there. In person he was uncannily like the image as seen on television or in the press – the same jowl, smile and expression that is somewhat equivocal in its effect.

As we sat having caviar and drinks before dinner, and after Nixon had made quite a good effort to recall the names of the various British Ambassadors to Washington whom he had known, Annenberg asked him about the book that he was writing. He needed very little encouragement to launch down the full sequence of chapters. 'There's one on the Middle East,' he said, 'and here I pay tribute to the British'. I smiled gratefully. He clearly was out to please. We moved to the dinner table and he continued with the book so intensely that he scarcely had time to eat. He looked very fit. He preferred to hold forth than to listen. He was eager to discuss the current political scene. To my surprise he said that he thought Kennedy would get the Democratic nomination. This was because the economy would go into recess by the third quarter of next year and Carter would be blamed for the high inflation and high unemployment. He said that the US public were not interested in foreign policy. Nixon said that Kennedy was 'dumb and unprincipled'. His election as President would be the worst thing for the USA. In fact he did not think he would be elected. He thought that it would be a Republican. Asked which Republican would be likely to get the nomination, Nixon said that he had not come to a view. He didn't really seem to be interested in any of the possible candidates, though he thought it might lie between Reagan and Bush. He seemed to think that Bush's trouble might be that he was 'too nice to be President' which I found interesting coming from him. He went on to say that people thought that Ike was just a nice guy with a warm smile. He, Nixon, knew better. He could be a terror. One of the traits of Nixon's speech and attitude was to talk fairly hostilely about someone and then to add – 'but I like him, he's a good man'.

Someone asked him what he thought of Kissinger's book and he replied that he had not read it. He showed no interest in getting drawn into a discussion about it.

Predictably, he was critical of the present US government's foreign policy which he regarded as soft towards the Russians. He was scathing about the response to the invasion of Afghanistan that had taken place in December 1979. He ridiculed 'the prohibition on taking part in high jumping in the Olympics in Moscow'.

I asked him what he would do in the face of the Soviet attack on Afghanistan. Here he was at his most disappointing. He had no specific ideas as distinct from a general diatribe about appearing weak and an exhortation to stand up to the Russians who were 'a) liars and b) only understand strength'.

When Nixon rose to leave for his two-hour return journey he said that he got up at 5 a.m. each morning to start work early on his book. He saw people in the afternoons when it didn't matter if he felt sleepy.

Someone commented on the Van Gogh which hung above the chimney-piece.

'I am afraid I know nothing about pictures,' Nixon said.

I was left wondering, as I often do, what it is about a person that leads him – or her – to become one of the rulers of their country. Nixon did not, judged admittedly by one meeting with him, have any of the obvious attributes of leadership – great self-confidence, vigour of mind and body, a shining personality or great charm. But then how rarely does one find this combination in any public leader; why that should be remains a mystery to me.

10 FEBRUARY
WASHINGTON

AMERICA'S NEW STRATEGIC AREA

When I saw Zbig this week, he told me of the theme dominant on his mind: the effect of the Soviet invasion of Afghanistan, the Soviet motives and their future intentions; and how to deter them from further adventures. I do not think that the Americans are very clear on how they are going to bring the Middle East and South-East Asian countries into some sort of defence arrangement – called first 'a doctrine', then 'a framework', and by Zbig 'a web'. They are also uncertain how they are going to concert policy with their European allies. The French are behaving in characteristically 'independent' fashion; relations between Paris and Washington are fractious. Helmut Schmidt has never been an admirer of Carter and takes little trouble to conceal it. The Americans are not impressed by the performance of the European Community in the aftermath of the Soviet invasion. All that goes on, at any rate seen from Washington, is bickering about the sale of butter to the Soviet Union and wrangling about the British contribution to the budget.

I sought to draw Zbig out on the US guarantee to the Persian Gulf and the proposed framework of security co-operation in the arc of crisis, leaving him in no doubt that I realised what an important departure this was in US foreign policy. It was being referred to as the Carter Doctrine.

Zbig confirmed that the main purpose of the guarantee had been to serve as a warning to the Soviet authorities to avoid both further direct aggression in the area and any stimulus to internal subversion. To my remark that there was imprecision, at any rate in the public mind, about the circumstances that would trigger the commitment and the way in which the USA might respond to a threat or an attack, Zbig said that he had discussed this aspect that very morning with the President. He had taken the line that the Soviets could not be allowed to dictate the terms or the terrain of a response. It was as well therefore not to be too precise. Thinking aloud he said that if for example the Soviets attacked Tabriz the US would not try to throw them out of Tabriz. There might be counter-moves elsewhere. Continuing to speculate Zbig said that a different and very difficult situation would arise if there was some insurrection that threatened the oil fields and refineries in Saudi Arabia and if at the same time the Saudi government had been overthrown and the successor government did not call for Western help. Nevertheless Zbig seemed to think that it would always be possible to imagine that someone in the area would call for outside help in such circumstances.

As Zbig saw it the President's guarantee to the Gulf had created a third strategic area. The first strategic area had been created in the forties by the US commitment to NATO. The second strategic area had come about in the fifties with the US response in the Far East. Now there was a third commitment to the Persian Gulf.

As to involving the countries of the area in a new framework of security, Zbig indicated that there might be a series of bilateral agreements or understandings between different Western countries and countries of the area. This would form a web without any particular shape. Anything comparable to NATO would be inappropriate. He asked me how I thought the US should go about this. The British had more experience of the area and of this sort of thing than did the Americans. He was sure that the countries concerned needed outside help. They did not want to be dominated by the Russians; but nor did they want to appear to be in some American orbit.

I replied that I thought that this was the sort of subject that would be discussed between Foreign Ministers shortly. In the meantime we would be happy to work over ideas with his staff.

Later the same day I called on Clark Clifford to hear about his mission to New Delhi to see Mrs Gandhi. Saying that he would be delighted to give me a rundown of his meeting with Mrs Gandhi, Clifford proceeded to recount at some length the remarks he had made to her. He had emphasised that, whatever might be thought or feared, the US government had no objections to India having close relations with the Soviet Union. Nor did it seek to bind India to any Western bloc. He spoke like an actor playing the part of a statesman, punctuating his remarks with an occasional touch of his fingers to his eyebrows or his cheekbones. It was an impressive performance that gave me time to look about the room at the leather furniture, the old prints, the well-bound books and the trophies of a lifetime devoted to the law and the public service. There was nothing Dickensian about his office which was spic and span. What was my surprise, however, when, having relayed to me the statement that he had made to Mrs Gandhi, Clifford put the tips of his fingers together and said that he would now be happy to answer any questions. He had made no attempt to give me an account of what Mrs Gandhi had said to him. I find, incidentally, that I am in danger of doing exactly the same thing in the accounts I send London of my talks here, say with Vance, Zbig or Christopher. I tend to give more space to what I have said than to what my interlocutors have said.

16 FEBRUARY
WASHINGTON

THE FEAR OF RUSSIA

There is much fear here that Russia could and might strike a blow in the Middle East and threaten the oil; and there is precious little the USA could do to stop them short of threatening nuclear war. A moment such as this is unlikely to recur again because the USA will be building up its military strength in all manner of ways.

The various steps that the US government has taken recently, including the grain embargo, the Olympic Games embargo and the Gulf guarantee, the creation of base facilities in the Middle East, the proposed web or framework of security in the area, and the embargo on high-technology sales to the Soviet Union have, it seems to me, the following purposes:

1 To warn the Soviets that they cannot act again as they have done by invading Afghanistan. The Americans had thought that their previous signals should have been sufficient to deter the Russians from such aggression and the fact that this did not prove to be the case explains why the new warnings now have to be so conspicuous (e.g. the ban on American participation in the Olympics).
2 To reassure the countries in the region that they can rely on US support.
3 To provide for the requirements of the US forces if they are to meet or deter a military threat – hence the search for bases, euphemistically described as facilities. The US hopes that other countries will collaborate in this; the UK in Oman, for instance.

There is much criticism in the USA at the present time of the irresolution of the European powers: the impression they give of fearing to stand up and be counted alongside the Americans, in contrast to American forthrightness in declaring itself ready to defend Europe when the latter was threatened. It is pointed out by government and press in Washington that Europe's interests are menaced in the Gulf through their dependence on oil just as much as are America's. The British government is acknowledged as a conspicuous exception in this respect.

Donna Hartman lunched with us today. She is wonderfully open and uncomplicated; and I remember how this stood out in Paris. I love her spirit, as I do that of Arnold Whitridge,[1] aged eighty-nine, who dined with us last night. I drove him and his daughter back to the hotel afterwards. As we reached the crossing at 16th Street he said, 'Do you know there is a restaurant along there where the waitresses serve you wearing nothing above the waist. Now don't you find that perfectly revolting?' I replied that it seemed to me to depend on what the above-the-waists looked like. He didn't agree and I was left wondering why on earth this old man should be bothering so much about it and should be getting so indignant.

2 MARCH
WASHINGTON
———

THE REPERCUSSIONS OF REX HARRISON

We have been to see William Douglas-Home's play, *The Kingfisher*, starring Rex Harrison and Claudette Colbert. It was originally going to be called 'The Hot Water Bottle'. We had supper afterwards with Rex and his wife (his sixth). It emerged that she was going to be in New York the following week, so I invited him to stay, which he accepted with alacrity. Mary was going to be away in the UK.

Caroline Gilmour was here, staying a few days on her way from seeing Christopher.[2] Despite her endemic back trouble, she was in fine form, and, as usual, highly appreciative of anything worth appreciating. We had the chance of a chat. She told me how well Ian was standing up to the rigours of ministerial life. He was not seeking a confrontation with

---

[1] Arnold Whitridge, historian whom we had known when he was Fulbright Professor of American Civilisation at Athens University 1949–51.
[2] Christopher Gilmour, her third son, later to be the founder of the eponymous and highly successful restaurant in London.

the PM on monetarism; but the press were doing their best to make it one. Ian was no good at ordering the food for the many official meals they had to give. He just wrote on the form: 'No onions. No garlic', which did not give them much inspiration or guidance.

I invited both Harrisons to tea on Sunday so that we could make arrangements for him to move in the following day. Sexy-Rexy, as Caroline calls him, explained that his requirements would be quite simple. He would send his wine and clothes on ahead of his arrival. 'Wine,' I expostulated. 'Don't you trust mine?' He explained that it was done to make things easier. He only drank Chassagne-Montrachet and Gewürtztraminer. He would be grateful if a cold supper could be left for him in the evenings. On Wednesday and Saturday he would like a hot lunch after the matinée, at 4.30 p.m.

He was a charming guest, noticing everything. On Tuesday he suddenly took a great interest in the portrait hanging in the upstairs sitting-room of Field Marshal Montgomery painted by Eisenhower. 'Look at those folds,' he said admiringly, pointing to Monty's rumpled sleeve. I seemed to remember having read somewhere that his hobby is painting.

We had a lot of theatre talk which I always love. American Equity are being difficult about allowing him to have an English actress play Eliza Doolittle in a revival of *My Fair Lady*.

On Thursday night I gave a dinner party for Teddy Youde[1] and Mark Russell[2] who are here for an inspection. In rather a mixed evening which included three Congressmen and their wives, two members of the National Security Council and a miscellany of officials and journalists, I did not think that the service was good. Mr Lightfoot[3] gave up announcing people when only half the guests had arrived. He also decided to disappear when the sweet should have been served a second time. I don't think the guests noticed; and they all seemed to enjoy the evening.

The next morning I mentioned these shortcomings to Suzanne Middleton, the social secretary, saying that I would be having a 'word' with Mr Lightfoot – he is always called that, never either John or Lightfoot – about it at midday. When I came across to the house for lunch I found a letter addressed to me from Lightfoot. It was in his exquisite hand. It said that he had heard from Miss Middleton that I had been dissatisfied with his services the previous night and that he therefore had no option but to submit his resignation forthwith.

---

[1] Edward Youde, member of Diplomatic Service. Ambassador to Peking 1974–8, Governor Hong Kong 1982–7.
[2] Mark Russell, member of Diplomatic Service. Chief Inspector 1978–82. Ambassador to Turkey 1983–6.
[3] John Lightfoot, our butler.

I had some difficulty in getting hold of him, but when I did I gave him the chance to let off steam which he obviously wanted to do. It began to dawn on me, as he complained about the feeling he had that he wasn't wanted, that he had been influenced by the plot of *The Kingfisher* for which Harrison had given him tickets. In that play the butler who has served Rex Harrison all his life feels rejected because Rex at a late age falls in love with Claudette Colbert. It became increasingly apparent that Lightfoot saw himself in the same plight as the butler in the play. I assured him that both Mary and I were fully aware of the wonderful service he gave the Embassy. We personally were both dependent on him. The Embassy would not be the same place without him. I admitted that it seemed to me that there was something wrong last night and that I had wanted to talk it over with him. I think that after more heart-to-heart talk we both felt better. Thank goodness he agreed to withdraw his letter otherwise Mary would never have trusted me in charge of the domestic arrangements again.

A couple of nights later I attended a supper party given by the Bradens for the Rex Harrisons. I told Rex of the evil effect that his play had had on my domestic staff. He was highly amused and rather flattered I think that it could have exercised such an influence.

That evening the snow came down and went on falling all night. I found myself snowed up in the Residence.

In my bachelor interlude, I attended two agreeable young dinners in Washington: one at the Marshall Brements[1] and the other at the Friendlys.[2] I spent a day in Detroit, lunched with Alsop and played two hours of tennis with Kay Graham and the Clayton Fritcheys.

5 APRIL

HOPE SOUND

———

EASTER WEEKEND WITH THE HEINZES; DINNER

FOR THE BRANDONS

We are here for Easter weekend having flown down from Washington in the Heinz company's tomato ketchup-coloured jet. It has been a lightning

---

[1] Marshall Brement, member of US Foreign Service since 1956. Specialist in Chinese and Russian affairs. Ambassador to Iceland 1981–5. His wife, Pamela, has written successful steamy novels.

[2] Alfred and Pie Friendly. He was a Soviet specialist, who worked for the *New York Times* and the US Government. She was a member of the distinguished South Carolina Pinckney family, one of whose early members signed the Declaration of Independence.

transformation in climate and vegetation and here we find palm trees waving in the hot wind, the smell of orange blossom and gardenia and all around the coast the lanquid air doth swoon. I am not surprised to hear that Prince Charles, who has been playing polo nearby, has been taken off to hospital suffering from the effects of heat. Yet in Washington a few hours back we left the daffodils only just coming out, the magnolias beginning to break but scarcely a leaf in sight and the landscape still that of a northern winter.

Bindy Lambton[1] is staying here; also the Quintons.[2] I asked Mary whether she can see anything in common between Quinton, Annan,[3] Kee, Brooks Richards, Derek Dodson[4] and me. Does she not notice the common tendency to showiness, eagerness to amuse, eclectic taste with particular response to architecture, clothes-consciousness, the horror of the dim, the non-hiding-of-lights-under-a-bushel manner typical of all old Stoics of J.F. Roxburgh's time, which we all are. I am not sure that she is gripped by the subject; not that I am at all one of nature's old-boys.

Roger Sherfield[5] who came to see me the other day described Geoffrey Howe as 'a typical Wykehamist'; and I suppose that is true – the down-playing of personal effect, the hard and even earnest search for truth, the indifference to panache, let alone fashion. It occurred to me that Roger himself is a pretty typical Wykehamist. Certainly I doubt whether a Stoic would have approved the architecture of the Washington Embassy new office building which Roger told me with pride that he had been responsible for.

We gave a large dinner party on Tuesday for a star cast. It was in honour of the Brandons,[6] for their move to Georgetown, for the tenth anniversary of their wedding and to commemorate Henry's thirty years in Washington. The Kissingers came and the Cutlers,[7] the Heinzes, the Clark Cliffords, the Aarons, the Marshal Shulmans, Joe Alsop, Nancy

[1] Belinda Lambton, wife of Antony Lambton.

[2] Anthony Quinton, philosopher. Fellow of All Souls College, Oxford; President, Trinity College, Oxford. An omnivorous reader with an elephantine memory. In 1952 he married Marcelle Wegier, a sculptress.

[3] Noël Annan, scholar and writer. Provost of King's College, Cambridge 1956–66; of University College London 1966–76. His wide knowledge, tastes and interests are displayed in his latest book, *Our Age*, published 1992. An outgoing personality with great vitality and enthusiasm.

[4] Derek Dodson, member of the Diplomatic Service. Ambassador to Hungary 1970–3, Brazil 1973–7, Turkey 1977–80.

[5] Roger Sherfield, Fellow of All Souls College, Oxon. Ambassador to Washington 1953–6. Joint Permanent Secretary Treasury 1956–9. Chairman UK Atomic Energy Authority 1960–4. He has subsequently held many high-level business appointments.

[6] Henry Brandon, syndicated columnist, *New York Times*. Previously correspondent *Sunday Times* 1939–83.

[7] Lloyd Cutler, lawyer, counsel to President of US 1979–81 and again in 1994.

Pierrepont,[1] Hélène David-Weill, Senator Mathias, David Buchan,[2] Kay Graham and the Yoders.[3] In a toast to the Brandons I said that Mary and I were also commemorating an important event in our lives, upon which a cake with one candle was carried into the room. We were celebrating one year of retirement.

It was intended to be, and it was, I think, an evening of amusement, Mary's food, particularly the quail's eggs in nests and the Pickwick Pie received acclaim all round, as did the Beychevelle 1964 in magnums. (Thursday's *Washington Post* has an article on Mary's technique of giving dinner parties, with a large and flattering photograph.)

On Thursday I had to attend and make a speech at an Oxford and Cambridge dinner. There must have been nearly three hundred people there, including many Congressmen. Everyone was ready for puerile jokes, which I did my best to provide. The one about Maurice Bowra at Parson's Pleasure, given me by Nick Witney, went down best, I thought. Dr Anthony Kenny,[4] Master of Balliol, was the other speaker. He sought to rally support for his plea that the government should reverse its policy of putting up the charges for foreign students attending British universities.

The evening showed me the valuable piece of real estate in Washington that Britain has through the many Americans who have been to Oxford or Cambridge on scholarships.

14 APRIL
WASHINGTON/NEW YORK

AN EVENING AT ELAINE'S

Another Iran hostages week with pressures on the allies to give more support to the Americans who have now broken off diplomatic relations with Tehran and imposed economic sanctions. I was asked to go on one of the morning TV shows which meant arriving at the studio at 6.45 a.m. I was struck, as usual, by the extreme topicality of the questions and the fleeting opportunity to engage in anything long term.

Derry has arrived. He told a story of John Pope-Hennessy crossing

[1] Nancy Pierrepont, an old friend from my previous time in Washington, 1947–9.
[2] David Buchan, journalist on the *Observer* and later the *Financial Times*; grandson of novelist John Buchan.
[3] Edwin Yoder, journalist; syndicated columnist, *Washington Post*. Pulitzer Prize 1979.
[4] Anthony Kenny, Master of Balliol College Oxon 1978–81. Warden, Rhodes House 1989, and president British Academy 1989. A brilliant and prolific philosopher.

New York Central Park one day on a public holiday. 'I don't mind the masses,' he said in his drawling voice, starting at the highest pitch and dropping down, 'so long as they are not enjoying themselves.'

The garden here in Washington is becoming a delight: the magnolias are magnificent; the daffodils wave their white hydra heads in the tubs on the terrace and the smell of new-mown grass pervades the air. We lunch out, admiring the trees just breaking into leaf. It is a pleasure simply to be outside on such days when there is no struggle against either heat or cold and the body is at one with the air.

I spent a good deal of yesterday with Kay Graham. At first two hours of tennis, now becoming a Sunday habit. I drove her to and from the indoor court at Arlington. We both played quite well so were pleased with ourselves. I then picked her up at around 7.15 in the evening to take her with me on the shuttle to New York, where we both had meetings the following day. A car met us in New York at La Guardia and we drove into the city admiring the clarity of the evening and the extravagance of the lights. Kay suggested that we should stop to have a drink at Elaine's.

I asked her, 'What is Elaine's?'

She said that I ought to know. I would like it. It is the in-place for writers, a bit tatty, but fun. 'We'll see everybody there,' she added.

I said, 'We'll see Lally.'[1]

Kay said, 'Perhaps.'

I said we won't get a table. After all you are not queen of New York. She said that she would because Elaine is a friend. So we stop at Elaine's and abandon the car. Inside I find a version of the Brasserie Lipp only less ordered. There are trad pictures on the walls, one of them of the Tower of London. The tablecloths are unsmart. Kay introduces me to Elaine who promises us a table. Kay says we can't sit in that room as I make my way next door where there seems to be space. She explains that it is not done to eat there and Elaine soon gives us a table in the correct room. We are next to one laid out for four and someone whispers that it is reserved for Woody Allen. He soon arrives with a girl and another couple, all looking gloomy. They show no mirth either at the beginning, middle or end of the evening. They drink a bottle of Lafite. Several people come up to greet Kay, from the world of journalism or films so I gathered, though I did not get their names.

'Oh, there's Lally,' Kay suddenly exclaims, and we see Lally making her way to a table on the other side of the room accompanied by her present paramour, Cockburn,[2] both of them trying, so I reckoned, not

---

[1] Lally Weymouth, Kay Graham's daughter, a journalist.
[2] Alexander Cockburn, British journalist, working in New York for the *Village Voice*.

to be seen by us. Kay waves at them and points, as if to beckon to them to join our table which induces me to say that they really don't want to do so. Kay swears that they do and persuades me to go over to invite them specifically, which I do, making my way past tables with people dressed down in a fairly elaborate way, the women having beautiful smooth hair and contrived casual clothes, the men in chequered open-neck shirts, the epitome of everything that one does not see in Washington. There is an air of emancipation, of wealthy bohemianism, of what I suppose must be real radical chic.

A Japanese man is sitting by himself at a large table in a white suit without a tie. I am told that he had a fight in the restaurant the previous night. He looks demure enough this evening but I presume he must be someone who is very important.

Lally at first resists my invitation, saying that she had a row with her mother that morning. Kay had indeed told me that when she had invited Lally to come to lunch the following day Lally had retorted by asking who the other guests were. This had so annoyed Kay that she had withdrawn the invitation. However, without much persuasion they agreed to come to our table and, as it turned out, we had a hilarious evening, thanks to Lally's quicksilver manner of speaking and inside knowledge of everyone who was having dinner at Elaine's. She asked me if I had forgiven her for chucking an invitation in Washington but she had been very busy with an article. She had telephoned me to apologise. I assured her that I had been deeply touched by that. She told me that her dinner in New York in a fortnight's time to which we had been invited is not only for George Weidenfeld but also for us. Her ways are very winning.

Kay stiffens up a bit and I can sense the mother–daughter tension that everyone talks about.

Cockburn talks about politics – about the possibility of a third party. His attention is focused on Kay while Lally natters away with me on politics, people, her daughter's broken ankle and her worry about the food for her dinner party.

I drop Kay off at her apartment overlooking the East River. She says she has trouble sleeping so worried is she by the financial responsibilities of her empire.

20 APRIL

WASHINGTON

———

VERNISSAGE IN NEW YORK; A PROTEST AT THE WHITE HOUSE

The weather in New York was perfect. We stayed in the Knickerbocker Club whence we could make sorties in the lively spring air of Central Park. Everybody and everything seemed vibrant with life and energy in the sparkling sunshine. Mary was in the highest spirits, saying how much better she felt there than in Washington. Alexandra and Derry are also in New York and having a particularly busy programme.

I opened a vernissage of Vanessa Bell's paintings, which are singularly ill-suited to the concrete Capri of New York but all the more interesting here for that reason. I asked the proprietor of the gallery what he wanted me to talk about and he said, 'Oh, something personal.' So I spoke about what it was like to be painted by Vanessa Bell at Charleston in the mid-twenties. I drew Angelica[1] to my side as the only member of the family present. When I first knew her – in 1925 – we called each other 'sticky-friends' because we were so close.

Back in Washington on Friday I saw Zbig. I complained that Father McManus, an avowed supporter of the IRA, had been received in the White House. Zbig professed not to know whom I was talking about. He undertook 'to do a note about it'. I asked him to do more, to give me an assurance that McManus would not be received again; it was as if Mrs Thatcher received at Number 10 a supporter of the Iranian 'students'. Zbig said that he could 'give that promise three years out of four but . . .'

We talked about the alliance. He was critical: there was no readinesss to show solidarity in standing up to the Soviets.

I find myself making several speeches a day at the moment; loquacity becomes more than a danger, a habit.

———

[1] Angelica Garnett, artist and author, daughter of Vanessa Bell and Duncan Grant, married David Garnett, the author.

26 APRIL
WASHINGTON

———

HOSTAGE DÉBÂCLE

The telephone rang at 6.50 yesterday morning. Mary answered. The *Evening News* from London wished to speak to me. I asked them to ring back later. I should have smelt a rat, but I did not. Then, soon after 7 a.m., Henry Kissinger rang. He wanted me to know, and to pass it on to Mrs Thatcher and Peter Carrington, that he supported the President's attempt to rescue the hostages even though it had failed. I had no idea what he was talking about but I thanked him and said that I would communicate with London.

I turned on the TV and the overseas service of the BBC and the story of the abortive rescue operation soon began to unfold. I could not help thinking that my office should have let me know in the course of the night what was going on as well as about the President's intention to broadcast at 7 a.m.

It was a case now of keeping one's eye on the box and dictating to London what was happening and why. I was asked by several TV channels to appear. I hesitated at first, not knowing how London was taking it: whether they would be cross at the USA acting militarily after requesting the European Community to apply sanctions, or whether they would say that a moment of crisis is not the time to criticise a friend. In the course of the morning I phoned George Walden and quickly got the mood. It was one of resolution and loyalty to Washington. So I accepted two TV requests and appeared on the box that evening. It may sound odd, and I may one day come badly unstuck, but at the moment the telly seems one of the easiest PR activities one can take part in. I was able to make categorical affirmations of support for the USA and sympathy for their setback, I hope not too patronisingly. I said that the British always lost every battle except the last. I mentioned this on the phone to Zbig this morning and he said that our stoicism in a crisis was a historical model to them all. His mood was one of foreboding. He hinted darkly at action the Americans might have to take that 'would ensure that such a thing never occurred again'. I cannot think what he is getting at. I had seen him at the White House exactly a week before the abortive rescue operation. He had given me no hint of the US intention to move. At one point he had said, à propos of his view that Afghanistan is more important than Iran, that it might be necessary to lose the hostages for the sake of a wider interest. Zbig is concerned about the Soviet threat to the Gulf and its oil.

We spent a night in Chicago this week involving an intense round of TV interviews and meetings with editorial boards. I gave a speech to the Council of Foreign Relations. Everyone asked me about Iran which is as much an obsession in Chicago as in Washington.

The Longfords have been here for Michael's wedding. We gave a large dinner party for them. Elizabeth looked very pretty and was amusing and saintly. As we were going to bed she said that Frank still asks every night at home, 'What time are they going to call us?' and every night she replies, 'Who's they?'

9 MAY

WASHINGTON

DINNER WITH JOE ALSOP; A VISIT BY CARRINGTON

A strange experience last night when watching at a dinner with Alsop a television interview with Nixon by Barbara Walters. At one moment Kay Graham turned to Kissinger and said, 'I wonder what he'd think if he knew that you and I were watching this programme together.'

During one of the commercials Kay asked me what I thought of it.

'Rather impressive,' I replied, truthfully.

'Yes, I am afraid so,' she commented.

Joe did not much like the idea of his dinner party being interrupted by television, particularly by Nixon. He thinks that the world would be a better place if television had never been invented – or Nixon born. He had taken a great deal of trouble with the food and wine. He complains that I have set an unnecessarily high standard in wine, far above what he is accustomed to. He loved the Gevrey-Chambertin 1971 magnums that I served at the small Sunday dinner for Carrington. As a result he had to borrow some Beychevelle from Susan Mary last night. She, incidentally, told me of her annoyance that Quentin Bell, for whom she had given a dinner the other evening, refused to be lionised. Anne Olivier, his wife, had been much more forthcoming. When the ladies of Washington prostrated themselves at Quentin's feet asking to be told 'everything about Woolf', as they call her, he refused to play. I rather sympathise with him, often finding myself being asked, as a small-talk gambit, what I think of Woolf. She is a cult figure in the USA at the moment. The other day in Philadelphia I sat next to a lady who asked me to tell her about 'Woolf and the Bloomingdale set'.

Reverting to the television programme I think that Kissinger was pleased that Nixon had put up such a good performance. It must be awkward for him when he is in the company of people who simply denigrate Nixon,[1] not that Kissinger ever gives much impression of being discomfited. He appears at present to be in the best of spirits and attracts as much attention everywhere as if it were he, rather than Muskie,[2] who were Secretary of State. He thought that Nixon's success on TV would redound to Reagan's advantage in that it contained a wounding critique of Carter, however much the viewer might have felt unsympathetic to Nixon.

A small lunch in the Embassy garden on Sunday, for which Kissinger had flown to Washington specially, consisted just of the Carringtons, Kissinger and ourselves. Nancy did not come. It was a beautiful day. The terrace of the Embassy garden provided a splendid luncheon platform. We drank Lafite 1970. Even Henry, who drinks little, could not resist it.

We talked, of course, of Reagan and of Henry's prospects of becoming Secretary of State if he wins in November. Clearly he does not rule that out. He had difficulty in naming anyone of importance whom Reagan consults on foreign policy. He considers Mrs Reagan to have a great deal of influence on everything – just as important as Mrs Carter's.

On the Iranian hostage rescue fiasco, he said that he would have done it earlier before the terrorists had established themselves and gained confidence.

Peter had arrived by Concorde the evening before – Saturday. He described a recent Community meeting on the budget. Mrs Thatcher had declaimed frequently about 'my oil ...' or 'my fish ...' telling the others that they must keep their hands off them. At one moment she had said, 'My God ...' upon which someone had interjected, 'Oh, not that too ...'

Peter recognises Mrs T's qualities: her courage; her leadership; her evenness of temper (apparently throughout the long Luxembourg wrangle she had never become cross, which somehow made her all the more irritating). But she seems to be irritating Schmidt and Giscard, the latter, however, appearing Olympian throughout.

On Sunday after the Kissinger lunch we drove to Middleburg for Peter to have a word with Vance who had resigned five days earlier, creating a sense of high personal drama in the aftermath of the failed hostage rescue operation. The two of them had a gossip by the swimming pool while the rest of us – the Marshall Shulmans, Dick Holbrooke,[3] Gay and

---

[1] Richard Nixon. Kissinger once said of him in my hearing, 'You can say anything about Nixon and it would be true.'

[2] Edmund Muskie became Secretary of State (1980–1) upon Vance's resignation.

[3] Richard Holbrooke, Assistant Secretary for East Asian and Pacific Affairs, Department of State in the Carter Administration. Partner, Lehman Brothers. Appointed Ambassador to Bonn, 1993.

Elsie[1] Vance, the Harrimans, Iona, Mary and I – sat about drinking tea and feeling rather out of it.

Vance had implored Peter to let everyone know during his talks in Washington how adverse would be the repercussions in Europe of another military operation. The same message was conveyed to me by people in the State Department. Those who were opposed to the military route required ammunition; any reports from Carrington of Europe's opposition would be a great help.

So over the next forty-eight hours Peter left everyone in no doubt about Europe's reaction. He also told the many important Americans he met – at the White House, at the State Department and on the Hill – how unpopular the Americans had made themselves in the Moslem world with their failed rescue operation, particularly because their planes had infringed Arab air space and territory (e.g. in Oman). He was surprised – much more than I was – by the apparent American ignorance, or indifference, on this point.

On Sunday night we gave a small dinner party for Peter, the Mondales, Kay Graham, the Brandons and the Heinzes. Monday started early enough with Peter live on television at 7 a.m. After breakfast here on the terrace we drove to the Hill for a call on Muskie.

When we returned to the car afterwards Peter turned to me and said; 'What a very nice man.' I think that he thought that my short biography of him, telegraphed before Peter's departure from London, had been ungenerous. At any rate they got off to a good start.

From there to the White House where the President was standing beaming on the terrace outside the Oval Room. They had about a quarter of an hour together. The others present were Brzezinski, Warren Christopher[2] and me. Peter gained a clear impression from the meeting that Carter was not contemplating a further military move in Iran.

As we left the Oval Room we waded our way through the President's entourage of closest advisers: Ham Jordan, Jody Powell, Lloyd Cutler, McPherson,[3] etc. They were panting to get in there and continue with the real work which, of course, was domestic politics. I was sure that their most hard-headed proposals would be greeted by Carter with the softest of smiles. In reacting against Carter's 'goodness' I realise I am becoming like the American public, and certainly like Joe Alsop.

Peter had quite a long chat with Zbig about Afghanistan and Iran. In addition to the other messages he wanted to get across, Peter told him

---

[1] Elsie, daughter of Gay and Cyrus Vance.
[2] Warren Christopher, Deputy Secretary of Department State 1977–81. Became Secretary of State 1993.
[3] Harry McPherson, lawyer and government official. Special Assistant to President Johnson 1965–9. Vice-chairman of Kennedy Center 1969–76.

of the great difficulty the European Community countries are having in applying sanctions to existing contracts.

Zbig is undergoing a lot of criticism just now but I can't help thinking that he is right about the Russians and about the Middle East, while knowing full well that politics here make reasonable policies unrealisable. Peter was impressed by him.

Peter has originality, frankness and gaiety. He's not like other Foreign Secretaries I have known. He is very natural. He has no pomposity whatever and no political bias or prejudice. He is certainly not right wing. He seems to me to hold his party in about the same degree of contempt as did Rab. He has a capacity for charming people he doesn't like. His face falls like Niagara whenever he wishes to express doubt. He is always ready with a joke. He has time and energy for unimportant people such as drivers, detectives, secretaries; yet there is nothing self-conscious or patronising about his friendliness. You do not feel that he is doing it to collect votes or because he thinks he ought to. He is of course in a wonderful position at the moment with no constituency – except the whole country. He is acknowledged in the UK at the present time and elsewhere as a colossal success at the job. Peter has an excellent head, a ready memory for what matters and a gift with people. He also knows enough about the past to be able to give a good analysis of a difficult problem, for instance of why the popular parallel between 1940 and today is inapposite despite Helmut Schmidt's insistence that it is. He has, I think a great sense of timing, including an understanding of when it is no good trying to do something.

He is a marvellous delegator. I asked him whether he would not like me to clear with him the telegram I was drafting for the Prime Minister on his, Peter's, impressions of the Washington visit. 'No,' he said, 'you know what I think.'

25 MAY

NEW ORLEANS

———

JAZZ

BRITAIN BACKTRACKING

A few minutes of repose as we fly back from two nights in New Orleans. I have been there to open an exhibition of treasures from Chatsworth. We were admirably looked after by the Honorary Consul, a young

American called Jimmy Coleman.[1] We dined with him last night at the French restaurant, Antoine, before going on to hear jazz at the Reservation Hall and the Paddock Room where large, middle-aged, or even elderly blacks were playing trumpets and trombones until their lungs and lips gave out. Coleman told me that the young blacks won't play jazz. They find it infra dig. So I fear New Orleans may cease to be the home of jazz and will come to rely increasingly upon oil refineries which already defile the banks of the Mississippi like giant and poisonous growths.

The French quarter of the city was no disappointment: lovely balconies and wrought-iron trellis-work interspersed with magnolia trees.

We had one official dinner but otherwise were on our own. Nobody seemed to want to interview me for press or television. It was certainly too hot for any such thing. We drove out to the Houmas plantation, a house with verandas built in 1840, prosperous in the days of slave and cheap labour. The present owner, Dr Croizat, who only has a few acres having sold off large chunks of the estate for refineries, opens it to the public every day. Crowds arrive in bus-loads and are shown round by local girls wearing *Gone With The Wind* costumes. Dr Croizat was delighted by our arrival as it encouraged him to make mint-juleps which he did with gusto.

At the official dinner I was tackled by the host about our backtracking on sanctions which has indeed been a nasty blow for us; we are all at once in the same doghouse as the French, having been very popular since the beginning of the hostage business thanks to Mrs T's forthright declaration of support for the Americans. 'We are your friends etc,' Mr Kaufmann complained, leaning across the table. He was offering an elaborate dinner in the Fairmont Hotel. The lighting was dimmed as illuminated dishes, including iced swans, were wheeled in and paraded before the guests. He said that three friends of his had asked him to kick the British Ambassador's shins when he saw him that evening, so disappointed were they by our retreat. I did my best to explain what had happened, laying particular stress on parliament's dislike of retroactive legislation, and drawing a parallel with the insistence of Congress in having the last word on foreign policy issues.

We have run into nasty criticism in the European Community for retreating on the decision and the French are having a field-day, eager to offset the adverse effects of Giscard's maverick meeting in Warsaw with Brezhnev. It is particularly galling when the *Washington Post* denigrates us as 'brave-talking Britain'. Indeed HMG is fast acquiring the reputation

---

[1] James Coleman, lawyer, businessman.

of being unable to deliver: first there was Mrs T's resounding call for a boycott of the Olympics – which the British Olympic Committee have rejected – and now there has been the no less resounding lead the government took over sanctions, only to have it reversed for fear of defeat in parliament.

At a briefing for NATO Ambassadors recently Muskie talked a lot about the different style that he, a politician as distinct from a diplomat, would show in dealing with foreign affairs – as though there were inevitably some sign of grace in this compared with the implied half-heartedness and lack of frankness of professional diplomats. It was not unlike the description I have just read of Mrs T in an American paper which likened her to a female bull, and one, moreover, which takes her own china-shop around with her.

This is a moment for us to lie low and batten down the hatches. If I am asked to appear on TV I will think twice about it because I doubt whether reason can get much of a hearing in the current acrimonious atmosphere.

I made a speech in New York last week to the Foreign Policy Association who were not hostile. It was the sort of gathering that I often meet in the USA and that is difficult to deal with: one or two very well-informed people, but mostly women in hats who are there principally to meet other women in hats. At the end I felt as I often do after speeches to American audiences, that I had spent too long in preparation and that the theme had been too elaborate when what would have done best would have been to stick to a few high-sounding clichés. I instinctively avoid using the words 'special relationship', knowing that if I refrain the Americans will be the more likely to use the phrase.

It made up for a lot to have Nancy and Jackie Pierrepont emerge unexpectedly from the audience at the end. I told them that their attendance had been a true act of kindness. In any case I love going to New York and much enjoyed the lunch I had at the Knickerbocker with the Griffiths and Tom Matthews. I also derived pleasure from being able to put at Tom's disposal so as to get him to the airport without the outbreak of travel fever to which he is prone, a Rolls Royce and chauffeur that had been provided for me.

We went to Philadelphia for a night to stay with the Annenbergs. A large and formal dinner party which left us over fed and over tired. They were very kind. She talked about Prince Charles and the need to find him a proper job. 'Mother is maternal about him,' Walter commented. Walter showed us the English azaleas that have not done well and that he will be uprooting to make a golf course. He seems to have the same need to make a golf course wherever he alights as 'less favoured people', to use his own phrase, have to make a lawn.

We went to a grand dinner at the National Gallery here this past week, given to mark the opening of the Post-Impressionist Exhibition, many of the pictures having come from London. On a beautiful evening we began the proceedings on the terrace of the seventh floor. I ran into Bunny Mellon[1] who was pacing out with I.M. Pei,[2] the Chinese-American architect, exactly where the crab-apple trees in large tubs should be placed. She and Paul Mellon have, not surprisingly, the status of demi-gods at the gallery, which is substantially financed by him. He has a large office there with a magnificent view of the Capitol. I gather he goes there quite regularly, presumably to talk to Carter Brown who has an office alongside. When they appear in the corridors a swathe is cleared for their passage and I felt that many Americans were readier to bow before them than before anyone else. All sorts of conflicting emotions about inherited wealth cut an equally sharp swathe in my mind.

I have spent two days recently in Atlanta and Tallahassee; the usual round of calls, speeches and receptions. Raymond Mason[3] of the Charter Oil Company brought me back to Washington in his private BAC 111 (a plane that normally seats one hundred people). He has just bought a hotel in Ireland because he wants to have somewhere reliable to stay.

Meanwhile we had three thousand people visiting the Embassy garden on Saturday afternoon to collect money for the Salvation Army.

31 MAY
WASHINGTON

KEITH JOSEPH IN A SCRAP WITH
PAUL JOHNSON

Sir Keith Joseph has been here for the night to address a seminar at the Center of Strategic and International Studies. The subject was Britain's new economic and industrial policy. He arrived from San Francisco looking a little tired, and, as he slumped into the back seat of the Rolls,

[1] Bunny Mellon, wife of Paul Mellon, Chairman Trustees of National Gallery, Washington; a man of assorted interests; a beneficent patron of the arts who also lists racing and fox-hunting amongst his recreations.
[2] I.M. Pei, an architect who came to the USA from China aged eighteen. He is the most acclaimed architect of his time with numerous major projects in many parts of the world, of which, for example, the East Building of the National Gallery, Washington, is universally admired, and the Pyramid at the Louvre no less universally, if often critically, discussed.
[3] Raymond Mason, company executive.

he said that he did not like flying and that he couldn't think how Foreign Secretaries managed.

He is sometimes referred to in the press as the Mad Monk, or as Mrs T's guru. The latter description was used of him by the chairman of the press conference which was given just before the dinner. From the twitch that was produced in his mobile, disturbed face, I do not think that he liked it. He does not, I should judge, on the basis of little experience, have the trait, frequent amongst politicians, of liking to be talked about in his presence. He is unlike a politician in many respects: he doesn't seem keen to communicate at all times and at great length on all subjects with his fellow men; he is not at all jolly or gregarious; he doesn't even give the impression of enjoying what he is doing.

He had been impressed – and hence depressed by comparison with the UK – by the vitality of American business, particularly in the micro-processing industry on the west coast. He spoke of the importance of 'venture capital'. He is against the government's intervention in industry.

He has a fanatical streak which, on occasion, however, shows a disarming seam even on the doctrinaire subject of monetarism about which we were chatting over a drink after his speech last night. He suddenly seemed to have doubts, protesting; 'I don't think there's an alternative to what we are doing.'

He also breaks from time to time into a surprising smile and even into a loud laugh, neither of which are predictable in his solemn, almost clown-like face. One of the questioners at the dinner appeared to be disturbed by this, interjecting in the middle of what was a long question that he noticed the minister was smiling, he did not know why. Indeed his facial expressions do not necessarily appear to match what he is saying or thinking; they remind me of an unsynchronised soundtrack in a film.

I did not find him at all didactic. He always spoke quietly. He was interested in people and asked why I had said in the short speech of introduction to him at the dinner that Anne Armstrong[1] who presided was likely to get high office if the Republicans won. 'What is her power-base?' he asked.

'Well,' I replied, 'she is a woman; and you well know how much that counts in politics.'

---

[1] Anne Armstrong, co-Chairman, Republican National Committee 1971–3. Ambassador to London 1976–7. Co-Chairman Reagan-Bush campaign 1980. Since then she has held many high-level business and foreign policy appointments and is the most glamorous and sought-after woman in public affairs in the USA in recent times.

He laughed in a way that was particularly explosive given how buttoned up he is.

He is very well mannered and so far as I gather exceptionally courteous and appreciative. He was put out, though he did not show it much, when someone got up after his speech; it was Douglas Cater,[1] who complained bitterly at the attack he alleged Joseph had made on the *Observer* newspaper during his remarks. Joseph said that he had intended no such thing, but if offence had been caused he apologised profusely and withdrew what he had said.

Cater persisted in taking and voicing offence. Joseph again apologised saying that Bob Anderson,[2] the owner of the *Observer*, was an old friend of his. His remarks had not been directed at any particular paper. Upon which Paul Johnson[3] rose and said that he regretted Joseph's apology and withdrawal. What he had said had been perfectly correct. The money doled out in wages by the new American owner of the *Observer* had completely upset wage levels in Fleet Street. Rather to my surprise, Cater did not return to the charge, perhaps because Paul Johnson's intervention had been loudly cheered.

Joseph's speech went down well. He is not an orator and I would not say that he has exceptional powers of advocacy or persuasion. But he is obviously genuine, can order his thoughts clearly, and he was saying what the Americans in the audience wanted to hear.

When we were driving home afterwards his comment on the incident of Cater and Johnson was to say that he always knew that Paul liked 'a scrap'.

However, I gather that the British press correspondents seized upon the row and reported it to London. For them it was the most interesting event of the whole conference.

Joseph had to leave early the following morning for New York where he was going to help find an apartment for his daughter who will be studying music at the Juilliard School which Joseph described as 'by far the best'. We had an exchange of words on the reports, just received, of the agreement, apparently reached by European Community Foreign Ministers on the vexed question of the UK budgetary contribution.

---

[1] Douglas Cater was special assistant to the President of the USA 1964–8. Vice-Chairman the *Observer* 1976–81.

[2] Robert Anderson, cattle rancher and successful and high-minded businessman. Chairman and chief executive Atlantic Richfield Company (now ARCO). Chairman the *Observer* 1981–3.

[3] Paul Johnson, prolific author. Editor *New Statesman* 1965–70. Member Royal Commission on the Press 1974–7. In addition to regular articles on the press he is the author of numerous books, including *A History of Christianity* 1976 and *A History of the Jews* 1987. Not afraid of political controversy, he has swung decisively from left to right.

'What a triumph for her determination,' he said ecstatically. There was not a word about Peter or his negotiating skill.

I gather from George Walden that Peter is still upset over the sanctions business in which he feels he has been shopped by the House of Commons. I am sure George is right that the trouble did not only arise from the House of Commons' dislike of retroactive legislation, but from their wish to 'cut down tall poppies'. Peter has been doing too well and has excited too much envy and resentment lately, something obviously that happens frequently in public life.

Art Buchwald has a column today on the sanctions theme: that what Muskie must learn is what any tourist who has been in Paris knows, and that is, if you want to get the French to do something, you have to indicate that you desire them to do the exact opposite.

I much enjoyed the conference on the British scene that preceded Joseph's speech to which I have referred. I had spent quite a time beforehand in preparing a fifteen-minute introduction to it. My compatriots, I find, but perhaps I am biased, are particularly good at keeping a conference going with interesting interventions that are not too lengthy. They certainly dominated this conference. It was particularly interesting for me to meet Sam Brittan[1] whom I read frequently in the *FT*. He, Paul Johnson, Hugh Thomas,[2] Peter Jenkins[3] and Norman Leyland[4] came to lunch yesterday and we continued the seminar. Paul J said that we should never forget that Mrs T is an eternal scholarship girl, eager to do well in the next exam.

Leyland said that he thought that the PM should make some friendly gesture towards the trade union leaders, such as inviting them to tea at Number 10. This would help prevent the growth of a bitter spirit of confrontation. To this Paul J rejoined that Mrs T's deliberate purpose was to try to break the belief of the trade union leaders that they had some special role in the state with the right of entry to Number 10. She intended to cut them down to size. She certainly would not have them to tea.

---

[1] Sam Brittan, since 1966 Principal Economic Commentator for the *FT*. Economics Editor, the *Observer* 1961–4. One of the most intelligible and influential journalists writing on economics today. Aphoristic in style he had recently delivered himself of the comment, that some British politicians could well heed, that '... there are none so theory-bound as those who think they are pragmatic.'

[2] Hugh Thomas, historian. Former member of the Diplomatic Service which furnished background for his first novel, *The World's Game*. Professor of History, University of Reading, 1966–76. Chairman Centre for Policy Studies 1979–91. Author, *inter alia*, of books that can be properly described as seminal: *The Spanish Civil War* and *The Cuban Revolution*. He is a liberated and shining spirit.

[3] Peter Jenkins, the best-informed and most influential political columnist in Britain during the last two decades until his sudden death in 1992.

[4] Norman Leyland, fellow of Brasenose College, Oxford, 1948–81.

I JUNE
VIRGINIA

LUNCH WITH BUNNY AND PAUL MELLON

We lunched today with the Mellons at their house near Middleburg in Virginia, certainly the most beautiful of all the luxurious houses we have been to. Bunny is a gardener and one with perfect gardening taste – or at any rate mine – that is to say she has no red flowers and plenty of thyme and tread-upons between the flagstones. She makes a speciality of growing myrtle and rosemary like small trees in pots with rounded, clipped foliage. She also grows tobacco in pots. I was full of enthusiasm as she showed me round before lunch.

The inside of the house is as beautiful as the garden. Every picture, every object, every piece of porcelain is perfect, yet there is no feeling that one is being overawed by it. There is no ostentation. The rooms are not vast, but comfortable. There are books everywhere.

She is building a separate library for gardening books, a white structure amidst crab-apple trees with expansive views of the Blue Mountains. There can be no more beautiful countryside in the USA than this. Inside, the new library is going to have white oak bookcases. Bunny's aim is to provide a centre to which scholars and students can come. Where, I ask myself, will these students stay? There is no accommodation nearby.

I ask Bunny where she spent most of her time. She replied that it was partly at Middleburg and partly in Antigua. She was rarely in Washington and occasionally in New York, New England and Paris. She asked me about the apartments in Albany in Piccadilly, indicating that she was tempted to have a residence there too; but she then hesitated, asking herself aloud when would she find the time to be there.

When we were all going round the garden afterwards (the Richard Helms[1] were also guests) Bunny pointed out a pagoda-like wooden structure and told us that it had been in that building that Derry and her daughter had cut the cake at their wedding.[2] Up to that point I had been photographing everything, but somehow I felt it would have been bad taste to have recorded the pagoda. It made me think, however, what a different life Derry would have had had he and Bunny's daughter stayed together, and how far removed it was from setting up house with Alexandra.

---

[1] Richard Helms, Director CIA 1966–73. Ambassador to Iran 1973–6.
[2] Derry Moore, my son-in-law, who had first married Eliza Lloyd.

Needless to say the food at lunch was as exquisite as everything else: all the vegetables home-grown, the ham home-cured, the wine Château Haut-Brion 1964.

Bunny spoke to me privately and enthusiastically about Joan[1] but said not a word about Garrett.[2]

8 JUNE

SHENANDOAH VALLEY, VIRGINIA

———

A HERO OF OUR TIME

We are staying the weekend in Lily Guest's[3] beautiful but stifling house here and sit out after dinner in darkness illuminated only by fireflies.

Liz Stevens[4] gives me an article to read by a Princeton student, published in the *Washington Post*, that says that the rise in oil prices in the seventies has brought about a greater change in the world balance of power than any event this century. This obviously is an exaggeration but it is a sign of how seriously people are taking the oil problem.

Leonard Cheshire has been staying with us in Washington. I am bowled over by his presence and personality – not only by his glorious past. He is not ebullient. He is intense and single-minded in vision. He is decidedly one-track; and it is an unself-seeking one, unless it be for a prime place in heaven. As we were leaving him after lunch to come here Mary was putting some papers into a bag to bring with her and, in response to some enquiry on his part, she said that what she had to do was of no importance, simply the preparation of menus and the ordering of food for the following week. 'Not at all,' Cheshire said, 'it will be recognised in the after-life.' He was being very serious about it.

When Mary told me this I could not avoid laughing. Indeed this is the reaction which his great solemnity is apt to produce though one is also very much aware of his complete honesty, dedication and selflessness. I long to break the spell of sanctity, to utter an expletive, to avoid getting into a fog of humbug which I fear is going to engulf me unless I make clear that I cannot live up to his ideals; that I like food and drink and have many other vices and cannot resist the pursuit of pleasure.

Leonard said that after his recent tour of the Far East – which he described to us – he was very tired. I was relieved by this revelation of

[1] Joan Drogheda, Derry's mother.
[2] Garrett Drogheda, Derry's father.
[3] Lily Guest, wife of Raymond Guest, race horse owner. Ambassador to Dublin 1965–8.
[4] Liz Stevens, daughter of Lily Guest, married George Stevens, film executive.

human weakness. In the Philippines he had had to lie down on the floor of the airport, fearing that he would not be able to continue the journey but then 'One recovers; one always does.' He asked if he could go to bed early and just have something very light to eat in his room instead of being out to dinner as was planned.

I asked in I suppose what was rather too jolly a fashion whether he would not like to borrow a book to read. 'What sort of thing would you like to read?' I asked.

'I have something,' he replied. 'You may think it odd. But I have *Vatican II* to read. I find it very thought-provoking.' He went on to say that he had had very little time to read since the war.

'Goodness, that's a long time,' I said somewhat fatuously. I remembered that as a boy he had been quite a scholar.

His father had evidently been a strong influence and example for him. At one moment he said, à propos of something, 'Oh, Father would have liked that.' He described admiringly his father's imperviousness to heat or cold. 'He was much tougher than I was,' he continued, 'he used to sleep and work all the year round with the windows wide open.'

I said that I had remembered his father playing tennis at Oxford, and he complimented me on my memory. His father had been very tall, which the son is not, and very lithe. He had lived to be over ninety and been a great law don. *Cheshire on Torts* had become a textbook classic.

Cheshire revealed other human sides to his otherwise ethereal and saintly character. He expressed a wish to play tennis explaining that following the removal of a lung soon after the war, his doctor had told him that he must never try to run or take exercise, instructions that he had followed. Twenty-five years later, however, he had seen another doctor in the course of some serious illness who had told him that he must take a lot of exercise in order to develop the surviving lung. So since then, i.e. since 1970, he had tried to play tennis twice a week. I recalled to myself, but didn't dare say it to Leonard because I thought he might take it amiss, that when Sue had been staying with us in Poland she had lamented the fact that he felt obliged to play tennis. She had indicated that she regarded this as a waste of time which he should be devoting to higher things.

Apart from wishing to play tennis, which he did on the Embassy court for nearly two hours – in singles – he was eager to watch the tennis finals on TV from Roland-Garros.

It was not clear to me how closely he followed the world news, though there was no doubt of his interest in sport; he asked me what had been the result of the rugger match between the Lions and the Springboks. He expressed admiration for the successful SAS raid on the Iranian Embassy in London. 'I must say that they made me proud to be an Englishman,' he said. There were other signs of a rather uncomplicated patriotism which rather surprised me as I thought that RAF heroes of the Second World War were almost theatrically keen to avoid heroics or admiration of heroics.

Mary was struck by his punctilious politeness and correctness of address. Seated watching the tennis on TV he not only stood up when she entered the room but he put on his jacket. During lunch he wore both a tie and a jacket though I wore neither. I told Mary that dressiness was one of the hallmarks of old Stoics as were, I hoped, good manners.

He talked one day about the administration of the Cheshire Homes in the USA. Mary had some suggestions to make because we had heard that all was not plain sailing. Indeed the Americans tended to resent foreign control over their charitable organisations which we did not think was surprising. He had written to me about this in advance of his arrival. We found that, intense and even fanatical though he may be, he is perfectly reasonable in discussion. Then, of course, with fervour goes great coolness of judgment, otherwise he would not have been the fantastic war pilot that he was.

In Cheshire's presence I kept wondering how far his personality impressed one because of what one knew of his past. Would he be so commanding if one was unaware of his Victoria Cross? The answer, I think, is obvious. He would probably not have performed such feats unless he had possessed exceptional qualities. He had been rather outstanding as a boy. I recalled the precision with which he played tennis and his ease in reaching the sixth form; also the irresponsible but controlled dash displayed when he came down to Stowe as an old boy in a fast racing car and managed to drive unscathed through the cricket screen, an accident of which I am sure he would be ashamed now were he to be reminded of it.

I also wondered about his daughter who was travelling with him in the USA and whom I have not yet met. He explained how he had financed her trip by signing brochures about the Lancaster bomber. It had taken him seventy hours and had earned enough money, so he assured us, to provide a good deal for the homes as well as for his daughter's journey. He was making her keep a diary and not encouraging her to watch TV. I shall look forward to meeting her tonight to see whether I can detect in her the expected seeds of rebellion.

Having met Gigi Cheshire I am not sure whether she is going to be a saint or a sinner. A look of longing came into her pretty face when we suggested that she should come back for the Commonwealth Ball the following Sunday. She had enjoyed the cook-out she had been to the night before. She had had no chance, throughout her trip, to wear her new evening dress. I supposed that her hosts everywhere had been frightened to lay on anything too frivolous for her. She gave no impression of wanting to react against her father upon whom her eyes were frequently fixed. Her views seemed demure and respectful.

I attended some function this week in the Vice-President's house. Mondale reprimanded me, half humorously, but only half, for giving his wife what he described as 'a book of pornography'. This was Nigel Nicolson's *Portrait of a Marriage*;[1] a book his wife had told me she was interested in reading.

We went to a gala evening at Wolf Trap this week as guests of Mrs Shous, a rich widow who has created and financed this organisation which she admitted to me was modelled on Glyndebourne.

The gala consisted of an incongruous hotchpotch of songs, ballet and individual turns, including a not totally comprehensible recitation by Elizabeth Taylor. At one moment the compère shouted in response to the whistling from what I thought was an otherwise very tolerant audience, mostly of young people, that if people thought that they were going on too long on the stage, they should realise that the singers were doing their best to entertain them. More whistles.

The seats were uncomfortable and by 1 a.m. I felt exhausted and depressed. I thought of Frances Partridge's[2] remark to me about Raymond Mortimer: that he had been quite ready to die as he felt so out of sympathy with the modern world.

Mrs White (P.D. James)[3] made much the same remark about the lowering of standards when she lunched with us this week: 'Or is it just that I am getting older?' she soliloquised. We assured her that it was not just that.

---

[1] *Portrait of a Marriage* was an account by Nigel Nicolson of the close but unconventional relationship between his parents, both of whom were homosexuals.

[2] Frances Partridge, author and close friend for over fifty years. Her diaries published in successive volumes beginning with *A Pacifist's War* are marked by original imagery and convey an authentic atmosphere of Bloomsbury. A nonogenarian, she is as fit as the fiddle she still plays, has retained undimmed all her faculties, continues to write, and to finish the crossword with alarming speed – but then she is the daughter of the first Wimbledon finalist, was runner-up in the English ballroom dancing championship and read moral sciences at Cambridge.

[3] Phyllis Dorothy James, the maiden name, under which Mrs C. B. White writes. She was a Civil Servant 1949–79 and has been a highly successful author of thrillers. She lived in the same building as my daughter, Alexandra.

3–5 JULY

BY TRAIN FROM DENVER TO SEATTLE

Crack trains, as Cyril Connolly liked to describe them, are pleasures of the past. We have gone back in time this week, having been provided with a private train, or rather a private coach attached to a public train, to take us from Denver to Seattle. Named the Arden, after the Harrimans' private house, the coach belongs to the Union Pacific Line. We will be coupled later today on to an Amtrack train.

We are wonderfully comfortable in our coach, each having a cabin and lavatory. We have a sitting-room, looking backwards down the line, with a sofa and armchairs in two-tone velvet, and little tables upon which Stanley, the black servant appointed to attend to our every need, places food and drink at frequent intervals in case we are tired of the platefuls of nuts that serve as a permanent temptation. What food it is! An excellent chef is working away in a galley the other side of the dining-room. On the first evening we had crab claws and a dip of some Pacific mayonnaise. The food has never looked back since.

What has struck me most about our journey has been the vastness of the landscape through which we travel, the unpeopled expanse of this part of the United States. The whole southern area of Wyoming and the breadth of Idaho seemed to pass in an unbroken pattern of high, arid, treeless plains, upon which cattle were occasionally to be seen, but humans never.

The Union Pacific has provided for each of us a guide-map to the most noticeable landmarks on the route. Sometimes there was no distinguishing feature that the cartographer could indicate on the landscape for hundreds of miles, except an occasional water tower or sugar-beet plant. During these long featureless stretches we switched on the TV set in our sitting-room and watched the tennis relayed from Wimbledon. A perfect diversion.

At Portland a couple called Vaughan[1] joined the train. He is a historian of the region. We passed the devastation caused by the Mount St Helen's volcano which has ruined the land and rivers around and has destroyed the symmetrical beauty of the mountain itself.

As we approached Seattle we had a magnificent view of Mount Rainier, an ice-cream cone dominating the landscape.

The Vaughans said that we should keep a lookout for Aubrey Morgan's

---

[1] Thomas J. G. Vaughan, editor-in-chief *Oregon History Quarterly* since 1954. Author of *A Bibliography of Pacific North West History* (1958).

house, so we piled out on to the rear platform and peered through the Mount St Helen's dust, thrown up by the train, until we whizzed past a little Union Jack waving in front of a white house. 'That's the Morgans,' the Vaughans said, gesticulating frantically. My memory shunted back to my earlier time in Washington when Aubrey had been with Oliver Franks, a genial shambling figure who, in his early days, had reputedly been something of a cricketer and, having married one of Dwight Morrow's daughters (Connie, the sister of Anne Lindbergh), had settled down in America, becoming honorary adviser to successive British Ambassadors and explaining humorously but also seriously how it was possible to be folksy with the locals, to scratch the backs of pigs, and call people by their first names on initial acquaintance without losing one's British identity. He himself is Welsh. We had dinner with him and Connie two evenings later at a Chinese restaurant in Seattle. Despite the bad stroke he has suffered he was little different from how I had remembered him from over thirty years previously. I think that both he and Connie were thankful for the chance to talk to people whose interests were not directly and solely concerned with the Mount St Helen's eruption. I kept wondering whether he had been happy cutting himself off so completely from the business of political life by isolating himself on a farm in this far western state.

13 JULY

WASHINGTON

———

CONTRASTED LUNCHEON PARTIES

We gave a lunch party this week for the black members of the Embassy staff who are responsible for moving furniture about and doing odd jobs such as plumbing and carpentry. There are twelve of them. I said a few words at the outset to thank them for their services over the years, carried out with such cheerfulness and efficiency. I spoke from the heart. Mary and I had been upset to find out that these black members of the Embassy had been in the habit of avoiding coming to the annual staff party at Christmas because they did not think that anyone else would talk to them. They are an indispensable part of our team, always being called upon to shift sofas and chairs out of this or that room for this or that reception. So we wanted to show gratitude.

After lunch Mary escorted them round the house, pointing out the finer features of the paintings by Turner and the exceptional qualities of the Chippendale furniture. The group looked on in amazement, less at the objects themselves than at Mary's K. Clark act. I had the impression that although they had been moving these things about for years they had not the faintest idea what they were, let alone their value. When she had finished telling them all about the treasures in the Embassy, the leader of the group, who is called Mr Washington, and known as 'Wash', said he wanted to say a few words. He wished to thank Mary very warmly for her hospitality and guided tour, but no less importantly he wanted to warn his colleagues 'to be very careful in future about the way you move the furniture now you know how valuable it is!'

I suspect in retrospect that it was a more useful lunch than the one we gave the following day which certainly lacked a single theme. It started out by being a party for Ronnie Grierson. Then I thought I would invite Mrs Hufstedler,[1] the Minister of Education who has recently been on an official visit to the UK. Reckoning that it was a long time since we had entertained the Saudi Arabians, I also invited them. The same went for the McNamaras. The Fritcheys always refuse, but as Grierson was staying with them I decided to try them again. The Brandons I knew to be friends of Ronnie, so in they went. Ambassador Owen would also, I thought, fit in well. The Sherman Coopers I like to include whenever the party is big enough for his deafness to be containable; and Lorraine likes to go out and she is a real friend, one of my oldest in Washington even if a little dotty nowadays. She told me afterwards that not knowing that Owen worked at the White House she had said to him at lunch that if Carter asked her advice she would recommend him to run his campaign for the Presidency on the following theme: 'Don't trust a man for the Presidency who has only served as a Governor. I am the living witness to the truth of that advice; but now I have also been President for years.'

I also invited the decorous correspondent of the *Wall Street Journal*, Karen House;[2] and of course, as we do for practically every lunch or dinner party, we realised we could not do without Joe Alsop who had expressed a wish to taste the fish that he knew we had brought back from Seattle.

Joe annoyed Clayton Fritchey a great deal at the lunch – and not for the first time – by monopolising Karen House's attention and ignoring his neighbour on the other side. Karen said to me afterwards, 'If Joe was not so intelligent he would be an awful man.' Certainly there are many bad sides to him but as Evangeline Bruce,[3] another regular attender when

[1]Mrs Seth (Shirley) Hufstedler, Secretary US Department of Education 1979–81.
[2]Karen House, Diplomatic Correspondent *Wall Street Journal* 1978–84; subsequently Foreign Editor. Pulitzer Prize winner for international reporting 1984.
[3]Evangeline Bruce was the widow of David Bruce, who had been US Ambassador to France 1949–52, to FRG 1957–9, to London 1961–9, to China 1973–4, to NATO 1974–6.

she is not in London, points out, he never makes a banal remark. Rude though he is there is nothing discriminating about it, so that the great have to bear the brunt of his tongue as do lesser fry.

One day this past week I went to Norfolk to be the guest of the Supreme Allied Commander Atlantic, Admiral Train.[1] I was flown there by helicopter only hours after returning from Seattle in what proved to be an unpleasant flight. Most of the morning at Norfolk was spent being briefed by different senior officers of varying nationalities. This was followed by lunch on the Admiral's barge that cruised about the harbour in and out of the US fleet. The sight of the *Nimitz* (ninety thousand tons, carrying five thousand people, the carrier replaceable at a cost of two billion dollars) impressed me more than anything that day. I could not help wondering at the USA's apparent inability to translate its power into political terms or to bring it to bear where it was most wanted at the present time. The existence of its navy – the ability to show the flag – should bring political dividends but this does not seem to be so. The fleet is kept 'over the horizon' in the Middle East, so as to avoid giving offence or creating an unfavourable impression.

Sean Donlon, the Irish Ambassador, came to see me to describe the efforts that have been made by the Irish National Caucus to get him removed. They nearly succeeded. His sentence is suspended. I think that he is being very courageous; it could be the end of his career in the Diplomatic Service. He is only in his thirties.

15 AUGUST

LONDON

———

MEETING HAROLD MACMILLAN AT

THE RITZ

I lunched yesterday with Alan Maclean and Harold Macmillan to talk about the latter's proposed trip to the USA. He is going there to launch Grove's new encyclopaedia of music and, perhaps more important in his

---

R. A. Butler told me when he was Foreign Secretary and David Bruce was Ambassador in London that he would always be ready to see him because 'he never wastes my time' – which struck me as being a good tip for Ambassadors. Since his death Evangeline has created a position for herself in Washington and London life and is at work on a study of Napoleon Buonaparte and Josephine.

[1] Admiral Harry Train, Commander-in-Chief US Atlantic Fleet and Supreme Allied Commander Atlantic 1978–82.

mind to make an exhortatory and farewell speech to the American people, a form of Fulton revisited. When I arrived at the Palm Court in the Ritz ten minutes early he was already there looking like an elderly lion. A stick at his side, he was sipping a martini. He apologised for not recognising me from far away, saying that his sight was not what it was. Shortly afterwards Alan arrived, accompanied by Byam Shaw[1] also from Macmillan's publishing house. We had not been assembled long before we got on to the subject of the visit. We discussed which speech Macmillan should make first and where. We considered who would be the ideal interviewer on TV. Macmillan ordered another martini and we continued discussing the programme. By now the martinis were beginning to have their effect and Macmillan was becoming eloquent. He was also becoming just a little repetitive and the waiters seemed to be as aware of this as I was and rather less tolerant. They produced enormous menus, dangled them before our eyes and suggested that we might wish to order lunch. The three of us studied the cards while Macmillan put his close up against his eyes, continuing to talk and waxing increasingly eloquent on the subject of his programme. He showed no interest in the food. Ordering yet another martini he said, 'Would you ask them not to hurry us.' Eventually he ordered, without any enthusiasm, a dish of macaroni cheese. The aim of the rest of us then was to avoid yet another round of drinks and to move into the dining-room. It must have been well after two when we got there.

Macmillan told a good story that, he suggested, indicated the different approach of Americans and British to politics, the latter showing the necessary vein of humour. After Kennedy had had his unsuccessful first meeting with Khrushchev in Vienna he came on to London where Macmillan met him for the first time as President. Talking about the tribulations of political life, Kennedy expressed concern at the abusive things being said publicly concerning his wife, Jackie. These evidently worried him.

In his most debonair and man-of-the-political-world fashion Macmillan apparently consoled him: 'These things happen; they are an inescapable part of public life; the President should not mind too much.' 'What would you think,' Kennedy retorted, 'if someone shouted out at a meeting that Lady Dorothy was a drunkard?'

With a theatrical pause and shifting his tongue to his cheek, Macmillan said that he had replied as follows to the President: 'I'd shout back – you should have seen her mother.'

---

[1]Nicholas Byam Shaw, Chairman Macmillan Publishers since 1990.

7 SEPTEMBER
WASHINGTON

––––––

MANY OPINIONS

Returned last week with some dread to the heat and humidity of Washington and to the combined monotony and volatility of the political scene in which Carter and Reagan alternate in holding the lead in the Presidential race. Suddenly Carter, who three months ago was judged by opinion polls to be a certain loser, is favourite again.

We dined the first evening with Lloyd Cutler at the F Street Club to meet Kingman Brewster, the Scottie Restons[1] and Minister Hufstedler. Scottie thought that the US system of government was unworkable so long as the press had such unlimited access and power, a viewpoint that was perhaps strange coming from one of the leaders of the journalistic profession. Lloyd spoke of the exaggerated application of the principle of the division of powers in the US constitution. He said that the trouble was not lack of leadership but the impossibility of governing when the President cannot get the legislation he wants through the Congress even though he was elected for that programme. This, of course, is the same as the view from the White House. Kingman, rather to my surprise, said that nothing was wrong with anything. If Congress would not pass something there was no point saying that it should become law. He was a strong supporter of the two-thirds majority vote needed in the Senate.

We gave lunch the following day for a young Tory MP, Christopher Patten,[2] a friend of the Gilmours, and for Clive James,[3] a friend of Diana Phipps. I had seen Clive previously at parties with Diana, but had never before experienced so much of his glitter, except from his writings. At lunch he was scintillating, and particularly eloquent on the tedium of a certain journalist. He described an occasion when he had seen this man

––––––

[1] James (Scottie) Reston; with the *New York Times* since 1943: director and columnist since 1973; co-publisher *Vineyard Gazette* since 1968. Respected and admired for his integrity, breadth of view and pursuit of truth, he has been a god in the pantheon of American journalism and has been regarded as an unfailing mentor to the younger generation of writers.

[2] Christopher Patten, Conservative MP 1979–92. At this stage he was Parliamentary Private Secretary to the Chancellor of the Duchy of Lancaster who was also Leader of the House of Commons.

[3] Clive James, an Australian with no inhibitions about good taste or convention, but with an exceptional gift for words which he spins and arranges, whether in print or on television, whether in prose or verse, whether humorously or in earnest, so as to make him one of the most original and widely read writers of our time.

and some other crashing bore at one and the same time which he said was like having him 'on stereo'.

Patten is a liberal Tory. He thinks that eventually there will be a struggle between the PM and Prior. He said that there were some good young Tory members of whom K. Clarke[1] was particularly silver-tongued. He did not think Heseltine negligible. He was enthusiastic about David Owen with whom he had recently shared a rail journey.

20 SEPTEMBER

WASHINGTON

OPENING OF THE GROUSING SEASON

Dinner last night with the Bradens, an event that marked the opening of the Washington grousing season. Other guests were the Kissingers, the Lane Kirklands, the McNamaras, some Admiral to whom Joan has taken a fancy, and Evangeline Bruce. Joan confided to me that Joe Alsop had originally been invited but he had then asked if he could bring his step-daughter which Joan had refused because it would make the numbers such as to necessitate a second table, whereas she wanted to keep the conversation to one table. 'Also,' she added, 'I had once wanted to bring my son to Joe's and he had refused.' I said that I was glad she had told me of this sweet revenge.

At the end of the evening Tom Braden said he had difficulty in suppressing a wish to give a toast to our deliverance from Joe who would have ruined all conversation had he been there. I reported this subsequently to Kay after we had had a game of tennis. She expressed concern that 'our English eccentric', as she calls Joe, was beginning to make himself *insortable*. 'But I love him,' she insisted.

I like the casual atmosphere of the Bradens' house – plenty of dogs, children, a gentle, courteous black butler and Joan radiating warmth regardless of the needs of conservation. She has so much energy that she doesn't have to have a depletion policy.

The conversation at dinner was mostly about Poland, with side-swipes by Henry at the whole of Carter's foreign policy, including the latest piece of news that the administration has ordered a long report on the

[1] Kenneth Clarke, Conservative MP since 1970. He is one of the post-war Cambridge school of political highflyers. At this stage of his career he was Parliamentary Under-Secretary of State for Transport 1979–82. Already showing a driving force that would make it likely that he would fly to the top.

USA's relations with Iran over the past forty years. On Poland, Henry, who gets more emphatic the bigger the gap since he was in office, was sure that the Soviets would not tolerate the creation of free trade unions in Poland. He supported the AFL-CIO decision to send money to Walesa and his supporters. He was scathing about Muskie whom he likens to McGovern. He was very very hardline on everything. I too am extremely realistic about Soviet policy and intentions, but somehow I don't quite go along with Henry's line which strikes me as prompted a lot by 'opposition' feelings. He told me that he was close to Reagan.

Joan said that she just couldn't bring herself to vote for Reagan, to which Henry rejoined that he had no patience with 'left-wing intellectuals'.

Bob McNamara hardly spoke. He blinked when Lane Kirkland, as part of his case for sending financial help to Poland, denounced the whole gnomic tribe of bankers.

I spent a night in hospital last weekend to have tests, which fortunately proved negative. I had not thought them necessary but doctors here are great believers in tests and mine said that 'a sword of Damocles' would otherwise hang over my head and that I must go through all the checking procedures. The staff of the hospital, male and female, were nearly all black; those who were white did not wear hospital or nursing garb, a renunciation that seemed to me less becoming than priests' abandonment of the dog-collar.

Characteristically, I was woken up at 5.50 a.m. to be told the time and informed I was not to have anything to drink, nor any breakfast. 'The procedure will begin at around 9 a.m.,' I was informed. The procedure was an arteriogram in which they inject iodine into the veins and take a series of X-rays. Not very painful, and the doctor in charge was considerate and warned me always what was going to happen. Not that I liked being inspected; and I was glad when it was over. I have decided to leave my body for medical science when I am dead.

28 SEPTEMBER

WASHINGTON

CARRINGTON IN THE USA WHICH TURNS A DEAF EAR TO IRAQ ATTACK ON IRAN

An extremely untidy week began in New York with a lecture by Peter Carrington at the Council of Foreign Relations followed by a dinner for him at the Heinzes. Other guests included Brooke Astor, Tony Parsons,[1] Evangeline Bruce, Nancy Kissinger, Ronnie Grierson and a French couple, the Hubert Faures (he works for a branch of United Technologies). I was seated between Drue and Madame Faure. Due told Evangeline afterwards, 'You could see how Nicko was lit up by a Frenchwoman.' Peter was not in the best of form, complaining about a stone in the kidney (which has now gone) and gastro-enteritis (still with him). The only apparent effect was to make him less jokey. I had breakfast with him the following morning, to discuss the Middle East, Poland and the Alliance. It was highly useful to have this chance of finding out how his mind was working. I also wanted to speak in Cassandra-like cadences about the likely problems for the Alliance after the Presidential election.

Back to Washington the following day to give a farewell reception for the Marshall Scholars. I delivered a little homily to the departing students, had my photograph taken with them and ate a great many cucumber sandwiches before taking the plane back to New York for another series of meetings. I stayed there at the Knickerbocker Club.

Muskie invited Carrington to a bilateral breakfast one morning in New York. Others present included Tony Parsons, Julian Bullard and Nick Fenn on our side; on the other, apart from Muskie, McHenry (the US representative to the UN), Billings whom Muskie has brought with him from Capitol Hill to the State Department; also Fonseth and George Vest. We were served a large breakfast of yellow blotting paper and brown parchment.

I have heard mutterings from the State Department that Muskie does not properly get through his work and spends too much time with Senators. There is talk that even if Carter is re-elected he will not reappoint Muskie who is in the dog-house with Carter's entourage for failing to sign the draft letter they had prepared for him at the Demo-cractic Convention renouncing all pretentions to the Presidency.

Peter led off at breakfast by giving Muskie a rough outline of what we were doing in Europe about the Arab-Israeli problem, concluding that it would not cut across what the US were involved in. Muskie muttered that he did not think that it would be unhelpful. Otherwise he hardly uttered throughout the breakfast.

Apart from Muskie's downbeat performance I was interested by one other feature of the breakfast. Peter Carrington had been briefed before-hand in the hotel about the two IRA terrorists who have recently been

---

[1]Anthony Parsons, member of the Diplomatic Service. Ambassador to Iran 1974–9; UK Permanent Representative to UN 1979–82; Special Adviser to the PM on Foreign Affairs 1982–3. An exceptionally fluent and persuasive speaker as shown by his influence at the UN during the Falklands War. He has written scholarly books about the Middle East and the Security Council.

fêted by the Governor of Massachusetts. It was suggested that he should lodge a complaint with Muskie, if only for the record. As things turned out he did not mention the subject. What was surprising was that when, the following day, John Fretwell called upon someone in the State Department the official there referred to representations the Secretary of State had made about it during breakfast with Muskie. The official was eager to give a considered response. Talking about this afterwards, John Fretwell and I could only conclude that the eavesdropping activities of US intelligence were even more rapid than we had expected.

Muskie's withdrawal symptoms have been increasingly to the fore. We have been saddled with a major crisis arising from Iraq's attack on Iran, greatly aggravated in the past twenty-four hours by the news we have received that Iraq has persuaded the Sultan of Oman, known as Qabous, to allow his country to be used as a staging-post for an air attack on Iran. Apart from the inevitable extension of the fighting that this could produce, it will be likely to involve HMG because of the presence in the Omani forces of about one hundred and thirty loan-service personnel from Britain, including the head of the Omani navy, a former British naval officer. They would be required to participate if, as was likely, the Iranians retaliated with an attack on the Omanis.

We heard about this new threat simultaneously through a telegram from Muscat and from the State Department. When the news arrived Peter was communing with nature on the terrace of the Embassy in Washington on a beautiful cool autumn morning prior to going out to Dulles airport to be flown by RAF VC-10 to Tokyo and Peking. With the help of a school map we went into a huddle to consider how best we might bring pressure to bear to prevent the Omanis becoming involved. At one point Carrington answered the phone beside him. 'It's a man for Mr Witney [my Private Secretary],' he said. Upon which Witney moved to the telephone and took the call. Afterwards he informed us that it was not 'a man' who had wanted to speak to him but 'Oman'.

Hearing this Peter told us how one day Lord Airlie had telephoned the House of Lords from Scotland.

'Airlie here,' he said.

To which the House of Lords attendant, evidently a Scot, retorted, 'It's early here too.'

Peter tried to ring Muskie, only to be told that Muskie was playing golf in Maine and could not be reached. Warren Christopher than rang. He was laconic. Peter tried to reach some of the experts in the UK but they were dispersed at various seats of learning. We were told by the State Department that so far as they knew the President, whose where-abouts were not divulged to us, had no intention of sending the Sultan, or anyone else, a message. The Secretary of State decided that we might as well get something off immediately to our man in Muscat to ask him to exert dissuasive pressure on the Omanis. Peter spoke to François-Poncet whose shrug could be felt down the telephone line.

Meanwhile time was running out and it was clear that Peter would not take off that morning (Saturday) for Tokyo, the more so since during the whole of the long flight he would be out of touch, as well as going in the wrong direction so far as the centre of critical events was concerned. So his departure was postponed, first for an hour, then for five hours, finally for twenty-four.

My life was somewhat complicated by the presence also in the house of the Chancellor of the Exchequer and Lady Howe. I was giving a financial lunch for Howe and Gordon Richardson which Miller,[1] Volcker and Cooper[2] would be attending; and, as we were wondering what to instruct our man in Muscat to do, or how to find out what the Americans were up to, these American guests started assembling on the terrace. While we lunched downstairs, Peter and Iona had lunch on trays upstairs.

We resumed our Gulf consultations after lunch, interspersing them with some short walks and a little tennis. From a telegram we learned, to our astonishment and consternation, that the Americans had been tipped off three days previously that the Iraqis were going to carry out their attacks on Bandas Abbas and the islands in the Gulf of Hormuz from Omani soil with the Sultan's approval. Why had they not told us? Why had they not started to react sooner in order to try to avert it? Why, I kept asking myself, was Muskie off the air when he knew that Carrington was in Washington?

It was impossible not to suspect that the Americans, or at any rate some of them, had deliberately kept things from us because they wanted the Iraqis to have a go, and feared, rightly, that we would have tried to deter them.

On Sunday Peter flew back to London rather than proceeding to Japan and Peking. The crisis was still unresolved except that, perhaps because of our interventions, the Omanis were not going to be involved.

I sent Carrington an account of the changes brought about by Iraq's attack on Iran as seen from Washington:
  i) *Some of the Gulf States were now showing greater readiness to accept help from the USA because of their fear of attack from either Iraq or Iran.*
  ii) *The Soviet Union might be finding the situation awkward if their arms client, Iraq, got into difficulties, whereas the Iranians would be bound*

---

[1]William Miller, chairman Federal Reserve Board 1978–9; Secretary of the Treasury 1979–81.
[2]Richard Cooper, Under-Secretary for Economic Affairs Department of State 1971–81.
  Professor of Economics at Harvard since 1981.

to resent the idea of being attacked with Soviet arms from Iraq. Nor would Moscow like the idea of the USA becoming involved in playing a hand in the Gulf.

iii) *For the United States the continued integrity and independence of Saudi Arabia is paramount. The Americans are probably ready to become involved in defence of Saudi Arabia provided there is a clear invitation. This is just the opening that they had been looking for. There could of course be difficulties with Congress.*

iv) *The US government is intrigued by the possibility of getting closer to Iraq.*

v) *Washington does not favour the dismemberment or disintegration of Iran because if this happened the Soviets would be tempted to move in.*

3 OCTOBER

WASHINGTON

GALBRAITH ENCOURAGES HOWE

I arranged a large luncheon party seminar for Howe this week: thirty-five people including economists (Samuelson[1] and Galbraith[2]), tycoons, and journalists. Gordon Richardson was also there.

Howe spoke very well and gave a good impression. After he had finished I encouraged others to express their views. Galbraith rose to his enormous height and said, 'I would not at all wish to discourage the Chancellor from continuing with his monetarist experiment. I would indeed deplore it if he stopped because Friedman[3] would then be able to say that the policy would have worked if only he had given it another six months.'

---

[1] Paul Samuelson, appointed Professor of Economics at MIT 1940. Consultant to US Treasury 1945–52, to Rand Corporation 1949–75. Author of report to President Kennedy on State of American Economy 1961. Nobel Prize for Economic Science 1970. Author of numerous learned books and articles.

[2] Kenneth Galbraith, with the Office of Price Administration 1941–3. Director Office of Economic Security Policy, State Department 1941. Professor of Economics, Harvard 1949–75. Ambassador to India 1961–3. Prolific, profound and entertaining author. In his Ambassador's journal he wrote of his appointment to India: 'I have considerable qualifications [for the post] ... an unquestioned willingness to instruct other people in their duty.' Of the State Department he wrote: 'I think I dislike most the uncontrollable instinct for piously reasoned inaction.'

[3] Milton Friedman, US Treasury 1941–3. Professor of Economics, University of Chicago 1948–83. In 1976 he was appointed Senior Research Fellow, the Hoover Institute of Stanford University, California. President's Economic Policy Advisory Board 1981–8. Nobel Prize winner for Economic Science 1976. He was the foremost apostle of monetarism in the West at this time.

12 OCTOBER

WASHINGTON

SPEECH TO THE PEOPLE WHO RUN
THE USA

In a speech to the annual conference of the Business Council at Hot Springs I should have stuck to a single, simple theme such as that of Mrs T's dislike of too much government which is what they would have liked to have heard about. Instead of which I embarked on Friday night, after prolonged drafting, upon a careful analysis of how different the international scene was now compared with a decade ago. One of the tycoons said to me afterwards, 'Gee, we found your speech had plenty of meat in it,' meaning, I suspect, that many of the audience had found it too heavy, or at any rate that their wives had.

Helped by Mrs Reg Jones, the wife of the chairman of the Business Council,[1] I observed the elite composition of the council; its members chosen, so Mrs Jones assured me, mainly from the British, Scandinavian, German and French sections of the population. She also told me – and this was confirmed from the positions they held – that those present, including the chairmen of Boeing, Coca-Cola, Bechtel, the Prudential, Eastern Airlines, Westinghouse, Ford, IBM, were 'the people who run America'.

13 OCTOBER

WASHINGTON

US POLICY FOLLOWING IRAQ'S ATTACK

Having received a message from London about the need for closer allied consultation on the Iraq-Iran problem I saw Muskie. He is involved in the Presidential election campaign but saw me one morning accompanied by Warren Christopher and George Vest.

As my diary records in some detail I told Muskie that London wanted to know more about America's ideas for an international naval force for

---

[1] Reginald Jones, born in England; naturalised American in 1925. With General Electric Company since 1939.

the Gulf in which they had asked for British participation. What were the suggested rules of engagement for the force and how long was it intended to remain in existence? The British government also was eager to learn of US intentions towards the Gulf as a whole. Was there evidence that the Saudi Arabian government was ready to welcome US involvement? What was the attitude to this of the Gulf States? I explained that to deal with these questions the British government urged that political talks should be held and that perhaps Warren Christopher would be prepared to go to London for the purpose.

From how Muskie replied I derived the impression that the idea of an international naval force had been advanced by the White House in order to meet a sudden emergency. He had not had time to discuss the proposal with his own officials.

When I came to report to London I indicated that the pace on this subject seemed to be set by the White House (Brzezinski) and the Pentagon who saw the present crisis as a means of establishing a permanent defence position for the USA in the Gulf. They wished to seize upon current Saudi fear, particularly of air-raids from Iran, in order to create the forward facilities necessary for the rapid deployment of US forces in the area. This would enable them in the last resort to establish a line to try to deter or block a Soviet military advance. They saw the initial Saudi invitation to them as the long-sought card of entry; and now that they had their foot in the door they were not going to be persuaded easily to take it out. They perceived a link between their growing connection with Egypt and their new relationship with the Saudis, the one helping the other and both offering a chance to overcome the handicap imposed on Middle East US policy by their commitment to Israel.

It was difficult, I concluded, to draw any useful conclusions before Presidential election day – the 'national dental appointment' as Meg Greenfield[1] describes it.

---

[1]Meg Greenfield, a Fulbright scholar and at Newnham College Cambridge 1952–3 where her moral tutor reprimanded her for frivolity to her life-long delight. She has written editorials in the *Washington Post* since 1968; and commanded the editorial page since 1979. Winner of the Pulitzer Prize for editorial writing in 1978 she has for long been one of the most sparkling figures in the journalistic world of Washington.

8 NOVEMBER
WASHINGTON

THE REAGAN LANDSLIDE

'Too close to call . . . It could go either way . . . Nothing to choose between the two, judged by all the polls . . .' These were the frequent sayings day and night in the weeks preceding the election. Now they look as stale as they were wrong.

We watched the election results with the Fritcheys at a party given for Pamela Hartwell. Not a totally successful evening, partly for mechanical reasons. Pamela kept muttering to me, as we failed to see or hear the results on the TV set which was ill-placed upon the floor and not working well, that prior to her election parties she always had the electricians in to make sure that the viewing arrangements were satisfactory. The main dampeners on the proceedings, however, were the early and resounding pro-Reagan results. Carter conceded before the voting had finished in California.

The Fritcheys' party was a gathering of Democrats – who constitute the hard-core of Washington social life. Although few had much liking or respect for Carter personally they felt slightly horrified by the extent of the swing and by the defeat of so many liberals in the Senate. I had read that Reagan himself found the results 'scary' when they started rolling in. Certainly nobody expected a landslide of that order.

Anne Armstrong who has been appointed deputy chairman of the Transition Committee told me on the telephone, when I called her in California, that not one of them had dared hope for anything so sweeping.

We now have the task of getting into touch with this Transition Committee when it sets up shop in Washington next week and of trying to answer London's insistent enquiries about the likely policies of the Reagan administration when it takes over on 20 January. There is much impatience abroad about the long interregum between the election and Inauguration Day, but with the far-reaching staff changes that occur upon a shift of party and with the absence of the continuity provided by our Civil Service procedure, the appointment of appropriate people to fill the thousands of posts in a new administration inevitably takes time. Dick Crossman likened the speedy process in Whitehall when one government is succeeded by another to the ease with which a mortician removes the corpse from a hospital bed so that its place can immediately be filled by another. It's not like that here.

We have Piru Urquijo[1] staying. Also the Bodley-Scotts. I told Piru that Bodley Scott had been a distinguished physician and had numbered the Queen among his patients ... 'It must have been Queen Victoria,' she quipped. We had a mixed bag for lunch yesterday including these guests, members of the London Symphony Orchestra, now performing here, the Saudi and Swedish Ambassadors, the Laughlin Phillips,[2] Selina Shirley[3] and Constantine Niarchos.[4]

28 NOVEMBER
WASHINGTON

MACMILLAN'S LAST VISIT TO THE USA

Harold Macmillan, who has been to stay, was just as entertaining as I had found him in Paris two and a half years ago. Rising slowly and unsteadily to his feet to address an audience of a hundred or so senior citizens at the Smithsonian on the subject of 'The Way Ahead', he began: 'Don't worry' – pause – 'Don't worry. As Adam said to Eve when they were leaving the Garden of Eden; we are living in a time of transition.' At this period of interregnum between Carter and Reagan the very word 'transition' is on everyone's mind and lips, so this opening sally produced great laughter. Later, when I congratulated him on the opening of his speech, he said, 'It's no good beginning a speech by saying how glad you are to be present or anything like that. You've got to wake them or make them sit up with some arresting statement.'

Incidentally, I heard another lively opening to a speech recently at the Annual Awards Ceremony for the Performing Arts at the Kennedy Center held soon after the Republican election victory. This was attended by the President, Mrs Carter and many political and theatrical stars. Art Buchwald,[5] well known for his liberal views, came on stage, his smile as usual like the Grand Canyon, 'Mr President and fellow Republicans ...' he bellowed.

---

[1] Jaime and Pirou Urquijo, he of the well-known banking family, she the granddaughter of the legendary Dr Marañon, had become close friends when we were living in Madrid.
[2] Laughlin Phillips, Foreign Service Officer 1949–64. President Phillips Collection since 1967. Married to the dynamic Jennifer Cafritz, thus making up a formidable tennis partnership.
[3] Selina Shirley, daughter of Earl Ferrers.
[4] Constantine, son of Stavros Niarchos.
[5] Art Buchwald, syndicated columnist whose articles appear in over five hundred newspapers worldwide. After forty years his columns still retain their satirical humour and bite.

Macmillan made a brilliant speech at the end of the dinner we gave for him at the Embassy. There was the usual theatrical uncertainty at the start and unsteadiness on his feet. His body only straightened up slowly and his head remained down. His voice for long quavering. This is how he began: 'In my profession you are called a politician when you are alive, and a statesman when you are dead. At the moment I am somewhere in between ...' He went on to speak about Churchill and Roosevelt and relations between our two countries, but he avoided clichés and struck a personal note. At one point he hesitated – he is a master of hesitation – and said that he did not nowadays represent anything except – another long pause – 'except affection for my mother's country'.

By the time he had finished, after not more than five or ten minutes, there were tears rolling down several cheeks, including those of Joe Alsop and Senator Tower.[1] When afterwards we mentioned this to Macmillan he laughed it off saying that the tears must have been thanks to alcohol.

It was a large dinner for forty-five or so, including the Harrimans, Anne Armstrong, Kissinger, Senator Tower (a new name to conjure with now that the Republicans are in the ascendant), Dr Winks[2] (of Yale where Macmillan had just spoken), Barbara Walters, Joe Alsop, Brooke Astor, the Heinzes, Kay Graham, Lally Weymouth (who was furious to find herself seated next to Drew Middleton[3] whom she regarded as a geriatric reactionary, but afterwards, without batting an eyelid, she said she had 'found adorable'). Among the other guests were Evangeline Bruce, George Will[4] (who is the man of the hour for having given the first Washington dinner attended by Reagan as President-elect), the Gunzburgs[5] (who are staying with us for a few nights), and Bob Silvers[6] (editor of the *New York Review of Books*). I have heard subsequently that Brooke Astor waylaid George Will and asked him how she could give a pre-inauguration party for Reagan, as he had done. Will said that

---

[1] John Tower, Republican Senator from Texas since 1961. Chairman Senate Committee on Armed Services.
[2] Robin Winks, historian. Assistant Professor then Professor at Yale since 1961. Master Berkeley College, Fulbright Scholar. Cultural Attaché US Embassy London 1969–71. Author of many books, particularly on Canadian and British history.
[3] Drew Middleton, journalist. War correpondent with various allied forces throughout the Second World War. Chief Correspondent *NY Times* to USSR 1946–7, Germany 1947–53, London 1953–63, Paris 1963–5, the UN 1965–8. Author of several books mainly on military matters. The Garrick Club gave a dinner to honour him as a venerable and trusted paragon of American journalism during and since the Second World War.
[4] George Will, political correspondent at this stage for the *Washington Post* and *Newsweek* magazine. He showed a marked pro-Republican bent.
[5] Minda and Alain Gunzburg, who were friends from Paris.
[6] Robert Silvers, associate editor *Harper's* magazine 1959–63. He has been editor of the *NY Review of Books* since 1963 and has made it a highly influential literary and political review publishing comprehensive surveys of current world problems as well as critiques of new books.

he would see to this and he proceeded to get into touch with the Reagans and fix an evening in New York. There is almost as much speculation and spilling of bad blood over Reagan's social life and the chances of horning in on it as over the appointments to his Cabinet.

Given the variegated guest list it was not surprising that I had difficulty over the *places à table* for Macmillan's dinner. Bill Walton,[1] who was staying with us and therefore saw early where people were to be seated, said that he could not possibly be next to Joe Alsop as the latter loathed him. We therefore had to make a last-minute switch. It suddenly emerged that Muffie Brandon would not be coming. Yet another adjustment had then to be made to the beautiful table plan.

I sat between Pam Harriman and Mrs Tower. At the end of dinner I made a speech before toasting Macmillan. I did not think that it was a complete success, I don't know why. I had taken trouble to prepare it which meant perhaps that it was too dense and lacked oxygen. Anyway I felt – and how sensitively one feels the reaction – that it fell a little flat.

I chatted with Macmillan afterwards – and it was then quite late – and he had had a long day, though he had been determined to stay at the dinner party as long as necessary since it would be impolite to leave early. He complained that it was impossible nowadays to lead the life of a gentleman adding, in answer to my question, that he regretted that women had to work. 'Women ought to sit about and look beautiful,' he commented. He likes to deliver himself of this sort of remark as well as opinions about the similarity between the aristocracy and the working classes due to the fact that they both like sport and women. But he takes a close interest in current events, particularly in America. He revealed a greater knowledge than I had expected or than I possess of the way revenue in the USA is collected as between the states and the federal government.

Upon returning from lunch with Alice Acheson[2] on the second day, where I gather he had been in spritely form and had made yet another moving speech, he told me that it had been most agreeable: 'Like lunching with the Whigs. That's what they're like, aren't they?' I did not dissent

I suggested that he might like an afternoon rest because he was due to participate at the Smithsonian from 5.30 p.m. on and it would be a long evening. But he said, 'No, I don't rest.'

It was clear that he wanted to talk. Mary said that he was always asking, as he sat in his sitting-room leaning on his silver-handled stick: 'Where is the Ambassador?' adding, 'In the old days he was always to

---

[1] Bill Walton was a friend from my earlier days in Washington. A painter and agreeable companion, he had been part of the White House set in Kennedy's time.
[2] Alice Acheson, widow of Dean Acheson.

be found in the library.' Part of his reason for wishing to talk is that he has difficulty in reading but he refuses to be operated on for his double cataract.

He said – twice I think – that he couldn't understand why modern politicians made such a fuss about being beaten at the polls. He was shocked that Muskie had burst into tears at being beaten. 'Why, in my day,' he said, 'if you lost, you accepted it and prepared for the next battle. I fought fourteen elections and lost six.' He expressed contempt for proportional representation saying that he recalled an Oxford election under that system in which the person who had come out bottom was declared the winner.

We talked about Ted Heath, who was about to come and stay with us. I muttered something about the widespread view that what Heath lacked was the influence of a good woman, to which Macmillan interjected, 'A bad woman would be better, I think.'

Macmillan's speech at the Smithsonian lasted fifty minutes. He spoke without a note giving many historical details and a broad sweep across the canvas of the past two hundred years. He answered questions afterwards brilliantly, being both humorous and detached without seeming cynical or uninterested. Asked whether he had ever discussed with Khrushchev the prospects of war and the way to avoid it he replied, 'Yes, often, both drunk and sober.'

He sat like some old dog, his head leaning forward, and when a question had been posed, there would be a long silence and one wondered whether he was going to utter anything at all. Then it all came out beautifully ordered and modulated, not at all deferential, but not abrasive either. What impressed the audience most, I think, was the range of his historical, political and economic knowledge. He was able to discourse on the benefits of the Age of the Antonines, to list in correct order the many constitutions that France had had since 1789, and to explain the pros and cons of high interest rates and to spell out the consequences for the future of a continued trade imbalance between the OPEC and non-OPEC countries; and to do so with clear conviction yet unpolemically and without rancour.

His main theme was how seldom political leaders are prepared to look ahead, yet it is 'that capacity that makes the statesman'. It is for that reason that Winston Churchill out-strode de Gaulle.

He concluded by deploring the extent to which religious faith had been lost.

The following morning he was a little tired, not surprisingly. I gave him a couple of cigars which cheered him up. On the journey out to Dulles airport we had another very agreeable chat. I thought to myself of a remark that Frank Longford had made to me once about the contrast between the high quality of Macmillan's company nowadays compared with the boredom for which he was renowned amongst his contemporaries before the war. 'He was thought a dull dog,' Frank insisted.

He wasn't at all dull as we talked in the car. I asked him how his mother from Indiana had come to meet his father. 'Well, it was an awful long time ago,' he said, '1880 or something. It was in Paris. He was her second husband. You know she never had an American accent. She came to Europe when she was very young.'

As I said goodbye I did not find myself wondering whether I would ever see the old boy again because somehow I thought I was bound to do so. There seemed to be still plenty of life in him. As he pointed out with some glee, Averell Harriman was two years older than he was. A few days after he had left, Julian Amery[1] came to lunch and told us how much Macmillan had enjoyed his stay. This pleased me a great deal.

6 DECEMBER

WASHINGTON

GEORGE WEIDENFELD AND PARTIES

I ran into Mike Nichols[2] at a party in New York for George Weidenfeld. He said, 'I've got a new idea for a TV commercial. There is a completely blank screen, but the sound of a big clock ticking and movement up and down like the undulations of a heart. Below a caption reads: "Somewhere someone every thirty seconds is giving a party for George Weidenfeld".'

George is now here in Washington spending the weekend with us. He is a delightful companion knowing a lot of gossip and bubbling with ideas. He had just had breakfast with Henry Kissinger whom he thought in poor form: bitter at the attacks on him from his own side and indignant over William Shawcross's[3] vendetta against him. I told George that Kissinger, like Heath, suffers from post-power frustration, which appears to be more corrupting than power itself.

---

[1] Julian Amery, Conservative MP 1950–92, with one interruption. Married Catherine, daughter of Harold Macmillan. Secretary of State for Air 1960–2; Minister of Aviation 1962–4; Minister for Housing 1970–2; Minister of State FCO 1972–4. A distinguished author, he has written the last three volumes of the life of Joseph Chamberlain. I have known him since we were at Summerfields together in 1930.
[2] Mike Nichols, American entertainer, stage and film director. Gives his leisure interest as: Arabian horse breeding.
[3] William Shawcross, writer, columnist, the *Spectator*. Author of *The Quality of Mercy: Cambodia, Holocaust and Modern Conscience* (1984) and a biography of Rupert Murdoch (1992).

The gala last night at the Kennedy Center was an American mixture of the good and very bad, the high and the very low: a bit of ballet; a song sung by Bernstein's daughter; a parade by the marines; Cagney on film, dancing Yankee Doodle Dandy; Galway playing the flute; a tape-recording of Carter addressing the Kennedy Center prize-winners; and the mass singing of 'Happy Birthday To You' to celebrate Lynn Fontanne's ninety-third birthday. The audience didn't seem to mind, or rather they positively enjoyed, the sharp contrasts of the programme. Their sense of discrimination was luckily in suspense.

13 DECEMBER
WASHINGTON

KAY GRAHAM ENTERTAINS THE REAGANS

We have attended a dinner given by Kay Graham for the Reagans. For us personally it began with a drama that arose in the course of the weekend of Thanksgiving Day which we spent with Kay on Martha's Vineyard. As we were being served the required turkey and sweet potatoes, and as Kay was putting logs on the fire she said how much the Reagans wished to avoid the practice followed by the Carters of having nothing to do with Washington or its inhabitants, particularly the cave-dwellers. To which I responded by saying, 'You know, what you ought to do, Kay, is to give a party for the Reagans.'

'Well,' she replied immediately, 'that's exactly what I am going to do.'

From then until the end of the weekend this dinner party which was to take place on 11 December was the main topic of our conversation. The principal subject for discussion was the guest list – one of the problems of which was whether or not we should be invited to attend. At an early stage in the weekend Kay said that she wanted to invite us but what was she to do about other diplomats? I suggested that she could ask the French whom she knew personally but if she was going to extend the list she would have difficulty in deciding where to stop without giving offence. Kay wondered about the Germans whom she did not know personally. Then what about the Israelis and the Saudis? And why, in those circumstances, leave out the Japanese? I implored her to do what she personally wanted and to forget about protocol. She wasn't, after all, a government and Reagan would not yet be in office at the time of the party, so it could not be called an official occasion. Whatever she did there would be resentment and envy. Kay said that she had difficulty in making up her mind. By the time she went to bed she had decided to invite the French, the Germans and us.

Early the next morning she had altered her mind by choosing to include the Saudis. A few hours later she said that she thought that, on balance and to save bitterness, she had better have the Israelis as well. When we were playing tennis, she stopped between points to say that the problem of which diplomats to invite was preying on her mind and that it had been doing so all night. When she left the island to fly to New York she was clearly still in great uncertainty about it.

Quite late that same evening – Sunday – when I was back working in Washington, dealing with Poland, I had a call from Kay in New York. In an apologetic tone of voice she said that after thinking it over she had come to the view that it would be better to have no diplomats. She hoped, therefore, that I would understand. To which I replied that of course I would go along with whatever she wanted. There was no need whatever to think that she was under any obligation to invite us. No personal offence of any kind would be caused. But, just as a matter of interest, what was it, I asked, that had caused her mind to tilt in this way? She said that she had been in such a state about the whole subject that she had consulted Henry Kissinger. He had taken the line that it would be quite wrong to invite diplomats to meet Reagan before he had become President and that if she invited one she would have to invite the lot. In response, I repeated that there was certainly no need or obligation to invite us. But I could not agree with Henry's arguments. Earlier I had disposed of a roadblock that somebody had tried to set up, saying that I could not meet Reagan before I had presented credentials. I pointed out that there was no question of having to present credentials whenever a new President assumed office; credentials were only presented once. Reagan, I said to Kay, was already meeting all manner of people prior to taking office. Of course he could not meet me officially, but the same applied to everyone else. I noticed from the press that George Weidenfeld and Fitzroy Maclean had been invited by Brooke Astor to meet him in New York. A private dinner at this stage in Georgetown, which is what she would be giving, seemed to me to cause no problems of protocol. The suggestion that if Reagan met one Ambassador he automatically had to meet all the hundred and fifty others was like saying that just because he accepted an invitation from the publisher of the *Washington Post* he would have to accept invitations from all other newspaper proprietors in the United States. It was, I insisted, for Kay herself to decide according to her own wishes. There was no requirement whatever to invite us, though naturally I would like to come, and I assured her that it would not cause a diplomatic incident if we were there.

Kay then said that Kissinger had thought there would be a problem of *places à table*. For instance would Mary and Antoinette de Laboulaye[1] (the wife of the French Ambassador) have to have places of honour? I said that I did not think she should bother about that. There would be no need to follow the rules of protocol because Reagan would not at that stage be President. Kay was obviously relieved to hear this. She promised to think the whole thing over again and get into touch with me.

She left a message later that night (I was out to dinner) to say that 'the dinner will be all right'. Next morning she rang early to say that she had at last made up her mind after consulting one or two other people (including Joe Alsop, so I heard later) and she would be inviting the French Ambassador and us – on the grounds that we were old personal friends.

Well, there we all were, assembling at Kay's house on R Street on Thursday evening. We filed into the small front room of the house, passing on our way the table-lists that showed Mary seated next to Reagan. She admits that she has been impossible ever since the dinner party as she begins every conversation by saying: 'As the President-elect said to me last week ...' I was seated between Mary Graham[2] and Mrs Gary Hart.[3] Bill Casey[4] was on Mary's other side and he did not seem to want to talk much.

I managed to buttonhole Meese[5] after the dinner and ask him about making arrangements for a visit to Washington by Mrs Thatcher soon after the inauguration. He was enthusiastic. She would be among the first of the allies the President would wish to receive. Would I get into touch about it with Richard Allen?[6] I asked him to speak to Allen and say that I would be doing this with his, Meese's, authority and he undertook to do this.

Meese went on to speak of his gratitude over the trouble taken for

---

[1]François de Laboulaye; French diplomat who had been born and brought up in Washington where he had known Kay Graham since childhood. Ambassador to Brazil 1968–71; to Japan 1972–5; to the USA 1977–82.

[2]Mary Graham, wife of Donald Graham who had been publisher of the *Washington Post* since January 1979.

[3]Gary Hart, Democratic Senator from Colorado since 1975. He was a potential candidate for the Democratic Presidential nomination until he became mired in an extra-marital scandal.

[4]William Casey, lawyer and government official. Under-Secretary of State for Economic Affairs 1972–3. Appointed Director of CIA 1981.

[5]Edwin Meese, lawyer and government official. Reagan's campaign Chief of Staff for Presidential Election 1980. Director Transition Committee 1980–1. National Security Council 1981–5. Attorney-General 1985–9. Gives his leisure interest as: collecting models of police patrol cars.

[6]Richard Allen, with National Security Council 1968–9. Head National Security Council and National Security Adviser 1981–2, when he resigned over a scandal in which he was shown with his wrist bedecked with watches.

him in London in the summer when he was shown how the raid on the Iranian Embassy had been carried out. His hobby is what he describes as 'police activities' about which he spoke to me with enthusiasm.

It looks as though he is going to be one of the most powerful men in Reagan's entourage, rivalled only by Weinberger[1] whom I have also seen since his appointment to the Pentagon.

I had no intention of trying to nobble the President himself personally about Mrs Thatcher's visit, or indeed about anything else; and I assured Meese that when I came to see him at the White House as I looked forward to doing from time to time, I would always be very economical of his time.

Having been invited at 7.30 p.m. sharp with a reminder that the President liked to depart early, I noticed that we stood around a long time before going into dinner and that this did not seem to bother Reagan at all. Indeed one of my impressions of the evening was that he probably doesn't mind all that much whom he is with so long as they are agreeable. After dinner he showed no inclination to rush away and, once again, he stood in the small front room chatting. It seemed to me that, in addition to Meese, Jim Baker[2] and Deaver[3] were evidently part of the inner entourage which certainly did not include Henry Kissinger. When Reagan, instead of leaving early, decided to sit down, everyone else who could find a seat did so too, hoping that they would learn something of the President-elect's interests and inclinations. Questions were put to him on a number of subjects of public concern but he made it quite clear he had no intention of being drawn. He told stories of his life in Hollywood, including a graphic account of how you best kissed while film-making. Bob McNamara, beside whom I was seated on a sofa, did not join in the merriment.

In the long wait before dinner Nancy Kissinger, tired and bored at standing up, had suggested that Irena Kirkland and I join her in the drawing-room. We had a good gossip there in the course of which I realised how far apart the Kissingers were from Reagan and his Californian set.

After the Reagans had left Kay's house, some of us stayed on: the

---

[1] Caspar Weinberger, educated at Harvard. Director Office of Manpower and Budget 1972–3; Secretary of Health, Education and Welfare 1973–5. Secretary of Defence 1981–7. He was the most respected and influential long-standing member of Reagan's Cabinet and someone with whom the British Embassy were lucky enough, thanks to his goodwill, to enjoy excellent relations.
[2] James Baker, Chief of Staff to US President 1981–5. Secretary of US Treasury 1985–8. Secretary of State 1989–92. He then became Chief of Staff to President Bush in an unsuccessful effort to secure his re-election to the White House.
[3] Michael Deaver was appointed to the White House staff in 1981 when he and his wife became among the Reagan's closest confidants and advisers.

Kissingers, the Donald Grahams, the Bradlees and Millicent Fenwick.[1] Henry was by now making a joke of his attempts to thwart our attendance at the party and he told the assembled company that by his action he had made an enemy of the British Ambassador; yet this hadn't prevented Kay from making a diplomatic gaffe. Alas, I had no repartee at hand and I was glad that there was no bitterness on anyone's part. Joe Alsop meanwhile was claiming credit for the *places à table* and the wine (Californian).

1981

20 JANUARY
WASHINGTON

PRESIDENT CARTER

On the eve of the inauguration of Reagan as President I have sent London a summing-up of President Carter – his personality and accomplishments in the White House. This summing-up is contained in the Appendix.

My conclusion was that history would be kinder to him than the present. Neither he nor his tenure of office will be regarded, even by the most revisionist, as great, but he will be seen to have had principles and to have stuck to them, and in so doing to have avoided war, spread the doctrine of human and civil rights and protected the natural resources of the country – not a very high monument, but not an ignoble one either.

24 JANUARY
WASHINGTON

THE CALIFORNIANS MIGRATE EAST

The Californians no longer have to dream of a snow-white Christmas now that they have exchanged Pacific Palisades for Pennsylvanian Avenue. We in Washington have been watching with fascination the

---

[1]Millicent Fenwick, member of House of Representatives 1975–83. Appointed Ambassador to FAO 1983. She was a fiercely independent, pipe-smoking politician.

arrival over several weeks of these flocks of exotic birds at a time of severe weather when the Potomac has been frozen over.

Reagan wants to have his close friends, of whom he has many, alongside him when he enters the new school; and they seem to want to be with him in this strange environment and, no doubt, to bask in some of the reflected glory emanating from the White House. We have been to several parties for him and are beginning to get the hang of the Californian world that will be running this country for the next four years at least. Revealing have been the asides about them expressed in the intimacy of the dinner table by those of the new government, for instance the Bushes and Baldridges,[1] who are not part of the inner Californian circle. Mrs Bush, a charming unspoilt grey-haired but buoyant extrovert, repeated to me last night what I have read several times in the papers, that she did not know the Reagans at all before the Republican Convention last summer, but that she now found them 'adorable'. She also told me, not I suppose altogether surprisingly, that she was against reform of the system of primaries because 'George would not have become a national figure or have won Iowa without the extended primaries.' She also told me that the American people were wise and the finest in the world. Mrs Baldridge, on the other side, was not going in for any political bromides. She asked me, as a diplomat, to advise her what to do about abortion. Reagan and many in the new administration were on record as favouring legislation to make abortion illegal – it was the Catholic/Conservative lobby – but she felt strongly the other way. What should she do to voice her views? I said that I certainly shared her opinions but it would require considerable thought how to impinge best on Reagan's mind without boring him or producing a counter-reaction. I enjoyed talk of this serious dilemma as I did my discussion at dinner on strategy with Brent Scowcroft,[2] until interrupted by Congresswoman Millicent Fenwick who came to smoke her pipe beside us and talk drivel.

Mrs Bush told me that she had just spent an hour with Mrs Reagan. She assured Mr Justice Powell[3] on her other side that she was not in the least a hard woman. Mrs Bush's main worry, so she told me, was the press and the tendency they were already showing to write derogatory things about Mrs Reagan. I implored Mrs Bush to persuade Mrs Reagan to make a resolution that she would cease minding what the press wrote about her because even if she were a combination of the Virgin Mary

---

[1] Malcolm Baldridge was appointed Secretary of Commerce 1981. His leisure interest was rodeo and he met an early death in a riding accident. He and his wife brought a free-and-easy, non-partisan air to Washington.

[2] Lieutenant-General Brent Scowcroft, Military Assistant at the White House 1972–7 and 1989–93.

[3] Lewis Franklin Powell, judge of the Supreme Court 1971–87.

and Cleopatra they would write horrible things. It was inevitable.

I find that the Californians are as baffled about whom they are meeting and why as the Washingtonians are. Last night I attended an Alfa Alfa dinner – an enormous men's dining club, like the Gridiron, that takes the mickey out of top politicians, preferably with them present, as they were last night, including the President himself. I don't think a day has gone by this past week when I have not shaken hands with Reagan or been quite close to him. I have seen far more of him than I did of Carter in eighteen months. But then he likes going out. Carter, for all his grinning, did not, I think, like people; or at any rate he had a chip about non-Georgians. Such gregariousness as he had related only to Georgia. At this Alfa Alfa dinner I was seated at the head table between the new Attorney General, French Smith,[1] and the Secretary of the Treasury, Regan.[2] I quizzed the former, whom I knew to be among the closest of the Reagans' confidants about the pecking order around the President and his methods of work and play. He, like so many in Reagan's entourage, is worried about the slight contempt in which Reagan is held abroad, particularly in Western Europe, where he is invariably referred to, and no doubt considered as, simply an ex-movie actor who is now playing a new part. French Smith did his best to disabuse me of that, saying that Reagan would be very capable of mastering the main problems quickly; he was a strange combination, he said, of extreme niceness and great firmness. He would do the nasty things if necessary. I suggested that Reagan ought to visit European capitals some time this year. There would be no other way that would be nearly so effective of getting his personality across.

There is no doubt that a new world is taking over here, a world that will not be very interested in specialist discussion, the weighing of argument, the impact of this or that course of action upon the welfare and happiness of the world at large. They are, I suppose, like the new industrialists of nineteenth-century England. They are not landed gentry. They are not mandarins. They are not, except for Reagan, politicians. Their common denominator is wealth. They are philistine and unphilanthropic. But they are not evil. They are not, for instance, like Senator Helms[3] who has already been trumpeting against what he considers to be insufficient conservative tendencies in policies and appointments.

---

[1] William French Smith, was US Attorney-General 1981–5. He and his wife, Jean, became good friends of ours.
[2] Donald Regan, chairman of board of Merrill Lynch 1973–81. Secretary of the Treasury 1981–5. Chief of Staff to the President 1985–7.
[3] Jesse Helms, was elected Republican Senator from North Carolina 1973. Member Senate Foreign Relations Committee 1981 where he soon became the scourge of the State Department.

They obviously, nearly all of them, are suspicious of Henry Kissinger who, incidentally, made a brilliantly funny speech last night at the Alfa Alfa dinner. He very definitely does not belong to their world. Senator Glenn,[1] to my mind quite an important Democratic figure emerging to the front of the political stage (if an ex-actor why not an ex-spaceman?) introduced Henry wittily by saying among other things that he might qualify as Amy Carter's successor as non-proliferation adviser in the White House. Glenn said à propos the wealth of the country's new rulers that 'millionaires were no longer a minority group.' Speaking on the same theme later David Rockefeller Junior suggested that the new motto on the White House should read: 'The buck starts here.' When Henry Kissinger rose to speak his first words were: 'Would you all sit down ...' as though everyone had been giving him a standing ovation which they certainly had not. He referred to his recent private trip to the Middle East where he had attempted to travel incognito. To assist this he had omitted his second name beginning with A when registering into a hotel.

Reagan turned up at the party and made a graceful and humorous speech completely appropriate to the occasion. Again Henry Kissinger was a suitable butt. The President said that everyone, including Henry, accepted the principle that all men are born equal; the only thing that had happened was that Henry had outgrown it quicker than other people.

The first time we ran into the migrating flock from California – characterised by rich plumage, some ignorance of the strange environment and a desire for friendship in their new surroundings – was at a dinner-dance given by the Dickersons,[2] ostensibly for the Deutsches[3] who are common friends of theirs and the Reagans. They found themselves having to invite so many people that they had to farm half the guests, nearly all of them Washingtonians, out to a club for the dinner, allowing them only to join the main party for dancing afterwards. We were among the favoured guests at the house where we found ourselves not only the sole foreigners but practically the only non-Californians. There they all were the *intimes* that we had been reading so much about:

[1] John Glenn, Democratic Senator from Ohio since 1975. As an astronaut he had made a three-orbit flight in 1962.

[2] Wyatt Dickerson; in real estate, married to Nancy, a well-known TV journalist. They lived on an estate in Virginia, formerly the childhood home of Jacqueline Kennedy Onassis. Not Reagan intimates, they nevertheless scored a coup by giving the party described here in which the President-elect and his Californian intimates were able to meet the cave-dwellers of Washington.

[3] Armand Deutsch; was described as 'philanthropist' when appointed to President Reagan's task-force on Arts and Humanities. One of Reagan's intimates, he had helped finance his rise to being Governor and then President.

Holmes Tuttle,[1] Justin Dart,[2] French Smith, the Wrathers,[3] and, of course, the Annenbergs. I have heard subsequently that the most *intime* of the *intimes* is Bill Wilson[4] whose wife spends an hour a day on the phone with Nancy Reagan. I do not know whether they were at the Dickersons, but they were certainly at the Annenberg lunch at the F Street Club where Mary sat next to him.

While I was chatting before dinner at the Dickersons to Justin Dart (who originally financed Reagan's entry into politics and who told me that he would not be going to the Embassy in London because he had 'too many things to do here') and to Holmes Tuttle (a car dealer who apparently sold Reagan a car some seventeen years ago and who decided then, by some strange process of causation, that Ronnie should give up films and go into business) there was a slight movement in the hall and one of them said to the other in a downbeat way, such I suppose as has been used in Beverly Hills every Saturday night for the past twenty years when the neighbours have arrived for drinks: 'Oh, there's Nancy and Ronnie.' And there indeed were the President-elect and the First Lady-elect. They were obviously delighted to see their friends and went around shaking hands, wreathed in smiles.

I sat next to Mrs Wagner (wife of the former Mayor of New York, a Democrat, but obviously acceptable in this gathering which was otherwise totally Republican except for one or two professional prostitutes like myself and the French Ambassador, the latter showing on his face a certain indignation from having been sent to dine elsewhere). On my other side at dinner was Mrs Deutsch, for whom as I have said the party was nominally being given. She is among the large and growing throng of women who are said to spend time talking to Nancy Reagan on the telephone.

There were toasts, the theme being the terrible parting involved in taking up the Presidency and the great consolation for Reagan in finding his Californian friends here to see him in.

We did a little dancing after dinner, everyone behaving self-consciously except Reagan himself who is obviously completely at home at such parties.

---

[1] Holmes Tuttle; also very close to Reagan from early days, he joined the White House staff 1982–88.
[2] Justin Dart; another member of President Reagan's kitchen Cabinet; he was Chairman of Dart Industries and served as Vice-Chairman of Reagan's National Council on Disability.
[3] John Deveraux 'Jack' Wrather jr; he made a fortune in oil, films and the media and was on the ground-floor when Reagan began his political career.
[4] William 'Bill' Wilson; one of the main chefs of Reagan's kitchen Cabinet, he began as a mechanical and metalurgical engineer. Reagan appointed him Ambassador to the Holy See.

The house was bulging at the seams with security men, many in mackintoshes and most with speakers in their ears.

On the Sunday before the inauguration we attended a lunch for the Reagans given by the Annenbergs. Walter made a speech and presented Mrs Reagan with a large sack of books about Dolly Madison. Again, Reagan was most gracious in his reply. He said that he was going to set apart a room in the White House where people could call him Ronnie, not 'Mr President'.

Bill Wilson, who, as I say, is one of the new Californian names to conjure with, sat between Mary and Kay Graham at the lunch. At one point he turned to Kay and said that he thought many things in recent times had been much exaggerated, that is to say blown up by the press out of all proportion. Kay asked him to what in particular he was alluding. He said, 'Watergate,' upon which Kay said, 'Well, I want you to know that I do not think so.' End of conversation.

2 FEBRUARY

WASHINGTON

JEANE KIRKPATRICK EXPLAINS HER APOSTASY;
KISSINGER IN A STATE

Today I attended a lunch given for Jeane Kirkpatrick,[1] the newly appointed US Ambassador to the UN. It was held in the crowded Sans Souci restaurant, which has about it a certain Parisian atmosphere. We listened to several rather long introductory speeches before Senator Moynihan introduced Mrs Kirkpatrick, saying that if she had enjoyed these lengthy lunchtime proceedings she would enjoy the UN (he is a former US Ambassador there).

A lifelong Democrat, Mrs Kirkpatrick explained her disillusion with recent Democratic policies and the reasons for her apostasy. She denounced the orthodoxy of 'perverted liberalism'. She said that a

[1] Jeane Kirkpatrick, political scientist, government official. Appointed Professor of Political Science, Georgetown University, Washington 1973. Member of the Reagan Cabinet and US Permanent Representative to UN 1981–5. She has said: 'My experience demonstrates to my satisfaction that it is both possible and feasible for women in our times to successfully combine traditional and professional roles, that it is not necessary to ape men's career patterns – starting early and keeping one's nose to a particular grindstone – but that, instead, one can do quite different things at different stages of one's life. All that is required is a little luck and a lot of work.'

genuine respect for human rights meant understanding that force reinforced legitimacy.

This is the prevailing mood. Supply-side economics means cutting taxes, which in turn means cutting government expenditure, which means cuts in Medicaid, less help for the disabled, for student and security benefits, for unemployment insurance, food stamps, training, health programmes, the arts, public broadcasting and school breakfasts and lunches.

I am sure there is going to be a great row ahead as people realise the difference between the talk and reality of tax-cutting. Mrs Thatcher and the British government are going to be picked on increasingly here as a warning of what monetarist policies can bring in practice because of the increased unemployment in the UK. So her visit is awaited eagerly by friend and foe.

Henry Kissinger telephoned me in a great state. I foresee him developing paranoia when it becomes increasingly clear that the new Republican administration wishes to keep him at arm's length. The hostility to him is not surprising if you think how little when he was in office he observed the maxim: 'Be considerate towards people on your way up; you may meet them again on your way down.' He had been told by irresponsible British journalists that the British government was inspiring a campaign against him on account of his recent trip to the Middle East. This had upset him very much. I assured him that Mrs Thatcher and Lord Carrington were his admirers and were not fair-weather friends. But of course when he attacked the Europeans for their Palestine initiative they naturally defended themselves. How sensitive he is – about himself.

7 FEBRUARY

WASHINGTON

——

PREPARATIONS FOR MRS THATCHER'S VISIT;

US HOSTAGES RELEASED; ESU GATHERINGS

We are becoming involved in details of Mrs Thatcher's visit, due at the end of the month. With Denis Thatcher, Carol Thatcher and both Carringtons coming with the Prime Minister there will altogether be five different programmes. We have been doing a lot of thinking about the dinner which Mrs Thatcher is going to give in the house for the President. There will be over a hundred guests for her dinner and thirty for her business/economic lunch. The demand on my Private Office for invitations is heavy.

At one moment the dinner looked as though it was going to be on the scrap-heap. I was told by the White House that we had jumped the gun, that they had never agreed to it and that Protocol Department at the State Department were saying that the President would not be able to accept return Embassy invitations so they had better avoid creating the precedent that would be set if Reagan were to come to the British Embassy. I was able to point out that Dick Allen of the National Security Council had welcomed the idea of the dinner when we had first discussed the programme, that it had been included in the agreed press announcement of the visit and that, anyway, we had already issued all the invitations. I have gathered that there has been a great deal of acrimonious toing and froing between the White House and State Department. But when Allen telephoned me to try to get me to say that I had pulled a fast one, he admitted that it was a *fait accompli* for which he blamed his inexperience, so the dinner has survived and I have never had to reveal to Number 10 how nearly it came to vanishing point. Nor, incidentally, did I ever tell Mary of the knife-edge we were on when she was already deep in details of the menu, flower-arrangements, and plans for televising the occasion.

The reaction of the American public to the long-delayed release of their hostages in Iran has demonstrated a distinctive national mood. It is as though there has been a widespread wish for a cause to inspire national unity and emotion and for a display of old-fashioned patriotism, a recoil from the humiliations and self-doubts of the Carter years. The return of the hostages after four hundred and forty-four days provided just that, so there was a ceremony on the lawn of the White House followed by Coca-Cola and cakes within, and a day or two later a ticker-tape parade in New York and a service of thanksgiving in the cathedral here at which the address of the leading hostage was applauded by the whole congregation. The return has generated an outpouring of national feeling. I must have heard the words 'God bless America' half a dozen times.

I have been reminded of how short the Americans are of national heroes. It seems to me odd, for instance, that they should at the moment be commemorating Edmund Hale, their first spy, whose statue stands outside the CIA building. The British captured and shot him in the War of Independence. He has now been eulogised as if he were a local version of Joan of Arc or Nurse Cavell.

I have been making calls on the new ministers. The most agreeble and useful was that on Cap Weinberger. He is extraordinarily friendly and sensitive.

I went to New York for the night to address the local branch of the English Speaking Union. I hope I am getting the right recipe for their audiences: one or two pure and not too subtle jokes, some remarks about local ESU activities and personalities; the dropping of a prominent name or two; and then a shower of unabashed sentiment – links, relations, ties, shores, common language, Shakespeare, Wordsworth, Churchill, the First World War and the Second World War, a tug at every chord short of singing 'Land of Hope and Glory'.

ESU gatherings are not, I find, embarrassed by schmaltz, unless laid on thinly. If that sounds cynical I have to say that I often find them moving.

18 FEBRUARY

WASHINGTON

———

TALKS IN LONDON ABOUT THE VISIT

I have been a few days in London to prepare for the Prime Minister's visit here which starts next week: calls on leading ministers and officials. I have a problem arising from the prevailing wanderlust in Whitehall: everyone wants to come over and meet their new opposite numbers even before they have been formally appointed.

Carrington raised one of his favourite subjects, that of who should succeed me in Washington. Apparently Mrs T also has acquired a taste for moving people about the world.

Saying that he rather favoured repeating what he had done with me, that is to say appointing someone who had just retired (say Parsons or Wright), he asked me whether I thought the wives mattered. I said that the new Californian world in Washington was very sociable. We met them frequently in the evenings. The important fact to bear in mind was that Mary was much more likely to get to know Reagan, Weinberger and Haig[1] on personal terms than I was because, in the nature of things, she would be sitting next to them at dinner and I would be with their wives.

Mrs T told me that she was a little worried by her forthcoming visit

---

[1] Alexander Haig, battalion and brigade commander 1st infantry division Vietnam 1966–7. Appointed to the White House 1969 and was Chief of Staff there 1973–4. Supreme Allied Commander Europe, SHAPE, 1974–9; Secretary of State 1981–2. He had the highest profile of any Cabinet minister at the outset of the Reagan administration but lost out in the battle for 'bureaucratic turf', as it was called. As Secretary of State he played a key part during the Falklands War, as will be shown in later diary entries.

to Washington. She did not quite see how it would go. She admitted to being nervous about it. She looked drawn – pale and rather distinguished. I did my best to reassure her, telling her how welcoming Reagan would be and how much he was looking forward to her arrival. I told her about the Californian gang who had come to Washington. We went through the programme. She was somewhat taken aback when I said that her after-dinner toasts would be televised. 'Then I shall have to think about them very carefully,' she said, adding, 'I shall want all the best historical advice I can get so as to get the allusions just right.'

We then discussed presents. She rushed out of the room to get some Halcyon boxes that she thought would be suitable for the Reagans.

As we became more and more involved in the plans of the visit, the worries seemed to flow off her and she became less taut. She didn't seem to want to leave the world ahead in which we had involved ourselves where she knew that she would be welcome and would be unmolested, to return to the beleaguered state in which she lives in London at present with a coal strike in the offing. It was noticeable how little we talked about the substance of her discussions with Reagan. She was rather clear that she wanted to see him alone for a few moments, and then in a restricted meeting – the fewer the better but she did not give me the impression that she had decided upon what subjects she wished to focus.

As I left her she thanked me for agreeing to put up Carol. She said that some people thought that mothers got on badly with their daughters, but she and Carol were on excellent terms.

25–28 FEBURARY

1 MARCH

MRS THATCHER'S VISIT TO WASHINGTON AND NEW YORK

The PM and the President had about half an hour together in the Oval Office on the first morning after the reception ceremony on the lawn of the White House where there was a guard of honour, a multitude of pressmen and where speeches were made by both of them. The tête-à-tête was followed by a meeting of four which included Haig and Carrington. Then at about 11.30 a plenary meeting was held in the Cabinet Room. I noticed that portraits of Lincoln, Coolidge and Eisenhower have taken over from Carter's spiritual fathers who hitherto hung on the walls – Truman and Jefferson, but also Lincoln. On the table stood a large jar of jelly-beans. Reagan explained to Mrs Thatcher that there are over thirty varieties including a peanut flavour. 'We haven't yet had time to take them out,' he quipped, referring of course to Carter's background as a producer of peanuts.

The PM spoke of the East–West relationship, the need to discuss fundamentals and tactics in the light of Brezhnev's speech, the Polish crisis and what is happening in Central and South America. The President said: 'The villain in Central and South America is the same as confronts the world at large.' He went on, his head shaking slightly, his voice quite deep and with a frequent smile, very charming and very unBismarckian: 'The US has tried a variety of programmes that were and look like our plan. But we looked like the Colossus of the north. We will now try a new approach to bring the continents together.' I didn't really know what he meant.

Reagan referred to his meeting before the Inauguration with Lopez Portillo, the President of Mexico. He said he had made clear that he wanted to hear the latter's views not just give his own. The meeting had been most warm. They had broken the barrier. Reagan then mentioned the Arab stallion that Lopez Portillo had given him as a present, no doubt an excellent investment judged by the personal pleasure Reagan had derived from it. The President said that he felt he had established a beach-head in Mexico: 'In the face of the suspicion that every Mexican child had about the United States.'

The PM seized the opportunity to ask whether the President would be going to the global summit in Mexico, fixed at the moment for 11–13 June. Might not his new relationship with Mexico be jeopardised if he did not go? This was followed by a discussion on dates and conditions in which Haig and Carrington also took part.

In general it seemed to me that the official meeting between the President and Prime Minister served the main purpose of such gatherings which is to focus the minds and attention of the leaders on the long-term issues of foreign policy – as distinct from day-to-day domestic business.

On the last morning the Reagans invited the Thatchers to go to the White House for a farewell cup of coffee on their way to the helicopter. This was intended, I am sure, as a gesture of friendship because they had already had plenty of opportunity for chitchat at the successive dinners at the White House and Embassy when they sat next to each other. Before the visit they had both decided, as I know from what they each said to me, that they liked each other: this was on the basis of their two earlier meetings, a few years back, and of their similar political and economic policies (government off the backs of the people; greater incentives to industry; everything for the individual) and of the warm message Mrs T had sent immediately the election results were known.

The media had been building up the visit as a 'love-in' or a 'honeymoon', even if monetarism as a doctrine and Britain's economy as a working model of that doctrine have come in for heavy criticisms in the US press in recent weeks. Brady, the White House Press Secretary, said after the visit was over that it had been 'difficult to prise them apart'. This was fortunate. Reagan said a lot of very generous things as did Mrs T – in after-dinner speeches at the Embassy, for instance. She is very good at rising to an occasion. She has acquired enough of the laudatory humbug necessary to keep international wheels turning, however much she likes to criticise the Foreign Office for wetness, for not standing up for Britain and for being sold-out to foreigners.

Denis plays a protective role at night. Apparently Mrs T does not like going to bed. During a recent visit to Rome she was eager after a long day to go out and visit some of the monuments by moonlight but Denis put his foot down. Not simply, I was assured, because such things did not interest him, but from fear that it would make her too tired. Likewise with us on the Friday night following the dinner for the President. It had been a long day, starting with two live TV programmes at 7 a.m. and 7.30 a.m., visits to two factories in the morning, a speech at Georgetown University at lunchtime, discussions at the Pentagon in the afternoon, followed by a press conference, a reception for the Commonwealth and then the party for the President. Rather to my disappointment the President did not ask Mrs T to dance though we had provided plenty of what we thought was appropriate music, such as 'Dancing Cheek to Cheek' and 'Smoke Gets in Your Eyes'. We began the after-dinner proceedings with some songs by Jim Symington[1] that seemed to suit the Reagans' tastes. We were sitting around on the verge of the large space that we had cleared in the middle of the drawing room – perhaps it was too large – the round tables at which we had dined having been removed. The Reagans remained chatting, rather than dancing. I am not sure why. It is possible that he may not have known in advance that dancing would be going to take place and did not therefore know whether it would have been in order to have started. Oddly, at the White House party the previous evening, he had accompanied the Thatchers to the door to say goodbye and had then returned to the party to dance with Mrs Reagan.

After the Reagans had left the Embassy party a number of guests departed but Mrs Thatcher stayed chatting and watching the dancing. She had said to me in London beforehand that she hoped people would not rush away, which was why we had arranged to have a band. Nobody

---

[1] James Symington, son of the highly respected Senator Stuart Symington. He took a part in Democratic politics; and in far from amateurish fashion could sing to his own accompaniment on the guitar.

asked her to dance. So I went up to her and said, 'Prime Minister, would you like to dance?' not an opening that would have been available to men in the courts of old, at Versailles or the Hofburg or, to move to more modern times when women Prime Ministers have become known, that would have been inspired by Mrs Golda Meir or Mrs Bandaranaike, or, surely, have been permitted by Mrs Indira Gandhi.

Mrs T accepted my offer without complication or inhibition, and, once we were well launched on the floor, confessed to me that that was what she had been wanting to do all the evening. She loved dancing, something, so I found out, that she did extremely well. Long afterwards I read that one of the few frivolous things she did as an undergraduate at Oxford was to learn ballroom dancing. The band showed great brio and I think Mrs T was happy. After the dance was over and we returned to the end of the room I hoped that someone else would ask her to dance, but alas, this did not happen. Were they all too shy, too much in awe? In retrospect, I realised that I should have encouraged Jim Symington to dance with her; or at any rate I should have arranged something rather than simply leaving it to chance. Meanwhile many others had moved to the dance floor and the party got into a swing. Denis approached and told Mrs T that she must go home to Blair House to bed. I asked her if she would like one more dance and she said she would like to waltz. 'Yes, come on,' she said, and we took the floor eagerly. It was with some difficulty that Denis eventually managed to extract her. She had expressed a wish to see some of the floodlit Washington monuments, but Denis put his foot down crying, 'bed'.

After her OSS speech in New York the following evening (at the end of which Denis was in tears of emotion) we repaired for a farewell drink to her suite in the Waldorf before having to leave to go to the airport for her take-off back to London. Mrs T was still in a state of euphoria from the applause she had received which was indeed very loud and genuine and she burst out: 'You know we all ought to go dancing again.' I think that even Michael Alexander[1] groaned at this; and Denis's foot came down heavily. The VC10 was after all waiting as if on tiptoe to take off at Kennedy airport.

Our dinner for the President and Prime Minister took a good deal of organisation. We could not seat more than a hundred and twenty people which meant that many were disappointed. The TV had to be there for the speeches. We arranged for a band of three to play background thirties

[1]Michael Alexander, a member of the Diplomatic Service, was Private Secretary (Overseas Affairs) to the Prime Minister 1979–81. He was later Ambassador to Vienna 1982–6 and Ambassador to NATO 1986–91. The son of a master chess player, he was an Olympic Gold Medallist for Fencing.

music during dinner and to be ready for dancing afterwards if any of the guests were so moved. Mary and John Lightfoot spent literally twelve hours a day for two days preparing the flowers for the evening. Long before the party, security men scoured the house, often accompanied by alsatian dogs. Not unnaturally when they saw all the undergrowth we had brought into the house from the garden for decoration they reacted predictably – which meant that several pots of daffodils had to be replaced. There were, it seemed, three quite distinct groups of security people: one for Mrs Thatcher; another for the Vice-President; and a third, the largest, for the President. I suppose they knew who each other were but we were certainly confused, struck particularly by the one feature they all had in common, namely listening-pieces in their ears. The impression given was that the house was teeming with strange people who indeed had taken it over. It seemed not only less private than usual, which isn't saying much, but even less secure. However, I was assured that despite Irish threats the security people could nowadays provide 100 per cent guarantee against assassination.

We had spent much time in the weeks before the visit tasting Californian wine. Mary had fined her choice of food down to the ideal menu for the President. About a dozen members of Chancery had been mobilised to help with the distribution of guests after their arrival. When the evening came we in the receiving line stood at the top of the stairs of the Embassy and a small covey of social journalists stood next to us, but roped off, their ears extended and pencils poised for recordable and preferably exaggerated expressions of greeting. Mrs T looked predictably fresh, despite her exhausting day. Denis was beside her. Beside him stood the Carringtons. Mary and I were slightly apart to field the guests as they left the line and to point them towards the drawing-room along the corridor past the battery of plants.

At exactly 8.20 p.m. the Thatchers descended to the front door to receive the Reagans. They accompanied them upstairs to introduce them to the Carringtons and us. We then proceeded along the corridor to join the other guests. The President was announced by a young member of the Defence Staff in uniform as he entered the Turner Drawing-Room. He shook hands and had a friendly remark for everyone. How excellent he is at that. I noticed that the press of people around him was diminishing so I introduced him to one or two of those who didn't seem to know him and then it suddenly became apparent that the room was empty, as we had asked everyone to be in their seats at the dinner tables by 8.40 p.m.; and I found myself standing alone with the President. Drinking a glass of the Californian wine that we were to have at dinner – Robert Mondavi, Cabernet Sauvignon 1974 – I decided to fill the gap by raising with the President the subject of Californian wine. It was apparent that he was both interested and informed. As Governor he had tried to encourage the producers to keep their wine longer before marketing it. He did not think that he had succeeded but he remained sure that the wine could benefit from longer laying down than was customary.

Mary and I then led the Reagans and Bushes into the dining-room to their seats and the dinner was under way. At my table the rather unusual food, which included quail pie, was much appreciated, at any rate by my neighbours, Mrs Weinberger and Mrs Casey. When it came to the speeches Mrs T used most of the text I had prepared for her, including the jokes, but interjected a long passage about the courage needed at two o'clock in the morning when you woke up aware of all the problems confronting you.

This, apparently, is a theme imparted by Airey Neave that she has used several times to describe the loneliness of politicians in the early hours of the morning worrying about the responsibility falling upon them. Later, Michael Deaver, who works in the White House and is close to the Reagans, vouchsafed to me, without any prompting, that the President had been moved by Mrs T's Embassy speech, especially the passage about two o'clock courage.

I was relieved when the VC10 finally took off late on Saturday evening from New York. It had not been easy to establish the visit in the President's programme long before he was inaugurated, and at the ideal time. Meese reminded me that it had all flowed from our initial conversation when we had met at Kay Graham's in early December. It had been quite delicate to secure all the items we wanted in the programme, including the dinner at the British Embassy. It had never been certain that with so tight a programme involving so many top people there would not be a last-minute hitch.

Although my reactions when it was over have been those of tiredness and anticlimax I realise that the visit has gone as was intended. Despite the UK's economic difficulties, the visit resulted in great exposure for Mrs T, even more than planned, and in more favourable media coverage for her and the UK than the circumstances really warranted. She returned to a very different type of reception in the UK where unemployment and bankruptcies accumulate, and there are widespread doubts within her Cabinet and party about her policies. I think that her acclaim in the USA may have helped to restore her.

Peter sent us a generous bread-and-butter letter.

9–13 MARCH

UNION PACIFIC TRAIN LAS VEGAS–OMAHA

We are back on this wonderful train as guests of Jim Evans,[1] spending four days 'inspecting' the line between Las Vegas and Omaha. For me the inspection consists of sitting in a comfortable chair in our private drawing-room reading and looking out of the window at the passing scene of mountains, high plateaux and scrub. We are a large party, mainly of business friends of the management, such as the Robinsons[2] (he is head of American Express) and a lawyer who managed 'our respective divorces' as Evans described the attorney to me in writing beforehand. The Robinsons have brought with them as their guest, David Ogilvy,[3] an Englishman who made a fortune in advertising in New York (e.g. Hathaway shirts identified with a man wearing a black eye-patch) and who has a château in France. He is setting a good standard as the eccentric Englishman suffering from no desire to please his hosts. Already Rosemary Evans is irate at his rudeness. At the outset of the journey he complained that his bed was above the wheels of the train which prevented him sleeping properly; with the result that the Union Pacific Company had to put on an extra coach. Their motto however is 'We can handle anything', to which must now be added: 'even David Ogilvy'.

At the large dinner party in the dining car of the train last night he sent back for re-cooking the vast and totally raw steaks; he then ordered English mustard, objecting to the French mustard that had been put on the table. I think he will prove a healthy antidote to the honeyed goodwill exuded by the other guests in the party who are inclined to describe everyone as 'so dear'. They even enthused last night over Las Vegas where we spent the evening 'on the town', driven there from our train in a bus in which an attendant served champagne.

John Bright advised Rosebery when he became Foreign Secretary to look at what Palmerston had done and to do the opposite. I was reminded of this when I visited Las Vegas. If you want my idea of an agreeable town look for the opposite of Las Vegas. Evelyn Waugh wasted his satirical talent on Forest Lawns when the vulgarity of Las Vegas offers to my mind a much richer field. All those flashing neon lights, the concrete hotels, the cocktail bars selling shrimps, and the full length of

---

[1] James Evans; chairman and chief executive officer, Union Pacific Corporation 1977–83.
[2] James Robinson; since 1977 had been chairman and chief executive officer, American Express.
[3] David Ogilvy; founder Ogilvy and Mather 1948, chairman to 1973. He had published *Confessions of an Advertising Man.*

the 'Strip' (the main street) devoted to gambling, with, I suppose, a bit of tatty sex thrown in. Marriage seems to be the other industry because apparently no advance notice is required. The Strip is full of wooden, hastily constructed churches announcing 'Weddings. Twenty-Four Hours'. I noticed one called 'Wee Kirk of the Heather'. We were taken by the bus to the main centre, to a vast structure called Caesar's Palace whose owner, called Wahl, wearing a check jacket proudly took us round. He said that he had eighteen hundred bedrooms and would shortly be putting up another tower with a further eight hundred. We ended the tour by being taken to a large suite of which he was particularly proud. It contained three baths which were in no way separated from the rest of the suite. There were two oval-shaped beds, surmounted each, not by a baldachin, but by mirrors. There was a bar surrounded by seats, as in an airport lounge. We asked rather absurdly how many people were meant to be accommodated, to be told, very practically, that that depended how many chose to be in each bed. The suite costs a thousand dollars a night. Everything shone of brass, silver and chrome. The curtain worked on a switch, as did the central bath.

It was a relief when the train pulled out of a siding early next morning making for Salt Lake City. Although the 'Home of the Church of Jesus Christ of the Latter Day Saints', as it is described, represents something that is in complete contrast to the gambling/materialist ethos of Las Vegas, I was struck by a strange similarity between these two towns. I think it was the fact that they were both so extreme that gave them something in common. We stopped in a siding at Salt Lake City. From there we went to the Visitors Centre in Temple Square where we ascended a ramp to be confronted with a colossal statue of Jesus Christ. It is placed in a vast dome depicting the universe, reminiscent of the dome in Caesar's Palace Las Vegas where there was a statue of similar size of the Emperor Caesar. The Mormon Jesus Christ looked like some funeral stonemason's reproduction of the statue of David in Florence. When we arrived at the Visitors Centre we were greeted by various leading Brothers of the Mormon faith – volunteer evangelists so we were told. Our first greeter was apparently very high up in the Brotherhood. We sat in a semicircle looking at a display of wilting poinsettias to be told the elements of the faith. We were shown some paintings of biblical scenes which reminded Mary of paintings of tractor drivers and norm-fulfillers in the Soviet Union. Our guide was a medical doctor who devotes all his spare time, so another Brother told us on one of the innumerable microphones on hand everywhere in the building, to telling good people like ourselves about the Mormon religion. What strikes me about it is the mixture of high religiosity with intense business acumen – something akin to the Quakers, who are different to the Mormons in all other ways. Brigham

Young wrote: 'My policy is to get rich; I am a miser in eternal things. Do I want to become rich in the things of this earth? Yes, if the Lord wishes me to have such riches, and I can use them to good advantage.' Certainly his house, the Beehive House, attests to his contempt for austerity. Strange to me is the moral code of the Mormons. Smoking and drinking (even coffee and tea are forbidden as being stimulants) are taboo; but not fornication. Although polygamy is now banned, Brigham Young, the George Washington of the movement, had sixteen official wives and apparently a good many others 'for security reasons' – whatever that may mean.

We saw a film entitled *Man's Search for Happiness* in which a muscular young man in shirt sleeves stares mistily into the distance and ponders on the meaning of life. We are shown shots of a baby being delivered, of the mother in painful ecstasy over delivery and of other babies in their cots. We are told that we did not suddenly come into existence at birth but that we have always lived. Accompanying a passage from Wordsworth about 'trailing clouds of glory' we are shown a lot of young men and women in white dressing-gowns gliding about and paying obeisances to a haloed figure of Christ. These same creatures appear at the end of the film and we realise that life on earth is a mere interlude between these eternal white clouds of glory. I shall never feel the same about dear Willie Wordsworth. I could not see much difference between the Mormon view of after-life and that of Christianity generally. It's the pre-life that is original. According to the doctor all memory of this pre-life has been blotted out at birth so that we 'might live by faith and further prepare for the everlastingness of life'.

While some of the Americans were gasping in ecstasy at the religious paintings, David Ogilvy was whispering subversively in my ear: 'Why don't you ask them about polygamy?' or 'I regard it as high-falutin' white slavery.' He pointed out that there's not a black face in the place. He was indignant that we were not allowed into the temple which is reserved for practitioners of the faith. 'What on earth are they concealing in there?' he speculated. 'Can it be mountains of pornography?'

30 APRIL–3 MAY
WASHINGTON

PRINCE CHARLES'S VISIT

It was the two-ring circus aspect of HRH's visit that appealed to me: the routine performance by day and evening of official duties – talking to people at receptions and at official lunches and dinners, speeches at public functions, showing interest and enthusiasm to hundreds of new people which Prince Charles does unflaggingly – and then the letting down of hair late at night, the removal of restraints so that HRH feels free to do the imitations which he performs brilliantly, and the revelations about what he likes and dislikes, the team-in-the-changing-room-after-a-match feeling.

We went to Andrews Field outside Washington to meet him and an event occurred there that has dominated press and TV treatment of the visit, as often occurs over some trifling incident e.g. when a photo was taken of a girl rushing up to the Prince on some Australian beach. Lee Annenberg, who is Head of Protocol, was planning to go up the steps and greet the Prince in the plane but a member of the advance royal party demurred, explaining that HRH did not like people entering the plane on arrival because he was often asleep, or, for one reason or another, not ready; and he preferred to be given time on board to collect himself. I had witnessed this self-collecting process when the Prince flew by helicopter to the *Nimitz*. He was wearing naval uniform and before leaving the helicopter had to put on his belt and sword. Having done so he shook himself and patted his sides, muttering as if checking off a list: 'Spectacles, testicles, wallet and watch.' I gather this is part of the royal routine, at any rate for male royals.

Lee therefore welcomed HRH at the bottom of the steps of the plane. She did so by extending him a deep curtsey. This was shown on television and in numerous press photographs. It stimulated a shower of abuse from practically every section of American opinion on the grounds that she was showing subservience and behaving in a manner unbefitting in a representative of a republic. Even those, and they were few, who thought that she had done nothing wrong by curtseying, complained that she had done it badly. Apparently Roger Mudd,[1] normally a serious TV commentator, devoted a programme of prime-time television to the

---

[1] Roger Mudd, correspondent. CBS 1961–80; Chief Washington correspondent NBC since 1980.

subject, contrasting Lee's clumsy curtsey with Mary's which he said was evidently much more graceful. In an anti-Annenberg frenzy the press have raked up details of Lee's matrimonial life, asserting that she has been married twice before, not once as she claims. They have published details of a second discreditable Las Vegas husband.

Late on the last evening we were discussing in light-hearted vein with the Prince how we could avoid a curtsey problem occurring when Lee came to see him off at the airport. The Prince resolved to grasp Lee with both hands and hold her upright, so that she would be absolved from the possibility of curtseying and thereby incurring the wrath of the American people, and also from deliberately not doing so which might appear discourteous after the curtsey extended upon the Prince's arrival. The plan was executed perfectly the next day and so far as I know there were no press comments or pictures.

Another small underlying drama occurred over invitations to the wedding.[1] The Prince told us that he could not invite anyone yet because no list had been drawn up so far. I said that Mrs Reagan was certainly expecting to come but that the President would not be able to do so. He could not make his first transatlantic visit as President just for the purpose of attending the wedding and it was too early for him to plan an extended transatlantic tour. Somehow I expected HRH to drop a pretty heavy hint about an invitation when he sat next to Mrs Reagan at dinner; but he didn't do so, though he told us afterwards, and mentioned it in his bread-and-butter letter, that having met and been enchanted by her he was determined that she should be there. A few days after the Prince had left I had a call from Michael Deaver at the White House. He is the member of the triumvirate (the others being Meese and Baker) who is closest personally to the Reagans. He said that he was trying to work out their forward programme; he realised it was awkward but could I give him some idea about the wedding. I told him personally what I thought the Prince wanted and, a few days later, I was able, on the basis of a letter from Edward Adeane, to confirm this, explaining that no official invitation would be issued until the end of May.

On the Prince's last evening we dined at the White House. Outside there was a crowd of demonstrators protesting about Northern Ireland. Had the visit come a week later when Bobby Sands died after a long hunger strike and the level of agitation rose by several decibels it would have made the execution of the Prince's programme very difficult. Passing a marine band playing some jovial and faintly familiar air, we were taken upstairs to be greeted by the Reagans in their private sitting-room. The

---

[1] The Royal wedding was due to take place on 29 July.

other guests included Cary Grant and his new (fourth) wife, Audrey Hepburn (and boyfriend, who had been formerly married, so we were told, to Merle Oberon), William Buckley,[1] Paul and Bunnie Mellon, Diana Vreeland,[2] the Louis,[3] the Annenbergs, Evangeline Bruce, Jerry Zipkin,[4] Robin Hambro,[5] David Niven's[6] son and his wife.

As the Reagans greeted them, the guests gasped at the wondrous change wrought in the interior decoration of the White House since Carter's departure. Naturally the Reagans were delighted as was Graber,[7] the decorator from Los Angeles, a friend of the Reagans, who has been at work in the White House. I noticed a fine octagonal table at the entrance to one of the private rooms. As we passed along the corridor to the dining-room we skirted the Reagans' private sitting-room where, as Muffie Brandon[8] explained to me, the Reagans have installed some of their own things. I noticed coloured photographs, one or two oil paintings of mountain scenery and fir trees, and various objects associated with horses or saddlery.

At dinner Mary was on Reagan's right and got on with him like a house on fire. At a separate table Mrs Reagan sat with the Prince on her right. On his right was Lee Annenberg. I was on Mrs Reagan's other side with Diana Vreeland on my left. However, the main point was that Mrs Reagan and the Prince hit it off perfectly. I am sure they talked about horses, though I have noticed that HRH is a bit bored, to put it mildly, with jokes about his frequent falls. He had to endure a good many of these at the Oxford-Cambridge dinner the night before. When the President had received him in the White House he made a crack on the same theme. The conversation had then moved on to terrorism, the attempt on the President's life, which he described, and his continued opposition to gun-control, followed by a discussion of Northern Ireland on which

---

[1] William Buckley; magazine editor, author. Editor-in-Chief *National Review* since 1955; syndicated columnist since 1962. Author of many books.

[2] Diana Vreeland, magazine editor. Editor Harper's Bazaar 1939–62; Editor-in-Chief Vogue magazine 1962–71. She was famous for her ingenuity in staging extravagant fashion exhibitions at the Metropolitan Museum NY.

[3] John Louis; Ambassadour to the UK 1981–3; previously director, international marketing, Johnson's Wax; and chairman of Combined Communications Corp, Chicago 1968–81.

[4] Jerry Zipkin, a frequent and agreeable attender at the Reagan court.

[5] Robin Hambro, American wife of Rupert Hambro. She worked for Covent Garden and subsequently for Christie's and is a successful designer of jewellery.

[6] David Niven was a close personal friend of the Reagans'.

[7] Ted Graber, a Beverly Hills designer who described his clients as 'the merchant princes who are today's royalty'. He was commissioned by Walter Annenberg to renovate Winfield House. According to the *New York Times*, Graber was hired by Nancy Reagan to integrate 'her own lacquered chinoiserie pieces with the White House's 19th century American antiques'.

[8] Mabel (Muffie) Brandon, wife of the journalist, and London *Sunday Times* columnist, Henry Brandon, was social secretary at the White House 1981–3.

both men expressed despairing concern. The Prince asked the President if he had any ideas for solving the problem, to which he replied that he had been wondering whether the Church leaders could play a role.

To return to the dinner, we had delicious food and good Californian wine. Mrs Reagan shows every sign of wanting to run an elegant White House – nearer to the Camelot of the Kennedys' era than to the homespun atmosphere of the Carters. The President made a speech which, rather to my surprise, he read, from a rostrum. The Prince replied, combining, as does his personality, humour with seriousness.

After dinner we returned to the bigger of the private sitting-rooms for some really bad songs which everyone seemed to enjoy. Then home quite early for a long gossip.

The next morning the Prince received members of the Embassy staff – office and domestic – thanked them in person and presented them with photos or presents. Once again I admired the great trouble he took. There was nothing skimped or peremptory about his manner of thanking, though I am sure in the circumstances he could have got away with a good deal less. He evidently wanted to do it properly, aware that the recipients would cherish a personal word almost as much as the photo itself.

Before they left I discussed with the Prince and Adeane[1] what sort of report they would like me to send on the visit. The answer was that they would like me to bring out that it was not just a social junket but that the Prince had met Bush, Haig and the President (twice). I myself was in no doubt that it had indeed served a useful public purpose.

7 MAY

WASHINGTON

TENSION OVER IRELAND

We are overwhelmed at the moment by Ireland. The death of hunger-striker Bobby Sands has aroused not merely the ire of the large Irish community but the widespread, scarcely sublimated, anti-colonial feelings which exist in this country, a conviction that HMG is in Northern Ireland for some imperial purpose and that in this particular case it is showing inflexibility over prison routine to such an extent

---

[1] Edward Adeane, Private Secretary and Treasurer to the Prince of Wales 1979–85; and Private Secretary to the Princess of Wales 1984–5. A Director of Hambros Bank since 1986. Remarkable for the dryness of his wit and his sense of duty.

that poor Bobby has been driven to his death. There have been inflammatory leaders in many papers and demonstrations against us in New York, Boston and San Francisco. The demonstrations in New York have continued uninterruptedly: crowds outside the entrance to our office there shouting and chanting and waving banners; in the office upstairs all this is audible and unpleasant; the staff have been getting worried; the atmosphere is brittle.

I am not surprised by the use the regular American-Irish lobby has made of the IRA's hunger strike. They have a built-in, unchangeable, undying attitude and they have votes, which means that they get a lot of support in Congress. I have been struck by the ignorance and bias even of educated Americans who have no Irish background. They know little of the problem in which, to be sure, they are not really interested.

What is going on reveals the hairy-heel effect of television. The camera responds much better to the young throwing bombs than it does to people going about their daily lawful business. The Americans have some eighty television reporters in Ulster at the moment, all of them eager to portray the smallest disorders, which, according to reports, they positively encourage.

I have had several murder threats from the IRA so police protection at the Embassy has been increased: men with motorbikes and handguns keep a particularly close watch on the swimming pool, a procedure that has seriously interrupted the nocturnal feeding and drinking habits of a family of racoons living in the woodpile behind the Embassy.

I have had to appear on US TV and radio. It is difficult to know if this has done much good. I believe that, uphill though it is, one has to take any chance that offers to try to explain the facts of the Irish dilemma to the American public. No doubt it would be more effective if I were a Catholic and spoke with an Irish accent. It does not matter that I am an official rather than a politician, a distinction that Nicholas Ridley,[1] who is staying with me, thinks must undermine the impact I make, though in fact such a distinction is blurred in the USA, or at any rate is very different from what it is in the UK.

---

[1]Nicholas Ridley, Conservative MP since 1959. At this stage he was Minister of State FCO. Interested in painting and architecture, he was particularly intrigued by the Embassy which had been built by his grandfather, Lutyens. Later I had close dealings with him when he was Minister of Transport and I was chairman of the Channel Tunnel Group.

7 JUNE

WASHINGTON

ISAIAH BERLIN WEEKEND

The Berlins are staying with Joe Alsop at his insistence. I think they
would like a change of hotel if only to escape from the late-night sessions
when the host's laughter is at its most Palmerstonian; and Joe, seated in
his upright chair, a glass of whiskey beside him and a chain of cigarettes
broken in two and inserted into a yellowing holder, likes to hold forth
about the awful ways of the modern world, protesting implausibly from
time to time, 'But I'm only an aged amateur art historian.' Isaiah is apt
to expostulate to me afterwards about Joe, but having done so he
invariably says, 'But I'm very fond of him.' Such is Joe's adulation for
Isaiah that he has said he will bequeath his library to Wolfson College
in Isaiah's memory.

The routine of a Berlin visit is always the same. Joe telephones me
weeks, even months, in advance to say that they are coming, that he
supposes we would like to give them lunch or dinner but that it must be
kept small because Isaiah does not like to meet a lot of new people
nowadays. There may be something in this last point even if Joe exag-
gerates, which he does partly, I suspect, from his wish to keep Isaiah as
much to himself as possible.

Before the latest visit, having received Joe's marching orders, I took
the precaution of telephoning Isaiah in Oxford to find out whether he
would be intrigued to meet one or two of the new gang who run
Washington. He said that he was not sure about Aline, but, as for himself,
he would certainly love the chance to make the acquaintance of some of
the fresh Californian rulers. So, without consulting Joe, on the principle
that having committed treason by approaching Isaiah direct I should not
aggravate the crime by ignoring his injunction to keep the party small, I
decided to invite the Weinbergers and the Meeses who immediately
accepted. The only other guests were Joe and Kay Graham – and Derry
who was staying with us.

I did not have time before the lunch to brief Isaiah about Meese, or
vice versa. Weinberger told me that Isaiah was a well-known and much
revered name to him; he greatly looked forward to the meeting. The
Washington Post had just published a social column describing a visit to
the Meeses' house, where he had 'a collection of model police-cars on a
shelf in his den'.

Our end of the table was as follows:

Mary	Meese	Kay Graham

Weinberger

Isaiah

Mrs Meese	N H	Mrs Weinberger

Isaiah was obviously out to enjoy himself and help others to do so. He bubbled away to Weinberger and Mrs Meese about everything under the sun. Mrs Meese was clearly astonished and once she realised what language he was speaking, enchanted. At one moment she said to me under her breath that she had never met anyone like that before. I replied that I doubted she had; and I proceeded, sotto voce, to try to explain the phenomenon of Isaiah.

The Weinbergers were eager to talk about A. L. Rowse. Apparently Rowse had met them in San Francisco, had talked a lot about Shakespeare and had been extremely friendly. Later in the day Isaiah said to me; 'I can see exactly how it came about. I shall tell Rowse when I see him about his highly placed admirers. He will be pleased, but also furious and certainly jealous that I have met them.'

Isaiah was polite whilst being honest about Rowse. Nevertheless I think that the Weinbergers were a little crestfallen. They are the nicest, least pretentious and most dignified of people and I was sure Isaiah had liked them.

The lunch enabled me to conduct a little business with Weinberger on the side, paving the way for John Nott's[1] visit. I was to play tennis later that afternoon with Kay who, after lunch, persuaded Weinberger to join us on the court. He agreed to do so. He did not prove to be a very good player. Kay said to me afterwards that there was an elaborate grid in Washington showing people's ratings as tennis players and as official

---

[1] John Nott, Conservative MP 1968–83. Another Cambridge high-flyer. General Manager S.G. Warburg 1960–6; Minister of State, Treasury, 1972–4; Secretary of State for Trade 1979–81; Secretary of State for Defence 1981–3.

contacts. The worse someone was in the former category the higher they had to be in the latter to achieve a good rating.

I think that in a macabre way Isaiah was even more fascinated to meet Meese than Weinberger because he is not the sort of American he has hitherto seen in high places: not at all like Sherwood,[1] or Harry Hopkins[2] or McBundy[3] or Kissinger. After lunch Meese came over to Berlin as we left the dining-room and said something about not having had the chance yet to meet him properly. So I suggested that they sat together in the drawing-room which they did, on the high-backed sofa. They presented an incongruous picture. Isaiah did all the talking: mostly about the past. Meese listened, exuding bonhomie. He did not say much. Nor, however, did he exude self-important confidentiality. He responded with plenty of laughter to Isaiah's sallies.

In his bread-and-butter letter Isaiah exclaimed how well he understood the comfort and confidence that Meese must bring to Reagan.

That night Joe gave a dinner for the Berlins. Other guests included Kay, Evangeline, Bob McNamara, the Weinbergers and the Fritcheys. Some way through the dinner Joe made the conversation general asking Weinberger about MX. To the minister's reply Clayton rejoined with a somewhat brusque intervention questioning the whole basis of the new US government's defence policy: 'How could the Soviets hit our missile sites? Why should they want to?' Weinberger started answering with extreme courtesy, to be interrupted by Clayton somewhat abrasively, upon which Joe said that he was not to speak like that in his house; whereupon Clayton got up, said that he was not going to stay in the house and stamped upstairs and out through the front door. Polly followed him shortly afterwards.

The dinner table was stunned (I recall that Mary Rothschild described to me the effect on her family of Mitterrand's electoral victory as having rendered them 'stoned' when she meant stunned). Dinner parties in Washington are less accustomed to rows than their counterparts in London. Weinberger, courteous as ever, apologised for having 'brought this on'. Joe cupped his chin in his hands and muttered something

---

[1] Robert Sherwood, American author and dramatist. Politically active, he was director of overseas operations in the Office of War Information and a speech writer for Roosevelt. He wrote a memoir, *Roosevelt and Hopkins* (1948), which was an important document on the Second World War.

[2] Harry Hopkins was an intimate friend and a special assistant to President Roosevelt who sent him on missions to the UK and Russia 1941–2. Few people with such uncertain health and indeterminate status as his can have exercised so much influence on national and international events.

[3] McGeorge Bundy; Special Assistant to the President for National Security Affairs 1961–6; president of the Ford Foundation 1966–79; appointed Professor of History NY University 1979. A man of the highest probity and intellectual vigour he has suffered from his involvement in decision-making over the Vietnam War.

disobliging about Clayton. Needless to say one of the Washington gossip writers has got hold of the story and published it in full, more or less accurately.

I sat on at Joe's the same evening chatting to Isaiah who confided to me that he does not like rows. Goodness knows now what we talked about but I expect it was Oxford gossip.

19 JUNE

———

IRISH DEMONSTRATORS DISRUPT PRINCE
CHARLES
IN NEW YORK

I have just been in New York for two nights for Prince Charles's visit there, which was intended to help raise money for Covent Garden (as well as for the Metropolitan Opera and the English Speaking Union). But an acute problem of security and Irish propaganda dominated the visit.

Policemen were everywhere, as were barricades, so that the crowd were never allowed within hollering distance. Mayor Koch himself has graciously complained about the cost – three hundred thousand dollars – that has fallen to the city of New York and that is unreimbursable from federal funds because HRH was not on a state visit. The press have made the point that the cost of the police etc, was more than the sum gained by Covent Garden for their appeal.

The aim of the authorities, spurred on by us, was to avoid not only the threat to life, but hostile demonstrations that could be embarrassing. It was not an easy task given that Koch has been making anti-British and pro-Irish speeches and when a fair (and I imagine blue-eyed) proportion of the city police are of Irish extraction. Mrs Reagan's presence by the Prince's side on most occasions added to the precautions, but given the present IRA campaign in New York (and elsewhere in the USA) there would have been a serious security problem for HRH anyhow. He arrived in Manhattan by helicopter, having flown to Kennedy airport by Concorde (the first time he had been in it, so he told me).

I drove with him from the heliport to the motor yacht, the *Highlander*, which we were to board for a trip round Manhattan. It was the first of several short car rides I was to take with him. He waved from time to time to those who cheered (mostly, he thought, black) and to those who looked glum. ('I've seen him before. I wonder why he thinks it necessary to spend so much of his time waiting just to turn his thumbs down at me.') He was astonished at the number of police and the crowd control that they felt necessary. 'I feel I'm in a gilded cage,' he said. I told him how convenient the Waldorf Astoria was as a hotel for the reception of a prisoner like himself. You could drive into an inner courtyard. There was no exposure to the street.

When, on his departure, we drove to the heliport he expressed relief that it was all over and thankfulness that, at any rate, he had helped Covent Garden to raise some money. The money motive was evident as much on the giving as the receiving end. People paid one thousand dollars for an evening of ballet and a subsequent ball. They thought they had a right at least to shake the Prince's hand. There were too many of them to enable this to take place in the time available. At the reception before the ballet the Prince proceeded down a red carpet besieged by ladies wanting to greet him. He is very good at that sort of thing and manages to suppress any sign of boredom. Several donors buttonholed me to ask me to introduce them. Initially I said that I would do my best and began to thread my way towards the Prince; but it was impossible to reach him, and if I did manage to get within range, I found that I was turned back by a security guard asking me peremptorily to move away.

Demonstrations took place during the ballet. Lee Annenberg, on my left, was next to the Prince. She muttered to me, waving her fan, that I mustn't worry about the hostile demonstration; it was only a few 'silly people'. After the third interruption I must confess that I began to wonder whether the silly people were going to continue their demonstrations throughout the performance. As it turned out that was the end of them. When the intermission came I thought there might be more trouble and we all stiffened our upper lips. But it went off peacefully. Mark Bonham-Carter,[1] whom I met at this juncture, said that he assumed that I had organised the whole thing to show how steady the company were. Certainly they had carried on dancing without missing a step despite the shouting. I said that the Windmill Theatre had been at its best when the bombs were falling on London.

---

[1] Mark Bonham-Carter is of the purest Liberal descent; he was Liberal MP 1958–9 and has been a working Liberal peer since 1986. First chairman Race Relations Board 1966–70; Chairman Community Relations Commission 1971–7; of the Anglo-Polish (Jablonna) Round Table Conference since 1971; director Royal Opera House, Covent Garden 1958–82; vice-chairman and a governor of the BBC 1975–81. Outspoken and unflinching in his judgments on people and politics.

4 JULY
LONDON AND COMBE

THEATRE AND GLOOM

Uncanny to be watching Angela Thorne portray Mrs Thatcher on the Whitehall stage in John Wells's play *Anyone for Denis*; and then, less than forty hours later, to find myself seated opposite her at Number 10. I felt that I was meeting her double.

I found her characteristically resilient, though worried by Ireland and the falling pound. Her final words were: 'Well, things often work out better than you think. They're not as bad as they seem ... I am off to Wimbledon this afternoon.'

We talked of the forthcoming summit. 'I must stick by Reagan,' she said, then adding, 'but I must say these very high American interest rates do worry me.'

It was apparent that she had not heard of the Friends of Ireland, the newly formed bipartisan group in Congress that seeks to avoid the extremism of Noraid and to attract Irish-American support away from them. I think that she understands the importance of the American dimension, however much she may resent it. Eighty-five per cent of the support the IRA receives, including arms, comes from the USA.

Once again I was impressed by her vitality and will. She is more beleaguered now than ever before. But she remains indomitable – and immaculate. There was not a hair out of place. There was no self-pity. I would not say that she was relaxed; that would give too calm an impression of her personality; but there was nothing flustered about her. Her personality is not exactly of a kind that seduces people, as if by a magic spell, to do things and make sacrifices on her behalf. It is done by the clarity of her appeal and the driving force of her will. She has no fear of committing herself though I think she is readier to change course in practice than she admits. She commands respect for her many great qualities – courage, integrity and endurance. Peter said the other night that he would be quite ready to go tiger-shooting with her. I have noticed that Peter is inclined at the moment to judge people by whether or not they are of a kind that he would like to go tiger-shooting with.

I attended a party at Syon[1] given by Douglas Fairbanks for the new US Ambassador, John Louis. The tempo of the evening's entertainment

---

[1] Syon House, on the Thames near Isleworth, one of the homes of the Duke of Northumberland and one of the greatest masterpieces of Robert Adam.

which started in the beautiful entrance hall, was stepped up by the sudden arrival of a large royal contingent: the Queen, Princess Margaret and the Kents. I was chatting to Clarissa Avon[1] when Fitzroy Maclean came up to me with a purposeful look saying that The Queen wanted to speak to me. 'Don't be funny', I retorted, thinking that it was a joke, some Titoesque leg-pull. He insisted that Her Majesty was demanding my presence. So over I went to the hollow space in the middle of the party where the Queen was holding court – very different from the density that surrounds a member of the Royal Family in a USA party. She wanted to talk about American opinion on Ireland and on how Prince Charles had got on during his apparently turbulent visit to New York.

We were chatting about this when Princess Margaret approached and, rather to my surprise, interrupted her sister's conversation with me. We had spoken on the phone earlier in the day about the cancellation of her visit to Washington on account of Irish trouble. Princess Margaret's comment was forthright. 'Serves 'em right', she said, striking what seemed to me an admirably self-assured and undefensive note. We spoke about the supper party I was intending to give for the ballet company, an evening that she would have attended had she come to Washington. 'Give them enough to eat,' she implored me. 'You see they take a lot of exercise and they can't eat beforehand.'

I assured her that Mary's sideboards would be groaning.

I failed to see Annie Fleming who was too ill to receive me. The Moores and I drove over from Combe to Sevenhampton to leave her a bunch of old-fashioned roses that I had picked in the garden. Alexandra was at the wheel, Derry at the back of the car was preparing the beans for dinner and I in the front was talking. Annie had said that if she had seen me in her desperately sick state she would have been unable to restrain her tears. I felt miserable for her unhappiness, for the pain and degradation she is having to endure which is so stark, as if in retribution for all the pleasure she has got out of, and given in, life. I am already thinking how much I shall miss her; and I feel ashamed that once when she was staying in Paris I made disparaging remarks about the way she was repeating herself. Brutally and priggishly I attributed this to drink. We had had a heart-to-heart talk about it. She had no reason to forgive me for this but not only did she do so but our relations became even closer

---

[1] Clarissa Avon has been a friend since long before she married the then Anthony Eden. Displaying disdain for the mediocre and having no desire to please, she nevertheless has her enthusiasms and loyalties; and she is eternally elegant and has an eye for the absurd. She made the immortal remark at the time of the Suez crisis when there was a constant flood of people at Number 10 that she thought that the canal must be flowing through the drawing-room there.

afterwards which was a tribute to her character and large-heartedness.

I also paid another sick visit, this time on Ted Brooks[1] in the Churchill Hospital in Reading where he is suffering from Weil's disease (alias the plague) caught from one of the numerous rats at Combe. He was able to tell me about the extent of the rat problem there this past winter and spring. So distressed was I by this that I later rang Barstable who runs Astor's farm. He was very much on the defensive. 'I'm sorry Ted Brooks has got Weil's but people in Combe seem to have gone overboard about the rats.'[2]

The news at home is unredeemably bad; economic decline, rising unemployment, hunger-strike deaths and violence in Ulster, riots in many towns in England. I find that the hopes I entertained exactly two years ago that we might be going to turn over a new leaf under Maggie have been dashed. Our plight is worse than two years ago because we appear to have tried something new and it has failed.

The Republicans in Washington no longer see us as a beacon of the true faith. We are now a spectre that haunts them. Yet, personally, I am not sure it's Maggie's fault or that it will not come right in the end. I so well recall people saying when the government took power in May 1979 that it would need time, that there would be great difficulties and that the most important and the most difficult moment would be when everyone started to say that the sacrifices being asked for were too high and that the policy therefore had to be changed. It is not, therefore, the moment to lose faith in her. When I told Peter that I would want to leave the Embassy in Washington in about a year I did not mean to say that I did not want to go on representing the present government in its difficult circumstances. 'A friend should bear a friend's infirmities'.

Peter, when he raised with me the future of the Washington job, said that from his point of view he would like me to continue beyond next year. This is what Palliser had said to me the previous day as being Peter's wish. I replied that I thought three years was enough. 'Enough from whose point of view?' Peter asked. I did not want to get drawn. I just said that I thought three years was about right. 'Not from our standpoint,' he retorted. I said how grateful I was that he should have shown such confidence but . . .

---

[1] Ted Brooks worked on John Astor's farm which was managed by Kenneth Barstable. In his spare time Ted helped me in my garden at Combe where he lives.
[2] To be sure we may have gone overboard, but the rats have not left the Combe ship. They remain a threat despite the efforts of the rodent control department of Newbury District Council whose help we enlist frequently; and notwithstanding the ferocious pursuit of a pack of Jack Russell terriers which came to hunt there.

13 JULY

WASHINGTON

A ROUND-UP OF US FOREIGN POLICY

Peter Carrington is coming here for a short visit on his way to Ottawa for a summit conference. I thought I would send him a review of the current state of US foreign policy.

I began by telling him that the decision-making process was as incoherent as ever. Haig is not firmly in the saddle. He does not have the President's trust as Weinberger does and is distrusted by the President's White House advisers. The latters' touch for foreign policy has hardly been reliable – except that they can be counted upon to oppose anything Haig suggests.

There has been much public criticism recently of the President's capacity as a formulator of foreign policy and the absence of some speech setting out his main objectives. Reagan has replied that there is no need to make a speech to prove that you have a foreign policy. It is, I think, clear to everyone that he attaches importance to restoring America's strength and taking a tough line with the Soviet Union as well as being seen to stand by America's friends. He does not try to have specialist knowledge on the details of foreign policy. He is still weakened in health by the attempt on his life in the spring.

The main theme of the new administration's foreign policy has been to correct a supposed shift in the global balance of power in favour of the Soviet Union (military superiority, Cuban proxies, Afghanistan, etc), relying on heightened military preparedness and tough language. However I think there has been some recent modification. There has been a desire to avoid the impression that Washington is seeking a confrontation with Moscow. Part of the reason for this change is the growing American fear of the rising tide of neutralism in Europe. To counter this the USA government wishes the world to know that it is serious about negotiating with the Russians on arms control.

Another modification of US policy may be some attenuation of the anti-UN, anti-human-rights, anti-liberal tone of early days. Jeane Kirkpatrick who, as US Ambassador to the UN, is a member of the Cabinet, has I think succeeded in persuading everybody in Washington of the importance of drawing a distinction between authoritarian and totalitarian regimes. The US are only excluded from having dealings with the latter. In general, however, the US government is eager to improve relations with the countries in America's backyard irrespective of the regimes there.

In practice the United States government is not cutting aid expenditure. It is sceptical, as is Congress, about multilateral institutions as a means of channelling aid. There are also doubts about the value to the US of wide-ranging discussions on economic matters whether in the UN or in any of its parts where the weight of opinion is skewed against free-market forces. The overall US approach to the developing world will be more hard-headed than it was under Carter. It will be clear that the aim is to help friends and to thwart the Soviets.

In the Far East the administration will continue to place prime importance on its relations with Japan and on its new-found friendship for China. Galling though it is for us, we have to reckon with the fact that when the US government talks of allies it has in mind Japan just as much as Europe.

In the Middle East it looks as though Haig's 'strategic consensus' is going to clock up just as short a shelf-life as the Carter doctrine. Nothing is emerging to put flesh and blood on the idea. Yet the gap remains: the Americans need some framework for their strategic requirements in the area and this will have to amount to something more than the simple attempt to buy their way in through ever more sophisticated arms sales which is what their current policy concentrates upon. They will not like it if European activity towards the Middle East looks like cutting across their own.

The Americans regard Europe as irresolute about defence. They are worried about political trends in France and Germany and about the continued economic weakness of the UK compounded now by violence in many English cities as well as in Northern Ireland.

22–27 JULY
ALASKA

A ROYAL WEDDING, OIL AND BEARS

It has been a visit devoted to two very different topics even if they both originated from one source, mother nature. I went to the BP oil field on the North Slope of Alaska, then on for a couple of days' fishing in the Aleutian Islands.

The North Slope harbours a paradoxical combination of surface barrenness and subterranean wealth. The flora and fauna of the Aleutian Islands form a natural kaleidoscope of silver birch and alder, trout, salmon, eagles, wolves and the king of the Arctic, the bear, the brown bear, busy at this time of the year catching, and gorging themselves with, salmon amidst rivers and lakes set amongst high mountains.

The Alaskans speak of themselves – I don't mean the Eskimos but the white settlers – as the inhabitants of the last new frontier. Per capita income in Alaska is said to be the highest in the world. The sparse towns in Alaska resemble those film-sets showing what the Middle West looked like in the last century.

Thanks to mass air travel and to the wanderlust of the Japanese, Anchorage has become a crossroads between East and West and North and South. I stayed in the Captain Cook Hotel. The vestibule was lined with souvenir shops selling Eskimo carvings and picture postcards of aeroplanes flying past mountain peaks. They seemed popular with the large number of female American travellers mooching about, accompanied by wan-faced husbands in baseball caps.

Dominating the entrance to the hotel was a stuffed polar bear and a sculptured head of Captain Cook.

I attended a gala evening at the hotel to commemorate the forthcoming wedding of Prince Charles and Princess Di – as she is invariably called here. The day had been declared British Heritage Day. This, together with my presence, provoked Irish demonstrations. But the nineteen-gun salute with which I was honoured (not twenty-one guns as had been originally announced because it was discovered that this would have put me into the royal category), together with the boisterous, straightforward loyalties of the frontiersmen of Alaska made short work of the Irish.

Many of the arrangements, including the gun salute and the release of balloons, were made by Mr Rod Muddle, the local British Airways manager. There were nearly a thousand people in the ballroom of the hotel wearing all manner of costumes. An expatriate Englishman dressed as a Beefeater whispered in my ear that he was over eighty years of age.

The evening was structured – to use the word by which it was described – to resemble the royal wedding ceremony. After we had had various routines, including accordion players, a Welsh male-voice choir, an Irish jig, the Anchorage Scottish Highland Pipe Band and some madrigal singers in Renaissance costume, we reached the climax which was the arrival of a bride and bridegroom who proceeded on stage to cut a wedding cake. While this was going on I slipped out of the ballroom to go to the lavatory which meant that I almost missed my cue: this was the arrival at my table of a young girl dressed, for some reason, as Queen Alexandra. At least that was how she was described in the programme. Her mission was to escort me on to the stage, accompanied by a mixed retinue comprising royal personages, explorers and pioneers, including Captain Cook who had announced himself to me at breakfast, pointing out that he was wearing an old Harrovian tie but would be unrecognisable in captain's uniform in the evening. I had asked him how long he had been at Harrow. To which he replied, only two terms, just after the Second World War. I supposed that that had given him a sufficiently British jaunty look to qualify him to play Captain Cook in the Anchorage pageant over thirty years later.

Thus this ill-assorted group found themselves on the stage of the hotel, everyone in some form of fancy dress except me. Queen Alexandra, who held me tightly by the elbow, beckoned me to the centre of the stage where there was a microphone. I had expected the master of ceremonies who had guided us throughout the evening to announce my presence. She had made sure that little had been left to the imagination, describing each successive act as the greatest ever; and I thought that she might give me the same sort of build-up. She had, however, withdrawn to the back of the stage behind the courtiers, the ladies in Jacobean dresses, Captain Cook and myself who formed a semicircle faced by a microphone and a thousand people in the body of the hall evidently waiting for some sort of toast to round off the ceremony. Impelled by a slight shove from Queen Alexandra I made towards the microphone and as I did so a ceremoniously-attired man advanced towards me bearing a tray with a glass of champagne. I made a short speech promising the whole company that I would report to the Prince himself on Anchorage's gala wedding party; and I was sure that HRH would read my report with interest on his honeymoon, provided that he had no other more pressing things to do.

The next morning I set off for the oil field; the flight to the terminal at the ice-free port of Valdez in the Arctic took about an hour. The terminal on the North Slope proved to be a series of pipes, tanks and turbines. I learned how BP had almost abandoned hope, after searching for oil for sixteen years, when ARCO suddenly found gas in a block adjacent to them.

I also heard of the difficulties caused by the permafrost. All the buildings and constructions have to be on insulated stilts so as not to sink into the permanently frozen ground. We lunched at the camp, an excellent meal. Apparently overeating is a problem for the four hundred Sohio (the name of BP's US subsidiary) inhabitants. What else is there to do in this strange environment? It is too cold and dark in the winter to be outside. The ground is not suitable for sport in summer. One clue to activity was divulged. I was told that the divorce rate is 100 per cent. The employees, who are of both sexes, work one week on (twelve hours a day) and one week off – or, as it was put to me, 'one week on, one week on'.

The roads are all on raised gravel platforms; and indeed everything has to be built on gravel – pipe stations, pump stations and living accommodation. Gravel is almost as much an industry as oil and a good deal more visible. At the end of the day I was covered in dust.

The oil field is in a completely flat area of tundra. Caribou roam about. There are seagulls. There are wild flowers, mostly Arctic poppy. The landscape consists of the sky, limitless gravel, and widely separated towers of oil rigs and smaller box-like structures containing oil shafts. The only movement is that of the occasional dusty truck ferrying field-workers to and fro.

On Saturday morning I flew in a small seaplane to the Aleutian Islands where I stayed in a log cabin at Kulik. Satisfactory though it was to be able to catch trout easily, despite bad casting on my part, the greatest excitement for me was the sudden appearance of a bear on the bank of the Kulik River. He stood on the edge of the river for a moment, looking round. As he stepped into the water for a little evening's fishing, I managed to take some photographs, struck by his lightness of colour which was like honey and by the way his ears stood up in furry semi-circles as on a toy teddy. His ears, indeed, were all that you could see of him when he swam, head down in the water, to fish.

For the rest of our stay at the camp our thoughts and conversation turned frequently to bears, much more so than to fish. We learned a good deal about their ferocity. No animal of the region threatens them. They are crazy for fish. The next day when we visited Brooks Falls and watched a bear in the river paddling about looking for salmon we were told of a recent Japanese visitor. He had been fishing in the Brooks River and, having caught a salmon, he put it in a sack on his back. A bear appeared on the bank, smelled the salmon and came running after him. Apparently bears have an amazing sense of smell. He made for the back of the Japanese fisherman who just managed to extricate the salmon and throw it to him.

The fishing camp on Brooks River has to shut down early in September because of the plethora of bears gorging salmon before hibernating for the winter. They stuff themselves full of fish and then go to sleep until the spring. In the transition between satiety and sleep they are very fierce and will attack humans if they think they are after their salmon.

During the course of a good deal of low-flying in the seaplane we saw many more bears (and moose and wolf and an eagle). Our pilot was particularly bitter about them because they had been trying at night to get into his cockpit and had badly scratched the windows of his plane.

Nobody seemed to think that there was the slightest chance of taming an Alaskan brown bear. Indeed everyone was against them and frightened of them. They are looked upon as scavengers.

Our pilot took us on an aerial tour of the valley of the Ten Thousand Smokes, the residue of the volcanic eruption of 1912 which has left a vast area deep in pumice stone (I took some pieces back to Mary who was delighted, making off with them like a squirrel to her bathroom).

As I left the Alaskan peninsula I had forgotten about oil, though it was BP who had been my hosts at the camp as well as on the North Slope and I felt grateful towards them. It was ironical to think that the area we had been in was too dangerous for children because of the presence there of the prototype of the child's best friend, the teddy bear. To spread this around would be almost as disruptive of human upbringing as to shatter the myth of Santa Claus.

Perhaps I was too busy setting up a giant TV screen in the Embassy, but I do not seem to have written anything about the breakfast party we gave to celebrate the royal wedding. I do, however, recall that the White House staff went on half shift that morning, so that many of them could be at the Embassy. Indeed, much of the Washington government machine came to a near standstill as so many people from all desks and benches came to the Embassy to watch the BBC recording of the ceremony that we showed two hours after the event. Mary and our British chef, Harry Simpson, had worked for days making sure that the breakfast tables would be groaning, as indeed they were, the menu including kippers flown from the UK and a large, tiered wedding cake. Down the long centre table she placed a row of Staffordshire figures in the shape of King Charles spaniels which she thought more appropriate for this particular occasion than silver.

22 SEPTEMBER
NEW YORK

LUNCH WITH HAIG AND CARRINGTON

I attended a lunch yesterday at the UN Plaza Hotel in New York seated between Carrington and Haig. Jeane Kirkpatrick was also present. Peter gave a subtle analysis of British policy on Southern Africa. He explains things in a dashing, unacademic manner yet it is very orderly and factual. We had an example of 'Haig-speak' on TV on Sunday when, in an interview, he answered a question about the threat to AWACS in Congress as shown by the long list of hostile signatures. He said that the list was 'replete with soft spots'. One knows what he means.

Raising objection to the European wish to try to engage the PLO in the Palestinian peace process, Haig referred to the great danger of an

Israeli attack on south Lebanon and the need to involve the Saudis in the maintenance of the present ceasefire in the Lebanon. He said that the Europeans were in danger of encouraging the Saudis to have a 'split vision'. Haig's cromagnon jaw was working away steadily at a large, completely raw steak, the finest fare from the UN Plaza kitchen. He gives an impression of great vigour despite the fairly recent heart operation. It was clear that he wanted to stick to the Camp David process and to try to head off the Europeans from playing any separate role such as would, in his opinion, divert the Arabs from the main task.

Peter has a gift for swift and witty repartee which is not dependent upon historical or literary allusions but upon informality and upon audacity. At a lunch today in New York given by the Foreign Policy Association and attended by over five hundred people he answered questions in customary debonair fashion. To one question about the likely effect of the formation of the SDP-Liberal alliance and whether it could be expected to take votes away from the Conservatives more than from Labour, he answered more or less as follows: 'I always thought one wasn't meant to interfere in the internal politics of another country but the answer is that we are not obliged to have an election for another two and a half years. A lot can happen between now and then – and I hope it does.' This was met by plenty of laughter.

Much of his statements to Haig at lunch were in the same light-hearted vein. Haig, though normally full of boyish banter did not respond; at least that was my impression. I found him not so much cool as dour. There were no polite preliminaries before we got down to business. He did not even ask Peter about his holiday. Perhaps I was being over-sensitive. He is a man of moods, at any rate following his triple bypass operation. At the beginning of lunch he turned to me amicably and asked, 'How is your bride?'

At one point Carrington asked Haig about his recent visit to Berlin where he had encountered hostile demonstrations. Haig gave a look of Charlton Heston dealing with apes and dismissed the protests as of no importance.

27 SEPTEMBER
WASHINGTON

TENNIS AT THE WHITE HOUSE

I had a revealing insight into the President's pace of life this afternoon, Sunday.

Deaver had asked me to play tennis at the White House at 3.30. I arrived a little late to find a tournament taking place. The players included Senator Laxalt,[1] Judge Webster,[2] two or three journalists and an athletic young man, a partner for me, who works at the White House in Nofziger's office. The court is well concealed both from the house and the road. From it you can catch a glimpse of the back of the White House and the roof upon which silhouettes of armed guards appeared immediately when the President arrived.

This happened after we had been playing for about an hour and a half. He came by helicopter. Deaver disappeared to greet him and, presumably out of deference to the President, we ceased playing and turned towards the helicopter, as if towards Mecca. Greatly to my surprise Deaver was back in the twinkling of an eye accompanied by both Reagans. They came to our court, shook hands with us all, took a seat by the ice-box containing Coke bottles, towels and sandwiches and proceeded to watch our somewhat erratic tennis.

They stayed until well after we had stopped playing which must have been a good two hours later. Conversation was of a light kind and I heard the President recounting the plot of a film he had just seen at Camp David, rather as Alexandra used to give us the plots of films she had seen. His main theme was to protest about the filthy language in the film which had evidently upset him. Nancy Reagan seemed to have been less disturbed. She asked tentatively after Mary. She told me of the video-tape they had received of the royal wedding and how this had enabled her to see things such as the horses that she had been unaware of at the ceremony; and she told me of a letter received from Prince Charles. It had dealt with their private joke about her plea that he should give up polo upon marriage.

The President listened, delivered a few cracks to Laxalt who was still playing (e.g. when the ball hit the netcord there were bantering references

---

[1] Paul Laxalt, elected Republican Senator from Nevada 1975. Chairman Campaign to Elect Reagan as President 1980.
[2] William Webster, judge US Court of Appeals 1973–8; director FBI 1978–87; director CIA 1987–91.

to the safety net, a subject of public discussion at the moment in the context of budget cuts) and offered me sandwiches. It was impossible to believe that he had a care in the world. Nor did he seem to think that he had to explain why he was sitting there. No exclamations came from his lips about the need to get back to work, or about the papers piling up for his attention. Yet I was aware that at that very moment every important Finance Minister of the world was in Washington for the annual IMF conference, that there was a run on almost every stock exchange and a great deal of intense discussion going on in smoke-filled rooms not a mile away on how to cope with the crisis. The President was unperturbed.

When eventually he did say goodbye he simply said to Nancy, 'Well, Nancy, we must be getting along,' for all the world like Darby telling Joan that they had better vacate the seat on the village green that they had been occupying for a long time. As he shook hands all round he spoke of the respective weights of muscle and fat in his body; and it was only when he felt his chest that I was reminded of the shooting exactly six months ago. He said that he had been riding at Camp David at the weekend. He was still wearing light-coloured leather cowboy boots, very pointed at the toes, blue rather wide trousers and an open-neck white shirt. Nancy, as usual, was neatly turned out. She mentioned the photo she had sent Mary, saying that the latter had asked for a picture of her in her prettiest dress.

I thought to myself that this was the sort of President the American public wanted at the moment – relaxed, non-interfering and with a general view of the national interest that was not afflicted by too much concern with detail.

1 NOVEMBER

WASHINGTON

———

HUMOUR AND THE MUSIC-HALL

We may have overstepped the mark in would-be humour the other evening; and I am reminded of the lack in the USA of political satire. I am assured by all Americans that it would be impossible for instance to have anything here resembling *Private Eye*. Sadly, wit and humour are not an indispensable weapon in American politics. Adlai Stevenson was the last politician to use them regularly and it may have had the effect of inducing people to take him less seriously than he deserved. Art

Buchwald, of course, is a brilliant satirist, but he is not in active politics.

The scarcity of satire is surprising given the laxity of the laws of libel.

Our troubles arose in the following way. We committed ourselves to laying on some entertainment in the Embassy to help collect money for the Cheshire Homes. Leonard Cheshire himself would be here for the occasion. We decided to present an Edwardian music hall to be put on by the Embassy players, a group who perform frequently in the rotunda of the Embassy. The music-hall would be given in the residence itself where we had a stage erected with curtains, footlights, etc.

Michael Pakenham agreed to write some topical patter for the master of ceremonies and accepted my plea that jokes should not be too bawdy or near the bone politically. He had done the same for the annual pantomime given in the British Embassy Club in Warsaw when we were there together some ten years earlier. Jokes and skits that he had devised about the Polish Secret Service and, for that matter, about the internal scene generally had gone down well with the various eavesdropping members of our Polish staff.

The music-hall took place on Friday evening with about a hundred guests. We began by singing old-time songs: 'Daddy Wouldn't Buy Me a Bow Wow'; 'Nobody Loves a Fairy When She's Forty'; and 'Knees Up Mother Brown'. We had a programme giving the words of the songs and the menu. Guests had been asked to come dressed in black tie or Edwardian costume, but, as we have found so often, it was only the British who dressed up.

At my table were Lee Annenberg, Cap Weinberger, the French Smiths, Minda Gunzburg, Peter McCoy,[1] Mrs Mike Deaver, Andrew Knight, K.K. Auchincloss[2] and Evangeline Bruce. After we sang a rousing number in which a man dressed as a sergeant-major conducted us singing 'Pack Up Your Troubles' and 'Tipperary', half the room singing one, the other half the other, the compère cracked a few fairly innocent jokes. We then had some tap-dancing followed by girls from the Embassy in a chorus line showing much versatility after which we were treated to some semi-clean fun. But then came the first political joke. The compère announced: 'Secretary of State Haig is just off on a world tour of friendly countries' – he paused before adding, 'He will be back tomorrow.'

I cast a sideways glance at the high-level visitors who were at my table and was unable to detect whether they were secretly delighted at this dig

---

[1] Peter McCoy a former auctioneer and management consultant who became Nancy Reagan's staff director. Following criticism of Mrs Reagan over the acquisition of china by the White House, McCoy was removed from this post and appointed Under-Secretary of Commerce for Travel and Tourism.

[2] K. K. Auchincloss, the wife of Douglas Auchincloss, formerly religious Editor of *Time Magazine*; an outgoing and generous personality.

at Haig or whether they were embarrassed but wanted to conceal it. I was sure, however, that Cap Weinberger was having trouble only in suppressing his mirth.

The menu included Pickwick pie and Christmas pudding with ginger ice-cream, which Lee and others evidently enjoyed.

In another series of jokes the compère certainly went too far given the sensitiveness of the White House on the particular subject mentioned. There has been a lot of public fuss about the gift of a dinner service to Mrs Reagan. The compère said that before setting off for a tour of the Far East Secretary of State Haig had asked Mrs Reagan, 'What do you think of Red China?' To which she had answered, so the compère told us, 'It's all right so long as it's on a yellow tablecloth.'

Our White House guests had to refrain from showing amusement over this.

When I came to say a word of thanks at the end of the show I said that I hoped that our Edwardian songs would be seen by the Attorney General as a contribution towards the appeal he had just made for a 'groundswell of conservatism'. I was told that he had beamed at this reference and been in no way put out, though Mrs French Smith had had doubts about some of the evening's jokes.

The next evening when we dined with the Phillips, Jennifer Phillips, who had been one of the guests at the music-hall, told me how risqué she thought the evening had been. She, of course, had enjoyed it: 'But for a foreign Ambassador to make jokes about another country, wasn't that going too far?' I think that she may have been reflecting the tone of some of the telephonic tittle-tattle that no doubt had been circulating in Washington after the party. However Peter McCoy, whom I saw at lunch today, expressed great enthusiasm for the evening and, in answer to my enquiry, said that anyone who had taken offence must lack a sense of humour.

At any rate we have given them something to talk about for a day or two, other than AWACS. But there is no doubt that jokes are a dicey business when told across frontiers.

8 NOVEMBER
WASHINGTON

A LONG DAY STARTING AT PITTSBURGH

We spent a night at the William Penn Hotel in Pittsburgh where I had come to open the British Festival. The Pittsburgh Symphony Orchestra under André Previn's direction were devoting a season to British music. The first concert included a violin concerto by William Walton in which a Korean girl, Miss Chung, gave a marvellous solo. Chatting with her afterwards as we ate little squares of English cheese, one of the more impressive side-shows of the British Festival and certainly more sustaining than the display of Hoffnung drawings, I learnt that she has recently bought a house in Chelsea where she intends to live.

André was his usual elfin but authoritative self. He asked me beforehand to let him know afterwards what I thought of the Tippett concerto about which he evidently felt some doubts. Over the Stilton and the Double Gloucester (spelt Glouchester on the menu) I said that I thought that we in the audience had rather lost our way but that we had greatly appreciated the Walton. I do not think that he found this observation any more interesting or profound than I had.

I was up early that morning to map out the speech I had to make at a midday lunch at the Pittsburgh World Affairs Council. I had had no time to concentrate on the speech during the week. I had hardly started to think about it when Nick Witney arrived to draw my attention to a *New York Times* press story giving a lurid account of a dressing-down that Haig was said to have given me on Wednesday over the proposed statements by European Community countries about participation in the Sinai force. This story had come from a briefing, allegedly off the record, that Haig had given Jewish organisations after his talk with me. It was distorted, particularly the report that Haig had given me an admonition to pass on to Carrington, 'to cool it'. Haig had certainly been worked up when he saw me. He had not, however, used this phrase or anything like it. I suppose that in talking to the Jewish organisations he had wanted to leave them in no doubt how tough he had been in condemning Europe's insistence upon stressing the importance of the Venice Declaration,[1] rather than Camp David. I am conscious that in dealing with

---

[1] Venice Declaration made by the European Community in June 1980 giving their views on an Arab-Israeli settlement to provide for Palestinian self-determination and security for Israel. It called for the PLO to be 'associated' with negotiations. The declaration was anathema to the US and Israeli governments.

the Americans nowadays about the West Bank problem, it has to be borne in mind that far from the United States being prepared to exert pressure on Israel, as the Europeans continue to think that they could and should do, it is the other way round. It is Israel which is pressurising the USA, which is not a free agent in deciding what it should do in the Middle East to safeguard American interests.

Relations between London and Washington are under some strain at the moment as a result of the idea Haig is promoting for a multilateral force for Sinai. The West Europeans see it as an attempt by Washington to undermine their initiative with the Arabs. I am sure Haig suspects the Europeans of trying to enhance their relations with the Arabs and to stultify the Camp David peace process.

To return to my morning at Pittsburgh, I decided to ring John Fretwell in Washington, asking him to telegraph the FCO imploring them not to overreact to the *New York Times* story – indeed, if possible, to ignore it. A newspaper story had also been published that morning that the US Department of Commerce was about to institute anti-dumping action against various European steel suppliers. Being in Pittsburgh I thought I might well get enquiries about this and about the likelihood of the British Steel Corporation being affected. So I also spoke to the Embassy on this fairly complicated subject.

Then soon after 9 a.m. I set off on my rounds, beginning with a half-hour radio interview. I was subjected to very intelligent questions about almost every subject under the sun, domestic and foreign. From there I went to the top of a skyscraper, to the world headquarters of Gulf Oil, to meet some of the leading members of the company with whom I discussed the world oil scene ('How soft is the market?') and Gulf's own particular problems ('Are you still in downstream difficulties?').

This was followed by a meeting at the sumptuous offices of the Mellon Bank where we talked mainly about the US economic and industrial outlook. Everything in that region depended upon motor cars and housing. With interest rates likely to remain high the prospects were not encouraging: there would be no upturn before mid-1982. When at lunch, later that day, I discussed the same subject with the ebullient, original head of Allegheny International, Robert Buckley,[1] he gave me a rather more revealing viewpoint. He said that interest rates were not the key factor. There was plenty of money about. What mattered was the understandable decision of manufacturers to hold off until next year when the various tax incentives (e.g. depreciation) of the Reagan administration would begin to make their biggest impact. The first quarter of 1982

[1] Robert Buckley, at this stage in his business career, was chairman of Allegheny a steel and metals company, which had an annual turnover of $1.5 billion.

would be difficult but Buckley was highly optimistic in the longer term.

Allegheny now own and control the Wilkinson Sword Company. Buckley was enthusiastic about the company, saying that it had increased output (mostly for export) by 40 per cent over the past year.

Buckley introduced me to the luncheon audience and I spoke for about half an hour, mostly about the Atlantic Alliance, anti-race demonstrations and the Middle East before answering questions. The first question, asked by a very old and fairly gaga judge, began with a long account of the career of a US diplomat Mr Norman Armour, who had been a friend of the questioner since their time together at Princeton. He gave a list of all the posts at which Mr Armour had served throughout his long career. I could not imagine what the actual question was going to be and when it came – 'I should like to ask the Ambassador whether in his career he ever served at the same post at the same time as Mr Armour?' – there was considerable laughter round the room. Later that afternoon Nick Witney expressed regret that the absurdity of this question had rather undermined the seriousness of the whole question and answer session. Secretly I was rather glad of it because it had used up a lot of the time, an attitude of mind that I realised was in conflict with Michael Stewart's high-minded doctrine that questions should be welcomed and taken seriously with the intention, not of evasion, but of imparting information.

We had a hectic drive through Pittsburgh traffic to catch our private plane back to Washington. I was in the office by 4 p.m. to take up the somewhat frayed threads of the Sinai force saga. At 6.45 p.m. I set off for the Soviet Embassy to attend the October Revolution party. Back to the house to change into a dinner jacket and collect Mary to attend a dinner at the State Department hosted by the Haigs. When Al shook hands with me in the receiving line before dinner he gave me a hearty shake of the hand, expostulating: 'Well ...' But that was as far forward as we took the problem of British involvement in the multilateral force – an American proposal – that evening.

At dinner I sat between a lady of ninety-four and a pretty girl from Florida in her thirties, both of whom had paid a thousand dollars for the privilege of being there in the ceremonial rooms of the State Department. Apparently they had also been lured by the prospect of hearing Haig speak and by the privilege of conversation 'with a live Ambassador'. How live they found me at the end of a long day I was hardly in a fit state to judge.

12 NOVEMBER
WASHINGTON

HAIG ON CARRINGTON

Most of my time recently has been taken up with the storm in US–UK relations that has arisen over the American proposal that we should join the Sinai force. This disagreement, which is not only between London and Washington but between the USA and Western Europe generally, is part of an overall difference over policy towards the Middle East. Sourness in the US–UK relationship has been stirred by the press report of Haig's admonition of Carrington.

I was called back to London by Concorde for a short visit to see both Carrington and the Prime Minister. They wanted to probe Haig's apparent animosity towards Carrington. I promised to do what I could to find out. On my return I saw Haig and said that I wanted to get to the bottom of the problem. We discussed personalities and Middle East policy. He said that he attached the greatest importance to working harmoniously with Carrington. He had no problem with him personally. He was grateful to me for having spoken to him frankly on the subject.

In reporting this meeting to Carrington I told him that I thought that my talk had cleared the air without causing any adverse side-effects. I suggested that no further action was needed by Carrington. He agreed with this and thanked me for what I had done. Thinking it over afterwards, I could not help pondering whether Haig had been fed some disinformation about Carrington. I liked and got on with him personally but I had to admit that he was apt to be susceptible to any Iago's approach.

6 DECEMBER
WASHINGTON

ON APPEARING ON AMERICAN TELEVISION

I have had two very different TV experiences on a recent visit to the Middle West. I have at last persuaded the Consul General there that TV is the easiest way of reaching a large audience. The old hands in the Service, particularly those who have served long in distant posts and do not know modern America, remain distinctly wary of the box, viewing it as though it were some wild animal. They believe instinctively in silent diplomacy. 'Least said the better,' is the habitual advice I receive when I ask what they recommend me to say on television on any subject. Then when I turn up at the local TV station to do a programme, and they accompany me they look worried as if I were about to undergo some appalling interrogation in which the slightest indiscretion or unintended disclosure could cause disaster.

The interview I had in Chicago was conducted by a very well-informed young man who asked me detailed questions on many of the burning topics of the day. As on many occasions during my swing this past week from New York to Philadelphia, Chicago and Minneapolis I was questioned about the prospects for the SDP Liberal alliance, a subject that has caught the imagination of the American public. I suppose that this owes something to its departure from the dreary catalogue of economic failures that has flowed out of Britain for so long.

At Minneapolis I was interviewed for the CBS local talk show by a young lady who was not in complete control. She did not seem to know when the programme was being recorded – 'running' I think is the technical term – or whether we were meant to be having a background or stocktaking chat rather than recording.

At any rate she began the proceedings by saying, 'I'm sorry to say, Sir Nicholson[1] that I don't know anything about your country except that you're having trouble in Northern Ireland and that Lady Di is going to have a baby.'

'Nothing else?' I asked in as matter-of-fact a voice as I could manage, adding that I quite agreed that those were very important facts.

'No, nothing else,' she assured me, saying, 'I'm sorry. You see I wasn't meant to be doing this programme.'

Later she asked me, as do many interviewers, what I did as an Ambassador. I was the first one she had ever met. But she had no idea what I did all day. The true answer, amounting to an account of meetings, briefings, draftings, attendance at official meals and functions, and looking after a string of visitors, would have sounded so unbelievably dull that I could not bring myself to embark upon it. Instead, I wanted to say, 'Well, I begin the day with a bath of champagne poured into a golden tub followed by an hour's massage to the sound of trumpets ...' but my eye caught that of the Consul General who was at his most ozymandian and I forbore to romanticise, contenting myself with some bromides about reporting, making contacts, trade promotion and public relations.

A girl making me up one morning for one of the breakfast programmes

---

[1] My successor was once introduced in similar circumstances as 'Sir 'Orible Wright'.

said, displaying a mastery of mixed metaphor: 'You're becoming quite an old hat.'

Earlier in my time in Washington, I was asked to take part in frequent television programmes about terrorism and the hunger strikers in Northern Ireland. Conscious that television, by showing to American audiences so many pictures of violence without much background information, was proving harmful to our interests, I did not think that I should avoid any chance of appearing and trying to explain what it was all about. Much American opinion tended to believe that 'a little flexibility' on the part of the British government would make a difference and would solve the problem of the hunger strikers.

The following is an account from my diary of what it was like after being summoned to appear on TV in Washington at that time in the early eighties.

I arrive at the studio half an hour before the programme is due to start. From the road the place looks shut despite the neon light inside the entrance. Eventually a young woman arrives, welcomes me, shows me to a shabby sofa and asks me to wait. A TV set has been left on though nobody is watching it. Ashtrays are full of cigarette ends; one or two plastic cups decorate the low glass-topped, much chipped table. There are no magazines. The receptionist, programme assistant or whatever she is, returns to say that Ted Copple, the interviewer, may appear soon or he may not. In any case he will be in a separate room for the programme, during which I will see him on the monitor. She adds that I will be going for make-up shortly. She disappears. Her occasional entrances and exits which are to continue throughout my time in the studio remind me of the way nurses in hospital come and go, telling one that the doctor will be around shortly, that a visit to the X-ray room is about to take place or that another nurse will soon appear to give an injection or something equally unpleasant. I have never grasped the purpose of these grim tidings in hospital but it cannot be to impart a feeling of peace, ease or confidence to the patient, any more than the spare information provided by the TV assistant can be expected to do anything to help gear the interviewee to what he has to say and how.

The make-up lady appears and asks me to follow her into a cubicle that is like an ill-equipped down-at-heel hair-dressing compartment. I have never been in a TV studio that has not looked down-at-heel, remarkably so when you think of the money being made there. For no good reason that I can make out there is nothing automatic about being made up for a TV programme. Sometimes one is made up, sometimes one is not. I suppose that it depends upon the hour of the day or night and whether a beauty specialist is available. Mary says that I badly need it otherwise I look so lined, like a prune. This must also be the view of Douglas Fairbanks who has written enclosing a tube of make-up that he advises me to use, adding that he has found it so good that he applies it to his own face every day.

While the greasepaint is being applied the programme's Ariel alights beside me and asks if I wish for some coffee which she then produces in a plastic cup that is very hot and pliable. I do my best to hold this without spilling it. There is no prospect of being able to drink it while the powder is whirling about and while my cheeks are being dabbed.

Then another wait in the entrance hall before being summoned to the electric chair. Various monitors are spread about the studio amidst the cameras and the wires. I thread my way gingerly through this maelstrom clasping the romboid plastic coffee cup. One or two assistants, mostly men, many of them black, are in the studio. They shout 'Hi' to me in friendly fashion. Ariel guides me to a small platform – stage would be too grand a term for this square, none-too-steady elevation – upon which there is a small table and a small chair. Several cameras are aiming at it like artillery. I notice that fortunately there is no bowl of plastic flowers or backcloth of mountain scenery such as sometimes features on these programmes. I dislike in particular the Tudor interior, red-brick chimney-pieces and furniture shown in one of the morning news programmes in which the interviewer and guests are compelled to sit in low chairs or sofas, their knees in consequence appearing to the viewer to be on the same level as their chins. I take my seat and someone approaches to insert a hearing device in my ear, and to attach a microphone to my tie, and then, as is always necessary with me, to straighten my tie. The monitors are showing the start of the programme in which the inter-viewer, who now appears on the screen, announces my forthcoming appearance. The attendant asks if I can hear him through my ear-piece. I say that I can. I ask where he is and am told that he is in another studio. Then there is a test for voice-level.

My mouth dries up as I wait, but by now the coffee cup is quite ungatherable, at any rate if I am to retain the ear-piece in my ear, the microphone on my tie and the make-up on my face. I try to focus on what I want to get across. I am aware that on TV you have to bang home the arguments straightaway, almost regardless of the question. The art is to catch the programme by the scruff of the neck before the interviewer has got hold of it.

I watch all the monitors which are like family photos reflected mul-titudinously in a series of mirrors. Suddenly one of the attendants says, 'You will be on soon.' He starts counting backwards, as for a space launch: 'Ten, nine ...' As he reaches 'one' all the screens show up with my face. How happy Narcissus would have been. In a bland voice the interviewer puts the first question and I am off, my voice a little thin and breathless, but the adrenalin flowing so that my wits are very much about me.

It is all over very quickly, much more so than one expects. But then, as I have said, there is no lolling about on telly. The end is rather an anti-climax: ear-piece and microphone removed, expressions of thanks from the staff, a word of appreciation from Ariel who is obviously eager to fly to the next visitor, a quick walk past the other studios and out of the door, to be greeted by Doug (my chauffeur) in much the same attentive manner as he displays on fetching one from hospital.

For a day or two you run into people in public places who come up to say that they have seen you on the programme. One lady approached me in the interval of *The Winslow Boy* at the Kennedy Center to say that I was 'a yummy person'. Mary thought that I had out-trumped her. She was recently dubbed by a complete stranger with the words 'You're a darling little lamb chop.'

12 DECEMBER

WASHINGTON

AN ANNIVERSARY DINNER FOR REAGAN

Having invited us ages ago to dine on 10 December Kay Graham divulged to me some time later, in the middle of a game of tennis, that the President and Mrs Reagan would be coming but that this was a great secret that I must keep to myself. The next instruction we received was to arrive on time – 7.30 p.m. If we got there a minute later the police would not allow us into the drive of Kay's house. When the time came on 10 December to enter the gates we were halted by guards. Police cars were ubiquitous. Soldiers armed with bazookas were silhouetted on the roof. A man brandishing a list asked for our names. 'British Ambassador and Lady Henderson,' I replied. He thumbed down the names until he reached what he thought must be ours: 'Nicko and Mary,' he announced triumphantly. As we heard this Mary and I looked at each other, delighted by this confirmation of the American passion for first names.

Guards thronged the hall of the house. I caught sight of Kay's invaluable secretary, Liz Hylton, who gave us our table numbers. We moved into the ante-room on the right so as to mingle with the other guests and to await the arrival of the Reagans. The company included a leavening of show business people, of whom I could immediately identify Mike Nichols and Kitty Hart. The press were well represented by Bill Paley,[1] Punch Sulzberger,[2] Joe Alsop, Donnie and Mary Graham (but not Lally), Meg Greenfield but not Ben Bradlee. Both Fritcheys and Polly's son, Frank Wisner,[3] were there and George Will and his wife. We also spotted Bob McNamara (who gave the impression at the outset that he expected to be shocked by the end of the evening), Dick Helms, Marella Agnelli,[4] Doug Dillon and the Deavers. There was nobody else there from the White House.

Kay told me later that the Reagans had not suggested any names themselves, but they had vetted all those submitted by her. She had taken great trouble in compiling a suitable list and had excluded all editorial journalists so that the President would not feel exposed.

The Reagans politely went round the room shaking hands with everyone. Then the President started chatting to a group. I edged into it only a few minutes before we went into dinner. Clayton Fritchey told me afterwards that he had been gently baiting the President over his animadversions about press leaks. Although I did not overhear the exchanges I did not get the impression that anything very trenchant had been said on either side. By the time I was in the group the President had embarked upon a story about how a psychiatrist had cured two children, one of excessive pessimism, the other of undue optimism. Before he had gone very far he put his hand on Mrs George Will's arm and asked her to forgive him as he was about to use words that were not very polite. This warning led me to expect some strong language. Not at all, the President proceeded to mention horse manure in order to illustrate some point of the story.

To begin with, Kay, the President and Mrs Agnelli had a triangular conversation. It was not long after the chestnut soup that conversation round the table became general, or rather that the conversation became a monologue with the rest of us listening. The President was giving an account of the film, *Reds*, that he had had shown privately at the White House. He had found it objective. He then launched into a series of stories, most of them relating to his time as a film actor. I was struck by how little events since then,

---

[1] William Paley, president of CBS 1928–46, chairman 1946–83. Co-chairman, board of *International Herald Tribune*.
[2] Arthur (Punch) Sulzberger, president and publisher *NY Times* 1963–92. Co-chairman board of *International Herald Tribune* since 1983.
[3] Frank Wisner has been a member of US Foreign Service since 1961; Ambassador to Egypt 1986–91; to the Philippines 1991–2. He is a worthy chip off the well-seasoned Wisner-Washington block.
[4] Marella Agnelli, wife of Giovanni Agnelli, the chairman of Fiat.

which means the best part of the last thirty years, seemed to be in the forefront of his mind or at any rate of his anecdotal repertoire. He told us of the difficulty he had experienced with the zip fastener of his trousers when playing the part of a soldier. Catching sight of Dick Helms, who is a former head of the CIA, he said that Helms would be interested to hear an Irish story about spies which he proceeded to relate.

He spoke of Tip O'Neill and of how the latter had responded to his, Reagan's, injured protest about something bitter that Tip had said about him. Tip had reminded him that politics stopped after 6 p.m. and friendship resumed. At this I mentioned the rule of the Other Club that runs: 'Nothing in the rules or intercourse of the Club shall interfere with the rancour or asperity of party politics.' I added that this had been written by Winston Churchill, upon which the President told a Churchill story.

From there he carried us to Elstree and to the time in 1949 when he had made a film in Britain, *The Burma Road*.[1] He spoke of the austerity and cold that he had experienced in England in those early post-war years. He told us of the courteous attendant who had had to climb a high flight of stairs to tell him whenever he was expected on the set. Reagan had implored him not to bother to come up each time but just to shout from the bottom of the stairs. The man had objected that 'that would be rather churlish' – a word that Reagan had evidently enjoyed, coming at any rate from that source.

We all laughed loudly at these stories, often before the punchline so eager were we to show appreciation. We made so much noise that the people at the other tables turned round and stared, some of them scarcely concealing envy at our luck in being at the President's table. Others bore expressions as if to say that they thought we were being excessively sycophantic.

Kay turned to Reagan and said, 'Mr President, you dined here a year ago, you have been President for ten months. What, looking back, has struck or surprised you the most in office?' (Kay told me later that on reflection she thought that this had been a dumb question because it had been similar to one that had been asked by Barbara Walters in a television interview the previous week.) Reagan answered laconically: 'Leaks.' He did not appear anxious to expand on the subject; nor evidently did he feel it awkward to mention the subject in a gathering that included many magnets from the media which greatly rely on leaks.

---

[1] *The Burma Road* was the title he gave, but he probably meant a film called *The Hasty Heart* which, according to the reference books, is the only film he made in England.

At dinner the President's table (there were two others) was made up as follows:

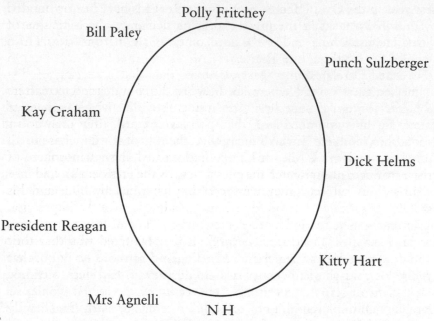

Polly Fritchey

Bill Paley

Punch Sulzberger

Kay Graham

Dick Helms

President Reagan

Kitty Hart

Mrs Agnelli

N H

Piecing together afterwards the jigsaw of the evening I have come to certain conclusions on what the President was getting at. He resents not so much the leak of secret information but the readiness of people in the administration, at whatever level, to run to the press if they fail to get their way in some intra-governmental argument, or if they feel that their authority is being questioned or is inadequately appreciated in the White House or on the Hill. Kay tells me that it is the frequent practice in this, as in previous administrations, for any minister or top official who has this feeling to ring up the *Washington Post* and spill the beans. This arises partly I think from the spoils system, from the lack of a permanent Civil Service and because those occupying the higher posts in an administration do not have a long-term commitment to the efficiency and integrity of government, regardless of party, and they are aware of the limited time-scale in which to exert influence and secure recognition for their service.

In contrast to the President's focus at the dinner on films I have recently seen a TV programme in which he was shown in earlier days in Hollywood as being difficult to restrain from talking politics. He was regarded by his associates as almost a bore on the subject. No doubt he has learnt enough about the Washington scene to realise that anything he says, even in a private house, goes whizzing round the town. In a recent interview with *US News and World Report* he has described

Washington as 'one gigantic ear'. He singled out 'the leaking of information and misinformation' as the main lesson he had learned from his first year in the Oval Office. Certainly the Reagans have been wounded by personal attacks in the press and in particular by the criticisms of their luxurious living and of the acceptance as a gift from friends of a large tea-set for the White House.

To return to the dinner party, I think that that gathering of distinguished guests would have wished to turn the conversation to matters of public concern so as to hear the President's views and his manner of discussing difficult problems of which there were many. Only a few hours before the dinner the United States government had issued a ukase to all Americans to leave Libya; this alone had created some atmosphere of crisis. However disappointed the guests were by the President's avoidance of all serious subjects, they were certainly charmed by him; and his friendliness seemed to be bestowed universally. He gave the impression of not knowing who all the other guests were. They were a crowd scene for his story-telling performance and all that mattered was that they should be appreciative, which indeed we were. There was no doubt that he enjoyed giving his audience pleasure. If he is impersonal he is certainly not at all aloof. He may prefer to spend an evening with his cronies or watching a film in the White House but he seemed to enjoy the friendly group which Kay had assembled. We were, after all, extremely deferential to him and there was no danger of anyone stopping him in the middle of a story by saying that they had heard it before.

After dinner a group surrounded the President. He continued with his stories and, stimulated perhaps by the proximity of Mike Nichols, these became exclusively concerned with his days in Hollywood. He described the manner in which a B film was made and how much the production of it cost. He told us how impossible it was to kiss when making a film without screwing up the girl's face. At one point I asked him if he had read any of David Niven's books which were full of excellent Hollywood stories. 'No,' he riposted, adding with a little shake of the head, turning to me on the floor where I was by now seated, 'you know, your lordship, I have to read all those memoranda.' I was neither surprised nor worried at this false ennoblement. It is a frequent occurrence in the USA to be wrongly addressed and I respond to any loud cry including 'lordship, Sir Nevile Henderson or Sir Harold Nicolson'.[1]

The butler came by from time to time bearing a bottle of champagne. On each occasion the President said, 'Oh, I really shouldn't, you know,'

---

[1] Perhaps the prize misnomer by Reagan was when he mistook Denis Healey for the British Ambassador, Oliver Wright. The error was compounded by the fact that Wright was no longer Ambassador but had been succeeded by Antony Acland.

while holding out his glass for it to be filled up. At dinner, incidentally, the President had shown no particular interest or knowledge concerning the food and wine.

By the time he left, which was around 11.30 p.m., I was sure that the President felt that he had had a wonderful evening. It seemed wrong to think of him going back to a pile of papers that his staff must have assembled for him. It surely must have done him good to be able to relax in this way at Kay's house; and had the public been aware of it I am sure that they would have been glad. The American people do not want their President to spend his evenings with his head in the files. However, I have to realise that his great capacity for delegation does mean, if it is to succeed, that he must be surrounded by people of great ability and integrity.

As a Christmas diversion I organised a competition in the Chancery – which, upon reflection, was highly irresponsible of me. I offered a case of good claret to whoever produced the best rendering of the Gettysburg Address in Al Haig's idiosyncratic and convoluted manner of speech which had come to be widely referred to as Haigspeak. Several members of the Chancery devoted considerable gifts of parody to the task and I received some truly hilarious versions of Lincoln's speech.

It then dawned on me that I might have lit a dangerous fuse. What if the winner's version was leaked to the Washington Post – always ready to report on undiplomatic incidents in the capital's diplomatic life – and published with the result that it became the talk of Washington? Al Haig would be bound to hear about it and might think that the British Embassy, particularly the Ambassador, could well devote their energy and talents to other less tactless pursuits. I, therefore, decided that I would play the Red Queen and say that all had won and all would get prizes, a bottle each. But I added that as there was no single winner there would be no prize-giving and no circulation of the texts, all of which I consigned to oblivion. Fortunately, I do not think there was a leak.

1982

——

3 JANUARY
WASHINGTON

——

A SMALL CHRISTMAS INCIDENT

A Christmas spent as usual writing the annual review, but interrupted this year by a great deal of toing and froing on account of the military crackdown in Poland, and, to a lesser extent, owing to the Israeli annexation of the Golan Heights. The Reaganauts, eager to show a tougher strain than the Carterites, have moved quickly to impose sanctions on the USSR, accusing them of responsibility for the declaration of martial law in Poland. The Europeans are sceptical of the value of sanctions. Naturally the media are playing up the rift between the two sides of the Atlantic.

Haig came to a Community Ambassadors' lunch that I gave just before the US announcement of their tough measures. He gave a good account of the reasoning behind US policy. The sanctions were required as retribution, and as punishment and warning. I am not sure that all my European colleagues understood all that he said in his inimitable Haigspeak, however well they all speak English, as they do.

Obviously we have a considerable advantage over our colleagues in language. I had to make one or two points on their behalf about US–European relations; and it was easier for me to do than it would have been for any of them. I also dare say that they saw an advantage in having me do it though some would not wish to admit this and it is certainly something better left unsaid. This is an aspect of our membership of the Community that I had not foreseen.

A tiresome little diplomatic event occurred just before Christmas. Mary belongs to a women's club composed of the wives of diplomats, Congressmen, members of the US government and one or two highly reputable journalists. The idea is that they should meet together from time to time; and once a year they invite husbands and a dinner is given in an Embassy. This year it was our turn and we decided to give a Christmas party with carols. To our surprise the Dobrynins said that they would be coming, as indeed did the Chinese.

The evening went off quite well. I was told later that it had provided Stoessel[1] with a useful opportunity to do some straight speaking to

---

[1] Walter Stoessel was a member of the US Foreign Service 1942–82. At this stage he was Under-Secretary of State for Political Affairs (1981–2), and was shortly to become the Deputy

Dobrynin without having to call him into the State Department which he didn't want to do. It also provided one or two others present with a chance to let off steam to Dobrynin and tell him what they thought of Soviet action in Poland. For once I felt myself a little on his side. For years he has had the run of Washington, hoodwinking them all with his bonhomie. I have been vexed by the way so many hostesses have been taken in by him over the years and how they have reached rosy views about Soviet policy as a result of this. But now it seems a bit obvious and crude to go for him at a social gathering when they have been duped by him for so long.

After dinner we all sat looking at the Christmas tree while a group sang carols. It certainly struck me as incongruous to have Dobrynin and the Chinese Ambassador honouring the birth of Christ in this fashion; but no odder, after all, than what our Ambassador has to do in attending parades celebrating the revolution and the execution of the Tsar and his family, or the Long March in China. I was a little annoyed when I read Scottie Reston's column in the *New York Times* a couple of days later. He said that it was ironical, just when we were all deploring the Soviet pressure on Poland, to see Dobrynin invited by the British Ambassador and Lady Henderson to sing carols in the British Embassy, including 'God Rest Ye Merry Gentlemen' and 'Peace on Earth and Mercy Mild'.

Alas that was not the end of it. Once something gets into the press it sticks. In his *Letter from America* at Christmas-time Alistair Cooke referred to the same event, a story he must have got from Reston's column.

But it's no good complaining about something that has been published and I certainly don't want to sour relations with Scottie Reston.

28 FEBRUARY

LONDON – WASHINGTON

——

DOMINANCE OF THE WINDSOR RIDE

Cap Weinberger came to supper to meet Yehudi Menuhin. At the age of five he had attended Yehudi's first public concert given in San Francisco when he was only six. Over dinner, Jane Weinberger mentioned to me 'that silly thing in the papers about Cap'. She was referring to the Atticus

---

Secretary of State. Ambassador to Poland 1968–72 (the time when I was there); to the USSR 1974–6; and to the FRG 1976–81. A correct and distinguished diplomat, his life was much enlivened by the spirited personality of his wife, Mary-Ann.

story in the *Sunday Times* about his friendship with Janet Morgan[1] whom he had met at Ditchley. She made light of it, saying that at the time the paper had said that he was dining intimately with the girl he was in fact having dinner with her, Jane, in a small restaurant near the Portobello Road. I was greatly relieved to hear that the Weinbergers were treating the story in this fashion because traditionally a rumour of this kind involving an English girl has proved to be damaging in the most un-Devonshire-house-set morality of the USA. I recall the prairie fire that consumed Vandenberg's Presidential nomination prospects at the Republican Convention at Philadelphia in 1948. It had been ignited by the gossip retailed by a note left under the door of each hotel bedroom alleging that the Senator was consorting with an English girlfriend.

I minded the harm that such gossip might cause to Weinberger officially – and incidentally to various bilateral projects – and the pain it could create for him personally. I find him highly sympathetic as an individual; and I understand totally his wish to be able to lead some semblance of a private life in the midst of his demanding public one.

Yehudi's concert took place at the Kennedy Center the following evening. Cap and I had a chat in the Presidential box ante-room before hand. He referred to Al Haig and the much-discussed account published in the *Washington Post* of Haig's obiter dicta at the morning staff briefing in the State Department. Haig was reported to have described Carrington as a 'duplicitous bastard', and to have made other unflattering remarks about his role in the Middle East. The story has attracted a great deal of egregious interest on both sides of the Atlantic. Cap quipped to me that he supposed the British empire would survive Haig's tough talk. This gave me the chance to probe him, ever so gently, on his views about Haig. He said that he was inclined to resort to barrack-room language. It was surprising really that his reported remarks had not been a good deal rougher, a thought that had struck me also, bearing in mind how people talk in the privacy, or presumed privacy, of their offices. Weinberger averred that his relations with Haig were a good deal better than the press made out. He had a high opinion of him. 'But he is entirely pro-Israel – that's the root of our problem.' Asked whether the reason for this lay in Haig's continued Presidential ambitions, Cap assented. As for himself, he insisted that he had no political ambitions. He had never wished to return to Washington. I said that this was just as well given the attacks on him for his Middle East policy. Cap seemed admirably

[1] Janet Morgan, writer and consultant. Lecturer in Politics at Exeter College, Oxon 1974–6; at St Hugh's College Oxon 1976–8. Member Central Policy Review Staff Cabinet Office 1978–81, since when she has held many business appointments. She has written books on a wide range of subjects including government broadcasting. She has published a biography of Agatha Christie. Her interests are as eclectic as her personality is lively.

unperturbed by the criticisms to which he has been subjected. He interjected that of those around Reagan only Clark[1] was in favour of a balanced, as distinct from an entirely pro-Zionist, policy.

I did not like to bother Cap on the subject that the Office had asked me to take up with him, the future of the Hawk contract. It is always a problem to know whether or not to use social occasions for raising matters of business. I tend not to do so; but sometimes one has no other opportunity, as I have found out over arrangements for the Presidential visit to the UK this summer. Had I not buttonholed Mike Deaver and Clark at parties I am not sure how the plans for the visit would ever have been worked out satisfactorily from our point of view.

London has been very patient with the contradictory messages I have kept sending about the President's wishes for his journey. They have been benign too when I have revealed, on the basis of what Clark told me at the end of a White House diplomatic dinner – the first for over twenty years – that the President had been misquoted, or, rather, that he had not been consulted about the programme. Contrary to what I had been told, for instance, he would be very pleased to address a session of the two Houses of Parliament, an item I had been strongly recommending (remembering de Gaulle's impact) in the face of opposition from others in the White House who had said that the President would not be able to find the time to give the preparation of such a speech the attention required. To Clark I said that Reagan was after all the Great Communicator. Clark in fact rang me when I was in South Carolina to tell me how eager the President was to seize the chance of addressing parliament. Would I, he asked, deal with him in future about the programme? It so happened that not long before this Haig had said exactly the same thing to me.

The one item in the programme that I thought everyone accepted with enthusiasm was the royal ride in Windsor Home Park. In the frequent exchanges with Deaver about the visit I had found that however doubtful he was concerning this or that proposal his eye invariably lit up at the prospect of the President's riding with the Queen. 'Carter couldn't have done a thing like that,' he said with a triumphant beam one morning when I was seeing him in the White House. 'Think of the photo opportunity,' he

---

[1] William Clark, member of the Supreme Court of California 1973–81. Deputy Secretary Department of State Washington 1981; Assistant to the President for National Security Affairs 1982–3; Secretary of the Interior 1983–5. He was one of those people who suddenly rocket to prominence in US public life and then no less dramatically disappear from view. Although inexperienced in international affairs, when he was at the White House he followed the practice of Kissinger and Brzezinski in trying to appropriate to it much foreign-policy decision-making – to the detriment of the State Department. We had much to do with him over the Falklands War when, whatever our differences, he was invariably calm and sociable.

added. It was therefore a shock to me – and to London – when, very late
in the preparations, I discovered that the President's ignorance about the
proposed programme extended even to 'the ride'. However, Clark put
this right, as he did the address to parliament.

It struck me that London, not least the palace, were long-suffering
about the degree of casual incompetence displayed by Washington over
the arrangements for the visit. When Michael Palliser came on a farewell
visit to Washington last week he was made aware of the prevailing chaos
here; and he left me in no doubt about London's concern. He said that
the Queen had commissioned him to find out more from me about the
President's riding wishes – and prowess. What sort of saddle? What sort
of horse? Clearly, too, the Queen was beginning to get anxious about
the glare of publicity in which this private ride was destined to take
place. There were going to be six hundred pressmen accompanying the
President on the journey and even more security men. I thought of –
Elinor Glyn's remark – or was it some other liberal-minded perceptive
Edwardian – that it doesn't matter what you do so long as you don't do
it in the streets and frighten the horses. This ride was going to be a
worldwide box-office draw.

It was evident to me that I would have to resort to unusual channels
to secure the necessary information. I therefore fed the questions to Mary
who fed them in turn to Nancy Reagan who then put them to the
President. The result is that by now we have the true answers from the
horse-rider's mouth. These cover all the necessary matters about seat,
saddle and horse.

This central subject I have discussed during a visit that I have paid to the
Lord Chamberlain's Office. After I had given my views the Comptroller of
the Queen's Household promised to raise the matter with Sir John Miller,[1]
the Crown Equerry. I was assured that they would have just the sort of
horse required, one that was accustomed to the razzmatazz of the Troop-
ing of the Colour, looked and was powerful, but behaved like a lamb,
and was responsive to the gentlest heel. The Lord Chamberlain's Office
showed great dignity despite their considerable surprise, as in a Bateman
cartoon wherein decorum is publicly shattered, when they heard that the
Windsor Castle banquet for the President would be televised. Never
before had a camera been in the place but then there had been no official
visit by a US President since Woodrow Wilson had been to London in
1919.

---

[1] John Miller; Crown Equerry 1961–87, a post that included the day-to-day running of the
royal stables. He was president of the Coaching Club 1975–82; and of the Royal Windsor
Horse Show Club 1985–90. He was certainly the person nearest the royal horse's mouth
one could reach. I had known him when we were at school together at Summerfields and
found him smilingly, inscrutably unchanged despite an interval of fifty years.

MRS. PATRICK CAMPBELL – ENGLISH ACTRESS

I swore to the Comptroller and to the Deputy Comptroller that this visit to Windsor was for the Reagans the highpoint of the whole European visit. Versailles might be grand, Rome romantic, but Windsor was the home of a surviving monarch, better than any film set. Johnny Johnston and the others in his office demonstrated that remarkable British quality, a stalwart attachment to tradition with an imaginative readiness to adapt if circumstances required it. Once the whole event was seen as something bordering on fantasy they were suffused with the desire to make it work. There was nothing censorious or governessy in their approach. Surprise, yes, but the surprise of school speech day when the guest of honour is an actor rather than a former colonial governor. Above all the belief that the show must be made to work. All of this subject to the overriding requirement which was emphasised to me frequently that the Queen's wishes must of course be respected.

On the walls of St James's Palace, where we were meeting, paintings hung depicting great occasions – Queen Victoria's Diamond Jubilee procession, for instance. She was seated in her carriage with the crowds close by acclaiming her. A pictorial record of Reagan's forthcoming visit would be a no less significant memorial, but alas, for security reasons, it would be much less dramatic to the eye: scenes of entering helicopters and being ushered into buildings, but without a state carriage drive through the streets of London. I nourish the private hope that the ride in Windsor Home Park may leave the early Tatler scenes looking modest.

When I lunched with John Coles,[1] the Private Secretary at Number 10, I managed to get across to him how much the President wanted to do whatever would be most helpful to Mrs Thatcher. When Clark conveyed this message to me I thought that it was very touching. Nobody can say that Mrs Thatcher's attachment to economics and applied science has brought political dividends so far at home or abroad. From being a beacon of hope after her election in 1979, Mrs T has become a symbol of failure, a warning, a lesson in what not to follow, as the US press keeps reminding us. So it is noble of Reagan, a tribute to the brotherhood of office, to the solidarity that joins those who suffer the slings and arrows of outrageous political fortune, that he should be so unequivocal in his readiness to back Mrs Thatcher in her present adversity and to 'help her' when he could perfectly well coast along on the royal level at Windsor Castle.

Coles told me that in fact Mrs T is setting much store by Reagan's visit. During a visit I paid to the FCO I mentioned this to Peter Carrington

---

[1] John Coles, Member of the Diplomatic Service. Private Secretary to Prime Minister 1981–4; Ambassador to Jordan 1984–8; High Commissioner to Australia 1988–91; Permanent Under-Secretary of State, Foreign and Commonwealth Office 1994.

who said that he thought she was justified. It would be a plus, despite Reagan's unpopularity over El Salvador.

I have had a wonderful week in London. I remember interludes like this from posts many years ago when I spent a few days at home and imagined that it could never be so good again: staying at Brooks's, and undertaking an intense round of official and social engagements. But it has been just as jam-packed and wonderful again this time.

I attended a conference one day about the US and British economic outlooks. Fairly depressing. No upturn in the USA before mid-year – that was the consensus. Those who spoke to me wanted to gossip about Haig's leaked remarks, or about my departure and likely successor, based on press reports. After a week of meeting many people in London I am confirmed in my view that it is time to go. Often when talking about my likely successor people ask me when and for how long they can come and stay before I leave.

The Moores gave a grand dinner for me one evening at Ledbury Road. I sat next to Tina Brown,[1] married to Harold Evans[2] with whom I had a long talk afterwards. He said that if Murdoch closed The Times there were plenty of potential buyers. Robert Kee and Sue Baring were there. Also the Mark Boxers. Anna was full of talk about her baby: 'After all, I have done everything else,' she said. Jacob Rothschild[3] was full of fun and mischief.

Lunch the next day with Robert and Derry chez Frances Partridge. Otherwise it has been mostly meetings. With Peter Carrington I talked about the alliance, suggesting that he should take an initiative with Haig and propose a study of the future relationship between the main allies. He doesn't much like general ideas, as Julian[4] confirmed over breakfast

---

[1] Tina Brown, editor Tatler 1979–83; editor-in-chief Vanity Fair 1984–92 when she became editor of the New Yorker. In 1981 she married Harold Evans. She has also written plays and books. The revitaliser of Vanity Fair and the New Yorker, she must be regarded as one of the outstanding journalists and editors of her generation.

[2] Harold Evans began his life as an editor on newspapers in the north of England, was editor of the Sunday Times 1967–81 and of The Times 1981–2. Editor-in-chief Atlantic Monthly 1984–6. Editor-director US News and World Report 1984–6. Editor-in-chief Condé Nast's Traveler magazine since 1986. He has written an excellent account of his newspaper life in London: Good Times, Bad Times (1983). He is a brillant editor whom Henry Kissinger consulted before publishing his volumes of autobiography.

[3] Jacob Rothschild, chairman J. Rothschild Holdings plc since 1971; Five Arrows since 1986. As chairman of Board of Trustees, National Gallery 1985–92 he made a terrific impact just as his time there greatly broadened his expereince and range of contacts and influence. An heir to the Rothschild tradition of banking and philanthropy, he has also inherited from the Hutchinson side of the family a taste for the arts and a streak of unconventionality and irreverence.

[4] Julian Bullard became a member of the Diplomatic Service in 1953 and his first foreign post was Vienna where we were serving at the time. We were together again in the 1970s in Bonn where he was minister. Early in 1982 he was Deputy to Permanent Under-Secretary of State and Political Director. Ambassador to Bonn 1984–8. A brillant and unassuming

the following day. I hope I was able to persuade Julian that something should be done to dissuade the Americans from their continual criticism about the alliance – their complaint that it is not doing something that in fact it was never intended to perform. People in London are little interested in institutions or I would think of sending a despatch on the subject from Washington.

Of all those I spoke to during the week in London I was most impressed by Hannay[1] who copes with our relations with the European Community. To my surprise he seemed to think that he would get some sort of settlement on the budget.

The grandest event during my stay was a dinner-dance at the Raynes,[2] a party for her fiftieth birthday.

13 MARCH
WASHINGTON

———

A LONGISH DAY

Thursday this week was one of the longer days I have spent recently, though such are the mysteries of the nervous system, or at any rate mine, that I was not in the least tired at the end of it.

The day began with the usual dreaded daily routine, that is to say morning exercises, an inadequate breakfast, a glimpse at the TV morning shows and a flip through the *Washington Post*, the *New York Times* and the *Wall Street Journal*. Then, accompanied by Robin Renwick,[3] I went to the White House at 9 a.m. to exchange letters between the President and the Prime Minister recording agreement on Trident II. Mcfarlane[4]

---

scholar and public servant. There was no member of the Service in his time who attracted more admiration and affection from colleagues.

[1] David Hannay, a member of the Diplomatic Service since 1959, UK Permanent Representative to the European Communities 1985–90. Since then he has been Ambassador to the UN where he has shown the necessary rapidity and assurance in exposition.

[2] Max and Jayne Rayne. He has been chairman, London Merchant Securities plc since 1960. On the board of many humanitarian and cultural institutions, the good he has done has been as stealthy as it has been generous.

[3] Robin Kenwick, member of the Diplomatic Service since 1963. First Secretary, Paris 1972–6; Political Adviser to the Governor of Rhodesia, 1980; Head of Chancery, Washington, 1981–4; Ambassador to South Africa, 1987–91; Ambassador to Washington since 1991. Having served with him in Paris and Washington I can attest the rigour of his mind and the gaiety of his spirit, qualities which have stood him in good stead in the United States.

[4] Robert Mcfarlane served in the Marine Corps 1959–79. Military Assistant to Henry Kissinger 1973–5; Special Assistant to President 1976–77; Counsellor State Department 1981–2; Deputy Assistant to President for National Security Affairs 1982–3.

greeted us, took us to the Map Room (adorned with only one map but used for the purpose apparently by Lincoln), made a short speech and offered us a glass of champagne. I would have appreciated the last more had I realised I would not be getting another drink until late that evening. Typically, arriving in the Rolls Royce in great state at the gates of the White House, we were asked our identity and kept waiting, an ignominious security process that the terrorists have managed to inflict on the world. Equally typically, the front lawn of the White House was filled with journalists and cameramen who appeared to have a free run of the place just as the Tass correspondent has a pass that enables him to wander at will in the State Department while the rest of us democratic mortals cannot move in the building without being accompanied.

From the White House back to the office for a short attendance at the regular morning meeting. From there to Dulles airport to take an executive jet to Hartford, Connecticut, where I was visiting the United Technologies Corporation (UTC).

I lunched at UTC with the chairman, Charles Gray, and members of his board. We talked about the aircraft industry and the future of defence contracts. Rolls Royce is a rival with Pratt and Whitney (which is part of the UTC empire) for the engine of one of Boeing's planes; but they are potential collaborators, together with the Japanese, for a new jet engine for a new one hundred and fifty seater plane. I do not find that this sort of thing embarrasses Americans any more than does straight sales-talk – a great relief. Americans have no qualms about putting all their goods in the shop window; they would think anything else barmy.

At this lunch with UTC I vaunted the qualities of Rapier, the AV8B etc, while Gray told me that he thought that future aircraft engines would have to last sixty years if they were to pay for themselves. A presentation took place after lunch about the various activities of the corporation with beautiful slides of aeroplanes taking off and landing. It wasn't altogether easy to keep the lids open.

In the early evening I gave a lecture to the local World Affairs Council. Then by air to New York in appalling weather for a dinner given by Brooke Astor for the Mouchys.[1]

We drank Haut-Brion which indeed it is the purpose of the Mouchys' current visit to the United States to promote. After dinner I chatted with

---

[1] Philippe Noailles, Duc de Mouchy, landowner; now married to Joan née Dillon whose grandfather in 1935 purchased Château Haut-Brion which Philippe now runs. Educated at Eton and bilingual in English and French he gave the drawling reply to a young Englishman who was ignorant of this and who had asked him whether he spoke English, 'Oh I get along as best I can.'

Brooke and Sidney Urquhart.[1] As usual nowadays a good deal of the talk was about *Brideshead Revisited*, the film of which is being shown on TV. I finally got to bed at the Colony Club around midnight.

27 MARCH

CALIFORNIA

THUS SPAKE SHAKESPEARE

I am intrigued by the parties given throughout the USA by the English Speaking Union (ESU) for visiting Ambassadors and touched by the spontaneous warmth of the members. They often inform me about important English-linked events in their lives. At the ESU party in San Diego one guest told me that she had an aunt living in Lincolnshire while another notified me that he had been in Scotland two years ago and was looking forward to going there again. I did my best to follow up on these openings. At all ESU parties I realise that one has to accept with resignation the assumption of all these kind people that England is permanently afflicted by fog or torrential rain and that if a mist or shower is threatening, wherever one may be in the United States, this must make one feel at home. Many are the questions about the royal family. At the present time I have to share the state of high euphoria that exists everywhere over the prospect of Lady Di's delivery.

President Eisenhower disclosed on some occasion that the best speech he had ever made in his life had been to the ESU. I am not able to make the same boast. I find myself concluding with a stock peroration in which I quote Wordsworth:

> We must be free or die, who speak the tongue
> That Shakespeare spake . . .

It may be galling but what right have I to complain if I find, amongst the crowds I meet, that as British Ambassador I am typecast as someone combining the qualities of Aubrey Smith, Sebastian Flyte and David Niven? That after all is exactly what people want to find, however much

---

[1] Sidney Urquhart, wife of Brian Urquhart, a highly respected official of the UN, where he had worked from the start in 1945; in the office of the UN Secretary-General 1949–56, and of the Under Secretary-General for Special Political Affairs 1954–71; Assistant Secretary-General UN 1972–4. Involved in many peace-keeping operations, described in his autobiography, *A Life in Peace and War*.

something may have gone awry with the casting of me for the role.

On the drive from Los Angeles to San Diego we passed pylons, refineries, power stations and skyscrapers situated alongside broken-down houses and enormous apartment blocks – the poverty adjacent to opulence which is to be found frequently in the USA. We visited a winery, Calloway, where we were given much scientific information about acidity, sugar and balance.

I gave a brief TV interview upon arrival in San Diego. Then lunch at the City Club with the usual salad, veal and ice-cream served with iced tea or coffee. I spoke for about forty minutes. With the San Diego journalists, as with those of the *Los Angeles Times* the day before, I was struck by their close interest in European affairs, notwithstanding the Pacific direction they were facing.

Our next stop was the San Diego zoo where we were given a rapid tour by bus by two young zoo-keepers, one male, the other female. The girl seemed to have a special rapport with the large brown bear who stood up on its hind legs at her bidding. She referred to most of the animals under her charge as 'guys'. Pointing to a couple of tapirs she said, 'See those guys asleep in the corner …'

I was as impressed by the lovely vegetation as by the animals, but also, of course, by the vast wealth obviously available to the zoo, thanks in part to their skill in providing shops for the public to buy all manner of goods from teddy bears to African drums. They make four million dollars per annum from retail sales.

Near the zoo we visited a reproduction of the Globe Theatre, recently built at a cost of several million dollars. It was beautifully done, a building in wood, rather than the concrete that is so prevalent elsewhere in the neighbourhood. The benefactions from private sources in the USA are staggering and I recalled my talk the previous day with Stephen Garrett,[1] the British director of the Getty Museum at Malibu. He told me how Getty had left a sum of money, now apparently amounting to 1.4 billion dollars, in trust for the museum, without giving any guidance on how it should be spent or who should have the responsibility for deciding. The annual income was around one hundred and forty million dollars, yet the running costs of the museum only amounted to about five million dollars. Garrett showed great awareness of the hostility that could be roused if the museum started using the balance to buy art on the scale that the money would permit. They were already purchasing a good deal as I learned when I went round the museum. I found it an

---

[1] Stephen Garrett, an architect, he was employed in the design and construction of the Getty Museum, Malibu. Director of the museum from its opening in 1974 to 1983. Later, director of the Long Beach Museum of Art and founding Director of the Armand Hammer Museum.

irresistible subject for private speculation how to advise Stephen Garrett on the means of separating the Getty Trust from some of its surplus funds. Surely, I thought to myself, some of the money should find its way to the UK where Getty lived for the last twenty-five years of his life. So far as I knew he had made no bequest for the benefit of any British institution.

THE FALKLANDS

The diary entries on the Falklands conflict are intermittent and incomplete, probably because I was too busy and tired to make them fuller. I published an account afterwards of the efforts made by the USA to try to bring about a diplomatic solution.[1] Unfortunately I was not allowed to reveal the nature or scale of the help given by the Americans in military supplies and intelligence. The American State Department was frightened of the effect this might have on its relations with Latin America which had been bruised by Washington's support for London during the conflict; and the Foreign Office, in consequence, opposed publication out of respect for this fear. More ignominiously, the British Ministry of Defence did not want anything published that might blur Britain's individual blaze of glory.

Aware of what the US Department of Defence and, in particular, of what Mr Caspar Weinberger had done to make essential materiel of war available to the British forces at the speed required, and disturbed by the injustice of concealing it, I wrote to Weinberger to explain what had happened. In a characteristically philosophical reply he said that he had read my article before hearing from me; and that he had to 'confess ("vanity, vanity, all is vanity") a certain mild surprise that the entire story of America and the Falklands was written without any passing reference to what our small department had tried to do both before and after the US took its strong position in support of Britain'. He expressed regret at the omission of information which he thought could have helped deter anyone from undertaking future adventures of this kind, apart from the boost it might give to the bilateral relationship. He said that, if I planned to write another piece covering some of the military relationship of the US and UK during the Falklands War, he would be glad to see if the State Department could be persuaded to have the truth appear, or,

---

[1] *Economist*, 12 November 1983. The text was subsequently reproduced in my book, *Channels and Tunnels*, Weidenfeld and Nicolson.

alternatively, he suggested that I should seriously consider simply ignoring them.

I thought that it would be better to get someone else to tell the story of the materiel help given by the Americans. All the information would be forthcoming from Weinberger and his staff. I therefore suggested that Simon Jenkins, then deputy editor of The Economist, *should take it on, which he undertook to do. He proceeded to obtain the facts and have them published in his paper.[1] This disclosed the scepticism of the US navy at the outset about the prospects for the success of the British task force. Britain was ill-equipped to fight a war in the South Atlantic. They lacked air surveillance; their satellite communications were inadequate. They were short of an effective air-to-air missile for the Harriers. They had no base in the South Atlantic. However, Weinberger and the US navy were ready to fill these gaps immediately as best they could. They also perceived that the logistics problem could be solved by the extensive use of the American Wideawake airbase on Ascension Island. This had been leased from Britain which had a right under the lease agreement to use it in an emergency. It was four thousand miles away from the Falkland Islands but this was half as far away as was the UK. Thanks to the close contacts between the navies of the two countries and, most of all, to the decisive intervention of Weinberger, an avalanche of supplies immediately started to pour into Ascension, e.g. aviation fuel, the new Sidewinder air-to-air missiles (which proved to be the most decisive weapon of the campaign), Stinger anti-aircraft systems, and weapons and ammunition of all kinds. Not least important was the help the Americans provided over intelligence and communications. For me the most dramatic moment occurred when Weinberger took me aside at a party at the British Embassy. He said that he would be prepared to make a US carrier available to us in the South Atlantic if the military situation required it – an offer of spontaneous and practical generosity that must be unique in the annals of the Washington–London relationship.*

It is impossible to exaggerate the contribution Weinberger made to our cause. As soon as the decision had been made to launch the task force – and a month before the USA openly declared its support for Britain – Weinberger, as he has written in his memoirs,[2] 'made it clear that we would supply them with everything they needed ... ' This flatly contradicts the statement in President Reagan's autobiography[3] that the USA provided no military assistance to the British other than the use of a military communication satellite during April.

---

[1] *Economist*, 3 March 1984.
[2] *Fighting for Peace*, Michael Joseph, 1990.
[3] Page 359, *Autobiography*, Hutchinson, 1990.

Weinberger has admitted that 'we all knew of the enormous military odds against Britain'. As he realised at the time, and has explained in his memoirs, the normal course for meeting requests for materials and supplies could not be followed if America was to be of any real assistance: 'I therefore directed that all British requests were to have immediate and first priority, and particularly that our staff examination be drastically reduced ... I also directed that each of these requests come directly to my desk, something that would otherwise not have happened. Finally, I directed that I be told within twenty-four hours of our receipt of a British request, whether it had been granted, if not, why not and when would it be granted?'.

Those most directly involved in the campaign, and the journalists and historians who have studied it closely in retrospect, have concluded that without American help the operation could not have succeeded as it did. Mrs Thatcher has written that 'without the Harriers ... using the latest version of the Sidewinder ..., supplied by Weinberger, we could not have retaken the Falklands'. Nobody minimises the fighting qualities displayed by the British forces in the campaign, but the hard fact is that they just did not have from their own resources the necessary equipment available in quality, quantity or in time. Weinberger is characteristically modest and generous on this subject, attributing the decisive factor to Mrs Thatcher's firm and immediate decision to retake the islands, despite the impressive military and other advice to the contrary. But he acknowledges that 'we certainly helped substantially in supplying resources more rapidly than would have been possible from elsewhere'. His conclusion is that the major factor in American assistance 'was the speed with which we fulfilled all British requests. I am told that not even during the Second World War were we able to, nor did we, respond so quickly to requests for military assistance. Speed was what they most needed'.

The political backing provided by the Americans was also crucial. Alexander Haig, the US Secretary of State, said to me repeatedly throughout the conflict that, however much the US government wanted and worked for a diplomatic rather than military outcome, which meant initially the adoption of a neutral attitude, it would not let its ally down as Washington had done over the Suez crisis.

Without seeking to describe the ups and downs of the diplomatic dialogue throughout the crisis, about which, as I say, I have already written an account, I must, in order to give the necessary background to the diary, pick out one or two nuggets from my frequent meetings with Haig. They may help to explain what was behind his policy which excited such controversy at the time, not least in the higher reaches of the British government. I do not attempt even to touch upon the hectic diplomatic activities at the UN where Tony Parsons was the British representative

*and managed to secure the passage of an all-important resolution,
(Resolution 502) immediately after the Argentinian invasion, calling for
their withdrawal from the islands.*

*When I saw Haig soon after the invasion I gave him a message
from Francis Pym, who was now Foreign Secretary, having succeeded
Carrington after his resignation (see entry for 10 April 1982). The
message emphasised Britain's determination to bring about the withdrawal of Argentinian forces and the restoration of British administration, by whatever means were necessary. It also referred to the
critical importance of the American role. Haig is a paragon of a fighting
man and this was reflected in the quick-fire manner of his response to
the message I had conveyed. But at the post he now occupied at the State
Department his business was peace, not war, and his rapid reaction was
directed to the need for urgent high-level mediation to head off military
conflict. The course of action that he immediately suggested to me was
mediation on his part to bring about negotiations which would lead to
some mixed administration to run the islands.*

*I saw that, to avoid any risk of misunderstanding, I must clarify
HMG's attitude. Our government could not enter into any negotiations
of the kind he was thinking about until Argentinian troops had been
withdrawn. The US administration would adopt the same stand if
American territory, say Puerto Rico, were occupied by Cuban troops.*

*Haig could not see how General Galtieri could survive if he was forced
to remove his troops without getting anything in return. I said that it
was not our purpose to help Galtieri survive. There had been few
international issues since 1945 about which the British had felt so
unanimously and so strongly. If it was asked why we bothered about a
mere two thousand people at the other end of the world, it was worth
remembering how bitterly the Americans had felt about their fifty-two
hostages held in Iran.*

*Assuring me that he fully understood the state of British public opinion
on this issue Haig wondered, thinking aloud, whether it would not be
possible to have some kind of interim administration appointed for the
islands. If the USA were going to serve as mediator they would have to
avoid taking sides. Haig admitted to me personally that at heart he was
not impartial. He was very aware of the strength of the 'Latino-Lobby'.
Mrs Jeane Kirkpatrick, the US Ambassador to the UN who had a seat
in the US Cabinet, was probably the most influential member of this
group. She did not consider that Argentina was an aggressor; it was
simply asserting a long-stated claim to the islands. Argentina was an
authoritarian but not a totalitarian regime. There was an important
distinction. Buenos Aires had been giving America support for its covert
operations in Central America and in anti-Communist causes throughout*

Latin America. Reflecting on this I realised that the Argentine junta may well have believed that in return for this the US government would acquiesce if it was to resort to force in the Falklands.

Haig was also sensitive to President Reagan's outlook on the matter. The President had described the Falklands as 'that little ice-cold bunch of land down there'. To a group of journalists he had said on 5 April that the USA were friends equally with Argentina and the UK.

There is no doubt that Haig reflected American public opinion in wanting a peaceful, rather than a military, outcome. He believed that it would be possible to bridge the gap between the Argentinian insistence that any settlement must in some way promote the transfer to them of sovereignty over the islands, and the British determination that Argentinian troops must be withdrawn and that nothing must infringe the right of the islanders to decide their own future. Hence Haig's shuttle diplomacy between London and Buenos Aires. He told me that he found Mrs Thatcher 'very tough', but added, 'I wish we had more like her.' As for Argentina, Haig described to me the irrational and chaotic nature of their leadership. They were guided by no coherent or consistent strategy.

On April 24, after much travelling and discussion, Haig conveyed to the British Government a plan for a negotiated settlement that he considered reasonable for both sides. His intention was to put it to the Argentinian Junta. In her memoirs, Lady Thatcher records that Francis Pym favoured concurrence in the plan; but that she did not like it at all. This produced a 'great crisis' – to use her words – in the Cabinet. She recalls that if Ministers had accepted Haig's proposals she would have resigned. Yet Ministers realised that to have turned them down would have been to have jeopardised the prospect of American support.

In this critical atmosphere the move the British Government decided upon – which, according to Lady Thatcher's memoirs, was John Nott's brain-wave – was a finesse of which Talleyrand would have been proud. Lady Thatcher replied to Haig by saying in effect, 'Pass', explaining that as the crisis had arisen from the Argentinian aggression and as the security council had thereupon called upon them to withdraw from the Islands, the next step for Haig should be to put his plans to Buenos Aires. Knowledge of their attitude would be important to the British Cabinet in considering Haig's ideas.

Haig did not demur to this. Making no effort to press for a substantial answer from London – for which London must surely have been grateful – he put his scheme to BA with a deadline. Long after this had expired the Junta replied baldly that their objective was 'sovereignty'. Haig construed this as a rejection. On April 30 he announced that negotiations had broken down and that the United States would support Britain. He listed various restrictions on trade with Argentina, including military exports, and declared that the President had directed that the US would respond positively to requests for military materiel from Britain.

Reagan, like Haig, was prepared to acquiesce in Britain's finesse. In a message to Lady Thatcher he said: 'I recognise that while you see fundamental difficulties in the proposal, you have not rejected it'. He also said that the US Government would not be releasing the text of the US plan because of the difficulty that that might cause London.

4 APRIL
WASHINGTON

OPENING OF THE FALKLANDS CRISIS

We are well and truly into a Falklands crisis and my involvement says something about US–UK relations generally.

Stoessel, Deputy Under-Secretary at the State Department, asked to see me last Monday, 29 March. He told me that he had just seen the Argentinian Ambassador. This was as a result of reports he had read about possible trouble in South Georgia where some Argentinians had landed. He knew that they had hoisted a flag and that the British were saying that they were there illegally and must either leave or secure the necessary documentation to regularise their presence. Stoessel said that the USA did not wish to take sides as between the UK and Argentina. They merely wished to counsel patience on both parties.

I expostulated to Stoessel that he could not tell me that the USA were going to be neutral when a country in the American hemisphere was threatening to occupy the territory of a foreign power. How would America react in the event of the occupation of part of the USA, say Puerto Rico, if the British government took the line that it was neutral?

Stoessel remained very bland. We went on to talk about methods by which the Argentinians might secure the necessary documentation.

I reported this to London where, by the next day, reports were beginning to arrive of intensive Argentinian military preparations. By Wednesday, 31 March these had become more conclusive, pointing to a clear intention to invade the Falkland Islands themselves on 2 April. Mrs Thatcher sent a message to the President asking him to intervene with the Argentinian President. I received instructions to see Haig which I did at around 7 p.m. on Wednesday, 31 March. He began by saying that he had heard that Carrington – who was by now in Israel – had been disappointed by the line Stoessel had taken with me. I explained why Carrington reacted this way, not mincing my words about the indignation caused in London by the lack of American support when the USA had been able to rely on backing from the UK when they had been in difficulty. I went on to give details of our latest intelligence about the likelihood of an Argentinian attack on Port Stanley.

I used some of the detailed intelligence material at my disposal without trying to get permission from London. I realised that they might well have refused or delayed and that the value of the material was in direct proportion to the speed with which it could be used. I did not believe that Haig would be persuaded of the seriousness of the Argentinian threat unless I could give him this hard evidence.

Haig exploded. It was an outrage. Why had he not been told about this? (His staff who were present at the interview remained silent.) Haig went on to say that of course the USA would do anything they could to try to head off the Argentinians. He would go into action immediately. It was all most dangerous. The British had loyally supported the USA; they must get the same help in return.

Tom Enders,[1] who was present, said that the US Ambassador in Buenos Aires had received a categorical assurance from the Argentinian Foreign Minister that the Argentinian government was not bent upon a confrontation. I said that the facts of the Argentinian fleet movements refuted this. Enders also said that Argentina had been helpful to the USA over El Salvador.

As I was leaving the State Department one of the young officials, who, so I have often found, tell one more interesting things than do their seniors, confided to me that the State Department was obsessed by El Salvador. The subject monopolises a great deal of its time and creates its own system of values. In that sense, he added, it is already like Vietnam.

What happened then was that Haig sent a message to Buenos Aires which received a dusty answer. By midday 1 April I was made aware that the Americans had become really worried. The intelligence was piling up. That afternoon the President had to spend several hours undergoing tests on his urinary tract but by early evening he put through a call to President Galtieri who refused to receive it.

My birthday was on 1 April and I had arranged a dinner party which

---

[1]Thomas Enders had served in the State Department since 1959, largely dealing with important economic matters. Ambassador to Canada 1975–9; to the EEC 1979–81. Assistant Secretary of State for Inter-American Affairs 1981–3, in which capacity his responsibility was to look after Washingtons interests in Latin America and at this time to ensure that the Falklands conflict did not damage them more than necessary.

was to be part entertainment and part hospitality for the Charterises who were staying with us and for Teddy Youde who was Governor-elect of Hong Kong. He had previously been Ambassador in Peking and was a Chinese expert. The Bushes who had served in China came to the party. We had decided to serve a Chinese menu, except for the birthday cake. Upon arrival George said that he might have to leave early as the President wanted him to go to Buenos Aires to try to forestall an Argentinian invasion on the islands. I replied that I had heard that Galtieri had refused to speak to the President. Bush said that the White House were trying again to get through.

It was a largish dinner party of thirty-two that included Stoessel (who was still very laid back about the whole subject), the Deavers, Kay Graham, Karen House (of the *Wall Street Journal*), Evangeline Bruce, Susan Mary Alsop and Drue Heinz.

Halfway through dinner I was called to the phone to speak to Haig urgently. He told me that Reagan had got through and had spoken for fifty minutes to Galtieri, but to no avail. Galtieri had rejected a visit by Bush. Haig asked me what we, the British, would now want the USA to do. They would be ready to consider anything, but he could see no way of averting the invasion. I said that they could make a strong public denunciation as soon as the Argentinians had landed. Haig replied that there would be no question about that. I said that I would consult London and get back to him.

I tried to ring Carrington but the Resident Clerk did not know where he was. I therefore decided to speak to the Prime Minister. It was 4 a.m. by her time. She said that she did not know what more the Americans could do. She was most grateful for what they had done. But she must leave it to me. I always had ideas. I asked her whether I should try to get through to Carrington, but she said no. He was dead tired, having started the day in Israel. I apologised for having disturbed her to which she replied graciously.

When I rang Haig back I did not have much to say except to ask for a denunciation which, to be sure, the State Department put out early the following morning as soon as it heard of the landings.

I returned to the dinner party and told Bush what I had heard and had been doing. I then had to give a light-hearted toast for which I did not feel in the mood. Bush replied with a reference to the Falklands crisis, the full importance of which I do not think most of the guests grasped. As can be imagined, the serving of the dinner had been subject to frequent interruptions. The cake was continually being carried in and out of the dining-room, the candles flickering in keeping with the precarious international scene.

After dinner I filled Stoessel in on what was happening. He seemed immensely detached. I suppose that's the impression British diplomats gave a century ago when we were a great power and some lesser country sought our support. I must say, however, that it is not at all the stance that Haig is adopting. He asked to see me the following morning, 2 April. He did not have much to say himself but I took the chance of telling him of further measures that we wished the Americans to take, e.g. stopping arms sales to Argentina.

10 APRIL

WASHINGTON

———

FALKLANDS PRESSURE

The pressure has, if anything, been worse this last week. Peter telephoned me at about 6.50 a.m. on the morning of Monday, 5 April to say that he had handed in his card. He personally did not think that he could have foreseen the invasion or done anything more but he had failed to convince the party of that, so he had decided that the only thing was to resign. 'Why not Nott, instead of you?' I asked, to which he replied that he, as Foreign Secretary, was responsible for policy.

I was not altogether surprised because we had heard of the venomous nature of the House of Commons debate on the previous Saturday and the call for the blood of the guilty men. I had also spoken to Brian Fall[1] on Sunday to get the atmosphere and did not like what I had heard. Nevertheless it was a terrible blow, as Peter has meant such a lot to me, both personally and officially. I would never have been here but for him. It would be quite different serving someone else. What an example of the unpredictable trajectory of public life. Until a few days ago Peter had been almost universally accepted as the star of the government, as carrying more weight in Cabinet than anyone else and as an outstanding Foreign Secretary. Then, whoops, within a few days, down in the pit of party and parliamentary obloquy. And all because of the Falklands – because he had not foreseen the totally irrational and irresponsible actions of the Argentinian military junta.

Brian Fall told me that the Office had tried hard to dissuade Peter from resigning, saying, among other things, that it would be misunderstood abroad – which it has been in the USA. They thought, when he had gone

---

[1] Brian Fall, member of Diplomatic Service since 1962. He was Principal Private Secretary to Foreign Secretary 1981–4; High Commissioner Canada 1989–92. Appointed Ambassador to the Russian Federation and to various republics of the former Soviet Union 1992.

home on Sunday evening, 4 April, that he had decided to stay on and fight, but then the next morning the press had been bloody, calling for heads to roll, so he had decided that the only way of uniting the party would be for him to go. Brian added that he thought Peter might have come to a different conclusion had he been in the House of Commons and been able to answer his critics there.

I had to appear on a TV morning show at 7.30 a.m. and naturally I was asked questions about the resignation, as about our naval movements, military intentions etc. That was ABC. Half an hour later I appeared on CBS. I decided that morning to devote the next few days to public, press and Congressional opinion. I undertook an uninterrupted programme of speaking engagements and interviews (see programme attached for 5 and 6 April). My aim was to get it across to the US public that this was not an act from Gilbert and Sullivan, which was how the press were representing it, but a serious transgression of the peace that, in its outcome, could have a direct impact on the Americans.

I think that it has been one of the most difficult and demanding moments of my life. Not surprisingly, given their preoccupations at home, London sent me no instructions on what line to take, or what to say. But that did not matter. I had the texts of the speeches being made there and listened to the BBC. I was in no doubt how deeply the FCO were in the dog-house for having failed to foresee the invasion; and also for having, over the years, toyed with the idea of negotiating about the future sovereignty of the Falkland Islands. In broaching this idea you run up against trouble at home from both sides; the left who won't have any truck with right-wing regimes (whether in Argentina or Spain); and the right, who are governed by a mixture of motives ranging from old-fashioned imperialism to vested commercial interests. But that does not affect the immediate problem created by the Argentinian invasion. Whatever one's thoughts about the long term it is the immediate problem of highly roused national spirits that prevails.

I decided here that the line to stick to was:

a) non-permissibility of the use of force to settle disputes, particularly in the American hemisphere riddled with territorial differences;
b) self-determination, a principle introduced by the Americans into the conduct of international affairs.

I have also likened our strong reaction to the attack on eighteen hundred sheep farmers to the indignation of the USA when fifty-two Americans were taken hostage in Tehran. I have had a public swipe at Jeane Kirkpatrick and Walter Stoessel for attending an Argentinian banquet in Washington on the night of the Argentinian invasion only a few hours after the US government had issued a strong condemnation.

I have put off going to Florida to stay with the Heinzes for the weekend. Nothing much has been happening here while Haig has moved between London and Buenos Aires, so I have had time to think out the questions that will arise here in public next week when our Maritime Exclusion Zone comes into effect. My main aim is to expose the unholy alliance between the Soviets and the Argentinians. The playing of the anti-Communist card is the best way to win any game here. The pro-Argentinians in the State Department and Jeane Kirkpatrick are saying that the USA must not take sides for fear of driving the Argentinians into the arms of the Bear. My answer is that they are already there. The Russians are observing our fleet and notifying the Argentinians of our movements. Cap Weinberger said this to me last night. But London seems inexplicably frightened of saying so.

Now, on Sunday morning, there is talk of Begin moving against south Lebanon, no doubt taking advantage of the diversion of world attention to the Falkland Islands.

Falklands Crisis: List of HM Ambassador's calls and interviews

Monday 5 April

07.30 ABC News – live television interview

08.00 CBS News – live television interview

11.00 Call on Congressman Zablocki, chairman of the House Foreign Affairs Committee

11.30 Call on Congressman Michel, Republican Leader in the House

13.30 Call on Vice-President Bush

14.30 Call on Secretary of Defence, Caspar Weinberger

18.45 Live television interview on *McNeil Lehrer Report*

23.30 Live television interview on ABC News *Night Line*

Telephone call was made during the day to Senator Baker

Mr Sanders, Senator Percy's Staff Director telephoned on Senator Percy's instructions

Tuesday 6 April

07.00 Live interview with National Public Radio

10.15 Recording of interview with Mr Peter Marshall, BBC London, by telephone

10.30 Interview with John Goshko of the *Washington Post*

12.00 Recording of three interviews with Mr Suchet for ITN Television; Mr Bell for BBC Television; and Mr Small for BBC Radio

13.45 Call on Secretary of State Alexander Haig

HM Ambassador spoke to assembled representatives of the press and television on leaving State Department

14.50 Call on Congressman James Wright, House Majority Leader

15.15 Call on Congressman Mike Barnes, chairman of the Sub-Committee on Latin American Affairs

15.30 Call on Mr Carbaugh (Helms's Foreign Policy Adviser at Helms's request)

16.00 Call on Speaker O'Neill

17.00 Interview with Cable News Network

17.30 Drinks with the British press

Dinner with Rowland Evans (Ed Meese present)

Telephone conversations in the evening with Haig and Weinberger

Letters were sent to all members of the House Foreign Affairs Committee and Senate Foreign Relations Committee

24 APRIL

WASHINGTON

A SURPRISING PROPOSAL FROM THE

WHITE HOUSE

We seem to be torn between an imperfect diplomatic solution which is the best the USA may be able to extract given the fact that the Argentinians are in possession of the islands (but a settlement that does not provide for cast-iron dependence upon the 'wishes' of the inhabitants such as Mrs Thatcher has committed herself to publicly) and a military alternative that is going to be extremely hazardous in military terms and may not in the end produce a long-term solution. At least that is how it looks to me now having had Francis Pym and the FCO team here engaged in forty-eight hours of talks with Al Haig.

The essential element in my view is to retain US support and secure their involvement in a final settlement. The oddest event during Pym's visit was the breakfast with Judge Bill Clark, the National Security Adviser, and its sequel. This happened in ideal physical surroundings on Friday morning. Pym had arrived by Concorde about twenty-four hours earlier. We breakfasted on the terrace in the sun to the smell of cherry and apple blossom, even finer than usual after the exceptionally cold and wet weather we have been having.

Clark began by wondering whether we would favour the idea of trusteeship for the islands under the Argentinians. When we said that we would not, but that we wondered whether the USA would be prepared to take on such a trusteeship themselves, he answered, yes. He went on to say that the President himself had been thinking of this idea. He knew that there had been precedents – in the Pacific. We asked for how long such a trusteeship would last. Clark seemed to think that the President had in mind five years. We asked what would happen afterwards and whether the USA would be prepared to guarantee whatever status the islanders decided upon. Clark replied that he thought the USA would guarantee any outcome, including independence, if that was what the islanders decided upon.

It was left that Clark would have another word with the President and then get back to us. Implicit in his remarks was the idea that Pym would see the President at some stage.

Haig put off for half an hour or so the meeting that had been arranged later that morning with Pym. He informed us that he had been called over to the White House. When he arrived back at the State Department he began by seeing Pym alone. The latter told me afterwards that he had been in a state of fury. He had been indignant that Clark should have floated this idea of a US trusteeship with us before even mentioning it to him. Was he not in charge of the negotiations? He knew that the Argentinians would not accept such a solution.

The only upshot of this incident was that it put a roadblock in the way of any visit by Pym to the White House to see Reagan. We never heard from Clark again. Pym was, I think, surprised by the whole business; but he is philosophical and equable. It brought home to him, in a way that nothing the Embassy sends in telegrams could do, what a strange place Washington is, no less strange now than under Carter.

(Nearly three years ago Pym happened to be on a visit to Washington at the time when the President was making his extraordinary TV broadcast about the malaise from which the whole country was suffering.)

After Pym left Washington we had a visit from Denis Healey. He was less abrasive than usual. He thought that the mood at home was becoming less jingoistic. He insisted that Labour had prevented a similar invasion in 1977 by moving four ships that deterred the Argentinians. I think that he believes that Labour will gain from the Falklands issue.

The American decision of 30 April to support Britain and provide military supplies was a turning point for us. But it did not put an end to Haig's desire to promote a negotiated settlement. On the contrary, with the increased likelihood of bloodshed in the South Atlantic his efforts were, if anything, intensified.

After the Argentine cruiser Belgrano *was sunk on Sunday, 2 May it was widely asserted that this had put an end to any chance of success for negotiations. It was even alleged that the attack on the* Belgrano *was carried out with the deliberate purpose of scuppering negotiations, in the belief that a short, decisive military solution would be best for Britain. Several debates on the* Belgrano *took place in the House of Commons. Mr Tam Dalyell MP was vociferous in asserting that Mrs Thatcher had ordered the sinking in order to thwart the latest peace plan which had been proposed by the Peruvians. He said twice in the House that I went white when I first heard the news of the attack on the* Belgrano. *How he came to this view I have no idea. I was dining at home on the evening of 2 May when Haig telephoned and told me in blunt West Point language what the British submarine had done to the Argentinian cruiser. It was the first I had heard of it. He suggested that we had better have a talk about it and I went down to see him at the State Department the following morning. Then, and in the following weeks, Haig continued to float various ideas for a peaceful settlement including a modified Peruvian plan. Of this, incidentally, British ministers had had no information when they reached their decision around midday on 2 May to authorise the attack on the* Belgrano.

In parenthesis it has to be admitted that Tam Dalyell was by no means the only, even if he was the most vociferous, opponent of the Belgrano *sinking. Many writers on the Falklands War, including the* Sunday Times *Insight Team, Max Hastings and Simon Jenkins in their book,* The Battle of the Falklands *and Desmond Rice and Arthur Gavshon in* The Sinking of the Belgrano *have also been critical. Apart from the conjecture that it destroyed the path of negotiations the assertion is made that the sinking was not necessary militarily and that it was carried out without the desired warning. I have to say, after studying the subject and taking* account of the views of Admiral Sandy Woodward who was commanding the task force in the South Atlantic at the time, that I do not think that allegations on these lines are warranted. This is borne out too by the detailed examination that has been made by Professor Lawrence Freedman, the Professor of War Studies at King's College London who has published two books on the Falklands War.

Anyway, the Americans were not at all deterred by the sinking from pursuing their attempts at a diplomatic solution. Haig sent Enders, the Under-Secretary in the State Department dealing with Latin America, round to see me to discuss amendments to the Peruvian plan. This was followed by a lengthy session that I had with Haig after which he put fresh proposals to London and Buenos Aires. Reluctantly, the British government accepted them. Argentina turned them down. Their aim at this stage appeared to be to move the whole issue to the United Nations which is what more or less happened.

4 MAY

WASHINGTON

THE GAP BETWEEN LONDON AND WASHINGTON

Pym was here for a second weekend running. Driving in from Dulles airport he told me about the very tough mood at home on the Falklands. There was a danger of getting out of touch with opinion. Last weekend when he was here he said that he failed to realise how feelings were hardening at home so that when he got back he himself felt light-years away from the sentiment there. He was determined to avoid this again.

The purpose of this last visit was largely, I think, to assuage parliamentarians who, in the House of Commons debate last week, were calling upon him to be more active diplomatically. So he was ready to fly across the Atlantic for talks with Haig and Pérez de Cuellar.[1] He received enormous press and TV coverage. His theme, which was that last week he had come here to visit a mediator and this week to visit an ally, made the Americans wince, at least so I thought. Enders, in the State Department, who has the reputation for being pro-Argentinian, has in my view been professionally helpful. I had a three-hour tense session with Al Haig last night in which he implored us to accept the US-

---

[1] Javier Pérez de Cuéllar, Peruvian diplomat, UN Secretary-General 1982–91.

Peruvian seven-point plan and declare a ceasefire. He torpedoed our proposals as being quite unnegotiable with either the Peruvians or Argentinians. I had to tell him once again how strongly Mrs Thatcher felt on some of the issues, e.g. respect for the wishes of the inhibitants of the islands and the restoration of the previous administration. Al said that if we were seen to be missing this chance for peace we would lose much US and world sympathy. I think he was also shaken by yesterday's news of the sinking of the *Sheffield* which destroyed with one missile our previous image of invincibility at sea. Al was in a very nervous state, barking at anyone who entered the room. He allowed Enders to join us; Enders was practical in suggesting language that might bridge the gap. Al kept insisting that it was not a question of language but of principle.

When I left the State Department late that night I had a useful lesson in humility. The security guard at the entrance to the building stopped me as I was going out and asked me to identify myself. He requested me to produce a pass which I did not have as I have been accustomed to entering without any such document. Within sight of his desk there was a crowd of about a hundred newspapermen and photographers swarming round the doors waiting for me to come out to photograph me and hopefully to hear a few indiscreet remarks. Nevertheless personal identification was necessary for the guard.

As I write, it looks as though there is still a long way to go before we can obtain a ceasefire and a set of proposals agreeable to both London and Buenos Aires. London at any rate now recognise they must show readiness to accept a compromise in negotiation if only to stop the fighting; though it is not in Mrs Thatcher's nature to compromise.

While the battle has been raging I have withdrawn from the TV screens, but I am under great pressure to appear and explain our negotiating flexibility. I shall have to wait until the British government has gone public on the issue. I have urged London strongly to offer a ceasefire even if the Argentinians refuse.

All this – which has been the most intense diplomatic and public relations activity of my life – has been going on against the extraordinarily inappropriate backcloth of preparations for the showcase on interior decoration to be displayed in the house. A marquee has been erected in the garden, casting a circus-like aura quite out of keeping with the gravity of the times when ships are being sunk and lives lost. But we will continue with the commercial aspect of the programme and downgrade the gala-dinner. I am going to describe it as a reception with supper. Princess Alexandra has already arrived and is longing to dance. At home, Pym, on the other hand, is naturally worried at the prospect of parliamentary questions. So we cancelled the dancing.

16 MAY
LONDON

PREPARATION FOR THE MEETING AT
CHEQUERS

On 16 May Tony Parsons and I were summoned to a meeting at Chequers to help draw up a British plan to be submitted to the Secretary General of the UN. This was to be our last offer before our forces landed on the Falklands.

I am here on a flying visit to take part in last minute discussions on the Falklands before the next phase of military operations. The issue is whether to press on with negotiations, which will involve considerable concessions on our part and give the Argentinians the time that they want and that they think is on their side; this course could also lead to what would virtually be an administrative takeover. Alternatively we could force a breakdown on an issue favourable to us from the international standpoint, e.g. over an interim administration and the need for it to take account of opinion on the island; but we would then face the prospect of military operations which could be very risky with heavy losses and which would not necessarily obviate the need for negotiations at some later stage.

I have discussed the subject at length with Antony Acland[1] and Tony Parsons. We shall be going to Chequers this morning where we shall see the PM. The right wing of the Tory Party are calling any shift from insistence on unconditional surrender a sell-out. Public opinion seems to be supporting a tough line, though I cannot help wondering how long this would be maintained in the face of heavy casualties. There is a military question that I cannot answer, whether we can evict, or force the surrender, of the Argentinian troops on the islands within a reasonably short space of time and without heavy casualties. If this is even a feasible possibility I am all in favour of it because I have come to the conclusion that the Argentinians are not going to negotiate except under extreme military pressure.

Incidentally, Acland revealed an amusing detail. He said that at some early stage of the crisis Mrs Thatcher had consulted a number of elder

---

[1]Antony Acland, member of Diplomatic Service since 1953. Principal Private Secretary of State 1972–9; Ambassador to Spain 1977–9; Permanent Under-Secretary of State 1982–6; Ambassador to Washington 1986–91. Later Provost of Eton. Correct in manner and appearance, he has a critical and independent approach to foreign affairs.

statesmen including Macmillan who had advised her to nominate someone uninvolved in the detail to apply his mind regularly to the problem (this is what Michael Palliser is now doing); and secondly to avoid having the Chancellor of the Exchequer anywhere near the decision-making process (Howe is not a member of the Falklands Ministerial Committee).

When I arrived at London airport after an overnight flight and was wheeling my trolley through the exit I was confronted by a throng of photographers and journalists. Feeling drowsy and jet-lagged I was not at my most self-possessed and I realised that there was something absurd about my trying to push the trolley through the crowd while this pack of newshounds were aiming cameras at me and holding microphones in front of my mouth. Questions were shouted at me such as: 'Tell us, Ambassador, is it peace or war?' The Foreign Office driver rescued me, seizing my luggage and leading me out of the maelstrom in the middle of which I abandoned the incongruous trolley.

I lunched that day at the Garrick with Tony Parsons and Antony Acland; then there was a meeting at the FCO in the afternoon to go through a draft Cabinet paper containing our bottom-line proposal. This was followed by a talk with the Secretary of State. The Prime Minister has made a jingoistic speech to the Scottish Tories.

I dined that night with Robert [Kee] at the Garrick. He also is highly Falklandised on account of the *Panorama* presentation and his row with the BBC. He is fairly hawkish; and it amuses me to think back to the anti-blimpish state of mind that we shared together in the thirties despite being anti-appeasement. Robert is now pleased to think that the British people are beginning to show again that spirit of bovine determination that we used to ridicule simply as insular complacency.

We both agreed that London, with holes in the roads and piles of bricks and corrugated iron on many abandoned building sites, the warning lights half fused, has a Third World look about it. I see that there is talk that the Falkland Islands crisis will awaken the British from their slumber. I wonder. But the mood is surprisingly resilient. The FCO, of course, are execrated all round, by the right for trying to 'sell out' the Falkland Islands years ago under a lease-back arrangement with the Argentinians; and by everyone for not having foreseen the Argentinian invasion. Accusations of treachery abound. I rather admired the line Pym was taking at a meeting with Acland, Parsons and me. He was expressing a moderate view which is not at all popular with the party or the press. I have been revolted by a *Times* leader on Wednesday that seemed to me to be toadying to the extremists. It thundered about our good fortune that the Argentinians had rejected the US-Peruvian plan which would have been a 'sell-out'.

My fear is not simply that the military operation has great risks but that if we succeed militarily by, for instance, sinking the Argentinian fleet or decimating their Falkland Islands garrison the Argentinians will spend the next thirty years preparing a war of revenge, and we shall have to devote disproportionate resources to defending these distant islands. Already we must have spent more on this operation than it would have cost us to maintain a force in the Persian Gulf for a generation, not to mention further east of Suez. Not that I would question the wisdom of Macmillan's advice to keep the Chancellor out.

The polls show a great increase in the PM's popularity as a result of the crisis.

17 MAY
LONDON

THE CHEQUERS MEETING

Tony Parsons, with whom I walked round St James's Park on Saturday afternoon, told me that he would definitely not be coming to Washington. Carrington had asked him to succeed me. He had never been enthusiastic and had only agreed to accept the post at Peter's personal request. As we moved back into the squalor of the Foreign Office – the lifts not working, half-empty milk bottles everywhere and a pervading air of dishevelment and decay – we wondered how and why we had both looked on the place with interest and enthusiasm only a decade or two ago; and we shuddered at the thought of ever having to work there again.

In the long day yesterday at Chequers the most useful moment for me was when the Chief of the Defence Staff, Admiral Lewin, took me aside to refer to some remarks I had made about the USA being interested primarily in success and speedy success at that, no diplomatic problems counting for much if there were military successes. He said that it was necessary to keep me better informed than I had been of the military scene. He went on to say that I should have no doubt about the favourable nature of the military prognosis. The Exocet missile hit on the *Sheffield* had been caused by bad luck. He gave me a technical explanation of how the Exocet had got through. Admiral Lewin was full of confidence that there would be no more accidents and that the re-occupation of the Falklands, while involving some casualties, was perfectly feasible.

The inner Cabinet meeting at Chequers comprised, apart from the Chief of the Defence Staff, Parsons and me, the Prime Minister, Whitelaw,

John Nott, the Attorney General, Frank Cooper,[1] Wade-Gery[2] (whom the PM addressed as Mr Wade-Gery throughout), Michael Palliser, Acland, Ian Sinclair (the FCO legal adviser), Cecil Parkinson (chairman of the Tory Party) and the Deputy Secretary of the Chiefs of Staff.

I reached Chequers at about 9.30 a.m. on the Sunday morning. Michael Palliser and Tony Parsons were already there. Nott was landing by helicopter as I drove through the gates thronged with photographers and pressmen. Mrs Thatcher came into the oak-panelled morning-room where we were forgathering. She hardly greeted us. I had somehow expected her to say a word to Tony Parsons and me about our arrival at the meeting. But no, we might for all the world be another couple of officials who had come down from Whitehall for the day. I realised that one had to make allowances for her Falklands preoccupation, but nevertheless from the start I was struck by the complete lack of any personal word. She spoke of the short night she had had since returning from Scotland. She suggested we went out on to the terrace to have some fresh air and coffee which we did while she read telegrams.

Most of the subsequent meeting, which went on from 10 a.m. to 4.30 p.m. with an interval for lunch was spent going through the text of the proposal that Tony Parsons was to present to the Secretary-General of the UN as our final negotiating position. If the Argentinians failed to accept it within forty-eight hours it would be assumed that they were not serious about negotiating and they could draw the conclusion that we would set about securing their withdrawal by other means. It was understood by all those round the table that the text had to be sufficiently firm to be acceptable to parliamentary and press opinion in the UK which was now a good deal harder than a month ago; yet not so extreme that UN opinion, and particularly that of the USA, would find it an unreasonable basis for a settlement.

The problem was, of course, that the PM veered the whole time towards being uncompromising, so that the rest of us, and in particular the FCO participants, constantly found themselves under attack from her for being wet, ready to sell out, unsupportive of British interests, etc. She emphasised again and again the virtues of democracy, the evils of aggression, the concession we had made to the Americans over the MFO[3]

---

[1] Frank Cooper, Permanent Under-Secretary of State, (i) Northern Ireland Office 1973–76 (ii) Ministry of Defence 1976–82. A forceful and outspoken civil servant.

[2] Robert Wade-Gery, Member Diplomatic Service since 1951; Deputy Secretary of the Cabinet 1979–82; High Commissioner to India 1982–7. One of the several Fellows of All Souls who in recent years have brought lustre to the Diplomatic Service.

[3] MFO; the Sinai Multilateral Force and Observers, to which the British contributed; it was an organisation outside the UN (because the Russians would not participate in something that flowed from the Camp David agreement) to oversee the withdrawal of Israeli troops from Sinai and observe the Israel-Egyptian frontier. As shown in the diary, Lady Thatcher

and observers to El Salvador.[1] Did not people realise that it was the Argentinians who had committed aggression? Did the Foreign Office have no principles? She said that while we were content to be dishonest and consult with dishonest people she was honest. Were the FCO prepared to hand over people who believed in democracy to a dictatorship? She would never abandon the Falkland Islands any more than she would fail to uphold the principle of self-determination which must, indeed, be written into the draft agreement, not just once but several times – though we told her that to do so would make everyone think that we were not serious because the Argentinians would reject it out of hand. They, the Falkland Islanders, Mrs Thatcher protested, were British weren't they? Well then, they would remain so. Did other countries not realise that we were doing their work for them in resisting aggression? Haig might like unclear language, but she insisted on clarity. This was accompanied by a stern look in Tony's and my direction.

We heard this speech frequently throughout the day as we worked our way line by line through the text. I was in no doubt that she really preferred the idea of a fight than the accusation of compromise.

From time to time I glanced out of the window to the peaceful scene of sheep grazing upon the Chilterns. It was a beautiful sunny day and the beech trees glistened.

Tony Parsons kept bringing her back to what would, he thought, be a reasonable negotiating position as seen by the Secretary-General and our friends in New York, a text upon which we could fairly break. I had to insist frequently upon the US's fear that we might appear intractable at this late stage and get involved in a very risky war into which they were afraid they would either be unavoidably dragged or in which they would be bitterly criticised by us for not joining in more whole-heartedly.

Right at the end of the meeting Nott protested about the American attitude. Did they realise the bitterness in the UK about them? There was strong criticism in the House of Commons. Would it be a good idea if a group of MPs, like the Bow Group, which he said had paid a successful visit to Washington recently, were to go over to tell their opposite numbers in Congress how unpopular they were. I asked him in what way the Americans had fallen short of expectations since they had

---

did not hesitate in other dealings with Washington, to draw on the credit gained by British participation in this project. The organisation pioneered the use of electronic surveillance equipment and it is possible to surmise that the lessons learnt from it could be useful in future Middle East frontier problems.

[1] Observers from several countries including the UK were sent to see whether the US-inspired elections in El Savador were conducted fairly. This was another example, however small, of what Britain could put into the kitty of the Anglo-US relationship; and it was capital again upon which Lady Thatcher had no inhibition of drawing.

declared their support for us on 30 April. Surely they had met all our demands for intelligence and equipment? With less than enthusiasm the PM referred to Reagan's recent telephone call to her urging us not to undertake military operations against the mainland. She exclaimed once again against 'ingratitude when we had provided observers for El Salvador'. But the Chief of the Defence Staff demurred at the suggestion that the Pentagon had failed to meet our requests for supplies. Whitelaw spoke up against sending backbench MPs over to Washington, loose cannons if ever there were such things. I said that to ventilate a sense of grievance publicly against the USA would be to delight the Argentinians.

I refrained from saying how closely I was in touch with Tower, Percy and other Senators because I sensed that this was resented.

Nott came up to me after the meeting was over to say that perhaps he had given the wrong impression. It was simply a feeling he had that some of the speeches were bad (which is true) and that there were people, e.g. Jeane Kirkpatrick, who were against us (also true).

At the meeting we went on to talk about the President's forthcoming visit to London. I suggested that if by then, by 6 June, we had been engaged in considerable hostilities and there had been widespread criticism in the UK of the US government for not doing enough and standing on the sidelines, the President might decide he had better not come. This produced an indignant reaction from the PM who asked me to remember that it was the Queen who had invited him and did I not realise how rude it would be to Her Majesty for the President not to come after all.

In the end we produced a text and a timetable. The PM had no difficulty in dispensing with the need for full Cabinet approval for the document, which gave Parsons an extra twenty-four hours. We are up against the deadline of the arrival of our task force in the islands. Once they get to the islands they could not bob about in a sea with forty-foot waves.

The PM is expecting a lot from the Americans on South Georgia. I don't think it is going to be easy, and I fear our relations may deteriorate in the next week or two. She is going to emphasise once again the importance of our contribution to US interests by providing two observers to the El Salvador elections. I can't see Reagan getting on to her on the phone again in a hurry whatever the promptings of Jeane Kirkpatrick.

On my return from the Chequers meeting I sensed a current in the White House running in favour of some last-minute intervention by the President. I therefore called upon Judge Clark at the White House and impressed upon him the inappropriateness of yet another American negotiating initiative at this juncture.

Following the Argentine rejection of the British proposal and the landing of our forces on the islands on 21 May Haig got into touch with me to say that the Argentinians were talking of breaking off relations with the USA. They were incensed by the military supplies that Britain was receiving from the USA. Haig then paid me a visit at the Embassy to underline the administration's concern. He spoke of the revanchism that would prevail in Buenos Aires if the battle was to be pursued to a final conclusion. He did not see that British interests would be served if we had to keep a large military force on the islands for an indefinite future, subject always to attack from the Argentine mainland.

I told Haig, on instructions, that the establishment of the British bridgehead would change our diplomatic position. We could no longer consider any idea for British withdrawal or the establishment of an interim administration. While understanding the British attitude, Haig felt obliged to emphasise the long-term issues at stake both for Britain and the USA. The dispute had already greatly jeopardised American interests in Latin America. He came across with further ideas about an interim administration, including the Americans and Brazilians to run the islands and to hold discussions about the future. I told Haig, immediately, without reference to London, that these ideas would be unacceptable there in current circumstances.

A meeting of the Rio Treaty powers took place in Washington on 27 May. Venomous attacks were made on the USA for their support of the UK over the Falklands. Haig put up a stout defence, telling me afterwards that whatever pressures I might feel under they were nothing to the five standing ovations against him that had taken place that day. He sketched out to me yet another idea, this time for what he described as an international umbrella organisation, which would eliminate the colonial tag. Besides supervising the government, it would consider the ultimate status of the islands.

Such was the anxiety in Washington about the consequences of an overwhelming British military victory that the President was persuaded to ring Mrs Thatcher. He had telephoned her on a similar theme two weeks earlier. Both calls went down extremely badly with Mrs Thatcher, and she made no bones about telling me so and asking me to inform the Americans of this in no uncertain terms. An account of these heads of Government telephone calls is contained in the following diary entry. Mrs Thatcher's very understandable view was that the British, having negotiated in good faith for weeks, during which time the Argentinians had shown no sign of being ready to talk business, were not prepared now, when they were back in the islands after considerable sacrifice, simply to pull out and make way for some umbrella or other organisation that included countries from Latin America.

American concern at the prospect of a bloody battle for Port Stanley and the consequences that would flow from it were reflected in a hand-wringing editorial in the Washington Post. *To me, Haig invoked Sir Winston Churchill's name saying that he had always shown magnanimity. To which I rejoined that Churchill had not talked of magnanimity until after victory had been achieved.*

In order to understand and commune with Haig I had to keep in mind all the time that he was a fighting man who had experienced war at first hand – in Vietnam. He was realistic and had no romantic illusions about war, such as, I suspect, he believed the Argentinian leaders nourished. He told me more than once how the Argentinian Admiral Jorge Anaya had spoken to him with pride of the prospect that his son, who was serving in the Islands as a helicopter pilot, might die 'for the Malvinas'. Unable to smother his feelings Haig had retorted that no one could know the meaning of war until he had seen, as he had done in Vietnam, the corpses of young men being put into body bags.

30–31 MAY

WASHINGTON

THE WIDENING TRANSATLANTIC GULF

When, on 25 May, Argentine Independence Day, we suffered heavy losses, including the *Coventry*, it looked as though the gamble might have been too high. But then, by the end of the week, only seven days after establishing our bridgehead at Carlos Bay, we had a considerable victory at Goose Green and Darwin and took over a thousand prisoners, giving us a considerable fillip.

Meanwhile I have been engaged in the difficult diplomatic task of trying to bridge the widening gulf between the non-negotiating mood in London and the growing feeling in Washington that we ought not to insist on a humiliating surrender on the part of the Argentinians; and that if we do so it will exacerbate the USA's relations with Latin America which are already seriously impaired by the 30 April decision to come down clearly on the British side.

Mrs T has not yet consigned me to the Tower; but I am told that her voice drops two dangerous decibels when she goes through my telegrams during inner Cabinet meetings. How much lower would it sink in patient but intolerant wrath if I included in my messages all Haig's pleas that she should, at this juncture, even before we have overcome the Argentinian garrison, show magnanimity.

Haig has telephoned me in a state of some impatience. He used his accustomed convoluted language: 'It's getting like duck soup down there.' He wondered whether the President, who was just back from California, should telephone Mrs Thatcher to explain why the US government thought it so important to make an appeal to London and Buenos Aires now, together with the Brazilians, with a view to achieving a ceasefire and avoiding a bloody battle and total defeat of the Argentinian garrison. I said that normally I thought these heads of government telephone talks were apt to lead to trouble and acrimony as had occurred over a previous call from Reagan, but as the PM would have read in detail Haig's ideas for a settlement I did not think a call could do any harm now.

How wrong I was. In particular, I overlooked the fact that Mrs Thatcher has obviously not applied her mind to Haig's proposals. Her thoughts are focused on the battle. She had seen Haig's plan as a sell-out, as a monstrous method of snatching victory from us in order to help the USA in its relations with the Latin Americans. This, and more, became all too clear to me when she telephoned me at around midnight London time. She spoke on an open line, but this in no way attenuated the criticisms she made of the Americans. She complained first that she had not been warned of the telephone call from the President. This I cannot understand because we told Number 10 what to expect about five hours in advance. Then she said that she had been 'dismayed', a word she repeated several times, 'dismayed by his attitude'. She went on to say that he had proposed 'another peace initiative'. She really was 'most upset' and she wanted me to tell the President how upset she was. 'It is pure Haigism.' This phrase was uttered in a withering tone, the speaker no doubt aware of the openness of the line. 'There's no possibility whatever in what they are thinking of,' she continued. 'We were prepared to negotiate before but not now. We have lost a lot of blood and it's the best blood. Do they not realise that it is an issue of principle? We cannot surrender principles for expediency.'

She said she was not impressed by the American threat to leave us on our own which she regarded as blackmail. She said that many Latin-American leaders longed for us to defeat the Argentinians, though they dared not say so. She had asked Reagan what he would think if some country invaded Alaska and then, when the Americans had thrown them out, they were called upon to withdraw in favour of a contact group. Mrs Thatcher's voice was particularly withering in speaking of Haig's proposed contact group. She told me three times that she had deployed the Alaskan analogy with the President.

Once again she expressed indignation about the President's call. It had 'horrified' her and she wanted me to get across to him how upset she was.

I said that there was a great gap, and perhaps it was my fault it had not been bridged. I would certainly do what I could to be sure that the White House understood the substantial difference between us; but I would not recommend complaining that the President had telephoned. It was in our interest that he should feel free to pick up the telephone when he wanted to exchange personal views with her. We should not discourage that. I think the PM accepted this, provided I made a row about the White House's failure to understand the substance of the issue.

I said something about the problem the US government saw in the future if we were still vulnerable to the charge of colonialism and if we had to keep a large force on the Falkland Islands indefinitely. Mrs Thatcher said that she quite realised we could not be there indefinitely in force. But – and here she strayed off again – someone would have to develop the islands and bring them to self-government. Now, however, after all that loss of blood there could be no question of just handing them over.

Mrs Thatcher was openly critical of the USA's inadequate support. I refuted this firmly saying that given post-Vietnam sentiment in the USA, their dislike of colonialism and their wish to get on to good terms with Latin America, we had been very lucky that they came down on our side on 30 April. That was not a decision that was self-evident or should be taken for granted – or whittled away by us now.

Mrs Thatcher concluded by saying that she wanted to discuss the whole problem calmly when she saw the President and Haig at Versailles at the end of the week, a meeting that was not going to be easy to fit in. She repeated her desire that I should not mince my words with the White House.

While I was having this long and difficult call from Mrs T I received a message that Haig was anxious for me to ring him as soon as possible. When I got through he said that he had heard of the Presidental-PM telephone conversation. He was full of admiration for the PM, as was the President: 'I wish there were more like her ...' But he said that he saw great difficulties ahead in our relations. Opinion was moving against us. I asked him if he meant in Congress or the media. No, he said, he meant the President and himself. In his characteristic way of saying two contradictory things in succession, he interjected immediately, 'Mind you, we are with you, make no mistake of that. We are on your side.' But, he went on, 'we can't accept intransigence.' If Mrs Thatcher insisted on that the US would have to reassess its attitude.

I asked whether we could not rely on them in the Security Council.[1]
Haig replied, 'Perhaps not.'

'Surely,' I rejoined, 'you would support us on Resolution 502?'

'Yes, we would do that,' Haig said. But, 'You must help the Argentinians to find a way out, short of total humiliation.'

I told him something of the mood in London which he admitted he
understood given the circumstances. I had not told him that Mrs T had
used to me on the phone the words 'we live in daily fear', referring to
the great threat from the missiles.

6 JUNE

COMBE

———

MRS T IN MILDER MOOD

Back for a briefing meeting at Number 10 prior to the President's visit
next week, I found the PM in a much quieter mood than she had shown
at Chequers a fortnight or so ago. She was prepared to consider for the
longer term something less than a return of full colonial rule for the
Falkland Islands backed by a commitment to defend the place ad infi-

---

[1] Pressure had been building up at the UN for a new Security Council resolution calling for an
immediate ceasefire; and this was tabled in early June by Panama and Spain and came to
a vote on 4 June. Anthony Parsons made clear the British position that Argentinian
withdrawal, as requested in the earlier resolution, 502, was an essential precondition to
any ceasefire agreement. London would therefore veto any such new resolution. Intense
discussion took place within the UN administration on how they should vote. Argentina
threaten to break off diplomatic relations with the USA if they joined Britain in vetoing.
Haig, as has been shown in the diary, was exerting pressure on Britain to be magnanimous
and had come forward with yet another plan to end the fighting. Nevertheless, before he
left for Paris he gave instructions that the US should join the UK in vetoing the resolution.
However the Latino faction in the US administration continued to beaver away and, with
the support of Haig's deputy, Walter Stoessel, they despatched a message to Haig suggesting
that the US should abstain rather than veto. Haig, who was miffed by what he regarded
as Britain's inflexible response to his latest plan, agreed to switch the vote. However, as a
result of delays in communication, this decision only reached the US delegation in New
York after they had cast their veto. Jeane Kirkpatrick decided nevertheless to make
something of it and she thereupon informed the Security Council that while she recognised
that governments could not change a vote once cast in the Security Council she wished to
notify them that her government wanted it put on record that had they been permitted to
do so they would have changed their vote from a no to an abstention.

It is difficult to know what was achieved by this except a demonstration of the vacillation
that afflicted the US administration on the Falklands. This was compounded by the
revelation made by Reagan, when questioned by an American journalist, that he did not
know anything about it.

The way this subject was handled by the US government was described as a 'snaffarou',
as mentioned in the diary entry for 8 June 1982.

nitum against an Argentinian war of revenge. I said that if we wanted to
keep the USA on our side and secure their support in providing security
for the islands we would have to keep open the question of ultimate
sovereignty and avoid the return of the Governor in a plumed hat.

I can't say that she liked it, but she listened. She cannot really believe
that if she thinks something right anyone else can think otherwise. She
said that she expected me to tell the Americans that they must teach the
Argentinians that they cannot behave like that. She thinks that the USA
have a duty to support us, although I think I made some impression in
telling her how much they had done already and how grateful we ought
to be to them. She has the rosiest view of the islands' future and talked
much of the development of the fishing industry and of the wildlife
possibilities. Peter Scott's name was dropped in the same tone of awe
that I remember my house matron at school using when she spoke of
Scott's prints of wild geese that adorned the walls of her surgery. Mrs T
seemed to think that many Latin American countries, including Argentina, would rush to pour money into the reconstruction of the islands;
and she appeared to envisage some sort of federation of South Atlantic
territories embracing St Helena, Ascension Island, South Georgia, the
Falkland Islands and some Antarctic territory, which would be able to
rely on USA protection.

In my efforts to inject some realism about the continuing bitterness of
the Argentinians and the inevitable attempts the Americans would make
to mend their fences with Buenos Aires and the Latinos generally, I got
precious little help from anyone else. Geoffrey Howe, the only other
minister present, was helpful. He foresees, of course, the appalling cost
of keeping a large military force indefinitely in the South Atlantic; and
he obviously realises that if we are to get the Americans to shoulder
some of the burden we will have to show flexibility about the islands'
future. 'Flexibility', is almost as odious a word to the Prime Minister as
is 'magnanimity'. She revealed how much she resents Haig's appeals to
her to be magnanimous before contemplating a final battle for Port
Stanley. She has persuaded herself that Haig has not been a good influence
on Reagan, urging him to make that telephone call proposing the offer
of a ceasefire before the Argentinians were totally defeated and humili-
ated. She asked me to explain once again how that unfortunate telephone
call had come about. Once again I said that rather than resenting it she
should be pleased that the president should have felt free to take her into
his confidence and consult her before making up his mind. He and Haig
had, after all, dropped their suggested plan as soon as she had expressed
opposition to it. I warned her against losing the Americans for the future,
and in the UN now, if our policies were insufficiently adaptable. Glaring
at me she said that she would be very reasonable in her conversation

with the President 'provided I get my way'. Once again I was reminded of *Henry V*: 'Then lend the eye a terrible aspect'.

Before the meeting ended Mrs T asked me to write her a speech for the President's lunch on Tuesday. 'With jokes?' I asked.

'Yes,' she said.

She was in a very good mood by now and, following the meeting, she joined Michael Palliser and me for a gossip in the corridor. She seemed relaxed, a consequence perhaps of the more favourable turn of the war.

8 JUNE

WINDSOR CASTLE

———

REAGAN'S VISIT

It is half past six in the morning in Augusta Tower in Windsor Castle. A light mist over the park heralds a sweltering day. A man on horseback rides smartly into the murk. I wonder whether the horse he is exercising is the one the President is going to ride with the Queen at 9.30 a.m. If so, he is presumably working off the animal's surplus energy so as to avoid accidents.

The castle is just awakening, with sounds being suppressed so as not to disturb the great. A servant wearing a white dress and with white hair enters to draw the curtains of our bathroom situated between our two bedrooms.

We were told last night very firmly that there could be no breakfast until 8.30 a.m. A cup of tea could be provided earlier. The men were expected to assemble for breakfast in the dining-room. Their wives, if they wished, and if, by implication, they were sufficiently decadent, could have trays brought to their rooms. I wonder how the Americans take these odd hours. They are accustomed to breakfasting at around 7 a.m. One of them told me last night that he would like to introduce into his life in the USA the idea of a private valet.

When I arrived yesterday I found a note on my dressing-table saying: 'Your valet is Adrian Pardey.' Some hours later Adrian turned up dressed in livery to ask me when I would like breakfast the following morning. When I said 7.15 a.m. he told me that I would have to wait until 8.30 a.m. The previous evening he had unpacked all my clothes and for that matter everything else. My pills were laid out in rows on the dressing-table making it look like an apothecary. From the tacky recesses of my sponge-bag he had extricated odd tube-ends of toothpaste and creams that were prominently displayed in the bathroom.

When, last evening, I lifted the telephone receiver to ask the switch-board to get me Alexandra the voice the other end said most mellifluously, 'Yes, Your Royal Highness ...' a remark that made me wonder which member of the royal family normally occupied my bed.

Philip Moore[1] has told me that the castle is used intensely in the month of April when the Queen invites members of the Cabinet and other dignitaries for dinner and to stay the night à la Jorrocks; a practice known as 'dines and sleeps'.

Having noticed a large box of chocolates in my room I told Sue Hussey, next to whom I was luckily seated at dinner, that the last time I had stayed at the castle, which was when President Heinemann of the FRG had been on a state visit in 1972, no such attentions had been paid. To which she answered, in typically bantering fashion, that I must realise that I was not then such a senior Ambassador.

Lying in bed I have noticed the elaborate high ceiling decorated in ornate plaster-relief. What a good idea to have so much to stare at when lying awake early in the morning waiting for breakfast, particularly when the aircraft have started coming in to land at Heathrow, streaming ceaselessly past the window.

After the private family dinner party last night (thirty-eight people) Haig told me that he was worried 'by all this gallivanting' when war was going on in the Middle East and in the South Atlantic. If Syria became more involved that would bring in the Russians. I forbore from saying that an Israeli attack on Lebanon had looked inevitable for months. Haig's anxiety is, I realise, partly the frustration Foreign Secretaries often have when accompanying their heads of government on foreign travel. It would have helped if Haig had been introduced to the reception line at the airport, but the Reagans were the only people presented by the Duke of Edinburgh. The Prime Minister incidentally spent the waiting time at the airport studying papers. She also expressed consternation at the lack of co-ordination between Haig and Jeane Kirkpatrick which has come to a head over a Security Council vote on the Falklands. Haig's ill-ease is compounded by his fear that the President does not really master the issues and that his immediate staff do little to ensure that he does so. This was evident when he and I were discussing the allied reactions to Mrs Thatcher's tough, no-negotiating stance on the Falkland Islands. He said that we were rapidly losing international support. I asked him whether the President had made this clear to Mrs Thatcher in their

[1] Philip Moore, Private Secretary to the Queen, 1977–86.

private talk in Paris last Friday. He regretted that he did not think that he had done so. I said that it was hopeless my telling Mrs Thatcher that the US government felt strongly the need for Britain to show magnanimity towards the Argentinians once we had demonstrated superior strength, if the President himself said nothing about it in prolonged private conversation with the Prime Minister.

At one point during the visit, I think it was during the drive from the Haig–Pym meeting at the FCO to Buckingham Palace to link up with the President's party which was arriving by helicopter from Windsor and was en route for Westminster, I had a word with Haig about the idea of Peter Carrington succeeding Luns at NATO. He was uncategorical in his answer. I think that this arose more from doubts whether the post would be in Peter's interest than from uncertainty about his fitness for it.

Haig did not speak about the 'snaffarou',[1] as it has been called, that has arisen over the USA veto in the Security Council and Mrs Kirkpatrick's statement in the Council that if it had been possible to do so she would have liked to change her vote to an abstention. It has had a bad effect here. While waiting at Heathrow for Reagan's arrival the PM spoke to me about it with consternation.

The Queen Mother was in characteristically jovial spirits. She wanted to tell me about her recent visit to Paris where she had opened a new wing of the Hertford Hospital, the appeal for which I had launched just before leaving Paris.

Prince Charles discussed the Falklands in some detail with Whitelaw and me. He had obviously been following closely events at the UN and with the Americans.

At her request I introduced Lady Irene Astor to Haig. Daughter of Field Marshal Haig, she claims a close kinship with Al. Incidentally, as we were driving past the Field Marshal's statue in Whitehall on the last morning, Haig told me that he had read all that had ever been written about the Field Marshal. 'Hell, he was no butcher,' he expostulated. 'Very intelligent man. Had to be to get to that position . . .' Al also spoke of his kinship with the Field Marshal.

After the private dinner at the castle we stood about being entertained by the pipers and by the Queen's eight corgis. No sooner had Sue Hussey confided to me that they would take orders from no one but the Queen than I perceived Sir John Miller, the Crown Equerry, who drives carriages with Prince Philip and is a dedicated horseman and bachelor, kneeling down on the floor and whispering to one of them. We suddenly perceived

[1] The 'snaffarou' is described in the footnote on p 468.

a cat in the next drawing-room. 'First time I have ever seen a cat in the castle,' said one of the Ladies-in-Waiting. 'It must belong to your maid,' someone said to us accusingly. A crisis was averted by one of the footmen shutting the door between the two rooms.

Mary and I bathed one afternoon in the solar-heated pool in the Orangery. 'Nobody wants an Orangery nowadays,' Prince Philip said to us when we were telling him later how much we had enjoyed our swim, 'so I decided to put a pool there.' The only other purpose to which the Orangery seems to be put nowadays is as a house for a vast polo practising machine, a wooden horse beneath netting.

There has been little discussion in the press about Reagan's visit. The Sunday papers did not hold a post-mortem. Of course he made no appearances before the press. For security reasons the routes in London were not publicised in advance. The public turnout was therefore minimal, mostly lines of policemen facing non-existent crowds.

I asked Roy Jenkins what he thought of the President's speech in parliament in which he had been laudatory about democracy and con-demnatory about Communism. Roy said that he did not think it had been very appropriate and everyone had been less interested in the substance than in the audio-visual prompters used by Reagan to enable him to give the impression of speaking without a text.

Earlier in the year Mrs T had attached enormous importance to Reagan's visit, convinced that it would help her politically. The Falklands issue came to change its relevance. She had suddenly become very popular. The lunch which the PM gave went well – it had to go quickly as she was due to answer questions in parliament.

The next morning we had a meeting at Number 10 after breakfast there. The two heads of government and Foreign Secretaries breakfasted together, the rest of us were put in a different room. We all joined up for a meeting afterwards. Mrs T was her usual dynamic self, retailing at the outset the points for discussion. She described the President's visit as having been 'a triumph'. We had been 'thrilled by the way he had strengthened the alliance'. She described his speech in parliament as 'fantastic', assuring him that it had got through to 'ordinary folk'. She told the President that 'we don't take freedom for granted' and she agreed with what he had said the day before that 'democracy is not fragile'. She went on to say that she hoped they could talk about the Falkland Islands, the Middle East and the Bonn summit in that order. In fact there was little discussion about the Falkland Islands, which I presume must have been discussed at the restricted breakfast, except for her plea for help over the logistic problems that would arise with the Argentinian prisoners. In the exchanges on Israel's invasion of the Lebanon Haig expressed the support of the United States for Security

Council Resolution 508 linking ceasefire with withdrawal. The President, looking extremely sleepy, muttered his support for 508, adding that he would have to beat Begin over the head when he came to Washington, though he would 'not betray him'. When the PM started machine-gun firing on the need for dialogue and detente and on the Harmel Report,[1] the president was unable to suppress a yawn, or rather several yawns.

I travelled with Reagan in the helicopter from Buckingham Palace to Heathrow. I was seated between Clark and Meese. Lord Somerleyton, the Lord-in-Waiting and leader of the British suite in attendance, sat opposite the President. The Americans cannot fathom the role of a Lord-in-Waiting in Attendance. Rather to my surprise Reagan came to life in the helicopter, but not in chatting or looking out of the window, despite the staggering view as we flew over the Houses of Parliament and up the Thames. Rather he was reading apparently with great interest the White House press summary from which he occasionally tore a page, handing it with evident annoyance to Clark. He was particularly cross at one story that alleged that he had had difficulty on the ride as he had ridden 'English', so it was said, for the first time. 'I always ride English,' he protested.

As I looked back on those two days I did not think that they could really have gone any better given the security restrictions that prevented all public contact. Everyone who saw Reagan on TV or met him personally liked him a great deal. He removed the false impression many people have derived of him of being a war-monger. He confirmed the widespread impression here about his fervent anti-Communism. I could almost see Michael Foot nodding his head as if to say there he goes again, when, during his speech in the Royal Gallery, Reagan launched into an anti-Communist tirade. Incidentally, I had a most agreeable word with Foot in the Waterloo Room at Windsor before the banquet. He was dressed one level down from the rest of us, in black tie. We talked about Jonathan Swift. He remembered our exchange of letters a decade or two ago on the subject.

A balance sheet of the efforts by the USA since early April shows that, if they failed to achieve their main purpose of avoiding bloodshed and finding a peaceful solution, their prolonged negotiations brought advantages to Britain. While the British task force was sailing to the South Atlantic something had to fill the diplomatic vacuum. Without Haig's toings and froings Argentinian intransigence would not have been

---

[1] Report submitted in 1967 by a committee under Belgian Foreign Minister, Pierre Harmel, on the future goals of NATO.

exposed, and if this had not happened America might not have been so ready to back us in the way they did.

Even when, by the end of April, it was clear that the Argentinian junta was not going to accept any reasonable solution, it was probably necessary, in order to hold American opinion, for Haig to continue with his efforts and for Britain to show its willingness to negotiate. I do not think London were justified in being intolerant of Haig's frequent attempts to find new solutions, even if, in the atmosphere of military conflict, their impatience was understandable.

I have already referred to the crucial importance that the USA's military supplies made to the battle in the islands. This should not lead to any underestimation of the significance of America's political support in which Haig himself played a prominent and heroic part.

How decisively helpful was Haig's role became all too clear when he was out of Washington and those opposed to US support for Britain immediately moved to exert themselves in the highest reaches of the US administration.

Unlike Lady Thatcher's views about him in her memoirs, Haig is generous and flattering about her in his; and he makes much of the wider significance of the stand the British took.

'Last and first' he has written in his book Caveat[1], 'the war was caused by the original miscalculation on the part of the Argentinian military junta, that a Western democracy was too soft, too decadent, to defend itself ... The British demonstrated that a free people have not only kept a sinewy grip on the values they seem to take for granted, but are willing to fight for them, and to fight supremely well against considerable odds ... The Falklands crisis was the most useful and timely reminder of the true character of the West in many years. Indeed, Britain's action in the Falklands may have marked a historic turning point in what has been a long and dangerous night of Western passivity ... In the Falklands, the West was given a great victory by Great Britain ... the free world may thank the men of the British task force and Mrs Thatcher, who was by far the strongest, the shrewdest and the the most clear-sighted player in the game.'

---

[1] Weidenfeld and Nicolson, 1984.

16 JUNE

WASHINGTON

———

RELIEF WITHOUT EUPHORIA

I returned to Washington on Monday 14th to be greeted immediately by
rumours of white flags flying over Port Stanley. By the evening the
surrender had been confirmed. I must say a great weight was lifted from
my mind removing all sense of jet-lag. I did two early TV broadcasts the
following morning on NBC and CBS, and two more during the day. I
did my best not to give the impression of crowing but just of expressing
relief as I referred to the acute problems around Port Stanley where there
are thousands of Argentinian prisoners.

The press have been surprised because no sounds of euphoria or the
popping of champagne corks have been heard from the Embassy. All I
am doing in that line is to give a party for all those who helped us at the
working level: that is to say in the State Department task force, the
Pentagon, the CIA and the various TV studios that I have frequented.

Al Haig, of course, is already showing signs of restlessness. He wants
us to make declarations about the future, about our readiness to involve
the Argentinians in some way in the running of the islands. I tell him
that just at the moment, in the immediate aftermath of battle, that sort
of thing is out of the question for us. He insists that we must avoid
slamming doors. He told me that some of the Prime Minister's remarks
in the House of Commons on Tuesday were 'too high in decibel content'.
I agree with him that foresight is needed, but please, give it a day or two.
We still have over ten thousand near-starving POWs on our hands and
there is no overall ceasefire so far with the Argentinians.

20–27 JUNE

WASHINGTON

———

THE PM'S VISIT; FRICTION OVER TRADE WITH THE
USSR

Nearly a week has elapsed since the surrender at Port Stanley. I am still
tingling with a sense of relief. The Americans are full of admiration and
applause now that it is over. I cannot forget the widespread scepticism

here, particularly amongst the military experts, about whether we could pull it off. It is heart-warming to have people approach one in a restaurant, for instance, to say how delighted they are.

There has been a characteristic example this week of the disjunction between the State Department and the White House. Haig telephoned to suggest that when the PM is in New York next week to make a speech on disarmament she should be invited to come down here to Washington to see the President. 'It is unthinkable that she should be in this country and not be invited to Washington,' he said, explaining that such a meeting would also provide the chance to caution her against too 'colonial' a line on the islands. I said that I saw no harm in the idea of an invitation to her but that it should not be linked to a discussion about the future of the Falkland Islands. That would turn her off. Al told me to do nothing until he had cleared it with the President. Obviously it was his idea.

The next evening he rang me to say that he had secured Reagan's agreement. Would I send an invitation? So I sent off a telegram.

On Saturday morning, Larry Eagleburger[1] rang to ask whether Thursday night would be a suitable time for the PM to come down from New York to Washington. The State Department was in the process of putting a formal submission to the White House. I replied that I thought she would have to be back in London by then in time for Parliamentary Questions but that I would let him know as soon as possible.

We got an answer out of London by Saturday afternoon that she would come here on Wednesday afternoon which I passed on to Larry. Thanking me, he said that I must understand that it was all provisional. The idea had not yet been submitted to the President. I told him that Al had told me that he had cleared it with the President.

The next event in the saga was a telephone call from Bill Clark at the White House. He had just received a memorandum from the State Department suggesting a visit by the Prime Minister and an invitation from the President. He thought that it was going to be very difficult because the President had so much on his plate with the Lebanon problem. He would be having a visit by Begin to Washington on the Monday. I told him that with Haig's authority, based, as he had told me, on a talk with the President, the invitation had already been extended.

'That's very awkward,' Bill mused in his slow, ruminative way.

---

[1] Lawrence Eagleburger, member of US Foreign Service since 1957; Ambassador to Yugoslavia 1977–81; Assistant Secretary of State for European Affairs 1981–2; Under-Secretary of State for Political Affairs 1982–4. Later Deputy Secretary of State and, when James Baker became campaign manager for Bush in 1992, acting Secretary of State. Suffering permanent ill-health he seemed to carry on joyfully and even rumbustiously, invariably getting to the heart of any problem and speaking his mind frankly but without acrimony.

'Yes,' I replied.

'What do you recommend?' he asked.

To which I said once again that the Prime Minister had in fact been invited. I added that if, nevertheless, the Americans thought that they must withdraw the invitation I was sure we could sort it out. The idea had not originally been that of the Prime Minister. She had not been intending to come here. But the Americans would have to give me a plausible reason for cancelling.

'I see,' Bill said even more slowly. 'The trouble is that this was not cleared with Mike Deaver. I have learnt that no engagement can be made without consulting Mike.' Whether ironically or not he added, 'I manage to get alongside him from time to time.' He said that the President would shortly be arriving back by helicopter.

One of the most vivid images I will take away from Washington is of the President leaving or arriving by helicopter and waving debonairly before stepping into or off the machine. He gives the impression of having no cares in the world, and Bill French Smith has told me that it is true that he does have the knack of switching off so that as soon as he has left the office he does not give affairs of state a moment's thought. Bill likens it to FDR's insouciance and says that without it he doubts whether the President could at seventy-one be showing so little sign of stress. This conversation took place at lunch yesterday to which the French Smiths came before he joined Al Haig and me for a game of tennis.

But to return to the invitation to the Prime Minister. I had heard nothing from the US side before receiving a telephone call from Number 10 on Sunday evening saying that the Prime Minister would shortly be returning from Chequers. She would want to discuss the US visit and would need to know, therefore, whether the proposal that she should reach Washington on Wednesday at 16.45 was acceptable.

I therefore rang Bill Clark who said that he would get Mike Deaver to speak to me. Shortly afterwards Mike rang, explaining that neither the President nor he had known anything about the invitation to the Prime Minister. I repeated Al's assurance to me that he had discussed it with the President. It did reveal something that had become apparent to me from my own experiences over the Presidential visit to the UK, that the President himself does not register if anything is said to him about programmes. He leaves that to others, or, to be more accurate, to Deaver; and the trouble is that Deaver and Haig are not on speaking terms. Nor is it much better at any other level between the White House and State Department.

Mike Deaver said, not altogether graciously, that as things had gone so far and Mrs T had actually been invited, there was no alternative but to go through with the visit. We proceeded to discuss times. We agreed, as I did also with Clark, that no reference would be made to London about these difficulties that had occurred in Washington over the visit. 'After all,' Clark said, 'that's what we are for, to sort these things out ...' I agreed.

As soon as Mrs Thatcher arrived in Washington she was received by the President who was accompanied by Bush, Haig and Clark as well as several NSC officials. On our side, apart from the Prime Minister were Whitmore,[1] Coles, Gillmore[2] and myself.

After the Prime Minister had thanked Reagan for the recent seizure of a cache of arms destined for the IRA he took the initiative over the extended ban on the export to the USSR of US energy equipment, notwithstanding existing contracts. He said that it was a matter of principle. After the crackdown in Poland he had decided, on 29 December 1981, that certain economic measures should be taken against the Soviet Union unless changes were made in Poland, e.g. releasing Walesa. He has threatened further steps if the repressions in Poland continued. He was now proceeding to carry out this threat. He certainly could not let up by allowing American pipeline equipment to be provided by John Brown on the grounds that this was part of a pre December 1981 contract. Reagan also dropped a bombshell by saying that he had learned that John Brown were quite happy with his decision and did not think that they would suffer a great deal on account of it.

Mrs T's eyes blazed and she launched into a fierce attack on the President's decision, pointing out that American exports to the USSR would grow this year because of the lifting of the grain embargo. Reagan said something about not making any new grain agreement with the Soviets, which led to a muddled discussion in which neither side knew the facts about whether this would or would not in practice curtail American grain shipments to the USSR.

At one point Clark extricated himself from the sofa where he was jammed with the other Americans and went over to the President's desk, taking out a piece of White House paper upon which he wrote to me a note saying that he hoped the PM would recognise that the President's decision was based on strong principle.

Throughout this Soviet pipeline imbroglio, Al Haig remained silent. We knew that he opposed the National Security Council's decision of the previous Friday extending the ban on exports to the USSR, that it

---

[1]Clive Whitmore, Principal Private Secretary to Prime Minister 1979–82; Permanent Under-Secretary of State Ministry of Defence 1983–8; Home Office since 1988.
[2]David Gillmore, member of Diplomatic Service 1970. Permanent Under-Secretary of State and head of the Diplomatic Service 1991–4.

had indeed been taken in his absence in New York where he was grappling with Gromyko. It was one of the sources of tension that led to his resignation.

The President had just started to say something about the Falklands when Mrs T interupted him to say that she wanted to give him an account of the present position. She described the state of the Argentinian prisoners: malnutrition, trench-foot, diarrhoea. We were spared nothing. She also spoke of the bad relations between officers and men. The former had insisted on being allowed to keep their pistols to defend themselves against their own troops.

Reagan asked whether it was true that some Argentinian soldiers had shot themselves, or been shot, in the foot. Mrs T replied that we had had no confirmation of this story.

She spoke of the problem of the land-mines the Argentinians had laid without keeping any plans of where they were. We were having difficulty in detonating them because they were plastic. The President offered to help. He also made another effort to get into the act, perhaps to deliver a warning about intransigence and the need for magnanimity, a word the Americans keep trying to put into Mrs Thatcher's vocabulary, quite unsuccessfully. She gave him no opening and was off again describing the battle and the sacrifices, so that by the time the President had to leave to keep his next engagement he still had not got a word in edgeways. Nor had Haig, though, I think that being less compliant than Reagan he could have done so if he had wished. Presumably, however, by now he was nursing his plans for resignation which would become public two days later. Why therefore bother to have a row with Mrs T as well as with the President?

As a result, when, at the subsequent press conference, Mrs T was asked whether the President had urged her to adopt a more flexible attitude on sovereignty for the Falkland Islands, she was able to answer, No, with complete honesty.

25 JUNE
WASHINGTON

HAIG'S RESIGNATION[1]

When I spoke to Haig about his resignation he said he did not want to single out any particular reasons. He profoundly disagreed with various directions that were being given to US foreign policy and he did not 'like the smell'. Obviously he was referring to the exacerbation of relations between himself and the White House. Reagan's entourage had from the day Haig was appointed contested his attempt to direct US foreign policy and be the sole spokesman. This had now come to a head.

We played tennis together on the Embassy court the day when Haig announced his intention to resign. Over the iced tea he soliloquised how the problem had become aggravated by personalities. Some of the people in the White House had been convinced that he was intending to run for high office. Even that week rumours on this score had been spread by the White House. There was no basis whatever for them. Having said this Haig told me, in answer to my question, that he would not be returning to United Technologies, though he knew that his place was still vacant there. His intention was to do a bit of speaking.

He said that during the Falklands crisis he had had great difficulty over policy.[2] He was not specific but I was sure from the way he spoke that what he was getting at was the influence exerted on the President by Jeane Kirkpatrick, Clark and other pro-Latinos. Haig expressed confidence that his departure would not jeopardise the interests of the United States or those of her allies. If he had had such fears he would not have left. Shultz,[3] he has assured me, was first rate. The White House

---

[1] On 25 June the President announced Haig's resignation, but he asked him to stay on to deal with the crisis that had arisen over Israel's invasion of the Lebanon until George Shultz's appointment to succeed him was approved by the Senate. By 5 July the position for Haig of not being Secretary of State and yet behaving as Secretary of State became untenable for Haig (and Shultz) and he withdrew from office.

[2] In his book *Caveat*, already mentioned, Haig wrote, p 298, '... my efforts in the Falklands ultimately cost me my job as Secretary of State ... the work I had done was perceived to be a failure, and those in the Administration who had been looking for an issue on which to bring me down recognised that I had given them one ... In my own mind, I regarded American diplomacy in the Falklands crisis as a success'.

Kissinger had pioneered the path of shuttle diplomacy and consciously or unconsciously Haig may have tried to emulate him. To the extent that he failed to avoid military conflict in the Falklands his enemies could point to failure. But so far as Britain is concerned there is no doubt that we owe a great deal to him for the US Government's decision of 30 April to come down on our side.

[3] George Shultz, Secretary of the Treasury 1972–4, Secretary of State 1982–9.

would be less inclined to give Shultz the trouble they had meted out to him.

After the tennis was over I accompanied Haig to his car. 'It's been one of the worst days of my life,' he muttered, 'the problem of decompression'.

I have had a separate talk with Eagleburger who was rather more explicit than Haig had been. He referred to a 'subterranean government', by which he meant the White House and some people in the Pentagon who sent messages to other countries that had the effect of undermining the policy of the United States. Eagleburger mentioned in particular the Falkland Islands issue on which he said that there had been covert policies and messages which had 'encouraged Argentinian recalcitrance'.

Referring to the differences that had arisen over the Soviet pipeline Eagleburger said that these had contributed to the crisis leading up to Haig's resignation. The crucial meeting of the NSC last week had been held while Haig was grappling with Gromyko in New York. This had rankled with him as he earlier had told me himself.

It says something about the nature of the government here at the present time that the President himself, having announced Haig's resignation, gave no explanation and went off by helicopter to Camp David. Pictures of him have been shown on television waving goodbye to be followed by pictures of Beirut under bombardment by air and artillery.

What it boils down to, I think, is that the resignation has come about as a result of an accumulation of differences on policy and a conflict of temperament. Haig is impetuous. He is also combative and even aggressive in defence of what he describes as his 'own turf'. It is inherent in the system that there will be conflict between the White House and the State Department on the conduct of foreign policy unless the Secretary of State is exceptionally compliant and passive. Even if, as is the situation at the moment, the President himself does not seek to direct day-to-day policy, those around him will believe that the US constitution does not permit the Presidency to abdicate its responsibility. Haig came to the State Department with an enormous reputation. The reasons for his constant clashes since then, the decline in his influence, and his inability to find a way through the inherent contradictions of the Washington decision-making process result not from lack of ability or of integrity but from his abrasive and volatile personality. The odd thing is that he has in practice achieved a large proportion of his objectives on policy but that this has not prevented a feeling of frustration and a belief on his part that he has in some way been undermined and circumvented.

26 JULY

WASHINGTON

———

A FAREWELL DINNER AT THE WHITE HOUSE

We dined last night at the White House. Nancy Reagan had spoken to Mary several weeks ago inviting us to a farewell dinner. Mary had replied that we were not giving or accepting farewell parties because, well, we never did. Upon which Mrs Reagan asked whether we would like a private dinner with them alone. We said that we would very much like one, so a date was fixed, a Sunday evening.

The only other official goodbye function we attended was a lunch given by the Vice-President. At this George Bush, with much solemnity, presented me with a toy helicopter to commemorate the many times he had overflown our house next door in his official chopper.

Later we got into a slight panic at the thought of ourselves alone with the Reagans for a whole evening. I therefore asked Mike Deaver (who is the closest of anyone in the White House to the Reagans) whether he and Carolyn could also be there. They, therefore, came along last night too.

We were invited at 7 p.m. and told to wear very informal clothes: sports jacket and slacks were specified. Doug drove us through the southeast gate entrance on the dot of 7 p.m. and we asked him to return at 8.45 p.m., thinking that that would be quite long enough for a private evening.

We had a heartening welcome at the door. Nothing was skimped on account of it being Sunday evening. A black footman opened the car and shook our hands. A young man, the equivalent, I suppose, of an equerry at Buckingham Palace, came from the house beneath the awning to receive us. I had not seen him before. He asked us to wait a minute or two in the Ambassadors' foyer, a large circular room on the ground floor which has a pretty, scenic wallpaper and fine antique furniture.

It was only a matter of minutes before the equerry was back saying that Mrs Reagan was ready to receive us if we would accompany him in the elevator to the second floor.

Nancy was there as we arrived. She wondered whether we would find it too hot to sit outside on the terrace. She loved the heat herself. We went through the oval-shaped sitting-room to the balcony that looks straight down to the Washington Monument and to the Jefferson Memorial. A minute or two later the Deavers arrived. I heard Nancy mutter that Ronnie would be here in a minute; he had forgotten. I thought to myself once again what an imposition it was that they should be giving us dinner on Sunday evening when they could be alone and he mugging up his papers for the heavy week ahead. We were meeting, I should record, at a time of considerable disarray for the Reagan administration: serious trouble over the budgetary deficit and the failure of the economic programme; tension in the Middle East where Israel, having attacked Lebanon, were in a quandary whether to enter Beirut and destroy the rest of the PLO there; friction within the Atlantic Alliance caused by US decisions on the pipeline and on steel imports.

When, a few minutes later, the President appeared on the balcony, wearing a white jacket and pink tie, he showed not an inkling of anxiety about these matters. We sat having drinks and chatting. The Reagans had spent the weekend at Camp David. They had been riding. The weather had been beautiful, better on Saturday than on Sunday, with a bit of 'coolit' in the air, as the President described it. We talked about the origins of Camp David as a Presidential retreat. The President was a little vague on the subject, but he thought that it had begun when, in FDR's time, the Americans had wanted to have secret talks with the British on intelligence matters.

In a non-sequitur he said, 'But you know what's inscribed in that Jefferson Memorial down there.' He went on to say that Jefferson's words, to which everyone could subscribe about all men having a right to liberty regardless of race or colour, were written there in stone, but not the words that had followed that statement about it being impossible for blacks and whites to live together under the same roof.

We had considerable discussion about Fagan's[1] break-in to Buckingham Palace. The Reagans had been much impressed by the Queen's sangfroid. We talked for a while about the great increase in security that had become necessary in recent times. We spoke with horror of the IRA bombings this past week in London. Reagan said that he did not want to sound callous but he could not help thinking how awful it had been to see all those horses blown up. I said that my compatriots would share those sentiments.

Reagan said apropos the Fagan intrusion incident, that it had produced a 'snide' reaction from the USA security authorities. Before and during his visit the previous month to the UK the British security officials had been dismissive of the elaborate precautionary arrangements that their American counterparts had wanted to make against the possibility of an assassination attempt. Such things don't happen here had been their attitude.

---

[1] A cat-burglar had managed to bypass the security system of Buckingham Palace and to reach the Queen's bedroom.

It was pleasant sitting there on the terrace even without there being any sense of privacy. We were visible from the neighbouring building, and indeed from the crowds who thronged round the fence at the far end of the garden staring up at us as if we were animals in a zoo. Someone with binoculars could have seen what we were drinking. Reagan made no pretence of his eagerness to find any excuse to get away from the claustrophobic atmosphere of the White House. He said that at the beginning of his time in Washington he had tried strolling in the garden but had had to abandon it when he realised how many security men were accompanying him. There was no privacy whatever. All he could do for exercise was to use the various machines installed in one of the rooms he showed us later after dinner. We spent some time there where he and Nancy gave demonstrations of weight-lifting and muscle-building. Reagan spoke a little wistfully of bathing in the Pacific when he could get there. The water, he said, was too cold for swimming north of the Conception line.

At dinner I referred to the Queen's proposed visit to California next spring and to her wish to visit the Reagans' ranch which she could do if the yacht came into Santa Barbara. I asked Nancy if she had seen the royal yacht. She said that she had not but that she longed to do so. There was a gleam in her eye. As usual when plans or engagements are being discussed, the President remained silent.

Otherwise he spoke a good deal, mostly anecdotally. I heard again of his four months in England making a film in the late forties. 'It's not the climate outside,' he said, 'that I minded; but the climate in the houses.'

We had one or two Hollywood stories, for instance, about C. Aubrey Smith and his cricket matches and about David Niven whom they had both greatly liked. There were scarcely any references to politics. The President deplored Larry Pressler's[1] criticism of Habib for whom he expressed great admiration, saying that he would much rather be playing golf than trying to settle the Middle East. He spoke about Arafat and the state of Israel. Otherwise the conversation was about trivia.

He spoke with great enthusiasm about the Bohemian Grove,[2] as I have heard others do, saying, as I have also heard others say, that nobody who has not been there can understand what it means. He singled out the theatrical performances. He said, not exactly priggishly, because he is not that, but in a manner that showed his preference for the correct, that the thousand or so men at the Bohemian Grove camp behave as if women were present, though none are!

---

[1]Larry Pressler, Republican Senator from South Dakota since 1979.
[2]Bohemian Grove, grandiose summer camp in California for grandees.

I had heard separately from both Susan Mary and Marietta that afternoon of Henry Kissinger's long telephone call to Nancy from the Bohemian Grove: he had described how in his camp there were Haig, Shultz, Helmut Schmidt, Isaac Stern and Lee Kuan Yew. There was only one toilet and one single room for all these distinguished campers. I recall someone describing to me as among the great joys of Bohemian Grove the freedom it gives you to walk about practically naked and urinate amongst the trees – pleasures sated for me by boy-scout weekends at school.

Nancy mentioned the tragedy of the death of Ed Meese's son in a motor accident. This touched off some reflex in the President's system. He proceeded to deliver a diatribe on small cars. Statistics showed that they were the cause of injuries and deaths that would have been avoided if people had been in bigger cars. I did not follow him down this track any more than I was prepared to touch on other subjects about which he feels strongly such as abortion and evolution. When people say that the present US administration is the most right-wing of this century they mean that it is influenced by Reagan's particular prejudices, the fruit, not, I think, of careful thought or discussion, but of his own experiences and whims. He is like Mrs T in having no sentimental or guilty feelings about underdogs. They come from more or less similiar backgrounds which are very different from the aristocratic surroundings that inspired the philanthropic do-gooding of Wilberforce or Shaftesbury or Frank Longford; theirs was an upbringing encouraging one later to think that others can look after themselves too, and that if they get into difficulties or remain underlings the fault lies in themselves, not in their stars, and that the more fortunate should not have any sense of guilt or reponsibility to help others.

Reverting to Reagan's obiter dicta, there was one revealing passage about the past. I suppose I must have been quizzing him about the problem of press conferences or off-the-cuff statements. He said that he had had a long training. For eight years, between 1954 and 1962, he had been employed by General Electric to go round the country addressing gatherings of the company's staff with a view to trying to encourage in them the sense of 'belonging'. He had found that the best way of doing this was to begin with some quite general remarks, but brief, and then to throw the meetings open to 'Q and A'. The President insisted on the therapeutic effect of 'Q and A'.

From there we moved to his entry into political life. He said that he had never thought of becoming a politician. He had always been happy to 'campaign for others', to use his own expression. Then these others had persuaded him to stand himself. 'Nancy and I talked it over one night,' he said without false modesty, 'and we decided we just could not let those people down out there.' I have noticed the prevalence of 'out there' as an expression used by public men to describe 'the people in the public domain'.

I did not get the sense of any belief on Reagan's part that this turning point in his life had occurred in response to some awareness of destiny or of some public call that had been latent, awaiting an answer. I did, indeed, have the feeling that there had not been anything more conscious or calculated than a response to a personal appeal by his friends who had decided that he was their man for public life.

We did not sit around for long drinking coffee after dinner. Nancy asked whether we would not like to see the top floor which she has completely redecorated. The President tagged along behind us, making an occasional remark about the carpets or the pictures, towards which he displayed, as he does about so many things, neither enthusiasm nor specialist knowledge, nor dislike nor resentment, but a benign, unsurprised acceptance expressed by little shakes of the head and equally fleeting anecdotes.

There were many more rooms than I had expected. None gave the appearance of much use. There was no suggestion that any of the Reagan children had customary rights to any particular room. There was no mention of any guest whom the Reagans had had to stay. During our tour of the house, as at dinner, Nancy made occasional references to the press campaign against her acquisition of various gifts of porcelain etc for the White House; but she did so in a manner that led me to think that she was now less bitter than previously about it.

We exchanged a fond farewell before making our way out as we had entered. I think Nancy has become genuinely attached to Mary and full of admiration for her taste and talents – and this Mary has reciprocated. The next day Nancy sent round an orchid named after her. With some difficulty we took this later to Combe along with six topiarised rose-maries. Reagan, at our parting, was his quintessential, friendly, joking, smiling self; not exactly impersonal, but like one of those one-way see-through mirrors: he could look at us, but there was no way in which we could peer back at him. He was forthcoming, but non-committal; and how indeed could he be anything else after all those years of meeting so many people? I think that he has a great gift in appearing to be, and in fact being, so friendly, so universally friendly, without this involving him in any expenditure of effort or sentiment. He is a difficult man to oppose because you cannot hold anything against him personally. He is without cynicism or malice. At one point in the evening Nancy singled out cynicism as a terrible flaw in character. She was shocked that some newspaper article had attributed appalling cynicism to them over some incident.

Mary and I came away from our evening at the White House feeling immensely grateful to the Reagans for taking the trouble to give us this sympathetic and very informal goodbye party. Looking back we were also touched by the warmth and personal friendship they had shown to us so unreservedly on many occasions during our time in Washington.

We left Washington on 31 July 1982 to return home.

It has been suggested that it would be fitting if these diaries were to be rounded off with some reflections, and even lessons, on the conduct of diplomacy in the modern age, together with some indication of how Mary and I have been affected by our years in the Service.

I am not sure that this book is the place for big thoughts. As stated at the outset, I think that the career can best be described by stories of particular experiences, such as those that these diaries have tried to relay, rather than by any attempt at institutional analysis. Nor do I think it appropriate here to do more than drop hints of the kind of pitfalls that may occur, as again I have aimed at doing, rather than prescribe rules on the basis of the past for a profession that is so highly susceptible to the vagaries and personalities of the moment.

As for the impact of the career on us personally, Mary thinks, and I can but agree with her, that this can best be summed up by reproducing the postcard shown below that we received from a perceptive friend upon our first retirement.

APPENDIX

SUMMING UP OF PRESIDENT CARTER'S PERSONALITY AND PRESIDENCY IN THE WHITE HOUSE 1976–80

A President can only make an impact and come near to achieving his goals if he has the ability to communicate, using the whole gamut of the modern instruments available. It was the failure of Carter to reach and persuade the public that was one of the main causes of his undoing.

Nevertheless his accomplishments deserve more than the low rating now accorded them after four years in office. From the outset he was determined to develop a national energy policy and he did this despite the obstruction from Congress and the indifference of the public. The single most important step was the decontrol of oil prices, an unpopular measure, which has nevertheless contributed much to the reduction in oil imports.

A lot is being said now on both sides of the Atlantic about the need to get the government off the backs of the people. In fact Carter stood for doing this as was shown, for example, by the deregulation of civil airlines. Here again there was a conflict of interest in which the government tried to hold the ring between the rights of the individual and the ambitions of the airlines.

Carter's concern for the environment, for the 'quality of this world within which we live', to quote from his farewell address to the nation, had an adverse effect upon the development of nuclear power. It was a reflection not simply of Carter's environmental concern but of his worry about nuclear proliferation.

The Clean Air Act and the Clean Water Act were among the most important contributions to the statute book in recent years and they are a tribute to Carter's firmness in sticking to his ideas however unpopular. The Environmental Protection Agency now has a staff of over twelve thousand full-time employees and spends over four billion dollars per annum.

The battle for human rights at home and abroad should certainly be blazened on Carter's escutcheon beneath his own words: 'America did not invent human rights ... human rights invented America.' Carter's devotion to human rights arose from grounds of both morality and expediency, qualities that were so inextricably entwined within him that it was difficult to see at any one time which was dominant. He certainly did not try to disentangle them himself.

There were early signs of the incompatability that others might feel about his motivations, even if Carter did not, particularly when he tried to persuade the Soviet government to accept new far-reaching strategic arms proposals, while at the same time expecting them to heed his lecture on the inalienable right of the individual to liberty. There is no doubt that in the conduct of East–West relations the Baptist preacher was as ineffective as he was earnest. Yet I believe that this public piety served the Americans well in some areas of the world, particularly in Africa and, with some reservations, in Latin America (not just in the context of the Panama Canal Treaties). Andy Youngism was a nuisance to the UK, and to many other countries, but I think that it had a helpful effect upon the way Africans and many of the other less favoured countries look upon the great power of America.

Apart from the Panama Canal Treaties, the normalisation of relations with China, the improvement of relations with Africa and Latin America, it seemed to me that Carter's most striking achievement was in the Middle East. The Camp David accords and subsequent Egyptian–Israeli Treaty, whatever their pros and cons, have altered fundamentally the situation in the Middle East. They might well not have come about without Carter's personal doggedness. He was prepared to take a risk that affected himself personally as well as the United States and, as over the decontrol of oil prices, I do not think that one can attribute this particularly to the prospects of domestic political advantage. The last year of Carter's Presidency was overshadowed by the Iran hostage issue. Although public opinion on this, and their judgment of Carter's role, fluctuated, I think that on election day the Iran hostages proved to be one of the counts against Carter in the minds of the voters. The way he handled the situation was widely regarded as a reflection of his vacillation, of his readiness to exploit the issue for political gain, and of his contribution to the country's poor standing abroad.

Carter's reaction to the Soviet invasion of Afghanistan may have far-reaching consequences. His response was rapid and forthright, reflecting both his own personal sense that the Soviets had undermined the common restraint upon which detente had been based and the public feeling that the Soviets had to be given a really severe warning if they were not to continue their adventures and not only extend Soviet political influence but also threaten fundamental United States economic and strategic interests. The Carter Doctrine, committing the United States to the defence of the Persian Gulf area in the event of a new security threat from outside, was in my view an important new undertaking, even though there was not the immediate military means to implement it. Since then the US government has been taking active steps to make ready its Rapid Deployment Force and improve its facilities in the Middle East, necessary for the defence of the Gulf.

An assessment of Carter's personal standing now is revealing about the USA in general at the present time and the extent to which the mood of the country has changed over the past four years. His election to the Presidency was largely a reaction against people and things: he was chosen because he was evidently not a racist, not a warmonger and not a crook; and we should remember, in passing, how warmly he was welcomed to Washington and how much hope was placed upon him. His election was a product of the time; he happened to fit the circumstances rather than the office. He was not equipped by nature to be a leader of a great nation, and I do not think that he had the qualities the Presidency requires, any more than the ability to grow with the responsibility.

Part of his failure as a communicator was his inability to inspire confidence whether by eloquence or personal integrity. He was impressive in small gatherings. The signal he gave to the American public and to the world at large was one of indecision and changeability in domestic and foreign policy. He was unable to create a clear-cut, comprehensive decision-making process. It was not in his being to gather around him a coterie of helpful and reliable friends. He had no base of support on Capitol Hill; nor in the business community nor amongst the media. For a man who wore goodness on his sleeve and a constant grin on his face it was surprising how isolated he was. I have never heard anyone say that he was endearing. Coming to Washington, a southerner with a chip the size and shape of a cathedral – to steal Koestler's analogy – Carter was determined from the outset to shun the establishment. Lifted to power, as he saw it, by the voice of the people, particularly of the underprivileged and unfavoured, he sought to appeal direct to them over the heads of the institutions, believing that in this way he could circumvent the checks and balances of the system.

He relied for advice on a small group, many of them Georgians, with little experience of national or international politics. Of those who had most influence upon him there is no doubt about the important role of his wife. He was extremely wrapped up in his family and it was typical of him that in his television debate with Reagan he should have prayed in aid of his daughter's views on nuclear proliferation. Dr Brzezinski also had Carter's ear and I think that he was creative in the thinking he did for the President. He was capable of articulating for him a concept of strategy which probably gave more of a framework than the piecemeal reactions to events either deserved or indicated. Against this it has to be admitted that Brzezinski, partly from a desire to emulate Kissinger, was far too much in the public eye, and too little ready to allow the State

Department to exercise the main influence on foreign policy; so that the lack of a single voice was even more apparent in America's foreign policy over this past term than in domestic policy.

Carter did not appear to be able to galvanise or use to best advantage the enormous machine of government that stood – or lay – at hand. He did not behave as a President. The Americans do not like pomp, but they expect their President to be respected. He was unable to be both informal and dignified. His person was without authority, yet it clearly hurt him when he was increasingly depicted by commentators and cartoonists as a small and shabby figure, ill-suited to great office.

INDEX

Aaron, David, 285, 331
Abbado, Claudio, 148–9
Abdy, Valentine, 252
Abrasimov, Pyotr Andreyevich, 42–3
Académie Française, 157, 178
Acheson, Alice, 369
Acheson, Dean, 280
Achillopoulo, Costa, 152
Acland, Sir Antony, 429n, 458–9
Adeane, Edward, 395, 397
Adenauer, Konrad, 48–50, 81
Afghanistan, 186, 321, 324–5, 327, 336, 339, 491
AFL-CIO (American trade union organisations), 359
Aga Khan IV, Prince Karim, 156
Agnelli, Marella, 426
Airbus Industrie Projet (AI), 154, 158–9, 166, 187–8, 208–11, 213–16, 220, 225–6, 238–9, 243
Airlie, David Ogilvy, 13th Earl of, 361
Alaska, 408–12
Aleutian Islands, 408, 411
Alexander, Sir Michael, 388
Alexandra, Princess, 457
Alfa Alfa club, 378–9
Alington, Giles, 70
Allegheny International (company), 419–20
Allen, Richard, 374, 383
Allen, Woody, 333
Alsop, Joseph: dines with NH, 292, 331, 354; recommends Hot Springs for Mary's illness, 295; on declining manners, 299; friendship with NH and Mary, 301; manner and behaviour, 301–2, 354–5; entertains, 308–9, 337; and NH's corruption by Annenberg, 323; and Carter, 339; and Bradens' dinner, 358; and Macmillan's Washington visit, 368–9; and Kay Graham's party for Reagans, 374, 376; Berlins stay with,

399, 401–2; at Reagan dinner, 426
Alsop, Stewart, 292n
Alsop, Susan Mary, 308, 337, 449, 486
Amateurs de Jardin, Les, 192, 217
American Farm Bureau, 321
Amery, Julian, Baron, 371
Anaya, Admiral Jorge, 465
Anchorage, Alaska, 409
Anderson, Robert, 345
Anglés, Jean-Paul, 116, 121
Anglo-German Foundation, 57–8
Annan, Gabriele, Lady (née Ullstein), 42n
Annan, Noël, Baron, 42n; at Stowe, 331
Anne, Princess, 50
Annenberg, Leonore (Lee), 307, 322–3, 342, 380–1, 394–6, 403, 416–17
Annenberg, Walter, 307, 318, 322–5, 342, 380–1, 396
Anstruther, Sir Ralph, 131
Apel, Hans, 63–4
Apple, Raymond Walter ('Johnny'), 270
Arab–Israeli war (1973), 75, 144
Arafat, Yasser, 485
Arbuthnott, Hugh James, 254
ARCO (oil company), 410
Arculus, Sir Ronald, 127
Argentina: and Falklands War, 445–7, 449–53, 456, 458–9, 461–4, 468, 475; invades South Georgia, 447; and long-term Falklands settlement, 469; prisoners of war, 473, 476, 480
Arizona Republic (newspaper), 322
Armour, Norman, 420
Armstrong, Anne, 344, 366, 368
Armstrong, Robert (Baron Armstrong of Ilminster), 55, 57, 70, 75, 78
Aron, Raymond, 124, 139, 183, 224
Ascension Island, 443
Ascherson, Neal, 25
Asher, Bernard, 153
Ashley, Sir Bernard, 291
Ashley, Laura, 291

Asquith, Herbert Henry, 1st Earl of Oxford and Asquith, 238

Astor, Brooke, 311, 360, 368, 373, 439–40

Astor, Lady Irene (*née* Haig), 472

Astor, John, 406n

Atlanta, Georgia, 343

Atlantic Alliance, 59, 89, 484

Attlee, Clement, 1st Earl, 70, 316

Auchinloss, K.K. (Mrs Douglas A.), 416

Audland, Christopher, 55

Auty, Richard, 234

Auvergne (France), 195–6

Avon, Clarissa, Countess of (*née* Churchill), 405

AWACS (airborne warning system), 412

Bahr, Egon, 41, 55–6, 80

Bahr, Frau Egon, 56

Baker, James, 375, 395, 477n

Baldridge, Mr & Mrs Malcolm, 377

Bamboo, Jackie, 241–2

Barclays International, 311

Bardot, Brigitte, 219

Baring, Susan Mary, 437

Barlow, Professor Harold Everard Monteagle, 16

Barrault, Jean-Louis, 254–5

Barre, Eve, 142n, 240–2

Barre, Raymond: Thatcher visits, 142–3; attends European Youth Orchestra concert, 148–9; forms 1978 government, 154; speaks at seminar, 193; on threat to living standards, 195; and Kay Graham, 251

Barry (Paris Embassy butler), 149

Baryshnikov, Mikhail, 222–3

Bayne, Sir Nicholas, 177–8, 244

BBC World Service, 212

Beaumarchais, Jacques de, 120n, 256

Beaumarchais, Marie-Alice de, 120, 256

Begin, Menachem, 212, 452, 474, 477

Beirut, 482, 484

Belfast, 274

Belgrade Conference (1978), 164

Belgrano (Argentinian warship), 455

Bell, Anne Olivier, 337

Bell, Quentin, 161–2, 337

Bell, Vanessa, 335

Benn, Anthony Wedgwood (Tony): Wilson on, 69; as Energy Minister, 97, 164n; meets Giraud, 164–6, 233; John Grigg on, 228–9; in Paris, 233; on NH's Paris despatch, 271

Beresford-Hope, Harold Thomas, 13

Berlin (Germany), 41–2, 44, 304

Berlin, Aline, Lady, 399

Berlin, Sir Isaiah, 212, 268, 292, 399–402

Bernard, Jack F.: *Life of Talleyrand*, 256

Berrill, Sir Kenneth, 126–7, 129, 216, 260

Bettencourt, André, 181–2, 230

Bevin, Ernest, 65, 70, 140, 173, 289, 316

Bevin, Florence, 173

Beytout, Jacqueline, 219

Billington, Rachel, 18

Billotte, General Pierre, 228

Bischler, Christine, 239, 250

Bismarck, Prince Otto von, 38

Blackstone, Tessa, Baroness, 127–9

Blake, Robert, Baron: *The Office of Prime Minister*, 99

Blumenfeld, Erik, 84

Blumenthal, Michael, 301–2

Bodley-Scott, Sir Ronald, 226, 367

Boeing aircraft company, 158–9, 166, 176, 208, 211, 215, 226, 439

Bohemian Grove, California, 485–6

Bonn: NH appointed Ambassador to, 37; NH leaves, 88–90

Bourges, Yvon, 256

Bowra, Sir Maurice, 332

Boxer, Mark, 305, 437

Brademas, John and Mary Ellen, 292

Braden, Tom and Joan, 308, 330, 358

Bradlee, Benjamin, 285n, 375, 426

Brady, James, 387

Brandon, Henry, 331–2, 334, 339, 369

Brandon, Mabel ('Muffie'), 331–2, 334, 339, 369, 396

Brandt, Willy: Ostpolitik, 26, 33, 38; as Chancellor, 38; character, 38–9; Heath meets, 39, 51–8, 59, 74, 144–5; and Callaghan's view of Europe, 65; lacks small talk, 74; popularity, 89; and Third World Commission, 251

Brantes, Madame de (Giscard's mother-in-law), 255

Bremen (Germany), 111, 209

Brement, Marshall and Pamela, 330

Bretécher, Claire, 157

Brewster, Kingman, 272, 299, 319, 357

Brewster, Mary Louise, 272

Brezhnev, Leonid: visits Warsaw, 20; Michelin on, 198; Giscard and, 256, 341; Thatcher discusses speech with Reagan, 386

Brideshead Revisited (TV film), 440
Bridges, Thomas Edward, 2nd Baron,
    54, 57, 70, 75, 78, 290
Bright, John, 391
Brimelow, Thomas, Baron, 60
British Aerospace: and airbus project,
    154, 158–9, 166, 175, 187, 210–11,
    215–16, 226
British Airways (BA): and airbus project,
    158, 176, 208, 211, 215
British Council, 106, 248
British Festival, Pittsburgh, 1981, 418
British Information Services, New York,
    285
British Olympic Committee, 342
British Overseas Trade Board, 225
British Petroleum (BP), 410, 412
British Ski Championships, 1979, 244–5
British Steel Corporation, 419
Brittan, Samuel, 346
Broad, Philip, 192
Broglie, Princesse Jean-Marie de, 194
Brooks, Ted, 406
Brooks's Club (London), 151, 437
Brown, Carter, 299, 343
Brown, George (*later* Baron George-
    Brown), 60
Brown, Harold, 279–80
Brown, John (company), 479
Brown, Pamela, 299
Brown, Tina, 437
Browning, Robert, 6
Bruce, David, 354–5n
Bruce, Evangeline, 354, 358, 360, 368,
    396, 401, 416, 449
Bryce, James, 288
Brzezinski, Zbigniew: telephones British
    Embassy, 277; NH meets in
    Washington, 280, 282–3, 303, 312–
    13, 325–7; on Carter's
    administration, 281; confidence, 281,
    qualities, 304, 313; and US attitude
    to IRA, 335; and failed Iran hostage
    rescue attempt, 336; Carrington
    meets, 339–40; and Iran-Iraq war,
    365; and White House foreign policy
    decision-making, 434n, 492; influence
    on Carter, 492
Buchan, David, 332
Buchwald, Art, 346, 367, 416
Buckingham Palace: intruder reaches
    Queen, 484
Buckley, Robert, 419–20
Buckley, William, 396, 440

Budd, Colin, 22
Bullard, Sir Julian, 360, 437–8
Bullitt, William, 4
Bullock, Hugh, 306n
Bundesbank: and 1972 monetary crisis,
    53–4
Bundy, McGeorge, 401
Burma Road, The (film), 427
Burnet, Sir Alastair, 240
Burns Night (1979), 249
Bush, Barbara, 377, 390, 449
Bush, George: as prospective
    Presidential candidate, 324; on
    Reagan, 377; entertained at Embassy,
    390; Prince Charles meets, 397; at
    NH's birthday party, 449; role in
    Falklands War negotiations, 449;
    1992 Presidential campaign, 477n;
    meets Thatcher in Washington, 479;
    farewell presentation to NH, 483
Business Council conference, Hot
    Springs, 1980, 364
Butler, Sir Michael Dacres, 230, 248n
Butler, Richard Austen, Baron (Rab),
    108, 177, 192, 311, 340, 355n
Butler, Rohan, 250
Byam Shaw, Nicholas, 356
Byrd, Harry, 307

Caccia, Harold, Baron, 221, 271
Cairn, Kirstie, 245–6
California: NH visits, 312–14, 440–2;
    Queen proposes visit to, 485
Callaghan, Audrey, Lady, 144–5
Callaghan, James (*later* Baron):
    antipathy to European Community,
    59–60, 62–65, 72–3, 146; expects
    support from Brandt, 61; at
    Dorneywood meeting with Genscher,
    67; meets Genscher in Germany, 73–
    4; invites Schmidt to Labour Party
    conference, 75–6; relations with
    Giscard, 94, 133–4, 235–6; succeeds
    Wilson as Prime Minister, 94, 98,
    109; at 1975 Paris energy conference,
    96–8; Maudling respects, 126; at
    1976 Rambouillet summit, 132–4;
    admits to tiredness, 134; relations
    with Schmidt, 134; temperance, 138,
    145; Giscard visits at Chequers, 144–
    7, 188, 220; and undermining French
    from within, 209; and airbus project,
    210, 213–15; and EMS, 213, 233; and
    Benn, 233; and 1978 Franco-UK

Callaghan, James – *cont*
  summit, 235–6; *Observer* interview,
  238; in Paris for 1979 European
  summit, 258–9; relations with Carter,
  283, 315; Jay likens to Moses, 289
Cambodia, 25
Cameron, Rory, 173
Camp David, 275, 413, 484; Accords
  (Egypt-Israel), 212, 419, 491
Canterbury, Archbishop of *see* Coggan,
  Donald
Carey, Hugh Leo, 284, 294
Carlisle, Kitty *see* Hart, Kitty Carlisle
Carlos Bay, Falkland Islands, 465
Carmoy, Hervé de, 237–8
Caroline, Princess of Monaco, 185
Carrington, Iona, Lady, 296, 339, 362,
  382, 389
Carrington, Peter Carington, 6th Baron:
  appoints DH to Washington, 8, 266–
  7, 269; as Foreign Secretary, 265–6;
  fatigue and overwork, 268–9; and
  NH's leaked despatch, 271; NH sees
  in New York, 295–6; qualities, 295–
  6, 340, 413; NH's sense of duty to,
  302; and Thatcher, 305, 404; Vance
  thanks for support, 312; visits USA
  with Thatcher, 316–20, 382, 386,
  389–90; 1980 visits to Washington,
  337–40, 360–2; meets Vance, 338–9;
  and failed US rescue bid in Iran, 339;
  and sanctions, 346; addresses Council
  on Foreign Relations, 359–60; and
  Kissinger, 382; on NH's successor in
  Washington, 384, 406, 460; attends
  Ottawa conference, 407; in New
  York, 412–13; on Southern Africa,
  412; relations with Haig, 418, 421,
  433, 437; and Reagan's visit to Britain,
  436; and US alliance, 437; resigns
  over Falklands, 445, 450–1; and US
  negotiations over Falklands, 448–9;
  as successor to Luns at NATO, 472
Carter, Amy, 379
Carter, Jimmy: Owen sympathises with,
  139; and human rights, 164; attitude
  to USSR, 186, relations with Thatcher,
  269, 287, 315, 317–19; and NH's
  appointment to Washington, 270; low
  esteem as President, 275–6, 281, 284,
  293, 324, 492–3; TV broadcast on
  energy, 280–1; NH presents
  credentials to, 281–3; relations with
  Callaghan, 283, 315; and Edward

Kennedy as prospective candidate,
  285; and Cuba/SALT II ratification,
  296; Brzezinski and, 313; and Iran
  hostage crisis, 321; 'doctrine' on
  Persian Gulf and Middle East, 325–6,
  408, 491; failed attempt to rescue Iran
  hostages, 336; Nixon on, 338;
  Carrington meets, 339; in 1980
  Presidential election, 357, 360; 1980
  election defeat, 366–7; NH's
  assessment of, 376, 490–3; social
  limitations, 378, 492
Carter, Rosalynn, 282, 285, 318–19,
  338, 367, 492
Casanova, Jean-Claude, 183
Casey, William, 374
Casey, Mrs William, 390
Caspari, Fritz, 47, 50
Casson, Sir Hugh, 156
Castle, Barbara, Baroness, 142
Cater, Douglas, 345
Cavaillé, Marcel, 105
Cazes, Roger, 106, 160, 223–4
Ceauşescu, Nicolae, 193
Center of Strategic and International
  Studies, Washington, 343
Central Policy Review Staff, 126–8
Cercle Interallié, 204
Cézanne, Paul: 1978 Paris exhibition,
  161–2; George V on, 168
Chaban-Delmas, Jacques, 218
Chad: French intervene in, 182–3
Chalmers, Ian, 30
Chamberlain, Neville, 4, 5
Channel Tunnel: 1975 cancellation, 94
Charles, Prince of Wales: visit to Berlin,
  41, 43; visits United World Colleges,
  237; commentary for film on Covent
  Garden, 300; polo-playing in USA,
  331; Lee Annenberg on, 342; 1981
  visit to USA, 394–7, 402–3, 405;
  wedding, 395, 409, 412, 414;
  discusses Falklands War, 472
Charteris, Sir Martin (*later* Baron), 45,
  117–18, 120, 449
Chatsworth: treasures exhibited in USA,
  290, 340
Chazot, Jacques, 185
Chequers (house), 67–9, 74–5, 77, 143–
  7, 188, 220, 458–61
Cheshire, Gigi, 350
Cheshire, Group Captain Leonard, VC,
  Baron, 27–8, 348–50, 416
Chicago, 299–300, 302, 337, 422

China: US relations with, 408

Chinese Embassy, Warsaw: NH organises table tennis match with, 30–2

Chirac, Jacques: admires Thatcher, 88; NH entertains, 102; Thatcher meets in Paris, 142–3; mellows, 150; and Vanneck's visit, 174–5; and French intervention in Africa, 185; at Rothschild dinner, 222; undermines Giscard, 241; and farewell present to NH, 260

Choiseul, Etienne François, duc de, 256

Christopher, Warren, 327, 339, 361, 364–5

Chrysler company, 211

Chung, Kyung-Wha, 418

Church, Frank, 279–80

Churchill, Clementine, Lady, 281n

Churchill, Sir Winston S., 4, 56, 77, 144, 152, 175, 206, 219, 265, 368, 370, 427, 465

Clark, William, 434–6, 454, 463, 474, 477–9, 481

Clarke, Kenneth, 358

Clay Cross (Derbyshire), 76

Clemenceau, Georges, 229

Clermont-Ferrand (France), 196–7, 199, 201–2

Cleveland, Grover, 289n

Clifford, Clark, 280, 304, 326–7, 331

Cockburn, Alexander, 333–4

Coggan, Donald, Archbishop of Canterbury, 303

Colbert, Claudette, 328, 330

Colchester, Nicholas, 71

Coleman, James, 341

Coles, Sir John, 436, 479

Colony Club, New York, 110

Combe (Berkshire): NH's cottage at, 69, 94, 301; Kingman Brewster rents cottage, 272; rats in, 406

Commonwealth: Callaghan favours, 59; Wilson on, 78–9

Commonwealth War Graves Commission, 189

Concorde aircraft, 120–1, 153, 208

Confédération Française Démocratique du Travail (CFDT), 166–7

Congleton, Christopher Patrick Parnell, 8th Baron, 245

Connolly, Cyril, 77, 173, 352

Conservative Party: 1970 election

victory and government, 24

Constancin, Poland: Sue Ryder Home in, 28

Cooke, Alistair, 432

Cooper, Alfred Duff (1st Viscount Norwich), 95

Cooper, Lady Diana, 95, 156n

Cooper, John Sherman, 297n, 354

Cooper, Lorraine, 279, 354

Cooper, Richard, 362

Cooper, Sir Frank, 461

Copple, Ted, 423

Corfu, 289

Council of Economic and Mutual Assistance (CEMA), 17

Council of Foreign Relations (USA), 337, 359

Courances (France), 231–2

Courcel, Geoffroy, baron de, 117, 124, 163, 224–5, 255–6, 306

Coucel, Martine, baronne de, 117n, 256

Couve de Murville, Maurice, 85

Couzens, Kenneth Edward, 230

Covent Garden: US fundraising for, 299, 300, 402–3

Coventry: Michelin plant at, 199

Coventry, HMS, 465

Cowles, Fleur, 172

Cradock, Sir Percy, 5

Crazy Horse Saloon (Paris), 261

Creasey, Lieut.-General Sir Timothy, 274

Cripps, Sir Stafford, 69, 259

Croizat, Dr, 341

Crosland, Anthony, 109–10, 121, 133–4, 309; death, 138n, 140

Crosland, Susan, 273

Crossman, Richard H.S., 70, 366

Crosthwaite, Sir Moore, 149

Cryer, Robert, 193

Cuban missiles crisis, 4

Cutler, Lloyd, 331, 339, 357

Cyrankiewicz, Jozef, 19

Czechoslovakia: invaded (1969), 14–18, 21–2, 32

Daily Mail, 98

Dalton, Hugh, 110

Dalyell, Tam, 455

Daninos, Pierre, 161

Darquier de Pellepoix (Vichy minister), 227

Dart, Justin, 380

Daudy, Philippe, 224–5

Daume, Willy, 39
Davenport, Nicholas, 238
David-Weill, Hélène, 182, 222, 332
David-Weill, Michel, 182n, 235
Davies, Howard, 103, 111, 124–5, 128, 153
Day, (Sir) Robin, 84
de la Haye Jousslin, Bertrand and Laure, 188–9, 255
Dearing, Ronald, 176
Death on the Nile (La Mort sur Le Nil; film), 227
Deaver, Carolyn, 416, 426, 449, 483
Deaver, Michael, 375, 395, 414, 426, 434, 449, 478, 483
Debré, Michel, 125
Deferre, Madame Gaston, 220
Dell, Edmund, 133, 175–7, 194
Deniau, Frédérique, 222
Dépêche du Midi, 105
Detroit, 330
Deutsch, Armand, 379
Deutsch, Mrs Armand, 380
Deux Magots (Paris restaurant), 224
Devonshire, Andrew Cavendish, 11th Duke of, 204
Devonshire, Deborah, Duchess of, 203
Diana, Princess of Wales (*formerly* Lady Diana Spencer), 395, 409, 412, 440
Dickerson, Wyatt, 379–80
Dickie, John, 98
Dillon, Douglas, 426
Dillon, Phyllis (Mrs Douglas Dillon), 311
Diocletian, Roman Emperor, 178
Dobrynin, Anatoly, 310, 431
Dodson, Sir Derek, 331
Dominik, Philippe Michel, 193
Donaldson, Frances, Lady: *Edward VIII*, 137
Donlon, Sean, 355
Donoughue, Bernard, Baron, 70
Dorneywood (house), 67
Douglas-Home, Sir Alec (*later* Baron Home of the Hirsel): as Foreign Secretary, 23; meets U Thant, 24; visit to Bonn, 37; Wilson on, 70; gives dog to Scheel, 116; on confidential documents, 271; Butler on, 311
Douglas-Home, William: *The Kingfisher*, 328, 330
Dreyfus, Pierre, 182
Drogheda, Alexandra, Countess of (*née* Henderson; NH's daughter): visits

Poland, 26–7; chauffeurs father from Chequers, 67; in Paris, 102; and father's remarks on garden exhibition, 192; engagement, 219; operation for cyst, 226, 244; wedding, 226, 239–42; on visit to Rothschild's, 252; celebrates NH's appointment to Washington, 270; telephones parents in USA, 277; in USA, 335; visits Ann Fleming, 405; entertains in London, 437
Drogheda, Derry Moore, 12th Earl of (*formerly* Viscount Moore): wedding, 226; on visit to Rothschild's, 252–3; on NH's departure from Paris, 261; in USA, 332, 335, 399; first marriage, 347; visits Ann Fleming, 405; entertains in London, 437
Drogheda, Garrett Moore, 11th Earl of, 239–40, 348
Drogheda, Joan, Countess of, 240, 252, 348
Drouas, Baronne, 225
Druon, Maurice, 178–9, 237
Dubček, Alexander, 17
Duffey, Joe, 293n
Dulles, John Foster, 206
Dumoncel, Maurice, 161, 178
Duncan, Sir Val (John Norman Valette), 126
Dunlop company, 200
Dunn, Mary, 161
Düsseldorf, 82

Eagleburger, Lawrence, 477, 481–2
East Germany (German Democratic Republic): relations with West Germany, 39
Eastern Europe: proposed British dialogue with, 21; West German policy on, 21, 26, 33, 38, 39, 89; Callaghan's policy on, 65
Echos, Les (French newspaper), 193, 219
Economist: publishes NH's leaked despatch, 271–2; publishes NH's account of Falklands War negotiations, 442n, 443
Eden, Anthony (*later* 1st Earl of Avon), 4
Edinburgh: Heinemann visits, 50
Edward VII, King, 175
Ehrlichman, John, 323
Eisenhower, Dwight D., 4, 289, 324, 329, 440

El Salvador, 437, 448, 462–3
Elaine's (New York restaurant), 333–4
Eliot, T.S., 179
Elizabeth I, Queen, 119
Elizabeth II, Queen: and President Heinemann's state visit, 45–7, 49–51; presents dog to Giscard, 116–18, 122–3; and Giscard's state visit, 120–2; refers to Concorde in speech, 120–1; entertains Giscard on visit to Callaghan, 144; Jubilee (1978), 179; and NH's appointment to Washington, 270, 272–3; at Syon House party, 405; and Reagan's visit, 434–6, 463; and palace intruder, 484; proposed visit to California, 485
Elizabeth, Queen Mother: at Windsor state banquet, 48; visits Paris, 129–32, 186, 472; and Reagan visit, 472
Emminger, Otmar, 53–4, 80
Enders, Thomas, 448, 457, 556
English Chamber Orchestra, 105–6
English Speaking Union, 299, 384, 402, 440
Ennals, David, Baron, 83
European Commission: Jenkins's Presidency, 108
European Community: and ministerial conferences, 5; British entry, 26, 37; Labour seeks to renegotiate British membership, 59–64, 66, 68, 71–3, 94; attitude to USA, 64; British referendum on, 81, 86–8, 94; Michelin's misgivings on, 199; effect on work of embassies, 243; UK budget contributions, 305, 318, 345; and Soviet invasion of Afghanistan, 325; and Iran sanctions, 340–1; and Sinai force, 418
European Council: Giscard develops, 93; 1978 Copenhagen meeting, 214
European Monetary System (EMS), 202, 209, 213–15, 218, 220, 230, 233, 236–7, 248, 305
European Parliament: direct elections to, 93, 125, 139, 235; powers, 235
European Unit (Committee of Permanent Under-Secretaries), 51
European Youth Orchestra, 147–9
Evans, Harold, 437
Evans, James, 391
Evans, Rosemary, 391
Evans, Rowland, 292
Evening News (London), 336

Evening Standard, 260
exchange rate mechanism (European), 202n
Express, L' (newspaper), 183, 227

Fagan, Michael, 484
Fairbanks, Douglas, Jr., 404, 424
Fairholt Street (London), 94
Falkender, Marcia Williams, Baroness, 68, 72
Falkland Islands: Argentinians invade, 451–2; sovereignty, 451, 469; trusteeship proposed, 454; Foreign Office policy on, 459; long-term plans for, 468–9, 480; land-mines in, 480
Falklands War, 1982: Thatcher gives account of, 9, 444; diplomatic negotiations over, 442–59, 474–5; and US policy, 442–8, 450–3, 459, 462–4, 466–7, 468n, 475, 481–2; military operations, 460, 464–5, 476–7; Thatcher's resolution on, 461–2
Fall, Sir Brian, 450
Faucigny-Lucinge, Jean-Louis ('Johnny'), Prince, 180, 242
Faure, Edgar, 178–9, 230–1
Faure, M. & Mme Hubert, 360
Fenn, Sir Nicholas, 259, 360
Fenwick, Millicent, 376–7
Feray, Thierry and Jean (brothers), 161
Fermor, Patrick Leigh, 14
Fermoy, Ruth, Lady, 131
Financial Times, 180, 192
Firyal, Princess, of Jordan, 240
Fleming, Ann, 314, 405–6
Fletcher, Air Chief Marshal Sir Peter, 158–9, 210
Fleury, Château de, 231
Foley, Thomas, 310
Fontainebleau (France), 194
Fontanne, Lynn, 372
Foot, Michael, 79, 474
Ford, Anna, 305n, 437
Foreign Policy Association (New York), 319, 342, 413
Foreign Press Association, 250
Fortescue, Adrian, 293
Foster, Sir John, 229
Four Power negotiations, 1972, 41
Fox, James, 224
France: economic prosperity, 93, 153; NH appointed Ambassador to, 93; 1978 elections, 152–5, 160;

France – *cont*
  anti-semitisim in, 157, 227; attitude
    to President, 216–17; Ambassadorial
    role in, 287
Franco, General Francisco, 13
Franco-British Council, 146, 225, 306
Franco-UK Summit (1978), 235
François-Poncet, Jean, 145–6, 188, 208,
  216, 220, 238, 254, 362
François-Poncet, Marie-Thérèse, 224,
  251
Frank, Paul, 63
Franks, Oliver, Baron, 353
Fraser, Lady Antonia (*later* Pinter), 15n,
  18, 305
Fraser, Sir Hugh, 18
Freedman, Lawrence, 456
Fretwell, Sir John, 31, 248, 361, 419
Fretwell, Mary, Lady, 31n
Friedman, Milton, 363
Friendly, Alfred and Pie, 330
Friends of Ireland (US Congress), 404
Fritchey, Clayton, 292, 330, 354, 366,
  401–2, 426
Fritchey, Polly, 292n, 301, 310, 330,
  354, 366, 401, 426
Froment-Meurice, Henri, 187, 226–7
Fürstenberg, Princess Ira, 220–1, 297,
  306

Gablentz, Otto von der, 64
Gaitskell, Hugh, 70
Galbraith, John Kenneth, 363
Galtieri, General Leopoldo Fortuno,
  445, 448–9
Galway, James, 372
Ganay, Jean-Louis de, 193n, 231–2, 256
Ganay, Philippine de, 100, 193, 231,
  256, 260
Gandhi, Indira, 326–7
Garaud, Marie-France, 180
Garbo, Greta, 229
Garnett, Angelica, 335
Garrett, Stephen, 441–2
Garrick Club (London), 459
Gaulle, Charles de, 81, 85, 107, 120,
  197, 201, 205, 210, 370, 434
Gaulle, Philippe de, 180
Gavshon, Arthur, 455
Gay, Michèle, 122–3
Genscher, Hans-Dietrich: visits Wilson,
  67, 73–4
George V, King, 168
Gérard, Chez (Paris bistro), 157

Getty Museum (Malibu) and Trust,
  441–2
Getty, Paul, 441
Geyr, Carlotta, 84
Gierek, Edward, 32–3, 256
Gilliat, Sir Martin, 129–30, 132
Gillmore, Sir David, 479
Gilmour, Lady Caroline, 83, 269n,
  328–9
Gilmour, Sir Ian, 229, 269, 305, 328–9
Giovanni (Embassy butler, Paris), 95,
  215–16, 234
Giraud, André, 164–6, 233
Giroud, Françoise, 106, 148, 150, 155,
  217, 224, 242
Giscard, Edmond (Valéry's father), 256
Giscard, May (Valéry's mother), 256
Giscard d'Estaing, Anne-Aymone, 120,
  134, 147, 257
Giscard d'Estaing, Valéry: Presidency of
  France and policies, 93–4; relations
  with Callaghan, 94, 97–8, 214, 235–
  6; relations with Schmidt, 94, 214,
  235, 250; NH presents credentials to,
  98; anti-British views, 100–2, 107–8;
  qualities and style, 101–2, 130;
  approves Jenkins's appointment to
  European Presidency, 109; state visit
  to Britain, 115–124, 132, 235; given
  dog by Queen, 116–18, 122–3, 135,
  257; and award of honours, 119; on
  France's economic superiority, 132,
  225; *Private Eye* on, 144; visits
  Callaghan at Chequers, 144–7, 188,
  220; daughter's marriage, 147; and
  1978 French election result, 154–5;
  retires Coucel, 163; protected by
  officials, 168; term of office, 180;
  intervention in Africa, 182, 185; and
  airbus project, 188, 211, 215–16;
  Auvergne origins, 195–6; on threat to
  living standards, 195; EMS proposals,
  202, 209, 213–15, 237; at 14 July
  parade, 210; and office of President,
  217–18; and 1978 Franco-UK
  summit, 235; farewell lunch for NH,
  255–8; relations with Thatcher, 338;
  meets Brezhnev in Warsaw, 341
Gladstone, William Ewart, 254
Gladwyn, Gladwyn Jebb, Baron, 190,
  267
Glenn, John, 379
Glyn, Elinor, 435
Goldschmidt, Betrand, 229

Gomulka, Wladislaw, 13, 15, 20, 32
Goodman, Arnold, Baron, 314
Goose Green, Falkland Islands, 465
Gorbachev, Mikhail, 4
Gordon-Lennox, Mary (Lady Nicholas),
    116n
Gordon-Lennox, Lord Nicholas, 116,
    119, 185, 260–1
Gosling, Miss (secretarial assistant), 130
Goulandris, Basil, 224
Graber, Ted, 396
Grace, Princess of Monaco, 169–73
Grafton, Fortune, Duchess of, 122, 131
Grafton, Hugh Denis Charles FitzRoy,
    11th Duke of, 131
Graham, Donald, 374n, 376, 426
Graham, Katharine (Kay): visits Paris,
    250–1; and Mathias, 279; social
    confidence, 280; on Joe Alsop, 301,
    358; plays tennis with NH, 330, 333,
    400; dines with NH, 332, 339, 399,
    449; and daughter Lally, 333–4;
    watches Nixon TV interview, 337; at
    Macmillan dinner, 368; entertains
    Reagans, 372–6, 390, 425–30; at
    Annenberg lunch for Reagans, 381;
    at Isaiah Berlin dinner, 401
Graham, Mary, 374, 376, 426
Grall, Alex, 106, 217, 242
Grant, Cary, 396
Grant, Duncan: visit to Paris, 161–2
Gray, Charles, 439
Greenfield, Meg, 365, 426
Greenwood, Allen, 158–9, 210
Gregory-Hood, Peter, 192
Grenoble (France), 246
Grierson, Ronald, 306, 354, 360
Griffith, Thomas, 289, 342
Grigg, John, 228–9
Grigg, Patsy, 228n
Grimond, Jo (later Baron), 83–4, 303
Gromyko, Andrei Andreevich, 480, 482
Groszkowski, Professor, 16
Guardian (newspaper): Mary Wilson
    reviews in, 77
Guest, Lily, 348
Guichard, Olivier, 125
Guiringaud, Claude de, 186
Guiringaud, Louis de, 138, 140–1, 148,
    154, 186, 194, 230
Guizot, François Pierre Guillaume, 8
Gulf see Persian Gulf
Gulf Oil (company), 419
Gulf States, 362

Gunzburg, Alain, 368
Gunzburg, Minda, 368, 416
Gymnich, Schloss (Germany), 53–5,
    72–3

Haig, Alexander: Mary meets, 384; and
    Mexico global summit, 386; Prince
    Charles meets, 397; insecure position,
    407; Middle East policy, 408, 412–
    13, 433; Carrington meets in New
    York, 412–13; satirised at Embassy
    party, 416–17; promotes
    multinational Sinai force, 418–20;
    relations with Carrington, 418, 421,
    433; manner of speech, 430–1, 433,
    462, 466; and US sanctions on USSR,
    431; Weinberger and, 433; and
    Reagan's visit to Britain, 434, 471;
    leaked remarks, 437; seeks negotiated
    settlement in Falklands War, 444–56,
    462, 464–8, 471, 474, 481; on
    Thatcher, 446–7, 475; and
    Argentinian threat to break off
    relations with USA, 464; appeals to
    Thatcher for magnanimity, 469; and
    Earl Haig, 472; meets Pym, 472; on
    UN Resolution 508, 473–4; and
    future of Falklands, 476; and
    Thatcher's 1982 visit to USA, 477–
    80; bad relations with Deaver, 478;
    plays tennis with NH, 478, 481; and
    US export ban on USSR, 479–80, 482;
    resignation, 480–2; qualities, 482; at
    Bohemian Grove, 486
Hailsham, Quintin McGarel Hogg,
    Baron, 72
Haines, Joseph, 70–1, 75, 78
Haldeman, Bob, 323
Hale, Edmund, 383
Hall, Sir Peter, 66
Hambleden, Patricia, Dowager
    Viscountess, 130
Hambro, Robin, 396
Hannay, Sir David, 438
Hardy-Roberts, Brigadier Sir Geoffrey,
    46
Hargrove, Charles, 256
Harlech, David Ormsby-Gore, 5th
    Baron, 207, 271
Harmel, Pierre: report on NATO, 474
Harriman, Averell, 280, 296, 303, 339,
    368, 371
Harriman, Pamela, 280–1, 314, 339,
    368–9

Harrison, Benjamin, 289n
Harrison, Rex, 328–30
Hart, Gary and Lee, 374
Hart, Dame Judith (*later* Baroness), 76
Hart, Kitty Carlisle, 311–12, 426
Hartford, Connecticut, 439
Hartington, Andrew ('Stoker'),
  Marquess of, and Amanda,
  Marchioness of, 290
Hartman, Arthur, 180
Hartman, Donna, 328
Hartwell, Lady Pamela, 251, 265, 306,
  366
Hase, Karl-Günther von, 47, 64
Hastings, Max, 455
Hasty Heart, The (film), 427n
Hawk contract, 434
Hay, Roy, 193
Haydon, Sir Robin, 275
Haye Jousslin, Bertrand and Laure de la
  see de la Haye Jousslin, B. and L.
Hayward, Max, 292
Healey, Dennis (*later* Baron): on NH's
  politics at Oxford, 78; and succession
  to Wilson, 99; view of office and
  position, 99–100; at 1976
  Rambouillet summit, 133; and
  Gordon Richardson, 168; at 1978
  Franco-UK summit, 236–7; in
  Washington, 302, 304–5; Reagan
  mistakes for Oliver Wright, 429n; on
  Falklands War, 445
Heath, (Sir) Edward: 1970 government,
  24; meets Brandt, 39–40, 51–8, 59,
  74, 144, 146; sailing, 40; enthusiasm
  for Europe, 59–60, 85; loses 1974
  election, 59n; brought down by
  unions, 72; lacks small talk, 74; on
  Arab money, 75; at Königswinter
  Conference, 83–5; visits to Paris,
  102–3, 194, 250–1; conducts
  European Youth Orchestra, 147–9;
  puts on weight, 149; on threat to
  living standards, 195; at Alexandra's
  wedding, 240–2; and NH's
  appointment to Washington, 268;
  qualities, 296; visit to Washington,
  370; post-power frustration, 371
Heinemann, Gustav W.: state visit to
  Britain, 45, 47–51, 471
Heinemann, Hilda, 47, 450
Heinz, Drue, 296, 331, 339, 360, 368,
  449, 452
Heinz, Jack, 296, 331, 339, 368, 452

Helms, Jesse, 378
Helms, Richard, 347, 426–7
Helsinki Conference (on security and co-
  operation in Europe), 58
Henderson, Alexandra (NH's daughter)
  see Drogheda, Alexandra, Countess
  of
Henderson, Faith, Lady (NH's mother):
  death, 269
Henderson, Mary, Lady: meets Reagan,
  7, 396; in Poland, 14, 18, 22; and Sue
  Ryder, 29; meets Gierek, 33; and
  decoration of Ambassador's house in
  Berlin, 42; at Windsor Castle, 45–6,
  48, 473; and decoration of Bonn
  Embassy, 52; in Bonn, 55, 70; Wilson
  thanks for hospitality, 71; makes
  fancy head-dress for NH, 74; and
  1975 Königswinter Conference, 83–
  4; at Paris Embassy, 96, 109, 251;
  entertains at Paris Embassy, 102,
  127–8, 179–80, 215–16, 255, 258; on
  provincial tours in France, 104, 106;
  locked out of Paris Embassy, 113–15;
  at Giscard's state visit, 119, 121; visits
  Duchess of Windsor, 135; and
  Thatcher, 142–3; at Aga Khan's
  dinner, 156; at Brasserie Lipp, 160;
  flower arrangements, 169, 171–2,
  240; and Rainiers, 169–72; on NH's
  wine expertise, 170; on turfing of
  Paris Embassy garden, 191; and Paris
  garden shrubs, 192; at Broglie ball,
  195; and Alexandra's engagement,
  219; and Alexandra's wedding, 226,
  239–40, 242; at Niarchos party, 230;
  and Lefort, 234; defends Macmillan
  ballet, 235; and Alexandra's operatio,
  244; on visit to Rothschild's, 252; and
  parting celebrations in Paris, 261; and
  announcement of NH's appointment
  to Washington, 270; leaves for
  Washington, 275; at White House,
  282, 396, 487; decorates Washington
  Embassy, 291; pneumonia in USA,
  291–2, 295, 298; in Dallas, 303; and
  Washington social life, 308, 339,
  380–1, 384, 420; in New York, 312,
  335; entertaining in Washington,
  318, 332, 369, 389–90, 412; and
  Lightfoot, 330; and influence of
  Stowe, 331; Leonard Cheshire and,
  348, 350; and Washington Embassy
  black staff, 353–4; and Kay Graham's

Henderson, Mary, Lady – *cont*
party for Reagans, 374; on Salt Lake City art, 392; greets Prince Charles, 395; and Nancy Reagan, 415; on NH's television appearance, 423; complimented by stranger, 425; in Washington club for diplomats' wives, 431; and Reagan's horse-ride on visit to Windsor, 435; and White House farewell dinner, 483; Nancy Reagan's fondness for, 487; impact of diplomatic life on, 489
Henderson, Sir Hubert (NH's father), 285–6
Henderson, Sir Nevile, 4
Henderson, Sir Nicholas: keeps diary, 5–6; dog, 14–15, 57, 95; ill with TB, 23–4, 37; plays table tennis against Chinese in Warsaw, 30–2; at fancy head-dress party, 74; posted to Paris, 93–6; makes jokes in speeches, 103; provincial tours and visits in France, 104, 110–11; locked out of Paris Embassy, 113–15; Paris valedictory despatch, 245, 260, 270–3, 293; appointed to Washington, 266–9; speechmaking in USA, 287–90, 297, 342, 384, 439–40; bronchitis, 289; exhausted by US duties, 302; tennis playing, 330, 333, 400, 414, 478, 481; influence of Stowe on 331; arteriogram, 359; decides on leaving Washington, 406; on political jokes and satire, 415–17; US television appearances, 421–5, 451–3; 1982 birthday party, 448–9; farewell dinner at White House, 483–8; leaves Washington and retires, 489
Henrion, Rosamée, 149
Hepburn, Audrey, 396
Herald Tribune, 139
Hertford Bridge Hospital (Paris), 241, 261, 472
Herwarth, Johann von, 50, 65
Heseltine, Michael, 358
Hibbert, Reginald Albert, 41, 43, 70
Hicks, David, 221
Hillenbrand, Martin, 42
Hillier, Harold, 191–3
Historia (magazine), 178
Hitler, Adolf, 3–4, 18
Hobbes, Thomas, 212
Hofmann, Harald, 47
Holbrooke, Richard, 338

Home of the Hirsel, Alec, Baron *see* Douglas-Home, Sir Alec
Hooper, Sir Robin, 271
Hope, Bob, 321, 323
Hope, Dolores, 323
Hopkins, Harry, 401
Hopkins, Joan, 128
Hormuz, Gulf of, 362
Hot Springs, Virginia, 295, 364
Houngbedji, Christoph, 215
House, Karen, 354, 449
House of Representatives Armed Services Committee, 278
Howe, Elspeth, Lady, 362
Howe, Sir Geoffrey (*later* Baron), 331, 362–3, 459, 469
Howell, David, 298
Howell, Denis, Baron, 176
Hoyer Millar, Sir Frederick (Derick), 212
Hu Yaobang, 310
Hufstedler, Shirley, 354, 357
Hughes, Howard, 197
Hugo, Victor, 124
Hume, John, 275
Hungary: 1956 rising, 21
Hunt, Sir John, 51, 57–8, 78, 144
Hunt, Pierre, 225
Hurrell, Anthony Gerald, 129
Husak, Gustav, 20
Hussey, Lady Susan, 48, 50, 122, 471–2
Hylton, Elizabeth, 425

India: and Western bloc, 326
inflation, 178
Institut Lane-Langevin, Grenoble, 246–7
International League for Animal Rights, 219
International Monetary Fund conference, Washington, 1981, 415
IRA *see* Irish Republican Army
Iran: US Embassy hostages in, 286, 310, 312–13, 315–16, 321, 332, 383, 445, 451; failed US attempt to rescue hostages, 336, 339; war with Iraq, 361–4
Iran, Shah of *see* Shah of Iran
Iranian Embassy, London: SAS raid on, 349, 375
Iraq: war with Iran, 361–4
Ireland: US attitude to, 275, 281–4, 294, 309–10, 395, 397, 402, 408, 423

Irish Republican Army (IRA): murder Sykes, 254; Conor Cruise O'Brien opposes, 273; US support for, 284, 335, 360–1, 398, 404; and hunger strikes, 397–8, 423; campaign in New York, 402; arms seized in USA, 479; London bombings, 484

Isherwood, Christopher, 42

Islamabad: US Embassy invaded, 312

Islamic revivalism, 312–13

Israel: and Lebanon, 413, 471, 473, 484; US attitude to, 418–19, 433–4, 485; and Sinai, 461n

Jablonna Conferences (Anglo-Polish), 19

Jacques (chauffeur), 169

James, Clive, 357

James, Sir Kenneth, 143, 149, 163, 224, 234

James, Phyllis Dorothy (Mrs C.B. White; later Baroness), 351

Japan: trade surplus, 146; US relations with, 408

Jarvis, Frederick Frank, 166

Javits, Jacob, 279

Javits, Marion Ann, 297

Jay, Peter, 8, 267–8, 285, 289, 291

Jefferson, Thomas, 484

Jellicoe, George, 2nd Earl, 247, 279

Jenkins, Dame Jennifer, 83–4, 109, 183

Jenkins, Peter, 283n, 346

Jenkins, Roy (later Baron Jenkins of Hillhead): on Adenauer's visit to Macmillan, 49; at Königswinter Conference, 83–4; Giscard's respect for, 98; and succession to Wilson, 99, 109; Presidency of European Commission, 108–10, 140; visits to Paris, 108, 183, 202; not offered Foreign Secretaryship, 109–10; on Crosland, 121; and Owen, 139–41; European diary 183; praises Guiringaud, 186; and EMS, 202, 209; on Macmillan, 207; on NH's appointment to Washington, 267; and Thatcher's view of EC budget payments, 305; on Reagan's speech to Parliament, 473

Jenkins, Simon, 443, 455

Jobert, Michel, 63, 85

John Paul II, Pope, 305

Johnson, Marigold, 306

Johnson, Paul, 345–6

Johnson, Samuel, 5

Johnston, Lieut.-Col. John, 120, 436

Jones, Jack, 76, 166

Jones, Mr and Mrs Reginald, 364

Jordan, Hamilton, 281, 339

Joseph, Sir Keith (later Baron), 273, 343–6

Jousslin see de la Haye Jousslin

Joxe, Louis, 124

Joyce, Robert and Jane, 292

Juan Carlos I, King of Spain, 130

Jürgens, Curt, 220–1

Karamanlis, Konstantinos, 224

Karol (driver, Poland), 22–3

Katowice, Poland, 33

Kaufmann (of New Orleans), 341

Kaye, Danny, 308

Kee, Cynthia, 269, 273

Kee, Robert: on Crosland, 110; at Alexandra's wedding, 240; NH dines with, 273, 459; at Stowe, 331; at Moores' dinner party, 437; on Falklands War, 459

Keeble, Curtis, 190

Keith, Sir Kenneth (later Baron), 159, 164, 166, 186–7, 208

Kennedy Center, New York: 1980 gala, 372

Kennedy, Edward, 273, 284, 294, 300, 313, 324

Kennedy, Jacqueline (later Onassis), 356

Kennedy, John F., 4, 207, 356

Kennedy, Ludovic and Moira, 151

Kenny, Sir Anthony, 332

Kent, Prince Edward, Duke, and Katharine, Duchess of, 405

Keynes, John Maynard, Baron, 285, 294

Khrushchev, Nikita S., 4, 356, 370

Kiel (Germany), 40, 67

King, William Lyon Mackenzie, 3

Kirkland, Irena, 299, 309, 358, 375

Kirkland, Lane, 299, 358–9

Kirkpatrick, Jeane: as Ambassador to UN, 381, 407, 472; Carrington meets in New York, 412; and Falklands War, 445, 451–2, 463, 468n, 471, 481

Kissinger, Henry: secret dealings with USSR, 41–2; and Jobert, 63; congratulates Callaghan on speech, 97; at Paris Queen's Birthday Party, 180; on difficulty of telephoning British Embassy, 278; status and position, 280; on Iraqi belief in

Kissinger, Henry – *cont*
  Washington coup, 281; and NH in
  Washington, 292, 358; on Nixon,
  306, 338; on Rhodesia, 309; NH
  entertains, 331; supports Carter's
  plan to free Iran hostages, 336;
  watches Nixon TV interview, 337;
  confidence, 338; criticises Carter's
  foreign policy, 358–9; at Macmillan
  dinner, 368; Weidenfeld on, 371; and
  Kay Graham's party for Reagans,
  373–4; excluded from Reagan's inner
  council, 375–6, 379, 382; Isaiah
  Berlin and, 401; and White House
  foreign policy decision-making,
  434n, 492; shuttle diplomacy, 481n;
  at Bohemian Grove, 486; *White
  House Years*, 305–6, 309, 324
Kissinger, Nancy, 292, 297, 309, 358,
  360, 375
Kitson, Sir Timothy, 39
Knickerbocker Club (New York), 306,
  335, 342, 360
Knight, Andrew, 268–9, 416
Knight, Sir Arthur, 249
Knox, John, 50
Koch, Edward Irving, 402
Königswinter Conference, 65, 79, 82–5,
  1974, 1975

Laboulaye, Antoinette de, 374
Laboulaye, François de, 374n
Labour Party: 1974 government, 59n,
  61–2; coolness on Europe, 59–66, 68,
  71–3; attitude to trade unions, 72;
  Schmidt attends 1974 conference,
  75–7; and airbus project, 211
Labouret, Vincent, 193
Lafite, Château, 252
Lambton, Belinda, Viscountess, 331
La Rochefoucauld, Duchesse de, 210
Larosière, Jacques de, 182, 304
Las Vegas, 391–2
Laughton, Charles, 308
Laval, Pierre: origins, 195–6
Lawford, Pat, 297
Lawson, Nigel, Baron, 302, 304
Laxalt, Paul, 414
Le Theule, Joël, 163, 175–6, 211, 215–
  16
Leathes, General Reginald, 245
Lebanon, 413, 452, 471, 473, 477, 484
Lee Kuan Yew, 486
Lefort, Bernard, 234

Lei Yang, 30
Len Aw Kay, 30
Leonetti, Madame (of Chez Gérard),
  157
Leppard, Raymond, 105
Lever, Diane, Lady, 87
Lever, Harold, Baron, 86–7, 257
Lever, Jeremy, 227
Lewin, Admiral of the Fleet Terence,
  Baron, 460
Leyland, Norman, 346
Libya, 429
Lightfoot, John, 329–30, 389
Ligne, Princesse de, 232
Lille: NH visits, 110–11
Linwood motor-car plant, 211
Lipp, Brasserie (Paris), 106, 160, 217,
  223–4, 232
Llewellyn, Sir John, 248
Lloyd, Eliza: marriage to Derry Moore,
  347n
Lloyd, Selwyn (*later* Baron Selwyn-
  Lloyd), 50
Lloyd George, David, 1st Earl, 5
Lodz (Poland), 22–3
Lon Nol, Marshal, 25n
London Symphony Orchestra, 367
Londonderry, 275
Longford, Elizabeth, Countess of, 15n,
  18, 306; at son Michael's Washington
  wedding, 337
Longford, Francis Aungier Pakenham,
  7th Earl of, 15n, 240, 306, 337, 370–
  1, 486
Lopez Portillo, José, 386
Los Angeles, 441
Los Angeles Times, 441
Lothian, Philip Henry Kerr, 11th
  Marquess of, 296
Louis, John and Josephine, 396, 404
Louis XIV, King of France, 216
Louvre, Magasin du (Paris), 225
Luns, Josef, 472
Lusaka: conference of non-aligned
  nations (1970), 25; Commonwealth
  Conference (1979), 286, 296, 317
Lyons, Humbert de, 256
Lyttle, John, 80

McCoy, Peter, 416–17
McDermott, Christa, 193n
McDermott, Patrick, 193
McFadzean, Frank, Baron, 208
McFarlane, Robert, 438

MacGinnis, Francis, 111–12
Macgougan, John, 166
McGovern, George, 359
McHenry, Donald F., 360
Mackintosh, John, 84
Maclean, Alan, 152, 205, 355–6
Maclean, Sir Fitzroy, 143, 373
Maclean, Robin (née Empson), 152n
McMahon, Sir Christopher (Kit), 230
McManus, Father, 335
Macmillan, Alexander, 2nd Earl of
    Stockton, 204, 207
Macmillan, Lady Dorothy, 143, 203,
    356
Macmillan, Harold (later 1st Earl of
    Stockton), 4, 49, 355–6; visit to Paris,
    203–7; visit to Washington, 367–71;
    advice on conduct of Falklands War,
    459–60
Macmillan, Kenneth, 233–4
McNamara, Robert: friendship with
    NH in USA, 301–2, 304, 354, 358–
    9; at Kay Graham's parties for
    Reagans, 375, 426; meets Isaiah
    Berlin, 401
McPherson, Harry, 339
Madrid: NH leaves post in, 13
Maire, Edmond, 167
Maitland, Sir Donald, 55, 243, 258
Makins, Roger see Sherfield, 1st Baron
Mallet, Robert, 6, 253
Mao Zedong, 310
Marcel (Paris Embassy gardener) see
    Pihée, Marcel
Margaret, Princess: at Windsor, 46;
    meets Giscard on visit to Britain, 119–
    20, 122; Ludovic Kennedy on, 151;
    and Townsend, 202; in Chicago, 299–
    300; Barbara Walters requests
    interview with, 306; at Syon House
    party, 405
Marin, Jean (i.e. Yves Morvan), 160
Marshall Plan, 65
Marshall Scholarships, 360
Marx, Groucho, 62
Mary, Queen of George V, 168
Mason, Raymond, 343
Massigli, Odette, 204n, 239
Massigli, René, 204, 206
Mathias, Charles, 279, 293, 332
Matthews, Charles, 279, 293, 332
Matthews, Thomas S., 141, 342
Maudling, Reginald, 124–6
Maugham, William Somerset, 173

Mauroy, Pierre, 110
Maze prison (N. Ireland), 274–5
Meany, George, 298–9
Meany, Irena, 299
Mecca: Grand Mosque occupied, 312
Meese, Edwin, 374–5, 390, 395, 399,
    401, 474, 486
Meese, Ursula, 400
Meletios, Monseigneur, 226, 228
Mellon, Paul, 343, 347, 396
Mellon, Rachel (Bunny), 343, 347–8,
    396
Mendès-France, Pierre, 102, 124,
    181–3
Mentzelopoulou, M. & Mme, 181, 230
Menuhin, Yehudi, Baron, 102–3, 432–3
Mérillon, Jean-Marie, 256
Mexico, 386
Meyer, Montague, 172–3
Michel (Paris Embassy security officer),
    251
Michelin, François: NH visits, 195–202
Middle East: US policy on, 325, 327,
    362–5, 408, 412–13, 421, 433–4,
    491–2
Middleburg, Virginia, 347
Middleton, Drew, 368
Middleton, Suzanne, 329
Midland Bank, 237
Milchsack, Dame Lilo, 65n, 83
Miller, Sir John, 435, 472
Miller, William, 362
Minimum Selling Price (MSP; oil), 97
Minneapolis, 422
Misérables, Les (club), 124, 182, 206
Mitchell, Sir Derek, 52–5, 99
Mitchell, John, 323
Mitford, Nancy, 160n, 204n, 239n
Mitterrand, François, 160, 185, 401
Mitterrand, Giselle, 159–60
Mitterrand, General Jacques, 159–60,
    187–8
Modiano, Colette, 161
Monaco, 169–74
Mondale, Walter Frederick, 140, 294,
    339, 351
Monde, Le (newspaper), 148, 163
Monetary Compensation Amounts
    (MACS), 248
Monnet, Jean: funeral, 257
Montagne, La (newspaper), 199, 201
Monte Carlo, 169–74
Montgomery, Field Marshal Bernard
    Law, 1st Viscount, 193n, 329

Moore, Alexandra, Viscountess *see* Drogheda, Alexandra, Countess of
Moore, Derry, Viscount *see* Drogheda, 12th Earl of
Moore, Sir Philip (*later* Baron), 471
Moorhead, William and Lucy, 292
Morgan, Aubrey, 352–3
Morgan, Connie (*née* Morrow), 353
Morgan, Janet (*later* Lady Balfour of Burleigh), 433
Mormons, 392–3
Morning Cloud (yacht), 40
Morrell, Lady Ottoline, 161
Mortimer, Raymond, 351
Mouchy, Duchesse Douairiére de, 193
Mouchy, Joan, Duchesse de (*née* Dillon), 439n
Mouchy, Philippe Noailles, Duc de, 439
Mountbatten, Admiral of the Fleet Louis, 1st Earl, 237, 300
Moyne, Walter Guinness, 1st Baron, 206
Moynihan, Daniel Patrick, 273, 294, 381
Mudd, Roger, 394
Muddle, Rod, 409
Muldoon, Robert, 294
Murdoch, Rupert, 437
Murray, Lionel (Len), Baron, 82, 166–7, 276
Muscat and Oman *see* Oman
Muskie, Edmund, 338–9, 342, 346, 359–62, 364–5, 370
Mutual Balanced Force Reduction talks, 58

Namibia, 185, 193
National Economic Development Council (Neddy), 153
National Gallery, Washington, 343
National Press Club, Washington, 278, 288, 290
National Security Council (USA), 479, 482
NATO *see* North Atlantic Treaty Organisation
Neave, Airey, 284, 390
Nelson, Philip, 155, 187, 193, 198–201, 239, 245–6
Nerina, Nadia, 234
New Orleans, 340–1
New York, 302, 306, 332–5, 342, 359–60, 384, 402, 412–13, 439
New York Times, 281, 418–19, 432, 438
New York Tribune, 272

Niarchos, Constantine, 367
Niarchos, Stavros, 220, 230–1, 306
Nichols, Mike, 371, 425, 429
Nicolson, Sir Harold, 289
Nicolson, Nigel: *Portrait of a Marriage*, 351
Nimitz, USS, 355, 394
Niven, David, 227, 396, 429, 485
Nixon, Richard M.: appoints Kissinger, 41n; Pedriel defends, 225; Longford on, 306; visits Annenbergs, 323–5; TV interview, 337–8
Noailles, Charles de, 188n, 189
Noraid, 404
Norfolk, Virginia, 355
North Atlantic Treaty Organisation (NATO): British attitude to, 26, 90, 154; Callaghan on, 65; and US policy on Middle East, 326
Northern Ireland: NH visits, 274–5; and UK–US relations, 282, 309, 395, 397, 408, 423
Nott, Sir John, 400, 446, 450, 461–3
Nouvel Observateur (newspaper), 250
Nureyev, Rudolph, 222

Oak Ridge (USA), 247
O'Brien, Conor Cruise, 173, 294
Observer (newspaper), 238, 272, 345
Oder-Neisee frontier, 19, 21
Odling-Smee, John, 126, 129
Ogilvy, David, 391, 393
oil and petrol: prices and consumption in USA, 276–7
Olympic Games: Munich, 1972, 39; Moscow, 1980, 324, 327, 342
Omaha, 391
Oman, 327, 339, 361–2
Oman, Qabous bin Said, Sultan of, 361
O'Neill, Sir Con, 60
O'Neill, Thomas (Tip), 283, 294, 309–10, 318, 427, 453
Ormsby-Gore, David *see* Harlech, 5th Baron
Ornano, Hubert, comte d', 231
Ornano, Isabelle, comtesse d', 224, 231
Ostpolitik, 26, 33, 38, 89
O'Sullivan, Mrs Donal, 48
Other Club (London), 427
Ottawa conference, 1981, 407
Owen, David (*later* Baron): appoints Jay to Washington, 8; visits Paris as Foreign Secretary, 138–42, 193–4; qualities and views, 139–40, 142; at

Owen, David – *cont*
Giscard-Callaghan meeting, 146; at 1978 Franco-UK summit, 236–7; on role of diplomats, 243; criticises Franco-German closeness, 250; work load at Foreign Office, 269; on NH's leaked despatch, 271; Patten praises, 358
Owen, Deborah, Lady, 138–9, 141
Owen, Henry, 293–4, 354

Pakenham, Michael: in Poland, 15, 18, 22–3; at Washington Embassy, 306n; wedding, 337; writes satirical skits, 416
Palestine Liberation Organisation (PLO), 412, 484
Paley, William, 426
Palliser, Marie, Lady (*née* Spaak), 87, 270
Palliser, Sir Michael: Youde succeeds in Downing Street, 22; and British membership of European Community, 63, 66, 87; predicts Wilson's departure, 72; appointed Permanent Under-Secretary, 88; and French reluctance over joint declaration, 117; at Chequers, 145; and British attitude to EMS, 218; and Lefort, 234; stays with Hendersons, 248; Giscard asks after, 258; and NH's appointmen to Washington, 267–8; and NH's staying on in Washington, 406; and Reagan's visit to Britain, 435; role in Falklands War, 459, 461, 470
Palm Springs, Arizona, 322–5
Palmer, Andrew Eustace, 95
Palmerston, Henry John Temple, 3rd Viscount, 391
Pardey, Adrian, 470
Paris: Embassy building, 93–6; NH posted to, 93; Embassy expenses challenged and investigated, 100, 126–9, 260; NH and Mary locked out of Embassy, 113–15; Embassy garden, 189–93, 213; 14 July parade in, 210; NH leaves, 259–61
Paris Match (magazine), 201–2
Paris Opéra, 233–4
Parker, Dorothy, 77
Parkinson, Cecil, Baron, 461
Parliament (British): Reagan's address to, 434–5, 473–4

Parsons, Sir Anthony, 5, 360, 384, 444, 458–9, 460–2
Partridge, Frances, 351, 437
Pass the Port (after-dinner stories collection), 249
Patronat (French employers' organisation), 167
Patten, Christopher, 357–8
Paul, Princess (of Yugoslavia), 256
Payne, Peter, 231
Pedriel, Claude, 225
Pei, I.M., 343
Pei Yuang Ying, 30–1
Pell, Claiborne, 279
Pepper (Rolls Royce official), 186
Percy, Charles ('Chuck'), 280, 463
Pérez de Cuellar, Javier, 456, 458
Performance Art, 248
Perkins Motors, 237
Persian Gulf: US guarantee to, 325–7, 491; and Soviet threat to oil, 336; and Iran–Iraq war, 362–5
Peru: proposed plan for Falklands, 456–7, 459
Peugeot-Citroën (company), 211
Peyrefitte, Alain, 178–9
Philadelphia, 342, 422
Philip, Prince, Duke of Edinburgh: in Munich, 44; and 1972 German state visit, 46, 49–50; at Giscard's state visit, 121–2; greets Reagans, 471; installs swimming pool at Windosr Castle, 473
Philippe IV (le Bel), King of France, 175
Phillips, Hayden, 83
Phillips, Jennifer, 417
Phillips, Laughlin, 367
Phipps, Diana, 240, 242, 357
Phoenix, Arizona, 321–2
Pierre-Brossolette, Claude, 100, 102, 115–19, 240, 242
Pierre-Brossolette, Sabine, 100, 119
Pierrepont, Jackie, 342
Pierrepont, Nancy, 332, 342
Pihée, Marcel, 179, 191–3, 213, 257–8
Pijasson, R., 252
Pilgrims (New York), 306
Pilkington Glass Company, 201
Pittsburgh, 418–20
Pittsburgh World Affairs Council, 418
Plowden, Edwin, 126
Podewils, Max, 54
Pöhl, Karl Otto, 55–8, 146
Poincaré, Raymond, 229

Pol-Roger, Odette, 152–3, 189, 193, 206, 219, 227, 252–4

Poland: NH posted to, 13–14; conditions in, 14–15, 32; secret service in, 17; fear in, 18–19; relations with Britain, 19; 25th anniversary of People's Republic, 20; 1956 rising, 21, 32; western frontier, 21; relations with West Germany, 26, 33; 1970/71 riots and demonstrations, 32; NH leaves, 33–4; 1980s crisis, 359, 386; Soviet martial law in 431–2, 479

Polignac, Princesse Edouard de, 237

Pompidou, Claude, 102, 251

Pompidou, Georges: and 1972 summit, 40; at 1972 summit, 59; Heath's relations with, 85; at Chequers, 145; origins, 196

Poniatowski, Prince Michel, 98

Pope-Hennessy, Sir John, 311, 332

Popular Front, 69

Port Darwin, Falkland Islands, 465

Port Stanley, Falkland Islands, 465, 469, 476

Post-Impressionist Exhibition, Washington, 1980, 343

Potocki, Count, 231

Potter, Beatrix, 256

pound sterling: declines, 130, 132, 134, 404

Powell, Carla, Lady, 84, 240

Powell, Sir Charles, 5, 84

Powell, Joseph (Jody), 281, 339

Powell, Lewis Franklin (Mr Justice), 377

Pratt and Whitney (aero-engines company), 439

Pressler, Larry, 485

Previn, André, 418

Price, Melvin, 278

Prior, James, Baron, 273, 292, 298, 305, 358

Private Eye (magazine), 71, 77, 125, 144, 286, 415

Property Services Agency: and Paris Embassy turfing, 190–1

Provisional Irish Republican Army (PIRA), 282

Pryce-Jones, Alan, 217

Pym, Francis, Baron: visits USA, 275–6, 278–80; as Foreign Secretary during Falklands War, 445–6, 454–7, 459; meeting with Haig, 472

Pym, Valerie, Lady, 278

Queen's Birthday Parties, 179–81

Quick Reaction Force, 277n, 304

Quinn, Sally, 285

Quinton, Anthony, Baron, 331

Quinton, Marcelle, Lady, 331

Radcliffe, Cyril, Viscount: confidentiality rules, 8

Rainier, Prince of Monaco, 169–71, 173–4

Rambouillet: 1976 bilateral summit, 132–5

Rapier engine, 439

Ravaud, René Robert, 186, 208

Ray, Cyril, 252

Rayne, Max, Baron, and Jayne, Lady, 438

Raynsford, Joan, 245

Reagan, Nancy: influence, 338; Mrs Bush on, 377; press comments on, 377–8; friends, 380; at Charles-Diana wedding, 395, 414; entertains at White House, 396–7; with Prince Charles in New York, 402; and bad language, 414; appearance and dress, 415; accepts gift of china, 417, 429; and husband's ride on visit to Windsor, 435; visit to Britain, 471–4; farewell dinner for NH and Mary, 483, 487–8; exercises in White House, 485; on death of Meese's son, 486; fondness for Mary, 487; redecorates White House, 487

Reagan, Ronald: meets Gorbachev in Reykjavik, 4–5; Washington social life, 7, 369, 378–81; as prospective Presidential candidate, 324, 338; contends 1980 Presidential election, 357; Kissinger supports, 359; elected President, 366–8; Kay Graham entertains, 372–6, 425–30; government, cabinet and administration, 377–8; Thatcher visits in Washington, 382–90, 477–80; Mary meets, 384; entertained at Embassy, 389–90; entertains Prince Charles at White House, 396; and terrorism, 396–7; and foreign policy, 407; puritanism over language, 414, 426; relaxed life-style, 414–15; filming in England, 427–8; on information leaks, 428–9; imposes sanctions on USSR, 431, 479, 484; addresses British Parliament, 434,

Reagan, Ronald – *cont*
   473–4; and Middle East, 434; visit to
   Britain, 434–6, 463, 470–4; and US
   role in Falklands War, 443, 446–7,
   449, 463, 464, 466–7, 468n, 469,
   471–2, 480; urinary problems, 448;
   and proposed trusteeship for
   Falklands, 454; TV broadcast on US
   national Malaise, 455; on Begin and
   invasion of Lebanon, 474; farewell
   dinner for NH, 484, 487–8; and
   official security, 484–5; on entering
   politics, 486–7; prejudices and strong
   views, 486
Reds (film), 426
Rees-Mogg, William, Baron, 271
Reform Club, London, 107
Regan, Donald, 378
Reilly, Sir Patrick, 227
Renaud, Madeleine, 254
Renger, Annemarie, 56
Renwick, Sir Robin, 438
Reston, James ('Scottie'), 292n, 357, 432
Reville, Durand, 124
Reykjavik conference (1987), 4–5
Rhodesia, Southern *see* Zimbabwe
Rice, Desmond, 455
Richards, Sir Brooks, 315, 331
Richardson, Gordon (*later* Baron
   Richardson of Duntisbourne), 168,
   307–8, 362–3
Richardson, Peggy, Lady, 168, 307–8
Richmond, Virginia, 290
Ridley, Nicholas (*later* Baron), 398
Rio Treaty powers: on Falklands War,
   464
Ripert, Edouard, 128
Ripley, Dillon, 308
Ritblat, John, 245
Roberts, Christopher, 39
Robertson, Mrs Walter, 290
Robin, M. & Mme Gabriel, 256
Robinson, James, 391
Robinson, John, 285
Robinson, John Armstrong, 57
Rocard, Michel, 141, 185
Roche, Paul, 161–2
Rockefeller, David, Jr., 308, 320, 379
Rohan, Duchesse de, 184
Rohwedder, Detler, 80
Rolls-Royce (company): and co-
   operation with France in aircraft
   industry, 154, 158–9, 164, 166, 186–
   7, 208, 215, 439

Roosevelt, Franklin Delano, 4, 206, 368,
   478
Rose, François and Yvonne de, 186
Rose, Kenneth, 124, 167–8, 225, 258
Rosebery, Archibald Philip Primrose,
   5th Earl of, 391
Rosnay, Joël de, 242
Rosnay, Stella de (*née* Jebb), 242
Rostropovich, Mstislav, 308
Rothschild, Cécile de, 193, 217, 229
Rothschild, Elie de, 193, 222, 227
Rothschild, Eric de, 161, 242, 252
Rothschild, Guy de, 221
Rothschild, Jacob, 4th Baron, 437
Rothschild, Liliane de, 193n, 217
Rothschild, Marie-Hélène de, 221–3
Rothschild, Mary de, 401
Rothschild, Nathaniel de, 227
Rothschild, Philippe de, 125, 194, 254
Rothschild, Philippine de, 150–1, 253
Rothschild, Victor, 3rd Baron, 217
Rousseau, Jean-Jacques, 6
Rowse, A.L., 400
Roxburgh, J.F., 331
Royal Ulster Constabulary: denied US
   arms, 274, 282–4, 309, 313, 318
Rubinstein, Aniela, 150
Rubinstein, Arthur, 148–50
Russell, Aliki, Lady, 13n
Russell, Sir John, 166
Russell, Sir Mark, 329
Russia *see* Union of Soviet Socialist
   Republics
Ryan, Nin, 311
Ryder, Susan (Mrs Leonard Cheshire;
   later Baroness), 27–9, 349

Sackville, Lionel Sackville-West, 2nd
   Baron, 289
Sadat, Anwar, 212, 225
Sagan, Françoise, 185n, 221–4
St Helen's, Mount, Washington State,
   352–3
St James's Club, (London), 151
St Malo: NH visits, 110
Saint-Phalle, Thérèse de, 225
Salisbury, Robert Arthur Talbot
   Gascoyne-Cecil, 3rd Marquess of, 2
Salote, Queen of Tonga, 156
SALT II, 296, 307
Salt Lake City, 392–3
Sampson, Anthony, 272
Samuelson, Paul, 363
San Diego, California, 440–1

Sandringham Sambo (labrador dog), 122–3, 134, 256–7
Sands, Bobby, 395, 397–8
Sarbanes, Paul-Spyros, 280
Saudi Arabia, 326, 363, 365
Sauvagnargues, Jean-Victor, 97, 125, 145
Sauzay, Philippe, 221
Scanlon, Hugh, Baron, 81
Scheel, Walter, 37, 47, 63–5, 116
Schilling, Wolf-Dietrich, 53
Schlesinger, James, 285–6, 296
Schmidt, Helmut: in hospital, 55, 58; Wilson visits, 66, 68, 71; visits Wilson at Chequers, 74–5, 77–8, 143–4; at Labour Party conference, 75–7; and Lever, 86–7; on German labour discipline, 89; qualities, 89, 144; and British membership of EC, 90; relations with Giscard, 94, 214, 235, 250; NH's contact with, 98; approves Jenkins's appointment to European Presidency, 109; EMS proposals, 202, 209, 213–15, 233; and airbus project, 215; at Paris Austrian Embassy party, 251; on British Paris Embassy, 259; relations with Thatcher, 269, 338; attitude to Carter, 325; draws parallels with 1940, 340; at Bohemian Grove, 486
Schulman, Horst, 293–4
Schultz, Miss (Duchess of Windsor's secretary), 135–7
Schumann, Carol, 261
Scotland: Giscard visits, 118–19
Scott, Sir Peter, 469
Scottish Nationalists, 97
Scowcroft, Brent, 377
SDP-Liberal Alliance (Britain), 413, 422
Seattle, 352–3
Seligman, Madron, 40, 240
Selwyn-Lloyd, Baron see Lloyd, Selwyn
Sen Tan Son, 30
Senate Foreign Relations Committee (USA), 279
Shah of Iran (Mohammed Reza Pahlevi), 310
Shawcross, William, 371
Sheffield, HMS, 457, 460
Sherfield, Roger Makins, 1st Baron, 331
Sherwood, Robert, 401
Shirley, Lady Selina, 367
Shore, Peter, 60
Shous, Mrs (Washington hostess), 351

Shriver, Eunice, 297
Shulman, Marshall, 304, 331, 338
Shultz, George, 480n, 481, 486
Sieff, Marcus, Baron, 271
Sihanouk, Prince Noradom, 25n
Silicon Valley (California), 313–14
Silkin, John, 133, 162–3, 235
Sills, Beverly, 307
Silvers, Robert, 368
Simpson, Harry, 412
Sinai: international force for, 277, 418–21, 461n
Sinclair, Ian, 461
Smith, C. Aubrey, 485
Smith, John, 236
Smith, Maggie, 172, 305
Smith, William French, 378, 416, 478
Smith, Mrs William French, 417
Snow, Charles P., Baron, 247
Snowdon, Antony Armstrong-Jones, 1st Earl of, 46
Snyders, Frans: painting at Chequers, 77, 144
Soames, Christopher (later Baron): owns horses, 42; as Ambassador in Paris, 100, 208; French oppose appointment to Presidency of European Commission, 108; as prospective Shadow Foreign Secretary, 126; Fortescue works with, 293
Soames, Mary, Lady (née Churchill), 42n, 178, 281, 313
Société Nationale d'Etude et de Construction Moteurs d'Aviation (SNECMA), 186, 208
Société Nationale Industrielle Aérospatiale (SNIAS), 187
Sohio (oil company), 410
Somerleyton, Savile William Francis Crossley, 3rd Baron, 474
Sommer, Ted, 84, 87
Soult, Marshal Nicolas, J de Dieu, 134
South Georgia, 447, 463
Soutou, Jean-Marie, 163–4, 194, 213, 226
Soviet Union see Union of Soviet Socialist Republics
Spangenberg, Dietrich, 47
Spiers, Ronald, 5
Staaden, Wendy von, 308
Stais, John, 270
Stalin, Josef V., 4
Stanley, Sir John, 142–3
Statham, Sir Norman, 60, 70

Steel, Sir David (MP), 303
Steel, Sir David (of BP), 193, 291
Stern, Isaac, 486
Stevens, Liz, 348
Stevenson, Adlai, 415
Stewart, Michael (Baron Stewart of
    Fulham), 25, 420
Stewart, Sir Michael, 266n
Stoessel, Mary-Ann, 432n
Stoessel, Walter, 431, 447–9, 451, 468n
Stoltenberg, Gerhard, 67
Stone, Sir (Dr) Joseph, 70
Stoppard, Tom: *Night and Day*, 305
Stowe School (and Stoics), 175, 331, 350
Strachey, Lytton, 155
Strasbourg: NH visits, 104–5
Stratford de Redcliffe, Stratford
    Canning, 1st Viscount, 3
Strauss, Robert, 293
Sue Ryder Foundation, 27
Suez crisis (1956), 4, 206
Sulzberger, Arthur ('Punch'), 426
Sunday Telegraph, 225
Sunday Times, 433
Svoboda, Ludvik, 20
Swift, Jonathan, 474
Sykes, Sir Richard, 254
Symington, James, 387
Syon House, near Isleworth, 404
Syria, 471

Talbot, Peter, 31
Tallahassee, Florida, 343
Talleyrand-Périgord, Charles Maurice
    de, 256, 446
Taylor, Elizabeth, 351
Taylor, Miss (formerly of Chequers), 77
Tehran: US Embassy siege and hostages
    in, 310, 312–13, 315–16, 321, 332,
    336, 383, 445, 451
Tesson, Philippe, 222
Thatcher, Carol, 382
Thatcher, Sir Denis, 286, 382, 387–9
Thatcher, Margaret (*later* Baroness):
    attitude to Foreign Office, 5; and
    Falklands War, 9, 444, 446–7, 449,
    454–5, 457–8, 460–2, 469–70, 475;
    elected Party leader, 82; and Chirac,
    88; visits Bonn, 90; appearance, 142–
    3; visits Paris, 142–3; Macmillan
    silent on, 205; 1979 election victory
    and government, 265; good relations
    with Schmidt, 269; relations with
    Carter, 269, 317–19; on NH's leaked

despatch, 271; Carter praises, 283;
    and US arms for RUC, 284; NH calls
    on in London, 286; manner and
    views, 287; meeting with Carter, 287;
    representation of views in USA, 289;
    at Lusaka Conference, 296; and EC
    budget, 305, 318, 346; and Prior, 305,
    358; Barbara Walters requests
    interview with, 306; December 1979
    visit to USA, 307, 309, 313, 315–20;
    qualities, 316, 338, 404; US view of,
    320, 322, 342; proprietorial
    pronouncements, 338; Paul Johnson
    on, 346; visits to Reagan in
    Washington, 374–5, 382–90, 477–80;
    and Kissinger, 382; monetarism, 382;
    ballroom dancing, 388; portrayed on
    stage, 404; and national problems,
    406; and Reagan's visit to Britain,
    436, 470–1, 473; Haig on, 446, 447,
    475; popularity increases during
    Falklands campaign, 460, 473;
    Reagan telephones during Falklands
    War, 464, 466–7, 469; and US attitude
    to Falklands War, 464, 466–7, 471–
    2; and long-term solution to Falklands
    problem, 468–9, 480; and Jeane
    Kirkpatrick's statement in UN, 472;
    resists Reagan's Soviet export
    embargo, 479; unashamed feelings
    about position, 486
Third World Commission, 251
Thomas, Hugh (Baron Thomas of
    Swynnerton), 346
Thorne, Angela, 404
Thornton, Sir Peter, 166
Thorpe, Jeremy, 303
Times, The, 146–7, 192, 459
Tomkins, Sir Edward, 87–8, 119
Toulouse: NH visits, 103, 104–6
Tourbien, Dr (Paris vet), 184
Tower, John, 368, 463
Tower, Lilla Burt, 369
Townsend, Marie Luce, 222
Townsend, Group Captain Peter, 202
trade unions: and Wilson's 'social
    compact', 72; and membership of EC,
    81; compared with German
    counterparts, 88; British visit to
    France, 166–7; in USA, 309;
    Thatcher's attitude to, 346
Trades Union Congress: visit to USA, 276
Train, Admiral Harry, USN, 355
Tramway Mont Blanc, 227

Travellers Club (Paris), 152, 213
Tree, Marietta, 486
Trevelyan, Kate (Mrs Robert Kee),
    110n, 240
Truman, Harry S., 217
Tsatsos, Constantine, 257
Tuttle, Holmes, 379–80
Tzu Jung Szeng, 31

U Thant, 24
Ullstein family, 42
Union of Soviet Socialist Republics:
    invasion of Afghanistan, 325, 327; in
    Middle East, 326–7, 336, 362–3,
    461n, 471; US high-technology sales
    embargo, 327; martial law in Poland,
    431–2; Reagan imposes sanctions on,
    431, 479, 482, 484; relations with
    Argentina in Falklands War, 452
United Nations: and Falklands War,
    444, 458
United Nations Security Council: and US
    hostages in Iran, 316; Resolution 502
    (on Falklands), 445, 468, 471–2;
    Resolution 508 (on Lebanon), 474
United States of America: Giscard's
    attitude to, 93; and European
    Commission, 140; attitude to
    President, 217; and Irish question,
    275, 281–4, 294, 309–10, 361, 395,
    397, 402, 404, 408, 423;
    preoccupation with energy, 276, 298;
    women's solidarity in, 300; and
    Tehran Embassy siege, 310, 312–13,
    315–16, 321, 332, 336, 383, 445,
    451; Middle East policy, 325, 362–5,
    421, 433–4, 491–2; 1980 Presidential
    election, 366; lacks political satire,
    415–16; role in Falklands War, 442–
    8, 450–3, 459, 462–4, 466–7, 468n,
    475, 481–2; and long-term settlement
    of Falklands problem, 469
United Technologies Corporation, 439
United World Colleges, 237
Urquhart, Sir Brian, 440n
Urquhart, Sidney, Lady, 440
Urquijo, Piru, 367
US News and World Report, 428
USSR see Union of Soviet Socialist
    Republics
Ustinov, Sir Peter, 102, 227
Utter, John, 135

Val d'Isère (France), 244–5

Valéry, François, 219
van der Vat, Dan, 81
Vance, Cyrus: relations with Carrington,
    269; as Secretary of State, 269, 275;
    approves NH's appointment to
    Washington, 270; offers resignation,
    281; and Thatcher's visits to Carter,
    283, 319; thanks UK for support,
    312–13; NH meets in Washington,
    327; resigns, 338
Vance, Elsie (daughter of Cyrus and
    Gay), 339
Vance, Gay (Mrs Cyrus Vance), 338
Vandenberg, Arthur H., 433
Vanneck, Sir Peter, 174–5
Varley, Eric, Baron, 164, 175–6, 211,
    215, 236
Vaughan, Thomas J. and Elizabeth Ann
    Perpetua, 352–3
Vaux-le-Vicomte (chateau, France), 184
Veil, Simone: invited to European Youth
    Orchestra, 148; birthday present for
    NH, 157; at Les Misérables, 206; at
    Alexandra's wedding, 240–2
Venice Declaration, 1980, 418
Verdy, Violette, 234
Vernier-Palliez, Bernard, 181
Vespasian, Roman Emperor, 178
Vest, George, 280, 282, 364
Viansson-Pontet, Pierre, 155
Victoria, Queen, 155
Vietnam War, 301–2
Vocke, Katarina, 55
Voguëe family, 184
Volcker, Paul, 301, 304, 362
Volkonsky, Prince Pierre and Princess
    Isabel, 191, 193
Vreeland, Diana, 396

Wade-Gery, Sir Robert, 461
Wagner, Barbara, 380
Wahl, Jacques, 255–6
Wahl, Madame Jacques, 256–7
Walden, George: and NH's appointment
    to Washington, 266–7, 270; and
    work load at Foreign Office, 268–9;
    on NH's leaked despatch, 271; in
    Washington with Thatcher, 318; and
    British support for Carter's Iran
    rescue attempt, 336; and Carrington
    on sanctions, 346
Waldheim, Kurt, 297
Waldner, Loulou de (Baronne Geoffroy
    de Waldner de Freundstein), 161

Walesa, Lech, 359, 479
Walker, John and Lady Margaret, 292
Wall Street Journal, 438
Wallace, Sir Richard, 260
Walters, Barbara, 296–7, 306, 317, 337, 368, 428
Walton, Bill, 369
Wan Su Mee, 30
Warner, Sir Frederick Archibald, 270, 306
Warner, Simone, Lady, 270
Warnock, Sir Geoffrey, 253
Warren, Sir (Dr) Brian, 39
Warsaw: Embassy building, 13; NH posted to, 13; NH builds Embassy tennis court in, 17
Warsaw Pact: and invasion of Czechoslovakia, 14–16, 22; proposes security conference, 21, 24
Washington, DC: NH appointed to, 266–9; Embassy life and conditions, 276–7; Ambassadorial role and activities in 287–8; Thatcher visits as PM, 315–19; black Embassy staff, 353–4
Washington, Mr ('Wash'; of Washington Embassy staff), 354
Washington Post (newspaper), 251, 285, 332, 341, 373, 399, 428, 433, 438, 465
Wass, Sir Douglas, 177–8, 218
Waugh, Evelyn, 16, 391
Webster, Judge William, 414
Wechmar, Rüdiger, Baron von, 55
Weidenfeld, Annabel, Lady see Whitestone, Annabel
Weidenfeld, George, Baron: marriage to Annabel, 150n; on city-baby-talk, 187; at Valentino gala, 220; 60th birthday celebrations, 296–7; party for Kissinger's book, 305–6; Lally Weymouth entertains, 334; New York party, 371; meets Reagan, 373
Weiller, Paul-Louis, 156
Weinberger, Caspar: position in Reagan administration, 375, 407, relations with NH, 383; Mary meets, 384; meets Isaiah Berlin, 399–401; at Embassy party, 416–17; meets Menuhin, 432; friendship with Janet Morgan, 433; relations with Haig, 433; gives help in Falklands War, 442–4, 452–3
Weinberger, Jane, 432–3

Well, Günther Wilhelm van, 64
Wells, John: *Anyone for Denis*, 404
Wells (of California semi-conductor company), 313–14
West Bank (Israel), 419
West Berlin, 304
West Germany (Federal Republic of Germany): East European policy, 21, 26, 33, 38, 39, 89; UK policy of friendship towards, 21; relations with Poland, 26, 33; NH appointed Ambassador to, 37–8; popular British attitudes to, 37–8; federal system, 38; and European monetary situation, 53–4; economic strength, 88–9, 132, 153, 206; NH leaves, 88–90; and British membership of EC, 89–90; democratic institutions, 89
Weston, Garfield, 231
Wexler, Anne, 293
Weymouth, Lally, 333–4, 368
White House, Washington: decor, furnishing and entertaining at, 282, 396–7, 487; security and lack of privacy in, 485
White, Mrs C.B. see James, Phyllis Dorothy
White, John, 246
White, Sam, 160, 260
Whitelaw, William, Viscount, 460, 463, 472
Whitestone, Annabel (*later* Lady Weidenfeld), 150
Whitmore, Sir Clive, 479
Whitridge, Arnold, 328
Whyte, William Erskine Hamilton, 270
Wilde, Oscar, 290
Wilkinson Sword Company, 420
Will, George, 368, 426
Will, Mrs George, 426
Williams, Marcia see Falkender, Baroness
Williams, Shirley, Baroness: visits Germany, 79–82; at Königswinter Conference, 83–4
Wilson, Sir Duncan, 24
Wilson, Harold (*later* Baron): accompanied by doctor abroad, 39; at Windsor Castle, 48; 1974 government, 59n, 61; and British membership of European Community, 66, 78–9; and Scotland–Brazil football match, 66, 69; visits Schmidt, 66, 68, 71; at Chequers,

Wilson, Harold – *cont*
68–9; reminisces, 69–70; manner, 71; and control of Labour Party, 72, 86; Schmidt visits at Chequers, 74–5, 77–8; sporting prowess, 74–5; on life at Oxford, 78; Cabinet shuffle, 86; retirement and succession, 94, 98, 109; health, 98–9; and Jenkins's move to European Commission, 108–9; skill as Prime Minister, 133; Macmillan on, 206; at Weidenfeld party, 306

Wilson, Mary, Lady, 68, 77, 306
Wilson, Peter, 311
Wilson, William ('Bill'), 380–1
Wilson, Woodrow, 435
Windsor: Reagan visit to and ride in, 434–6, 470, 472, 474
Windsor Castle: formal reception at, 45–9; NH stays in, 470–3
Windsor, Wallis, Duchess of, 135–7
Winks, Robin, 368
Winskill, Air Commodore Archibald, 50, 131
Wisner, Frank, 426
Witney, Nicholas, 283, 332, 418, 420
Wolfschanze (Hitler's HQ, East Germany), 18
Woodward, Admiral Sir John (Sandy), 456

Woolf, Virginia, 337
World Affairs Council, 439
Wormser, Olivier, 85, 107–8
Wrather, John Deveraux ('Jack'), 380
Wright, James, 292
Wright, Sir Oliver, 23, 384, 429n
Wrightsman, Charles and Jayne, 307
Wroclaw (Poland), 27
Wyrouboff, Nicolas, 96, 100, 193
Wyrouboff, Sabine, 96, 100, 192, 260
Wyszyński, Cardinal Stefan, Archbishop of Warsaw, 28

Yoder, Edwin, 332
Yom Kippur War *see* Arab–Israeli War (1973)
Youde, Sir Edward, 22, 329, 449
Young (Ministry of Defence official), 126, 129
Young, Brigham, 392–3
Young, Gerry, 73

Zaire: disorder in, 182–3, 185, 193–4
Zervudacki, Nolly and Mrs, 151, 240
Zimbabwe (*formerly* Southern Rhodesia), 269, 287, 305, 309, 316–18
Zipkin, Jerry, 396
Zorba (NH's dalmatian), 14–15, 57, 74, 95, 132, 184, 239, 250

Mr James Callaghan, with his humble duty to

Your Majesty, has the honour respectfully to submit

for Your Majesty's approval that Sir Nicholas Henderson

KCMG be appointed Your Majesty's Ambassador to France.

James Callaghan

FOREIGN AND COMMONWEALTH OFFICE
27 May 1975